Handbook of Research on Sustainable Consumption and Production for Greener Economies

Richa Goel
Amity University, India

Sukanta Kumar Baral
Indira Gandhi National Tribal University, India

A volume in the Advances in Business Strategy and Competitive Advantage (ABSCA) Book Series

Published in the United States of America by
IGI Global
Business Science Reference (an imprint of IGI Global)
701 E. Chocolate Avenue
Hershey PA, USA 17033
Tel: 717-533-8845
Fax: 717-533-8661
E-mail: cust@igi-global.com
Web site: http://www.igi-global.com

Copyright © 2023 by IGI Global. All rights reserved. No part of this publication may be reproduced, stored or distributed in any form or by any means, electronic or mechanical, including photocopying, without written permission from the publisher. Product or company names used in this set are for identification purposes only. Inclusion of the names of the products or companies does not indicate a claim of ownership by IGI Global of the trademark or registered trademark.

Library of Congress Cataloging-in-Publication Data

Names: Goel, Richa, 1980- editor. | Baral, Sukanta Kumar, 1966- editor.
Title: Handbook of research on sustainable consumption and production for greener economies / edited by Richa Goel, and Sukanta Kumar Baral.
Description: Hershey, PA : Business Science Reference, [2023] | Includes bibliographical references and index. | Summary: "Sustainable Consumption and Production for Greener Economies examines the critical factors that can encourage sustainable consumption production patterns and a green economy. The major barriers hindering consumers and producers from moving towards sustainable consumption, sustainable consumption behavior and production patterns, the green economy, and more are explored. Covering topics such as green economy, sustainable consumption, and resource management, this book is ideal for government officials, policymakers, researchers, academicians, and more"-- Provided by publisher.
Identifiers: LCCN 2023013630 (print) | LCCN 2023013631 (ebook) | ISBN 9781668489697 (hardcover) | ISBN ISBN 9781668489710 (ebook)
Subjects: LCSH: Sustainable development. | Environmental economics. | Environmental policy--Social aspects.
Classification: LCC HC79.E5 S86463 2023 (print) | LCC HC79.E5 (ebook) | DDC 338.9/27--dc23/eng/20230411
LC record available at https://lccn.loc.gov/2023013630
LC ebook record available at https://lccn.loc.gov/2023013631

This book is published in the IGI Global book series Advances in Business Strategy and Competitive Advantage (ABSCA) (ISSN: 2327-3429; eISSN: 2327-3437)

British Cataloguing in Publication Data
A Cataloguing in Publication record for this book is available from the British Library.

All work contributed to this book is new, previously-unpublished material. The views expressed in this book are those of the authors, but not necessarily of the publisher.

For electronic access to this publication, please contact: eresources@igi-global.com.

Advances in Business Strategy and Competitive Advantage (ABSCA) Book Series

Patricia Ordóñez de Pablos
Universidad de Oviedo, Spain

ISSN:2327-3429
EISSN:2327-3437

Mission

Business entities are constantly seeking new ways through which to gain advantage over their competitors and strengthen their position within the business environment. With competition at an all-time high due to technological advancements allowing for competition on a global scale, firms continue to seek new ways through which to improve and strengthen their business processes, procedures, and profitability.

The **Advances in Business Strategy and Competitive Advantage (ABSCA) Book Series** is a timely series responding to the high demand for state-of-the-art research on how business strategies are created, implemented and re-designed to meet the demands of globalized competitive markets. With a focus on local and global challenges, business opportunities and the needs of society, the **ABSCA** encourages scientific discourse on doing business and managing information technologies for the creation of sustainable competitive advantage.

Coverage

- Core Competencies
- International Business Strategy
- Business Models
- Balanced Scorecard
- Outsourcing
- Tacit Knowledge
- Strategy Performance Management
- Foreign Investment Decision Process
- Strategic Alliances
- Resource-Based Competition

IGI Global is currently accepting manuscripts for publication within this series. To submit a proposal for a volume in this series, please contact our Acquisition Editors at Acquisitions@igi-global.com or visit: http://www.igi-global.com/publish/.

The Advances in Business Strategy and Competitive Advantage (ABSCA) Book Series (ISSN 2327-3429) is published by IGI Global, 701 E. Chocolate Avenue, Hershey, PA 17033-1240, USA, www.igi-global.com. This series is composed of titles available for purchase individually; each title is edited to be contextually exclusive from any other title within the series. For pricing and ordering information please visit http://www.igi-global.com/book-series/advances-business-strategy-competitive-advantage/73672. Postmaster: Send all address changes to above address. Copyright © 2023 IGI Global. All rights, including translation in other languages reserved by the publisher. No part of this series may be reproduced or used in any form or by any means – graphics, electronic, or mechanical, including photocopying, recording, taping, or information and retrieval systems – without written permission from the publisher, except for non commercial, educational use, including classroom teaching purposes. The views expressed in this series are those of the authors, but not necessarily of IGI Global.

Titles in this Series

For a list of additional titles in this series, please visit: www.igi-global.com/book-series

Strategic Management and International Business Policies for Maintaining Competitive Advantage
Ailson J. De Moraes (Royal Holloway University of Londo, UK)
Business Science Reference • © 2023 • 340pp • H/C (ISBN: 9781668468456) • US $250.00

Handbook of Research on Digital Natives as a Disruptive Force in Asian Businesses and Societies
Omkar Dastane (UCSI Graduate Business School, UCSI University, Malaysia) Aini Aman (Universiti Kebangsaan Malaysia, Malaysia) and Nurhizam Safie Bin Mohd Satar (Universiti Kebangsaan Malaysia, Malysia)
Business Science Reference • © 2023 • 400pp • H/C (ISBN: 9781668467824) • US $295.00

Handbook of Research on Sustainability Challenges in the Wine Industry
Bartolomé Marco-Lajara (University of Alicante, Spain) Armand Gilinsky (Sonoma State University, USA) Javier Martínez-Falcó (University of Alicante, Spain & Stellenbosch University, South Africa) and Eduardo Sánchez-García (University of Alicante, Spain)
Business Science Reference • © 2023 • 435pp • H/C (ISBN: 9781668469422) • US $295.00

Opportunities and Challenges of Business 5.0 in Emerging Markets
Sumesh Dadwal (Northumbria University, UK) Pawan Kumar (Lovely Professional University, India) Rajesh Verma (Lovely Professional University, India) and Gursimranjit Singh (Lovely Professional University, India)
Business Science Reference • © 2023 • 357pp • H/C (ISBN: 9781668464038) • US $250.00

Embracing Business Sustainability Through Innovation and Creativity in the Service Sector
Pankaj Kumar Tyagi (Chandigarh University, India) Vipin Nadda (University of Sunderland, UK) Vishal Bharti (Chandigarh University, India) and Ebru Kemer (Niğde Ömer Halisdemir University, Turkey)
Business Science Reference • © 2023 • 329pp • H/C (ISBN: 9781668467329) • US $250.00

Strengthening SME Performance Through Social Media Adoption and Usage
Sikandar Ali Qalati (School of Business, Liaocheng University, Shandong, China) Dragana Ostic (School of Finance and Economics, Jiangsu University, China) and Rohit Bansal (Vaish College of Engineering, Rohtak, India)
Business Science Reference • © 2023 • 291pp • H/C (ISBN: 9781668457702) • US $250.00

Bankruptcy and Reorganization in the Digital Business Era
Fahri Özsungur (Mersin University, Turkey) Nevzat Tetik (Inonu University, Turkey) and Ersin Kanat (Zonguldak Bulent Ecevit University, Turkey)
Business Science Reference • © 2023 • 300pp • H/C (ISBN: 9781668451816) • US $250.00

701 East Chocolate Avenue, Hershey, PA 17033, USA
Tel: 717-533-8845 x100 • Fax: 717-533-8661
E-Mail: cust@igi-global.com • www.igi-global.com

List of Contributors

Arun, Korhan / *Tekirdag Namik Kemal University, Turkey* 74
Baral, Sukanta Kumar / *Indira Gandhi National Tribal University, India* 141, 198, 247
Batule, Radhakrishna / *Vishwakarma University, India* 230
Biju, A. V. / *University of Kerala, India* 160
Bisoyi, Bhubaneswari / *Sri Sri University, Cuttack, India* 327
Blekhman, David / *California State University, Los Angeles, USA* 27
Bouarar, Ahmed Chemseddine / *University of Medea, Algeria* 58
Büyükselçuk, Elif Çaloğlu / *Fenerbahçe University, Turkey* 121
Chandel, Sunandani / *Kerala Agricultural University, India* 358
Chawla, Yukta / *Mahatma Jyotiba Phule Rohilkhand University, India* 213
Chummun, Bibi Zaheenah / *University of KwaZulu-Natal, South Africa* 91
Das, Biswajit / *KIIT School of Management, KIIT University, India* 327
Efe, Omer Faruk / *Bursa Technical University, Turkey* 42
Goel, Richa / *SCMS Noida, Symbiosis International University (Deemed), Pune, India* 398
Kalshekar, Burhan Abdur Rasheed / *Gharda Institute of Technology, India* 384
Kanade, Tarun Madan / *Vishwakarma University, India* 230
Khandelwal, Ayush / *Mahatma Jyotiba Phule Rohilkhand University, India* 213
Krishnan, Akamsha / *Amity University, Noida, India* 178
Kulkarni, Sunil Jayant / *Gharda Institute of Technology, India* 283, 384
León, Jeffrey / *Ean University, Colombia* 27
Makhlouf, Asma / *University of Medea, Algeria* 58
Malia, Abhiraj / *KIIT School of Management, KIIT University, India* 327
Mehra, Pooja / *Amity University, Noida, India* 301
Mehta, Shivani / *Amity University, Noida, India* 178, 265
Mijalkovski, Stojance / *Goce Delcev University, North Macedonia* 42
Mouloudj, Kamel / *University of Medea, Algeria* 58
Mouloudj, Smail / *University of Medea, Algeria* 58
Nayak, Arpita / *KIIT School of Management, KIIT University, India* 247
Ocampo, Pablo Cesar / *Ean University, Colombia* 27
Ozmutlu, Saniye Yildirim / *Tekirdag Namik Kemal University, Turkey* 74
Patil, Ameya / *Dr. Vishwanath Karad MIT World Peace University, India* 344
Patnaik, Atmika / *King's College, UK* 247
Patnaik, B. C. M. / *KIIT School of Management, KIIT University, India* 247
Pradhan, Prajnya Paramita / *KIIT School of Management, KIIT University, Bhubaneswar, India* 327

Satpathy, Ipseeta / *KIIT School of Management, KIIT University, India*	247, 327
Sawhney, Anahita / *Amity University, Noida, India*	301
Saxena, Harshit / *ICAR-IVRI University (Deemed), India*	213
Sengupta, Rajeev / *Dr. Vishwanath Karad MIT World Peace University, India*	344
Sharma, Nikita / *Amity University, Noida, India*	265
Shibu, C. / *Kerala Agricultural University, India*	358
Singh, Pushpam / *Indira Gandhi National Tribal University, India*	141
Sreelekshmi, G. / *University of Kerala, India*	160
Swain, Adyasha / *Jönköping University, Sweden*	107
Tiwari, Saurabh / *University of Petroleum and Energy Studies, India*	398
Vats, Preeti / *Kerala Agricultural University, India*	358
Yadav, Madhuri / *Indira Gandhi National Tribal University, India*	141, 198
Yalkı, İrem / *İstanbul Okan University, Turkey*	1
Zeqiri, Kemajl / *University of Mitrovica, Kosovo*	42

Table of Contents

Preface xx

Chapter 1
Industrialization Impact on Climate Change: An Examination of NICs 1
    İrem Yalkı, İstanbul Okan University, Turkey

Chapter 2
Context Good Practices in Energy Matrix Focused Towards a Hydrogen Economy: Colombia
Becoming the Colossus of the Hydrogen Economy and Sustainability in the Region 27
    Pablo Cesar Ocampo, Ean University, Colombia
    Jeffrey León, Ean University, Colombia
    David Blekhman, California State University, Los Angeles, USA

Chapter 3
Application of Multi-Criteria Decision-Making Methods for the Underground Mining Method
Selection 42
    Stojance Mijalkovski, Goce Delcev University, North Macedonia
    Omer Faruk Efe, Bursa Technical University, Turkey
    Kemajl Zeqiri, University of Mitrovica, Kosovo

Chapter 4
Exploring Intention to Purchase Energy-Efficient Home Appliances: An Extension of the Theory
of Planned Behavior 58
    Ahmed Chemseddine Bouarar, University of Medea, Algeria
    Kamel Mouloudj, University of Medea, Algeria
    Asma Makhlouf, University of Medea, Algeria
    Smail Mouloudj, University of Medea, Algeria

Chapter 5
The Critical Impact of Sustainability Innovations on Green Supply Chains 74
    Saniye Yildirim Ozmutlu, Tekirdag Namik Kemal University, Turkey
    Korhan Arun, Tekirdag Namik Kemal University, Turkey

Chapter 6
Can Green Products and Services in the Insurance Industry be a Sustainable Measure? 91
Bibi Zaheenah Chummun, University of KwaZulu-Natal, South Africa

Chapter 7
Smart Non-Invasive Approach for Workspace Rating Assessment: A Post-Occupancy Evaluation Approach for University Buildings 107
Adyasha Swain, Jönköping University, Sweden

Chapter 8
Where Are We and What Should We Do in Cleaner Production Transformation? 121
Elif Çaloğlu Büyükselçuk, Fenerbahçe University, Turkey

Chapter 9
Artificial Intelligence Retrofitting for Smart City Strategies in the Context of India's Growing Population 141
Pushpam Singh, Indira Gandhi National Tribal University, India
Madhuri Yadav, Indira Gandhi National Tribal University, India
Sukanta Kumar Baral, Indira Gandhi National Tribal University, India

Chapter 10
Green Bonds for Mobilising Environmental Finance: A Conceptual Framework for a Greener Economy 160
G. Sreelekshmi, University of Kerala, India
A. V. Biju, University of Kerala, India

Chapter 11
Factors Affecting the Purchase Intention of Indian Youths: Special Reference to the Textile and Clothing Industry 178
Akamsha Krishnan, Amity University, Noida, India
Shivani Mehta, Amity University, Noida, India

Chapter 12
Can Asia Accomplish the Sustainable Development Goal for Water and Sanitation by 2030? 198
Madhuri Yadav, Indira Gandhi National Tribal University, India
Sukanta Kumar Baral, Indira Gandhi National Tribal University, India

Chapter 13
Achieving a Picturesque Global Green Economy by Sustainable Consumption and Production (SCP): Green Economy and Sustainable Development 213
Ayush Khandelwal, Mahatma Jyotiba Phule Rohilkhand University, India
Yukta Chawla, Mahatma Jyotiba Phule Rohilkhand University, India
Harshit Saxena, ICAR-IVRI University (Deemed), India

Chapter 14
Constructing New Greener Infrastructures, Retrofitting, and Exploiting the Potential of Smart Technologies 230

 Tarun Madan Kanade, Vishwakarma University, India
 Radhakrishna Batule, Vishwakarma University, India

Chapter 15
Green Manufacturing: Opening Doors to Greener Economy 247

 Arpita Nayak, KIIT School of Management, KIIT University, India
 Ipseeta Satpathy, KIIT School of Management, KIIT University, India
 B. C. M. Patnaik, KIIT School of Management, KIIT University, India
 Sukanta Kumar Baral, Indira Gandhi National Tribal University, India
 Atmika Patnaik, King's College, UK

Chapter 16
Factors Influencing Green Purchase Intention Among Food Retail Consumers: An Empirical Study on Uttar Pradesh 265

 Nikita Sharma, Amity University, Noida, India
 Shivani Mehta, Amity University, Noida, India

Chapter 17
Conversion of Cellulosic Raw Feed Stock Into Cellulose Nanocrystals (CNC): Methods, Characterization, and Novel Applications 283

 Sunil Jayant Kulkarni, Gharda Institute of Technology, India

Chapter 18
Inching Towards Sustainability in Developing Countries: An Analysis of the Food Industry – A Case Study of India 301

 Anahita Sawhney, Amity University, Noida, India
 Pooja Mehra, Amity University, Noida, India

Chapter 19
Greener Economy for Sustainable Development Through AI Intervention: Demystifying Critical Factors 327

 Prajnya Paramita Pradhan, KIIT School of Management, KIIT University, Bhubaneswar, India
 Abhiraj Malia, KIIT School of Management, KIIT University, India
 Biswajit Das, KIIT School of Management, KIIT University, India
 Bhubaneswari Bisoyi, Sri Sri University, Cuttack, India
 Ipseeta Satpathy, KIIT School of Management, KIIT University, India

Chapter 20
Green Finance Products and Investments in the Changing Business World 344

 Rajeev Sengupta, Dr. Vishwanath Karad MIT World Peace University, India
 Ameya Patil, Dr. Vishwanath Karad MIT World Peace University, India

Chapter 21
Scaling Up of Wood Waste Utilization for Sustainable Green Future 358
    C. Shibu, Kerala Agricultural University, India
    Sunandani Chandel, Kerala Agricultural University, India
    Preeti Vats, Kerala Agricultural University, India

Chapter 22
Preparation and Extraction of Alpha Cellulose and Synthesis of Microcrystalline Cellulose From Agro-Waste (Pineapple Leaves) 384
    Sunil Jayant Kulkarni, Gharda Institute of Technology, India
    Burhan Abdur Rasheed Kalshekar, Gharda Institute of Technology, India

Chapter 23
Industry 4.0, Sustainable Manufacturing, Circular Economy, and Sustainable Business Models for Sustainable Development 398
    Saurabh Tiwari, University of Petroleum and Energy Studies, India
    Richa Goel, SCMS Noida, Symbiosis International University (Deemed), Pune, India

Compilation of References 416

About the Contributors 472

Index 479

Detailed Table of Contents

Preface xx

Chapter 1
Industrialization Impact on Climate Change: An Examination of NICs 1
    İrem Yalkı, İstanbul Okan University, Turkey

This study aims at investigating the industrialization impact on environmental degradation in the newly industrialized countries (NICs). In order to measure climate change, the ecological footprint indicator is used. As GDPpc, energy use, and fossil fuel consumption are inextricably linked with industrialization, they are taken as the industrialization indicators. In addition to the industry level, also industry % of GDP is examined to determine the industrial structure of the countries. The study uses descriptive analysis to present the relationship between industrialization and climate change. The statistics show that energy use in NICs is at high levels, and fossil fuel consumption is dominant. Thus, the situation causes environmental degradation as these indicators act together. As the share of the NICs indicators has increased gradually over the years, the policies of these countries have significant importance. Therefore, they have to make urgent policies to transition to green economies.

Chapter 2
Context Good Practices in Energy Matrix Focused Towards a Hydrogen Economy: Colombia Becoming the Colossus of the Hydrogen Economy and Sustainability in the Region 27
    Pablo Cesar Ocampo, Ean University, Colombia
    Jeffrey León, Ean University, Colombia
    David Blekhman, California State University, Los Angeles, USA

This chapter of the book consists of documenting the different practices in relation to the energy matrix through a systematic analysis of deductive literature in which hydrogen fuel is a fundamental element in the energy transition in a hydrogen economy in Colombia. During the investigation it was observed that Colombia is becoming one of the countries that is betting on the leadership of energy transformation in Latin America, followed by Chile, Brazil, Uruguay, and Mexico. Colombia hopes to become the colossus of the hydrogen economy and sustainability in the region.

Chapter 3
Application of Multi-Criteria Decision-Making Methods for the Underground Mining Method
Selection... 42
    Stojance Mijalkovski, Goce Delcev University, North Macedonia
    Omer Faruk Efe, Bursa Technical University, Turkey
    Kemajl Zeqiri, University of Mitrovica, Kosovo

In mining, there are many complex problems that need to be solved in a limited period of time. When solving these complex tasks, it is necessary to take into account many parameters, all in order to determine the optimal solution for a given problem. The application of multi-criteria decision-making methods (MCDM) is very widely used to solve such complex problems. One of the most complex problems in mining is the underground mining method selection. In order to choose the most appropriate method of mining excavation, it is necessary to take into account a large number of influential parameters according to which we will compare mining methods. This paper will discuss the problem of underground mining method selection using the EDAS method. Also, a comparison of the obtained results will be made for a specific example, when applying several methods for multi-criteria decision-making. After comparing the obtained results, the most suitable mining method for a specific example will be determined.

Chapter 4
Exploring Intention to Purchase Energy-Efficient Home Appliances: An Extension of the Theory
of Planned Behavior... 58
    Ahmed Chemseddine Bouarar, University of Medea, Algeria
    Kamel Mouloudj, University of Medea, Algeria
    Asma Makhlouf, University of Medea, Algeria
    Smail Mouloudj, University of Medea, Algeria

The corporations' irrational behavior and individuals' alike had a disastrous effect on the environment due to increasing energy consumption and causing a massive squandering of natural resources. That prompted researchers and practitioners worldwide (in developed and developing countries) to consider and pay immense attention to saving energy behavior. Hence, this chapter seeks to identify the factors that affect the intention to purchase energy-efficient home appliances in Algeria. Data were collected using a convenience sample; consumers in three cities were invited to participate in a questionnaire survey. The analysis was ultimately conducted on 193 valid questionnaires. The findings revealed that attitude, subjective norms, perceived behavioral control (PBC), and environmental awareness positively impacted the intention to purchase energy-efficient home appliances. Therefore, this chapter provides relevant policy recommendations on stimulating consumer's intention to purchase energy-efficient home appliances.

Chapter 5
The Critical Impact of Sustainability Innovations on Green Supply Chains 74
    Saniye Yildirim Ozmutlu, Tekirdag Namik Kemal University, Turkey
    Korhan Arun, Tekirdag Namik Kemal University, Turkey

The prevailing business methods have a strong focus on environmental sustainability. To that aim, the rising concern about environmental issues in the supply chain has sparked the growth of green supply chains. Organizations are also highly interested in planning and implementing green strategies. In that case, the innovative approach is labeled as the primary driver of change from traditional to green in the supply chain. Therefore, environmental sustainability innovations are examined in this chapter as the forces behind the green supply chain in organizations. 172 waste management and recycling companies are the samples of the study, where path analysis with partial least squares-based structural equation modeling was conducted to test the hypotheses. The findings demonstrate a strong connection between green supply chains and improvements in resource conservation, energy reduction, managing environmental communication, and pollution.

Chapter 6
Can Green Products and Services in the Insurance Industry be a Sustainable Measure? 91
Bibi Zaheenah Chummun, University of KwaZulu-Natal, South Africa

Nowadays sustainability is classified as a prominent issue, more specifically in the business world. Sustainability has a bearing on every industry at all levels. The insurance sector is not an exception and shows a remarkable interest in matters related to sustainability. Sustainable insurance businesses require multi-dimensional interventions of eco-innovation and creativity. Increasing contradictions between economic growth and environmental issues have become an important issue for businesses worldwide. The societal and technological responses to climate change threats are rapidly developing and there is still a lack of efficient financial strategies to mitigate sustainable risks. To achieve insurance business success, many insurers focus constantly on their growth in increasing their market share and retaining better risks. Insurers should always look for new ways to differentiate themselves from their competitors. In developing and offering new green products and services-related to potential sustainability, green insurance movement is the new wave and can be the solution.

Chapter 7
Smart Non-Invasive Approach for Workspace Rating Assessment: A Post-Occupancy Evaluation Approach for University Buildings 107
Adyasha Swain, Jönköping University, Sweden

This study describes the development and examination of a customized post-occupancy evaluation (POE) software application to improve FM and students' exposure to and use of real-time data. To adapt that facility management could involve students in class activities and enhance their perception of the validation process, it is necessary to demonstrate that gathering info in real-time and exploiting is feasible. A mobile application was built to gather information on occupants' perceptions and likewise, real-time realignment of the data store. Physical parameters were used to guide the selection of lighting and space usage parameters that corresponded with perceived indoor conditions. During the pilot project, an immediate representation of the gathered data was given, illustrating how the POE app functions and what more statistical assessment can be done further. The prototype's use in a real-world university building demonstrates the system's adaptability, viability, and capacity for gathering and analyzing real-time building performance data.

Chapter 8
Where Are We and What Should We Do in Cleaner Production Transformation? 121
Elif Çaloğlu Büyükselçuk, Fenerbahçe University, Turkey

Until recently, production models developed according to market conditions focused on reducing costs and increasing profitability at the expense of the destruction of natural resources and the deterioration of ecological balance and human health. However, today, with the effects of the deterioration in the ecosystem reaching sensible dimensions and being accepted as a global threat, a new production approach is needed.

Due to environmental pressures, new markets and scarce resources, development, and economic growth are being tried to be redefined. Traditional production methods and environmental technologies are no longer sufficient to provide resource efficiency and increase environmental performance. Therefore, the need for new systems, processes and technologies has arisen for the restructuring of the industry and the creation of green business models. In this chapter, it is discussed how the cleaner production approach will contribute to this transformation, considering the green transformation efforts in question and considering the current situation of the Turkish industry.

Chapter 9
Artificial Intelligence Retrofitting for Smart City Strategies in the Context of India's Growing Population 141
    Pushpam Singh, Indira Gandhi National Tribal University, India
    Madhuri Yadav, Indira Gandhi National Tribal University, India
    Sukanta Kumar Baral, Indira Gandhi National Tribal University, India

Artificial intelligence has gained momentum by assimilating into almost every aspect of the country's development, and smart city innovation is one aspect among them. It is a possible solution for issues related to rapid urban growth. This chapter addresses the top five smart city countries: Singapore, Zurich, Oslo, Taipei City, and Lausanne, implementing artificial intelligence in their smart city strategies. The study analyzed how those strategies can be applied to India's smart city by retrofitting artificial intelligence. The study used quantitative data from secondary sources such as government websites, journals, articles, and online books. R programming was applied to show the statistical performance of those five countries and area-based developmental projects of India. The study's findings will be beneficial for assisting decision-makers, professionals, and academicians in making more informed choices by providing insight into potential opportunities associated with the widespread implementation of artificial intelligence.

Chapter 10
Green Bonds for Mobilising Environmental Finance: A Conceptual Framework for a Greener Economy 160
    G. Sreelekshmi, University of Kerala, India
    A. V. Biju, University of Kerala, India

Sustainability in production and consumption requires infrastructure, pointing to the enormous financial prerequisite. Green bonds are an innovative means for channelling capital toward the environment and sustainability. Through a methodical evaluation of the literature, global green bond frameworks, and issuances to date, this chapter attempts to develop a comprehensive understanding of green bonds, as well as their importance in achieving sustainable development. The authors examine the potential of green bonds in unleashing sustainability focusing on the UN SDG 12, titled "responsible consumption and production." The results suggest that green bonds have huge potential in financing green infrastructure that enables responsible production and consumption. The interdependencies of the sustainability pillars result in overall sustainability with the benefits derived from green bond issuances.

Chapter 11
Factors Affecting the Purchase Intention of Indian Youths: Special Reference to the Textile and Clothing Industry 178
    Akamsha Krishnan, Amity University, Noida, India
    Shivani Mehta, Amity University, Noida, India

The objective of the study is to identify the factors affecting purchase intention of consumers while purchasing green clothes and textiles using theory of planned behavior (TPB) and theory of reasoned actions (TRA). Furthermore, the study intends to investigate gender disparities in green purchasing intentions. The study employs a quantitative and qualitative method, with sample size of 384 youths through a self-administer five-point Likert scale-based questionnaire. For data analysis, exploratory factor analysis, and multiple regression analysis, and a Mann-Whitney U test has been adopted. The empirical findings reveal that the female consumers are more likely than male consumers to purchase green items. The results of the study will provide better understanding of different factors that can influence purchase intention towards sustainable fashion and offer some useful insights to help the marketers and firms.

Chapter 12
Can Asia Accomplish the Sustainable Development Goal for Water and Sanitation by 2030? 198
    Madhuri Yadav, Indira Gandhi National Tribal University, India
    Sukanta Kumar Baral, Indira Gandhi National Tribal University, India

The SDGs are a global call to action to eradicate poverty, protect the natural environment, and ensure everyone lives in prosperity and peace. Asian countries to achieve the United Nations SDGs, particularly SDG 6 are concerned with providing all sanitation and water systems that are addressed sustainably. To evaluate a composite index (CI) for SDG 6 in Asia, data has been taken for water stress, basic drinking water, and sanitation facilities for 41 of the 48 Asian countries. According to the findings, the countries that scored highest in the assessment, such as Kuwait, United Arab Emirates, Turkmenistan, Bahrain, Saudi Arabia, Qatar, and Israel, and might be achieved SDG 6. Whereas the three countries (Cambodia, Afghanistan, and Timor- Lee) that showed low scores in both indicators of SDG6 also had lower overall points in the water and sanitation and water stress-related SDG Composite index. The SDGs provide a framework for sustainable development and guide policies and programs at the global, nationwide, and regional levels.

Chapter 13
Achieving a Picturesque Global Green Economy by Sustainable Consumption and Production (SCP): Green Economy and Sustainable Development 213
    Ayush Khandelwal, Mahatma Jyotiba Phule Rohilkhand University, India
    Yukta Chawla, Mahatma Jyotiba Phule Rohilkhand University, India
    Harshit Saxena, ICAR-IVRI University (Deemed), India

The necessity for investments or financing of sustainable consumption and production is highlighted by the green economy. However, unsustainable patterns of consumption and production are the root causes of the triple planetary crisis of climate change, biodiversity loss, and pollution. SCP system aims to build recovery plans and improve production and consumption patterns toward a sustainable future. Now, SCP is accelerating opportunities in green jobs, managing resources that are scarce and valuable, expanding the market for more sustainable products and increasing the contribution of economic activities, and also contributing substantially to poverty alleviation and the transition towards low-carbon and greener economies. Hence, this chapter gives insights into promoting eco-friendly resources, efficient energy utilization, and approaches for achieving global sustainable economic growth.

Chapter 14
Constructing New Greener Infrastructures, Retrofitting, and Exploiting the Potential of Smart Technologies 230

    Tarun Madan Kanade, Vishwakarma University, India
    Radhakrishna Batule, Vishwakarma University, India

Humans made a common habit and became dependent on others, the main dependency is on mother nature and making the most of its benefits which are provided in the forms of food, clean water, clean air, climate regulation, materials, etc. The known fact that all these commodities are free of cost and in unlimited supply available, humans are using them in abundant quantity without giving anything in return for retaining it, and this is not at all appreciated by intellectual humans. This is giving rise to humans who are nature lovers creating some alternative or substitute for such nature. This can be termed as natural building or rebuilding the green environment. Day-to-day innovations in science gave rise to smart technologies which can be used in building and maintaining green infrastructure. As known to all that the GI can be implemented in multiple sectors at various locations, the authors will be highlighting the sites where it can be implemented, which related technology will be used in deploying such GI, and what will be their benefits to humans.

Chapter 15
Green Manufacturing: Opening Doors to Greener Economy 247

    Arpita Nayak, KIIT School of Management, KIIT University, India
    Ipseeta Satpathy, KIIT School of Management, KIIT University, India
    B. C. M. Patnaik, KIIT School of Management, KIIT University, India
    Sukanta Kumar Baral, Indira Gandhi National Tribal University, India
    Atmika Patnaik, King's College, UK

The goal of this work is to provide an overview of the different advantages of green manufacturing to society, it is a step taken towards a greener economy. This analysis comprises approximately 47+ published research articles on this topic. The evaluation covers papers from prominent publications as well as general management journals with significant links to the topic. This chapter makes a significant contribution to theory by giving insights into the advantages of green manufacturing and its impact on a greener economy, and it draws on various works of literature and numerous theoretical perspectives to get a more thorough understanding of green manufacturing's influence on society, the environment, and the economy. The chapter also addresses the integrated perspective's consequences for philosophy and practice. This study states the advantages of green manufacturing adoption by some of the organizations in our society.

Chapter 16
Factors Influencing Green Purchase Intention Among Food Retail Consumers: An Empirical Study on Uttar Pradesh 265

    Nikita Sharma, Amity University, Noida, India
    Shivani Mehta, Amity University, Noida, India

The main objective of the study is to investigate the factors influencing the green purchase intention of Indian food retail consumers using the theory of planned behavior (TPB). Additionally, the study also aims to determine the effect of green consciousness and health consciousness over green purchase intention among Indian food retail consumers and give suggestive measures for effective implementation of green policies and green practices of the consumers. The study is conducted based on the quantitative as well as qualitative approach, with data collected from 384 Indian consumers of Uttar Pradesh through a self-administered five-point rating questionnaire. Exploratory factor analysis, and regression analysis are adopted for the data analysis to identify the predictors of green purchase intention of the consumers, highlighting the importance of subjective norms, environmental knowledge, green consciousness, and health consciousness, which are positively and significantly influenced the green purchase intention with consumer attitude being least significant variable in the study.

Chapter 17
Conversion of Cellulosic Raw Feed Stock Into Cellulose Nanocrystals (CNC): Methods, Characterization, and Novel Applications 283
    Sunil Jayant Kulkarni, Gharda Institute of Technology, India

Over the period, cellulosic biomass and wood were used as a source of energy, clothing, construction material. Cellulose can be modified into microcrystalline and nanocrystalline form for better mechanical and antimicrobial properties. Wood contains 40 to 60% cellulose whereas cotton, 90%. In nanotechnology, the material is disintegrated to have at least one dimension in nanoscale (1 to 100 nanometre). Nanosized particles have unique properties. Nanocellulose can be isolated from cellulosic materials that are abundantly available in nature. Cellulose nanocrystals can be obtained by alkaline treatment, bleaching, hydrolysis, and dewatering route. The crystallinity index of derived CNC varies from 52 to 99%. Sugarcane peel fiber was reported to have a maximum of 99.2% crystallinity. Combination of CNC with other materials, this can yield better and desired properties. Water sensibility and permeability can be minimized for their application in films by adding citric acid in the structure.

Chapter 18
Inching Towards Sustainability in Developing Countries: An Analysis of the Food Industry – A Case Study of India 301
    Anahita Sawhney, Amity University, Noida, India
    Pooja Mehra, Amity University, Noida, India

Sustainable development stands on three core elements: environment, economy, and social equity. The environment is under constant pressure from a long list of hazards. Even though there have been various innovations and developments of new practices to reduce the pressure and tackle the negative externalities, there still seems to be a long way to go. This chapter lays its entire focus on the sustainable consumption and production patterns of the food industry in the developing countries, while paying special attention to India and the impacts it has on the human habitat. The current state of the environment calls for the innovation of methods which lead to an efficient future. To understand more of this, a study was run on the people of Delhi, NCR so as to understand their current degree of awareness about sustainability, their consumption behaviours, and the importance laid on sustainability. The impact of factors like price, nutrition, taste, availability, convenience, sustainability, brand reputation, and packaging were also highlighted.

Chapter 19
Greener Economy for Sustainable Development Through AI Intervention: Demystifying Critical Factors.. 327

    Prajnya Paramita Pradhan, KIIT School of Management, KIIT University, Bhubaneswar, India
    Abhiraj Malia, KIIT School of Management, KIIT University, India
    Biswajit Das, KIIT School of Management, KIIT University, India
    Bhubaneswari Bisoyi, Sri Sri University, Cuttack, India
    Ipseeta Satpathy, KIIT School of Management, KIIT University, India

This research chapter deals with understanding the concept of the sustainable ecosystem through the development of a greener economy, and managing the environment for socio-eco environmental growth. The chapter introspects to understand the implication of AI intervention for an eco-friendly economy. It's an exploration into the faces of inclusive growth and equitable equality in life betting natural disasters and environmental degradation towards a greener economy. It explores the cause and effect of climate change for promoting sustainable consumption and production growth and exploration of the potential of AI. The research essentially reviews, analysis, and explores qualitatively and quantitatively the concern of ensuring the consumption of sustainable order through a pattern of production under the ambit of SDG 17. Eventually, it will identify the essential critical factors that can combat the obstacle to greener economy for sustainable consumption by eradicating the restraining forces and measuring barriers that the producer and the consumer encounter towards sustainable peace.

Chapter 20
Green Finance Products and Investments in the Changing Business World....................................... 344

    Rajeev Sengupta, Dr. Vishwanath Karad MIT World Peace University, India
    Ameya Patil, Dr. Vishwanath Karad MIT World Peace University, India

There is a promulgation in the 21st century that those projects which are green should be given preference for financing, amid growing climate change concerns. As a result, green finance, which deals with financing sustainable projects, is in vogue. This study seeks to understand various investments in green finance as well as the green finance products such as green bonds and green insurance, along with vouching the use of weather derivatives for sustainable finance projects. The factors determining green finance are also incorporated, along with green fintech. The study finds that though investments in green finance are increasing, it is not enough. Government policy and support, innovativeness, and further awareness will determine the further investments in sustainable projects. The combination of fintech and green finance can help society to transition to near zero emissions, and protect the planet.

Chapter 21
Scaling Up of Wood Waste Utilization for Sustainable Green Future.. 358

    C. Shibu, Kerala Agricultural University, India
    Sunandani Chandel, Kerala Agricultural University, India
    Preeti Vats, Kerala Agricultural University, India

Utilization of wood waste for sustainable production is becoming increasingly important in the current environmental and economic scenario. Various types of wood waste are generated by different industries. The current practices of wood waste recycling and reuse exhibit several benefits and limitations. The various technological innovations include the production of biofuels, engineered wood products, nanomaterials, animal bedding, and other potential applications. The importance of using wood waste for sustainable production includes various technological, environmental, economic, and social implications. Thus, the scaling of wood waste utilization for sustainable green production is a new age tool that offers immense potential for achieving sustainable development goals.

Chapter 22
Preparation and Extraction of Alpha Cellulose and Synthesis of Microcrystalline Cellulose From Agro-Waste (Pineapple Leaves) 384
    Sunil Jayant Kulkarni, Gharda Institute of Technology, India
    Burhan Abdur Rasheed Kalshekar, Gharda Institute of Technology, India

Microcrystalline cellulose (C6H10O5) is purified, white free-flowing powder partially depolymerized cellulose prepared by treating alpha cellulose, obtained as a pulp from fibrous plant material. There are various fibrous materials such as rice husk, wheat husk, coconut husk, and cotton yarn, which contain cellulose can be used as a raw material. The chemical composition of these materials detects 65-70% cellulose content. The motive of our project is to highlight the significance of 3R's: Reduce, Reuse, and Recycle. There are many agricultural waste materials in our environment which can be recycled and transformed into new products. This project admitted this policy and chose the agricultural waste material of pineapple leaves. First pretreatment was done of the raw materials. Then they were given various chemical treatment such as acid hydrolysis, bleaching, etc. After successful extraction of alpha cellulose and microcrystalline cellulose, samples were sent for analysis which was FTIR the results showed the good quality of product was successfully extracted.

Chapter 23
Industry 4.0, Sustainable Manufacturing, Circular Economy, and Sustainable Business Models for Sustainable Development.. 398
    Saurabh Tiwari, University of Petroleum and Energy Studies, India
    Richa Goel, SCMS Noida, Symbiosis International University (Deemed), Pune, India

Current international issues include the emergence and application of Industry 4.0 (I4.0), a cutting-edge manufacturing system powered by information technology (IT), as well as the development of a sustainable society. The implications for sustainable development (SD) from the perspectives of sustainable manufacturing (SM), sustainable business models (SBM), and the circular economy (CE) have received a lot of attention. I4.0 adoption and implementation, sustainable supply chains, and smart factories are frequently the subjects of studies on sustainable manufacturing. Two recently developed research areas that concentrate on I4.0 adoption and implementation as well sustainable supply chains are the circular economy and sustainable business models. This chapter combines recent research developments in the disciplines of I4.0 and sustainability with the aid of the literature on the CE, SM, and SBM.

Compilation of References 416

About the Contributors 472

Index.. 479

Preface

Welcome to the new edition of *Handbook of Research on Sustainable Consumption and Production for Greener Economies*. As editors, we present this book as a valuable resource that addresses the pressing challenges and offers potential solutions to promote sustainable practices and transition towards greener economies.

Over the past fifty years, ensuring sustainable consumption and production patterns has become a global concern. The approval of Sustainable Development Goal 12, which aims to ensure sustainable consumption and production, highlights the need for systemic goals across societies. However, various barriers hinder the adoption of sustainable practices, and the increasing world population, coupled with changing consumption and production patterns, places immense pressure on the environment. Furthermore, natural disasters and environmental shocks have a significant impact on both health and the pursuit of greener economies. Addressing these challenges requires a comprehensive understanding of the interplay between various factors and the development of effective strategies.

In this new edition, we delve into the critical factors that encourage sustainable consumption and production patterns and offer insights into building greener economies. The book explores the barriers preventing individuals, consumers, and producers from adopting sustainable practices and proposes strategies to overcome them. It examines sustainable consumption behavior, production patterns, the green economy, and showcases successful examples of innovative sustainable business models.

The book emphasizes the importance of inclusive and equitable quality education, which promotes lifelong learning opportunities for a greener economy. It explores the links between gender inequality and environmental degradation, recognizing the role of gender equality in driving sustainability. Furthermore, the sustainable management of water resources and access to safe water and sanitation are crucial components of greener practices. The book also highlights the significance of energy efficiency and the increased use of renewable energy sources in mitigating climate change.

To achieve sustainable consumption and production, sustained, inclusive, and sustainable economic growth is vital. Constructing new greener infrastructures, retrofitting existing structures, and harnessing the potential of smart technologies are key steps towards greener economies. Additionally, the sound global management of natural resources and the environment plays a critical role in reducing inequities among countries.

Preserving and promoting the sustainable use of terrestrial ecosystems and combating desertification are crucial in fostering greener economies. Furthermore, promoting peaceful and inclusive societies supports sustainable consumption and product development. Lastly, revitalized and enhanced global partnerships that bring together governments, civil society, and the private sector are instrumental in driving collective action towards greener economies.

Preface

This new edition of "Sustainable Consumption and Production for Greener Economies" provides a comprehensive exploration of the challenges and solutions surrounding sustainable practices. By studying and implementing the insights presented in this book, individuals, organizations, governments, policymakers, and researchers can contribute to the development of greener economies and a more sustainable future.

We extend our gratitude to the authors for their dedicated research and contributions to this important subject matter. We also thank the contributors, reviewers, and publishing team for their valuable efforts in bringing this book to fruition.

Together, let us address the challenges and strive towards sustainable consumption, production, and greener economies.

Industrialization Impact on Climate Change an Examination of NICs

In this chapter, author İrem Yalkı focuses on investigating the impact of industrialization on environmental degradation in the Newly Industrialized Countries (NICs). The study utilizes the ecological footprint indicator to measure climate change. Key indicators such as GDP per capita, energy use, and fossil fuel consumption, which are closely associated with industrialization, are examined to assess the level of industrialization in these countries. The industrial structure of the NICs is also analyzed, considering the industry's contribution to GDP. Descriptive analysis is employed to establish the relationship between industrialization and climate change. The findings indicate that energy use in the NICs is significantly high, with a dominant reliance on fossil fuel consumption. Consequently, these indicators contribute to environmental degradation. The chapter emphasizes the increasing importance of policies in NICs as these indicators continue to rise over time. Urgent policy interventions are required to facilitate the transition to green economies and mitigate the adverse environmental impacts of industrialization in these countries. The insights provided in this chapter can inform policymakers, researchers, and stakeholders interested in addressing the environmental challenges associated with industrialization in the NICs.

Context Good Practices in Energy Matrix Focused Towards a Hydrogen Economy: Colombia Becoming the Colossus of the Hydrogen Economy and Sustainability in the Region

Authored by Pablo Ocampo, Jeffrey León, and David Blekhman, this chapter delves into the good practices and initiatives related to the energy matrix, with a specific focus on the transition towards a hydrogen economy in Colombia. The chapter presents a systematic analysis of deductive literature, highlighting the pivotal role of hydrogen fuel in driving the energy transition. Throughout the investigation, it becomes evident that Colombia is emerging as a leading player in energy transformation in Latin America. The country, along with Chile, Brazil, Uruguay, and Mexico, is actively investing in and pursuing the development of a hydrogen economy. Colombia's commitment to sustainability and its efforts in embracing hydrogen as a strategic energy source position it as a colossus of the hydrogen economy and sustainability in the region. This chapter documents various practices and initiatives undertaken in Colombia to support the transition towards a hydrogen economy. It sheds light on the country's leadership in energy transformation and its potential to become a key player in promoting sustainable energy practices in Latin America. By showcasing Colombia's experiences and successes, this research provides valuable insights and inspiration for policymakers, researchers, and industry professionals seeking to explore and implement similar approaches in their own contexts.

Application of Multi-Criteria Decision-Making Methods for the Underground Mining Method Selection

Authored by Stojance Mijalkovski, Omer Efe, and Kemajl Zeqiri, this chapter delves into the application of multi-criteria decision-making methods (MCDM) in the context of underground mining method selection. Mining poses numerous complex problems that require timely solutions, and considering multiple parameters is crucial to determine the optimal solution for a given problem. The authors highlight the significance of MCDM in addressing these complex tasks and discuss its widespread usage in solving mining-related problems. The chapter specifically focuses on the underground mining method selection, which is recognized as one of the most intricate challenges in mining. Selecting the most suitable method of mining excavation requires considering a multitude of influential parameters that serve as a basis for comparing mining methods. The authors examine the implementation of the EDAS (Evaluation based on Distance from Average Solution) method in solving the problem of underground mining method selection. They also present a comparison of results obtained through the application of several methods for multi-criteria decision-making, offering insights into their effectiveness. By comparing the obtained results, the chapter concludes by determining the most suitable mining method for a specific example. This research provides valuable guidance and recommendations for decision-makers in the mining industry, aiding them in making informed choices for underground mining method selection through the application of MCDM techniques.

Exploring Intention to Purchase Energy Efficient Home Appliances: An Extension of the Theory of Planned Behavior

Authored by Ahmed Chemseddine Bouarar, Kamel Mouloudj, Asma Makhlouf, and Smail Mouloudj, this chapter focuses on understanding the factors influencing the intention to purchase energy-efficient home appliances in Algeria. The detrimental effects of corporations' and individuals' irrational behavior on the environment, including increased energy consumption and depletion of natural resources, have prompted global researchers and practitioners to prioritize energy-saving behaviors. Using a convenience sample, data were collected through a questionnaire survey administered to consumers in three cities. The analysis was conducted on 193 valid questionnaires, allowing the authors to identify key factors influencing the intention to purchase energy-efficient home appliances in Algeria. The findings of the study indicate that attitude, subjective norms, perceived behavioral control (PBC), and environmental awareness have a positive impact on the intention to purchase energy-efficient home appliances. These factors play crucial roles in shaping consumers' behaviors and decisions regarding energy-efficient appliances. By uncovering the determinants of consumer intention to purchase energy-efficient home appliances, this chapter provides valuable insights for policymakers and practitioners. The research offers relevant policy recommendations aimed at stimulating consumers' intention to invest in energy-efficient appliances, thereby promoting sustainable consumption patterns and reducing energy consumption in Algeria. Researchers, policymakers, and professionals in the field of sustainable energy will find this

Preface

chapter beneficial in developing strategies and interventions to encourage the adoption of energy-efficient home appliances and foster environmentally conscious consumer behavior.

The Critical Impact of Sustainability Innovations on Green Supply Chains: Green Supply Chains

This chapter, authored by Saniye Yildirim Ozmutlu and Korhan Arun explores the critical impact of sustainability innovations on green supply chains. The authors highlight the increasing focus on environmental sustainability in business practices and the consequent growth of green supply chains. They emphasize the importance of planning and implementing green strategies in organizations. The chapter specifically examines environmental sustainability innovations as the driving force behind the transition from traditional supply chains to green supply chains. The authors conducted a study involving 172 waste management and recycling companies to investigate this relationship. They employed path analysis with partial least squares-based structural equation modeling to test the hypotheses. The findings of the study reveal a strong connection between green supply chains and improvements in resource conservation, energy reduction, managing environmental communication, and pollution. This underscores the significance of sustainability innovations in driving positive environmental outcomes within supply chains. The chapter provides valuable insights for organizations seeking to develop and implement green supply chain practices. It highlights the importance of sustainability innovations as catalysts for positive change and offers empirical evidence supporting the link between green supply chains and environmental improvements. Researchers, practitioners, and professionals in the field of supply chain management and sustainability will find this chapter informative and relevant. It contributes to the existing literature by examining the critical role of sustainability innovations in shaping green supply chains and offers practical implications for organizations striving for environmental sustainability in their supply chain operations.

Can Green Products and Services in the Insurance Industry be a Sustainable Measure?

Authored by Bibi Zaheenah Chummun, this chapter explores the potential of green products and services in the insurance industry as a sustainable measure. With sustainability gaining prominence across industries, including insurance, there is a growing interest in integrating sustainable practices into business operations. The chapter highlights the significance of sustainability in the insurance sector and the need for multi-dimensional interventions, such as eco-innovation and creativity, to foster sustainable insurance businesses. The increasing contradictions between economic growth and environmental concerns have become a global issue, necessitating efficient financial strategies to mitigate sustainable risks. To achieve success in the insurance business, insurers must continuously strive to differentiate themselves from competitors. One avenue for achieving this is through the development and offering of new green products and services. The green insurance movement represents a new wave in the industry, where insurers can align their offerings with potential sustainability goals. By embracing green products and services, insurers can contribute to sustainable practices and provide solutions for the environmental challenges faced by individuals and businesses. This chapter sheds light on the opportunities and benefits of adopting green products and services in the insurance industry. It provides insights into how insurers can leverage sustainability as a competitive advantage, contributing to the overall sustainability agenda.

The research presented in this chapter serves as a valuable resource for insurance professionals, policymakers, and researchers seeking to explore sustainable measures within the insurance sector.

Smart Non-Invasive Approach for Workspace Rating Assessment: A Post-Occupancy Evaluation Approach for University Buildings

This chapter, authored by Adyasha Swain, presents a non-invasive approach for assessing the workspace rating of university buildings through a customized post-occupancy evaluation (POE) software application. The author focuses on improving facility management practices and enhancing students' exposure to and utilization of real-time data. The chapter begins by discussing the need to involve students in facility management activities and enhance their understanding of the validation process. The author emphasizes the importance of gathering and utilizing real-time data to demonstrate the feasibility of student involvement and improve the perception of indoor conditions. A mobile application is developed to collect data on occupants' perceptions in real-time and ensure the availability of up-to-date information for analysis. The selection of lighting and space usage parameters is guided by physical parameters that correspond to perceived indoor conditions. The chapter showcases the pilot project, providing an immediate representation of the gathered data and demonstrating the functionality of the POE app. The author discusses the potential for further statistical assessment based on the collected data. The application prototype is tested in a real-world university building, highlighting its adaptability, viability, and capacity to gather and analyze real-time building performance data. The author emphasizes the significance of this approach in improving workspace ratings and informing facility management decisions. This chapter serves as a valuable resource for researchers, facility managers, and professionals in the field of building performance assessment. It offers insights into the development and implementation of a non-invasive approach for workspace rating assessment, particularly in university buildings. The chapter demonstrates the potential of real-time data collection and analysis in enhancing facility management practices and student engagement. Overall, the chapter contributes to the advancement of post-occupancy evaluation methodologies and presents a practical approach for assessing workspace ratings in university buildings. It highlights the benefits of utilizing real-time data and emphasizes the importance of student involvement in facility management processes.

Where are We and What Should We do in Cleaner Production Transformation?

In this chapter, Elif Çaloğlu Büyükselçuk examines the current state of cleaner production transformation and outlines the necessary steps to be taken in this process. The author emphasizes the need for a new production approach that prioritizes environmental sustainability, in contrast to traditional models focused solely on cost reduction and profitability. The detrimental effects of resource depletion, ecological imbalance, and threats to human health have necessitated a shift towards a more sustainable production paradigm. Recognizing the global significance of these environmental challenges, there is a growing realization that development and economic growth must be redefined to address environmental pressures, emerging markets, and limited resources. The chapter highlights the limitations of traditional production methods and environmental technologies in achieving resource efficiency and environmental performance. It argues that new systems, processes, and technologies are required to reshape industries and establish green business models that align with sustainable practices. The cleaner production approach is discussed as a crucial framework for driving this transformation. The chapter explores how

Preface

cleaner production practices can contribute to sustainability efforts, considering the specific context of green transformation in Turkey and the current state of the country's industry. This chapter serves as a guide for understanding the importance of cleaner production in achieving environmental sustainability goals. It provides insights into the challenges and opportunities associated with the transition towards cleaner production methods and offers recommendations for policymakers, industry stakeholders, and researchers seeking to drive sustainable change. Researchers, practitioners, and policymakers interested in sustainable production and industrial transformation will find this chapter informative and valuable. It contributes to the existing literature by examining the role of cleaner production in addressing environmental concerns and offers a perspective on the current situation and future trajectory of cleaner production practices, particularly within the Turkish industry.

Artificial Intelligence Retrofitting for Smart City Strategies in the Context of India's Growing Population

Authored by Pushpam Singh, Madhuri Yadav, and Sukanta Kumar Baral, this chapter focuses on the integration of artificial intelligence (AI) into smart city strategies, particularly in the context of India's growing population. The rapid urban growth in India poses various challenges, and AI has emerged as a potential solution to address these issues. The chapter explores the implementation of AI in smart city strategies in five leading smart city countries: Singapore, Zurich, Oslo, Taipei City, and Lausanne. By analyzing the strategies employed in these countries, the authors highlight their applicability to the Indian smart city context. The study utilizes quantitative data gathered from secondary sources such as government websites, journals, articles, and online books. The authors employ R programming to showcase the statistical performance of the five countries and compare them with area-based developmental projects in India. By examining the findings of the study, the chapter provides valuable insights for decision-makers, professionals, and academicians involved in smart city planning. The research offers a deeper understanding of the potential opportunities associated with the widespread implementation of AI in the Indian context. This knowledge will aid stakeholders in making more informed choices and developing effective strategies for smart city development, ultimately contributing to the sustainable and efficient management of India's growing urban population.

Green Bonds for Mobilising Environmental Finance: A Conceptual Framework for a Greener Economy

Authored by Sreelekshmi G and Biju A V, this chapter delves into the concept of green bonds and their significance in mobilizing environmental finance to promote a greener economy. With sustainability contingent upon adequate financial resources, green bonds have emerged as an innovative mechanism for directing capital towards environmental and sustainable initiatives. The chapter employs a systematic evaluation of the existing literature, global green bond frameworks, and previous issuances to develop a comprehensive understanding of green bonds and their role in achieving sustainable development. Specifically, the authors focus on the potential of green bonds in supporting the objectives outlined in UN Sustainable Development Goal (SDG) 12, which pertains to responsible consumption and production. The findings of the study indicate that green bonds hold immense potential for financing infrastructure that facilitates responsible production and consumption practices. By investing in projects aligned with sustainability principles, green bond issuances contribute to the overall sustainability agenda and generate various benefits. The interdependencies among the pillars of sustainability are highlighted, showcasing the holistic impact derived from the utilization of green bonds. This chapter provides valuable insights into the realm of green finance and its potential to drive positive environmental outcomes. It offers a conceptual framework for understanding the mechanisms and implications of green bonds, ultimately supporting the transition towards a greener economy. Professionals, researchers, policymakers, and practitioners involved in sustainable finance, environmental economics, and green investment will find this chapter informative and relevant to their work. The conceptual framework and analysis presented in this chapter contribute to the existing knowledge on green bonds and their role in promoting sustainable development.

Factors Affecting Purchase Intention of Indian Youths: Special Reference to Textile and Clothing Industry

Authored by Akamsha Krishnan and Shivani Mehta, this chapter focuses on identifying the factors that influence the purchase intention of Indian youths when buying green clothes and textiles in the context of the textile and clothing industry. The study employs the Theory of Planned Behavior (TPB) and Theory of Reasoned Actions (TRA) to understand consumer behavior and investigates gender disparities in green purchasing intentions. Combining quantitative and qualitative methods, the study gathers data through a self-administered questionnaire using a five-point Likert scale. The sample size consists of 384 youths. The collected data is analyzed using exploratory factor analysis, multiple regression analysis, and the Mann-Whitney U test. The empirical findings of the study reveal that female consumers demonstrate a higher likelihood of purchasing green items compared to male consumers. This indicates a gender disparity in green purchasing intentions among Indian youths. The study provides valuable insights into the various factors that influence purchase intention towards sustainable fashion, shedding light on consumer behavior in the textile and clothing industry. The results of this research contribute to a better understanding of the factors that shape purchase intentions related to sustainable fashion among Indian youths. The chapter offers useful insights for marketers and firms operating in the textile and clothing industry, helping them tailor their strategies and offerings to align with the preferences and intentions of the target market. Researchers, practitioners, and professionals in the field of sustainable fashion and consumer behavior will find this chapter beneficial in understanding the dynamics of green purchasing intentions among Indian youths and devising effective strategies to promote sustainable choices in the textile and clothing industry.

Can Asia Accomplish the Sustainable Development Goal for Water and Sanitation by 2030?

Authored by Madhuri Yadav and Sukanta Kumar Baral, this chapter explores the feasibility of Asian countries achieving the Sustainable Development Goal (SDG) for water and sanitation, specifically SDG 6, by the year 2030. The SDGs serve as a global call to action to address poverty, protect the environment, and ensure prosperity and peace for all. The chapter focuses on Asian countries' efforts to meet SDG 6, which aims to provide sustainable access to sanitation and water systems for all. To assess the progress in this regard, the authors develop a composite index (CI) for SDG 6 in Asia. The CI takes into account indicators such as water stress, access to basic drinking water, and sanitation facilities. Data from 41 out of the 48 Asian countries is analyzed to evaluate their performance. Based on the findings, the chapter

Preface

highlights the countries that have scored highest in the assessment, including Kuwait, United Arab Emirates, Turkmenistan, Bahrain, Saudi Arabia, Qatar, and Israel. These countries demonstrate potential to achieve SDG 6. Conversely, countries like Cambodia, Afghanistan, and Timor-Leste show lower scores in both SDG 6 indicators, indicating significant challenges in water and sanitation access. Their overall performance in the water and sanitation domain and the water stress-related SDG Composite index is comparatively lower. The chapter emphasizes that the SDGs provide a comprehensive framework for sustainable development and serve as guiding principles for policies and programs at the global, national, and regional levels. By examining the progress and challenges faced by Asian countries in achieving SDG 6, this research contributes to the understanding of the region's efforts towards sustainable water and sanitation practices, ultimately aiding decision-makers and policymakers in developing targeted strategies to meet the SDGs by 2030.

Achieving Picturesque of Global Green Economy by Sustainable Consumption and Production (SCP): Green Economy and Sustainable Development

Authored by Ayush Khandelwal, Yukta Chawla, and Harshit Saxena, this chapter focuses on the need to address higher consumer classes and rising consumption levels within the framework of sustainable consumption and production (SCP). The authors highlight the importance of investments and financing in sustainable practices, as emphasized by the concept of the green economy. The chapter sheds light on the adverse effects of unsustainable consumption and production patterns, which contribute to the triple planetary crisis of climate change, biodiversity loss, and pollution. By discussing the SCP system, the authors delve into the development of recovery plans and the improvement of production and consumption patterns towards a sustainable future. The chapter also explores how SCP accelerates opportunities in green jobs, manages scarce and valuable resources, expands the market for sustainable products, and contributes to poverty alleviation and the transition towards low-carbon and greener economies. Through this comprehensive analysis, the chapter provides valuable insights into promoting eco-friendly resources, efficient energy utilization, and approaches for achieving global sustainable economic growth.

New Greener Infrastructures, Retrofitting, and Exploiting the Potential of Smart Technologies

In this chapter, Tarun Kanade and Radhakrishna Batule address the concept of sustainable consumption and production as a means to achieve greener economies. The authors emphasize the need to shift from a dependency on natural resources without providing anything in return, towards the construction of new greener infrastructures and the retrofitting of existing ones. The chapter starts by discussing the common habit of humans relying on nature's benefits, such as food, clean water, clean air, and climate regulation, without giving back or appreciating the value of these resources. This unsustainable approach is criticized, and the authors advocate for the development of alternative solutions and the rebuilding of the green environment. The authors highlight the role of smart technologies in constructing and maintaining green infrastructure. They explore the innovations in science that have given rise to these technologies, which can be utilized in various sectors and locations. The chapter focuses on identifying suitable sites for implementing green infrastructure, determining the relevant technologies for deployment, and highlighting the benefits that these technologies can bring to humans and the environment. Overall, this chapter provides insights into the importance of sustainable consumption and production for achieving greener economies. It emphasizes the need to move away from resource depletion and towards the development of new greener infrastructures. The chapter also explores the potential of smart technologies in this context, showcasing their role in constructing and maintaining sustainable infrastructure. Researchers, policymakers, and professionals interested in sustainable development, green infrastructure, and smart technologies will find this chapter valuable. It offers a comprehensive overview of the concepts, challenges, and opportunities associated with sustainable consumption and production, and provides practical insights into constructing new greener infrastructures and leveraging smart technologies for a sustainable future.

Green Manufacturing: Opening Doors to Greener Economy

In this chapter, the authors Arpita Nayak, Ipseeta Satpathy, B.C.M. Patnaik, Sukanta Kumar Baral, and Atmika Patnaik present an overview of the advantages of green manufacturing and its role in fostering a greener economy. The analysis is based on a comprehensive review of more than 47 published research articles, encompassing both specialized and general management journals. The findings of the study contribute to existing theoretical knowledge by highlighting the positive impact of green manufacturing on society, the environment, and the economy. The chapter emphasizes the importance of adopting green manufacturing practices and explores their implications for philosophy and practical implementation. By showcasing the experiences of organizations that have embraced green manufacturing, this chapter provides valuable insights and serves as a general review of the field. Overall, it underscores the significance of green manufacturing as a catalyst for sustainable economic growth and offers a valuable resource for researchers and practitioners interested in this domain.

Factors Influencing Green Purchase Intention Among Food Retail Consumers: An Empirical Study On Uttar Pradesh

Authored by Nikita Sharma and Shivani Mehta, this chapter focuses on investigating the factors that influence the green purchase intention of Indian food retail consumers, specifically in the context of Uttar Pradesh. The study employs the Theory of Planned Behavior (TPB) to understand consumer behavior and explores the impact of green consciousness and health consciousness on green purchase intention among Indian food retail consumers. The chapter also provides suggestive measures for the effective implementation of green policies and practices by consumers. The study adopts a mixed-methods approach, collecting data from 384 Indian consumers in Uttar Pradesh through a self-administered questionnaire using a five-point rating scale. The data is analyzed using exploratory factor analysis and regression analysis to identify the predictors of green purchase intention among consumers. The empirical findings highlight the significance of subjective norms, environmental knowledge, green consciousness, and health consciousness as key factors positively and significantly influencing green purchase intention. Interestingly, consumer attitude is found to be the least significant variable in the study. These results shed light on the specific factors that shape the green purchase intention of food retail consumers in Uttar Pradesh. The chapter provides valuable insights for policymakers, marketers, and practitioners in the food retail industry, offering guidance on the effective implementation of green policies and practices. By understanding the factors that drive green purchase intention, stakeholders can tailor their strategies and initiatives to encourage sustainable choices among consumers. This research contributes to the existing body of knowledge on green consumer behavior in the Indian context, specifically within the food

Preface

retail sector. Professionals and researchers in the fields of sustainable marketing, consumer behavior, and environmental sustainability will find this chapter informative and relevant to their work.

Conversion of Cellulosic Raw Feed Stock into Cellulose Nanocrystals (CNC): Methods, Characterization and Novel Applications

Authored by Sunil Kulkarni, this chapter focuses on the conversion of cellulosic raw feedstock into cellulose nanocrystals (CNC) and explores the methods, characterization techniques, and novel applications of CNC. Cellulosic biomass, such as wood and cotton, has been historically utilized for energy, clothing, and construction materials. However, by modifying cellulose into microcrystalline and nanocrystalline forms, its mechanical and antimicrobial properties can be significantly enhanced. The chapter highlights that wood typically contains 40 to 60% cellulose, while cotton has a higher cellulose content of around 90%. In the field of nanotechnology, materials are disintegrated to achieve at least one dimension in the nanoscale range of 1 to 100 nanometers, leading to unique properties associated with nanosized particles. Nanocellulose, derived from abundant cellulosic materials found in nature, can be isolated through processes such as alkaline treatment, bleaching, hydrolysis, and dewatering. The resulting cellulose nanocrystals exhibit varying crystallinity indexes, ranging from 52 to 99%. Notably, sugarcane peel fiber has been reported to have a maximum crystallinity index of 99.2%. The chapter further explores the combination of cellulose nanocrystals with other materials, highlighting the potential for achieving improved and desired properties through such synergistic approaches. For example, the addition of citric acid in the structure of CNC-based films can minimize water sensitivity and permeability, expanding their applications. By providing insights into the methods of obtaining cellulose nanocrystals, their characterization techniques, and the possibilities for their utilization in various novel applications, this chapter contributes to the understanding and exploration of CNC as a versatile nanomaterial. Researchers, scientists, and industry professionals seeking to leverage the unique properties of CNC in their work will find this chapter informative and valuable.

Inching Towards Sustainability in Developing Countries: An Analysis of the Food Industry—A Case Study of India

This chapter authored by Anahita Sawhney and Pooja Mehra focuses on the concept of sustainable development and its three core elements: environment, economy, and social equity. The authors highlight the constant pressure on the environment and the need for innovative practices to reduce negative externalities. The specific context of the food industry in developing countries, with a special emphasis on India, is examined to understand the implications for sustainable consumption and production patterns. The study conducts research on the people of Delhi, NCR, to assess their awareness of sustainability, consumption behaviors, and the importance they place on sustainable practices. Factors such as price, nutrition, taste, availability, convenience, sustainability, brand reputation, and packaging are analyzed to determine their impact on consumer choices. By providing insights into the current state of sustainability in the food industry, this chapter aims to contribute to the development of more efficient and sustainable practices. The findings and recommendations from this case study can inform policymakers, industry stakeholders, and consumers in developing countries seeking to advance sustainability in the food sector.

Greener Economy for Sustainable Development Through AI Intervention Demystifying Critical Factors

In this chapter, the authors Prajnya Pradhan, Abhiraj Malia, Biswajit Das, Bhubaneswari Bisoyi, and Ipseeta Satpathy delve into the concept of a sustainable ecosystem and its relationship with the development of a greener economy. The focus is on managing the environment in a way that promotes socio-economic growth while addressing environmental challenges. The chapter explores the implications of AI intervention in fostering an eco-friendly economy, aiming for inclusive growth and equitable equality in the face of natural disasters and environmental degradation. It investigates the cause and effect of climate change and its impact on promoting sustainable consumption and production. The potential of AI is examined in the context of achieving the goals outlined in SDG 17. Through a qualitative and quantitative analysis, the chapter reviews and explores the concerns surrounding sustainable consumption patterns and production practices. The ultimate objective is to identify critical factors that can overcome barriers and obstacles to creating a greener economy for sustainable peace. This chapter provides valuable insights and recommendations for policymakers, researchers, producers, and consumers interested in driving sustainable development through AI intervention.

Green Finance Products and Investments in the Changing Business World

In this chapter, the authors Rajeev Semgupta and Ameya Patil, delve into the growing significance of green finance in the 21st century and its implications for sustainable projects. The focus is on understanding various investments in green finance and exploring green finance products such as green bonds, green insurance, and weather derivatives. The chapter also examines the factors that determine the success of green finance initiatives, including government policies, support mechanisms, innovation, and raising awareness. Additionally, the authors highlight the potential of green fintech in facilitating the transition to a low-carbon economy and protecting the environment. Overall, this chapter provides valuable insights into the evolving landscape of green finance and its role in driving sustainable development.

Scaling up of Wood Waste Utilization for Sustainable Green Future

This chapter by Shibu C, Sunandani Chandel, and Preeti Vats focuses on the utilization of wood waste for sustainable production and its significance in achieving a greener future. The authors highlight the increasing importance of wood waste utilization in the current environmental and economic scenario. The chapter begins by discussing the various types of wood waste generated by different industries and the need for effective recycling and reuse practices. The authors explore the benefits and limitations of current wood waste management practices. Technological innovations in wood waste utilization are highlighted, including the production of biofuels, engineered wood products, nanomaterials, and animal bedding, among other potential applications. These innovations offer opportunities for sustainable production and contribute to environmental, economic, and social implications. The authors emphasize the importance of utilizing wood waste for sustainable production, citing its potential to address technological advancements, environmental challenges, and socioeconomic considerations. They argue that scaling up wood waste utilization is a crucial tool for achieving sustainable development goals. This chapter serves as a comprehensive resource for researchers and practitioners interested in wood waste utilization and its potential for sustainable production. It provides insights into the various technological

Preface

innovations, benefits, and implications of scaling up wood waste utilization. The chapter emphasizes the role of wood waste in promoting a greener future and offers practical guidance for implementing sustainable practices in wood waste management. Overall, the chapter contributes to the understanding of wood waste utilization as a means to achieve sustainability and provides valuable insights into its applications and implications in the context of a sustainable green future.

Preparation And Extraction of Alpha Cellulose and Synthesis of Microcrystalline Cellulose from Agro-Waste (Pineapple Leaves)

This chapter authored by Sunil Kulkarni and Burhan Kalshekar focuses on the preparation and extraction of alpha cellulose and the synthesis of microcrystalline cellulose from agro-waste, specifically pineapple leaves. The authors emphasize the significance of the 3R's (Reduce, Reuse, Recycle) policy in utilizing agricultural waste materials to create new products. The chapter begins by discussing the raw materials that contain cellulose, such as rice husk, wheat husk, coconut husk, and cotton yarn, highlighting their cellulose content of around 65-70%. The authors then explain the importance of pineapple leaves as the chosen agricultural waste material for their project. The process starts with pretreatment of the raw materials, followed by various chemical treatments including acid hydrolysis and bleaching. The aim is to extract alpha cellulose and microcrystalline cellulose from the pineapple leaves. The extracted samples are then subjected to analysis, specifically Fourier-transform infrared spectroscopy (FTIR), to assess the quality of the product. Through this chapter, the authors showcase the successful extraction of alpha cellulose and microcrystalline cellulose from pineapple leaves, highlighting the potential of utilizing agro-waste for the production of valuable cellulose-based materials. This work contributes to the promotion of sustainable practices and the utilization of waste materials for the creation of new products. The chapter serves as a valuable resource for researchers and practitioners interested in cellulose extraction and the synthesis of microcrystalline cellulose from agricultural waste, specifically pineapple leaves. It provides insights into the process, analysis, and potential applications of these cellulose derivatives, emphasizing their role in sustainable and environmentally friendly practices.

Industry 4.0, Sustainable Manufacturing, Circular Economy, and Sustainable Business Models for Sustainable Development

In this chapter, authors Saurabh Tiwari and Richa Goel explore the intersection of Industry 4.0, sustainable manufacturing, circular economy, and sustainable business models in the context of sustainable development. It highlights the significance of Industry 4.0 as a modern manufacturing system driven by information technology (IT) and its implications for a sustainable society. The focus is on understanding how these concepts contribute to sustainable development from various perspectives. The chapter delves into the concept of sustainable manufacturing and its relationship with Industry 4.0, examining topics such as I4.0 adoption, implementation, sustainable supply chains, and smart factories. It also discusses the emerging research areas of circular economy and sustainable business models, exploring their connection with Industry 4.0 and sustainable manufacturing. By synthesizing recent research developments in Industry 4.0 and sustainability, the chapter aims to provide insights into the role of circular economy, sustainable manufacturing, and sustainable business models in achieving sustainable development. It draws upon literature on these topics to present a comprehensive overview and identify potential synergies and opportunities for integrating these concepts. This chapter serves as a valuable resource for researchers, practitioners, and policymakers interested in understanding the relationship between Industry 4.0, sustainable manufacturing, circular economy, and sustainable business models in the pursuit of sustainable development.

In conclusion, this edited reference book provides a comprehensive exploration of various topics related to sustainability and the transition towards greener economies. The chapters within this book delve into key areas such as green finance, green manufacturing, sustainable consumption and production, industrialization's impact on climate change, utilization of wood waste, workspace rating assessment, and the critical impact of sustainability innovations on green supply chains, among others.

Throughout the chapters, the authors present valuable insights, empirical evidence, and theoretical perspectives that shed light on the challenges and opportunities associated with achieving sustainability goals. They discuss the importance of adopting sustainable practices in different sectors, highlight innovative approaches and technologies, and examine the role of various stakeholders in driving the transition towards greener economies.

One overarching theme that emerges from the chapters is the recognition of the urgent need for change. The current environmental and economic landscape calls for a paradigm shift in how we produce, consume, and manage resources. The concepts of sustainability, circular economy, cleaner production, and green business models are no longer mere buzzwords, but crucial pathways to ensure a sustainable future for our planet and future generations.

The chapters also underscore the interconnectedness of sustainability issues and the need for multidisciplinary approaches. They emphasize the importance of collaboration among academia, industry, policymakers, and society as a whole to tackle the complex challenges we face. The insights and recommendations provided by the authors serve as valuable guidance for stakeholders in implementing practical solutions and driving systemic change.

As editors, we are grateful to the contributing authors for their rigorous research, thought-provoking analyses, and valuable contributions to this edited reference book. We believe that the diverse perspectives presented in this collection will inspire further research, policy development, and practical initiatives aimed at advancing sustainability and greener economies.

We hope that this edited reference book serves as a valuable resource for researchers, policymakers, industry professionals, and individuals interested in understanding and promoting sustainable development. By disseminating knowledge, encouraging dialogue, and fostering collaboration, we can collectively work towards a greener, more sustainable future.

Together, let us strive to create a world where economic prosperity, social equity, and environmental well-being go hand in hand, paving the way for a sustainable and thriving planet for generations to come.

Richa Goel
Amity University, India

Sukanta Kumar Baral
Indira Gandhi National Tribal University, India

Chapter 1
Industrialization Impact on Climate Change:
An Examination of NICs

İrem Yalkı
İstanbul Okan University, Turkey

ABSTRACT

This study aims at investigating the industrialization impact on environmental degradation in the newly industrialized countries (NICs). In order to measure climate change, the ecological footprint indicator is used. As GDPpc, energy use, and fossil fuel consumption are inextricably linked with industrialization, they are taken as the industrialization indicators. In addition to the industry level, also industry % of GDP is examined to determine the industrial structure of the countries. The study uses descriptive analysis to present the relationship between industrialization and climate change. The statistics show that energy use in NICs is at high levels, and fossil fuel consumption is dominant. Thus, the situation causes environmental degradation as these indicators act together. As the share of the NICs indicators has increased gradually over the years, the policies of these countries have significant importance. Therefore, they have to make urgent policies to transition to green economies.

1. INTRODUCTION

Climate change is one of the main threats that concern all countries over the last few decades. When the trend of environmental degradation in the world is analyzed during the 1961 – 2018 period, it is clearly seen a dramatic increase in the number of countries that have an ecological deficit. Based on the GFN (2023) ecological footprint vs biocapacity dataset, it is calculated that 89 of 132 countries had a higher biocapacity than their ecological footprint, while 43 countries had a higher ecological footprint than their biocapacity in 1961. The year 1970 is a turning point in this comparison due to the World's total ecological footprint exceeded its biocapacity. In this year, 79 of 141 countries had a higher biocapacity than their ecological footprint, and 62 had the opposite scenario. The gap between biocapacity and eco-

DOI: 10.4018/978-1-6684-8969-7.ch001

logical footprint, with a few exceptions, continues to deepen every year. In 2018, only 50 of 182 countries had a higher biocapacity than their ecological footprint. In other words, nearly 73% of countries in the world are facing environmental degradation. Even these simple statistics reveal why the issue becomes a crucial topic and concerns the whole world.

According to IPCC (2014) *"human activities are changing the climate"*. Energy-related CO_2 emissions are the main reason for climate change. In the same report, it is stated that CO_2 emissions originated from fossil fuel combustion and industrial processes are 78% of the total GHG emissions increase from 1970 to 2010 and a similar contribution is indicated for the 2000-2010 period. Thus, it is proof that the industrialization process causes climate change so countries have to make a choice between economic growth and combating climate change. So far, most high-income countries have begun their industrial process before climate change becomes a crucial concern and they have not taken into consideration the environmental degradation while aiming to achieve their economic growth targets. Moreover, it is observed that most of the newly industrialized countries follow the same path which makes industrialization a priority, and after the process has been completed the environment could become a topic (Okereke et al., 2019). So, it is expected that, after countries become developed they could have able to sustain their economic growth by enabling transmission to green economic activities (Rahman et al., 2021). This transmission requires decoupling industrialization from environmental impacts so the traditional type of manufacturing based on fossil fuels has to be changed. Not only this necessity but also the Paris Agreement limitation to CO_2 emissions, not to exceed 1.5^0C above pre-industrial levels UNFCCC (2015) forces countries to change their industrial processes. While it is observed that positive developments have been occurring in developed countries in order to adopt this transmission, the newly industrialized countries have been behind to take the necessary steps.

Thus, this study aims to examine the industrialization impact on climate change for the newly industrialized countries (NICs) by using descriptive analysis as a methodology. The NICs are listed as Brazil, China, India, Indonesia, Malaysia, Mexico, the Philippines, South Africa, Thailand, and Turkey. The NICs have particular importance as they are the newly industrialized country group it consists of some of the world's largest energy consumers so they cause a vast amount of CO_2 emissions (Rahman et al., 2021). Also, this country group has the 48.15% of the world's population in 2021. The population density of the NICs is not a new matter, when the population data is analyzed, it is seen that the lowest share is 46.55% and the highest share is 50.22% between the years 1960 – 2021 (The World Bank, 2023a). Considering the population density of the countries, the energy consumption levels of these countries are also of vital importance in terms of energy transformation.

To analyze the NICs industrialization process, the indicators are taken into account in the study as follows: GDP per capita, energy use, fossil fuel energy consumption, industry, and industry % of GDP. All of the indicators related to industrialization are taken from the World Bank (2023b-c). These indicators and ecological footprint indicators are evaluated together and it is clearly seen that they are in line with each other. Thus, this relationship provides to design policies. For this purpose, primary policies to prevent environmental degradation are also recommended.

The structure of the study is organized as follows: Section 2 reviews the relevant literature. Section 3 explains the relationship between industrialization and climate change then Section 4 explains the data and methodology then presents the statistics related to industrialization and climate change indicators. Section 5 concludes the statistical results and makes policy recommendations.

2. LITERATURE REVIEW

In the past few decades, environmental degradation has occurred as one of the biggest global challenges that affect all countries. The term environmental degradation started by referring to global warming. However, in recent years, it has started to be expressed as climate change, as environmental effects are not limited to global warming and affect many more factors. Thus, primarily this study seeks to contribute to the literature by taking into consideration all the factors related to environmental degradation. When environmental degradation is on the matter, most of the studies (Dong et al., 2019; Ghazali & Ali, 2019; Liu & Bae, 2018; Mahmood et al., 2020; Nasir et al., 2021; Rahman et al., 2021; Raihan et al., 2022; Q. Wang et al., 2018; Q. Wang & Su, 2019; Z. Wang et al., 2020; Zhu et al., 2017) use CO_2 emissions as the environmental indicator. But especially while investigating the industrialization impact on the environment, all the aspects of environmental degradation must be taken into account, not only CO_2 emissions, as industrialization also gives damage other factors related to the environment, such as the land, and ocean. For this reason, the ecological footprint (EF) indicator is taken as the environmental degradation in this study. The ecological footprint involves six environmental factors and these factors are; built-up land, carbon, cropland, fishing grounds, forest products, and grazing land (GFN, 2023). As it is calculated by including different aspects of pollution, the EF indicator is a more extensive and accurate indicator to represent the environmental degradation. To the best of knowledge, only a limited number of studies (Aluko et al., 2021; Ibrahim & Vo, 2021) use ecological footprint. Second contribution to the literature is that this study focuses not only on one country. As it is known that China is the leading countries that rapidly growth and cause CO_2 emissions, and many studies (Chien et al., 2023; R. Wang et al., 2019; S. Wang & Altiparmak, 2022; Zheng et al., 2016) concentrate on the country. However, given the importance of the NICs, it is essential to analyze the situation of these countries. Therefore, this study investigates all the newly industrialized countries and their trends together. Thus, this study aims to make a contribution to this literature gap by considering the ecological footprint and the NICs together. Since there are many studies that analyze climate change and industrialization together, only current studies that deal with the subject empirically are included in this part of the study.

Q. Wang et al. (2018) analyze the decoupling effect of economic growth from the CO_2 emissions for China and India between the years 1980 – 2014. The study also analyzes the effects of urbanization, industrialization, GDP per capita, and carbon emissions intensity to decoupling. For the decoupling effect, the study uses Tapio decoupling model, and for the other effects, the co-integration analysis and the impulse response function are applied. The model of the study established that the decoupling elasticity is the dependent variable, and urbanization, industrialization, GDP per capita, and carbon emission intensity are taken as the explanatory variables. The study divides the time period into four phases for the decoupling analysis and emphasizes that China and India have different decoupling statuses for the phases, and the countries individually do not have a particular decoupling status as well. The countries decoupling status differs within the periods. Co-integration estimate results show that in China, urbanization is the main factor of decoupling in the positive direction. GDP per capita follows urbanization but this time, in the negative direction. Industrialization and carbon emission intensity have a positive impact on decoupling elasticity as well. Similar to China, the order of the effects is the same in India, but the urbanization and GDP per capita effects are the opposite. Urbanization has the most remarkable effect but the effect is negative and GDP per capita has a positive effect on decoupling elasticity. Following them, industrialization and carbon emission intensity have positive effects as China. Then, the study analyzes the explanatory variables' paths on decoupling elasticity by using the impulse response function for the short and long run. The results of industrialization in China, the effect of industrialization is higher in the short run compared to the long run. In India, industrialization shows irregular positive and negative fluctuations and its effect gets smaller. Nasir et al. (2021) examine the impacts of economic growth, energy consumption, industrialization, trade openness, and financial development on environmental degradation in Australia for the years 1980 - 2014. The study takes CO_2 emissions to represent the environmental degradation factor, then to evaluate the other factors mentioned above, it is taken as respectively GDP per capita, energy use per capita, industry value added per capita, trade value per capita, and financial development indices. The study uses two different approaches which are EKC and STIRPAT to investigate the short and long run relationship. The results of the study denote that there is a causal relationship between all factors with CO_2 emissions in the short run, and the two approaches support the same result as well. Also, it is seen that the EKC did not occur for the country. In the long run, different findings are observed. While, financial development, energy consumption, and trade openness have a positive effect on CO_2 emissions in the long run, industrialization does not have a significant effect on CO_2 emissions. And as a result, it is stated that the situation should not be considered as the effect of industrialization on CO_2 emissions in the short run cannot lead to the long run. Mahmood et al. (2020) did research the effects of industrialization and urbanization on the CO_2 emissions per capita for the years between 1968 – 2014 in Saudi Arabia by using cointegration tests. The results of the study reveal that both factors have an impact on CO_2 emissions. In addition to this result, the study indicates the effect of industrialization is inelastic, while the urbanization effect is elastic. Also, the relationship between industrialization and CO_2 emissions is asymmetry, which means that increasing industrialization has a more significant effect on CO_2 than decreasing industrialization. In light of this information, the study recommends the Saudi government to strict policies for the environmental degradation. Q. Wang & Su (2019) investigate the decoupling of economic growth from CO_2 emissions using the Tapio decoupling index model in China between 1990 – 2016. Then, the study continues to analyze the effects of GDP, urbanization, industrialization, energy consumption structure, and technical progress between decoupling elasticity in the long term with the co-integration and Granger causality tests. Based on the decoupling results, approximately 70% of the years show weak decoupling, while strong decoupling is seen for 5 years, and expansive negative decoupling is seen for 3 years. In the long term, GDP and energy consumption structure positively effect decoupling elasticity, whereas the other factors have a negative effect. Also, it is expressed that the most significant negative factor is the technical progress so that it can be used as a tool for policymakers. The causality test results show that two-way Granger causality exists between decoupling elasticity and GDP, industrialization, energy consumption structure, and technical progress. For the urbanization, there is an unidirectional causality from decoupling elasticity to urbanization. With these findings, the study recommends the government to support the sustainable development and establish policies, which reduce CO_2 emissions taking into consideration the particular situation of China. Raihan et al. (2022) analyze the dynamic impacts of economic growth, renewable energy use, urbanization, industrialization, technological innovation, and forest area on CO_2 emissions from 1990 to 2019 in Bangladesh. To test the impacts, the Dynamic Ordinary Least Squares (DOLS) is used, and also the study investigates the causal relationship between the variables by using the Granger causality test. The DOLS results reveal that economic growth, urbanization, and industrialization variables have a significant and positive impact on CO_2 emissions, whereas renewable energy use, technological innovation, and forest area have a significant but negative impact. The study performs a detailed causality test among the variables and based on these outcomes, multi-directional policy recommendations take place for each variable. Dong et al. (2019) aim to explore the relationship between urbanization, industrialization, and CO_2 emissions from 1960 to 2013 for 14 developed economies by using the panel threshold regression model. The study divides the countries' CO_2 process into three stages, which are CO_2 intensity, per capita CO_2, and total CO_2 reached a peak. For every stage, the effects of urbanization and industrialization on CO_2 emissions are specified. The summarized results express that urbanization and income level both have a significant double-threshold effect on CO_2 emissions. In the case of urbanization, in the low urbanization stage, there is no significant correlation between them, but for the mid-urbanization stage, there is a significant and negative effect. Furthermore, when the level of urbanization moves on to the mid-urbanization stage, the effect turns into a promotional effect. For the income level, industrialization causes an increase in CO_2 emissions. The promotional effect is seen at the low and intermediate-income levels, whereas at the high-income level, the effect starts to lose its power and becomes weaker.

As can be seen from these studies, different results were observed on the subject according to countries and years. In addition, due to the special importance of the subject, more research is needed.

3. THE IMPACT OF INDUSTRIALIZATION ON CLIMATE CHANGE

3.1. Why Industrialization is a Matter of Environmental Degradation

Countries had to increase their energy use in order to enhance their economic growth. Energy sources could be classified as two main types as renewable and non-renewable. For non-renewable energy, it can also be defined as fossil fuels. And the main source for the CO_2 is using fossil fuels (Azam et al., 2021). Thus, it can be stated that when environmental degradation is the matter, there is no doubt that human activities are responsible for environmental crises. The main reason for the environmental degradation, or climate change, is the accelerating increase of CO_2 emissions since the industrial revolution. The industrial revolution led to more production and consumption activities, so aiming to meet the demand, production based on fossil fuels began to increase. As fossil fuels are the main cause of CO_2 emissions, industrialization is respected as one of the primary reasons for environmental degradation. Besides, increasing CO_2 emissions is not the only environmental impact that industrialization causes, it is also responsible for the loss of biodiversity, life on land, life below water, and so on. It puts pressure on the limits of the Earth. Apart from the direct effects, industrialization also has indirect effects such as an increase in population and urbanization that lead up to environmental degradation. So, as it signifies these three factors are strongly related to each other.

In Figure 1, the relationship between industry and its causal links is given. According to the study of Patnaik, (2018), it is organized for Puducherry region, but it is possible to interpret this picture in general by not limiting the industry effect to this region merely. As it clearly indicates that industry causes not only CO_2 emission problem, but also many other environmental degradations. Due to the limitations of the study, merely the environmental impact of the industry is examined in this study. However, as can be seen in Figure 1, industrialization has multiple dimensions. In order to solve the industrialization-related problems, it is crucial to investigate the root of the problems. Therefore; governance, law, incentives, technology, knowledge, and socio-cultural factors should be evaluated together aiming at making policy decisions.

Figure 1. The relationship between industry and its causal links
Source: *Patnaik. (2018).*

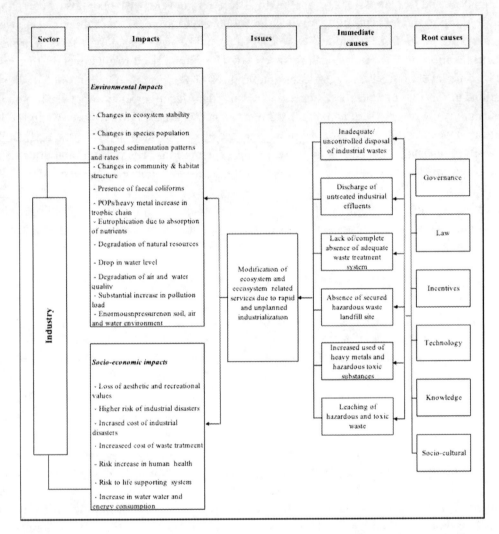

As it is mentioned in the literature section of the study, the effect of industrialization on CO_2 emissions has been studied widely. The results of the studies indicate that the effect of industrialization shows an alteration for each country or region at different times as well. Another crucial point for this situation is that if the country is a developed or developing country (Haraguchi et al., 2019). On the other hand, the Worlds' trends are the best guide while examining the linkages between ecological footprint and its causes. Thus, Figure 2 shows the relationship between the annual growth of industrialization, energy use, GDP, and ecological footprint series belonging to the World, and the period is between 1995 – 2014, due to accessing the available data for all the indicators. The indicators are represented as IND, EnU, GDP, and EF respectively, as it is represented in Figure 2.

Figure 2. The annual growth of IND, EnU, GDP, and EF in the world
Source: *It is calculated by the author using the World Bank and GFN datasets.*

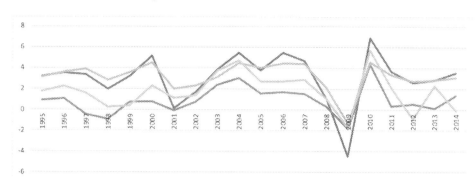

It is clearly seen that the tops and bottoms of all the indicators move together and follow the same trend over time in the graph. In addition to following the same trends, the striking ups and downs of the trends have almost exactly the same depths for the same years. Particularly, a sharp decrease was seen in industrialization more than the other indicators in 2009. But also, the other indicators showed a severe decline. Thus, it is out of the question to consider industrialization, energy use, GDP, and ecological footprint separately. This graph is proof that these indicators are strongly related and dependent on each other. Therefore, if the matter is to combat climate change, policies depending on energy use have to be assigned. As it is stated at the beginning of this chapter, GDP growth becomes with industrialization, and for industrialization, it is necessary to use energy. So, this process could be evaluated as an infinitive loop. The vital point here is whether the energy use is fossil fuels or not. This graph is crucial to see the World's trend, related to these indicators, it specifies the relationship between them, and relying on these trends policies can be made. In addition to this composition, it must be indicated that a positive development was observed in 2013. The EF started to decrease, whereas the other indicators continued to increase. So, the opposite direction between EF and other indicators is a critical point, which gives the idea that something can change through an encouraging process. But, on the other hand, it is not sufficient, it can only be counted as an improvement and it should be monitored if it continues in this trend, so the gap between them widens.

3.2. The Importance of the Relationship Between the Industrialization Process and Climate Change in NICs

Aiming at a high economic growth rate, most of the developed countries reached their peak levels of CO_2 emissions and remained constant or show a decrease (Aluko et al., 2021). Now, the turn comes to developing countries. Developing countries have been following the trends that developed countries experienced. The biggest share of the environmental degradation belongs to developing countries. Thus, NICs have a particular place in this situation. If these countries continue to act like the developed countries used to, it is inevitable to see environmental disasters. So, it is necessary to see the picture of the NICs' environmental situation and industrialization process together. Also, the other related factors' effect on these indicators has to be investigated. Therefore, environmental and industrialization-related indicators are presented for the NICs.

Figure 3. The NICs share of GDP, IND, and EF in the world
Source: *It is calculated by the author using the World Bank and GFN datasets.*

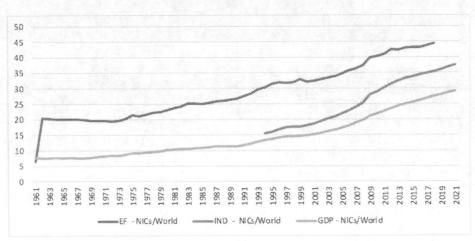

Figure 3 represents the NIC s share of GDP, IND, and EF share in the World following a positive and increasing trend. In 1961, the NICs' share of GDP in the World was 7.64%, and in 2018 it became 27.45%. The NICs' share of IND available data began in 1994, so in 1994 the value was 15.45%, then it was observed at 35.50% in 2018. Lastly, in 1961, the NICs' share of EF in the World was 6.63%, then, in 1962, a sudden and sharp leaping occurred and the share reached 20.45%. Continuing the increase in 2018, the share hit 45.55%. Thus, these increasing trends evidently blare out that NICs are in a critical position in the World. This situation also reveals the importance of the policies to be determined by these countries. So, this graph exhibits the significance of the NICs in the World.

4. DATA, METHODOLOGY, AND EXAMINATION FINDINGS

4.1. Methodology and Data

The study uses descriptive analysis to investigate the relationship between industrialization and climate change. To represent the trends of the indicators, the time series of the indicators are graphed. While interpreting the indicators, it is not sufficient to refer only the indicator itself. It is also necessary to indicate the percent change by the years, to see the turning points and fluctuations evidently and by this representation, it is possible to link them to the cases that cause these increases or decreases. Thus, in this study, the indicators and their annual % growth are taken place in this part. All the interpretations are based on these two different types of statistics linked to the same indicator.

The datasets are selected from two different databases. To represent climate change, the ecological footprint indicator is used. It is represented as EF and it consists of built-up land, carbon, cropland, fishing grounds, forest products, and grazing land factors. The ecological footprint is expressed as the unit of gha in total. In addition to EF, the per capita of the indicator is taken into consideration in order to see the change depending on the increasing population. These data sets are collected from the Global Footprint Network database. GDP per capita, energy use, fossil fuels energy consumption, industrialization, and industry % of GDP datasets are gained from the World Bank. They are represented as GDPpc, EnU, FFEC, IND, and IND %of GDP respectively. GDPpc is formed of GDP constant 2015 US$. Energy use is stated as a unit of kg of oil equivalent per capita. Fossil fuel energy consumption is the % of total energy consumption. Industrialization is expressed in terms of US$, and it is 2015 constant, the values include construction as well.

Except for GDPpc dataset, the other indicators datasets are not taken place as growth rate, therefore in the study, all the indicators are gained as raw data, and based on these raw datasets, the annual growth of the indicators are calculated by the author.

4.2. The Examination Representations and Findings

In this section of the study, the indicators, and their related factors are examined. In the first instance, the examination starts with the environmental indicators and then continues with the industrialization factors.

The ecological footprint per capita can be evaluated as the most accurate indicator to denote the environmental degradation, due to taking into account the increasing population impact. As it is clearly seen in the Figure 4 below, for all the countries that take place in the graph, their ecological footprint per capita indicators show an increasing trend. If their increasing levels are compared it is easy to observe that they do not follow the same trend, even though they are all on an uptrend. If it is desired to try the classify the trend similarities of the countries among themselves in general, it can be pointed out that China has a particular and devastating increasing trend, which does not resemble any other country. Generally, it can be expressed that the overall trend of India, Indonesia, and the Philippines have similar trends that display less fluctuations compared to the other countries. On the other hand, Malaysia, Mexico, South Africa, Thailand, and Turkey show more variations in different times of their trends. In Brazil, the trend is in between these situations. It has more fluctuations than the first group, but a smoother trend than the second group of countries.

While interpreting the ecological footprint per capita indicator, the biocapacity per capita indicator cannot be held separately. It is the only way to observe the turning points the ecological footprint exceeds the biocapacity of the country. The vital treat about the biocapacity is that it is hellacious to increase the capacity. Through the instrument of technology and innovation, it is possible to use the resources more efficiently but it has limitations to increase the capacity, thus the option is not a sufficient one that can be relied on. On the contrary, associated with the rapidly increasing population, the biocapacity per capita shows tendency to decrease. Thus, it is crucial to determine the year, in which the ecological footprint exceeds the biocapacity, in other words, an ecological deficit occurs.

According to the GFN (2023), ecological footprint vs biocapacity (gha per capita) dataset, 1970 is the year the World's ecological footprint equals its biocapacity then the equilibrium turns to start devastation for biocapacity. Based on the available data in 1961, the biocapacity per capita (BCpc) was 3,15 while the ecological footprint per capita (EFpc) was 2,28. The values for the same indicators were 1,58 and 2,77 respectively in 2018. Furthermore, 2018 is the year that the gap between BCpc and EFpc becomes the maximum level. While the BCpc is decreasing, EFpc continues to increase, therefore the range is getting deeper every year. For the NICs, Brazil and India exhibit opposite exceptions. BCpc of Brazil is higher than its EFpc for all the years, whereas India presents a reverse situation. If the countries are listed depending on their turning points in chronological order; it is seen that China, the Philippines, and South Africa were the first countries to experience the situation among the NICs in the year 1964. Then Mexico and Turkey followed them in the year 1977. At this place, Turkey sets out an unusual structure.

Figure 4. The ecological footprint, per capita in the NICs and in the world
Source: *It is compiled by the author using the GFN (2023) dataset.*

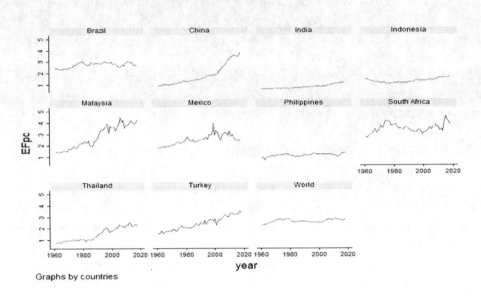

When a country's EFpc value exceeds its BCpc, the width expands without some exceptions as they are the usual fluctuations. But it is not usually observed the BCpc exceeds the EFpc. Exceptionally, after Turkey's EFpc exceeded its BCpc in 1977, the following two years, BCpc became higher than EFpc again then in 1980, it maintains the ecological deficit. The remained countries come along with different turning points. Thailand, Malaysia, and Indonesia came to the ecological deficit levels in the years 1988, 1993, and 2000 respectively. As it is obvious from the statistics given above, the NICs' transition to an ecologic deficit state occurs since a long time period. The latest year observed was 2000, which is 23 years ago. Thus, for NICs, the environmental degradation is a major threat.

It is mentioned that EFpc is an accurate indicator to see the picture of environmental degradation. But also, EF data has to be interpreted to visualize the general degradation.

In Figure 5, the ecological footprint, total gha in NICs except for China and the World is given. Owing to the values of the World and China are enormously high, the other countries' trends are seen as stable, but actually it is not the case. This structure occurs since the values of the World and China cause deviation, and it cannot be reflected in the graph. In order to avoid this situation, they are not included in the graph. Although the graphs are still seen as stable, it also shows that India follows China, with an increasing trend.

The turning points for the BC and EF are the same years as the BCpc and EFpc for all the countries except Thailand. In Thailand, the turning point for the BCpc and EFpc was in 1988, but for BC and EF this situation occurs one year later in 1989. Due to the unit size of the EF being high, aiming at avoiding to express complicated values, the percentage of the changes are given for this indicator. The ratio of exchanges are determined as taken the base year is 1961 and the change is depending on the year 2018.

All the exchange ratios are examined as the base year 1961, and the change is calculated for the year 2018. Starting with the World, the ratio of exchange is 200.76%. All the countries' exchange ratios are higher than the World's ratio. The closest ones are 203.71%, 246.41%, 314.61%, and 366.90% belong

Figure 5. The ecological footprint, total in the NICs
Source: *It is compiled by the author using the GFN (2023) dataset.*

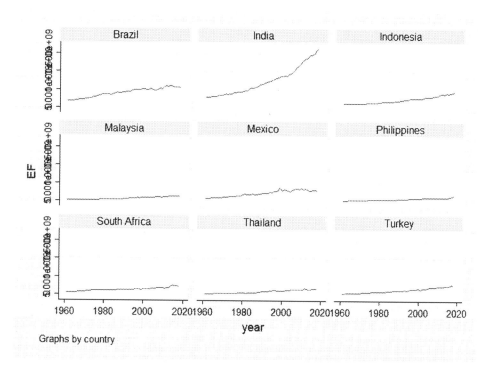

to countries Brazil, Indonesia, Mexico, and South Africa respectively. Then India, the Philippines, and Turkey follow them with ratios of 467.23%, 506.23%, and 526.21% respectively. The ratio is 688.84% in Thailand and 790.66% in China. The massive change is seen in Malaysia with 1005.87%. As these incredible rates of change clearly demonstrate, there is evidence to be a tremendous shift in the ecological footprint. Moreover, changes of this magnitude have occurred compared to just 58 years ago. So, this perspective shows that urgent policies must be developed to prevent this scene.

In order to determine the appropriate policies, it is necessary to specify the root of the problem. Since the weights of the factors that cause the ecological footprint of each country are different, it is also crucial to analyze the countries in this respect. Therefore, the types of ecological footprint per capita are given for the most recent available data which is 2018, in Figure 6. The values of all factors are expressed as the global hectare- gha unit of measure.

As seen in Figure 6, the ecological footprint per capita of Malaysia was the highest a value of 4.26gha. South Africa and China followed Malaysia with 3.80gha, and after them, Turkey took place with 3.35gha. These four countries were above the World's value which was 2.77gha. Brazil, Mexico, Thailand, Indonesia, the Philippines, and India were below the EFpc of the World by the values 2.59gha, 2.38gha, 2.35gha, 1.72gha, 1.47gha, and 1.21gha respectively. When the values are examined, it draws attention to the last three countries, Indonesia, the Philippines, and India EFpc values were less than 2gha, whereas the general tendency was around 3gha and more. However, if the environmental degradation of countries is considered only in terms of CO_2, this order changes. The top CO_2 emitters were the same countries with the EF, but the first three of the countries' alignment was not the same. The fourth country which was Turkey keeps the same order. In the CO_2 indicator itself, South Africa was the leading country with a value of 3.07gha. China and Malaysia came after South Africa with a value of 2.68gha and 2.55gha. Then Turkey came with a value of 2.02gha. The countries that take place below the World were; Thailand, Mexico, Brazil, Indonesia, and the Philippines. Their CO_2 values were; 1.45gha, 1.23gha, 0.70gha, 0.70gha, 0.68gha, and 0.63gha respectively. For the World, the value was 1.69gha.

Figure 6. The types of ecological footprint of countries in 2018
Source: *GFN (2023).*

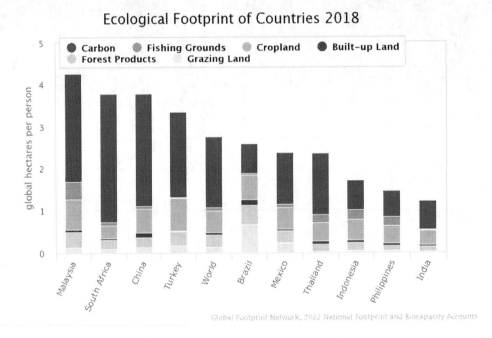

From the perspective that the factors among the total EF are examined, diverse results emerge. In Figure 7, the share of EF factors in NICs in 2018 is given as expected, for all the countries the highest share belongs to CO_2 emissions. In Brazil's ecological footprint distribution, unlike other countries, the ratios of the factors were relatively close to each other. The highest ratio was 27.18% which belongs to CO_2 emissions, then grazing land and cropland had ratios of 25.35% and 22.93% respectively. The forest products had a high ratio of 17.99, and this was the highest value among the NICs as well. In India, cropland had a remarkable share with 28.08% after CO_2 emissions which was 55.93%. Forest products was also a substantial factor with 9.78%. The CO_2 emissions share in Indonesia was the second lowest one among the NICs with 40.93%. The same scenario in India is also seen in Malaysia. The CO_2 emissions was higher than Indonesia with 59.97%, but on the other hand, the cropland share was lower by the value of 16.63%. Then, fishing grounds and forest products followed them with 10.15% and 8.45% respectively. In Mexico, half of the EFpc was CO_2 emissions with 51.61%. The other factors that became after CO_2 emissions were, cropland with 22.03%, forest products with 11.56%, and grazing land with 9.54%. When examining the Philippines, the same scenario in India and Malaysia was also seen. The CO_2 emissions ratio was relatively lower by the value of 43.06%. The cropland share was close to CO_2

emissions, it was observed as 28.80%. Then fishing grounds and forest products were the other factors with a value of 14.23% and 7.42% respectively. When forming an estimate of South Africa, it is seen that the country had a different position from the other countries. South Africa had the highest CO_2 share which is 80.83%, and the following share was 8.01% which belongs to cropland. Thailand and Turkey had quite similar ratios. Their CO_2 ratios were 61.66% and 60.47% respectively. Then, it is seen that cropland was the second contributing factor with the values of 18.82% and 23.01%. Forest products took place as the third factor, again respectively with the values of 7.34% and 9.58%. The case of China was similar to the Philippines, starting with very high CO_2 emissions which was 70.57. Then the following problem was cropland and its share was 15.0%. Finally, the Worlds' CO_2 share was observed as 60.89%, and the other main two problems were cropland and forest products. The values were 18.50% and 10.25% respectively.

Figure 7. The share of EFpc factors in the NICs and in the world in 2018
Source: *It is calculated by the author using the GFN (2023) dataset.*

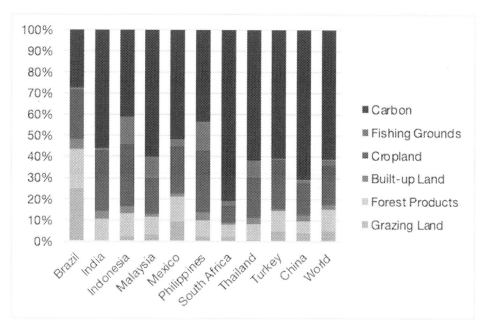

As the CO_2 emissions is the major problem, it is also seen that it is not the only environmental problem. Figure 7 is proof that, the countries have to deal with the other problems as well. In addition to this, it is remarkable to see the relationship between cropland and forest products. They are usually the second and third threats seen among the NICs. It can be concluded that the emerging factors following CO_2 emissions are cropland and forest products. Fishing grounds is another one that is seen in three countries. Grazing land and built-up land are the rarer factors.

After analyzing ecological-related indicators, the other indicators are evaluated, starting with GDP per capita. In Figure 8, GDP per capita in terms of US$ and in Figure 9, GDP per capita % growth are given for the NICs and the World.

As shown in Figure 8, although the growth rates are at different levels, GDP has an increasing trend in all countries. In 1960, the GDPpc of China, India, Indonesia, Thailand, the Philippines, and Malaysia were lower than the other countries in NICs. Then, Brazil and Turkey took place after them but all these countries' GDPpc levels were lower than the Worlds'. In this year, solely two countries had higher GDP values than the World. These countries were South Africa and Mexico. Yet, none of the countries could maintain this position. Mexico lost its position above the World's GDPpc level in 2009, while South Africa lost it in 1972.

When the trend similarities of the countries are examined in general, it can be shown that the trends of India, the Philippines, and Indonesia are very similar to each other. In severalty, Mexico and Brazil have a close trend. As it is seen the trend in South Africa is not similar to any of the NICs. The following trend is in between these mentioned two groups, and it is not as smooth as the first mentioned one, on the other hand not fluctuating as the second ones. The rising velocity of Thailand is not high, but it started a higher increasing trend after the 1980s. Conversely; China, Malaysia, and Turkey follow a massive increase, additionally China's trend seems a unique trend as its shape is upslope. Furthermore, only Turkey and China had a higher GDPpc than the World in 2021. Malaysia remained below the Worlds' level of GDPpc but the difference is mere.

Figure 8. GDPpc in the NICs and in the world
Source: *It is compiled by the author using the World Bank (2023) dataset.*

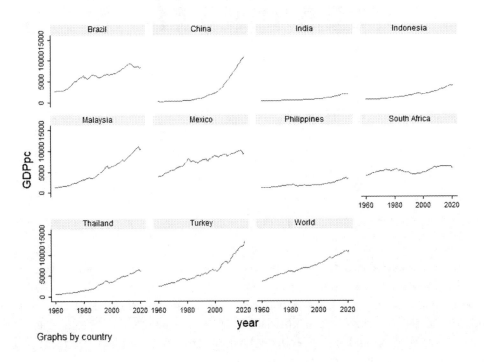

Figure 9 could be evaluated as the continuation of Figure 8 in order to express its annual growth rate. Since, the trends are interpreted in Figure 9, merely the growth rates are indicated.

The striking growth rate belongs to China, as it is seen in Figure 9. The growth rates were observed at approximately 10% between 2003-2011, then the rate started to fall down. Though, these decreases have still been high rates compared to other countries. The rates were shown approximately 6% up to 2020 when the Covid-19 effects occur. In 2020, the growth rate was 1.99% whereas, for the other countries eventuated as negative values except for Turkey. The Covid-19 affected all the countries' production processes thus, the growth rate was confronted with a negative impact. As seen in the graphs, all the countries' growth rates experienced this sharp decrease and then started to increase the following year.

Figure 9. GDPpc % growth in the NICs and in the world
Source: *It is compiled and calculated by the author using the World Bank (2023) dataset.*

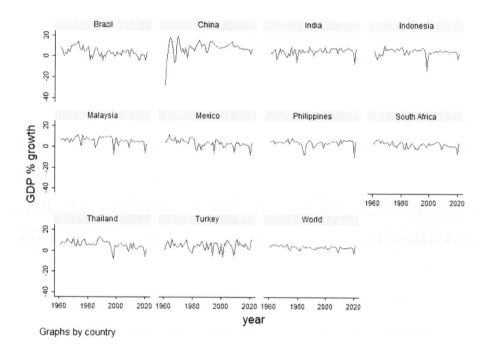

In order to achieve high GDP growth rate targets, industrialization used to be a necessity as a traditional production process. As a consequence of that the main input of production becomes a crucial factor, which is energy use. Figure 10 demonstrates the energy use, and Figure 11 shows its annual growth rate below.

When the energy use values of the countries are examined, the high values of South Africa and the rapid increase in Malaysia immediately draw attention. South Africa has a distinctive structure with the highest level of energy use until 2012. At this point, Malaysia exceeded South Africa and became the country with the highest energy use. Furthermore, in 1971, solely South Africa was above the Worlds' energy use, whereas the other countries remained below. When the matter is energy use of the countries, as seen clearly in Figure 10, not many countries are above the Worlds' line. South Africa always holds its place above the World. In 1993, Malaysia exceeded the Worlds' energy use, then China and Thailand became the other two countries with the years in 2010 and 2013 respectively. On the other hand, in 1981, Mexico exceeded the Worlds' value, with ups and downs until 1986, after this year it continues to remain below again. Malaysia stands out for its incredibly rapid rise. In addition, Thailand's rising trend is similar to Malaysia's, but the energy use level is less than Malaysia, therefore it takes a lower place in the graph. The increasing trend in Turkey is also noteworthy. It is seen that China has a different trend compared to other countries. It follows a more stable path until 2002, but then it exhibits a sharp increase. The Philippines, India, and Indonesia display a very similar trend until the 1990s'. After this year, Indonesia's trend started increasing compared to the others. These three countries are the ones that use energy at the lowest levels among the NICs.

Figure 10. Energy use in the NICs and in the world
Source: *It is compiled by the author using the World Bank (2023) dataset.*

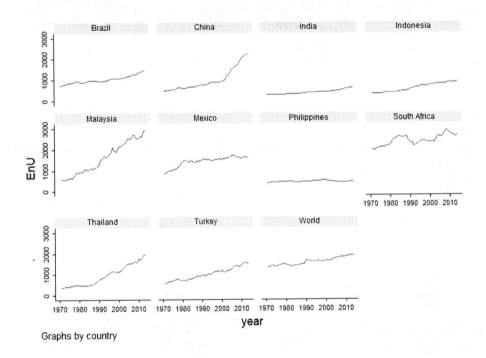

The highest growth rates belong to Malaysia as it is seen in Figure 11. It is the only country that exceeded the 20% level. Although most countries' rates of increase are close to each other, their energy use values were not at the same level, thus this situation causes the trends of the countries to become different. To sum up, these growth rates in Figure 11 reflect the countries' energy use values based on their beginner levels and cause the trends to become as in Figure 10.

Energy use graphs are given above, but investigating energy use alone is not a sufficient source of information to make a meaningful assessment. Since the effect of energy on the environment is caused by fossil fuels, it is necessary to know the ratio of fossil fuels in energy consumption. So that, Figure 12 and 13 represent the fossil fuels energy consumption % of total, and its growth rate.

Figure 11. Energy use % growth in the NICs and in the world
Source: *It is compiled and calculated by the author using the World Bank (2023) dataset.*

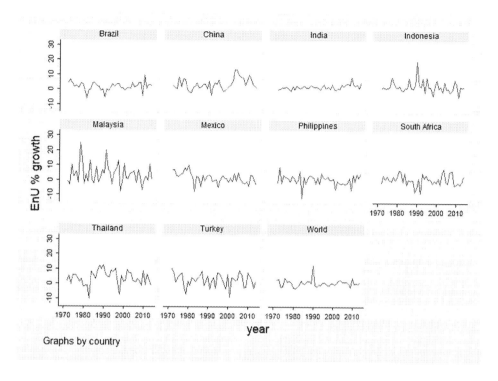

Figure 12. Fossil fuels energy consumption % of total in the NICs and in the world
Source: *It is compiled by the author using the World Bank (2023) dataset.*

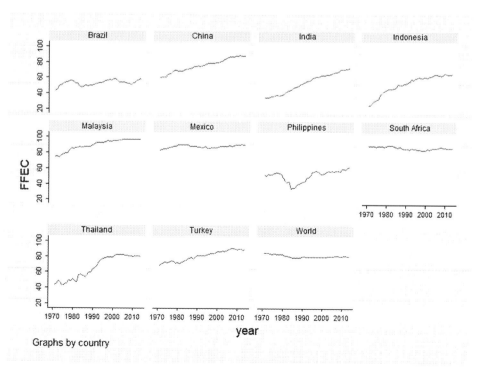

As seen in Figure 12, energy use is dominated by fossil fuels. To begin with the World, devastating values are observed. The share of fossil fuels was around 80%, and only 14 years of 44 years were below 80%, but when it is mentioned as below 80%, it is only a maximum 2% downfall. In other words, the lowest share for the World was 78.72%. The fossil fuel share of the Philippines exhibits a different structure compared to other countries and also has the lowest share in general among them. In 1971, the share began at 51.68%, then in 1978, it started to decrease until 1982. In 1983, it showed a 2.71% increase, then a sharp decline occurred with 21.01%, which can be seen clearly in Figure 13. Continuing with the lowest ones, Indonesia was in sight with 24.68% in 1971. But tracking an increasing share, the value was observed at 66.09% in 2014. India was the second lowest country in 1971 with 35.11%. Although their annual growth rates are different as seen in Figure 13, they follow an increase, and the share of fossil fuels in India hit 73.58%. Thailand and Brazil became after them with the share of 43.21% and 43.65% respectively in 1971. Though, they follow different trends. As shown in Figure 13, Thailand's trend is more volatile than Brazil's. In 2014, the share of fossil fuels was valued at 59.11%, which was the lowest percentage among the NICs for the same year. On the other hand, Thailand experienced a striking rise with 19.42% in 1983 and continued to rise with lower percentages. When it comes to the year 2014, the share was 79.84%. In addition to this, Thailand is the country, which started at a lower percentage share with the countries mentioned above, and hit the highest share among them, and also became at the same level with the World. The share of China was 59.90% in 1971. China's trend reached 87.67% in 2014, with no sharp fluctuations, showing a continuous upward trend except for a few years. One of the exceptions owned to the last year with a percentage of 0.64%. The countries' trends that began with a high percentage of the fossil fuel share, are seen more smooth compared with the starting lower percentages. As their shares are already high, the increasing levels do not have a much options so this causes their trends more stable than the others. Turkey, Malaysia, Mexico, and South Africa can be counted as these kinds of countries for the FFEC indicator. Among these four countries, Turkey and Malaysia show a higher increase. They began at 68.90% and 75.23% in 1971, then became the levels of 89.54% and 96.63% in 2014 respectively. Furthermore, the highest share in 2014 belongs to Malaysia. Mexico and South Africa had the highest two values with 83.19% and 89.64% in 1971. Mexico reached 90.28% in 2014, whereas it was 86.79% in South Africa. South Africa is the sole country, which ends with a lower percentage based on the beginning year.

Figure 10 is proof that energy use of all the countries rate of rise are differ, although all of them show a upslope trend. In addition to this information, Figure 12 exhibits the increasing the share of fossil fuels in the energy consumption. When these statements are considered together, a threatening picture occurs.

The industry, including construction in the NICs, is given in Figure 14. Although, this graph does not involve China and the World. The occasion not to include these graphs, China and the World have exorbitant values, thus making the range so high. In these circumstances, the other countries' values cannot be seen clearly, and not possible to follow their trends and interpret them as well. The same situation occurred as it is experienced in Figure 5.

To illustrate the gap between them, the highest value in Figure 14 is 726887958330.329US$, and this value belongs to India in 2021, whereas in China the value is 6239406525346.22US$, and in the World it is 23463868380996.6US$. So, if their values are added, due to the widening range, the other countries' trends become straight lines. To illustrate the graphs, China and the World do not take place in Figure 14.

As it is signified above, China is an outlier in the industry, and in Figure 15, the high growth rates can be seen. China's industry shows an upslope trend when it is drawn. The graphs are evidence that all the countries' industry levels have increased over the 50 years.

Figure 13. Fossil fuels energy consumption % growth in the NICs and in the world
Source: *It is compiled and calculated by the author using the World Bank (2023) dataset.*

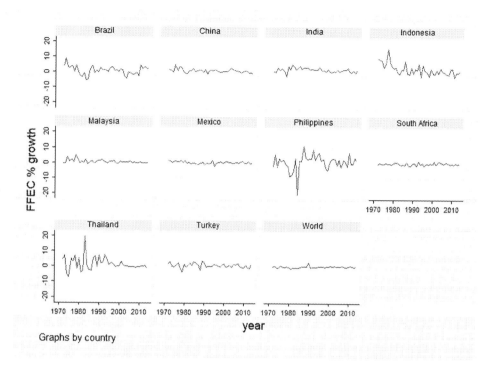

Figure 14. Industry, including construction in the NICs
Source: *It is compiled by the author using the World Bank (2023) dataset.*

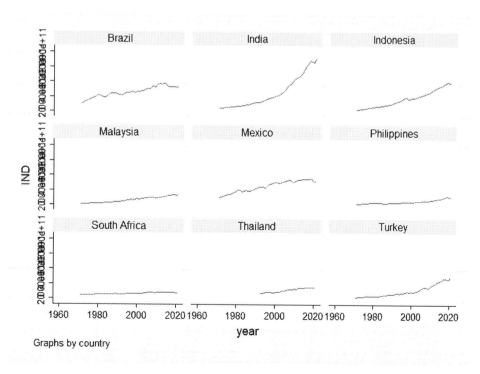

To begin with, the countries that attract the attention, India comes to the forefront. India also follows a different trend compared to other countries, as it can be clearly observed a severe increase. Mexico and Brazil have a similar trend, and also, after China and India, they owned the highest industry values until 2016. In 2016, Indonesia forged ahead of them and became the third country. Indonesia and Turkey follow a similar trend as well. Showing an increasing trend Turkey took place in the sixth highest industry level. Thailand dataset begins in 1993 and comes after Turkey. Then, Malaysia, the Philippines, and South Africa follow them. South Africa has the lowest level and also the smoothest trend among them. Each country's industrialization process starts at different times of period and follows different stages. These changes in reflections could be monitored in Figure 15 for all the countries and in the World. As Figure 15 represents the changes, the problem mentioned above the width is not a matter for the percentages.

Figure 15. Industry, including construction % growth in the NICs and in the world
Source: *It is compiled and calculated by the author using the World Bank (2023) dataset.*

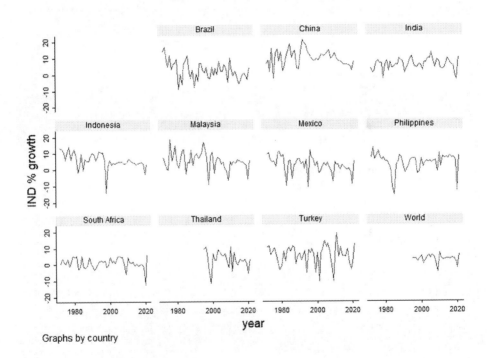

Besides the value of industrialization, determining its share in GDP is a very important source of information about the economic structure of the country. This structure is a component that countries must take into account when determining their economic policies. Therefore, in Figure 16, the industry % of GDP in NICs and in the World is given, also Figure 17 illustrates its annual growth rate.

The trends in Figure 16 show a different distribution compared to the trends discussed above. The limits of the distribution have a narrower area than the others. The values of Brazil and Malaysia assign the limits of the distribution. The minimum value is 17.70% and maximum value is 48.53% belong to Brazil and Malaysia for the years 2020 and 2004 respectively. In 1991, the World share was 32.08%, and four countries share were below this percentage. However, the share of Turkey and Brazil were 31.54%

Figure 16. The industry % of GDP in the NICs and in the world
Source: *It is compiled by the author using the World Bank (2023) dataset.*

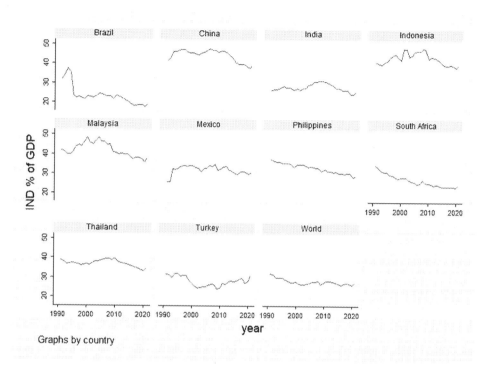

and 31.77% respectively, so it cannot be straightly lower than the World's share. On the other hand, Mexico and India had remarkably lower values, which were 25.75% and 26.44%. The other six countries' shares were above the Worlds' share. South Africa, the Philippines, and Thailand were the closest ones with 34.22%, 37.66%, and 38.66% respectively. The share of Indonesia and China were so close to each other with 41.20% and 41.49% respectively. Lastly, Malaysia had the highest share among the countries with the 42.11%. Since the distribution of sectors in an economy shows the economic structure of that country and changing this structure is possible with long-term policies. Thus, generally, the economic sectoral shares of countries do not change excessively except for general fluctuations. So, in light of this information if the industry share of the GDP of the countries are examined for the year 2021. The comparison is based on the year 1991, 30 years later in 2021, the share of the World decreased and was observed at 27.60%. This year, three countries were below the Worlds' share. The lowest share belongs to Brazil with a value of 18.86%. Then South Africa and India followed Brazil with shares of 24.50% and 25.89% respectively. The Philippines' share was higher than the Worlds', but the value was so close with 28.89%. Then Mexico and Turkey followed the Philippines with shares of 30.83% and 31.11% respectively. Thailand and Malaysia, also had high shares with 34.78% and 37.76%, but the highest shares belonged to China and Indonesia with shares of 39.43% and 39.86% respectively. When the industrialization percentages of countries in 2021 are compared to 1991, it can be noticeable that except Mexico, all the countries' shares declined. While these decreases are mostly not very high values, the decrease in Brazil was substantially striking. South Africa and the Philippines also showed a significant decline.

Figure 17. Industry % of GDP % growth in the NICs and in the world
Source: *It is compiled and calculated by the author using the World Bank (2023) dataset.*

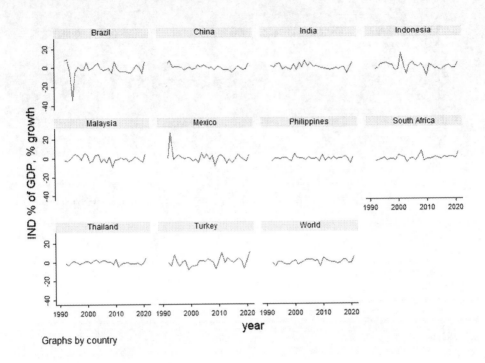

As it is mentioned above, the limit of the distribution is narrow, in the graph the range is between 0 and 50. So, even the small-scale fluctuations can be observed apparently. In Figure 17, all these changes could be seen. It is clearly observed that the trend positions are forwarded to the upslope after 2020, and in Figure 17, the level of the increase can be monitored for each country. While the scene is, the decline of the industrialization shares for the countries, this situation could be a threat for them, due to the share of the industry starting to increase. Thus, the trends should be followed if they are on an increasing path.

5. CONCLUSION

This study aims to examine the industrialization impact on climate change. The ecological footprint indicator, which covers the environmental degradation to the widest extent is used to investigate all the effects of environmental degradation. Industrialization cannot be evaluated without its determinants. Since, GDP pc, energy use, and fossil fuel consumption are significantly related with industrialization, their trends are also examined. The statistics show that the industry share in GDP, in seven of the NICs except for India, South Africa, and Brazil are seen above the world's share in 2021. Besides, India and South Africa were respectively 1.70% and 3.08% below the world's percentage which was 27.59%. For Brazil, the percentage was 8.73%, so it is clearly seen that Brazil's situation is an exception with an outlier value in NICs for the industry share in the GDP indicator. On the contrary, Indonesia, China, and Malaysia had dominated the industry share in the GDP with the highest shares, respectively 39.85%, 39.42%, and 37.75% for the same year. On the other hand, the industry growth rate is not high as the previous years. But, the industry share in GDP still remains dominant. As energy is the main source of industry, the energy consumption based on fossil fuels is analyzed and it is clearly seen that the NICs' economic growth relies on fossil fuels. Especially, Malaysia has the highest fossil fuel energy consumption share which is 96%, whereas the world's percentage was 80.91% in 2014. In line with the fact, fossil fuel consumption and climate change are strongly related to each other, Malaysia had the highest ecological footprint per capita. The effects of this state are directly seen in the environmental data of the NICs as they become the largest CO_2 emission emitters, and cause environmental degradation.

There is no doubt that CO_2 emissions is the primary driver of climate change and governments' priority is policies related to this problem as it has to be. On the other hand, it is not paid attention to CO_2 emissions a few decades ago, so the reflection of this situation should not be experienced for other factors. It is obvious that other problems are arising and there is no chance to neglect them. If the aim is to combat climate change, all the related factors about the environment must be taken into consideration. Otherwise, it is inevitable to go through a similar process that now facing CO_2 emissions. Of course, governments and policymakers have to make strict policies aiming at decreasing CO_2 emissions, but besides that, the other environmental-damaged factors cannot be ignored. To sum up, to fight the climate change, the focus is on the CO_2 emissions, but the other related factors must be taken into account without wasting time. When the other ecological footprint factors are determined, the results show that cropland is another crucial ecological concern for the NICs. Solely, South Africa had a share with 8.01%, the other countries' share limitations is between 15% and 29.04% in 2018. Fishing grounds is a significant environmental issue for the Philippines, Indonesia, and Malaysia.

Considering all this information and the data, it is concluded that the NICs have to take urgent action to realize green economic transmission. To reduce their ecological footprint, they must urgently reduce their dependence on fossil fuels and transition to renewable energy. In addition to this, cropland, and the other ecological degradation factors have to be taken into consideration by the policymakers. The composition of energy use is the main factor to determine the country's ecological footprint, and on the other hand, revealing this situation is crucial, so it is known how the problem could be solved. But the vital factor is the time. By not acting soon enough, it cannot be prevented to reach the inevitable point.

5.1 Limitations and Future Research Opportunities

This study uses descriptive analysis to present the industrialization impact on environmental degradation. As it is seen in the studies that analyze the impact of industrialization is a crucial threat to climate also urbanization factor comes to the fore when NICs are on the matter. But this study limits its research area only based on the impact of industrialization. Thus, the study takes into account the indicators that represent industrialization. For future research direction, urbanization could be added as a crucial factor. Moreover, an econometric analysis could be done within the same framework.

REFERENCES

Aluko, O. A., Osei Opoku, E. E., & Ibrahim, M. (2021). Investigating the environmental effect of globalization: Insights from selected industrialized countries. *Journal of Environmental Management, 281*, 111892. doi:10.1016/j.jenvman.2020.111892 PMID:33433368

Azam, A., Rafiq, M., Shafique, M., Zhang, H., Ateeq, M., & Yuan, J. (2021). Analyzing the relationship between economic growth and electricity consumption from renewable and non-renewable sources: Fresh evidence from newly industrialized countries. *Sustainable Energy Technologies and Assessments*, *44*, 100991. doi:10.1016/j.seta.2021.100991

Chien, F., Chau, K. Y., & Sadiq, M. (2023). Impact of climate mitigation technology and natural resource management on climate change in China. *Resources Policy*, *81*, 103367. doi:10.1016/j.resourpol.2023.103367

Dong, F., Wang, Y., Su, B., Hua, Y., & Zhang, Y. (2019). The process of peak CO2 emissions in developed economies: A perspective of industrialization and urbanization. *Resources, Conservation and Recycling*, *141*, 61–75. doi:10.1016/j.resconrec.2018.10.010

GFN, Global Footprint Network. (2023). *Ecological Deficit/Reserve dataset*. GFN. https://data.footprintnetwork.org/

Ghazali, A., & Ali, G. (2019). Investigation of key contributors of CO2 emissions in extended STIRPAT model for newly industrialized countries: A dynamic common correlated estimator (DCCE) approach. *Energy Reports*, *5*, 242–252. doi:10.1016/j.egyr.2019.02.006

Haraguchi, N., Martorano, B., & Sanfilippo, M. (2019). What factors drive successful industrialization? Evidence and implications for developing countries. *Structural Change and Economic Dynamics*, *49*, 266–276. doi:10.1016/j.strueco.2018.11.002

Ibrahim, M., & Vo, X. V. (2021). Exploring the relationships among innovation, financial sector development and environmental pollution in selected industrialized countries. *Journal of Environmental Management*, *284*, 112057. doi:10.1016/j.jenvman.2021.112057 PMID:33581497

IPCC. (2014). Climate Change 2014 Part A: Global and Sectoral Aspects. In Climate Change 2014: Impacts, Adaptation, and Vulnerability. Part A: Global and Sectoral Aspects. Contribution of Working Group II to the Fifth Assessment Report of the Intergovernmental Panel on Climate Change. Retrieved from papers2://publication/uuid/B8BF5043-C873-4AFD-97F9-A630782E590D

Liu, X., & Bae, J. (2018). Urbanization and industrialization impact of CO2 emissions in China. *Journal of Cleaner Production*, *172*, 178–186. doi:10.1016/j.jclepro.2017.10.156

Mahmood, H., Alkhateeb, T. T. Y., & Furqan, M. (2020). Industrialization, urbanization and CO2 emissions in Saudi Arabia: Asymmetry analysis. *Energy Reports*, *6*, 1553–1560. doi:10.1016/j.egyr.2020.06.004

Nasir, M. A., Canh, N. P., & Lan Le, T. N. (2021). Environmental degradation & role of financialisation, economic development, industrialisation and trade liberalisation. *Journal of Environmental Management*, *277*, 111471. doi:10.1016/j.jenvman.2020.111471 PMID:33049616

Okereke, C., Coke, A., Geebreyesus, M., Ginbo, T., Wakeford, J. J., & Mulugetta, Y. (2019). Governing green industrialisation in Africa: Assessing key parameters for a sustainable socio-technical transition in the context of Ethiopia. *World Development*, *115*, 279–290. doi:10.1016/j.worlddev.2018.11.019

Patnaik, R. (2018). Impact of Industrialization on Environment and Sustainable Solutions – Reflections from a South Indian Region. *IOP Conference Series. Earth and Environmental Science, 120*, 012016. doi:10.1088/1755-1315/120/1/012016

Rahman, M. M., Nepal, R., & Alam, K. (2021). Impacts of human capital, exports, economic growth and energy consumption on CO2 emissions of a cross-sectionally dependent panel: Evidence from the newly industrialized countries (NICs). *Environmental Science & Policy, 121*, 24–36. doi:10.1016/j.envsci.2021.03.017

Raihan, A., Muhtasim, D. A., Farhana, S., Pavel, M. I., Faruk, O., Rahman, M., & Mahmood, A. (2022). Nexus between carbon emissions, economic growth, renewable energy use, urbanization, industrialization, technological innovation, and forest area towards achieving environmental sustainability in Bangladesh. *Energy and Climate Change, 3*, 100080. doi:10.1016/j.egycc.2022.100080

The World Bank. (2023a). *Climate Change dataset*. The World Bank. https://data.worldbank.org

The World Bank. (2023b). *Economy & Growth dataset*. The World Bank. https://data.worldbank.org

UNFCCC. Conference of the Parties (COP). (2015). *Adoption Of The Paris Agreement - Conference Of The Parties Cop 21*. UNFCC. https://doi.org/FCCC/CP/2015/L.9/Rev.1

Wang, Q., & Su, M. (2019). The effects of urbanization and industrialization on decoupling economic growth from carbon emission – A case study of China. *Sustainable Cities and Society, 51*, 101758. doi:10.1016/j.scs.2019.101758

Wang, Q., Su, M., & Li, R. (2018). Toward to economic growth without emission growth: The role of urbanization and industrialization in China and India. *Journal of Cleaner Production, 205*, 499–511. doi:10.1016/j.jclepro.2018.09.034

Wang, R., Zheng, X., Wang, H., & Shan, Y. (2019). Emission drivers of cities at different industrialization phases in China. *Journal of Environmental Management, 250*, 109494. doi:10.1016/j.jenvman.2019.109494 PMID:31514002

Wang, S., & Altiparmak, S. O. (2022). Framing climate strategy of the oil industry of China: A tailored approach to ecological modernization. *Zhongguo Renkou Ziyuan Yu Huanjing, 20*(4), 324–331. doi:10.1016/j.cjpre.2022.11.003

Wang, Z., Rasool, Y., Zhang, B., Ahmed, Z., & Wang, B. (2020). Dynamic linkage among industrialisation, urbanisation, and CO2 emissions in APEC realms: Evidence based on DSUR estimation. *Structural Change and Economic Dynamics, 52*, 382–389. doi:10.1016/j.strueco.2019.12.001

Zheng, J., Jiang, P., Qiao, W., Zhu, Y., & Kennedy, E. (2016). Analysis of air pollution reduction and climate change mitigation in the industry sector of Yangtze River Delta in China. *Journal of Cleaner Production, 114*, 314–322. doi:10.1016/j.jclepro.2015.07.011

Zhu, Z., Liu, Y., Tian, X., Wang, Y., & Zhang, Y. (2017). CO2 emissions from the industrialization and urbanization processes in the manufacturing center Tianjin in China. *Journal of Cleaner Production, 168*, 867–875. doi:10.1016/j.jclepro.2017.08.245

ADDITIONAL READING

Herman, K. S. (2022). Beyond the UNFCCC North-South divide: How newly industrializing countries collaborate to innovate in climate technologies. *Journal of Environmental Management, 309*, 114425. doi:10.1016/j.jenvman.2021.114425 PMID:35183940

Herman, K. S., & Xiang, J. (2022). How collaboration with G7 countries drives environmental technology innovation in ten Newly Industrializing Countries. *Energy for Sustainable Development, 71*, 176–185. doi:10.1016/j.esd.2022.09.011

Shahzad, U., Doğan, B., Sinha, A., & Fareed, Z. (2021). Does Export product diversification help to reduce energy demand: Exploring the contextual evidences from the newly industrialized countries. *Energy, 214*, 118881. doi:10.1016/j.energy.2020.118881

Wu, P.-I., Qiu, K.-Z., & Liou, J.-L. (2017). Project cost comparison under the clean development mechanism to inform investment selection by industrialized countries. *Journal of Cleaner Production, 166*, 1347–1356. doi:10.1016/j.jclepro.2017.08.090

KEY TERMS AND DEFINITIONS

Climate change: This refers to the broadest range of changes that are occurring on the planet. The term involves all the environmental factors.

Environmental degradation: This means damage to the environmental resources.

The ecological footprint: This is the total deterioration of the environment caused by human activities.

The ecological footprint per capita: Measures the total deterioration of the environment caused by human activities per person.

CO_2 emissions: The main contributors to GHG emissions and also the primary cause of climate change.

Cropland: States whether the land that is suitable for crops, in other words, the suitable area for agriculture.

Energy consumption: Expresses all the activities that cause energy use.

Industrialization: The process of producing goods by using machines. The mechanization process also provides efficiency.

Chapter 2
Context Good Practices in Energy Matrix Focused Towards a Hydrogen Economy:
Colombia Becoming the Colossus of the Hydrogen Economy and Sustainability in the Region

Pablo Cesar Ocampo
https://orcid.org/0000-0003-3768-2052
Ean University, Colombia

Jeffrey León
Ean University, Colombia

David Blekhman
California State University, Los Angeles, USA

ABSTRACT

This chapter of the book consists of documenting the different practices in relation to the energy matrix through a systematic analysis of deductive literature in which hydrogen fuel is a fundamental element in the energy transition in a hydrogen economy in Colombia. During the investigation it was observed that Colombia is becoming one of the countries that is betting on the leadership of energy transformation in Latin America, followed by Chile, Brazil, Uruguay, and Mexico. Colombia hopes to become the colossus of the hydrogen economy and sustainability in the region.

INTRODUCTION

It is pertinent to mention how sustainability and its multiple factors gathered in a single word would be the hallmark of the EAN University in Bogotá Colombia where sustainopreneurship (innovation and entrepreneurship for sustainability) may be a concept that has risen from the prior concepts of ecopreneurship and social entrepreneurship through sustainability entrepreneurship. The concept implies utilizing creative business organizing to unravel issues related to sustainability to make environmental and social sustainability a vital purpose and objective while at the same time respecting the boundaries set to preserve the life support frameworks within the process. In other words, it could be a business with a cause where world issues are turned into business openings by the arrangement of sustainability innovations (Verma, 2021), also sustainable production and consumption can be defined as the production and use of products and services in a manner that is socially beneficial, economically viable and environmentally benign over their whole life cycle (Publication of the Institution of Chemical Engineers Official Journal of the European Federation of Chemical Engineering, 2023)

The chapter consists of the following topics: conceptualization of sustainability about factors such as entrepreneurship and innovation, it also deals with the energy matrix in Colombia and Latin America, and the criteria considered by the OECD and other environmental agencies. Prospective towards decarbonization programs by 2050. How the electrolysis process works, the necessary technology for obtaining green hydrogen used for the transport sector, contributing to the decarbonization process, good practices from European and American countries and multinationals, and, of course, Colombia, are mentioned. They are on this mission of contamination, and it culminates with different types of hydrogen. It is pertinent to clarify that this research project is more oriented to the context of the energy matrix, factors to be considered theoretically than an application in the field.

To contextualize the energy matrix, hydroelectricity makes up most of the energy matrix of the countries of Latin America and the Caribbean region (LAC). Considering the concern about reducing Greenhouse Gas (GHG) emissions from hydroelectric plants and hydrogen production from fossil sources, green hydrogen (H_2) appears as an energy vector capable of reducing this impact. Improving the efficiency of the plant and the production of renewable energy, the element is an interesting alternative from an ecological and economic point of view (Nadaleti et al., 2022)

The Latin American and Caribbean region (LAC) represents 9% of the world's population, approximately 6.5% of the world's gross domestic product (GDP), 6% of global energy consumption, and 5% of world energy-related CO_2 emissions [1]. The LAC consists of 42 countries, which are characterized as emerging countries. Among these, representing 72% of the regional population are Brazil, Mexico, Argentina, Colombia, and Venezuela, the five countries account for 82% of the GDP, 80% of the energy consumption, 82% of electricity use, and 80% of CO_2 emissions (Nadaleti et al., 2022)

In recent years, governments around the world have been increasing their attention to energy supply policies. These policies are focused on three main energy goals that define the energy trilemma: security of supply, affordability, and environmental sustainability (Ang et al., 2015); (Pupo-Roncallo et al., 2019). which will not entitle these ideas not to be however compatible. It has been previously documented that some countries may rely on cheap coal to guarantee its supply, and this has a direct impact on

environmental sustainability. Also, others may prefer the use of clean energy sources at a higher cost. A true tradeoff between these factors is necessary when assessing energy goals and policies to achieve a low-carbon energy transition and more efficient energy systems. In addition, a change is needed in how energy is produced and consumed to observe a positive impact in terms of environmental protection and economic development (Organization for Economic Cooperation and Development of the Country, 2011)

In the last 20 years, more than 85 modeling tools for energy planning have been worked on. These theoretical constructs grounded in models have made contributions in the formulation of strategies for renewable energies.

(De Moura et al., 2018) simulated three long-term future scenarios for the integration of the South American electrical system using the Open Energy Sources Modeling System (OSeMOSYS). Also, Octaviano et al (2014) improved MIT Economic Projection and Policy Analysis (EPPA) model to evaluate different alternatives to reduce CO2 emissions for Brazil and Mexico.

A particular case was the case of Colombia, in which electricity generation has been dominated by hydroelectric power for decades and, in 2017, approximately 53.7 TWh were generated produced by this source, representing 86% of the total production (Colombian electrical information system (SIEL). 2022)

This operationalization of the Colombian energy mix is different from that of the vast majority of countries in the world. However, this also implies a high risk due to the great dependence on the recourse to climatic variations. A clear example is the energy crisis in 1992e93, 2009e10 and 2015-16 due to El Niño and La Niña -NA- southern oscillation (ENSO), and the recent increase in the cost of energy.

Some models for countries with an electrical mix similar to that of Colombia have been developed for Brazil (Schmidt et al., 2016b); (Schmidt et al., 2016a); Norway (Hagos et al., 2014) and New Zealand (Mason et al., 2010). The need for research oriented towards the development of a diversified energy matrix has been raised by the Energy Mining Planning Unit (UPME) (Mining and Energy Planning Unit (UPME)., 2015). According to (Pupo-Roncallo et al., 2019) According to (Pupo-Roncallo et al., 2019) little evaluation of the integration of renewable energies in developing countries has been investigated. For the case of Colombia, there have been no limited studies on this topic and models represent the entire energy system (this includes heat, gas, electricity, transport, residential and industrial sectors) using a high temporal resolution model. Furthermore, no previous study has estimated the RES penetration limit in the Colombian electricity system power system.

According to (Pupo-Roncallo et al., 2019) the region represents 28% of world energy production, especially biofuels and renewable hydroelectricity (IRENA., 2017). The hydroelectric potential is of sum reaching an importance of 614,977 MW, around 20% of the global potential (Connolly et al., 2010). Brazil has the largest hydroelectric resource, which represents 42% of the regional potential. Followed by Colombia (16%), Peru (10%), Mexico (9%), Venezuela (7%) and Argentina (7%). The region uses about 21% of the hydroelectric potential.

Depending to (International Energy Agency (IEA), 2021) nowadays the world faces an unprecedented threat, the increase in greenhouse gas (GHG) emissions due to the indiscriminate burning of fossil fuels and deforestation are causing global warming where the consequence corresponds to a lack of control of the climate, putting lives, livelihoods and ecosystems at risk.

On the other hand, the historic 2015 Paris Agreement Its objective was to avoid the most devastating effects of climate change and limit global temperature rise to no more than 2°C above pre-industrial levels. To achieve this goal, countries are to reach net zero emissions by mid-century, one point representing the balance between the unavoidable greenhouse gas emissions and their removal from the atmosphere, through reforestation or carbon capture and storage technologies and Colombia cannot be the exception. According to the International Energy Agency (IEA), it argues that developing and deploying clean energy technologies is key to achieving net zero before the agreed deadline of 2050.

In addition to the above, in practical terms, achieve global net zero requires demanding measures through public and private projects a two-pronged approach:

- Reduce man-made emissions and remove carbon of the atmosphere.
- Many countries have already committed to reaching some kind of net zero by 2050, and a measure that the world accepts the effects of COVID-19, the understanding of society and the response to the looming climate crisis will accelerate.

That is why this energy matrix project within the Latin American context analyzes, conceptualizes how developed countries, both in the American and European continents and others, develop and deploy clean energies, implies a lot more than just a technological advance. It must be clear that the energy matrix includes solar, wind, bioenergy and other clean energy sources, the economy of electrical power systems, infrastructure, energy storage, batteries for electric vehicles, smart home technologies, data security and privacy, to name just a few. All of the above are components essential to ensure that clean energy plays the required role. Also, a successful transition to net zero require the involvement of corporations, government policies and intergovernmental, and the participation of the public.

According to Yang et al (2022) the following was stated:

Decarbonising energy and industrial sectors, among the other sections of the economies, is an urgent undertaking for the world to mitigate catastrophic climate change. In the campaign for decarbonisation, hydrogen has received increasing attention as an option to deliver zero- or low-carbon energy and feedstock to replace fossil fuels, particularly through applications in the heavy emitters such as utilities, transport, chemical, steel and cement industries. On the other hand, producing hydrogen at scale, for industrial and/or residential/commercial use, introduces technological, social and economic challenges in different regions and sectors that are yet to be thoroughly explored. As many policy makers and industrial leaders are actively seeking to advance their strategies with respect to hydrogen, robust evidence and discussions are much needed to foster rational decisions. (p1)

Achieving net zero greenhouse gas emissions by 2050 will require the rapid development and deployment of clean energy technologies. Research is essential to the success of this clean energy transition. This report examines the state of play in clean energy research over the last 20 years and provides expert insights into potential pathways forward.

According to (California Fuel Cell Partnership, 2022) has published that the current problem is that diesel combustion engines can contribute to more than 40% of the It is pertinent to ask the following question: ¿How can the scientific literature regarding sustainability assessment of hydrogen supply chain be structured and which research gaps?

How can the scientific literature on hydrogen supply chain sustainability assessment be structured and what gaps in the research?

Diesel combustion trucks can contribute up to more than 40% of the pollution particles for this aspect.

California has launched the "Norcal zero project" to commercialize fuel cell electric heavy duty trucks.

Hyundai Motors 30 fuel cell electric heavy-duty trucks will remplace high emission trucks entering and exiting between Oakland-to-Oakland port from 2023. This is the largest hydrogen electric truck related business introduced in the United States.

Based on this funding a consortium formed by non -profit center for transportation and the environment (CTE) and Hyundai motor has established a hydrogen ecosystem ranging from hydrogen supply to vehicle supply.

Building on this funding, a consortium made up of the non-profit Center for Transport and Environment (CTE) and Hyundai Motor has established a hydrogen ecosystem ranging from hydrogen supply to vehicle supply. Also, it is important to have a suitable lease and financing, fleet operation and follow up management.

There'll be 30 new drayage trucks that will use hydrogen fuel only we purify the air as we move forward handover California. Furthermore, Switzerland in 2021, during this period, more than 1013 tons of carbon dioxide avoidance was achieved across Swiss. And today, hydrogen is about 2x the price of diesel, without government subsidies or incentives, but as station construction cost decrease, as the supply chain matures, as production ramp up on a large scale to match the transport demand.

Depending to (California Fuel Cell Partnership, 2022) by 2045 all trucks in California will be electric using Fuel Cell Electric Truck FCET technology. Heavy duty trucks represent only 2% of vehicles on California roads. These trucks account for more than 9% of the state's greenhouse emissions, 32% of its nitrogen oxides and 3% of its particulate matter emissions. According to (California Fuel Cell Partnership, 2022) has published that the current problem is that diesel combustion engines can contribute to more than 40% of the It is pertinent to ask the following question: ¿How can the scientific literature regarding sustainability assessment of hydrogen supply chain be structured and which research gaps?

It is required to synchronize from the launch of vehicles with the infrastructure of hydrogen fuel and the production of renewable hydrogen.

Only until 2025 is it expected that this logistics will be sufficient to keep the entire automotive sector running with this type of fuel, the sustainability of the market must be considered.

There is a commitment to involve this transition from diesel trucks to electrification by 2024, such as starting with delivery vans.

One of the test models corresponds to the class 8 tractor, where it must face challenges aimed at climate change, health and economy.

Trucks contribute to 40% of the carbon emissions generated by vehicles, pollution is observed in the areas surrounding highways, on the other hand, we are faced with hotter days, intense forest fires, droughts, rising sea levels, worsening of air quality.

California Air Resources Board (CAR)

As a complementary and viable alternative to battery electric trucks (BETS), full cell electric truck (FCETs), the latter is the most appropriate offers greater advantages.

- Economic viability is within reach.

It is necessary to take into account how these technologies influence the cost of ownership, the return on investment and the rate of adoption by cargo operators and improvements in air quality. politics is the main accelerator of growth, where work is done to revolutionize cargo movement, creating mandatory deadlines to adopt these changes. It is imperative to work on the expansion of the hydrogen supply chain.

It is required to trigger the initiation of the market and lead to build accelerated and sustained growth.

- Reaching the tipping point. Achieve a full and sustainable transition to zero emissions, cargo movement while meeting aggressive schedules.
- The pathway to 2045 and beyond the vast logistics supply chain. PTO and overnight idling applications are required for long distance travel. Diesel trucks have an integral unit for this, the challenge is how the electric leverages these needs, and the battery electric truck will be part of the charging solution. However, the Fuel cell electric truck (FCET) is above the Battery electric truck (BET).
- Something that caught my attention corresponds rapid and complete transition requires one to one replacement.

The fastest and most efficient transaction to zero emission trucks requires using technology that can sustain existing business, minimal operational disruption models and FCET and BET are the only technologies. FCET excel in the criteria of payload capacity, range and fueling.

One of the effective practical cases using the use of electric cell batteries has been the forklifts in the distribution centers, they have demonstrated this capacity. the reduction of refueling times is the key, on the other hand, we must work on improvements in fuel refueling. Use the infrastructure of diesel fuel stations for H2.

Changes are required in the infrastructure of the BET stations, characterized by the layout width for trucks that can be loaded daily and where the loading rates are in megawatts and where the cost of electricity is more rational for the operators.

California State University Los Angeles United States (CSULA) introduced catalytic converters of the use cathodic.

It is necessary for producers or manufacturers to work on the generation of hydrogen fuel cells.

CSULA is the first to receive seal of approval for sale of hydrogen on per Kg basis as of January 2015.

It is very important in this type of infrastructure to ensure the verification of leaks and determine the pressures within the vehicle tank flows and temperature, pre cool hydrogen minus 20C° compressors called hydra where they have the function of increasing pressures from 6200 to roughly 10000 PSI.

CSULA Hydrogen station Specs, production 60kg/day, pressure 350-700bar, capacity 15-20 fuel cell vehicle per day.

Professor Blekhman from CSULA has been researching topics related to cooling (testing, limits, improvements), applied research, station capacity, guidelines for other stations, data adquisition, business case, research, energy performance, energy analysis and best practice.

Observing the different initiatives of both the American and European continents, some research topics that are important for the democratization of projects in a hydrogen economy are presented below.

Project will:

Develop industry connections
Evaluate European Regulations
Perform industry assessment
Develop evaluation questionnaire
Arrange travel for evaluation
Collect data
Determine unique operational details in Scandinavia, compare to station in California.
Catalogue, summary

Context Good Practices in Energy Matrix Focused for an H Economy

Sister station
Sister station close to the sea and the ports
Best practices refer to Gothenburg: Woikoski station
Electrolysis by wind power.
To check practices around Noruega & Dinamarca
Station Operational Status systems (SOSS)

To Apply market orientation (MO) to hydrogen supply chain orientation (my doctoral topic research.

To need to know where, when and if hydrogen is available:
1000 station gas vs 1000 h2 by 2030
key storage purpose of entities
Another important reference to (Ogbonnaya et al., 2021) considered:

As the political will to adopt and scale-up clean energy technologies (CETs) increases across the globe, there is an urgent need to facilitate the technological transition by developing novel CETs or optimizing the existing ones. Of all the renewable energy resources available to mankind (including solar, hydro, wind, geothermal, biomass, tidal, etc.), solar energy appears to be the most sustainable because it is inexhaustible, ubiquitous across the globe, and it is not subject to price controls, unlike fossil fuels. Because of this, renewable energy technologies (RETs) that use solar energy as a prime mover will continue to attract research and development attention because they can be deployed across the globe. One of such RETs is integrated photovoltaic-fuel cell (IPVFC) system, which uses photovoltaics and fuel cells to majorly generate power and hydrogen, using solar energy as the prime mover. (p1)

Web Page Hyzon motors (Julio 8 del 2022) (Hyzon Vehicles, 2022) https://www.hyzonmotors.com/vehicles. A global supplier of zero-emissions hydrogen and fuel cell powered commercial vehicles, announced that the California Air Resources Board (CARB) has certified its Class 8, 7, and 6 Repowers as exempt from emission requirements, enabling the company to sell fuel cell electric trucks in California. Hyzon's Repower program allows customers to exchange their used diesel trucks for conversion to fuel cell electric using Hyzon's proprietary fuel cell technology.

It is necessary for producers or manufacturers to work on the generation of hydrogen fuel cells.

CSULA is the first to receive seal of approval for sale of hydrogen on per Kg basis as of January 2015.

It is very important in this type of infrastructure to ensure the verification of leaks and determine the pressures within the vehicle tank flows and temperature, pre cool hydrogen minus 20C° compressors called hydra where they have the function of increasing pressures from 6200 to roughly 10000 PSI.

CSULA Hydrogen station Specs, production 60kg/day, pressure 350-700bar, capacity 15-20 fuel cell vehicle per day.

Professor Blekhman from CSULA has been researching topics related to cooling (testing, limits, improvements), applied research, station capacity, guidelines for other stations, data adquisition, business case, research, energy performance, energy analysis and best practice.

Observing the different initiatives of both the American and European continents, some research topics that are important for the democratization of projects in a hydrogen economy are presented below.

MEMBRANE ELECTRODE ASSEMBLY

Web page Hyzon Membrane Assembly (Julio 8 del 2022) https://www.hyzonmotors.com/in-the-news/hyzon-to-build-us-first-commercial-scale-mea-production-line, (Hyzon Motors, 2022)

The Membrane Electrode Assembly (MEA) is the heart of the fuel cell, as electricity is generated in its layers. Innovating across these layers impacts not only the fuel cell's power density, but also its cost, as the layers contain precious metals. One layer, the cathode catalyst, has been developed in-house to optimize the surface area while increasing cell reversal tolerance, leading to greater durability under varying environmental circumstances. Through this and other innovations, Hyzon's MEA has industry-leading power density, as determined by a 3rd party. Additionally, Hyzon's manufacturing improvements are expected to reduce MEA costs by enabling large-scale, roll-to-roll production.

Blue hydrogen: that which is also obtained from fossil fuels, but without the release of carbon dioxide (CO_2). Green hydrogen: that which is obtained from non-conventional sources of renewable energy, such as biomass, wind energy, solar energy and geothermal heat, among others.

One of the many problems lies in the permanence of hydrogen.

Furthermore, hydrogen has several uses within that is the manufacture of ammonia, explosives 55%, oil refining 25% and 10% ethanol. World production of H_2 (48% natural gas, 30% oil, 18% coal, 4% water (twice as expensive).

On the other hand, the German community already has a colossal train that works with hydrogen batteries. According web page (June 26, 2022) (Berlin from Siemens Mobility GmbH and Niederbarnimer Eisenbahn (NEB), 2022)

The order placed with Siemens Mobility also includes a service and spare parts supply agreement (TSSSA) covering the entire term of the transport contract.

Guidehouse report on hydrogen imports to Germany - "a German hydrogen import strategy should consider the following aspects:

- To establish European and international hydrogen partnerships to ensure a sufficient supply of hydrogen.
- To diversify hydrogen supply countries and transportation routes to increase security of supply.
- To build and finance transportation infrastructure for short-term and long-term hydrogen imports to accelerate hydrogen market development.
- To establish and align standards and regulation for hydrogen production and transportation to ensure sustainability and provide necessary certainty for investors.
- To continue and expand hydrogen support instruments to close the financing gap for early hydrogen projects and ensure bankability.
- To support research and development in technology and innovation throughout the hydrogen value chain to achieve rapid cost reductions.
- To support international emblematic projects of green hydrogen and derivatives".

Finally, and as evidenced in the different previous practices, the world is faced with a new technology based on H_2 in a hydrogen economy and Colombia -a region cannot serve outside these disruptive changes that seek a harmonized market orientation. with the needs of the interest groups based on the decarbonization of the different organizational processes focused on a hydrogen economy.

Context Good Practices in Energy Matrix Focused for an H Economy

There are a number of companies linked to the issue of the massification of hydrogen and its infrastructure, such is the case of the company CEREs. At more than 75 members strong, the Ceres Policy Network (BICEP) represents some of the most recognizable brands in the U.S., who have become leading advocates in the fight against the climate crisis at both the state and federal level."Electrification of medium- and heavy-duty vehicles would not only help protect public health and the climate, but would also provide economic benefits to manufacturers, suppliers, and fleet owners across the country." (Ceres. Org 2022)

Collaboration between companies, Ceres Policy Network 'Business for Innovative Climate and Energy Policy' (BICEP) is a coalition of 75 of the U.S. most recognizable brands including IKEA, HP, Microsoft, Nestle and Unilever. Alliances such as this, with stated commitments to fleet electrification and huge collective purchasing power send a strong message to both automotive manufactures and policy makers, encouraging support at a state and federal level. Source IDTechEx_Samplepages_Electricand-FuelCellTrucks20232043.pdf

According to (Wyatt, 2022).Though battery-electric models currently make up only a small fraction of total global truck sales (around 0.4% in 2021), it is already clear that the transition from diesel combustion engines to zero-emission technologies is well underway.

Efforts to decarbonize road transport have seen most manufacturers, including Tesla, Daimler, VW, Scania and Volvo invest in battery-electric trucks. A smaller minority of OEMs, notably Toyota and Hyundai have chosen to focus their efforts on fuel cell vehicles. Despite issues with their efficiency and the availability of H2 as transport fuel and H2 refuelling infrastructure, fuel cells' energy density advantage mean they remain in the conversation for zero emission long haul trucking applications where a large daily milage is required, though deployment is dependent on the production cheap low carbon hydrogen. IDTechEx believe that BEV trucks will be the dominant zero-emission truck technology, as improving battery energy density and charging optimization will increase the length of duty-cycle they can deliver. Unlike electricity, H2 fuel offers no operational saving to offset high CAPEX costs. FCEV will be an expensive option for longer range requirements (Wyatt, 2022)

Concerns around greenhouse gas emission and local air quality are pushing vehicle manufacturers around the world toward zero-emission powertrain solutions and the phasing out of fossil fuel powered combustion engines (Idtechex, 2022)

The use of hydrogen technologies is not a utopian concept. Its adoption has already started and with it, the fourth industrial revolution.

The report explains the role of hydrogen in the so-called hydrogen economy, emphasising the advantages of its adoption, and showing the current limitations which are hindering its evolution. Then, several solutions to facilitate hydrogen economies' adoption are explained (Idtechex, 2022)

Beginning with the definition of the hydrogen economy, the importance of hydrogen as an energy carrier will be explained, highlighting its use in multiple sectors, not simply as energy storage material. The importance of hydrogen as an energy vector is driven by the possibility of adopting it in a large variety of sectors, hence coupling different sectors together, while allowing their decarbonization, due to its employment, without the emission of green-house gas (GHG) (Idtechex, 2022)

Besides its consumption, hydrogen can also be produced from several different sources, both renewable and not.

From this general picture it's possible to understand the two main reasons why hydrogen will be used as energy vector:

1. It allows a country to be, to some extent, independent from large energy imports
2. While reducing the GHG emissions

Figure 1. The color of hydrogen defined the environmental impact for its production
Source (Idtechex, 2022)

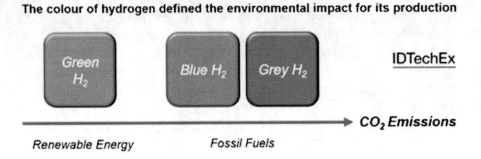

It is worth presenting the types of hydrogen, Gray hydrogen, produced from fossil fuels, mainly natural gas and carbon, without subsequent carbon capture and storage.

- Blue hydrogen, blue hydrogen is the name produced from fossil sources that incorporate capture and storage of CO2 emissions. The Energy Transition Law Blue hydrogen is defined as hydrogen that is produced from fossil fuels.

especially due to the decomposition of methane (CH_4) and which has a system of carbon capture, use and storage (CCUS), as part of its process of production. Blue hydrogen is included within the Unconventional Sources of Energy (FNCE).

- Green hydrogen, corresponds to renewable hydrogen. According to article 5 of the Colombian Energy Transition Law 2099 of 2021, is defined as hydrogen green to hydrogen produced from Unconventional Renewable Energy Sources (FNCER), such as biomass, small hydroelectric projects, wind power, geothermal heat, solar, tidal, among others.

Because of these reasons, several governments have already started to work on the implementation of a hydrogen economy(Gobierno de Colombia, 2021)

Besides the advantages of an integrated hydrogen economy, several barriers must be overcome first. Hydrogen reduction cost is without doubts the most pressing task. Moreover, infrastructures need to be adapted to hydrogen distribution, while policy and regulations must be implemented to ease the integration of hydrogen in current economies. From the technical side, hydrogen technologies like fuel cells and electrolysers, have to be improved to reduce the cost and ease their adoption by the market.

Reaching a complete hydrogen economy will be a long process, but it has already started (Idtechex, 2022).

Electrolyzers

The Hydrogen TCP is an international collaborative R&D programme created under the auspices of the IEA in 1977. In this session, we will learn more about the current and planned activities of the Hydrogen TCP that will address challenges faced by hydrogen technologies in the different steps of the value chain. What are the main challenges and drawbacks that limit the massive scale-up and deployment of hydrogen technologies? How are they being addressed? What is needed? (Conference Agenda 2021, 2021)

According to Klippenstein (2022) said "Hydrogen is not the solution, the efficiency is too low." That's what many people believe and say. Efficiency is important, but it is not the only factor to be taken into account in an energy system. Size, weight, geographical aspects of the production site and the place where energy is needed, availability of materials e.g. for batteries, geopolitical aspects, seasonality, available infrastructure, approval procedures, legal aspects etc. are other factors that have to be taken into account as well.

On the other hand, in Colombia, work is being done for the regulations that conform to the renewable energy sector and such is the case of Decree 348 of 2017 that adds to the sole regulatory decree of the administrative sector of mines and energy (Decree 1073 of 2015) in Regarding the establishment of public policy guidelines on efficient energy management and delivery of surplus small-scale self-generators, establishes the obligation on the part of the MME Ministry of Mines and Energy to define and implement the energy policy guidelines on of measurement systems and the graduality in their fundamental implementation in technical studies for this purpose; It also defines the parameters to be considered a small-scale self-generator, among which are the installed power limit defined by UPME (currently 1MW), which is energy produced for self-consumption without the need to use assets from the STN National Transmission System. o SDL Local Distribution System, the amount of surplus generated based on self-consumption is not limited and the property or operation of the assets may be owned or owned by third parties (World Bank Group et al., 2017)

In cohesion with the above, the Indicative Action Plan for Energy Efficiency 2017-2022 (UPME-PAI, 2016) was adopted through Resolution 41286 of 2016, in which it is formulated as the rethinking of the energy efficiency policy in the country, and includes numerous studies developed mainly by UPME. Among them, the characterization studies of industrial energy consumption in the CIIU 10-18 (UPME - INCOMBUSTION, 2014) and CIIU 19-31 (UPME-CORPOEMA, 2014) sectors, the energy efficiency policy proposal (UPME-EE Policy, 2015) among others. It also seeks to continue the Program for the Rational and Efficient Use of Energy and Non-Conventional Sources (PROURE), which was formulated until 2015, and integrate the new regulatory framework established by Law 1715 of 2014 and the emission reduction commitments acquired by the country, particularly at COP 21. The Indicative Action Plan (PAI) is directly articulated with the emission reduction commitments of COP 21, especially in the line of action of the Ministry of Mines and Energy (MME) in reducing emissions for efficiency Likewise, some of its lines of action, particularly in transportation, contribute to the goal of this sector and in general to the country goal.

In relation to the Sustainable Development Goals, the execution of the Indicative Action Plan goals contribute directly to the seventh objective that refers to guaranteeing access to affordable, safe, sustainable and modern energy for all, in particular to target 7.3 From here by 2030, double the global rate of improvement in energy efficiency, as well as the channeling of investments in R+D+i in clean and efficient technologies. The main objective of the PAI is to define the strategic and sectoral actions that allow achieving the goals in terms of energy efficiency, this taking into account the most cost-effective indicative goals, the construction of economic, technical, regulatory and information conditions to promote a market of energy efficiency, institutional strengthening, the establishment of adequate procedures for the application of incentives, the harmonization of goals, and the consolidation of a culture of sustainable and efficient management of resources in the energy chain. Based on the update studies of the new Colombian energy balance BECO, the characterization of energy consumption for the transportation, industrial, commercial, public and services, and residential sectors is presented. Based on this information, the Energy Demand Situation in Colombia Page 39 of 135 indicative goals 2017-2022 were set for each of the sectors as shown below. As can be seen below, the national energy saving goal for all sectors was 9.05%, the highest being the transport sector with more than half of the total goal, 5.49%, followed by industry, 1.71% tertiary and residential., 1.13% (Unidad Planeación Minero Energetica, 2016)(World Bank Group et al., 2017)

The first two low-emission hydrogen pilot projects in Colombia were put into operation in Cartagena, Bolivar department, confirming the country's progress at full speed in the energy transition carried out by Ecopetrol, using hydrogen for oil refining testing the sedan Toyota Mirai and the second hydrogen generation project carried out by the Promigas company, framed in the hydrogen route launched by the government in 2021, where the objective was to produce between 1 to 3 gigawatts of electrolysis for green hydrogen in the medium term. according to the climate action law.

The first electrolyser has been installed at the Ecopetrol refinery (Reficar) that has an Ecopetrol farm as its source. According to former President Duque, Colombia is seen as the leading exporter of green hydrogen in Latin America and the Caribbean. 3.5 years ago, Colombia had 28 megawatts in non-conventional renewables and 2,500 megawatts was completed, with sources such as the sun, the wind, ending in 2022 and with 4,500 megawatts in production, making Colombia one of the countries that has done so expeditiously. the path to energy transition. On the other hand, the second electrolyser is being installed with a private company (PROMIGAS).

Another project that is being carried out in the Andes-southwest of the department of Antioquia is being implemented six months ago, a project called Hevolution, developed by the OPEX company, where it is desired to test hydrogen that supplies vehicles with this fuel, for this case it is testing a Hyundai Nexo SUV, which works with hydrogen where through an electrolyser in which the raw material is water and this through a chemical process separates hydrogen from oxygen resulting in electricity that will be stored in batteries. Something that draws attention is how taking a shower in the morning can consume 45 liters of water and how this amount of resource can generate hydrogen for an average of 700 km, a distance between Medellin and the Colombian Atlantic coast.

Electric vehicles that are ending their useful life are being replaced by hydrogen fuel cell technology (Full Cell Electric Vehicle, FCEV), batteries that convert hydrogen into water to generate electricity. In January 2023 OPEX a company opens the first green hydrogen plant with a capacity of one ton per day, the idea is that the first beneficiaries are the buses and trucks that have this technology. The international renewable energy agency (IRENA) included Colombia as one of the countries with the best price offer for this type of fuel. This fuel has three times more energy than gasoline and does not burn carbon dioxide. Colombia is forecast to be the fourth country out of 34 countries with the best price for this fuel, considering that by the year 2050 one dollar/kg. Specifically, research is being carried out so that it costs between 70-120 cents according to IRENE. Decree 895 of 2022, is characterized with tax incentives for the generation of electrical energy with Non-Conventional Energy Sources up to 50% in income taxes for 15 years. Another of the interesting and important factors of hydrogen is the supply time, which can be from 5 minutes for a family vehicle to 8 to 20 minutes for a truck that will transport 35 tons or perhaps more (Ministerio de Hacienda y Crédito Público de Colombia, 2022).

Finally, as could be seen through the article, there is everything to be done and more in Colombia regarding the use of hydrogen as fuel. What is evident is that there is a government trend towards the application of this type of fuel in transportation. On the other hand, it is necessary to work in the field of security for the manipulation of this element of the periodic table, which will surely substantially reduce the carbon footprint and generate greater environmental and sustainable awareness. Europe and the US are working hard on how to improve the efficiency of this fuel, however it is a good start that Colombia is a benchmark that is working on the issue of energy transition.

Another novelty, in the month of April of the year 2023 in Bogota, Colombia, South America, the first bus that works with green hydrogen called Marcopolo Attivi 3RH2FC was presented, created by the main mobility companies such as Marcopolo-Superpolo- alcaldía Mayor de Bogotá, TransMilenio S.A., the Ecopetrol Group, the Fund for Non-Conventional Energies and Efficient Energy Management, (FENOGE), the National Auto Parts Factory (FANALCA) and Green Móvil. The main technology it has is an electrolyzer with a capacity of 165 kilowatts to supply an average of 17 buses in an average of 8 minutes and that gives it a range of 450 km and that wants to be linked to the main mass transportation company transmilenio.

It is a reality that Colombia has been coming out of a productive slowdown in the field of the energy matrix and where it is becoming an interesting emerging country because it has been one of the pioneers in starting decarbonization processes, however work must continue for future research is worth focusing on the safety of hydrogen handling both in the upstream and downstream processes, this would be the entire value network, on the other the market orientation approach to determine exactly the needs of the interest groups and finally this type of initiative is not part of a single actor, universities, government entities, businessmen, and regulatory entities are required, because the more stakeholders understand the project, the more benefit it will be for reducing operating costs and fewer greenhouse effect remittances.

REFERENCES

Ang, B. W., Choong, W. L., & Ng, T. S. (2015). Energy security: Definitions, dimensions and indexes. In *Renewable and Sustainable Energy Reviews* (Vol. 42, pp. 1077–1093). Elsevier Ltd. doi:10.1016/j.rser.2014.10.064

Berlin from Siemens Mobility GmbH and Niederbarnimer Eisenbahn (NEB). (2022). *Press Joint press release from Siemens Mobility GmbH and Niederbarnimer Eisenbahn.* NEB.

California Fuel Cell Partnership. (2022). *California Fuel Cell Partnership Envisions 70,000 Heavy-Duty Fuel Cell Electric Trucks Supported by 200 Hydrogen Stations in-State by 2035.* CA Fuel Cell Partnership.

Ceres.org. (2022). *Major companies and investors call on the federal government to strengthen proposed truck emissions standards.* Ceres.

Hydrogen Tech. (2021). *Conference Agenda 2021.* Hydrogen Tech. https://www.hydrogen-worldexpo.com/2021-conference-agenda/. Https://Www.Hydrogen-Worldexpo.Com/2021-Conference-Agenda/

Connolly, D., Lund, H., Mathiesen, B., & Leahy, M. (2010). A review of computer tools for analysing the integration of renewable energy into various energy systems. *Applied Energy, 87*(4), 1059–1082. doi:10.1016/j.apenergy.2009.09.026

David Wyatt. (2022). *Electric Truck Deployment Ready for Acceleration in 2023*. Idtechex.

de Moura, G. N. P., Legey, L. F. L., & Howells, M. (2018). A Brazilian perspective of power systems integration using OSeMOSYS SAMBA – South America Model Base – and the bargaining power of neighbouring countries: A cooperative games approach. *Energy Policy, 115*, 470–485. doi:10.1016/j.enpol.2018.01.045

Gobierno de Colombia. (2021). *Hoja de ruta del hidrogeno*. Gobierno de Colombia.

Hagos, D. A., Gebremedhin, A., & Zethraeus, B. (2014). Towards a flexible energy system – A case study for Inland Norway. *Applied Energy, 130*, 41–50. doi:10.1016/j.apenergy.2014.05.022

Hyzon Motors. (2022, July). *Hyzon to Build First Commercial Scale MEA Production line*. Hyzon. https://www.hyzonmotors.com/in-the-news/hyzon-to-build-us-first-commercial-scale-mea-production-line

Hyzon Vehicles. (2022, July). *Camiones Hyzon*. Hyzon.

Idtechex. (2022). *The Hydrogen Economy, Fuel Cells, and Hydrogen Production Methods*. Idtechex. Https://Www.Idtechex.Com/En/Research-Report/the-Hydrogen-Economy-Fuel-Cells-and-Hydrogen-Production-Methods/744

International Energy Agency (IEA). (2021). *Pathways to Net Zero: The Impact of Clean Energy Research*. IEA. https://www.iea.org/reports/net-zero-by-2050

Mason, I. G., Page, S. C., & Williamson, A. G. (2010). A 100% renewable electricity generation system for New Zealand utilising hydro, wind, geothermal and biomass resources. *Energy Policy, 38*(8), 3973–3984. doi:10.1016/j.enpol.2010.03.022

Matthew Klippenstein. (2022). *Hydrogen is not the solution, the efficiency is too low. Canadian Hydrogen and Fuel Cell Association*. CHFCA.

Mining and Energy Planning Unit (UPME). (2015). *Integracion de las energías renovables no convencionales en Colombia*. UPME.

Ministerio de Hacienda y Crédito Público de Colombia. (2022). *decreto 895 del 2022*. MHCP.

Nadaleti, W. C., de Souza, E. G., & Lourenço, V. A. (2022). Green hydrogen-based pathways and alternatives: Towards the renewable energy transition in South America's regions–Part B. *International Journal of Hydrogen Energy, 47*(1), 1–15. doi:10.1016/j.ijhydene.2021.05.113

Ogbonnaya, C., Abeykoon, C., Nasser, A., Turan, A., & Ume, C. S. (2021). Prospects of integrated photovoltaic-fuel cell systems in a hydrogen economy: A comprehensive review. In Energies (Vol. 14, Issue 20). MDPI. doi:10.3390/en14206827

Organización para la Cooperación y el Desarrollo Economico del Pais. (2011). *Harnessing Variable Renewables*. OECD., doi:10.1787/9789264111394-

Institution of Chemical Engineers. (2023). Sustainable production and consumption. *Journal of the European Federation of Chemical Engineering, 39*.

Pupo-Roncallo, O., Campillo, J., Ingham, D., Hughes, K., & Pourkashanian, M. (2019). Large scale integration of renewable energy sources (RES) in the future Colombian energy system. *Energy, 186*, 115805. doi:10.1016/j.energy.2019.07.135

Rahul Verma. (2021). Sustainable and Responsible Entrepreneurship and Key Drivers of Performance. Sustainopreneurship Rahul Verma (Delhi University, India). doi:10.4018/978-1-7998-7951-0.ch005

Schmidt, J., Cancella, R., & Pereira, A. O. Jr. (2016a). An optimal mix of solar PV, wind and hydro power for a low-carbon electricity supply in Brazil. *Renewable Energy, 85*, 137–147. doi:10.1016/j.renene.2015.06.010

Schmidt, J., Cancella, R., & Pereira, A. O. Jr. (2016b). The role of wind power and solar PV in reducing risks in the Brazilian hydro-thermal power system. *Energy, 115*, 1748–1757. doi:10.1016/j.energy.2016.03.059

Unidad Planeación Minero Energetica. (2016). *U*. UPME-PAI.

World Bank Group, Enersinc, & Korea Green Growth Partnership. (2017). Energy Demand situation in Colombia. World Bank.

Chapter 3
Application of Multi-Criteria Decision-Making Methods for the Underground Mining Method Selection

Stojance Mijalkovski
Goce Delcev University, North Macedonia

Omer Faruk Efe
Bursa Technical University, Turkey

Kemajl Zeqiri
University of Mitrovica, Kosovo

ABSTRACT

In mining, there are many complex problems that need to be solved in a limited period of time. When solving these complex tasks, it is necessary to take into account many parameters, all in order to determine the optimal solution for a given problem. The application of multi-criteria decision-making methods (MCDM) is very widely used to solve such complex problems. One of the most complex problems in mining is the underground mining method selection. In order to choose the most appropriate method of mining excavation, it is necessary to take into account a large number of influential parameters according to which we will compare mining methods. This paper will discuss the problem of underground mining method selection using the EDAS method. Also, a comparison of the obtained results will be made for a specific example, when applying several methods for multi-criteria decision-making. After comparing the obtained results, the most suitable mining method for a specific example will be determined.

DOI: 10.4018/978-1-6684-8969-7.ch003

INTRODUCTION

With the rapid development of industry in developed and underdeveloped countries, as well as the general increase in living standards, there is an increasing demand for various mineral raw materials, especially for metals and non-metals, as well as for other useful raw materials that represent the basic industry. The increasing demand for useful mineral resources encourages their exploration and the opening of many mines in the world. Apart from the above, the growing environmental awareness of humanity and the impending collapse of the planet Earth are strongly in favor of underground exploitation. Therefore, it can rightly be said that good times are yet to come for the underground exploitation of useful mineral raw materials.

The mining is such an area where many complex problems are encountered that require a solution in a relatively short time. When solving tasks, it is necessary to take into account as many influential parameters as possible, all so that the obtained solution is the most adequate. One of such complex problems is the underground mining method selection. The correct choice of mining method for a specific ore deposit is of great importance, because it has a direct impact on the total costs for the operation of the mine itself.

The mining method selection and the preparation of the stope consists of a series of procedures, the application of which solves the problem. The selection and dimensioning of the stope structure consists in fully harmonizing the dimensions of the stope with the selected equipment, with a constant analysis of its stability, which implies the selection and dimensioning of the support structure as needed. In the case of caving mining methods, it is necessary to make a forecast of the impact of the hanging wall and the terrain surface. At the end, a cost and risk analysis is performed for all solutions, i.e. is. economic assessment of effects as an authoritative criterion for choosing the optimal variant.

Empirical and numerical methods are used in the engineering part to solve the problem of massif management, which includes stability analysis, selection and dimensioning of the support and prediction of the impact of stope on the surrounding massif and the surface. Empirical methods are represented by rock mass classifications, and numerical methods are represented by the finite element method as the most frequently applied and most powerful method for rock mass modeling and simulation of geomechanical processes in the massif.

The selection and design of the excavation method are the most problematic and complex procedure, which is the ultimate skill of mining engineering. To make this decision, it is necessary to have the most reliable data about the ore deposit. Therefore, when solving the problem of underground mining method selection, it is necessary to take into account several influential parameters. Some of the influencing parameters can be calculated or measured (quantitative), while some parameters cannot be calculated or measured (qualitative). The qualitative parameters are defined by descriptive ratings, and then they need to be transformed into numerical values so that they can be used for calculation.

The parameters that influence the underground mining method selection can be divided into three groups: mining - geological, mining - technical and economic parameters (Bogdanovic et al., 2012). Below are the most important parameters for each of the groups:

- mining and geological parameters, such as: geometry of deposit (depth below surface, general shape, plunge, ore thickness), rock mechanics characteristics (ore zone, footwall and hangingwall, i.e. rock substance strength, fracture shear strength, fracture spacing, structures, stability, stress), ore variability (grade distribution, ore uniformity, ore boundaries), quality of resource, etc.

- mining and technical parameters, such as: applied equipment, annual productivity, environmental impact, health and safety, mine recovery, ore dilution, machinery and mining rate, flexibility of methods, and
- economic parameters, such as: ore value, ore body grades, mineable ore tons, operating cost and capital cost.

A large number of influential parameters when mining method selection unequivocally points to the conclusion of the great complexity of this problem. Therefore, the selection and design of mining methods should be handled by a mining engineer with extensive practical experience in mining, with solid knowledge of special disciplines, especially ventilation and transportation.

The mining method selection and construction of the stope is a multi-phase and long-term process that is carried out in several steps at different stages of engineering decision-making. Only after preliminary geological investigations based on weak geological data, a method is selection and construction of the stope, technology is adopted, costs are analyzed and, based on this, a decision is made for further research. This procedure is later repeated often and several times, with a larger number of reliable data about the deposit, until the start of mining, and it often happens that during excavation, the mining method is changed, based on new knowledge about the deposit or changed external conditions.

The enumerated parameters that influence the mining method selection are not all of the same weight, some change, and some are constant. Some parameters in some cases exclude the method or technology, in other cases, some of them have no effect, etc. The basic parameters for underground mining method selection and construction of the stope are the natural conditions of the deposit and its environment, on the basis of which, in addition to other data, the mining method selection and construction of the stope, the mining technology is adopted, the work is organized for the designed production capacity, the costs of mining are defined and analyzed. This is usually done for several possible mining variants, sometimes diametrically opposed. The decision on which mining method will be applied is made in the economic analysis process, whereby as a rule, the mining method that provides the fastest return on investment and the highest profit is chosen.

MAIN FOCUS OF THE CHAPTER

In this study, research was conducted in order to solve the existing problems in the underground mining method selection, using multi-criteria decision-making methods. There is limited data on this topic in the existing literature. In this study, the EDAS method was used to select mining method, the results obtained were compared with the results obtained when applying other methods for multi-criteria decision-making, all in order to obtain the most suitable mining method.

METHODOLOGY

The procedure for underground mining method selection can be divided into two steps: rational and optimal selection (Mijalkovski et al., 2021) (Figure 1).

Figure 1. Procedure for underground mining method selection

```
                         Start
                           │
                           ▼
          ┌─────────────────────────────────┐
          │ Defining the problem:           │
          │ Mining and geological parameters│
          └─────────────────────────────────┘
                           │
                           ▼
          ┌─────────────────────────────────────────┐
          │ Rational mining method selection with   │
          │ numerical methods                       │
          └─────────────────────────────────────────┘
                           │
                           ▼
          ┌─────────────────────────────────┐
          │ Rational mining methods:        │
          │  1. Sublevel Caving             │
          │  2. Shrinkage Stoping           │
          │  3. Sublevel Stoping            │
          │  4. Cut and Fill Stoping        │
          └─────────────────────────────────┘
                           │
                           ▼
          ┌─────────────────────────────────────────┐
          │ Input data for optimal selection:       │
          │ Mining - technical and Economic parameters│
          └─────────────────────────────────────────┘
                           │
                           ▼
 ┌────────────────────────────────────────────────────────────────┐
 │ Optimal mining method selection with multi-criteria            │
 │ decision-making methods (MCDM)                                 │
 └────────────────────────────────────────────────────────────────┘
                           │
                           ▼
                   ┌───────────────┐
                   │  EDAS Method  │
                   └───────────────┘
                           │
                           ▼
            ┌─────────────────────────────┐
            │ Optimal mining method:      │
            │ Sublevel Caving             │
            └─────────────────────────────┘
```

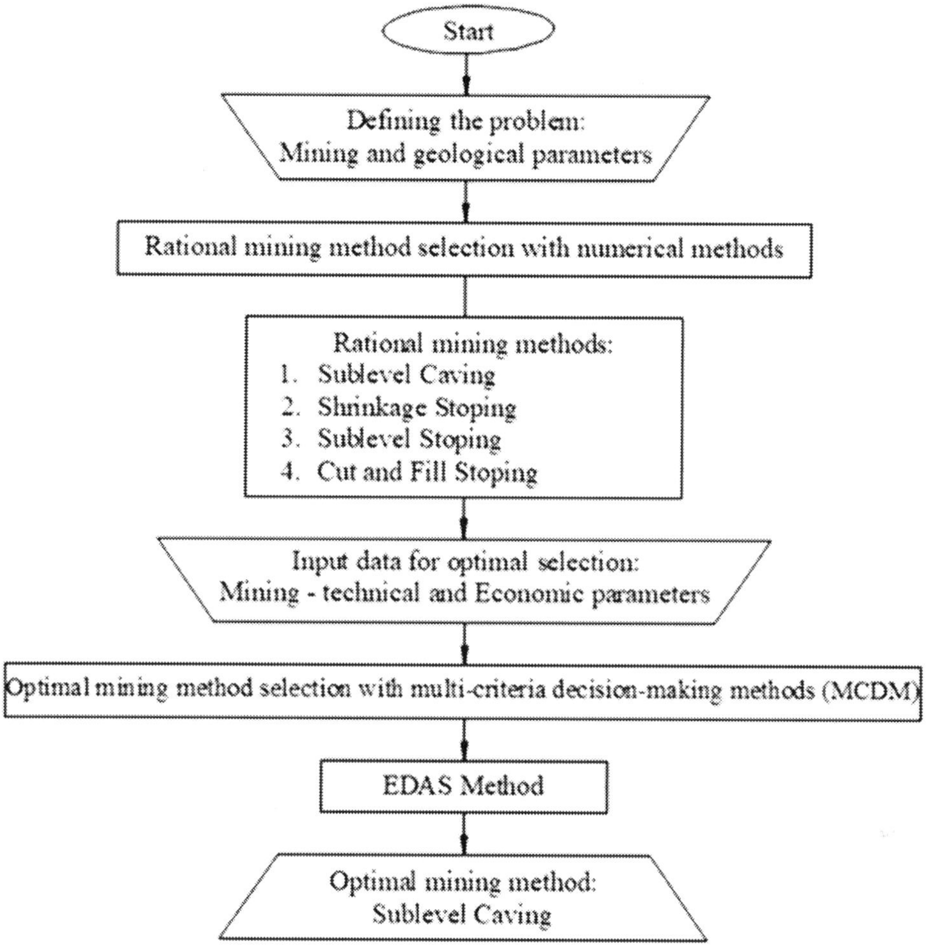

In the first step, i.e., during the rational mining method selection, all mining methods for underground exploitation are taken into account and the selection is made according to mining-geological parameters, such as: rock quality, geometry of deposit, ore variability (Mijalkovski et al., 2012a). The purpose of the rational mining method selection is to single out the mining methods that can be applied in a specific case, thereby reducing the number of mining methods that will be considered in the second step, that is, in the optimal mining method selection.

Several procedures have been developed for mining method selection according to mining-geological parameters, such as the procedure according to Hartman, Laubscher, Nicholas, UBC, etc. For the ore deposit that will be considered in this paper, a rational mining method selection was made according to the Nicholas procedure (Mijalkovski et al., 2022a) and UBC procedure (Mijalkovski et al., 2022b). In this paper, we will use a mining method selection according to the UBC procedure, and according to this procedure, the four best ranked mining methods are: Sublevel Caving, Shrinkage Stoping, Sublevel Stoping and Cut and Fill Stoping. The best ranked mining methods will represent alternatives for multi-criteria decision making in the second step.

In the second step, i.e., in the optimal mining method selection, the four best ranked mining methods according to the first step are taken into account and their selection is made according to mining-technical and economic parameters.

There are several multi-criteria decision-making methods (MCDM) that can be successfully applied for the optimal underground mining method selection, such as: AHP, PROMETHEE, ELECTRE, VIKOR, TOPSIS, EDAS and other.

The several methods for multi-criteria decision-making (MCDM) have been applied in previous research on the underground mining method selection, such as: Mijalkovski et al. in 2012 (Mijalkovski et al., 2012b), used integrated AHP and PROMETHEE method for mining method selection. Bogdanovic et al. in 2012 (Bogdanovic et al., 2012), used the PROMETHEE and AHP methods to select an appropriate mining method in the Coka Marin mine in Serbia. Mijalkovski et al. in 2020 (Mijalkovski et al., 2020), used Fuzzy TOPSIS method for risk assessment at workplace in underground lead and zinc mine. Mijalkovski et al. in 2021 (Mijalkovski et al., 2021a), used PROMETHEE method for mining method selection for underground mining. Mijalkovski et al. in 2021 (Mijalkovski et al., 2021b), used VIKOR method for mining method selection for underground mining. Ali et al. in 2021 (Ali et al., 2021), used TOPSIS and modification of the UBC method for selection mining methods via multiple criteria decision analysis. Mijalkovski et al. in 2022 (Mijalkovski et al., 2022), used TOPSIS method for underground mining method selection.

The EDAS method will be used in this paper to underground mining method selection. This method is one of the more recently developed methods in the group of methods for multi-criteria decision-making. The EDAS method has not been used so far for the underground mining method selection, and for that reason it will be applied in this paper. The result obtained by the EDAS method will be compared with other methods for multi-criteria decision-making (TOPSIS, VIKOR, AHP, PROMETHEE etc.).

There are several authors who have used the EDAS method to solve certain problems, such as: Ghorabaee et al. in 2015 (Ghorabaee et al., 2015), used Multi-criteria inventory classification using a new method of evaluation based on distance from average solution (EDAS). Ghorabaee et al. in 2016 (Ghorabaee et al., 2016), used Extended EDAS method for multi-criteria decision-making: An application to supplier selection. Kahraman et al. in 2017 (Kahraman et al., 2017), used intuitionistic fuzzy EDAS method: an application to solid waste disposal site selection. Ghorabaee et al. in 2017 (Ghorabaee et al., 2017), used stochastic EDAS method for multi-criteria decision-making with normally distributed data. Aggarwal et al. in 2018 (Aggarwal et al., 2018), used evaluation of smartphones in Indian market using EDAS. Stevic et al. in 2018 (Stevic et al., 2018) used Fuzzy EDAS method for selection of Carpenter Manufacturer.

EDAS METHOD

Estimation based on the distance from the average solution, or EDAS for short, was developed and presented by Mehdi Keshavarz Ghorabaee, where this distance is calculated in the positive and negative direction of the average solution, separately and appropriately for selected useful or non-useful criteria (Ghorabaee et al., 2015). In this case, it is necessary to create an inactive solution, with the largest values of the positive distance from the average solution and the smallest values of the negative solution that give the best solution from the average solution (Aggarwal et al., 2018). When it comes to individual judgments among decision makers in group decision making with uncertainty, it must be taken into account that not all decision makers have the same level of knowledge and experience. They may differ in terms of skills and areas of research. What sets the EDAS method apart is that the result is obtained from the average solution, which eliminates the risk of expert bias towards alternatives. The result obtained from the average solution normalizes the data, which greatly limits the chances of deviation from the best solution. In this way, a better and more accurate solution is obtained than what is obtained by the TOPSIS and VIKOR methods, when solving a specific real problem.

The steps to solve this method are given below:

Step 1: Selection of the most important criteria, which describe the alternatives;
Step 2: Constructing a decision matrix (X);
Step 3: Determination of the average solution by all criteria:

$$AV_j = \frac{\sum_{i=1}^{n} X_{ij}}{n} \quad (1)$$

Where n is the number of alternatives.

Step 4: Calculating Positive Distance from Average (PDA) and Calculating Negative Distance from Average (NDA):

If the jth criterion is useful:

$$PDA_{ij} = \frac{max\left(0, \left(X_{ij} - AV_j\right)\right)}{AV_j} \quad (2)$$

$$NDA_{ij} = \frac{max\left(0, \left(AV_j - X_{ij}\right)\right)}{AV_j} \quad (3)$$

If the jth criterion is useless:

$$PDA_{ij} = \frac{max\left(0, \left(AV_j - X_{ij}\right)\right)}{AV_j} \quad (4)$$

$$NDA_{ij} = \frac{max\left(0, \left(X_{ij} - AV_j\right)\right)}{AV_j} \quad (5)$$

Where i is alternative.

Step 5: Determination of the weighted sum of PDA and NDA for all alternatives:

$$SP_i = \sum_{j=1}^{m} w_j PDA_{ij} \qquad (6)$$

$$SN_i = \sum_{j=1}^{m} w_j NDA_{ij} \qquad (7)$$

Where w_j is the weight of the jth criterion.

Step 6: The normalize the values for SP, SN, NSP and NSN:

$$NSP_i = \frac{SP_i}{max_i(SP_i)} \qquad (8)$$

$$NSN_i = 1 - \frac{SN_i}{max_i(SN_i)} \qquad (9)$$

Step 7: Calculation of grade (AS) for all alternatives:

$$AS_i = \frac{1}{2}(NSP_i + NSN_i) \qquad (10)$$

Where $0 \leq AS_i \leq 1$.

Step 8: Ranking of alternatives according to decreasing grade values (AS). The alternative with the highest AS value is ranked best.

APPLICATION

In this paper, an underground mine of lead and zinc, which is currently actively working and a new section is being opened, will be considered, where it is necessary selecting the appropriate mining method. The ore body is a platy-tabular, with an average ore thickness of 12m, an average plunge of 36°, the depth below surface is about 580m and the grade distribution is erratic.

In the mining work so far, mining methods have been applied, which were obtained as the best ranked mining methods according to the UBC procedure (Mijalkovski et al., 2022b), that is, according to the rational mining method selection and will represent alternatives for the optimal mining method selection, with the application of the EDAS method (Table 1). For the optimal selection, we will use eight mining-technical and economic parameters, which will represent the criteria by which the alternatives will be compared (Table 2). Each criterion has a different impact on the alternatives, i.e. a different weight. In this work, the weights of the criteria were defined in consultation with a group of 10 experts in the field of underground exploitation, in order to reduce subjectivity in decision-making to a minimum. Each expert gave his opinion on the weight of the criteria, and then the mean value was calculated and further calculations were done with it using the EDAS method. Table 2 shows the goal the criteria aim for (min or max) and the criteria's classification category (qualitative or quantitative). Some criteria can be measured or calculated (quantitative), and some criteria cannot be measured or calculated (qualitative). Criteria that cannot be measured or calculated are defined by a descriptive score and in order to be used for further calculations, they need to be transformed into numerical values. The transformation from descriptive ratings of numerical values can be done using a qualitative scale, an interval scale, a linear scale, a bipolar transformation scale, etc. In this paper, an interval scale was used to transform qualitative into quantitative values.

Table 1. Alternatives

Alternatives	Symbol
Sublevel Caving	A_1
Shrinkage Stoping	A_2
Sublevel Stoping	A_3
Cut and Fill Stoping	A_4

Table 2. Criteria

Criteria	Symbol	Weights	Definition
Effect of mining	K_1	0,095	This criterion is quantitative and tends to the maximum. The value for this criterion is taken from the literature, according to each alternative.
Ore recovery	K_2	0,145	This criterion is quantitative and tends to the maximum. The value for this criterion is taken from the literature, according to each alternative.
Terrain degradation and other environmental impacts	K_3	0,065	This criterion is qualitative and tends to the minimum. Qualitative grades are assigned to each alternative.
Occupational safety and health conditions	K_4	0,125	This criterion is qualitative and tends to the maximum. Qualitative grades are assigned to each alternative.
Cost of one ton (1 t) of ore	K_5	0,180	This criterion is qualitative and tends to the minimum.
Coefficient of ore dilution	K_6	0,085	This criterion is quantitative and tends to the minimum. The value for this criterion is taken from the literature, according to each alternative.
Value of mined ore	K_7	0,195	This criterion is quantitative and tends to the maximum. The values are obtained by a separate calculation for each alternative.
Coefficient of preparation works	K_8	0,110	This criterion is quantitative and tends to the minimum. The value for this criterion is taken from the literature, according to each alternative.

After the analysis to evaluate the criteria for each alternative solution, a multi-criteria model was defined based on theory and our assessment (Table 3).

Table 3. Input model for EDAS method

Alternatives	Criteria							
	K_1	K_2	K_3	K_4	K_5	K_6	K_7	K_8
Goal	max	max	min	max	min	min	max	min
A_1	30.000	75.000	9.000	9.000	3.000	22.000	77.300	2.560
A_2	10.000	85.000	3.000	7.000	7.000	12.000	88.200	17.550
A_3	22.000	80.000	5.000	5.000	7.000	18.000	81.600	23.900
A_4	15.000	94.000	3.000	7.000	9.000	6.000	93.300	8.650
Weights of criteria	0.095	0.145	0.065	0.125	0.180	0.085	0.195	0.110

Table 4. Determine the average solution (AV_j)

Average solution	Criteria							
	K_1	K_2	K_3	K_4	K_5	K_6	K_7	K_8
AV_j	19.250	83.500	5.000	7.000	6.500	14.500	85.100	13.165

Table 5. Calculate the positive distance from average (PDA)

Alternatives	Criteria							
	K_1	K_2	K_3	K_4	K_5	K_6	K_7	K_8
Goal	max	max	min	max	min	min	max	min
A_1	0.558	0.000	0.000	0.286	0.538	0.000	0.000	0.806
A_2	0.000	0.018	0.400	0.000	0.000	0.172	0.036	0.000
A_3	0.143	0.000	0.000	0.000	0.000	0.000	0.000	0.000
A_4	0.000	0.126	0.400	0.000	0.000	0.586	0.096	0.343
Weights of criteria	0.095	0.145	0.065	0.125	0.180	0.085	0.195	0.110

Table 6. Calculate the negative distance from average (NDA)

Alternatives	Criteria							
	K_1	K_2	K_3	K_4	K_5	K_6	K_7	K_8
Goal	max	max	min	max	min	min	max	min
A_1	0.000	0.102	0.800	0.000	0.000	0.517	0.092	0.000
A_2	0.481	0.000	0.000	0.000	0.077	0.000	0.000	0.333
A_3	0.000	0.042	0.000	0.286	0.077	0.241	0.041	0.815
A_4	0.221	0.000	0.000	0.000	0.385	0.000	0.000	0.000
Weights of criteria	0.095	0.145	0.065	0.125	0.180	0.085	0.195	0.110

Table 7. Weighted sum of PDA

Alternatives	Criteria							
	K_1	K_2	K_3	K_4	K_5	K_6	K_7	K_8
Goal	max	max	min	max	min	min	max	min
A_1	0.053	0.000	0.000	0.036	0.097	0.000	0.000	0.089
A_2	0.000	0.003	0.026	0.000	0.000	0.015	0.007	0.000
A_3	0.014	0.000	0.000	0.000	0.000	0.000	0.000	0.000
A_4	0.000	0.018	0.026	0.000	0.000	0.050	0.019	0.038

Table 8. Weighted sum of NDA

Alternatives	Criteria							
	K_1	K_2	K_3	K_4	K_5	K_6	K_7	K_8
Goal	max	max	min	max	min	min	max	min
A_1	0.000	0.015	0.052	0.000	0.000	0.044	0.018	0.000
A_2	0.046	0.000	0.000	0.000	0.014	0.000	0.000	0.037
A_3	0.000	0.006	0.000	0.036	0.014	0.021	0.008	0.090
A_4	0.021	0.000	0.000	0.000	0.069	0.000	0.000	0.000

Table 9. Calculate normalize the values of SP, SN, NSP, NSN and AS

Alternatives	SP_i	SN_i	NSP_i	NSN_i	AS_i
A_1	0.274	0.129	1.000	0.260	0.630
A_2	0.050	0.096	0.184	0.447	0.315
A_3	0.014	0.174	0.049	0.000	0.025
A_4	0.151	0.090	0.549	0.481	0.515

Table 10. Ranking of alternatives

Alternatives	AS_i	Rank
A_1	0.630	1
A_2	0.315	3
A_3	0.025	4
A_4	0.515	2

As we can see from Table 10 and Figure 2, the best-ranked alternative is A_1, i.e., the most suitable method of mining excavation for the specific case is the Sublevel Caving. The second ranked alternative is A_4, i.e., Cut and Fill Stoping. The third ranked alternative is A_2 (Shrinkage Stoping) and the last ranked alternative is A_3 (Sublevel Stoping).

Figure 2. Ranking of alternatives

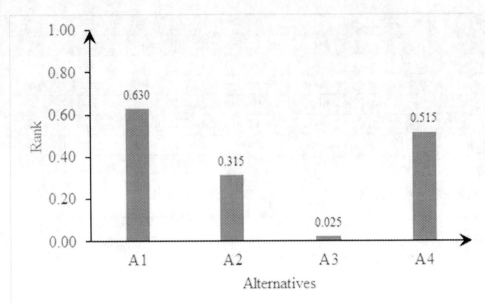

During the analysis for the final mining method selection for the mine that is the subject of consideration in this paper, several multi-criteria decision-making methods were applied. The resulting ranking of mining methods is mostly unchanged or changes slightly in the ranking order.

Table 11 shows the ranking of mining methods obtained according to the EDAS, TOPSIS (Mijalkovski et al., 2022) and VIKOR (Mijalkovski et al., 2021b) methods, as the most characteristic methods for multi-criteria decision-making. From Table 11, we can notice that the ranking according to the EDAS and TOPSIS method is identical, and according to the VIKOR method there is a slight change in the order of ranking. When we compare the results obtained according to the three methods for multi-criteria decision-making, we can state that the best ranked mining methods are Sublevel Caving and Cut and Fill Stoping.

Table 11. Ranking of alternatives according to EDAS, TOPSIS, and VIKOR methods

Alternatives	EDAS	TOPSIS	VIKOR	Average	Rank
A_1	1	1	4	2.00	0.50
A_2	3	3	1	2.33	0.43
A_3	4	4	3	3.67	0.27
A_4	2	2	2	2.00	0.50

In order to obtain the optimal mining method, we additionally applied several multi-criteria decision-making methods: AHP, PROMETHEE II, AHP – PROMETHEE and ELECTRE I. Table 12 shows all the obtained rankings of mining methods and it can be stated that according to the newly applied methods, the best ranked is Cut and Fill Stoping.

Table 12. Final ranking of alternatives

Alternatives	EDAS	TOPSIS	VIKOR	AHP	PROMETHEE II	AHP – PROMETHEE	ELECTRE I	Rank
A_1	1	1	4	4	2	2	2	0.44
A_2	3	3	1	2	3	3	1	0.44
A_3	4	4	3	3	4	4	1	0.30
A_4	2	2	2	1	1	1	1	0.70

When comparing the results obtained according to all the methods for multi-criteria decision-making applied so far and after analyzing the average ranking, it can be concluded that the most optimal mining method is Cut and Fill Stoping (Figure 3).

Figure 3. Final ranking of alternatives

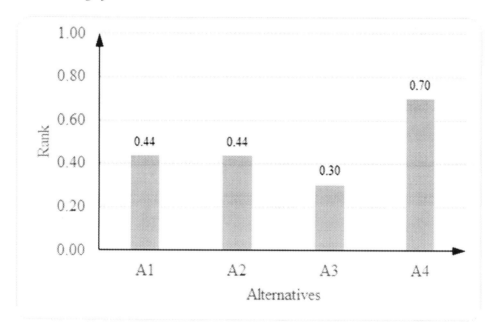

FUTURE RESEARCH DIRECTIONS

The question of underground mining method selection will always be relevant, because the financial operation of the mine it depends on the correct mining method selection. In the future, this issue will be elaborated by applying Fuzzy methods for multi-criteria decision-making, which represents a higher level for studying this issue and making the final mining method selection.

CONCLUSION

The applied mining method in a given underground mine has a direct impact on the total costs of the exploitation of the mine itself, whereby a great responsibility for the correct mining method selection arises from this.

The problem of mining method selection has been studied by many authors, and several procedures for mining method selection have been proposed and developed, taking into account the most influential parameters. According to the opinion of the majority of authors who dealt with this problem, two steps can be distinguished for the mining method selection: rational and optimal mining method selection. The complexity of this issue stems from a large number of influential parameters, which need to be taken into account when mining method selection. All these influences parameters can be divided into three groups: mining - geological, mining - technical and economic parameters.

Multi-criteria decision-making methods make it possible to take into account a large number of criteria when solving a certain problem, that is, when choosing the best-ranked alternative. This possibility of multi-criteria decision-making can also be applied when mining method selection, where more influential parameters will be taken into account. In previous research, several methods for multi-criteria decision-making were applied, all with the aim of choosing a mining excavation method for the same real case. The obtained results do not differ much from each other, that is, there is little change in the order of mining methods. When the EDAS and TOPSIS methods are applied, the top-ranked mining method is Sublevel Caving. Whereas, when the VIKOR method is applied, the top ranked mining method is Shrinkage Stoping. After comparing the results obtained according to the three methods for multi-criteria decision-making, we came to the conclusion that two mining methods were obtained as the best ranked: Sublevel Caving и Cut and Fill Stoping. In order to obtain the optimal mining method, we applied several more methods for multi-criteria decision-making: AHP, PROMETHEE II, AHP - PROMETHEE and ELECTRE I, according to which the Cut and Fill Stoping was ranked best. After comparing the results obtained according to all methods for multi-criteria decision-making applied so far, we can conclude that the most optimal method of mining excavation is Cut and Fill Stoping.

REFERENCES

Aggarwal, A., Choudhary, C., & Mehrotra, D. (2018). Evaluation of smartphones in Indian market using EDAS, *International Conference on Computational Intelligence and Data Science (ICCIDS 2018), ScienceDirect,* (*vol. 132*, pp. 236-243). Science Direct. 10.1016/j.procs.2018.05.193

Ali, M. A. M., & Kim, J. G. (2021). Selection mining methods via multiple criteria decision analysis using TOPSIS and modification of the UBC method. *Journal of Sustainable Mining, 20*(2), 49–55. doi:10.46873/2300-3960.1054

Bogdanovic, D., Nikolic, D., & Ilic, I. (2012). Mining method selection by integrated AHP and PROMETHEE method. *Anais da Academia Brasileira de Ciências, 84*(1), 219–233. doi:10.1590/S0001-37652012005000013 PMID:22441612

Ghorabaee, M. K., Amiri, M., Zavadskas, E. K., Turskis, Z., & Antucheviciene, J. (2017). Stochastic EDAS method for multi-criteria decision-making with normally distributed data. *Journal of Intelligent & Fuzzy Systems, 33*(3), 1627–1638. doi:10.3233/JIFS-17184

Ghorabaee, M. K., Zavadskas, E. K., Amiri, M., & Turskis, Z. (2016). Extended EDAS method for multi-criteria decision-making: An application to supplier selection. *International Journal of Computers, Communications & Control, 11*(3), 358–371. doi:10.15837/ijccc.2016.3.2557

Ghorabaee, M. K., Zavadskas, E. K., Olfat, L., & Turskis, Z. (2015). Multi-criteria inventory classification using a new method of evaluation based on distance from average solution (EDAS). *Informatica (Vilnius), 26*(3), 435–451. doi:10.15388/Informatica.2015.57

Kahraman, C., Ghorabaee, M. K., Zavadskas, E. K., Onar, S. C., Yazdani, M., & Oztaysi, B. (2017). Intuitionistic fuzzy EDAS method: An application to solid waste disposal site selection. *Journal of Environmental Engineering and Landscape Management, 25*(1), 1–12. doi:10.3846/16486897.2017.1281139

Mijalkovski, S., Despodov, Z., Mirakovski, D., Adjiski, V. & Doneva, N. (2022b). Application of UBC methodology for underground mining method selection, *Underground mining engineering, 40*(1), 15-26.

Mijalkovski, S., Despodov, Z., Mirakovski, D., Adjiski, V., Doneva, N., & Mijalkovska, D. (2021a). Mining method selection for underground mining with the application of PROMETHEE method. *3st International Multidisciplinary Geosciences Conference (IMGC 2021), Mitrovica, October 2021*, (pp. 84-91). Science Direct.

Mijalkovski, S., Despodov, Z., Mirakovski, D., Adjiski, V., Doneva, N. & Mijalkovska, D. (2021b). Mining method selection for underground mining with the application of VIKOR method. *Underground mining engineering, 39*(2), 11-22.

Mijalkovski, S., Despodov, Z., Mirakovski, D., Hadzi-Nikolova, M., Doneva, N. & Gocevski, B. (2012b). Mining method selection by integrated AHP and PROMETHEE method. *PODEKS-POVEKS 2012, Stip,* 121-127.

Mijalkovski, S., Despodov, Z., Mirakovski, D. & Mijalkovska, D. (2012a). Rational selection of mining excavation methods. *Natural resources and technology, 6*(6), 15-23.

Mijalkovski, S., Efe, O. F., Despodov, Z., Mirakovski, D., & Mijalkovska, D. (2022). Underground mining method selection with the application of TOPSIS method. *GeoScience Engineering, 68*(2), 125–133. doi:10.35180/gse-2022-0075

Mijalkovski, S., Peltechki, D., Zeqiri, K., Kortnik, J., & Mirakovski, D. (2020). Risk assessment at workplace in underground lead and zinc mine with application of Fuzzy TOPSIS method. *Journal of the Institute of Electronics and Computer, 2,* 121–141.

Mijalkovski, S., Peltecki, D., Despodov, Z., Mirakovski, D., Adjiski, V. & Doneva, N. (2021). Methodology for underground mining method selection. *Mining science, 28,* 201-216.

Mijalkovski, S., Zeqiri, K., Despodov, Z., & Adjiski, V. (2022a). Underground mining method selection according to Nicholas methodology. *Natural Resources and Technology, 16*(1), 5–11. doi:10.46763/NRT22161005m

Stevic, Z., Vasiljevic, M., Zavadskas, E. K., Sremac, S., & Turskis, Z. (2018). Selection of Carpenter Manufacturer using Fuzzy EDAS Method. *The Engineering Economist*, *29*(3), 281–290.

ADDITIONAL READING

Brans, J. P., & Vincke, P. (1985). A Preference Ranking Organisation Method: (The PROMETHEE Method for Multiple Criteria Decision-Making). *Management Science*, *31*(6), 647–656. doi:10.1287/mnsc.31.6.647

Massam, B. H. (1988). Multi-Criteria Decision Making (MCDM) techniques in planning. *Progress in Planning*, *30*, 1–84. doi:10.1016/0305-9006(88)90012-8

Miller, T. L., Pakalnis, R., & Poulin, R. (1995). UBC Mining Method Selection. Singhal R.K. et at. (Eds), Mine planning and equipment selection. (MPES), 163-168. Balkema, Rotterdam.

Opricovic, S., & Tzeng, G. H. (2004). Compromise solution by MCDM mehods: A comparative analysis of VIKOR and TOPSIS. *European Journal of Operational Research*, *156*(2), 445–455. doi:10.1016/S0377-2217(03)00020-1

Parıda, P. K. (2019). A general view of TOPSIS method involving multi-attribute decision making problems. [IJITEE]. *International Journal of Innovative Technology and Exploring Engineering*, *9*(2), 3205–3214. doi:10.35940/ijitee.B7745.129219

Roy, B. (1968). Classement et choix en presence de points de vue multiples (La methode ELECTRE), *Revue Francaise D Informatique de Recherche Operationnelle*, *2*(8), 57–75.

Saaty, T. L. (2008). Decision making with analytic hierarchy process. *International Journal of Services Sciences*, *1*(1), 83–98. doi:10.1504/IJSSCI.2008.017590

KEY TERMS AND DEFINITIONS

Alternative (A): Different options in the context of certain actions, which are present for decision makers.

Analytic Hierarchy Process (AHP): It is a multi-criteria decision making technique developed by Thomas Saaty.

Criteria (C): Properties used to evaluate alternatives.

ÉLimination Et Choix Traduisant la REalité - "Elimination and Choice Translating Reality" (ELECTRE): It is a multi-criteria decision making technique developed by Bernard Roy.

Estimation based on the Distance from the Average Solution (EDAS): It is a multi-criteria decision making technique developed by Mehdi Keshavarz Ghorabaee.

Multi Criteria Decision Making (MCDM): MCDM is a research discipline that explicitly considers multiple criteria in decision-making process.

Preference Ranking Organization METHod for Enrichment Evaluations (PROMETHEE): It is a multi-criteria decision making technique developed by Brans.

Technique for Order Preference by Similarity to Ideal Solution (TOPSIS): It is a multi-criteria decision making technique developed by Hwang and Yoon.

University of British Columbia (UBC): It is a mining method selection algorithm developed by Miller, Pakalnis and Poulin.

VIsekriterijumskog KOmpromisnog Rangiranja - "Multi-Criteria Optimization and Compromise Solution" (VIKOR): It is a multi-criteria decision making technique developed by Serafim Opricovic.

Chapter 4
Exploring Intention to Purchase Energy-Efficient Home Appliances:
An Extension of the Theory of Planned Behavior

Ahmed Chemseddine Bouarar
University of Medea, Algeria

Kamel Mouloudj
University of Medea, Algeria

Asma Makhlouf
University of Medea, Algeria

Smail Mouloudj
University of Medea, Algeria

ABSTRACT

The corporations' irrational behavior and individuals' alike had a disastrous effect on the environment due to increasing energy consumption and causing a massive squandering of natural resources. That prompted researchers and practitioners worldwide (in developed and developing countries) to consider and pay immense attention to saving energy behavior. Hence, this chapter seeks to identify the factors that affect the intention to purchase energy-efficient home appliances in Algeria. Data were collected using a convenience sample; consumers in three cities were invited to participate in a questionnaire survey. The analysis was ultimately conducted on 193 valid questionnaires. The findings revealed that attitude, subjective norms, perceived behavioral control (PBC), and environmental awareness positively impacted the intention to purchase energy-efficient home appliances. Therefore, this chapter provides relevant policy recommendations on stimulating consumer's intention to purchase energy-efficient home appliances.

DOI: 10.4018/978-1-6684-8969-7.ch004

INTRODUCTION

Over the past few decades, energy demand and consumption have rapidly increased due to the destructive changes in the energy industry and service industry and people's lifestyles worldwide (Akroush et al., 2019). Furthermore, irrational consumption behavior and habits have inflicted the environment with a massive deterioration (Bansal & Sharma, 2018), such as climate change and wasted resources (Hua & Wang, 2019; Wang et al., 2019). This has o led to an increased use of sustainable products (Goel et al., 2022). Joshi et al. (2020, p. 40) pointed out that "increasing environmental concerns have resulted in consumers indulging in conserving energy by curtailing energy usage rather than switching to energy efficient practices." However, the high demand for energy resulting from technologically advanced electrical and electronic appliances has strengthened the importance of energy efficiency to conquer energy deficiency and environmental concerns (Ali et al., 2021).

So, more producers are manufacturing eco-friendly products to tackle the adverse effects, and governments are encouraging residents to use energy-saving products, specifically energy-efficient appliances manufactured to save energy in daily life (Hua & Wang, 2019). Energy-efficient appliances help reduce energy consumption and meet consumers' utilitarian needs (Fatoki, 2020; Waris & Hameed, 2020a; 2020b). Therefore, household energy conservation is key to reducing emissions (Karlin et al., 2014).

Algeria is one of the world's largest countries producing and exporting energy, as it holds a considerable energy reserve and possesses the tenth-largest gas reserves and the third-largest shale gas reserves globally (Abada & Bouharkat, 2018). It is also a major natural gas-producing country in Africa and the second-largest natural gas exporter to Europe; it is also among the three largest oil producers on the African continent (Anon, 2014). However, fossil fuels remain the primary source of electricity generation and the third-largest CO_2 emitter in Africa, which is mainly susceptible to climate change (Bouznit et al., 2020). Therefore, understanding human eco-friendly decisions is pivotal to overcoming global environmental challenges, as influencing behavior makes a significant difference (Klöckner, 2013). In the hope of alleviating global climate change, Algeria is developing a strategy based on combining sustainable development with international climate-related commitments; besides, it is increasingly promoting renewable energy adoption in the electricity sector (Bouznit et al., 2020).

The theory of planned behavior (TPB) is considered one of the most modern utilized theories to predict human behavior. The TPB has proven its robustness in predicting behavior in different spheres, including save energy consumption (Mouloudj et al., 2023). It has also proven its soundness in several contexts, including those in developing countries. The TPB stems from the theory of reasoned action (TRA), which assumes that consumers are rational and employ all available information to assess the potential implications of their actions before making any decisions to perform a particular behavior or not (Ramkissoon & Nunkoo, 2010). According to Ajzen (1991), behavioral intention is a function of three constructs—namely, "attitude toward the behavior, perceived behavioral control (PBC), and subjective norms"—and each predicts behavioral intentions.

The intention to purchase energy-efficient appliances using TPB has been explored by Ali et al. (2021), who found that attitudes, PBC, policy information campaigns, and previous experience significantly influence the intention. Recently, Gangakhedkar et al. (2023) conducted a meta-analytic review of 30 researches that have used TPB investigate intentions to purchase energy efficient household appliances. They have found that all the three TPB constructs have medium to large relationship with the intention. In this context, additional variables have been incorporated into the TPB to improve the model's predictability (e.g., Ali et al., 2021; Asif et al., 2023; Bhutto et al., 2021; Fatoki, 2020; Harun et al., 2022; Li et al., 2019; Waris & Ahmed, 2020).

Mouloudj et al. (2023) showed that adding environmental awareness to the original TPB model extensively strengthened the explanatory power of the intention to save energy, indicating that environmental awareness was a strong predictor of intention. Paul et al. (2016) confirm the suitability and strength of the extended TPB in predicting green product purchase intention in the light of TPB in developing country cases. In addition, other researchers have combined the TPB with several different theories to identify the factors that influence energy-saving appliance purchase intentions. For example, Hua & Wang (2019) merged the technology acceptance model (TAM) and TPB. Wang et al. (2019) integrated the norm-activation theory model and TPB. Ali et al. (2019) combined the TPB and the technology readiness index (TRI).

The present study includes environmental awareness, which is considered a significant predictor of behavioral intentions to purchase green products (Mouloudj & Bouarar, 2021), energy-efficient appliances (Teoh et al., 2022; Wang et al., 2017), and intention to create green start-ups (Bouarar et al., 2022). The purchasing behavior of green products, in general, and energy-saving products, in particular, is influenced by many psychological, cultural, social, and economic factors. In developed countries, the popularity and utilization of these particular appliances are increasing due to the high level of environmental awareness. As for the Algerian context, energy-saving household appliances are relatively new on the market, and the level of environmental awareness is somewhat low among Algerian consumers.

Additionally, despite the large body of literature on the intention to purchase energy-efficient home appliances, hardly any research has been focused on this topic in the context of Algeria as a developing country. To fill this lacuna, this paper aims to: (1) determine the impact of TPB constructs and environmental awareness on the intention of the consumer to purchase energy-efficient home appliances; (2) develop and validate a model that extends a TPB to include environmental awareness; and (3) answer the call by Hua and Wang (2019), who suggested future studies to measure the intention to purchase energy-efficient appliances. The paper is structured as follows. Section 2 presents literature reviews and hypothesis development. Section 3 explains the methodology. Section 4 presents the main results and discussions. Section 5 includes implications and directions for future research.

THEORETICAL FRAMEWORK AND HYPOTHESES

Intention to Purchase Energy Efficient Home Appliances

Energy efficiency plays a vital role in developing sustainable energy and alleviating the effects of the energy sector on the environment. Energy-efficient appliances are deemed useful, advanced, innovative, and helpful to the household in providing better service and mitigating the burden of housework and chores (Hua & Wang, 2019). Energy-efficient home appliances include appliances that consume less energy due to their specific design to save energy; these appliances are often more expensive than the old ones. Home appliances consumers from an energy-saving perspective can be categorized into three categories: (1) those interested in saving energy; (2) those reluctant to the idea of saving energy due to their distrust in manufacturers' claims; and (3) those uninterested in saving energy behavior due to the lack of awareness about energy saving, and their unique interest in prices and quality as being the most relevant criteria in their purchasing behavior. Accordingly, understanding the purchasing intention toward energy-efficient home appliances is the cornerstone to attracting and convincing more consumers.

Mouloudj and Bouarar (2023) define intention as "the extent of the individual's willingness to complete the behavior". In this study, the purchase intention is defined as the possibility that a consumer performs a purchase energy-efficient home appliance. Intention to purchase energy-efficient appliances can get influenced positively by many factors, including policy information campaigns and prior experiences (Ali et al., 2021), societal norms (Joshi et al., 2019), moral norms (Fatoki, 2020), environmental knowledge (Li et al., 2019), social relationships, level of education and age (Wang et al., 2017), perceived benefits (Akroush et al., 2019), social interaction and quality (Harun et al., 2022), environmental concern, environmental attitude, and environmental trust (Issock et al., 2018), functional value (Issock & Muposhi, 2023), and consumers social responsibility (Jamil et al., 2022). Abu-Elsamen et al. (2019) found that risk perceptions (performance and financial) negatively correlate with the intention to purchase energy-efficient household products. However, Joshi et al. (2019) found that price sensitivity and risk perceptions positively correlate with the intention to purchase energy-efficient appliances.

On the other side, various potential barriers to purchasing energy-efficient appliances have been identified. Those barriers are low electricity costs, lack of trust in energy-efficient labels and products, low awareness about energy-efficient and energy conservation and absence of incentives to retailers (Dianshu et al., 2010), low level of awareness on energy-efficient appliances, and distrust claims made on labels of energy-efficient appliances (Joshi et al., 2019). Therefore, identifying factors influencing energy-efficient home appliances purchasing intention may significantly help overcome these barriers.

Attitudes Towards Energy-Efficient Home Appliances

Attitude refers to "the human propensity to behave positively or negatively towards the attitude in question" (Mouloudj & Bouarar, 2021). In psychology, Ajzen (1991, p. 188) defines attitude as "the degree to which a person has a favorable or unfavorable evaluation or appraisal of the behavior in question." The consumer's attitude is a direct antecedent intention to behave in a certain way (Kotler et al., 2016). One of these behaviors is the consumer's inclination to save energy, which influences his attitude (Wang et al., 2014). Attitudes can depict people's appraisement of energy-saving appliances or the purchasing behavior of energy-saving (Wang et al., 2017). Mouloudj and Bouarar (2021) confirmed that attitudes significantly affect the intention to purchase green products. Several empirical research find that attitude toward energy-efficient household products positively relates to purchase intention (Abu-Elsamen et al., 2019; Ali et al., 2019; Ali et al., 2021; Fatoki, 2020; Zhu & Thøgersen, 2023). Akroush et al. (2019) explored the influencing factors for the purchase intention of energy-efficient products and proved that attitude has the most significant effect. According to Waris and Ahmed (2020), there is a positive relationship between attitude and a consumer's tendency to purchase energy-efficient home appliances due to the low electricity consumption of these appliances and the reduced carbon emissions. However, Božić (2021) found evidence that attitudes toward climate change do not affect the actual purchase of electric cars among European consumers. Also, Harun et al. (2022) reported that attitudes had insignificant impact on intentions to purchase energy-efficient appliances in Malaysia. Recently, Asif et al. (2023) found that attitudes do not have a significant effect on purchase intentions of energy efficient appliances among Pakistani consumers. Thus, it can be expected that the consumer's attitude influences purchase intention. In this regard, the following hypothesis is formulated:

H1: Attitude has a positive impact on the intention to purchase energy-efficient home appliances.

Subjective Norms

Referring to the TPB presented by Ajzen, subjective norms are one of the three determinants of intention to behave in a particular manner, which are defined as "perceived social pressure to perform or not to perform the behavior" (Ajzen, 1991, p. 188). Social pressure is usually imposed by people who are essential to the individual, such as family members, friends, or co-workers. There is consensus in the energy efficiency literature regarding the low impact of subjective norms on a consumer's purchase intention among all constructs in the TPB.

In China, Zhu & Thøgersen (2023) reported that subjective norms had insignificant impact on intentions to purchase energy-efficient appliances. Subjective norms were found to be insignificant in influencing consumers' intentions to purchase energy-efficient appliances (Ali et al., 2021; Fatoki, 2020), similar to what was reported by (Bhutto et al., 2021; Tan et al., 2017). The results were also consistent with those of Li et al. (2019), which indicated that the impact of subjective norms on residents' willingness to buy energy-efficient appliances was not significant. Nevertheless, the previously discussed findings were counterintuitive to the results of Hua and Wang (2019), who found that subjective norms significantly impacted buying attention. These results have been further supported by Waris and Ahmed (2020) and Harun et al. (2022), who emphasized the positive influence of subjective norms on a consumer's intention to purchase energy-efficient appliances. Therefore, the discussion above leads to the following hypothesis:

H2: Subjective norm has a positive impact on the intention to purchase energy-efficient home appliances.

Perceived Behavioural Control (PBC)

PBC was added to the TRA as a third determining factor of intention to clarify the circumstances wherein individuals cannot take full control over their behavior. Conceptually, PBC refers to the individuals' judgments regarding the extent of their ability to perform a particular behavior in the presence of the necessary resources and opportunities. Ajzen (1991, p. 183) defined PBC as "a person's perception of the ease or difficulty of performing the behavior of interest." The level of perceived difficulty of implementing the behavior in question is influenced by multiple factors. These factors include previous experiences, knowledge (Azjen, 1991), required skills and abilities, time availability or its insufficiency, premium prices, and cooperation by other individuals (Ajzen, 2020). Within the context of buying energy-efficient appliances, the result shows that PBC in terms of devices' availability and reasonable prices has a significant impact on consumers' purchase intentions (Ali et al., 2021; Zhu & Thøgersen, 2023). The same result was reached by Hua and Wang (2019), who assumed that the more consumers believed in their ability to own and use energy-efficient appliances, the more willing they were to purchase them. These findings were consonant with those achieved by Waris and Ahmed (2020), who confirmed a positive impact of perceived effectiveness on intentions to purchase energy-efficient appliances. Fatoki (2020) reported that PBC had a positive effect on purchasing intentions for energy-efficient appliances in South Africa. Galván-Mendoza et al. (2022) found that PBC influences female employees green behavior and is affected by environmental knowledge. Therefore, the following hypothesis is formulated:

H3: PBC has a positive impact on the intention to purchase energy-efficient home appliances.

Environmental Awareness

According to Mouloudj & Bouarar (2021, p. 875), environmental awareness refers to "the first level of environmental knowledge the individual owns about the causes and effects of environmental damage." Environmental awareness is a sense of taking full responsibility for improving the environment and resisting all actions that may threaten its safety. Arguably, a consumer's environmental awareness reflects the consumer's concept of environmental protection and his attention to solving ecological-related issues such as reducing energy consumption. The study of Lillemo (2014) sought to explore the relationship between energy-saving behavior and environmental awareness. The result reveals that people with a higher level of environmental awareness are more likely to make decisions towards energy saving, such as reducing the indoor temperature when they are out. Yue et al. (2020) found that environmental concern has a significant influence on green consumption intentions in China.

Some studies have found that environmental awareness has direct positive influences on intentions to purchase energy-efficient household products (Abu-Elsamen et al. 2019; Teoh et al., 2022). Fatoki (2020) showed that environmental concern has a significant effect on the intention to purchase energy-efficient appliances. Another study has shown that residents who are more concerned about the environment have a higher ecological purchase intention (Arisal & Atalar, 2016). Galván-Mendoza et al. (2022) found that environmental knowledge influences employees green behavior. These findings contradict the research conclusions of Zhang et al. (2020), who found that environmental awareness has no significant effect on consumers' attitudes toward purchasing energy-saving appliances. In this regard, the following hypothesis is formulated:

H4: Environmental awareness has a positive impact on the intention to purchase energy-efficient home appliances.

RESEARCH METHODOLOGY

Sample and Procedure

The data collection methodology for the current study is survey research. The questionnaire includes demographic information about participants (gender, age, monthly income level, education level, and marital status). The selection of the sample was based on a non-probability convenience sampling, which included those who expressed a willingness to participate in the study. The convenience sampling method is rapid, helpful, readily available, and cost-effective, making it a useful and appealing option to most marketing researchers (Mouloudj & Bouarar, 2021). Like most marketing studies, individuals above 18 years old are the most suitable to fill out questionnaires associated with energy-saving products. The questionnaire was distributed in three cities located in central Algeria, namely Medea, Bouira, and Blida. Paper-form copies of the questionnaire were distributed with the help of some appliance retailers. Data has been collected from May 1st, 2021, to July 10th, 2021.

Totally, out of 300 questionnaires distributed, 212 questionnaires were retrieved. However, the analyses were ultimately conducted on 193 questionnaires, since 19 copies were either incomplete or incorrect. Respondents' demographic analysis revealed that most of them were males (71.5%), and half of the total respondents (53.87%) were between 35 and 50 years old. Regarding monthly income, it ranged between 35,000 and 55,000 dinars for nearly 98 (50.78%) respondents. For the educational level, nearly one-third of respondents 67(34.72%) have a secondary school level or less, and 81(41.97%) have a university degree. Finally, concerning marital status, most of the respondents (58.08%) were married.

Measurement

The adopted questionnaire employed reliable and validated scales based on previous studies. The attitude was measured using three items scale from Akroush et al. (2019); and Waris and Hameed (2020a). Subjective norms measures were adapted from Fatoki (2020) and Mouloudj et al. (2023). PBC has been measured using three items adapted from Bouarar et al. (2021). Environmental awareness measures were adapted from Mouloudj and Bouarar (2021); Bouarar et al. (2022); and Mouloudj et al. (2023). The purchase intentions scale was adapted from Akroush et al. (2019). Ahead of the questionnaire distribution process, three academics in environmental marketing were invited to review the questionnaire, to assure content validity. Minor revisions were introduced based on the provided suggestions. A pilot test of the questionnaire was also conducted on 20 respondents. All items except "I think the environment is getting worse" and "If I can choose between energy-efficient home appliances and conventional home appliances, I prefer energy-efficient home appliances one" were added for the final analysis. The items of the questionnaire were scored on a five-point Likert scale; "(1) strongly disagrees to (5) strongly agree". The questionnaire was initially in English and then translated into Arabic. The two versions of the questionnaire were distributed according to the participants' will. The constructs measurement is shown in Table 1.

Table 1. Measurement of constructs

Constructs	Measurement Item	Reference
Attitude	ATT1 Purchasing energy-efficient home appliances are a good idea.	Akroush et al. (2019); Waris and Hameed (2020a)
	ATT2 Energy-efficient home appliances can save electricity and this is important to me.	
	ATT3 I have a favorable attitude towards purchasing energy-efficient home appliances.	
Subjective Norm	SN1 Most people who are important to me think I should buy energy-efficient home appliances.	Mouloudj et al. (2023); Fatoki (2020)
	SN2 Most people whose opinions I value would prefer that I buy energy-efficient home appliances.	
	SN3 The extent of influence from the people or the group (friends, colleagues, etc.) can strongly affect my decision.	
Perceived Behavioral Control (PBC)	PBC1 I have resources, time, and opportunities to buy energy-efficient home appliances.	Bouarar et al. (2021)
	PBC2 I am confident that if I want, I can buy energy-efficient home appliances.	
	PBC3 To buy or not to buy energy-efficient home appliances is entirely up to me.	
Environmental Awareness	EC1 By buying energy-efficient home appliances, I influence environmental protection.	Mouloudj and Bouarar (2021); Bouarar et al. (2022); Mouloudj et al. (2023)
	EC2 I think I have a responsibility to protect the environment.	
	EC3 I think environmental problems will affect human life.	
Intentions	INT1 I like to purchase energy-efficient home appliances.	Akroush et al. (2019)
	INT2 I will pay more money on energy-efficient home appliances.	
	INT3 I will recommend other people to purchase energy-efficient home appliances.	

RESULTS AND DISCUSSION

The internal consistency reliabilities of all constructs of TPB, environmental awareness, and purchase intentions measures are given in Table 2. The minimum coefficient was 0.835; which was above the accepted threshold of 0.60 suggested by Malhotra (2010). According to Mouloudj and Bouarar (2023), "the normality test is an important assumption to perform a multiple regression analysis". The analysis showed that the values of skewness and kurtosis ranged between -1.393 to -0.541; and +0.270 to +3.213 respectively. These values are within the range suggested by Byrne (2016); i.e. ±2 and ±7 respectively. Therefore, the data is normally distributed.

Table 2. Reliability analysis, skewness, kurtosis, tolerance, and VIF

Constructs	Cronbach's Alphas	Skewness	Kurtosis	Tolerance	VIF
ATT	0.835	-1,292	3,213	,579	1,727
SN	0.946	-1,034	1,159	,652	1,535
PBC	0.935	-1,023	1,039	,655	1,526
EA	0.912	-,541	,270	,609	1,643
INT	0.869	-1,393	2,761	-	-

Another issue that can affect the multiple regression models is the multicollinearity. Therefore, the authors checked the values of "the variance inflation factor" (VIF) and tolerance. According to Hair et al. (2013), when the tolerance values exceed 0.20 and when the VIF values are less than 5, the multicollinearity problem does not arise. Accordingly, the values shown in Table 2 indicate that there is no problem of multicollinearity.

The descriptive statistics results in table 3 show that respondents have strong positive attitudes toward energy-efficient home appliances (Mean=3.94) and they have a great intention to purchase energy-efficient home appliances (Mean=3.97), while the respondents' awareness towards environmental problems is low (Mean=2.52).

Table 3. Descriptive statistics and correlation matrix

Constructs	Mean	SD	ATT	SN	PBC	EA	INT
ATT	3,943	,649	1				
SN	3,528	,776	,450**	1			
PBC	3,611	,806	,486**	,507**	1		
EA	2,526	,619	,579**	,464**	,409**	1	
INT	3,975	,744	,718**	,613**	,630**	,673**	1

The current study employed Pearson correlation by SPSS 26 for assessing the correlations. The results show that there is a significant positive relationship between attitude towards energy-efficient home appliances and purchase intention ($r = 0.718$; $p< 0.01$). Additionally, the findings show that the subjective norm is significantly positively correlated with purchase intention ($r = 0.613$; $p< .001$). Similarly, PBC is significantly and positively correlated with purchase intention ($r = 0.630$; $p< 0.01$), and finally environmental awareness has a significant positive correlation with purchase intention ($r = 0.673$; $p< 0.01$).

The hypotheses were tested using multiple regression analysis. The regression equation was run in SPSS 26. The multiple regression model with all constructs gave $R^2 = 71.5$ per cent, F = 117.944, ($p<0.001$).

Table 4. Multiple regression results for intention to purchase energy-efficient

Model	B	t	Sig.	Results
(constant)	,059	,309	,757	-
ATT	,398	6,777	,000	H1 supported
SN	,196	4,228	,000	H2 supported
PBC	,226	5,085	,000	H3 supported
EA	,334	5,569	,000	H4 supported

Dependent Variable: Intention to purchase . Independent variables: Attitude (ATT), Subjective norm (SN), Perceived behavioral control (PBC), Environmental awareness (EA). Notes: Model summary: $R = 84.6\%$; R Square $= 71.5\%$; Adjusted R Square $= 70.9\%$; $F = 117,944$; $P = 0.000$ (p<0.05).

The findings of this paper demonstrate that a positive attitude towards buying energy-efficient home appliances have a positive impact on the intention to buy it ($\beta =0.398$; $t=6.777$) at the .001 level (p. 05), the same outcome was posited by many researchers in the green marketing literature (Mouloudj et al., 2023). Hypothesis 1 is supported. This means that strengthening consumers' attitudes towards the adoption of energy-efficient products will increase their purchase intention. This result is consistent with the study carried out by Bhutto et al. (2021) and Hua and Wang (2019); they found that the effect of attitude on energy-efficient product purchase intention was higher than the subjective norm and PBC. Prior studies have explored the relationships between attitude with purchase intention, which found a positive relationship between attitude and energy-efficient home appliances purchase intention (Ali et al., 2021; Bhutto et al., 2021; Fatoki, 2020; Issock et al., 2018; Jamil et al., 2022; Li et al., 2019; Waris & Hameed, 2020b; Zhu & Thøgersen, 2023), energy-efficient products purchase intention (Abu-Elsamen et al., 2019; Akroush et al., 2019), intention to save energy (Mouloudj et al., 2023), as well as with the intention to purchase green products (Mouloudj & Bouarar, 2021).

In the same vein, the results show that subjective norm exerts a strong positive impact on the intention to purchase energy-efficient home appliances ($\beta =0.196$; $t= 4.228$). Thus, hypothesis 2 is supported. This means the social pressure helps to form the intention to purchase energy-saving appliances. In other words, the consumer under pressure from surrounding people is more likely to form a positive intention to purchase these appliances. This finding is supported by the studies of Bhutto et al. (2021); Hua and Wang (2019); and Waris and Ahmed (2020), which indicates that subjective norms have a positive and significant effect on energy-efficient appliances purchase intention. However, the finding of this paper is counterintuitive to the findings of Ali et al. (2021) and Fatoki (2020), which showed that subjective and moral norms were not significant predictors of intention to purchase energy-efficient appliances.

Besides, findings showed that PBC has a significant and positive impact on intention to purchase energy-efficient home appliances ($\beta = 0.226$; $t = 5.085$). Thus, hypothesis 3 is supported. This suggests that the high level of PBC should intensify the intention to buy energy-efficient home appliances (perform the behavior). According to Ajzen (2020, p.315), "a favorable attitude and a supportive subjective norm provide the motivation to engage in the behavior but a concrete intention to do so is formed only when perceived control over the behavior is sufficiently strong". Consumers with the capacity to afford, possess, and use the energy-efficient appliance, are more expected to purchase it than those who lack enough resources (Hua & Wang, 2019; Paul et al., 2016). This finding is consistent with the finding of Waris and Hameed (2020b) who found that the perceived consumer effectiveness has a positive effect on energy-efficient appliances purchase intention. Similarly, Ali et al. (2019); Ali et al. (2021); Asif et al. (2023); Bhutto et al. (2021); Fatoki (2020); Hua and Wang (2019); Li et al. (2019); and Zhu and Thøgersen (2023) discovered that PBC positively influences energy-efficient appliances purchase intention.

Finally, findings indicate that environmental awareness has a strong direct impact on the intention to purchase energy-efficient home appliances ($\beta = 0.334$; $t = 5.569$). Thus, hypothesis 4 is also supported. This suggests that environmental awareness is a fourth factor affecting willingness to adopt energy-efficient appliances. Individuals can decide to adopt a pro-environmentally behavior to preserve the environment and environmental quality value without giving preference to their personal comfort (Cattaneo, 2019). In addition, Urban and Scasny (2012) found out that people with powerful environmental concerns are more likely to reduce energy consumption and may place some energy-saving structures in their houses. This finding is consistent with the finding of Wang et al. (2017) who found that environmental awareness exerts a significant effect on the purchase intention of energy-efficient appliances. Also, Fatoki (2020); Issock et al. (2018); Li et al. (2019); and Waris and Hameed (2020b) shown that environmental concerns have a positive influence on energy-efficient appliances purchase intention.

LIMITATION AND DIRECTIONS FOR FUTURE RESEARCH

This research, like any other, is not without limitations. First, the sample size in this study is relatively small. Thus, future studies should enlarge the sample size. Second, the current study used convenient sampling, and this restricts the ability to generalize the results of the study. Thus, it is recommended that future research utilize random sampling to generalize results. Third, this study focused on consumers' intentions to purchase energy-efficient home appliances; thus, we recommend future research to tackle actual conservation behaviors to effectively understand the transition from intentions into behaviors. Fourth, the current study incorporated environment awareness into the TPB; future studies may include other variables such as awareness of energy-saving products, consumer trust in environmental claims, perceived risks, past experiences, religious commitment, and any other variables that can strengthen the explanatory power of the extended model.

Theoretical and Managerial Implications

This study provides important theoretical and managerial implications. Theoretically, this paper adds to the research body of literature about the factors that influence the intention to purchase energy-efficient home appliances in Algeria as a developing country. As well, the study extended the TPB and suggested adding other variables to the original model. In addition, this model can be extended to study the energy savings of other products, such as electric cars and smart devices.

From a managerial perspective, this study provides important recommendations for practitioners. First, the results indicate that consumer attitudes have a strong impact on energy-saving appliances, which means the necessity to strengthen positive attitudes and adjust negative ones through the provision of high-quality information from highly trusted parties. This sort of information can be obtained via comparative advertisements, social media, brochures, retailers, and opinion leaders. Second, the study also revealed that subjective norms play a key role in forming positive intentions towards energy-saving appliances, and since Algerian society is a Muslim society with a predominantly Arabic culture, it presumes that important people involved in buying energy-saving behaviors will help propagate this behavior among people; therefore, corporations are required to employ opinion leaders (such as experts, religious scholars, and celebrities) in their promotional activities. Third, perceived behavioral control has a significant impact on the intention to purchase energy-saving appliances; accordingly, any barriers that may prevent the purchasing behavior must be removed. Financial barriers can be overcome by providing consumers with the possibility of an installment sale option. Technical barriers can also be overcome by simplifying the use, functioning, and maintenance of these appliances, along with providing after-sales services. Perceived risks can be overcome by providing assurance and appropriate information to potential consumers.

Finally, various stakeholders, such as government agencies, companies, and environmental protection associations, ought to intensify awareness campaigns on environmental issues in general and devote more efforts to rationalizing energy consumption in particular by highlighting the personal benefits of switching to energy-saving appliances (such as washing machines, refrigerators, heaters, etc.). This can be done by: (1) programming television programs with energy experts to explain the benefits of energy-saving; (2) invigorating the role of mosques in raising awareness of environmental hazards and the necessity to save energy and avoid irrational usage; and (3) incorporating within educational programs and curricula at all educational levels lessons that emphasize the importance of saving energy. Families' awareness of the financial benefits of saving energy as a result of using energy-saving appliances may significantly lead to the formation of positive attitudes towards purchasing these particular appliances, increasing their willingness to pay more money to obtain them.

CONCLUSION

Energy-efficient appliances help reduce energy consumption and meet consumers' utilitarian needs (Waris & Hameed, 2020b). To understand energy-efficient home appliances purchasing intention the TPB was extended by incorporating environment awareness. For this purpose a paper form questionnaire was distributed to a convenience sample of 300 consumers in three Algeria provinces, 193 valid questionnaires were retrieved. The results indicate that respondents have a positive attitude, and most of them have good intentions to purchase energy-saving appliances. However, most respondents were found to have low awareness of environmental awareness. The results also indicate that the three constructs of the TPB along with environmental awareness have a positive and significant impact on energy-efficient home appliances purchasing intention, and the four factors combined explain 71.5% of the purchase intention variance.

This research received no specific grant from any funding agency in the public, commercial, or not-for-profit sectors.

REFERENCES

Abada, Z., & Bouharkat, M. (2018). Study of management strategy of energy resources in Algeria. *Energy Reports*, *4*, 1–7. doi:10.1016/j.egyr.2017.09.004

Abu-Elsamen, A. A., Akroush, M. N., Asfour, N. A., & Al Jabali, H. (2019). Understanding contextual factors affecting the adoption of energy-efficient household products in Jordan. *Sustainability Accounting. Management and Policy Journal*, *10*(2), 314–332. doi:10.1108/SAMPJ-05-2018-0144

Ajzen, I. (1991). The theory of planned behavior. *Organizational Behavior and Human Decision Processes*, *50*(2), 179–211. doi:10.1016/0749-5978(91)90020-T

Ajzen, I. (2020). The theory of planned behavior: Frequently asked questions. *Human Behavior and Emerging Technologies*, *2*(4), 314–324. doi:10.1002/hbe2.195

Akroush, M. N., Zuriekat, M. I., Al Jabali, H. I., & Asfour, N. A. (2019). Determinants of purchasing intentions of energy-efficient products: The roles of energy awareness and perceived benefits. *International Journal of Energy Sector Management*, *13*(1), 128–148. doi:10.1108/IJESM-05-2018-0009

Ali, M. R., Shafiq, M., & Andejany, M. (2021). Determinants of consumers' intentions towards the purchase of energy-efficient appliances in Pakistan: An extended model of the theory of planned behavior. *Sustainability*, *13*(2), 1–17. doi:10.3390u13020565 PMID:34123411

Ali, S., Ullah, H., Akbar, M., Akhtar, W., & Zahid, H. (2019). Determinants of consumer intentions to purchase energy-saving household products in Pakistan. *Sustainability (Basel)*, *11*(5), 1–20. doi:10.3390u11051462

Anon. (2014). *4Country Analysis Brief: Algeria*. U.S. Energy Information Administration, Washington.

Arisal, I., & Atalar, T. (2016). The exploring relationships between environmental concern, collectivism, and ecological purchase intention. *Procedia: Social and Behavioral Sciences*, *235*, 514–521. doi:10.1016/j.sbspro.2016.11.063

Asif, M. H., Zhongfu, T., Irfan, M., & Işık, C. (2023). Do environmental knowledge and green trust matter for purchase intention of eco-friendly home appliances? An application of extended theory of planned behavior. *Environmental Science and Pollution Research International*, *30*(13), 37762–37774. doi:10.100711356-022-24899-1 PMID:36574131

Bhutto, M. Y., Liu, X., Soomro, Y. A., Ertz, M., & Baeshen, Y. (2021). Adoption of energy-efficient home appliances: Extending the theory of planned behavior. *Sustainability (Basel)*, *13*(1), 250. doi:10.3390u13010250

Bouarar, A. C., & Mouloudj, K. (2021). Using the theory of planned behavior to explore employee's intentions to implement green practices. *Dirassat Journal Economic Issue*, *12*(1), 641–659. doi:10.34118/djei.v12i1.1118

Bouarar, A. C., Mouloudj, S., Makhlouf, A., & Mouloudj, K. (2022). Predicting students' intentions to create green start-ups: A theory of planned behaviour approach. In *SHS Web of Conferences* (*Vol. 135*). EDP Sciences. 10.1051hsconf/202213501002

Bouarar, A. C., Mouloudj, S., & Mouloudj, K. (2021). Extending the theory of planned behavior to explain intention to use online food delivery services in the context of COVID -19 pandemic. In C. Cobanoglu, & V. Della Corte (Eds.), Advances in global services and retail management (pp. 1–16). USF M3 Publishing.

Bouznit, M., Pablo-Romero, M. P., & Sánchez-Braza, A. (2020). Measures to promote renewable energy for electricity generation in Algeria. *Sustainability (Basel)*, *12*(4), 1–14. doi:10.3390u12041468

Božić, L. (2021). Attitudes towards climate change and electric car purchase–The case of European consumers. *Market-Tržište*, *33*(SI), 81-94. doi:10.22598/mt/2021.33.spec-issue.81

Byrne, B. M. (2016). *Structural Equation Modeling with AMOS: Basic Concepts Applications, and Programming*. Routledge. doi:10.4324/9781315757421

Cattaneo, C. (2019). Internal and external barriers to energy efficiency: Which role for policy interventions? *Energy Efficiency*, *12*(5), 1293–1311. doi:10.100712053-019-09775-1

Dianshu, F., Sovacool, B. K., & Vu, K. (2010). The barriers to energy efficiency in China: Assessing household electricity savings and consumer behavior in Liaoning province. *Energy Policy*, *38*(2), 1202–1209. doi:10.1016/j.enpol.2009.11.012

Fatoki, O. (2020). Factors influencing the purchase of energy-efficient appliances by young consumers in South Africa. *Foundations of Management*, *12*(1), 151–166. doi:10.2478/fman-2020-0012

Galván-Mendoza, O., González-Rosales, V. M., Leyva-Hernández, S. N., Arango-Ramírez, P. M., & Velasco-Aulcy, L. (2022). Environmental knowledge, perceived behavioral control, and employee green behavior in female employees of small and medium enterprises in Ensenada, Baja California. *Frontiers in Psychology*, *13*, 1082306. doi:10.3389/fpsyg.2022.1082306 PMID:36600723

Gangakhedkar, R., Kaur, J., & Karthik, M. (2023). Purchase intention on energy efficient household appliances-a meta-analysis of the studies based on theory of planned behaviour. *International Journal of Sustainable Economy*, *15*(1), 1–25. doi:10.1504/IJSE.2023.127733

Goel, R., Singh, T., Sahdev, S. L., Baral, S. K., & Choudhury, A. (2022). Impact of AI & IOT in sustainable & green practices adopted in hotel industry and measuring hotel guests' satisfaction. In 2022 *10th International Conference on Reliability, Infocom Technologies and Optimization (Trends and Future Directions) (ICRITO)* (pp. 1-5). IEEE. 10.1109/ICRITO56286.2022.9965152

Hair, J. F., Hult, G. T. M., Ringle, C., & Sarstedt, M. (2013). *A Primer on Partial Least Squares Structural Equation Modeling (PLS-SEM)*. Sage Publications.

Harun, S. A., Fauzi, M. A., Kasim, N. M., & Wider, W. (2022). Determinants of energy efficient appliances among Malaysian households: Roles of theory of planned behavior, social interaction and appliance quality. *Asian Economic and Financial Review*, *12*(3), 212–226. doi:10.55493/5002.v12i3.4463

Hua, L., & Wang, S. (2019). Antecedents of consumers' intention to purchase energy-efficient appliances: An empirical study based on the technology acceptance model and theory of planned behavior. *Sustainability (Basel), 11*(10), 1–17. doi:10.3390u11102994

Issock, I. P. B., Mpinganjira, M., & Roberts-Lombard, M. (2018). Drivers of consumer attention to mandatory energy-efficiency labels affixed to home appliances: An emerging market perspective. *Journal of Cleaner Production, 204*, 672–684. doi:10.1016/j.jclepro.2018.08.299

Issock, I. P. B., & Muposhi, A. (2023). Understanding energy-efficiency choices through consumption values: The central role of consumer's attention and trust in environmental claims. *Management of Environmental Quality, 34*(1), 250–270. doi:10.1108/MEQ-01-2022-0012

Jamil, K., Dunnan, L., Awan, F. H., Jabeen, G., Gul, R. F., Idrees, M., & Mingguang, L. (2022). Antecedents of consumer's purchase intention towards energy-efficient home appliances: An agenda of energy efficiency in the post COVID-19 era. *Frontiers in Energy Research, 10*, 863127. doi:10.3389/fenrg.2022.863127

Joshi, G., Sen, V., & Kunte, M. (2020). Do Star Ratings Matter?: A qualitative study on consumer awareness and inclination to purchase energy-efficient home appliances. *International Journal of Social Ecology and Sustainable Development, 11*(4), 40–55. doi:10.4018/IJSESD.2020100104

Joshi, G., Sheorey, P. A., & Gandhi, A. V. (2019). Analyzing the barriers to purchase intentions of energy-efficient appliances from a consumer perspective. *Benchmarking, 26*(5), 1565–1580. doi:10.1108/BIJ-03-2018-0082

Karlin, B., Davis, N., Sanguinetti, A., Gamble, K., Kirkby, D., & Stokols, D. (2014). Dimensions of conservation: Exploring differences among energy behaviors. *Environment and Behavior, 46*(4), 423–452. doi:10.1177/0013916512467532

Klöckner, C. A. (2013). A comprehensive model of the psychology of environmental behavior—A meta-analysis. *Global Environmental Change, 23*(5), 1028–1038. doi:10.1016/j.gloenvcha.2013.05.014

Kotler, P. T., Bowen, J. T., Makens, J., & Baloglu, S. (2016). *Marketing for Hospitality and Tourism*. Pearson Education.

Li, G., Li, W., Jin, Z., & Wang, Z. (2019). Influence of environmental concern and knowledge on households' willingness to purchase energy-efficient appliances: A case study in Shanxi, China. *Sustainability (Basel), 11*(4), 1073. doi:10.3390u11041073

Lillemo, S. C. (2014). Measuring the effect of procrastination and environmental awareness on households' energy-saving behaviors: An empirical approach. *Energy Policy, 66*, 249–256. doi:10.1016/j.enpol.2013.10.077

Malhotra, N. K. (2010). *Marketing research: An applied orientation* (6th ed.). Pearson.

Monika, B., & Sharma, K. (2018). Environmental consciousness and consumer lifestyle. *Business Analyst Journal, 39*(2), 57–76.

Mouloudj, K., & Bouarar, A. C. (2021). The impact of word of mouth on intention to purchase green products: An empirical study. *Revue Algérienne d'Economie de gestion, 15*(1), 871-890.

Mouloudj, K., & Bouarar, A. C. (2023). Investigating predictors of medical students' intentions to engagement in volunteering during the health crisis. *African Journal of Economic and Management Studies*. doi:10.1108/AJEMS-08-2022-0315

Mouloudj, K., Bouarar, A. C., & Mouloudj, S. (2023). Extension of the theory of planned behaviour (TPB) to predict farmers' intention to save energy. *AIP Conference Proceedings*, *2683*, 020002. doi:10.1063/5.0125022

Paul, J., Modi, A., & Patel, J. (2016). Predicting green product consumption using the theory of planned behavior and reasoned action. *Journal of Retailing and Consumer Services*, *29*, 123–134. doi:10.1016/j.jretconser.2015.11.006

Ramkissoon, H., & Nunkoo, R. (2010). Predicting tourists' intention to consume genetically modified food. *Journal of Hospitality Marketing & Management*, *20*(1), 60–75. doi:10.1080/19368623.2010.514557

Tan, C.-S., Ooi, H.-Y., & Goh, Y.-N. (2017). A moral extension of the theory of planned behavior to predict consumers' purchase intention for energy-efficient household appliances in Malaysia. *Energy Policy*, *107*(C), 459–471. doi:10.1016/j.enpol.2017.05.027

Teoh, C. W., Khor, K. C., & Wider, W. (2022). Factors influencing consumers' purchase intention towards green home appliances. *Frontiers in Psychology*, *13*, 927327. doi:10.3389/fpsyg.2022.927327 PMID:35846659

Urban, J., & Scasny, M. (2012). Exploring domestic energy-saving: The role of environmental concern and background variables. *Energy Policy*, *47*, 69–80. doi:10.1016/j.enpol.2012.04.018

Wang, Z., Sun, Q., Wang, B., & Zhang, B. (2019). Purchasing intentions of Chinese consumers on energy-efficient appliances: Is the energy efficiency label effective? *Journal of Cleaner Production*, *238*, 117896. doi:10.1016/j.jclepro.2019.117896

Wang, Z., Wang, X., & Guo, D. (2017). Policy implications of the purchasing intentions towards energy-efficient appliances among China's urban residents: Do subsidies work? *Energy Policy*, *102*, 430–439. doi:10.1016/j.enpol.2016.12.049

Wang, Z., Zhang, B., & Li, G. (2014). Determinants of energy-saving behavioral intention among residents in Beijing: Extending the theory of planned behavior. *Journal of Renewable and Sustainable Energy*, *6*(5), 1–18. doi:10.1063/1.4898363

Waris, I., & Ahmed, W. (2020). Empirical evaluation of the antecedents of energy-efficient home appliances: Application of the extended theory of planned behavior. *Management of Environmental Quality*, *31*(4), 915–930. doi:10.1108/MEQ-01-2020-0001

Waris, I., & Hameed, I. (2020a). An empirical study of purchase intention of energy-efficient home appliances: The influence of knowledge of eco-labels and psychographic variables. *International Journal of Energy Sector Management*, *14*(6), 1297–1314. doi:10.1108/IJESM-11-2019-0012

Waris, I., & Hameed, I. (2020b). Promoting environmentally sustainable consumption behavior: An empirical evaluation of purchase intention of energy-efficient appliances. *Energy Efficiency*, *13*(8), 1653–1664. doi:10.100712053-020-09901-4

Westbrook, R. A. (1987). Product/consumption-based affective responses and post-purchase processes. *JMR, Journal of Marketing Research, 24*(3), 258–270. doi:10.1177/002224378702400302

Yue, B., Sheng, G., She, S., & Xu, J. (2020). Impact of consumer environmental responsibility on green consumption behavior in China: The role of environmental concern and price sensitivity. *Sustainability (Basel), 12*(5), 2074. doi:10.3390u12052074

Zhang, Y., Xiao, C., & Zhou, G. (2020). Willingness to pay a price premium for energy-efficient appliances: Role of perceived value and energy efficiency labeling. *Journal of Cleaner Production, 242*, 1–12. doi:10.1016/j.jclepro.2019.118555

Zhu, B., & Thøgersen, J. (2023). Consumers' intentions to buy energy-efficient household appliances in China. *ABAC Journal, 43*(1), 1–17. doi:10.14456/abacj.2023.1

KEY TERMS AND DEFINITIONS

Behavioral Intentions: This is the extent to which the consumers are willing to purchase energy-efficient household appliances in the future.

Eco-Friendly Product: A product that takes into account environmental considerations when designing, producing, storing, distributing, consuming, and disposing of it.

Energy-efficient Household Appliances: Refers to all appliances used in homes that have the ability to reduce greenhouse gas emissions, and use less energy such as water and electricity; and include washing machines, refrigerators, freezers, dishwashers, dryers and air cleaners, etc.

Environmental Knowledge: This is the amount of information that consumers have about ecological challenges and their capability to comprehend and estimate its negative consequences on the environment.

Green Consumer Behaviors: All conscious decisions to buy products that have little or no impacts on the environment, such as buying an electric car.

Irrational Human Behavior: Includes all intentional acts that involve engaging in socially, environmentally, healthily, or economically irresponsible behavior such as such as harming the environment by wasting medicines.

Sustainable Business: Refers to the optimal use of natural resources and minimizing environmental damage during the implementation of business.

Chapter 5
The Critical Impact of Sustainability Innovations on Green Supply Chains

Saniye Yildirim Ozmutlu
Tekirdag Namik Kemal University, Turkey

Korhan Arun
Tekirdag Namik Kemal University, Turkey

ABSTRACT

The prevailing business methods have a strong focus on environmental sustainability. To that aim, the rising concern about environmental issues in the supply chain has sparked the growth of green supply chains. Organizations are also highly interested in planning and implementing green strategies. In that case, the innovative approach is labeled as the primary driver of change from traditional to green in the supply chain. Therefore, environmental sustainability innovations are examined in this chapter as the forces behind the green supply chain in organizations. 172 waste management and recycling companies are the samples of the study, where path analysis with partial least squares-based structural equation modeling was conducted to test the hypotheses. The findings demonstrate a strong connection between green supply chains and improvements in resource conservation, energy reduction, managing environmental communication, and pollution.

INTRODUCTION

Environmental sustainability is carefully balancing the human environment with environmental factors such as soil conservation, water resource management, climate change, and fossil fuel use (Es'haghi et al., 2022). This is primarily motivated by the notion that the environment is finite and that every environmental modification must have a net positive value (Dragulanescu & Dragulanescu, 2013). Additionally, the advancement of sustainable development depends on resolving organizational issues by utilizing

DOI: 10.4018/978-1-6684-8969-7.ch005

knowledge, expertise, and a shared global ethic to satisfy basic requirements (Sachs, 2015; Staniškis, 2022b). From this definition, the notion of sustainability needs innovation.

Sustainable innovation is the innovative activities firms engage in to become sustainable (Adams et al., 2016). Tiwari and Thakur (2021) defined eight subscales for the accommodation sector: sustainability management, food waste and purchase management, environmental communication and pollution management, resource and energy conservation, transportation energy conservation, water recycling, wastewater management, and guestroom sustainability.

A green supply chain focuses on environmental thinking (C. Chang & Chen, 2013; R.-D. Chang et al., 2017; Stekelorum et al., 2021). Green supply chain management also entails the selection of "green" suppliers as well as the desire of suppliers to contribute to a green supply chain (Roehrich et al., 2017).

According to the literature, green supply chain initiatives correlate highly with sustainability (Stekelorum et al., 2021). Thus, it naturally comes to mind that environmental sustainability is positively related to the green supply chain. However, literature is scarce on green logistics performance regarding sustainability innovation. Furthermore, it is crucial to recognize sustainable innovation management's role in managing a green supply chain (Kusi-Sarpong et al., 2019). Therefore, this chapter discusses the relationship between environmental sustainability innovation and green supply chain management.

Although the study of sustainability is expanding, and firms are under more pressure than ever to incorporate the three sustainability metrics—economic, environmental, and social—into their operations, little attention has been paid to sustainability in connection to green supply chains (Kleindorfer et al., 2009; Vlachos et al., 2019). Therefore, we explore the research question to what extent does environmentally sustainable innovation drive green supply chain performance?

LITERATURE REVIEW

Although there are several, the broadest definition of sustainability considers the resilience and long-term viability of our ecosystems, society, and economy (Chang et al., 2017; Sharma, 2014). Environmental sustainability refers to human behavior in its relationships with the environment (Keong, 2020). According to environmental sustainability, the environment may still be able to sustain human existence, all current ecosystems, and life in general despite resource depletion brought on by human activities (Brinkmann, 2020a). Thus, maintaining the ecological integrity of the natural system while maximizing its economic usage might be considered environmental sustainability in the current context (Choy, 2015).

Utilizing ecologically friendly goods and services is considered going green. Utilizing goods or services sustainably implies staying within the resources of future generations (Yanarella et al., 2009). From an organizational perspective, the key characteristics of business sustainability may include economic factors, environmental issues, social demographics, stakeholder concerns, resilience, and strategy (Ahi & Searcy, 2013). Given the nature of the term "green supply chain," which unmistakably highlights this aspect of sustainability, the emphasis on environmental issues was to be expected.

Within sustainability, businesses might choose to go green by utilizing innovation and cutting-edge technology (Brinkmann, 2020b). Implementing new or updated practices, structures, and tactics to lessen environmental harm is part of the specialized innovation process known as sustainability innovation (H. ur R. Khan & Khan, 2020). Alternatively, environmental sustainability is the current state of sustainability, where organizations can choose to use innovation and new technologies to go green within the sustainability parameters (Brinkmann, 2020b). For example, according to Watanabe et al. (2016), a sustainable manufacturing system encompasses all stages of production and a product's lifecycle, from getting raw materials to selling finished items to customers.

From an economic standpoint, sustainability entails finding ways to lessen human activity's effects on the environment significantly. Businesses began to take on increased responsibility for environmental sustainability during the 1970s ecology movements (Bellucci et al., 2019). It is workable to distinguish between "strong" and "weak" versions of sustainability in the contexts of business and society. Regarding the degree of change necessary to achieve sustainability, these views diverge. While proponents of "weak" sustainability contend that only minor changes to the current system are necessary to achieve sustainability, proponents of "strong" sustainability assert that fundamental, structural reform is necessary (Bini & Bellucci, 2020; Charlton & Howell, 2007). Organizational management should seek to maximize its benefits to both society and itself, and management is accountable for everything from deep ecology to sustainable resource use (Schuler et al., 2017). Sustainability management perspectives change depending on whether they have instrumental value (economic benefits) or intrinsic value (organizational goals and vision). The first stage entails making money while using resources sustainably. The second involves protecting the ecosystem by conserving resources. The third involves respecting the entire ecosystem even if it conflicts with organizational goals. The fourth and final stage entails entirely relying on nature and rejecting any process that harms it (Schuler et al., 2017). Sustainable management thus has a positive impact on the green supply chain. Moreover, our economies must adopt new strategies for reinventing entire production, consumption, and sustainable supply chain systems (Edwards et al., 2023). Consequently, not only sustainability but also innovations in sustainability also positively increase green supply chain effectiveness.

Organizations can only learn about the effectiveness of the green supply chain through their connections to the community in terms of communication. The way that environmental manager interprets sustainability and how they communicate on a scheduled basis significantly impacts how other employees within the organization formulate and carry out various sustainable policies and programs (Ageron et al., 2012; Schuler et al., 2017). Moreover, talent and IT management are strategic for environmental sustainability (Benitez-Amado et al., 2015).

Resource use and energy conservation are also crucial in environmental sustainability (R.-D. Chang et al., 2017; Tiwari & Thakur, 2021). Some of the crucial steps the organizations take to complete their greening process include implementing market-oriented approaches to renewable energy, preserving energy through the promotion of energy-saving and energy-efficient policies, and optimizing the energy structure through the promotion of renewable energy sources (Keong, 2020). Achieving sustainability will also need changing unsustainable practices and unrestrained consumption. It is feasible to build a green supply chain in the framework of sustainable development.

Hypothesis Development

In the broadest sense, transportation energy conservation refers to the area of the sustainable supply chain that deals with transporting and storing goods along the green supply chain. The evaluation and selection of environmentally friendly logistics service providers, modes of transportation, and distribution techniques may be among the green logistics objectives at the strategic design level. At the tactical and operational levels, effective inventory management, delivery schedule consolidation, and green routing are typically the top priorities (Fahimnia et al., 2015).

Briefly, environmental sustainability will increase green supply chain effectiveness. Thus, sustainable innovations are hypothesized to positively change the supply chain's green.

H1: Supply chain innovations positively and significantly affect the green supply chain.

However, in this paper, sustainable innovations are measured through their dimensions adapted from Tiwari and Thakur (2020). Energy and resource conservation, corporate social responsibility, culture innovation, blending local culture to increase innovation value, and sustainability management are all examples of sustainability innovations. Energy conservation includes using environmentally friendly building materials, resource conservation includes recycling, corporate social responsibility includes respecting and protecting the natural environment, and sustainability innovation includes combining local culture to increase innovation value (Horng et al., 2017).

Sustainability is continuously changing and improving targets for many organizations (Gaziulusoy et al., 2013). A multidisciplinary approach is also used in sustainability management to connect concerns in the economic, political, social, and ecological issues across temporal and spatial dimensions (Williams et al., 2017). Interdependence between organizations and the environment is crucial from a systemic sustainability management perspective since businesses depend on the natural environment for inputs. Through feedback loops, organizational actions directly impact the environment (Starik & Kanashiro, 2013). Therefore, understanding interconnections is vital for organizational managers to achieve sustainability (Metcalf & Benn, 2013). In order to attain its objectives, sustainability management guides the business toward making changes to the structure and arrangement of its supply chains (Varsei et al., 2014). However, in everyday business practice, sustainability has to be operationalized (Johnson & Schaltegger, 2016). Piercy and Rich (2015) found that management practices are fundamental in sustainability management. The authors noted that many sustainability outcomes and environmental advantages are satisfied by workplace sustainability management methods including staff training. These tools include supplier monitoring, transparency, workforce treatment, and community participation.

H1a: Sustainability Management increases green supply chain effectiveness.

The potential for green supply chain operations ranges from proactive environmental program measures to reactive monitoring (Kashmanian, 2015; Srivastava, 2007). Environmental performance is a concern for socially conscious businesses and environmentalists, making it more applicable to research and practice (Llach et al., 2016). These practices need prompt supply chain and factory communication of sales and manufacturing data (Preuss, 2005). Organizations can also use automatic systems like EDI (electronic data transfer). EDI allows businesses to minimize lead times, which is crucial for sustainability because it is significantly faster than traditional lines of communication (Jia et al., 2015; Mukhopadhyay & Kekre, 2002).

The effectiveness of the green supply chain has been studied in the previous study by analyzing behavior and purpose to accomplish a specific job through persuasive communication (Patnaik, 2022; Pejić-Bach & Dogru, 2022). Environmental communication is frequently used in sustainability as a tool for performance monitoring and public outreach (Zhou et al., 2021). Additionally, supply chain collaboration and the growth of knowledge on community communication, which are the cornerstones of supply chain projects, are driven by technology improvement in information and communication (Chen et al., 2021; Sureeyatanapas & Yang, 2021). This chapter establishes the necessity of appropriate incentives to motivate consumers for prompt product returns. It underlines how crucial close coordination with internal and external stakeholders is to successfully integrate environmental operations. The cornerstones of a green supply chain are identified as being communication and the reuse of used goods (Mahapatra et al., 2021).

H1b: Managing Environmental communication and pollution increases green supply chain effectiveness.

The logistics sector and tech-based companies have very different levels of R&D expenditure, the number of new product inventions, successful innovation adoption and product commercialization, etc. (Liu, 2019; Mena et al., 2007; Prakash, 2019). In a supply chain, the green strategy entails conserving energy and reusing the materials to create and apply environmental policies (Sánchez-Flores et al., 2020). The World Economic Forum (WEF) model incorporates reductions by simply using energy more efficiently and lowering the greenhouse gas intensity of internal operations and supply chain activities (Staniškis, 2022a). The findings indicated a link between sustainable supply chain management techniques and organizational success, with internal environmental management, green warehousing and construction, green purchasing, and customer collaboration on environmental issues ranking top (Diab et al., 2015).

H1c: Resource use and energy conservation increase green supply chain effectiveness.

Distribution of goods is a crucial logistical and operational challenge many businesses constantly encounter in today's business environment(Rattanamanee & Nanthavanij, 2019). Energy use and savings, gas emissions, mode of transportation, and cost are additional green supply chain metrics (Sánchez-Flores et al., 2020; Vanalle et al., 2017). Green mobility, whether internal or external, improves environmental performance and reduces supply chain costs, giving businesses a competitive edge by utilizing renewable energy sources, increasing customer happiness, and developing a favorable brand image (Khan et al., 2018). The same authors looked at how green purchasing, distribution, and transportation affected organizational performance in Pakistani businesses. The results showed a good and significant association between green distribution and transportation operations and the overall improvement of organizational performance.

H1d: Transportation energy conservation increases green supply chain effectiveness.

Twelve green performance indicators are grouped into four categories because of a thorough literature analysis. These aspects include reverse logistics management, green shipping policies, stakeholder cooperation in green shipping, and green design and promise (Lirn et al., 2019). Environmental sustainability, however, also shows that the only innovations with a chance of succeeding in green supply chains are those that satisfy the needs of stakeholders in terms of the economy and the environment (Acciaro et al., 2014). So, this research will evaluate which dimensions of sustainable innovations will satisfy the demands of green supply chains.

METHODOLOGY

Sample

The universe of our study consists of waste management and recycling companies in Turkey. With waste management gaining a more prominent economic dimension, the necessity of following competition policies and protecting the environment has gained importance in Turkey, as in many other countries. As a result, waste management in Turkey has been the subject of various regulations since the 1930s. The Ministry of Environment, Urbanization, and Climate Change handle deciding policies and preparing programs for protecting the environment and preventing pollution in Turkey.

Figure 1.

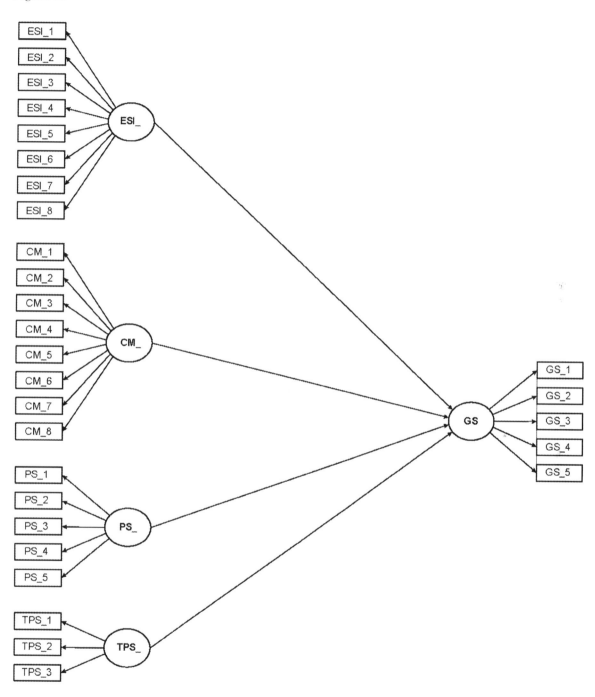

The European Union Council Directive defines waste management as "collection, sorting, transportation, recovery, recycling, and disposal of waste, as well as the supervision of these operations and after-use care of disposal areas" (https://stats.oecd.org). In addition to solid, liquid, and gaseous wastes, there is a wide variety of waste, such as packaging (paper, plastic, metal, glass, wood, composite packaging, etc.).

Companies that undertake the management and recycling of these wastes ensure that each has distinctive characteristics and that this diversity's environmental, economic, physical, and biological effects are effectively managed. Waste management is among the top policies that serve the purpose of protecting the environment. A large part of the environmental pollution problem is caused by waste. Reducing waste production and maximizing the use of natural resources are the main objectives. To minimize the amount of waste generated, waste should be recovered or converted, and those that cannot be recovered or converted should be disposed of with minor damage. The waste hierarchy in the 4th article of the European Union Waste Framework Directive puts waste management activities in a specific order as prevention, reuse (preparation for reuse), recycling, recovery, and disposal, and the relevant targets are determined per this order. (http://eurlex.europa.eu). Waste industries have begun to be regulated by legislators due to the acceptance of the necessity of waste management, the limited nature of natural resources and the necessity to protect them as much as possible, and a large amount of waste generation.

Businesses operating in the fields of waste management and recycling need to cooperate, make agreements, or come together to serve a common purpose under the umbrella of an undertaking union. As can be seen, the waste problem is not only environmental and human but also an issue that should be given immense importance in administrative circles, policy practitioners, and executives.

The study universe comprises 1235 waste management and recycling companies registered with the Chamber of Commerce and Industry in Turkey and operating in 2022. All companies within the universe's scope were contacted, and 624 companies stated that they would like to participate in our research voluntarily. A questionnaire designed for research was sent to these companies. The questionnaires were collected online with the managers using the "surveymonkey" program. In addition, each company's senior/top manager was contacted. The administrators who participated in the survey were asked 29 questions about the scale items used in the research. A total of 172 waste management and recycling companies (624 questionnaires were sent for practical purposes, of which 172 were 28% complete) filled out the questionnaire. The sample size for the investigation was supported for normal distribution with 5% precision and 95% confidence interval (Israel, 2013).

Measures

The study used the environmental sustainability innovation measures scale (4-dimensional) developed with 24 items, adapted from the research conducted by Tiwari and Thakur (2021). The dimensions of the measure are sustainability management consisting of 8 items, environmental pollution management consisting of 8 items, resource use and energy savings, consisting of 5 items, and transportation energy savings, consisting of 3 items.

The sustainability management dimension is about the company's written environmental policy, setting up a committee to ensure environmental management, creating reports to assess environmental impacts, participating in sustainability conferences and scientific events, evaluating greenhouse gas emissions or carbon footprints, obtaining information about environmental policies, and supplying external services. It also includes such elements like "receiving consultant support, adopting any nationally or internationally recognized sustainability certificate program, and developing a detailed program to reduce environmental impacts."

Environmental pollution management dimension: The company provides environmental training to its employees and enables them to participate in these activities, to ensure and support the protection of local habitat and biological diversity, to take participatory roles in supporting the prevention of environmental pollution, to organize meetings to discuss issues related to the environment and environmental management, the ISO 14000 environmental management system, or other nationally or internationally accepted environmental management systems, to provide training to its employees on environmental education and the prevention of environmental pollution, to obtain information about environmental pollution in the workplace, and to intervene to prevent environmental pollution.

Resource usage and energy conservation dimensions: to encourage recycling with the company's collaborators and employees, to provide products and services through solar energy, wind energy, or other renewable energy sources in all workplace areas, to pay attention to energy consumption in the transportation services it provides to its employees, to purchase renewable energy from national and international companies, and to obtain renewable energy loans. It consists of scale items such as buying a "green label."

The transportation energy conversation dimension consists of scale items such as the company's use of alternative fuel or hybrid vehicles in transportation service provision. These alternative transportation incentives will save energy for its employees and purchase renewable energy from a national or international service provider in transportation service delivery.

In the study, a 5-item green supply scale, adapted from the research of Stekelorum et al. (2021), was used. The "Green supply chain" scale consists of items like "Eco-labeling of products consists of scale items such as ensuring cooperation with suppliers for environmental targets, conducting environmental audits in the internal management of suppliers, obtaining ISO 14000 certification from suppliers, and evaluating environmentally friendly practices of second-tier suppliers."

Descriptive Statistics

Two questions about waste management and recycling companies and two questions about the information of their managers—four basic descriptive questions in total—were asked to the participants. According to the descriptive analysis results, when the activity structure of the waste management and recycling companies participating in the research and operating in Turkey is examined, 28 companies (16.3%) continue their activities as national, 98 companies (57%) continue their activities as international, and 46 companies (26.7%) continue their activities as global companies. As can be seen, more than half of the companies within the scope of the research continue their activities as international companies. When waste management and recycling companies are examined, 21 companies (12.2%) are from the health sector, 16 companies (9.3%) are from the logistics sector, for a total of 36 companies (21.5%) are from the service sector, and 29 companies are from the food sector.(16.9%), 25 companies (14.5%) from the textile industry, that is, 54 companies (41.4%) in total, and 81 companies (47.1%) from the other sectors. When the education areas of the managers within the scope of the research are examined, there are 35 people (20.3%) in the field of business, 14 people (8.1%) in the field of economics, 30 people (17.4%) in the field of logistics, 45 people (26.1%) in the field of engineering, and 48 people in the field of other sciences. (27.9%) seem to have completed their education. When the age range of the managers working in the companies covered by the research is examined, there are nine managers (5.2%) between the ages of 18 and 29, 88 managers (51.2%) between the ages of 30-39, 60 managers (34.9%) between the ages of 40 and 49, and 59 managers (50.2%) between the ages of 50 and 59.12 managers (7%) and three managers (1.7%) aged 60 and over are working. Findings show that more than half of the managers are between the ages of 30 and 39, and the managers must be dynamic, experienced, and young.

RESULTS AND DISCUSSION

To study the path, partial least squares based on structural equation modeling are utilized. Path models are diagrams visually depicting the hypotheses and variable relationships investigated when SEM is used.

Data Quality Assessment

How well a measure correlates with other measures of the same construct is known as convergent validity. In order to evaluate the convergent validity of reflective conceptions, researchers look at the outer loadings of the indicators and the average variance extracted (AVE) (Fornell & Larcker, 1981; Hair, 2019). Variables met the validity criteria: convergent validity with average variance extraction (AVE) greater than .50.

The composite reliability ranges from 0 to 1; higher values denote higher reliability levels. It usually has the same meaning as Cronbach's alpha. For example, in exploratory research, composite reliability values between 0.60 and 0.70 are acceptable, but in later stages of research, values between 0.70 and 0.90 can be considered satisfactory (Table 1). With variation inflation factor (VIF) values of 5.0, the data showed no signs of multicollinearity (Hair et al., 2019). A new criterion for discriminant validity is the heterotrait-monotrait ratio of correlations (HTMT) (Table 2). The criterion HTMT .90 entails that one regards HTMT values smaller than 0.90 as evidence for discriminant validity (Henseler et al., 2015). A stricter criterion is HTMT .85, which requires that HTMT values be smaller than 0.85 to support discriminant validity.

Table 1. Data quality

	Cronbach's alpha	Composite reliability (rho_a)	Composite reliability (rho_c)	The average variance extracted (AVE)	variation inflation factor (VIF)
CM_	0.897	0.903	0.918	0.582	4.987
ESI_	0.945	0.946	0.955	0.725	4.634
GS	0.822	0.829	0.875	0.584	
PS_	0.878	0.884	0.911	0.672	4.809
TPS_	0.924	0.929	0.952	0.868	3.577

GS: Green supply chain, PS: Resource use and energy conservation, TPS: transportation energy conservation, ESI: Environmental sustainability management, CM: Managing environmental communications and pollution.

In recent simulation research, the HTMT outperformed the Fornell-Larcker criterion (Voorhees et al., 2016). Furthermore, an HTMT score significantly less than 1 or less than 0.85 demonstrates the discriminant validity of a pair of components (Table 2).

If one or more emergent variables are present in a structural equation model, composite-based SEM is useful for explanatory purposes. The analyst's focus areas are the R-square, the statistical inference of path coefficients, and effect sizes. Path coefficients are the variables used to characterize direct linear correlations between components. For example, the parameters in Table 3 are path co-efficient.

Table 2. Heterotrait-Monotrait ratio of correlations (HTMT)

	Heterotrait-monotrait ratio (HTMT)
ESI_ -> CM_	0.831
GS -> CM_	0.856
GS -> ESI_	0.797
PS_ -> CM_	0.922
PS_ -> ESI_	0.865
PS_ -> GS	0.822
TPS_ -> CM_	0.794
TPS_ -> ESI_	0.814
TPS_ -> GS	0.669
TPS_ -> PS_	0.939

GS: Green supply chain, PS: Resource use and energy conservation, TPS: transportation energy conservation, ESI: Environmental sustainability management, CM: Managing environmental communications and pollution.

Table 3 shows that sustainability management and transportation energy conservation variables are not significantly affecting the green supply chain of waste management and recycling companies in Turkey. On the other hand, environmental communication, pollution, resource consumption, and energy conservation have a significant and beneficial impact on the effectiveness of the green supply chain.

Interestingly, not every dimension of environmental sustainability innovation affects green supply chains. Thus, only some of the hypotheses are accepted.

Table 3. Path coefficients

Relationships	Path coefficients (PC)	Sample mean (M)	Standard deviation (STDEV)	T statistics (|O/STDEV|)	P values
CM_ -> GS	0.391	0.396	0.179	2.191	0.028
ESI_ -> GS	0.200	0.194	0.145	1.380	**0.168**
PS_ -> GS	0.364	0.365	0.144	2.517	0.012
TPS_ -> GS	-0.156	-0.157	0.109	1.440	**0.150**

GS: Green supply chain, PS: Resource use and energy conservation, TPS: transportation energy conservation, ESI: Environmental sustainability management, CM: Managing environmental communications and pollution.

Communicating openly with stakeholders about environmental efforts, difficulties, and successes can help get feedback, control expectations, and educate them on the practical difficulties and potential for collaboratively developing affordable, ecologically friendly solutions (Mahapatra et al., 2021). **H1a**, environmental sustainability positively increases green supply chain performance, is rejected. We may have reached a prominent level of executive knowledge of the need to move toward corporate sustainability. However, surveys consistently show that, for the most part, this understanding needs to translate into broad and effective action (Edwards et al., 2023). Because externally driven innovation is as vital as inter-organizational innovation (Achillas, 2019). Thus, it comes to mind naturally that Turkish companies need to be able to manage innovation for sustainability. The lack of long-term investment strategies is a systemic management strategy weakness that has a detrimental effect on evaluating clean technology. Overall investments are accordingly oriented on quick financial returns, which prevents the introduction of innovation at any level of the organization. This result is coherent with the recent study by Kusi et.al. (2019). To encourage sustainable supply chain management and development, industrial managers considered "financial availability for innovation" the most crucial sub-criteria, followed by "green manufacturing and operational capabilities development." Thus, in developing countries like Turkey, the failure of environmental sustainability management is related to economic factors. To successfully integrate green supply chain operations, businesses must stress open communication and collaboration with internal and external stakeholders (Reefke & Sundaram, 2021). Cost-effective innovations in environmental sustainability may need to be improved by adequate communication.

H1b is accepted-Managing Environmental communication and pollution increases green supply chain effectiveness. The difficulty of producing trustworthy reports is one of the significant problems with sustainability impact-oriented results. For external communication (to investors, consumers, future employees, communities, etc.), this reporting must be just as reliable and validated as other public statements that a company makes (so subject to litigation and transparency claims) (Falsarone, 2022). The acceptance of H1b shows that organizations in Turkey focus on external communication processes and that the community sees their reports as dependable.

H1c is accepted. This hypothesis concerns resource use and energy conservation, increasing green supply chain effectiveness. Innovation in the sustainability of energy conservation positively affects the green supply chain. This result parallels the previous literature that innovations promote environmental protection and energy conservation activities (Lirn et al., 2019).

Using alternative fuels for transportation, planning routes to cut down on miles traveled and save energy, adopting eco-friendly packaging materials, increasing vehicle efficiency, promoting eco-driving, switching from road to rail transportation, and working with partners to maximize vehicle utilization are some examples of green logistics activities (Sureeyatanapas et al., 2018; Sureeyatanapas & Yang, 2021). However, **H1d** -Transportation energy conservation increases green supply chain effectiveness- is rejected in this research. So, waste management companies in Turkey have been more focused on internal operations and waste management than logistics operations.

A systemic lack of management strategies that harms the evaluation of clean technology is the failure to implement long-term investment programs. The result is a need for more innovation introduction at any organizational level because total investments depend on early economic return (Achillas, 2019). Thus, this point of view is valid for sustainability management in Turkey; our results found no significant effect between sustainability management innovation and green supply chain ($p > 0.168$).

CONCLUSION

How little attention has been given to sustainability innovation is revealed by past literature on environmental management, sustainability, and innovation (Adams et al., 2016; Doherty et al., 2014). More organizations are embracing sustainable paradigms daily due to variables like worldwide competitiveness, diversifying consumer needs, and quickly evolving technology. By using current innovation methods and supporting the viability of current business models, the sustainability innovation outcome is a decrease in harm per unit of a business process. Since most large organizations have a network of suppliers, sustainability-based innovation needs to reach beyond the factory walls into the supply chain network (Modak, 2018). The path analysis between dimensions shows that some are positive, and some have no significant effect.

The most important results are that sustainability management innovation needs more focus, and transporting energy conservation needs long-term investments.

In conclusion, environmental sustainability is crucial to balancing human activities with environmental factors. Sustainable innovation is the process of implementing new or modified procedures, strategies, and frameworks to reduce environmental harm. Green supply chain management is highly correlated with sustainability, and the relationship between environmental sustainability innovation and green supply chain management is discussed in this chapter. The hypothesis development section proposes that supply chain innovations, sustainability management, environmental communication, and pollution management, resource use and energy conservation, and transportation energy conservation increase the effectiveness of green supply chains. The methodology section describes the sample of waste management and recycling companies in Turkey. This chapter highlights the importance of sustainability and innovation in achieving a green supply chain and the need for further research.

FUTURE RESEARCH DIRECTIONS

Sustainability is no longer considered a cost-versus-economic-growth trade-off but rather a must for a business to grow and stay competitive. Future research should take green practices into account throughout the supply chain since research on sustainability innovation from a supply chain management viewpoint may provide knowledge generation and assistance to practitioners, industrial businesses, and academics.

Opportunities abound around empirical case studies from a supply chain-wide green environmental sustainability strategy. Future research on green practices in poor countries will also focus on their potential for sustainable development. Raising supply chain performance can be aided by studies on the effects of sustainability innovations on supplier performance and bettering logistical operations. To understand how environmental regulations, global standards, and new trends affect the performance of the green supply chain throughout supply chain, extensive study is also required. The metrics and benchmarks used in sustainable innovation, which will promote performance improvement, are another factor to consider.

Sustainable innovation methodologies are still required for research on the potential benefits of increased sustainable performance in the sector, particularly from green supply chain initiatives. Future studies should look into how well organizations do in terms of sustainable innovations. The adoption of green supply chains and the effects they have on performance should also be emphasized. This may entail employing techniques for assessing advancements in sustainability and developing eco-friendly management systems.

REFERENCES

Acciaro, M., Vanelslander, T., Sys, C., Ferrari, C., Roumboutsos, A., Giuliano, G., Lam, J. S. L., & Kapros, S. (2014). Environmental sustainability in seaports: A framework for successful innovation. *Maritime Policy & Management*, *41*(5), 480–500. doi:10.1080/03088839.2014.932926

Achillas, C. (2019). *Green supply chain management*. Routledge, Taylor & Francis Group.

Adams, R., Jeanrenaud, S., Bessant, J., Denyer, D., & Overy, P. (2016). Sustainability-oriented Innovation: A Systematic Review: Sustainability-oriented Innovation. *International Journal of Management Reviews*, *18*(2), 180–205. doi:10.1111/ijmr.12068

Ageron, B., Gunasekaran, A., & Spalanzani, A. (2012). Sustainable supply management: An empirical study. *International Journal of Production Economics*, *140*(1), 168–182. doi:10.1016/j.ijpe.2011.04.007

Ahi, P., & Searcy, C. (2013). A comparative literature analysis of definitions for green and sustainable supply chain management. *Journal of Cleaner Production*, *52*, 329–341. doi:10.1016/j.jclepro.2013.02.018

Bellucci, M., Simoni, L., Acuti, D., & Manetti, G. (2019). Stakeholder engagement and dialogic accounting: Empirical evidence in sustainability reporting. *Accounting, Auditing & Accountability Journal*, *32*(5), 1467–1499. doi:10.1108/AAAJ-09-2017-3158

Benitez-Amado, J., Llorens-Montes, F. J., & Fernandez-Perez, V. (2015). IT impact on talent management and operational environmental sustainability. *Information Technology and Management*, *16*(3), 207–220. doi:10.100710799-015-0226-4

Bini, L., & Bellucci, M. (2020). Accounting for Sustainability. In L. Bini & M. Bellucci, Integrated Sustainability Reporting (pp. 9–51). Springer International Publishing. doi:10.1007/978-3-030-24954-0_2

Brinkmann, R. (2020a). Connections in Environmental Sustainability: Living in a Time of Rapid Environmental Change. In R. Brinkmann, Environmental Sustainability in a Time of Change (pp. 1–8). Springer International Publishing. doi:10.1007/978-3-030-28203-5_1

Brinkmann, R. (2020b). *Environmental Sustainability in a Time of Change*. Springer International Publishing. doi:10.1007/978-3-030-28203-5

Chang, C., & Chen, Y. (2013). Green organizational identity and green innovation. *Management Decision*, *51*(5), 1056–1070. doi:10.1108/MD-09-2011-0314

Chang, R.-D., Zuo, J., Zhao, Z.-Y., Zillante, G., Gan, X.-L., & Soebarto, V. (2017). Evolving theories of sustainability and firms: History, future directions and implications for renewable energy research. *Renewable & Sustainable Energy Reviews*, *72*, 48–56. doi:10.1016/j.rser.2017.01.029

Charlton, C., & Howell, B. (2007). Life cycle assessment: A tool for solving environmental problems? *European Environment*, *2*(2), 2–5. doi:10.1002/eet.3320020203

Chen, C., Chen, Y., & Jayaraman, V. (Eds.). (2021). *Pursuing Sustainability: OR/MS Applications in Sustainable Design, Manufacturing, Logistics, and Resource Management* (Vol. 301). Springer International Publishing. doi:10.1007/978-3-030-58023-0

Choy, Y. K. (2015). From Stockholm to Rio+20. *The International Journal of Environmental Sustainability*, *11*(1), 1–25. doi:10.18848/2325-1077/CGP/v12i01/55037

Diab, S. M., AL-Bourini, F. A., & Abu-Rumman, A. H. (2015). The Impact of Green Supply Chain Management Practices on Organizational Performance: A Study of Jordanian Food Industries. *Journal of Management and Sustainability*, *5*(1), 149. doi:10.5539/jms.v5n1p149

Doherty, B., Haugh, H., & Lyon, F. (2014). Social Enterprises as Hybrid Organizations: A Review and Research Agenda: Social Enterprises as Hybrid Organizations. *International Journal of Management Reviews*, *16*(4), 417–436. doi:10.1111/ijmr.12028

Dragulanescu, I.-V., & Dragulanescu, N. (2013). Some Theories Of Environmental Sustainability. *Romanian Statistical Review*, *61*(12), 14–23.

Edwards, M., Benn, S., & Dunphy, D. (2023). Leadership for Sustainable Futures. In R. T. By, B. Burnes, & M. Hughes, Organizational Change, Leadership and Ethics (2nd ed., pp. 215–232). Routledge. doi:10.4324/9781003036395-15

Es'haghi, S. R., Rezaei, A., Karimi, H., & Ataei, P. (2022). Institutional analysis of organizations active in the restoration of Lake Urmia: The application of the social network analysis approach. *Hydrological Sciences Journal*, *67*(3), 328–341. doi:10.1080/02626667.2022.2026950

Fahimnia, B., Bell, M. G. H., Hensher, D. A., & Sarkis, J. (Eds.). (2015). *Green Logistics and Transportation: A Sustainable Supply Chain Perspective*. Springer International Publishing. doi:10.1007/978-3-319-17181-4

Falsarone, A. (2022). *The Impact Challenge: Reframing Sustainability for Businesses* (1st ed.). CRC Press. doi:10.1201/9781003212225

Fornell, C., & Larcker, D. F. (1981). Evaluating structural equation models with unobservable variables and measurement error. *JMR, Journal of Marketing Research*, *18*(1), 39–50. doi:10.1177/002224378101800104

Gaziulusoy, A. I., Boyle, C., & McDowall, R. (2013). System innovation for sustainability: A systemic double-flow scenario method for companies. *Journal of Cleaner Production, 45*, 104–116. Scopus. doi:10.1016/j.jclepro.2012.05.013

Hair, J. F., Babin, B. J., Anderson, R. E., & Black, W. C. (2019). *Multivariate data analysis*. http://search.ebscohost.com/login.aspx?direct=true&scope=site&db=nlebk&db=nlabk&AN=2639357

Henseler, J., Ringle, C. M., & Sarstedt, M. (2015). A new criterion for assessing discriminant validity in variance-based structural equation modeling. *Journal of the Academy of Marketing Science*, *43*(1), 115–135. doi:10.100711747-014-0403-8

Horng, J.-S., Liu, C.-H., Chou, S.-F., Tsai, C.-Y., & Chung, Y.-C. (2017). From innovation to sustainability: Sustainability innovations of eco-friendly hotels in Taiwan. *International Journal of Hospitality Management*, *63*, 44–52. doi:10.1016/j.ijhm.2017.02.005

Israel, G. D. (2013). *About*. Institute of Food and Agricultural Sciences (IFAS), University of Florida. https://edis.ifas.ufl.edu/pd006

Jia, P., Diabat, A., & Mathiyazhagan, K. (2015). Analyzing the SSCM practices in the mining and mineral industry by ISM approach. *Resources Policy*, *46*, 76–85. doi:10.1016/j.resourpol.2014.04.004

Johnson, M. P., & Schaltegger, S. (2016). Two Decades of Sustainability Management Tools for SMEs: How Far Have We Come? *Journal of Small Business Management*, *54*(2), 481–505. doi:10.1111/jsbm.12154

Kashmanian, R. M. (2015). Building a Sustainable Supply Chain: Key Elements: Building a Sustainable Supply Chain. *Environmental Quality Management*, *24*(3), 17–41. doi:10.1002/tqem.21393

Keong, C. Y. (2020). *Global environmental sustainability: Case studies and analysis of the united nations' journey to sustainable development* (1st ed.). Elsevier.

Khan, H. ur R., & Khan, Z. R. (2020). Green Product Innovation and Financial Resource Availability: Multi-Actor Model Approach. In S. A. R. Khan (Ed.), *Advances in Logistics, Operations, and Management Science* (pp. 111–133). IGI Global. doi:10.4018/978-1-7998-2173-1.ch006

Khan, S. A. R., Zhang, Y., & Golpîra, H. (2018). The Impact of Green Supply Chain Practices in Business Performance: Evidence from Pakistani FMCG Firms. *Journal of Advanced Manufacturing Systems*, *17*(02), 267–275. doi:10.1142/S0219686718500166

Kleindorfer, P. R., Singhal, K., & Wassenhove, L. N. (2009). Sustainable Operations Management. *Production and Operations Management*, *14*(4), 482–492. doi:10.1111/j.1937-5956.2005.tb00235.x

Kusi-Sarpong, S., Gupta, H., & Sarkis, J. (2019). A supply chain sustainability innovation framework and evaluation methodology. *International Journal of Production Research*, *57*(7), 1990–2008. doi:10.1080/00207543.2018.1518607

Lirn, T.-C., Wong, C. W. Y., Shang, K.-C., & Li, Y.-T. (2019). Identifying Green Assessment Criteria for Shipping Industries. In X. Liu (Ed.), *Environmental Sustainability in Asian Logistics and Supply Chains* (pp. 21–44). Springer Singapore. doi:10.1007/978-981-13-0451-4_2

Liu, X. (Ed.). (2019). *Environmental Sustainability in Asian Logistics and Supply Chains*. Springer Singapore. doi:10.1007/978-981-13-0451-4

Llach, J., Alonso-Almeida, M. D. M., Martí, J., & Rocafort, A. (2016). Effects of quality management on hospitality performance in different contexts. *Industrial Management & Data Systems*, *116*(5), 1005–1023. doi:10.1108/IMDS-06-2015-0235

Mahapatra, S., Cole, D., Pal, R., & Webster, S. (2021). Towards a Unified Understanding and Management of Closed Loop Operations. In C. Chen, Y. Chen, & V. Jayaraman (Eds.), *Pursuing Sustainability* (Vol. 301, pp. 219–237). Springer International Publishing. doi:10.1007/978-3-030-58023-0_9

Mena, C., Christopher, M., Johnson, M., & Jia, F. (2007). *Innovation in Logistics Services*.

Metcalf, L., & Benn, S. (2013). Leadership for Sustainability: An Evolution of Leadership Ability. *Journal of Business Ethics*, *112*(3), 369–384. Scopus. doi:10.100710551-012-1278-6

Modak, P. (2018). *Environmental management towards sustainability*. Taylor & Francis. doi:10.1201/9781315156118

Mukhopadhyay, T., & Kekre, S. (2002). Strategic and Operational Benefits of Electronic Integration in B2B Procurement Processes. *Management Science*, *48*(10), 1301–1313. doi:10.1287/mnsc.48.10.1301.273

Patnaik, P. (2022). Personalized Product Recommendation and User Satisfaction: Theory and Application. In M. Pejic-Bach & Ç. Doğru (Eds.), (pp. 35–67). Advances in Logistics, Operations, and Management Science. IGI Global. doi:10.4018/978-1-7998-7793-6.ch002

Pejić-Bach, M., & Dogru, C. (Eds.). (2022). *Management strategies for sustainability, new knowledge innovation, and personalized products and services*. Business Science Reference. doi:10.4018/978-1-7998-7793-6

Piercy, N., & Rich, N. (2015). The relationship between lean operations and sustainable operations. *International Journal of Operations & Production Management*, *35*(2), 282–315. doi:10.1108/IJOPM-03-2014-0143

Prakash, G. (2019). Exploring Innovation and Sustainability in the Potato Supply Chains. In X. Liu (Ed.), *Environmental Sustainability in Asian Logistics and Supply Chains* (pp. 97–120). Springer Singapore., doi:10.1007/978-981-13-0451-4_6

Preuss, L. (2005). *The green multiplier: A study of environmental protection and the supply chain*. Palgrave Macmillan.

Rattanamanee, T., & Nanthavanij, S. (2019). Multiple-Trip Vehicle Routing with Physical Workload. In X. Liu (Ed.), *Environmental Sustainability in Asian Logistics and Supply Chains* (pp. 261–274). Springer Singapore. doi:10.1007/978-981-13-0451-4_15

Reefke, H., & Sundaram, D. (2021). Decision Support for Sustainable Supply Chain Management. Pursuing Sustainability: OR/MS Applications in Sustainable Design, Manufacturing, Logistics, and Resource Management, 43-70.

Roehrich, J. K., Hoejmose, S. U., & Overland, V. (2017). Driving green supply chain management performance through supplier selection and value internalisation: A self-determination theory perspective. *International Journal of Operations & Production Management*, *37*(4), 489–509. doi:10.1108/IJOPM-09-2015-0566

Sachs, J. (2015). The end of poverty: Economic possibilities for our time. Penguin Books.

Sánchez-Flores, R. B., Cruz-Sotelo, S. E., & Ojeda-Benitez, S. (2020). Green Practices in Supply Chain Management to Improve Sustainable Performance. In S. A. R. Khan (Ed.), (pp. 45–71). Advances in Logistics, Operations, and Management Science. IGI Global. doi:10.4018/978-1-7998-2173-1.ch003

Schuler, D., Rasche, A., Etzion, D., & Newton, L. (2017). *Guest Editors' Introduction:* Corporate Sustainability Management and Environmental Ethics. *Business Ethics Quarterly*, *27*(2), 213–237. doi:10.1017/beq.2016.80

Sharma, S. (2014). *Competing for a sustainable world: Building capacity for sustainable innovation*. Greenleaf.

Srivastava, S. K. (2007). Green supply-chain management: A state-of-the-art literature review. *International Journal of Management Reviews*, *9*(1), 53–80. *Scopus*. doi:10.1111/j.1468-2370.2007.00202.x

Staniškis, J. K. (2022a). Socio-Environmental-Economic Transformations Towards Sustainable Development. In J. K. Staniškis, E. Staniškienė, Ž. Stankevičiūtė, A. Daunorienė, & J. Ramanauskaitė, Transformation of Business Organization Towards Sustainability (pp. 81–165). Springer International Publishing. doi:10.1007/978-3-030-93298-5_3

Staniškis, J. K. (2022b). Sustainability Challenges in an Business Organisation. In J. K. Staniškis, E. Staniškienė, Ž. Stankevičiūtė, A. Daunorienė, & J. Ramanauskaitė, Transformation of Business Organization Towards Sustainability (pp. 3–14). Springer International Publishing. doi:10.1007/978-3-030-93298-5_1

Starik, M., & Kanashiro, P. (2013). Toward a Theory of Sustainability Management: Uncovering and Integrating the Nearly Obvious. *Organization & Environment*, *26*(1), 7–30. doi:10.1177/1086026612474958

Stekelorum, R., Laguir, I., Gupta, S., & Kumar, S. (2021). Green supply chain management practices and third-party logistics providers' performances: A fuzzy-set approach. *International Journal of Production Economics*, *235*, 108093. doi:10.1016/j.ijpe.2021.108093

Sureeyatanapas, P., Poophiukhok, P., & Pathumnakul, S. (2018). Green initiatives for logistics service providers: An investigation of antecedent factors and the contributions to corporate goals. *Journal of Cleaner Production*, *191*, 1–14. doi:10.1016/j.jclepro.2018.04.206

Sureeyatanapas, P., & Yang, J.-B. (2021). Sustainable Manufacturing and Technology: The Development and Evaluation. In C. Chen, Y. Chen, & V. Jayaraman (Eds.), *Pursuing Sustainability* (Vol. 301, pp. 111–140). Springer International Publishing. doi:10.1007/978-3-030-58023-0_5

Tiwari, V., & Thakur, S. (2021). Environment sustainability through sustainability innovations. *Environment, Development and Sustainability*, *23*(5), 6941–6965. doi:10.100710668-020-00899-4

Vanalle, R. M., Ganga, G. M. D., Godinho Filho, M., & Lucato, W. C. (2017). Green supply chain management: An investigation of pressures, practices, and performance within the Brazilian automotive supply chain. *Journal of Cleaner Production*, *151*, 250–259. doi:10.1016/j.jclepro.2017.03.066

Varsei, M., Soosay, C., Fahimnia, B., & Sarkis, J. (2014). Framing sustainability performance of supply chains with multidimensional indicators. *Supply Chain Management*, *19*(3), 242–257. doi:10.1108/SCM-12-2013-0436

Vlachos, I., & Huaccho Huatuco, L. ShakirUllah, G., & Roa-Atkinson, A. (2019). A Systematic Literature Review on Sustainability and Disruptions in Supply Chains. In X. Liu (Ed.), Environmental Sustainability in Asian Logistics and Supply Chains (pp. 85–96). Springer Singapore. doi:10.1007/978-981-13-0451-4_5

Voorhees, C. M., Brady, M. K., Calantone, R., & Ramirez, E. (2016). Discriminant validity testing in marketing: An analysis, causes for concern, and proposed remedies. *Journal of the Academy of Marketing Science*, *44*(1), 119–134. doi:10.100711747-015-0455-4

Williams, A., Kennedy, S., Philipp, F., & Whiteman, G. (2017). Systems thinking: A review of sustainability management research. *Journal of Cleaner Production*, *148*, 866–881. doi:10.1016/j.jclepro.2017.02.002

Yanarella, E. J., Levine, R. S., & Lancaster, R. W. (2009). Research and Solutions: "Green" vs. Sustainability: From Semantics to Enlightenment. *Sustainability (New Rochelle, N.Y.)*, *2*(5), 296–302. doi:10.1089/SUS.2009.9838

Zhou, H., Yang, Y., Chen, Y., Zhu, J., & Shi, Y. (2021). DEA Application in Sustainability 1996–2019: The Origins, Development, and Future Directions. In C. Chen, Y. Chen, & V. Jayaraman (Eds.), *Pursuing Sustainability* (Vol. 301, pp. 71–109). Springer International Publishing. https://stats.oecd.orghttp://eurlex.europa.eu, doi:10.1007/978-3-030-58023-0_4

Chapter 6
Can Green Products and Services in the Insurance Industry be a Sustainable Measure?

Bibi Zaheenah Chummun
University of KwaZulu-Natal, South Africa

ABSTRACT

Nowadays sustainability is classified as a prominent issue, more specifically in the business world. Sustainability has a bearing on every industry at all levels. The insurance sector is not an exception and shows a remarkable interest in matters related to sustainability. Sustainable insurance businesses require multi-dimensional interventions of eco-innovation and creativity. Increasing contradictions between economic growth and environmental issues have become an important issue for businesses worldwide. The societal and technological responses to climate change threats are rapidly developing and there is still a lack of efficient financial strategies to mitigate sustainable risks. To achieve insurance business success, many insurers focus constantly on their growth in increasing their market share and retaining better risks. Insurers should always look for new ways to differentiate themselves from their competitors. In developing and offering new green products and services-related to potential sustainability, green insurance movement is the new wave and can be the solution.

INTRODUCTION

Eco-innovative and creativity initiatives are practically used in different contextual settings and generate different results accordingly. The insurance setting has seen the urgent call for the requirement of innovative and creative financial strategies and this has not been witnessed as nowadays for the purpose of sustainable well-being. The insurance cover niche is increasingly placing a lot of emphasis on sustainability, given the fact that the effect of climate change on profitability of the industry as a whole has taken its toll (Collier, Elliott & Lehtonen, 2021). Climate change is related to an anthropogenic (man-

DOI: 10.4018/978-1-6684-8969-7.ch006

made) climatic change that leads to an increase in temperatures globally caused by gases emissions like methane and carbon dioxide, also called greenhouse gases. According to a study undertaken by Ernst & Young in 2008, climate change could lead to an increase in environmental challenges, mortality rates and a negative impact of resources control, economic losses, and a lack of profitability (Ernst & Young, 2008). It is undeniable that we have not witnessed events such as an increase in storms, floods, heatwaves and these have caused more than €145 billion as economic losses during the last decade in the European Union showing a trend of an increase of almost 2% annually in economic losses (Eurostat, 2022) . In Africa, an analysis of unpredictable climatic risks events revealed that extreme weather events due to climate change has killed almost 4,000 people and affected the lives of 19 million people since the inception of 2022 in the continent (Carbon Brief, 2022).

Identifying, determining, understanding and controlling the risks are the bedrock of the insurance market (Chummun, 2012). The insurance companies have potential to widen the economic transformation in assisting governments to reach sustainability goals (Muhamat, Jaafar, Basri, Alwi, & Mainal, 2017). As time has elapsed, the providers of insurance have progressively been placing most of their priority on sustainability measures, hence highlighted the need for green sustainable behaviours and green products.

In advocating for the drive and promotion of sustainability, insurers can quantify risk, hence can reduce risks further. The United Nations Environment Programme Finance Initiative (UNEPFI) Principles for Sustainable Insurance (PSI) is a guideline that the UNEPFI released on how the insurance providers should handle sustainability challenges. In order for insurers to better understand risk, vulnerabilities and risk management in a risky-made environment, the policy can easily guide and assist insurers in their self-alignment strategies with environmental, social and governance standards (The United Nations Environment Programme Finance Initiative) [UNEPFI, 2012]. The policy is equipped with four main principles; to embed environmental, social, governance issues relevant to the insurance business in the decision making process; to work together with their clients and business partners to raise awareness of ESG issues, manage risk and find solutions across society on ESG issues; to work together with regulators, governments and other key stakeholders in order to provide actions and last not least to show accountability and transparency in regularly disclosing publicly the process in actioning these principles (UNEPFI, 2012). All the risks have several different dimensions. However the environmental, social and governance profile of a risk is a set of dimension which has only become known recently in the analysis of risk analysis in the insurance segment. On a comparative basis, other types of perils and risks for instance financial risks, the application and understanding of the ESG issues are still at a preliminary stage. Insurance providers in the market place who used and applied these standards managed to cope and increase their customer portfolio and this new trend of doing business could demarcate the providers of insurance cover from their competitors in going green which is a sustainable practice as a new trend in enhancing economic losses and the society as a whole.

Therefore, the main aim of the study is to investigate how green products and services lead to sustainability. The first section looks at insurance and its role in sustainable development. The challenges of not having green products and services and the role and importance of offering those products in an eco-friendly environment to generate sustainability is highlighted in section two. Section three gives a snapshot of the benefits of offering green products. Section four provides an overview at the relationship between green initiatives and sustainability. Section five highlights the future research directions of green products and services and how it lays the foundation for future research. Also, the author gives some insightful recommendations based on the findings identified in this paper. Finally, a conclusion follows.

BACKGROUND

Sustainable insurance businesses require multifaceted interventions of innovation and creativity. Whilst many providers of insurance globally have put a lot of concerted efforts to enhance the economic losses, others have not fully grasp the opportunities available to address sustainability in the sector, nor they have applied their full competencies and skills to tackle the issues showcased by the United Nations (UN) Sustainable Development goals (SDGs). Globally much concern has been demonstrated in order to implement sustainable measures among insurance businesses.

Sustainable products relate to those which generate social, economic and environmental benefits while safeguarding the health of the public and the environment across the whole value chain, from the raw materials extraction which is used to make the final product until their disposal. By the same token, green insurance sustainable products relate to those that comprise of their whole design, manufacturing and utilisation of these green products and services affiliated with their manufacturing and use. If there is a claim the insurers indemnify the policyholder against the consequences of that claim for instance in a potentially occurring climate change risk event, the policyholder is indemnified against the environmental consequence of that climate change related event. Further, in the context of this definition green services and products possess certain attributes that entail green/sustainable behaviour. Later in the chapter the author will give scenarios of what is considered as green insurance sustainable products.

One cannot say that all countries react similarly to the adoption of green insurance innovations. For instance, Hsu and Chao (2020) claimed in a report that the urban infrastructure related investment in Asia was classified as green, as the investment cost was exorbitant and factored an extra 9.2 million American Dollars. The authors added that the report also mentioned that there was another extra of 1.2 million Dollars that was invested in the non-green project related investments and that sum of money was more than the return expected (Hsu and Chao 2020).

One does not only derive the environmental benefits where green insurance providers provide green building insurance cover but also receive added-value, for instance discounts on insurance premiums. Therefore the investors are more likely to embark on this particular approach. The insurance industry is becoming highly volatile and it is a big portfolio of the economy as part of financial services for the sector not to do much. Insurance premiums accounted for 6.13% of the world's GDP, spreading between below 3% in the African continent and compared to 6.5% in the European countries (SwissRe, 2020). Considering the impact of claims payments in various sectors of the multifaceted economy, the effect of insurance cover can amount to almost 10% of the world's Gross Domestic Product. By the same token, insurance related assets comprise an important share or reserve of wealth. On a comparative note the insurance assets in Europe accounted for 13.2% of total household wealth, while the insurance assets of biggest 100 insurers amounted to 7.2% of household wealth worldwide (Sovereign Wealth Fund Institute) [SWFI, 2021]. Therefore it would be less of an effort to not fully deploy and leverage the insurers' financial authorities to tackle climate change.

Further, there is a progressive contradictions between environmental challenges and economic development growth and this has become an important issue of concern to the state, regulators and insurance providers across the world. Nowadays, technological and societal replies to the climatic change and other risky events are continuously showing up. However, it is noted that there is limited solutions such as lack of efficient insurance strategies under financial services in reducing sustainable risky events (Sun, Kexin & Shi, 2020). In an attempt to reach financial objectives such as business success in the industry, many providers of insurance put their efforts consistently as to work on their development way forward in retaining favourable risks and also to enhance their respective share of the market (Chummun & Bisschoff, 2014). The providers of insurance must always be on the look-out for new measures in differentiating their strategies from those of their competitors. By introducing and devising new services and products in the market which are associated with the potential climatic change and the affiliated sustainability, offering green movement in terms of green products and services could be a useful answer.

The climatic change has definitely put so much of focus on resources that are limited or missing. The volatility aspect in weather patterns are more acute, among other impacts. Subsequently the customers' expectations have changed accordingly. This has probed an urgent requirement for new reliable products and services. One should not forget the effect of climatic change on the process of underwriting here and this include green products or sustainable policies that are presently being offered by both the insurers and reinsurers. There are some policies that were identified and offered by reinsurers and insurers on the market in order to give an answer to the possible effect of climatic change related risky events. However, the number of green products and services have only grown up over time in order to substantiate sustainability or green-related behaviours from customers that are normally expected in the assistance journey to confront climate change.

The term sustainable insurance is used interchangeably with green insurance in the context of the study and is a systematic approach which grow in an economy where all insurance activities in the value chain with all stakeholders, are implemented in an accountable and responsible way by identifying, determining, analysing, controlling and monitoring uncertainties and opportunities connected with environmental, governance and social challenges.

Sustainable insurance seeks to mitigate risk, improve overall business performance, come up with innovative solutions and partake in the development of social, environmental and economic matters. The principles of sustainable insurance (PSI) provide a roadmap globally on how to grow insurance solutions and develop the risk management strategies in order to promote hygienic sanitation, renewable energy, food security, sustainable communities and economies. In 2020, the world premiums accounted for almost $4 trillion and the global assets exceeded $24 trillion for insurers related to the sustainability of their business operations, comprising of both short term and long term investments (SwissRe, 2020). The PSI lays the foundation upon which the sector of insurance lies and that puts sustainability at the forefront of risk management strategies for the well-being of everyone.

Green insurance relates to a creative and innovative aspect of business sustainability practice promotion in the market. Green insurance, specifically referred to as "environmental pollution liability insurance" can be related to the refund of a case involved with pollution incidents' caused losses and promotes "corporates' environmental risk control performance" (Chen, Meifang & Dazhi, 2021). Furthermore, it is utilized to stimulate emission-reducing inventions that adapt to the world's everchanging climates (Wang, Pu-yan, Da-heng & Zheng-hui, 2017).

Nowadays, green insurance encompasses various insurance products that are available in most green economies, including green building insurance, global weather insurance, green car insurance, and renewable energy insurance can be used to achieve sustainability (Zona, Roll & Law, 2014). Central banks and global regulators recognise green insurance policies that play a prominent role in mitigating climate change (Ramani 2020). Insurance providers can speed up the economic transformation and assist governments to reach sustainability goals in getting recourse to green insurance that can be used to strengthen the promotion of environmentally friendly products and to subsequently develop efficient inspection, examination, assessment and approval processes systems in the insurance operations.

Before the relationship of green insurance and sustainability will be highlighted later in the chapter, it is important first and foremost to explore the role of insurance in promoting sustainable development which is taken care in the next section of this chapter.

INSURANCE AND ITS ROLE IN SUSTAINABLE DEVELOPMENT

It is a fact that in this quick changing business landscape and competitive world, a comprehensive and wise effort are definitely needed. Sustainable development is related to the development in accomplishing the requirements of the stakeholders. Across the world, especially emerging economies such as the African continent demonstrate much interest towards sustainable development strategies as they recognize that the coming generation as well as the present one should not suffer from limited resources which is important for survival and welfare.

The term sustainable development has come in most business operations especially after second world war. The continuously changing behaviours and expectations of many people about sustainability has urged many companies to embrace business practices that are sustainable and insurance and is not excluded from the formula. Since the start of the past decade the corporate world has been upfront in informing the communities through campaigns and social media, about climatic change related risks and recently, risky events such as floods, droughts, global warming increasing pressures on fresh water and ecosystems have taken place vividly. Insurance providers have also been seen to be progressively realising the urgent need to customise their products and services that tackle the requirements of an increasingly changing worldwide business landscape.

Insurance cover plays a prominent role in the development of a sustainable business company through its range of products and services. In insuring the community, businesses against the risks, the standard and quality of living community and also increases the confidence of stakeholders to take on challenges and seize the opportunities that are available in the market place (Chummun & Singh, 2019).

Sustainable businesses operate, taking into account, in the interest of all, make sure that a long term welfare is associated with the economic, environmental and social system. Sustainability in the context of this paper relates to maintaining a proper equilibrium between the insurance sector and the community at large, undertaking business activities and operations in an attempt of using resources efficiently for the ultimate development and welfare of the society.

Sustainable insurance forms part of this approach. "Insurance provides an important underpinning for economic activity by addressing a wide variety of risks that many types of business are confronted with. By recognising these several risks and adopting solutions for sustainable development, the insurance sector has a wide consortium of increasing growth opportunities"(International Insurance Society, 2012).

In the present context, economies are more prone to face sustainable development in their respective business operations only if their insurance cover market is properly developed. The insurance market development is strongly linked to a well performed financial services sector and one cannot deny that without private and public sector investment in insurance, it is almost impossible for the insurance sector to develop properly (Han & Donghui, 2010). Sustainability is a buzzword and terms like corporate sustainability and sustainable development are used interchangeably. The term sustainability relates to the business activities which are normally considered as voluntary and that factor in the involvement of environmental, social, economical and governance concerns in the day to day business operations (Marrewijk, 2003).

The next section of this chapter takes into consideration of the main challenges or the key issues that impact on the growth of green business which are encountered by stakeholders dealing in green insurance products.

A SNAPSHOT OF CHALLENGES IN OFFERING GREEN INSURANCE/SUSTAINABLE PRODUCTS

As providers of insurance, the industry plays a critical role in advocating environmental, social and governance (ESG) sustainability or sustainable development. Collaborating with the UN Sustainable Development Goals (SDGs) adoption, there is a progressive urgency and pressure across all sectors including the insurance sector to address sustainability challenges and find solutions .

Environmental, social and governance (ESG) issues also known as sustainability issues pose a shared risk to the insurance providers and provide a strong motivation for collaboration and innovation (Busch & Friede, 2018). Some ESG issues have important consequences relating to financial issues for instance ecosystem degradation, pollution and climate change (Thistlethwaite & Wood, 2018).

Nowadays there is an increased interest in the use of green and sustainability-related products in the insurance arena to access the capital market where insurers are frequent issuers of instruments that qualify as regulatory capital. The growing importance of ESG factors for investors is reflected in the green and sustainability-related capital market for insurers. The providers of insurance can better access the growing demand for green and sustainability portfolios as the green insurance business model broadens. However, there are some noted challenges that dominate the insurance industry in this regard.

Credit or counterpart risk can occur if an insurer defaults due reasons related to decisions in terms of regulation and supervisory associated with ESG aspects that affect negatively the business model of the insurance company such as a carbon dioxide (CO_2) tax (Principles for Responsible Investment) [PRI, 2022]. Further, the expectations of the market in terms of this regulatory ESG measures is more likely to lead to the price risk also known as the market risk related investments that are classified as non-sustainable through depreciation. Many insurance providers have scarce understandings/knowledge of the green insurance journey. Their expectations lie in the sense that they have to be compliant to certain norms for instance pollution norms, however they do not take into account that they are missing out on opportunities of using green as a vehicle for competitive advantage. Green initiatives are perceived as expensive and do not have a payback value for insurance companies as it is a new trend in the sector.

Also, liquidity risk can happen in case of a natural catastrophe where a significant number of customers withdraws funds from their accounts to finance losses. Besides climate risks being the dominant issue, ESG risks, including water scarcity and their impact on assets, are increasingly assessed by financial firms as well (United Nations Environment Programme) [UNEP, 2020].

Another challenge which is related to insurers is that the development of a green and sustainability product class could increase reputational risks around related events. For example, investors in a green-labelled product may not receive payments because of problems that a bank or insurer faces from losses after an investment fails due to the ESG risks, for instance from losses due to pollution.

However, there are also other weaknesses which need to be mitigated if not removed so that the insurance providers can unlock their full potential related to their financial capacity, such as non-transparent regulatory and supervisory matters on capital requirements (Golnaraghi, 2018), a lack of transparency on the sources of data, lack of reliable information and the unavailability of investment opportunities related to the infrastructure in the market place (Gatzert & Kosub, 2017).

The move or trend heading towards sustainable insurance cover is generated through the recognition of many insurers facing substantial challenges for instance, a rise in greenhouse gas emissions resulting in drought, extreme weather instability flooding, climate change, global warming, drought and extreme weather conditions. It is important to note that the essence of sustainable insurance relies on the strong collaboration between the United Nations as advisory bodies and the players that consist of the insurance companies on a worldwide basis. The insurance players need also to collaborate with their existing and potential customers to promote and market green initiatives such as green products and services.

Nowadays the analysis of risk and pre-risk as well as post risk management strategies lie at the forefront of the insurers' sustainability matters. Unlocking understanding and liaising with different types of risks require specific expertise of the insurance sector.

The relationship between sustainability challenges and the insurance sector is strongly connected and the recognition thereof is appreciated by the society. Taking into account what has been reached as milestone in the insurance niche in the dimensions of sustainability, it is worthwhile to know how uncertainties or risks and sustainability are related and how the insurance industry comes into the game of addressing the different types of risks.

THE BENEFITS OF OFFERING GREEN/SUSTAINABLE PRODUCTS AND SERVICES

While having challenges, insurance providers offering green sustainable products and services have also some inherent direct and indirect benefits which will be explained in this section. The following is a brief summary that provides the involvement of the insurance industry in environmental sustainability matters.

Insurance companies which provide financial help to the community at large are involved in the management of all types of environmental losses, natural or man-made, give loss prevention advice as they have competencies, skills in the risk management strategies and handle claim matters as being experts in the field. The adoption and use of technology as well as the online insurance business reduce the amount of paper work which save the environment. It also improves the standard and quality of living of the community through innovative insurance products and services such as weather-indexed insurance products and crop insurance.

The indirect benefits offered by insurance companies with regard to green sustainable products and services relate to the encouragement and promotion of environmentally/ecological friendly behaviours of customers in providing related protection for a new green project .

The direct benefit offered by an insurance company is by offering green insurance products and services that can create value and competitive advantage compared to their competitors such as follows:

- **An increase in the market share**

For instance in giving discounts on premiums for electric vehicles(EVs)/hybrid versions, insurance companies can increase their penetration/entry in this expanding niche of the insurance automobile market.

- **First- mover advantage**

In view of the government encouraging insurers to enter the green insurance market in giving incentives in this regard, the new sector of renewable energy can be seen expanding if not booming, for instance nowadays technology and innovative intensive nature of the sector play a major role in these energy renewable projects. Insurers who penetrate in the sector at a much earlier stage can have the first mover advantage over their competitors in similar industries.

- **Green insurance marketing advantage**

Alongside green insurance or green movement comes green marketing. Insurers who are proactive in offering green products and services can build their own brand name, become corporate responsible and can benefit from marketing and branding strategies.

- **Favourable adverse selection**

It has to be noted that existing or potential customers who are sustainable or environmentally-user friendly are more receptive in the way they conduct themselves for instance such as driving their private vehicles or wearing the safety belts or hats while working. Further these conscious customers are likely to add security features in their homes or yards, hence they position themselves as better risk for green insurance cover.

It is therefore important for the stakeholders to be made aware of the relationship between green initiatives and sustainability in the insurance sector, which is highlighted in the next section of this chapter.

- **Green insurance products can assist to counter climatic change**

Insurance providers are important players in the financial services market that collect premiums in terms of savings. With the coming of financial markets' globalisation, the role and importance of financial agents/intermediaries has grown up considerably. Classified as investors, they perceive climate change as a benefit. Unfortunately for some, climate change can be very risky. As subscribers invest massively in sustainable goods such as wind turbines, the need to insure these products is crucial and subsequently insurance companies have the competencies and acumen to cover those risks. Therefore, the insurance policies advocate for the use of sustainable technologies' items.

- **Green insurance policies cover costly technological projects**

The insurance companies normally cover the small to big projects at different levels. For instance, one main issue nowadays is energy consumption and production. It is known that solar energy has a lot of energy sources . However, the technology equipped with it is costly to harness it. Although having such uncertainties, the insurance providers can cover such risks.

- **Loss prevention**

Loss prevention is one of the strategies used by stakeholders in the insurance market place. However, climate change is embedded with massive losses and risks. Insurers who engage in catering financially the customers green projects tend to increase their resilience. For instance, when houses are built in flood related areas on stilts, the losses or damages can decrease during a flood risky event. Insurance companies can advocate sustainable incentives that bring down the losses or the providers can support a better planning and do not encourage risky regions development.

GREEN INITIATIVES AND SUSTAINABILITY IN THE INSURANCE NICHE

An important trend in the financial market over the past decade is the inclusion of sustainability in the insurance niche. Insurance companies, investors and risk managers play a critical role for the promotion of environmental, social, and governance practices. The interest of insurance companies in sustainability has grown over the past decade. The insurance industry across the world is reacting to the challenges related to sustainability with actions taken strategically on both investment and underwriting of insurance operations. The largest insurance companies factor in the environmental, social and governance component into the provision of insurance coverage, underwriting strategies, reallocating capital towards green assets. A growing number of insurance supervisors and regulators are starting to incorporate sustainability into the way they oversee the sector. For example, the Prudential Regulation Authority (PRA) in the UK and the European Union's European Insurance and Occupational Pensions Authority (EIOPA) have made it clear that they expect insurance companies to be sustainable (Prudential Regulation Authority) [PRA, 2019].

There are a lot of possible avenues to include sustainability into the insurance cover. Sustainability in the insurance arena can be related to lowering insurance premiums for example, electric vehicles (EVs) as a measure for green initiatives, agreeing with the authorities about the criteria that are eligible for deciding the tax incentives measures that are associated with green sustainable insurance, advocating for new designed green products and also encouraging investments in insurance projects that comply with the criteria of green as a sustainable measure. Green sustainable insurance can also be in terms of new products that are intended to tackle climate change such as weather-indexed insurance, crop insurance or insurance products that lead to customers' green behaviours and sustainability. Moreover, sustainability-related practices are predicted to be incorporated into the operations of businesses and ventures across the industries and jurisdictions. For example, insurance companies may require companies to uphold environmental, social and governance practices principles to be eligible for certain insurance policies and can be a condition of a pre- requirement for the project.

RECOMMENDATIONS: TYPES OF GREEN INSURANCE PRODUCTS AND SERVICES THAT CAN BE RECOMMENDED TO ENTAIL SUSTAINABILITY

Although very few big insurers have started offering green insurance products and services and that also with some limitations in their cover, others are emerging economies in the market place or have limited capital . The following are some recommendations that the insurance companies may consider adopting in their decision-making process with regards to green insurance products and services.

- **Green property /building insurance**

The green property/ building insurance encourages developers of property in building green and sustainable buildings which consists of specific green specifications, design which may involve environmentally friendly or more energy-efficient materials to preserve the environment and at the same time protect losses from climate risk. In an event of a covered loss, the green property/building insurance caters for the utilization of environmentally, ecological user-friendly or better renewal energy related materials upon the undertaking of repairs . For those policyholders who comply with the green measures, the companies often offer discounts on their insurance premiums.

- **Renewable energy insurance**

Renewable energy cover has an important benefit cover against climate change. However, the cover is a bit costly as it is uptight with risks. In an attempt to mitigate the risks associated, support its growth and sustainability and reduce their risks, insurers generally offer renewable energy cover policies to people and manufacturing operating companies. For instance, while the project is in its development phase, insurance companies, in the event of a valid claim, will cover construction and engineering risks while others will cover for business revenue loss and interruption support.

- **Global Weather Insurance**

Global weather-indexed cover has for the last number been offered to fill in the vaccum that has been left over by the main conventional insurance cover falling under the short-term classified property insurance policies. The subscribers are generally the insureds or the farmers that are covered against any risky-related weather uncertainties such as climate change and global warming. This is a benefit insurers who intend to hedgerow against a particular weather component like rainfall that could exceed a certain threshold.

- **Directors & officers insurance cover**

The insurance companies can take into account offering an option to the customers between environmental or global warming insurance protection to officers and directors mainly due to the progressive cases of litigation against companies that are involved in the contribution of climate change.

- **Property loss mitigation Insurance**

For the owners of houses who make use of mitigation strategies such as materials or techniques, devices, and can bring down the losses arising from after a catastrophe, insurance companies can offer discounted premiums to the owners.

- **Pay as You Drive (PAYD) Insurance**

The essence of the Pay as You Drive (PAYD) insurance is that the lesser drivers travel drive it is known that the probability of accidents and pollution happening are less. In this context a device such as a tracker sensor is normally fitted in the vehicle to monitor the kilometres driven. The less people drive the more discounted premiums they benefit from the insurance providers.

- **Insurance for environmental/pollution liability**

The insurance cover can cater for a consortium of risks, for instance pollution legal liability arising from the ruling of the court, and commercial liability. The losses can be due to several hazards that have an effect on large companies to relatively smaller contractors.

- **Political Risk Insurance- carbon emission**

The stakeholders including parties such as lenders, sponsors of projects and investors are offered insurance protection arising from risks events with regard to government interference, license or registration cancellation, riot, political violence and war that could stop the manufacturing, certification, production and final delivery of carbon substances.

- **Marine environment liability insurance**

The marine environment insurance can cover a ship wreck losses or damages. For instance, in August 2020, the Wakashio vessel/ship wreck which happen on the South-East coast of Mauritius injected an excess of 1000 tons of oil into the lagoons/sea destroying coastal marine biodiversity and livelihoods. The Bunker convention for oil pollution stipulates that it is the owners' responsibility to cater for the damages caused by the leakage of oil. Further, the limitation clause of liability for maritime insurance claim also stipulates that the owners should have enough cover. Hence the insurer can pay out the estimated amount of claim related damage.

- **Green building cover against negative advertising**

This cover secures whenever a property or building project experiences poor advert. The insurance money is deployed and caters for this adverse publicity. These are often handled by management specialists who assist, advise and guide the employees in doing damage control with regard to the restoration of other services to keep the corporate's goodwill.

- **Food perishable mitigation insurance**

This type of product advocates for the utilization of devices or techniques which is used to mitigate losses related to the produce quantity and enhance quality of those produce in the event of distribution from the farm to the retail outlets. For instance, the technological devices are set to monitor and control the conditions and temperature of those goods as they travel throughout borders assuming the remaining shelf-life. This is an important information that is used to optimise the quality and mitigate the unnecessary waste that may be perishable.

FUTURE RESEARCH DIRECTIONS

It has come to realization that only a small proportion of the world-wide population is collaborating to bring the solution to the wicked green insurance issue prevalent globally. However, this is not enough, many more stakeholders in the insurance industry can work together to solve the green issues. Eco-innovation and green creativity are a must to solve green issues in offering green products and services that can be made affordable to the masses and are important in the assistance of solving green issues by tailor-making the respective green policies both affordable and accessible to all. One can easily say nowadays that the hit of various waves of the COVID virus pandemic has seriously imposed some restrictive protocols for instance social distancing measures, curfews, among others without forgetting the transitional shift in the new ways of pursuing insurance business for instance embarking on remote online measures for both emerging and developed economies. Those changes are impacting on the stakeholders of the insurance industry who do not embrace change so easily about new ways of doing insurance business such as offering green insurance products to incorporate sustainability. The limited skills, knowledge, competencies, misconception of price risk, credit risk and liquidity risk embedded in the new insurance sector nowadays require attention for the insurance niche to change for the better in the cover market which is highly volatile. It is imperative that the state regulators and other stakeholders embark on new measures for doing insurance business such as offering new green insurance products that are tailored-made to match the needs of customer expectations.

It is important to note that researchers investigate or explore the different insurance sectors of economies to find out if they have embarked or involved in the green products and services business. Henceforth, the researchers or scholars could analyse the challenges, benefits, the costs and the outcomes/results culminating from green insurance business. It is also important to come to realization of the profitability aspect and competitive advantage component of green insurance products and services, the essence of being in business The urgent need is mainly due to the impact of climate change on the insurance companies' risk management strategies and the increased pressure and trend to adopt green products and services that benefit the environment at large.

It is important to facilitate the new processes to different stakeholders at all levels such as green insurance businesses related technologies, practices of ESG standards on both an online and face-to-face ways . This training project can be a time-consuming assignment that has to be undertaken by regulators/government to educate the insurance providers which in turn can facilitate their customers. Further, the providers of insurance have a big assignment to make sure that the facilitation and training are done well and ethically to the various stakeholders about new ways and measures to do insurance business through green movement. Therefore, the state and other players in the financial services niche can include those suggested components of active training in order to green- create and eco-innovate the insurance products and services in an attempt to develop and grow the niche insurance area with the ultimate aim of entailing sustainability at all levels and that lays the foundations for future research in the insurance niche of any economy.

CONCLUSION

This paper gives a snapshot of the importance and role of green insurance products and services as a form of green creativity and eco-innovation. The chapter also emphasises the spirit of working together which can bring sustainability . The content of this chapter adds to the literature and brings contribution to knowledge in the field of green insurance cover and sustainability. Simultaneously, it provides the bedrock for future research in the important discipline of green insurance as a measure of sustainability. This chapter is useful to decision-makers, regulators, government officials, researchers, corporate leaders, academics and the public at large.

The urgent attention that is needed for green insurance creativity in the insurance niche has never been given priority until present in this challenging times and this has been discussed in the background of this chapter. Insurance and its role and importance in its sustainable development has been discussed in section one. Furthermore, the challenges such as liquidity, market risk, regulatory capital which are linked to the interruption of green cover business have been taken care in section two of this chapter. The insurance landscape or providers of insurance have been impacted globally due to many risks such as climate change which is one of the main set-backs urging the need for green insurance business across the sector worldwide. Resultantly risky events have affected many insureds in the insurance arena probing the urgent need for green sustainable insurance in addressing the wicked green problems in the world. The insurers think that such a trend could lead to the next insurance revolution wave or new global crucial trend in the financial services industry. The wicked green problem and its disruptions tend to continue and have been recorded already, thus highlighting the adoption of green insurance market across all value chain. Section three takes into account the indirect as well as the direct benefits of green sustainable insurance products and services. Ploughing some concerted efforts and adopting a new measure in informing the stakeholders about the green creativity initiatives in the insurance sector can be a concerted effort and at the same time a time-consuming assignment for the cover providers. This inevitably needs a fast creative route for training and learning way forward for both the providers and the consumers. Section four takes into account the relationship between green initiatives and sustainability. Section five of the chapter gives an overview and lays the foundation of future research directions. Ultimately, the author gives some useful recommendations in favour of some green insurance products and services as a measure for sustainability. These innovative solutions can be of benefit to both the cover providers and existing as well as potential customers in the time of this proven-wicked green issue we are all facing.

REFERENCES

Busch, T., & Friede, G. (2018). The robustness of the corporate social and financial performance relation: A second-order meta-analysis. *Corporate Social Responsibility and Environmental Management*, 25(4), 583–608. doi:10.1002/csr.1480

Carbon Brief. (2022). *Climate loss and damage in Africa: Massive costs on the Horizon.* Carbon Brief. https://www.carbonbrief.org/analysis-africas-unreported-extreme-weather-in-2022-and-climate-change

Chen, H., Meifang, Y., & Dazhi, C. (2019). Research on Institutional Innovation of China's Green Insurance Investment. *Journal of Industrial Integration and Management*, 4(1), 1–17. doi:10.1142/S2424862219500039

Chummun, B. Z. (2012). *Evaluating business success in the Microinsurance industry of South Africa* [Doctoral dissertation, North-West University].

Chummun, B. Z., & Bisschoff, C. A. (2014). A theoretical model to measure the business success of Microinsurance in South Africa. [KRE]. *Journal of Economics, 5*(1), 87–96. doi:10.1080/09765239.2014.11884987

Chummun, B. Z., & Singh, A. (2019). Factors Influencing the Quality of Decision-Making Using Business Intelligence in a Metal Rolling Plant in KwaZulu-Natal. *Journal of Reviews on Global Economics, 8*, 1108–1120. doi:10.6000/1929-7092.2019.08.96

Collier, S. J., Elliott, R., & Lehtonen, T. K. (2021). Climate change and insurance. *Economy and Society, 50*(2), 158–172. doi:10.1080/03085147.2021.1903771

Ernst & Young. (2008). *Strategic business risk 2008: Insurance.* E&Y. https://www.ey.com/GL/en/Newsroom/News-releases/Media---Press-Release---Strategic-Risk-to-Insurance-Industry

Eurostat. (2022). *Losses from climate change: €145 billion in a decade.* Eurostat. https://ec.europa.eu/eurostat/web/products-eurostat-news/-/ddn-20221024-1

Gatzert, N., & Reichel, P. (2020). *Awareness of climate risks and opportunities: empirical evidence on determinants and value from the US and European insurance industry.* Working Paper, Friedrich-Alexander University Erlangen-Nürnberg, Nuremberg

Golnaraghi, M. (2018). *Climate change and the insurance industry: taking action as risk managers and investors. Perspectives from C-level executives in the insurance industry.* The Geneva Association. https://www.genevaassociation.org/sites/default/files/research-topics-document-type/pdf_public//climate_change_and_the_insurance_industry_-_taking_action_as_risk_managers_and_investors.pdf

Han. L. & Donghui, L. (2010). *Insurance Development and Economic Growth, the Geneva Papers on Risk and Insurance-Issues and Practice, 35*(2), 183-199.

Hsu, K., & Jen-Chih, C. (2020). Economic Valuation of Green Infrastructure Investments in Urban Renewal: The Case of the Station District in Taichung, Taiwan. *Environments (Basel, Switzerland), 7*(8), 56. doi:10.3390/environments7080056

International Insurance Society. (2010), *Sustainable Insurance Society.* International Insurance Society. http://www.iisonline.org/forum/markettrends/sustainable-insurance/e-insurance/

Marrewijk, V. M. (2003). Concepts and Definitions of CSR and Corporate Sustainability: Between Agency and Communion. *Journal of Business Ethics, 44*(2), 95–105. doi:10.1023/A:1023331212247

Mills, E. (2009). A Global Review of Insurance Industry Responses to Climate Change. *The Geneva Papers on Risk and Insurance. Issues and Practice, 34*(3), 323–359. doi:10.1057/gpp.2009.14

Muhamat, A., Jaafar, M., Basri, M., Alwi, S., & Mainal, A. (2017). Green Takaful (Insurance) as a Climate Finance Tool. *Advanced Science Letters, 23*(8), 7670–7673. doi:10.1166/asl.2017.9549

Principle for Investments. (2022). *Statement on ESG in credit risk and ratings.* UNPRI. https://www.unpri.org/credit-risk-and-ratings/statement-on-esg-in-credit-risk-and-ratings-available-in-different-languages/77.article

Prudential Regulation Authority. (2019). *Enhancing banks' and insurers approaches to managing the financial risks from climate change, policy statement 11/19*. PRA. https://www.bankofengland.co.uk

Ramani, V. (2020). *Addressing Climate as a Systemic Risk*. Ceres. https://www.ceres.org/sites/default/files/reports/202006/Financial%20Regulators%20FULL%20FINAL.pdf

Sovereign Wealth Fund Institute. (2021). *Top 100 Insurers*. Sovereign Wealth Fund Institute. https://www.swfinstitute.org/fund-rankings/

Sun, Y., Kexin, B., & Shi, Y. (2020). Measuring and Integrating Risk Management into Green Innovation Practices for Green Manufacturing under the Global Value Chain. *Sustainability (Basel)*, *12*(2), 545. doi:10.3390u12020545

SwissRe. (2020). *Insurance Sustainable Development Goals (iSDGs)*. SwissRe. https://www.swissre.com/institute/conferences/sustainability-leadership-in-insurance/sustainability-leadership-ininsurance-live-session-3.html#abouttheevent

The United Nations Environment Programme Finance Initiative. (2012*). Principles for Sustainable Insurance a global sustainability framework and initiative of the United Nations Environment Programme Finance Initiative*. UN. https://www.unepfi.org/psi/wp-content/uploads/2012/06/PSI-document.pdf

Thistlethwaite, J., & Wood, M. O. (2018). Insurance and climate change risk management: Rescaling to look beyond the horizon. *British Journal of Management*, *29*(2), 279–298. doi:10.1111/1467-8551.12302

United Nations Environment Programme Finance Initiative. (2012). *PSI Principles for sustainable insurance*. UN. https://www.unepfi.org/psi/wp-content/uploads/2012/06/PSI-document.pdf

Wang, C., & Pu-yan, N. (2017). Green insurance subsidy for promoting clean production innovation. *Journal of Cleaner Production*, *148*, 111–117. doi:10.1016/j.jclepro.2017.01.145

Zona, R., Roll, K., & Law, Z. (2014). *Sustainable/Green Insurance Products,* pp. 165–72. Casualty Actuarial Society E-Forum.

KEY TERMS AND DEFINITIONS

Carbon emissions: Pollution that gets injected into the environment from carbon monoxide and carbon dioxide and is generally caused by automobiles or vehicles.

Eco-friendly: Environmentally related actions which produce very little harm to the planet earth.

Economies: Countries which are on the route to development and growth for the welfare of their people or already developed.

Environmental impact: The impact of a variable on the environment.

Green creativity: Unleashing the potential of the mind to create new innovative ideas.

Green insurance: This is a cover type that assists protecting the environment/ecology and addressing climate change.

Green: This is a term used to describe the behaviour, policies, products, people that can work to reduce environmental damage.

Innovation: Introducing change into the systems.

Insurance Providers: This can include insurers, institutions offering insurance cover on the marketplace to existing and potential customers.

Participation.: Engagements or involvement that encourage stakeholders to work together to enhance the welfare, the standard of living and boost economic growth and development.

Sustainability: The environmental practices, processes which give protection to natural resources that are needed by everyone for a better quality of life.

Sustainable insurance: The cover attempts to mitigate risk, find out innovative and creative solutions, enhance the performance of business and also environmental, social and governance standards.

Chapter 7
Smart Non-Invasive Approach for Workspace Rating Assessment:
A Post-Occupancy Evaluation Approach for University Buildings

Adyasha Swain
Jönköping University, Sweden

ABSTRACT

This study describes the development and examination of a customized post-occupancy evaluation (POE) software application to improve FM and students' exposure to and use of real-time data. To adapt that facility management could involve students in class activities and enhance their perception of the validation process, it is necessary to demonstrate that gathering info in real-time and exploiting is feasible. A mobile application was built to gather information on occupants' perceptions and likewise, real-time realignment of the data store. Physical parameters were used to guide the selection of lighting and space usage parameters that corresponded with perceived indoor conditions. During the pilot project, an immediate representation of the gathered data was given, illustrating how the POE app functions and what more statistical assessment can be done further. The prototype's use in a real-world university building demonstrates the system's adaptability, viability, and capacity for gathering and analyzing real-time building performance data.

1. INTRODUCTION

Post-occupancy evaluation (POE) has evolved among the most crucial components of assessing a facility's performance over time. An exacting strategy and precise performance criteria are used to determine the discrepancy between the actual functioning of buildings-in-use and performance requirements (Cochran Hameen et al., 2020). While grading systems for energy and environmental performance shifted

DOI: 10.4018/978-1-6684-8969-7.ch007

their focus from architecture and construction to building management, POE has gained traction in the construction industry. Despite the long-standing argument that many construction industry experts know building construction without being required to implement the POE process and assure the performance of buildings, building performance research and POE have been formed in the field of architecture and construction in higher education (Abisuga et al., 2019).

By employing a student-centered POE strategy, students can obtain first-hand experience with building-user interactions and how these exchanges affect building efficiency. To increase students' exposure to and usage of real-time data, a post-occupancy evaluation (POE) software built was developed and tested. Traditional post-occupant evaluation (POE) techniques can be used in conjunction with subjective and objective techniques. Conversations, walk-through inspections, and occupant evaluations are examples of subjective techniques, whereas objective techniques include physical evaluation of the surroundings (Altomonte et al., 2020). Recent POE projects appear to make the most use of occupant surveys, whether standard or customized. Large samples for surveys can be collected employing a survey via the internet or a questionnaire that you administer yourself, making them ideal for defining the traits of an enormous population. When compared to methods that require communication with another person, like a physical or teleconference interview, they also improve the likelihood of truthful responses. Yet, the nature and methods of gathering both subjective and objective data have altered as a result of virtually universal internet access and internet-connected mobile devices. A multi-platform IEQ questionnaire was created for use in non-desk environments in connection with a residential studies project in Australia (Parkinson et al., 2013; Tartarini et al., 2022). It was touted as the primary field application of this technology and one of the first survey platforms to directly support mobile devices. This survey doesn't require any additional software, but since it finally refers survey participants to a mobile-friendly internet survey, it might be viewed as a tool that is more focused on research than on user-friendliness.

As a result, many different gadgets are used to connect to the internet, including laptop computers, smartphones, and tablets. Active internet users prefer to provide peer feedback in a visual style, especially those who are younger. Following these circumstances, we created a POE application that collects non-intrusive real-time data on occupant building evaluations.

2. BACKGROUND

IoT, cloud computing, big data, and artificial intelligence are examples of the ongoing technical advancements that have steadily enveloped people with technology (Tien, 2017). In order to construct technologically sophisticated and intelligent settings, it is essential to establish intuitive interfaces and systems with some level of intelligence, the capacity to identify and respond to human needs in a discrete and frequently imperceptible way. As a result, the paradigm known as intelligence services were created. Ambient intelligence is used in conjunction with a digital environment to help people become conscious of their actions, wants, feelings, and gestures (Cook et al., 2009).

For instance, the necessity to address all of the associated disciplines—physics, engineering, design, technology, architecture, human behavior, and health—has led to an increase in interest in safety settings in risky environments. The study of informatics provides an understanding of each discipline and how it influences the practice of a solution because it is a multidisciplinary field of study by nature. The key is that it contains a rich variety of information that sufficiently addresses each of the knowledge areas discussed. Comparable scenarios are depicted in the study of human-building interaction, which calls for a wide range of data as support for any decisions regarding the infrastructure and its parameters (Henricksen & Indulska, 2006).

A well-planned transition can go awry if one of four interconnected domains—technology, data, process, or organizational change capability—performs poorly. The genuinely important tasks, like creating and communicating a compelling vision, developing a strategy and adapting it as needed, and toiling through the details, all revolve around people. In particular, digital change calls for expertise. It is critical to assemble the best team possible of data, technological, and process professionals that can work together (Lonsdale et al., 2015).

The untapped potential of cutting-edge technology like the Internet of Things, blockchain, data lakes, artificial intelligence, cloud platform services like IaaS, PaaS, and SaaS, and Digital Twin Solutions, is astounding from a technological standpoint. Even if many of them are becoming simpler to use, it is quite challenging to understand how specific technology aids in disruptive potential, adapt that technology to the particular requirements of the organization, and integrate it with existing systems. To make matters worse, the majority of firms have a sizable amount of technical debt — legacy technologies that are challenging to replace — and a person's familiarity with new technologies may limit the prospects for new developments in a project (Saarikko et al., 2020).

Due to the rigors of transformation, significantly improved data quality and analytics are required. Unfortunately, the majority of data in many organizations today do not meet fundamental standards. Understanding additional categories of unstructured information, utilizing proprietary data, utilizing the vast volume of external data, and incorporating everything around each other are almost certainly all parts of the evolution process, while simultaneously discarding enormous quantities of information that hasn't ever been (and will never be) utilized.

3. PROBLEM STATEMENT

The majority of space utilization prediction methods used in workspace design and user simulation manually assign space types to user activities that correspond according to the activities' spatial requirements (Jakubiec & Reinhart, 2012; Reinhart et al., 2006). Because workspace planning and analysis of space utilization do not take into account how occupants interact with their space, it's possible that a facility space can't support all of the tasks allocated to it.

For instance, prior energy-efficient lighting approaches in universities used to be heavily centered on parameters related to aesthetic needs, but today we need a new, evidence-based approach that takes into account the real users, such as user behavior and customers (Amirazar, 2021). This aids in the identification of a problem, such as the wellness of a student or worker, or issues of a student, the proper solutions, and the environment a student should be exposed to for workplace productivity, by gathering real-time data over a period of time and analyzing it. After identifying the issue, the best available data are sought out in the literature to support the hypothesis. The validity, quality, and generalizability of the evidence are next critically evaluated.

This causes the focus to shift to technical crucial areas that require additional research attention and pose many open-ended questions, such as what lighting solution can be applied in the healthcare or academic industry introducing new business models for commercialization and innovation, data collection and its analysis; for example, how are the devices or possible alternatives detect an activity? These behaviors—are they typical or abnormal? Are such actions demanding your attention? Do those students need a natural setting? The best available research is then reviewed, along with clinical knowledge and resources, and integrated into clinical practice. This supports the Post Occupancy Evaluation's goal of generating value for stakeholders by allowing recommendations to be made for better-informed decision-making.

The operating system's validation and verification, which need time-consuming processes, are additional issues. It is quite difficult for a human to understand a system's desired behavior. Simply said, the state space, which is made up of numerous sensor and actuator data, is too large to analyze the behavior of the accessible system as a whole. Because of its dispersed structure, large-scale distributed IoT systems are often challenging to test and validate in terms of behavior. This is caused by several things, such as the fact that specifications are sometimes ambiguous and complex, which causes misinterpretation and undesirable behavior. Second, it is almost impossible for a person to rationally evaluate the accuracy of a system made up of hundreds or thousands of distinct parts. When attempting to resolve a problem, it can be challenging to observe all the related components because the system is geographically scattered across a large area. There must be a solution developed for the challenging optimization challenge.

Yet, the information technology revolution that has been revolutionizing practically every other part of smart society is placing challenges on another area of research that can be investigated, university buildings. These new growing technologies include the Internet of Things and cloud services. The difficulty is in collecting a variety of data from devices every second, analyzing that data for exact results, and figuring out how to mix traditionally constructed environments with automated build environments. In order to effectively and efficiently make decisions for the FM in value creation to user innovation, it will be necessary to properly analyze the bottleneck for the system that has been imagined.

To support the reliability and accuracy of such predictions, it can be enhanced by modeling occupants' space preferences and their effects, this article explores how real-world studies on educational facilities can be used to infer the relationship between space utilization and space preference, space denial, and satisfaction level. Because numerous student activities regularly demand a space selection and because the area is seldom made available to pupils for their activities, this type of university facility can offer a strong case for this study (Henricksen & Indulska, 2006). The following questions were used to collect and analyze empirical data to fulfill the purpose of this study:

1. What percentage of tasks attributes the students to choose their workspace?
2. What percentages of students are uneasy in each quadrant of various spaces, and why do they feel that way?
3. In what ways does students' satisfaction with their use of space change as a result of space rejection?
4. What features of a space affect students' acceptance or rejection of that space?

These four inquiries probe why students select a particular area, how students reject the location, and why these decisions and rejections are related to a particular space feature within the lighting parameter.

4. RESEARCH DESIGN IDEATION

There are various definitions of what it means to be well. Health, happiness, and prosperity are described as its experiences. Good mental health includes having the capacity to manage stress. Well-being is simply feeling good. "Health is a state of complete physical, mental, and social well-being, not merely the absence of disease or infirmity" (WHO 2020). It can't just be that there are no illnesses or unpleasant emotions. For instance, health is not always the same as disease-free status. The relationship between this issue and the social and professional environments in terms of culture and demographics is also taken into account. Well-being in the workplace, in the community, and all other spheres is crucial.

It is a subjective feeling, though. In some circumstances, not everyone experiences the same things. It is how a person perceives their place in the environment concerning their expectations, and standards, as well as the current cultural and ethical framework in which they now reside. It's an expansive idea that is deeply influenced by a person's physical and mental health, as well as their ideals, relationships with others, and interactions with important aspects of their environment. It can be stated simply as the general well-being of people, highlighting negativity and embracing good aspects of life. Also, people react differently to various well-being elements.

According to the Human Interaction perspective, technology is centered on how a user can engage with it by using a variety of graphical user interfaces made possible by smartphone technology in a variety of situatedness settings. The fundamental approach could involve planning and designing the user interface, user testing, analysis of feedback, and iterative process until a consensus is reached. Here, the planning may include the following ideas.

1. Perceptual, including potential decision-making based on visual, auditory, effective top-down functionality, and avoiding misunderstanding.
2. Cognitive, where actions might be focused on realistic illustrations that the user could comprehend.
3. Simplicity, where decisions might be made by substituting sensory information for psychological context in the interface to capture the user's attention.
4. Situational decision-making, where action on the interface may be dependent on several applications.

For a better understanding of the causes of space acceptance and rejection, and to relate the findings to space qualities in a qualitative way. This study combined a time-use survey (TUS) with a post-occupancy evaluation (POE) (Lonsdale et al., 2015; Saarikko et al., 2020). Nevertheless, present approaches rarely consider how people use their space, even though this is frequently a crucial element in deciding how much space is used in many structures. In actuality, people's choices about where to live are far more intricate and broader, necessitating the consideration of several variables, including individual heterogeneity, interactions, and social, psychological, and physical aspects of human behavior (Jakubiec & Reinhart, 2012).

These elements come from several academic fields. In psychology, emphasis has been placed on two topics: first, discrete spatial layouts created specifically for the mental map are unique to each person, and second, spatial perception is how people process spatial data. Researchers in social geography have been considering how spatial interaction affects spatial preference. provided an approach for predicting space utilization based on agents that model occupant behavior while simulating space consumption. Because it is strongly related to both space use and occupant satisfaction with space use, it is crucial to comprehend occupants' space preferences throughout the design phase. Generally speaking, a place that creates a lot of satisfaction on the best and most likely option is just one visit or subsequent visits (Reinhart et al., 2006).

This highlighted the significance of occupant satisfaction with their space selection in a structure. Yet, the consequences of occupants' space selection, abandonment of initially preferred areas, and space satisfaction have not been thoroughly investigated using concrete data.

4.1 Time Use Survey (TUS) and POE

The general assumption among building users is that they look for a floor space based on the preferences that they had previously been happy with. Nonetheless, it has frequently been observed that many facility users are disappointed with their surroundings and feel some discomfort in the location they have selected. Space rejection is one cause of discontent. For a variety of reasons, such as if the space is currently filled by another user or is inaccessible, a building user's first choice of space may be denied. It is difficult to meet the varying needs of building users, which can change depending on different activities and users. On the other hand, architects are expected to maximize occupant happiness in addition to space efficiency (Amirazar, 2021).

The following information on space selection has to be obtained to support this project and provide architects with important empirical data and thoroughly evaluated: How users choose the location for their activities in buildings, what these events are, how comfortable they are with the spaces they have selected, and how space ambiance influences occupant satisfaction, and the motivations behind inhabitants' selection of and rejection of space. The combined TUS and POE methodology was used in this work. A TUS quizzes participants on their everyday activities, including where and when they took place at each time step (Garling et al., 1984).

Understanding space choice at the spatial level throughout time for particular activities, it is useful to use the data from TUS. Unfortunately, a TUS by itself does not offer comprehensive information about the characteristics of space, making it it's difficult to link space happiness to space characteristics (Harvey, 1993). Using a mix of two approaches, detailed data on spatial preference and satisfaction will be gathered, that complement one another (Fleming & Spellerberg, 1999; Kim et al., 2018).

The proposed evident-based real-time data collecting, data processing, and publishing components make up the POE platform. To gather qualitative data on occupant perceptions and to instantly update the central database, a smartphone application is deployed. These components are summarised below. In their study, the authors provide more information regarding the system conception and creation process cause in their paper, 'The Need for Digital Twin Strategy Framework in a Smart Building Ambience for Ease of Evaluating Interaction Between Facility Entities and its Occupants'.

4.2 Ideation of the Application

For the prototype implementation from real case scenarios at Jönköping University, the lighting living lab rooms' pilot prototype was created. Figure 1 shows the location and mapping of the six rooms used for the experiment purpose (31113A, 31113B, 31114A, 31114C, 31114D, and 31114F), as they are approached from the School of Engineering Department's entrance for real-time implementation review by the students on campus in these areas. For a better explanation of the region utilized for pilot experiments, it can be viewed using the link provided below.

By including students from different departments, the creation of a guide map for the prototype served the primary purpose of proving the project's viability and enabling the application's scalability. So, generalizing it to the general public using the facilities without literally providing any context. When you click the link, it will take you to the allocated space area that is used from the building entry to the living lab entrance area. This area is indicated with a blue icon and is also shown in the accompanying images. For easier navigation, the walkway is marked with a green icon, which denotes the facility's amenities such as the lift and sign board images, guiding users to the designated rooms for feedback.

Link: https://www.google.com/maps/d/edit?mid=1MSFHrVMqsxLt_c5NxUvhUf2wThenyhrA&usp=sharing

Figure 1. Location of the 6 rooms at the campus for the prototype implementation of the project

4.3 Mobile Application: DOALE

According to early studies in the field of sociology of work by Herzberg determined that there are several additional important aspects of the workplace environment through his examination of factors that affect employee motivation, which can also influence an occupant's motivation towards a task and they can be either neutral, positive, or negative (House & Wigdor, 1967). Thus, this key notion of influence on performance is not noticed and the threshold effect that has an impact on motivation can be identified by their propensity to switch from having no effect to having a negative effect. This notion led to the notion of environmental stress. Stress, in general, is a set of physiological and psychological changes that happen in the aftermath of a perceived danger or challenge (Herzberg, 2017). It is the result of how a person and their environment interact. If an occupant can deal with the severity of the situation, then the resultant motivated performance is a supported result. Here the notion of support incorporates how the situation can be characterized as stressful. It can be defined as those occasions where components of the physical environment conflict with the attainment of performance objectives, affecting performance. Thus, satisfaction, functional comfort, and physical environment perception can be influenced by the physical environment and put limitations on a user's performance (Smerek & Peterson, 2007). An in-depth investigation is required to connect these ideas. From an environmental parameter perspective, subjective data is a variable of data that is difficult to capture and collect in a virtual space. This perspective generated the ideation of the application.

The design ideas for POE and Human Computer Interaction (HCI) were taken into consideration when creating the DOALE mobile application (Digital Occupancy Assessment for Lighting Evaluation)

(Edirisinghe & Woo, 2019). Physically comparable characteristics of perceived indoor conditions, such as lighting condition parameters, were chosen to create an app to record occupants' subjective evaluation data. The mobile application's primary goal was to enhance non-invasive response rates; as a result, instead of creating a survey that would exhaust participants, a faster survey was created. On a scale of one to four, the participants were asked how happy they were with the lighting as a whole in the space utilized. Two parts of a single, four-point Likert scale with emojis were used to categorize respondents' levels of overall satisfaction (1 = very satisfied and 4 = very unhappy), to prevent respondents from answering in the negative. In the second section of the survey, respondents score the atmosphere and lighting parameters of the room on a 7-point Likert scale for in-depth subjective knowledge (Akpınar, 2014; Schaumann et al., 2016).

For the real-time feedback response from the occupants regarding the environmental factors and their personal feelings, the Android POE app was designed using the JAVA programming language. The ideation of the application is shown in Figure 2 below where a total of 8 splash screen was designed. Splash screen 1 to 3 demonstrates the purpose of the app. Whereas splash screen 4 to 7 demonstrates how the feedback is acquired from the occupants regarding the space of the lab rooms.

1. Splash screen 1: Demonstrates the initial home screen of the University building used in the prototype.
2. Splash screen 2: Demonstrates the building space area in 3D used for the prototype implementation for the students.
3. Splash screen 3: Demonstrates the information about the usage of the Android application built for the students.
4. Splash screen 4: Demonstrates the feedback technique from the occupants of the six rooms individually.
5. Splash screen 5: Demonstrates the feedback requirement from the occupants from each quadrant of space occupied.
6. Splash screen 6: Demonstrates the feedback requirement from the occupants for the overall assessment of comfort regarding the room used.
7. Splash screen 7: Demonstrates the questionnaire with scaling from low to high for more in-depth knowledge about the subjective assessment.
8. Splash screen 8: Demonstrates the user of the application regarding their responses being recorded for research purposes.

Strategically a space is further subdivided into 4 quadrant spaces for acquiring detailed information about the geospatial location of an occupant and their personal feelings in that space occupied by them in a room. As this is the initial test bed development phase for validating the subjective feelings of an occupant, importance was given to the primary creation of an Android app for acquiring real-time response and data management for room only.

While the interiors of each of the six rooms were created by several lighting businesses, the initial concept was used in the living lab which comprised of these rooms. Each room had a unique seating arrangement, unique lighting, and was oriented towards a different side of the university structure. The sunlight entering the space changed because the windows were on various sides. The prototype was ideal for being created on these 6 rooms because it can demonstrate 6 case scenarios.

The concepts of good user-centered design placed a high value on accessibility (as an investigative device), usability, and interactivity. Special attention was also paid to the direct manipulation capabilities, overall structure, and navigation design cues that improve users' perceptions through engagement and pleasure based on the intended users and the application domain. Less text is used in the design, which instead emphasizes room layouts with the right amount of explanation and guidance, to inspire users to contribute their perception using symbols that describe their emotions (Woo & Edirisinghe, 2018).

For instance, as shown in Figure 2 below, the main splash screen introduces the prototype by showing a picture of the department building where the lab space is designated, while the subsequent splash screen shows the rooms' layout in a 3D image so that the occupants can completely understand it. Also, allowing the audience to more readily comprehend the queries, the good scenarios are symbolized by positive feelings and the negative situations are symbolized by negative emotions.

Figure 2. Splash screens of the POE application deployment for acquiring feedback

4.4 Data Storage

The MySQL database was used for back-end operations such as updating surveys, retrieving stored questions from the database as question lists, and retrieving answers provided by respondents from the smartphone application as answer lists for a specific period instance log. Figure 3 depicts the flow diagram for backhand task formulation, whereas Figure 4 depicts the admin panel for the data analysis and its visualization in time frame segments and the responses by the users who have utilized the room in a specific time frame.

The initial data flow architecture for collecting subjective data occupants' perspectives in real-time is represented, where the data ingestion from the smartphone could be manifested from the response given as the feedback to MySQL Database for data storage in tabular format for easy querying of the database for analysis purpose. The initial database management system strategy for the implementation relies on SQL (Structured Query Language) and is known as MySQL. In addition to data warehousing the application is also used for logging purposes technique. Everything from a single piece of information to an entire store's worth of data can be stored in a cloud storage system. A programming language like PHP can be used in conjunction with a MySQL database for hosting accounts to quickly display categorized and searchable information to an API user.

Figure 3. Data flow architecture for POE application implementation for feedback purposes

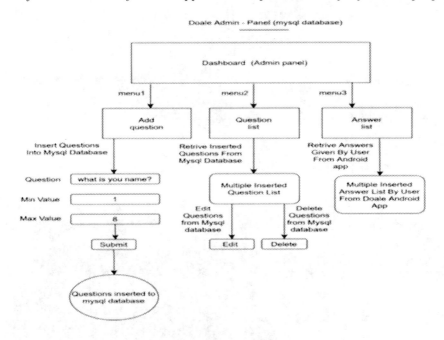

5. CONCLUSION AND DISCUSSION

As a subjective method, the current POE protocols use a standardized web-based poll. Most surveys inquire about how satisfied or how the inhabitants perceive their indoor illumination settings. Yet, the nature and methods of gathering both kinds of subjective and objective data have altered as a result of internet access and mobile technology. People now have easier access to a variety of information thanks to the internet, which also serves as a vital tool for communication. Most young adults who use the internet frequently like to quickly and visually communicate their feedback to friends. Due to these reasons, prototype POE research was created. and carried out as a part of university assignments during the research studies to improve their expertise with live information collection and usage in the management of building facilities.

In the living lab rooms, data on occupant perceptions were gathered using a smartphone app. During the pilot project, an immediate representation of the gathered data was given, illustrating how the POE application functions and what more statistical analysis can be investigated. Evaluation of the improved POE software and to work keeping student's perspectives and interaction, this pilot research was shorter and easier to complete than traditional POE protocols. It was established that by gathering information in real-time, facility management, gets students involved in academic tasks and enhances their learning in evaluating facility space in its operational phase. This could be done by using the app to collect data, immediately after, the data overview of the data that was collected. Although the current system architecture does not immediately analyze correlations in statistics between sensor data and occupant feedback, it is anticipated that additional detailed live reporting methods will be able to close the current methodological void in the collecting of POE data and its application to building facility management.

Figure 4. Live feedback response storage visualization

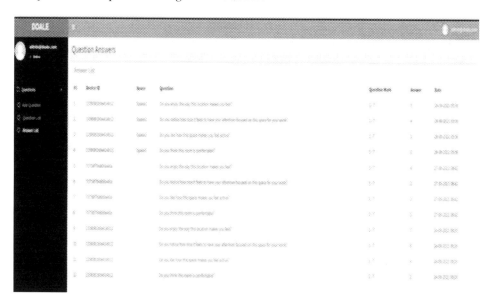

6. FUTURE WORK

There is still much to learn about how occupants view a building's physical environment, which has an impact on how well it performs. the use of occupancy metrics, including people's presence and mobility inside a place, how they interact with architectural elements like windows, and how they use control systems like lighting. The objective assessment comprises monitoring adaptive interactions between the occupants and the control systems as well as collecting occupancy data using occupancy sensors. While subjective evaluation extends beyond the method of observing individual behavior or acquiring information about the structure, it senses the interaction between the occupant and the building.

The idea of non-invasive evident base practice can be supported by several technologies. Yet, because of its dispersed character, it is difficult and time-consuming to assess and confirm how an extensive distributed IoT system behaves in a building from the perspective of its occupants. Every technology used today faces unique difficulties, and it is occasionally impossible to combine one technology with another.

It will take adequate system implementation to complete the development of an IoT real-time system for the lab, which is currently in the early stages. On the upcoming evidence-based validation development phase:

- The method for the objective assessment of occupant behavior and interaction with the building must be integrated with the data model architecture, which includes the GSR, HR, and occupancy sensor.
- The Android application has to be improved so that feedback from users can be properly gathered and cross-validated with lab results.
- To obtain more data on lighting quality, more light sensors must be integrated.

Microsoft Azure Digital Twin service which is an IoT platform as well as a platform as a service (PaaS) serves as a better contender for the development of the system later in the development phase of the whole system, as time is invested into the data management by easy plugins with various other service saves a lot of time. As with many requirements, some clouds work better for some project specifications than others. There are a variety of models, varieties, and services available to meet the requirements. To begin with, it must be decided regarding the cloud computing architecture or type of cloud deployment that will be used to execute the cloud-based services complimenting this prototype implementation for better evidence-based as well as non-intrusive practice.

REFERENCES

Abisuga, A. O., Wang, C. C., & Sunindijo, R. Y. (2019). A holistic framework with user-centered facilities performance attributes for evaluating higher education buildings. *Facilities*, *38*(1/2), 132–160. doi:10.1108/F-07-2018-0083

Akpınar, E. (2014). The use of interactive computer animations based on POE as a presentation tool in primary science teaching. *Journal of Science Education and Technology*, *23*(4), 527–537. doi:10.100710956-013-9482-4

Altomonte, S., Allen, J., Bluyssen, P. M., Brager, G., Heschong, L., Loder, A., Schiavon, S., Veitch, J. A., Wang, L., & Wargocki, P. (2020). Ten questions concerning well-being in the built environment. *Building and Environment*, *180*, 106949. doi:10.1016/j.buildenv.2020.106949

Amirazar, A. (2021). *Evidence-Based Human-Centric Lighting Assist Tool towards a Healthier Lit Environment* [Doctoral dissertation]. The University of North Carolina at Charlotte.

B. (2023, March 23). *What is Azure Digital Twins? Azure Digital Twins*. Microsoft Learn. https://learn.microsoft.com/en-us/azure/digital-twins/overview

Cochran Hameen, E., Ken-Opurum, B., & Son, Y. J. (2020). Protocol for post-occupancy evaluation in schools to improve indoor environmental quality and energy efficiency. *Sustainability (Basel), 12*(9), 3712. doi:10.3390u12093712

Cook, D. J., Augusto, J. C., & Jakkula, V. R. (2009). Ambient intelligence: Technologies, applications, and opportunities. *Pervasive and Mobile Computing, 5*(4), 277–298. doi:10.1016/j.pmcj.2009.04.001

Edirisinghe, R., & Woo, J. (2019). Drive towards real-time reasoning of building performance: Development of a live, cloud-based system. In *Advances in Informatics and Computing in Civil and Construction Engineering: Proceedings of the 35th CIB W78 2018 Conference: IT in Design, Construction, and Management* (pp. 661-668). Springer International Publishing.

Fleming, R., & Spellerberg, A. (1999). *Using Time Use Data*. Statistics New Zealand.

Garling, T., Book, A., & Lindberg, E. (1984). Cognitive mapping of large-scale environments: The interrelationship of action plans, acquisition, and orientation. *Environment and Behavior, 16*(1), 3–34. doi:10.1177/0013916584161001

Harvey, A. S. (1993). Guidelines for time use data collection. *Social Indicators Research, 30*(2-3), 197–228. doi:10.1007/BF01078728

Henricksen, K., & Indulska, J. (2006). Developing context-aware pervasive computing applications: Models and approach. *Pervasive and Mobile Computing, 2*(1), 37–64. doi:10.1016/j.pmcj.2005.07.003

Herzberg, F. (2017). *Motivation to work*. Routledge. doi:10.4324/9781315124827

House, R. J., & Wigdor, L. A. (1967). Herzberg's dual-factor theory of job satisfaction and motivation: A review of the evidence and a criticism. *Personnel Psychology, 20*(4), 369–389. doi:10.1111/j.1744-6570.1967.tb02440.x

Jakubiec, J. A., & Reinhart, C. F. (2012). The 'adaptive zone'–A concept for assessing discomfort glare throughout daylit spaces. *Lighting Research & Technology, 44*(2), 149-170.

Kim, T. W., Cha, S., & Kim, Y. (2018). Space choice, rejection and satisfaction in university campus. *Indoor and Built Environment, 27*(2), 233–243. doi:10.1177/1420326X16665897

Lonsdale, K., Pringle, P., & Turner, B. (2015). *Transformative adaptation: What it is, why it matters and what is needed*. Academic Press.

Parkinson, T., Candido, C., & de Dear, R. (2013). *Comfort Chimp": a Multi-Platform IEQ Questionnaire Development Environment. CLIMA 2013: Energy Efficient*, Smart and Healthy Buildings.

Reinhart, C. F., Mardaljevic, J., & Rogers, Z. (2006). Dynamic daylight performance metrics for sustainable building design. *Leukos, 3*(1), 7–31. doi:10.1582/LEUKOS.2006.03.01.001

Saarikko, T., Westergren, U. H., & Blomquist, T. (2020). Digital transformation: Five recommendations for the digitally conscious firm. *Business Horizons, 63*(6), 825–839. doi:10.1016/j.bushor.2020.07.005

Schaumann, D., Pilosof, N. P., Date, K., & Kalay, Y. E. (2016). A study of human behavior simulation in architectural design for healthcare facilities. *Annali dell'Istituto Superiore di Sanita, 52*(1), 24–32. PMID:27033615

Smerek, R. E., & Peterson, M. (2007). Examining Herzberg's theory: Improving job satisfaction among non-academic employees at a university. *Research in Higher Education*, *48*(2), 229–250. doi:10.100711162-006-9042-3

Tartarini, F., Miller, C., & Schiavon, S. (2022). *Cozie Apple: An iOS mobile and smartwatch application for environmental quality satisfaction and physiological data collection.* arXiv preprint arXiv:2210.13977.

Tien, J. M. (2017). Internet of things, real-time decision making, and artificial intelligence. *Annals of Data Science*, *4*(2), 149–178. doi:10.100740745-017-0112-5

Woo, J., & Edirisinghe, R. (2018). Enhancing students' experience in real-time data collection and utilisation: A cloud-based post-occupancy evaluation app. ASA.

Chapter 8
Where Are We and What Should We Do in Cleaner Production Transformation?

Elif Çaloğlu Büyükselçuk
Fenerbahçe University, Turkey

ABSTRACT

Until recently, production models developed according to market conditions focused on reducing costs and increasing profitability at the expense of the destruction of natural resources and the deterioration of ecological balance and human health. However, today, with the effects of the deterioration in the ecosystem reaching sensible dimensions and being accepted as a global threat, a new production approach is needed. Due to environmental pressures, new markets and scarce resources, development, and economic growth are being tried to be redefined. Traditional production methods and environmental technologies are no longer sufficient to provide resource efficiency and increase environmental performance. Therefore, the need for new systems, processes and technologies has arisen for the restructuring of the industry and the creation of green business models. In this chapter, it is discussed how the cleaner production approach will contribute to this transformation, considering the green transformation efforts in question and considering the current situation of the Turkish industry.

1. INTRODUCTION

The world economy, which continues to grow in an uncontrolled way, brings an intense consumption pressure on raw materials and energy resources, and causes environmental problems to increase. Especially in the period from 1980 to the present, there has been a significant increase in the use of global resources and, accordingly, environmental problems. In addition to ensuring economic growth and prosperity, countries need to take more effective decisions in the long term to prevent the adverse impacts of these economic activities on the environment and to protect natural assets.

DOI: 10.4018/978-1-6684-8969-7.ch008

With population growth and more consumption, production has gradually increased. The basis of the production approach is the linear economy model based on fossil fuels. In this model, economic activities based on carbon emissions, which are based on growth, first brought the world to the climate crisis, and then overcome the deepening problems of the crisis, the consequences of the destruction of nature such as weather events (hot and cold air waves, storms, floods, droughts, forest fires, etc.), loss of biodiversity. By confronting humanity with the last global health threat, the Covid-19 pandemic. All of the five hottest years on record were experienced after 2015, 25 percent of all plant and animal species on the planet are in danger of extinction (OECD, 2020), and as a result of record increases in greenhouse gas emissions and heavy destructions, the planet's oceans, glaciers, forests, etc. It has been demonstrated by many different studies that vital variables are moved to irreversible limit points (Ripple et al. 2021).

Today, economic development and growth are tried to be redefined due to environmental pressures, new markets and scarce resources. It is obvious that traditional production methods and environmental technologies are no longer sufficient to ensure resource efficiency and increase environmental performance. To struggle these problems, the restructuring of the industry and the emergence of sustainable business models are important. At this point, new methods, systems, processes and technologies that use resources more efficiently are needed. Sustainable production/business models, low-carbon and resource-efficient industry and green growth should be targeted in the upcoming period.

If there is a quality interaction between the environment and the economy, the concept of sustainability can be mentioned in countries. However, ensuring that this relationship between economic activities and the environment is effective is a challenging process that is not easy. As a result of human activities all over the world, the environment has come under great pressure, and it has become inevitable for this issue to become a global problem. In recent years, biological environmental risks and damages have clearly proven their existence. The basis of these losses is based on some indices such as energy, investment and employment used in industrial and economic activities (Zahra et.al, 2019).

In the first part of the study, a conceptual framework was drawn on cleaner production and green (or clean) technologies. Then, the issue of cleaner production practices in the industrial sector, especially in the manufacturing industry, was revealed. In the third part, the existing situation in the era of cleaner production in Turkey is explained. In this context, information on national legislation, relevant organizations, activities, and projects carried out, practices in the industrial area, particularly in the manufacturing industry, and a general assessment were presented. In the fourth chapter, the steps to be taken towards the green transformation of the industry in Turkey are discussed.

2. CONCEPTUAL FRAMEWORK

2.1. Cleaner Production Concept

When it comes to production processes, the concept of sustainability comes to the fore with the adverse effects of these processes on the environment. They should be handled within the framework of the United Nations' production-related sustainability indicators. These; biodiversity, air quality, greenhouse gases, deforestation, desertification, ozone layer, drought, agriculture, toxic chemicals, non-renewable materials, dangerous waste, water, and waste amount. Considering these indicators, sustainable production can be defined as the production of materials without greenhouse gas emissions, without the use of toxic and non-renewable materials, or the development of transformation technologies that will not produce waste (Yavuz, 2010).

Cleaner production is described as "reducing risks to people and the environment by the continuous application of a holistic and preventive environmental strategy to products and processes" (UNEP, 1996). Cleaner production refers to the prevention of environmental impacts at the source before they occur, and contrary to the "pollution control" approaches that try to eliminate environmental problems after they emerge, environmental issues are addressed in urban, agricultural, and industrial, etc. All kinds of human activities need to be included in the design processes. Pollution control sees pollution as an inevitable result of design and production processes, and since it tries to solve this problem (waste treatment and disposal) after pollution occurs, it brings significant additional costs to organizations. Whereas cleaner production, resource efficiency, prevention of pollution at source, environmentally friendly product, etc. With its approaches, it provides organizations with an increase in environmental performance as well as a decrease in production costs (TTGV, 2010).

According to Pang and Zhang (2019), green or cleaner production is a concept that was introduced in developed countries in the 1990s. With this concept, nations aimed to minimize the negative effects of all production processes and systems on the environment and to maximize resource efficiency. Orji and Wei (2016) define green production as the efficient design of new product development and all manufacturing operations to minimize negative impacts on the environment. Green production is a sustainable form of production and integrates the life concept cycle. In this cycle, it is aimed to minimize the depletion of resources in production, distribution, maintenance, and disposal processes by including green designs (Orji and Wei, 2016).

According to Shrivastava and Shrivastava (2017), green production is a concept that combines product and process design that influences production planning and control activities. With this concept, it is aimed to determine, measure, evaluate and manage the environmental waste flow. Green production is also known as cleaner production, environmentally friendly production and sustainable production. Whatever the name, the goal is the same, that is, to design, make and deliver products that minimize adverse effects on the environment through the process of manufacturing, use and discard (Seth et al., 2016).

The United Nations Industrial Development Organization - UNIDO, on the other hand, accepts cleaner production strategies as a guide to be used in the optimization of industrial production processes and a protective and integrated strategy to be applied to the entire production phase. With a cleaner production strategy, efficiency can be increased by more efficient use of raw materials, energy and water; better environmental performance can be achieved by reducing waste at the source and emissions to the atmosphere; the environmental impacts of products throughout their life cycle can be reduced by designing environmentally friendly products that are also cost effective. In this way, more competitive advantage will be provided to businesses in underdeveloped and developing countries and their opening to international markets will be supported (UNIDO, 2008).

The elements of the cleaner production system are schematized as follows in the report prepared by UNIDO and UNEP (2010), which is a guide document for cleaner production centres operating in various parts of the world (Figure 1).

Figure 1. Elements of cleaner production (UNIDO-UNEP, 2010)

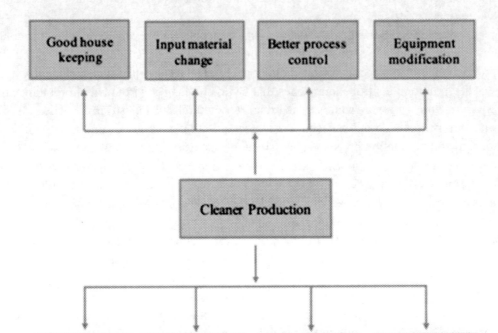

2.2. Clean Technologies

Technology, by its nature, is seen as the cause of both economic growth and global environmental problems. On the other hand, in many parts of the world, the spread of new technologies also leads to a marked improvement in the condition of the natural environment. Technology has created an important area in the fight against climate change by making the production and use of energy, which is one of the biggest emission causes, more efficient and enabling renewable energy (UNIDO, 2016). The belief in the potential of technological change to produce new solutions for current pollution and natural resource scarcity within the framework of climate change is overwhelming (Bretschger, 2005).

As can be seen in the solution of other environmental problems, technology is increasingly coming to the fore in an effective global climate change management. Encouraging the development and dissemination of environmentally friendly technologies in developing countries for the reduction of emissions in the fight against climate change is of critical importance and it is anticipated that a significant contribution will be made to the solution of climate change in this way.

Clean technologies, without leaving any waste that harms the environment, even without producing any new waste, using the waste of other productions as raw materials, without harming nature and living things in nature, even the natural environment and historical texture, without producing toxic waste and poison, without creating greenhouse gases such as methane and carbon dioxide, Production made by working with nature, by taking advantage of natural resources, by considering future generations and other elements of nature, is environmentally friendly production. If the production technology is such that it produces the desired product with the least energy and with the highest efficiency, without leaving any waste that may harm the environment, by consuming the least natural substance in the production process, "environmentally friendly production" close to the ideal will be realized (Yücel, 2011).

According to the waste management hierarchy, the highest priority within the scope of cleaner production is on prevention of pollution through source reduction and reuse techniques or closed-loop recovery. Cleaner production technology covers all activities that reduce waste at its source and/or eliminate (zero discharge) (MoSIT, 2015a).

However, the technology diffusion process does not work as fast and effectively as it should. As technology diffusion studies have shown, widespread adoption of green product-generating innovations or cleaner and energy-efficient technologies can take decades. Therefore, it is very important not only to develop innovations by encouraging R&D, but also to ensure that these innovations are adapted and used by companies in the process of technological change (Battisti, 2008).

Clean technologies: pollution control technologies (end-of-pipe technologies), off-site recycling and waste treatment technologies (such as technologies that clean a contaminated soil), and technologies that try to prevent waste at the source and are integrated into production (clean technologies-pollution prevention technologies) (Radonjic & Tominc, 2007). To date, the greatest developments in the field of environmental technologies have been in pollution control technologies (Hammar & Lofgren, 2010).

A study was conducted to evaluate energy efficiency in developed and developing countries between 1990 and 2014. In this study, it is stated that the basis of sustainable environment can be laid with the use of zero-carbon or low-carbon energy sources (Sun et. al., 2019). Clean technologies diminish the amount of waste and pollutants produced during the manufacturing process or the entire life cycle of the product.

Clean technologies, on the other hand, are technologies that enable organizational and technological change to prevent pollution before it occurs and affect the production process. According to the OECD, clean technologies are "products that extract and process raw materials as efficiently as possible, produce products with reduced or zero impact, minimize material use during production and damage to water, air and soil, and produce products that can be reused or recycled. It is defined as the technologies that increase the durability and produce the output with the least energy input (Radonjic & Tominc, 2007). Clean technologies, which cover areas such as equipment modification, input change, by-product use, better process control, on-site recycling and recovery, product modification or reformulation, are generally used in the same context as "anti-pollution technologies" (Luken et al., 2008). With the use of clean technologies during production, serious resource efficiency can be achieved, and environmental impacts can be reduced.

Environmental technology and resource efficiency as green technologies is a cross-industry consisting of six leading markets. These leading markets are (UNEP, 2017);

- Material efficiency
- Energy efficiency
- Environmentally friendly energy generation, storage, and distribution
- Sustainable mobility
- Waste management and recycling
- Sustainable water management

3. CLEANER PRODUCTION PRACTICES IN THE MANUFACTURING INDUSTRY

Today, the manufacturing industry faces the challenge of complying with strict environmental regulations due to global warming, waste management problems, and scarcity of natural resources. Increasing environmental concerns and awareness are the driving force pushing manufacturers all over the world to adopt green production practices (Ghazilla et al., 2015). The governments also play an important role in establishing regulations and penalties to avoid harming the environment (Li et al., 2016). In addition, due to global competition, companies have to struggle with environmental pressures in order to maintain their long-term business goals (Johansson & Winroth, 2010).

Emissions from industry correspond to approximately 40% of global emissions (Napp et al., 2014). Since 1970, industrial sector emissions have doubled worldwide. Considering the annual changes in emissions from industry, it is seen that it increases more than other final sectors (such as transportation). The manufacturing and production sectors account for 20% of the world's carbon emissions (World Economic Forum, 2022). In addition, too many chemicals and toxic substances are used in the production process (Li et al., 2016). These companies consume energy and natural resources and cause the emergence of greenhouse gases, which is an economic, environmental and social problem (Mittal & Sangwan, 2014). Considering all these data, the need to carefully evaluate the obligations and opportunities that the climate change process will bring on the industry emerges.

An increasing number of companies have started to work towards the implementation of green production due to increasing concerns about pollution increase, depletion of natural resources and global warming (Mittal & Sangwan, 2014). This is a positive situation for companies because green production prevents pollution and saves energy through the discovery and development of new processes that reduce the formation of hazardous substances in the design and production stages (Shrivastava and Shrivastava, 2017).

Firms have applied green production first to coercive factors such as government regulations and then to gain competitive advantages. Various factors that motivate firms to adopt green manufacturing practices are government regulations, organizational policies, availability of greener technologies, tax exemptions, competitive advantage, etc. (Sangwan & Choudhary, 2018). Among the green production practices of the companies, reducing the use of energy and raw materials and solid wastes, reusing products, using renewable materials and training employees on product management practices can be given as examples (Ghazilla et al., 2015). A company that has already successfully implemented green production should control four basic factors: the amount of energy and resource consumption, the scope of green energy, the amount of hazardous waste and the number of recycling of hazardous waste (Prasad et al., 2016).

It has been determined that there are serious increases in greenhouse gas emissions in the atmosphere due to the energy sources used in manufacturing processes. In particular, the use of fossil fuels increases air pollution and adversely affects natural life. This has revealed the necessity for enterprises to use renewable energy sources in all their processes. As a result, they should allocate more shares to investments especially in R&D and technological activities (Avunduk, 2021).

Using less resources and/or energy to produce the same product is a good strategy that provides significant economic gain through reduced production cost. Therefore, it is accepted that the costs of green manufacturing initiatives will repay themselves with the money to be saved through a more efficient system and therefore will positively affect the return of investments (Deif, 2011:28). Green production is a production method that minimizes waste and pollution through product and process design. The main purpose of green production is sustainability (Maruthi & Rashmi, 2015). But green production is not the same as sustainability, but both are related and often used interchangeably. While green production is often associated with products or practices or processes that do not harm the environment, sustainability is mostly about the holistic approach of the company and considers the whole business, including production and supply chain management (Seth et al., 2018).

According to DCED (2012), green industry is a two-pronged strategy aimed at:

- Greening existing industries: Regardless of the industry, size or location of the industry, all industries continuously reduce the environmental impact of their processes and products, use resources more efficiently, progressively reduce hazardous materials, replace fossil fuels with renewable energy sources, increase corporate responsibility and contribute to the environment, climate and people. to reduce the risks.
- Creating green industries: Creating green industries that provide all kinds of environmental goods and services, helping address the consequences of pollutants and reduce adverse environmental factors.

The greening of the industry can be followed by increasing resource efficiency. Raw material inputs constitute a cost for the industry, showing that they can constitute 65 percent of the total cost in the food and beverage industry and 70-80 percent of the total cost in the steel industry. It encompasses resource efficiency, manufacturing, product design, value acquisition, and supply circle management. According to the studies, it has been determined that the producers can reduce the amount of energy used in production by 20% to 30% (Manyika et al., 2012).

As industries turn green, new jobs will emerge. Thanks to renewable energy sources, the number of green studies is also increasing. The concept of green production is supported by the use of scrap and energy efficiency activities in industries such as steel, paper, cement, and aluminum (UNIDO, 2011).

4. CURRENT SITUATION IN TURKEY

The concept of "cleaner production" in Turkey was first used in 1999 by the Scientific and Technological Research Council of Turkey (TÜBİTAK) and the Technology Development Foundation of Turkey (TTGV), Science-Technology - Industry Discussions Platform, Cleaner Production-Clean Product Environmentally Friendly Technologies Study. Group came to the agenda with the Industrial Sector Report. In this context, it has been proposed to build a cleaner production center, but the said center has not yet been established on a national scale. In the meantime, both the strategic importance of the subject and the need for cleaner production consultancy services and R&D studies of the Turkish industry have increased rapidly (TTGV, 2010).

After the European Union announced its green transformation targets, it is seen that the leading actors of international trade started to announce similar targets. As a matter of fact, the United States of America, with its decision to rejoin the Paris Climate Agreement, has revealed that it aims for global leadership in the fight against climate change. In this direction, ensuring the green transformation that will support the transition to a sustainable, resource-efficient and green economy is of great importance in terms of maintaining and improving Turkey's integration with the global economy. Since nearly half of its exports are to the EU and the United Kingdom, it is clear that the targeted policy changes should also cover the fields of industry, agriculture, energy and transportation in connection with the country's foreign trade.

In this period, when Turkey has clearly demonstrated its commitments by signing the Paris Climate Agreement, with the Green Reconciliation Action Plan studies carried out under the coordination of the Ministry of Commerce, sectoral analyses, studies on the field, as well as standards, incentives and supports, accelerate the transformation that will be experienced in the country's industry and therefore in the trade in the coming period. puts great effort into it. The European Green Consensus can be considered as a brand-new opportunity for Turkey, which will be a tool of transformation aiming at sustainable development.

In this context, Green Transformation Policies and Measures in the Medium Term Program covering the years 2022-2024 are listed as follows (SBB, 2021):

- New approaches supporting green transformation and transition to circular economy in the fields of industry, trade, transportation, environment and energy will be implemented within the framework of support and credit incentive mechanisms, taking into account external financing opportunities; The competitiveness of exports will be increased in line with climate change policies in the field of international trade, by supporting investments that increase efficiency, especially in recycling technologies, and aim to limit the increase in greenhouse gas emissions.
- In order to accelerate green transformation, R&D studies will be supported, and necessary technologies for green production will be developed and expanded.
- By completing the green industrial zone certification system with the Green OIZ, the creation of environmentally sensitive, sustainable industrial and circular economy areas will be accelerated.
- Regulations in the financial sector will be improved to support green transformation.
- Green bond and sukuk issuances will be encouraged by preparing a guide in line with international standards for the financing of environmentally sensitive investments.
- In order to minimize the negative effects of global climate change, investments in environmentally friendly production that use energy and production resources efficiently will be supported.
- Zero waste practices will be expanded to include households, and measures will be taken to decrease the import of waste that is not needed in critical areas of production.

Under the Paris Agreement, it is recognized that the new global climate regime requires mitigation and adaptation efforts by all actors, including all industries and businesses. As stated in Turkey's Intended National Determined Contribution (INDC), increasing energy efficiency in industrial facilities, and supporting energy efficiency projects are part of the national roadmap to combat the negative effects of climate change.

Turkey has recently been encouraging industries to take a greener path to compete and supports this strategy through several national and international policies. Turkey's 10th Development Plan includes actions aimed at ensuring sustainable development in essence with a green growth perspective. In addition, the National Climate Change Action Plan can be considered as the first strategy for green growth, which intends to decrease Turkey's energy consumption by 20% by 2023.

One of the important components of the European Green Deal, which is built on two main elements, green and digital transformation, is the Carbon Border Adjustment Mechanism proposed against the risk of carbon leakage, and this mechanism is expected to directly affect Turkey's trade and manufacturing industry. In this respect, special attention should be paid to reducing the carbon intensity of emission-intensive sectors, especially metal industry and cement industry, in terms of Turkish industry.

Turkey is already laying the groundwork for the implementation of some projects and practices by prioritizing climate change in the New Economic Program covering the years 2021-2023 and the Presidential Annual Program for 2021. It is stated in the New Economic Program that "Necessary studies and preparations will be made by coordinating the public, private sector, non-governmental organizations and universities with the aim of ensuring compliance with the European Green Deal in Turkey's exports to the EU in the context of the EU Customs Union" (MoTF, 2020).

The policies that Turkey will implement for harmonization with the European Green Deal have to be effective in many areas. Since the European Green Deal aims to protect and increase the competitiveness of the member states, in order to adapt to the changing world, Turkey also needs to keep up with the innovations in legislation and practice in order to make its conditions suitable for competition.

Turkey's Green Deal Action Plan lists the actions planned to be carried out under nine headings, including 32 targets and 81 actions. These are (MoT, 2021):

- Carbon regulations at the border,
- A green and circular economy,
- Green financing,
- Clean, economical and safe energy supply,
- Sustainable agriculture,
- Sustainable smart transportation,
- Combating climate change,
- Diplomacy,
- The European Green Deal is listed as information and awareness activities.

The importance of the concepts of sustainable production and sustainable consumption was mentioned in the plan and a union of government, producer and consumer should be formed.

In this process, investments to be made in environmental management systems and cleaner production practices by both the private and public sectors will not only increase the environmental performance of industrial organizations but will also positively affect their economic performance and corporate prestige, and contribute to growth and productivity increases.

In this context, in a way that can serve the purpose of ensuring sustainability and increasing efficiency in production and at the same time contributing to increasing the international competitiveness of enterprises; A new approach that envisages developing integrated policies for the adoption of a sustainable production approach in all branches of industry needs to be put forward. Projects should be developed to raise awareness of enterprises, especially SMEs, on sustainable production, to have knowledge about good practice techniques and to reflect these techniques in their production processes. Legislation should be developed to provide financial support to businesses for the development of cleaner production / resource efficiency practices, and production processes should be encouraged to make improvements and technological changes that will not cause environmental damage.

In addition, in order to determine integrated policy implementations, the establishment of information and communication networks that will allow quantitative and qualitative monitoring and evaluation of industry-environment interaction and meeting the need for data and analysis in this direction are inevitable requirements.

It can be said that 85% of the relevant legislation in Turkey has become compatible with the EU legislation, however, since the EU legislation is a constantly renewed legislation, compliance with the legislation should be constantly taken into consideration. However, it is necessary to make legislative changes by evaluating the practices in other developed countries of the world apart from the EU and considering the opinions, suggestions and needs of the industrialists. Depending on the developing technology, the concept of sustainable industry is a concept that is constantly developing in the world, so new conditions and situations need to be constantly supported by legislation and policy revisions. It is another important issue to start and follow the implementation after the legislation is enacted, in other words, to have enforcement mechanisms (Fidan, 2020).

Some of the national legal regulations, including national legislation, national plan, program, strategic plan, performance program and actions related to cleaner production, pollution prevention, recovery, reuse, waste reduction, are listed in the Table 1.

Table 1. Legal regulations and national plan/program/documents on cleaner production

Program/Plan/Document	Purpose	Scope
National Cleaner Production/ Eco-Efficiency Program (2014-2017)	It is the dissemination of cleaner production/eco-efficiency practices that will contribute to the sustainable growth of the manufacturing industry and to increase international competitiveness.	To raise awareness, to ensure inter-institutional coordination and to increase the level of cooperation, to develop human resources and institutional capacity, to strengthen the policy infrastructure, to provide technical support, financial support and incentives to enterprises.
10th Development Plan (2014-2018)	In addition to stable and inclusive economic growth, international competitiveness, environmental protection and sustainable use of resources are aimed.	Within the scope of cleaner production, the programs of Increasing Production Efficiency and Increasing Energy Efficiency stand out in the 10th Development Plan.
Turkey Industrial Strategy Document (2011-2014)	In the action number 44 included in the document; It is aimed to implement a national eco-efficiency program throughout Turkey.	It covers the establishment of an "Eco-Efficiency Center" in a region where the country's industry and organized industrial zones are concentrated.
Productivity Strategy and Action Plan (2015-2018)	The Plan aims to strengthen policy-making processes and increase traceability in productivity-related fields, to disseminate practices and technologies that will contribute to the transformation process into a sustainable production infrastructure in the industry and to increase international competitiveness.	Dissemination of technologies in the field of sustainable production; Increasing the awareness and knowledge level of enterprises. Preparation and dissemination of sectoral guides and guide documents for the dissemination of sustainable production practices in the sub-sectors of the manufacturing industry. Creating platforms that can contribute to increasing cooperation and knowledge sharing in the field of sustainable production; Managing national and international cooperation networks.
Energy Efficiency Strategy Document (2012-2023)	In the light of the lessons learned as a result of the evaluation of the activities carried out within the scope of energy efficiency in the document, the difficulties encountered in various application points and the global trends in the energy sector, it is inevitable that Turkey's road map in the field of energy efficiency should be prepared with a strategic and dynamic perspective. is said to be.	Among the strategic objectives set in the Energy Efficiency Strategy Document are the following; • Reducing energy intensity and energy losses in industry and services • Ensuring market transformation of energy efficient products • Encouraging investments to increase energy efficiency • Reducing energy demands and carbon emissions of buildings • Promoting sustainable environmentally friendly buildings using renewable energy sources.

continues on following page

Table 1. Continued

Program/Plan/Document	Purpose	Scope
Energy Efficiency Law (18.04.2007)	The purpose of the law is to increase efficiency in the use of energy resources and energy in order to use energy effectively, to prevent waste, to alleviate the burden of energy costs on the economy and to protect the environment.	The law covers the procedures and principles to be applied to increase and support the efficiency of energy in production, transmission, distribution and consumption stages, in industrial enterprises, buildings, electrical power generation facilities, transmission and distribution networks and transportation, to raise energy awareness in the society, and to benefit from renewable energy sources.
The Law on the Use of Renewable Energy Resources for the Purpose of Electricity Generation (18.05.2005)	This Law covers the procedures and principles regarding the protection of renewable energy resource areas, certification and use of electrical energy obtained from these resources.	In the Law, renewable energy sources include non-fossil energy sources such as hydraulic, wind, solar, geothermal, biomass, gas obtained from biomass (including landfill gas), wave, current energy and tides. "Renewable Energy Source Certificate" (YEK Certificate) is given by the Energy Market Regulatory Authority (EMRA) to the legal entity holding the generation license in order to determine and follow the source type in the purchase and sale of electrical energy produced from renewable energy sources in the domestic and international markets. It is regulated by the "Regulation on the Procedures and Principles Regarding Issuance of the YEK Certificate".
Regulation on Increasing Efficiency in the Use of Energy Resources and Energy (27.10.2011)	The Regulation includes detailed and up-to-date regulations for the implementation of the Energy Efficiency Law, authorizing universities, professional chambers and energy efficiency consultancy companies in directing and disseminating energy efficiency services and studies; to energy management applications; It covers the procedures and principles regarding the duties and responsibilities of energy managers and energy management units.	The Regulation includes training and certification activities related to energy efficiency, studies and projects, supporting projects, voluntary agreement applications, demand side management, increasing the efficiency in electricity generation, transmission, distribution and consumption, utilization of waste heat from thermal power plants and biofuel and hydrogen. rules on encouraging the use of alternative fuels are regulated.

5. GREEN TRANSFORMATION OF TURKISH INDUSTRY

Sustainable industrial policy draws a framework for the industry for sustainable development and sustainable growth. Within the framework of sustainable industrial policy, a renewable energy resource that uses resources sustainably, makes use of efficient production methods, tries to keep its damage to the environment at a minimum, refrains from the use of harmful chemicals, aims to reduce greenhouse gas emissions that cause climate change, gives importance to waste recovery, reuse and recycling. There is an industry that rises its diversity and an industry that develops technology for all of these (UNIDO, 2016).

The definition of "green" also means optimizing the production cost primarily for the manufacturing industry. To succeed this, it is essential to transform the existing industrial product pattern and bring new products with this feature to the industry. In this context, it is also important to reduce the energy density by producing the same product with less energy. In a country like Turkey, which is more than 70 percent dependent on imports, efficiency in energy use must be ensured. In addition, energy production from domestic and industrial wastes and the use of renewable energy sources will reduce foreign dependency in energy, while reducing total resource costs, thus increasing the competitiveness of the producer. The use of domestic machinery and equipment to the maximum extent in the production of renewable energy production technologies that will provide this will trigger the transformation needed (MoSIT, 2015b).

In this context, it is aimed to;

- Develop new products with high employment opportunities and market value,
- Ensure efficiency and sustainability in production,
- Expand the use of clean technology, especially to SMEs,
- Reveal the industry's need for environmentally sensitive technology change,
- Expand the use of methods such as recycling and recovery in the Turkish industry (Fidan, 2020).

The necessary measures for the green transformation of the industry are explained in the Green Deal Action Plan announced by the Turkish Ministry of Commerce. Increasing energy efficiency in reducing greenhouse gas emissions in Turkey and expanding the use of renewable energy sources and low-carbon energy sources are mentioned in this plan.

The plan also includes activities on impact analysis and action plan preparation for Border Carbon Regulation. The action plan for priority manufacturing industry sectors that may be subject to Border Carbon Regulation should be determined, modelled their effects on energy-intensive sectors under different conditions, and measured the precautions to be taken on a sectoral basis. There should be a coordination of the Ministry of Industry and Technology and the Ministry of Environment, Urbanization and Climate Change about this issue. One of the most important sub-headings in the action plan is a green and circular economy. The EU announced the "Circular Economy Action Plan" on 11 March 2020. This plan covers the preparation of circular economy action plans on a national basis and the determination of the steps to be taken in this regard (MoT, 2020). With this plan, it is necessary to establish legal regulations for sectoral-based cleaner production strategies, as well as a national action plan and implementation calendar to apply EU Integrated Pollution Prevention and Control (IPPC) legislation. It is clear that it is important to use water, energy, and raw materials effectively and efficiently in all sectors, especially in the textile and leather sector (TSKB, 2021).

Organized industrial zones in Turkey are one of the areas where green transformation can be started. Within the scope of the Organized Industrial Zones Law No. 4562 and its related Regulations, various supports are provided through the loan mechanism in order to create planned investment areas such as OIZs for industrialization, which is one of the main tools of development policy, and to make these areas ready for investment. According to the 2021 annual report of the Ministry of Industry and Technology, these supports aim to make the Turkish industry planned and environmentally friendly and to reduce the initial investment costs of investors (MoIT, 2022).

Active organized industrial zones (OIZs) in Turkey have predominantly completed their factor-oriented status by providing basic infrastructure and public services and are transitioning to an efficiency-oriented position that will enable them to improve the quality of their services and increase their attractiveness for foreign direct investments. While green structures maximize the efficiency potential of OIZs, on the other hand, they aim to reduce resource consumption, waste production and greenhouse gas emissions that increase with the increase in OIZ activities.

With the "Turkey Organized Industrial Zones Project" financed by the World Bank, it is aimed to increase the efficiency, environmental sustainability and competitiveness of the Organized Industrial Zones (OIZs) selected and to set an example for other OIZs at the same time. In this context, a Loan Agreement amounting to USD 300 million was signed with the World Bank Group in 2021. The following activities will be supported by the project as loans (MoIT, 2022);

- Supporting OIZ basic infrastructure investments by using green solutions as much as possible (road, water, rainwater, sewer lines, telecommunication and internet networks, natural gas networks, power lines, OIZ buildings, waste water treatment plants, environmental laboratories and logistics facilities)
- Supporting green infrastructure investments in the OIZ (advanced infrastructure investments, investments in energy supply from renewable sources, energy efficiency of administrative buildings, advanced wastewater treatment, recycling and/or reuse of waste materials for production inputs, LED street lighting)
- Supporting OIZ innovation centers investments.

The first target regarding climate change and energy independence includes effectively reducing greenhouse gas emissions, strengthening the capacity to adapt to climate change, reducing the rate of fossil fuel use and reducing foreign dependence on energy (Choi, 2012). The South Korean Government attaches importance to the development of environmentally friendly green technologies, the development of the industrial structure, the creation of a technical structural basis, making the existing sectors environmentally friendly, and their support and dissemination (Ateş & Ateş, 2015). Considering that Turkey is also a foreign-dependent country in energy, the abundance of energy-intensive industrial sectors and the need to engage in greenhouse gas emission reduction activities to a large extent, the "green growth" strategy implemented by South Korea and the main strategies and policy guidelines developed are important for Turkey. It is considered to be a benchmarking example.

The share of electricity generation in Turkey's total greenhouse gas emissions, which was announced as 506 million tons of CO_2 equivalent in 2019, is 140 million tons (28%). Electricity is vital for many industries. This situation shows that the transformation to green in Turkey should start in the field of energy. This transformation indicates that an annual investment of 13.5 billion dollars should be made soon in order to decarbonize electricity generation in Turkey. Regarding coal, it is thought that this target can be achieved soon with the achievements to be achieved by drawing the roadmap as soon as possible and establishing a domestic Emission Trading System (Aşıcı, 2021).

One of the key points is the effective and efficient use of electrical energy. Therefore, the transition to low-carbon energy systems is inevitable. For this transformation, the use of renewable energy sources should be expanded, the losses in transmission and distribution networks and the energy obtained from fossil fuels should be reduced. The industry sector constitutes approximately 25.3% of the energy consumption in Turkey (MoEUCC, 2021). Including the cement sector, the manufacturing of basic metal (27%) and non-metallic mineral products (23%) is the sectors with the highest energy consumption. These sectors are followed by the manufacture of chemistry, textile and paper products.

According to a research report made by Shura in 2019, it was determined that 10 billion dollars were invested to increase energy efficiency in Turkey between 2002-2018. It has been determined that these investments are made especially in the iron-steel, cement, glass, ceramics, and refinery products sectors. However, it was mentioned in the report that energy efficiency applications are relatively limited in small and medium-sized enterprises. It is necessary to expand them in these enterprises as well. According to the same report, it was stated that investments were made in the cement sector for activities aimed at obtaining energy from waste, energy efficiency and heat recovery. When the iron and steel sector is examined, it has been determined that investments have been made in activities for the recovery of heat and gases, as well as energy and fuel efficiency. In the textile sector, investments were made for resource efficiency to support energy efficiency (Shura, 2019).

At this step, it is essential to direct the enterprises to the efficient use of energy and the development of renewable energy production technologies by applying the right environmental policies and making the right regulations. With the transition to cleaner production processes, there will be an increase in productivity in many sectors. Sectors such as iron-steel, cement, chemistry, automotive, textile, electrical-electronics, white goods, furniture and paper production within the manufacturing industry have a major impact on global greenhouse gas emissions. Increasing efficiency in the use of energy and materials, reducing pollution and waste, and increasing the rate of recycling and reuse in these industrial branches, where it is very difficult to qualify as green in Turkey, will transform these areas into an environment-friendly structure and support green growth. In addition to using less materials and energy in the transition to green growth, protecting existing jobs by transforming them into green jobs and creating new employment opportunities will contribute to the social benefits of positive changes for the environment.

The green growth model will accelerate the transformation process in the manufacturing industry in terms of reducing resource costs, creating new economic areas with high added value and increasing production efficiency. The definition of "green" also means optimizing the production cost primarily for the manufacturing industry. In order to achieve this, it is necessary to transform the existing industrial product pattern and bring new products with this feature to the industry. In this context, it is also important to reduce the energy density by producing the same product with less energy. In a country like Turkey, which is more than 70 percent dependent on imports, efficiency in energy use must be ensured. In addition, energy production from domestic and industrial wastes and the use of renewable energy sources will reduce foreign dependency in energy, while reducing resource costs, thus increasing the competitive power of the manufacturer. The use of domestic machinery and equipment to the maximum extent in the production of renewable energy production technologies that will provide this will trigger the transformation needed (MoSIT, 2015b).

One of the exemplary projects carried out within the scope of the green transformation of the industry is the "Promotion of Energy Efficient Electric Motors in Turkey" (Tevmot Project) carried out by the Ministry of Industry and Technology and UNDP. Within the scope of the project, studies are carried out to replace inefficient motors with efficient motors in 100 SMEs operating in the manufacturing industry in 7 selected OIZs. Since the main goal of the project is to propose a sustainable and widespread energy efficiency finance mechanism with the experience to be gained from the pilot implementation, studies are carried out to expand the support mechanism (UNDP, 2021).

Another important project is the LCA project carried out by the TÜBİTAK Marmara Research Center, Environment and Cleaner Production Institute and the Ministry of Industry and Technology. With the project, in order to provide economic and environmental benefits in the Turkish industry, to comply with international environmental agreements and to make calculations such as environmental footprint; Efforts are underway to develop a national database consisting of data representing country conditions in terms of technology, geography and time and form the basis of Life Cycle Assessment studies, and to establish a National LCA Platform. Necessary studies have been carried out to add data sets for steel, cement, lime, freight transport (road, air, sea, rail) product groups produced in electric arc furnace facilities in 2021 to the energy and water data sets completed in the past. As a result of these studies, a total of 308 data sets were included in the database by the end of 2021 (MoIT, 2022).

The content analysis study conducted by Avunduk (2021) revealed that the two most researched topics at the global level in the last three years are green technology innovation and environmental regulations and government incentives. The use of green technologies should be ensured by conducting R&D studies in enterprises. The dissemination of these activities in enterprises can be achieved more quickly with the incentives and legal regulations to be made by the government for the environment. Yiğit (2014), also stated that the supply of environmentally oriented innovations in Turkey may increase with the driving force of more regulation and policy factors. Similarly, Yıldız (2016) emphasizes that the support given to initiatives by various international funds or organizations that give importance to green is at a limited level, and therefore it is beneficial for the government to take steps to support projects involving green technologies through incentive practices. Sun et al. (2019) also argue that the adoption of green technology needs strong support and funding from reliable government agencies to change the country's paradigm. In this context, it is very important to increase government support in order to increase green technology investments in the industry in Turkey.

5. CONCLUSION

Today, serious environmental damage has occurred as a result of rapidly developing technologies and increasing industrial activities. Many of the developed countries have realized that the classical environmental protection approach is not an effective environmental management system. For this reason, these countries have started to search for new and alternative technologies. In particular, the concept of green or clean production, which was introduced with the sustainable development plan, is seen as the most effective way to solve environmental problems (Yücel, 2011).

Scarce and valuable resources such as raw materials, energy and water constitute the basic inputs of economy as well as life. The sustainability of life and economy is directly dependent on these resources, and the effects of the use of these resources are also felt on both ecology and the economy. Resource use not only causes increased pressure on natural resource reserves and adversely affected the environment, but also affects national and international trade and market prices. While the expansion in international commodity markets and the unsustainable inefficient use of resources in many markets have increased price volatility, the increase in world population and welfare has also increased the demand for resources and resource prices. Megatrends indicate that the world population will increase further to exceed 9 billion and the number of middle-class consumers will triple. This shows that the increasing trend in the current demand for resources will continue in the future and the impact of resource use on the economy will be many times greater than what is felt today.

Cleaner production has been on the agenda of both developed and developing countries since the 1990s. When country examples are examined, it is seen that the development of the concept of cleaner production is realized through the stages of raising awareness, building capacity, establishing partnerships and creating information sharing networks, establishing financial mechanisms and making necessary policy reforms (TTGV, 2010).

Cleaner production and technology are one of the main investment areas today. Products that consume less energy and cause less harm to the environment are preferred. That's why companies are doing R&D and innovation studies in this field, trying to produce products that have the lowest carbon emissions and consume the least energy.

Technological change has a critical importance for the industry as in other sectors, among the long-term and cost-effective solutions to environmental problems. It has been revealed that strategically successful technology acquisition significantly affects the competitive advantages of companies (Arifin, 2015). In addition, technological change and innovation is an important area in the fight against climate change in industry.

Climate change affects the industry in many ways and is expected to affect it. Among these, the scarcity of resources in the supply of raw materials and resources and the problems to be experienced in access to resources, increase in the costs of resources, tightening national and international obligations can be listed. Climate change is closely related to all business and management processes of companies. Mitigation measures in industry often provide side benefits such as competitiveness, cost reduction, new business opportunities, better environmental compliance, health benefits, better working conditions and waste reduction.

The European Union aims to zero net greenhouse gas emissions by 2050, to reduce industrial production and global greenhouse gases, as well as to protect production and employment. In order to achieve this goal, with the European Green Deal announced in 2019, it has designed a 'green order' transformation in many main and sub-sectors from agriculture to industry, from energy to transportation. While the Union is taking steps towards the goal of 'climate neutral', it also wants to activate the Carbon Border Adjustment Mechanism in order to eliminate the negative effects of these steps on the economy. With this mechanism, it will be possible to demand an extra amount of money from countries that do not have carbon pricing for exports to the EU. With the Carbon Border Adjustment Mechanism, the EU is trying to minimize the damage to their competitiveness by protecting companies that will suffer the cost disadvantage to protect the climate (Aşıcı, 2021). In the light of these developments, it is clear that Turkey, which makes almost half of its exports to the EU, will be directly affected by the 'green transformation' that the EU will implement. For Turkey to make the transition to 'green production' sustainable without experiencing economic losses, it is necessary to plan and support the sectoral effects of the Green Deal and the smooth transition to compliance.

When we evaluate the development of Turkey on the path of sustainable growth, it is easily possible to say that the principles of sustainability have been largely integrated into development policies and national documents, and within this framework, a high level of political ownership is shown. Turkey can develop new and high value-added products and industries that will provide employment by using environmentally friendly technologies in the future. Thus, it can be ensured that all segments of the society and future generations benefit from the welfare created by a highly competitive industrialization process, while observing their rights.

REFERENCES

Arifin, Z., & Frmanzah. (2015). The Effect of Dynamic Capability to Technology Adoption and its Determinant Factors for Improving Firm's Performance; Toward a Conceptual Model. *Procedia: Social and Behavioral Sciences*, 207, 786–796. doi:10.1016/j.sbspro.2015.10.168

Aşıcı, M. A. (2021). *Avrupa Birliği'nin Sınırda Karbon Uyarlaması Mekanizması ve Türkiye Ekonomisi*. IPM-Mercator.

Ateş, S. A., & Ateş, M. (2015). Sosyo-Ekolojik Dönüşüm Karşısında Türkiye: Bir Alternatif Olarak Yeşil Büyüme. *Siyaset Ekonomi ve Yönetim Araştırmaları Dergisi*, 3(4), 69–94.

Avunduk, Z. B. (2021). Üretim Yönetiminde Yeşil İnovasyon:(S) SCI Dergilerinde Yayımlanan Makalelerin İçerik Analizi. *Yönetim Bilimleri Dergisi*, 19(Özel Sayı), 187–210. doi:10.35408/comuybd.974854

Battisti, G. (2008). Innovations and the Economics of New Technology Spreading within and across Users: Gaps and Way Forward. *Journal of Cleaner Production, 16*(1), 22–31. doi:10.1016/j.jclepro.2007.10.018

Bretschger, T. (2005). Economics of Technological Change and the Natural Environment: How Effective Are Innovations as a Remedy for Resource Scarcity? *Ecological Economics, 54*(2-3), 148–163. doi:10.1016/j.ecolecon.2004.12.026

Choi, S. D. (2012). *The Green Growth Movement in the Republic of Korea Options or Necessity.* Sustainable Development Network. World Bank.

DCED. (2012). *Green Industries for Green Growth.* Enterprise. https://www.enterprise-development.org/wp-content/uploads/Green_Industries_for_Green_Growth.pdf

Deif, A. (2011). A system model for green manufacturing. *Advances in Production Engineering & Management, 6*(1), 27–36.

Fidan, E. T. (2020). Türkiye'de Sürdürülebilir Sanayi Politikalarının Uygulanması ve Kamu, Sivil Toplum Kuruluşları ve Özel Sektörün Sürdürülebilir Sanayi Politikalarına İlişkin Yaklaşımlarının Değerlendirilmesi. *Verimlilik Dergisi*, (2), 73–100.

Ghazilla, R. A. R., Sakundarini, N., Abdul-Rashıd, S. H., Ayub, N. S., Olugu, E. U., & Musa, S. N. (2015). Drivers and barriers analysis for green manufacturing practices in Malaysian SMEs: A Preliminary Findings. *Procedia CIRP, 26*, 658–663. doi:10.1016/j.procir.2015.02.085

Hammar, H., & Lofgren, A. (2010). Explaining Adoption of End of Pipe Solutions and Clean Technologies: Determinants of Firms' Investments for Reducing Emissions to Air in Four Sectors in Sweden. *Energy Policy, 38*(7), 3644–3651. doi:10.1016/j.enpol.2010.02.041

Johansson, G., & Winroth, M. (2010). Introducing Environmental Concern in Manufacturing Strategies Implications for the Decision Criteria. *Management Research Review, 33*(9), 877–899. doi:10.1108/01409171011070305

Li, K., Zhang, X., Leung, J. Y. T., & Yang, S. L. (2016). Parallel Machine Scheduling Problems in Green Manufacturing Industry. *Journal of Manufacturing Systems, 38*, 98–106. doi:10.1016/j.jmsy.2015.11.006

Luken, R., Van Rompaey, F., & Zigova, K. (2008). The Determinants of EST Adoption by Manufacturing Plants in Developing Countries. *Ecological Economics, 66*(1), 141–152. doi:10.1016/j.ecolecon.2007.08.015

Manyika, J., Sinclair, J., & Dobbs, R. (2012). *Manufacturing the Future: The Next Era of Global Growth and Innovation.* Mckinsey Global Institute.

Maruthi, G. D., & Rashmi, R. (2015). Green Manufacturing: It's Tools and Techniques that can be implemented in Manufacturing Sectors. *Materials Today: Proceedings, 2*(4-5), 3350–3355. doi:10.1016/j.matpr.2015.07.308

Mittal, V. K., & Sangwan, K. S. (2014). Prioritizing Barriers to Green Manufacturing: Environmental, Social and Economic Perspectives. *Procedia CIRP, 17*, 559–564. doi:10.1016/j.procir.2014.01.075

MoIT (Turkish Ministry of Industry and Technology). (2022). *T.C. Sanayi ve Teknoloji Bakanlığı 2021 Yılı Faaliyet Raporu*. T.C. Sanayi ve Teknoloji Bakanlığı.

MoSIT. (2015a). (*Turkish Ministry of Science, Industry and Technology*). İklim Değişikliği ve Sanayi. T.C. Bilim, Sanayi ve Teknoloji Bakanlığı.

MoSIT (Turkish Science, Ministry of Industry and Technology). (2015b). *Türkiye Sanayi Stratejisi Belgesi 2015-2018*. T.C. Bilim, Sanayi ve Teknoloji Bakanlığı, Ankara.

MoT (Turkish Ministry of Trade). (2020). *Yeşil Mutabakat Eylem Planı*. T.C. Ticaret Bakanlığı.

MoTF (Turkish Ministry of Treasury and Finance). (2020). *Yeni Ekonomi Programı 2021-2023*. T.C. Hazine ve Maliye Bakanlığı.

Napp, T., Gambhir, A., Hills, T. P., Florin, N., & Fennell, P. S. (2014). A Review of the Technologies, Economics and Policy Instruments for Decarbonising Energy-Intensive Manufacturing Industries. *Renewable & Sustainable Energy Reviews*, 30, 616–640. doi:10.1016/j.rser.2013.10.036

OECD. (2020). *Biodiversity and the economic response to COVID-19: Ensuring a green and resilient recovery*. OECD. https://www.oecd.org/coronavirus/policy-responses/biodiversity-and-the-economic-response-to-covid-19-ensuring-a-green-and-resilient-recovery-d98b5a09/

Orji, I., & Wei, S. (2016). A detailed calculation model for costing of green manufacturing. *Industrial Management & Data Systems*, 116(1), 65–86. doi:10.1108/IMDS-04-2015-0140

Pang, R., & Zhang, X. (2019). Achieving Environmental Sustainability in Manufacture: A 28-Year Bibliometric Cartography of Green Manufacturing Research. *Journal of Cleaner Production*, 233, 84–99. doi:10.1016/j.jclepro.2019.05.303

Prasad, S., Khanduja, D., & Sharma, S. K. (2016). An Empirical Study on Applicability of Lean and Green Practices in the Foundry Industry. *Journal of Manufacturing Technology Management*, 27(3), 408–426. doi:10.1108/JMTM-08-2015-0058

Radonjic, G., & Tominc, P. (2007). The Role of Environmental Management System on Introduction of New Technologies in the Metal and Chemical/Paper/Plastics Industries. *Journal of Cleaner Production*, 15(15), 1482–1493. doi:10.1016/j.jclepro.2006.03.010

Ripple, W., Wolf, C., Newsome, T., Barnard, P., Moomaw, W., & Grandcolas, P. (2019). World Scientists' Warning of a Climate Emergency. *Bioscience*, 1–5. doi:10.1093/biosci/biz088

Sangwan, K. S., & Choudhary, K. (2018). Benchmarking Manufacturing Industries Based on Green Practices. *Benchmarking*, 25(6), 1746–1761. doi:10.1108/BIJ-12-2016-0192

SBB (T.R. Presidential Strategy and Budget Department). (2021). *T.C. Cumhurbaşkanlığı Strateji ve Bütçe Başkanlığı*. Orta Vadeli Program. https://www.sbb.gov.tr/wp-content/uploads/2021/09/Orta-Vadeli-Program-2022-2024.pdf

Seth, D., Shrivastava, R. L., & Shrivastava, S. (2016). An Empirical Investigation of Critical Success Factors and Performance Measures for Green Manufacturing in Cement Industry. *Journal of Manufacturing Technology Management*, 27(8), 1076–1101. doi:10.1108/JMTM-04-2016-0049

Shrivastava, S., & Shrivastava, R. L. (2017). A Systematic Literature Review on Green Manufacturing Concepts in Cement Industries. *International Journal of Quality & Reliability Management, 34*(1), 68–90. doi:10.1108/IJQRM-02-2014-0028

Shura. (2019). *Türkiye'de Enerji Dönüşümünün Finansmanı*. Sabancı Üniversitesi. https://shura.org.tr/turkiyede_enerji_donusumunun_finansmani/

Sun, H., Edziah, B. K., Sun, C., & Kporsu, A. K. (2019). Institutional Quality, Green Innovation and Energy Efficiency. *Energy Policy, 135*, 111002. doi:10.1016/j.enpol.2019.111002

TSKB. (2021). *Türk Sanayicisinin Yeşil Dönüşümü*. TSKB. https://www.tskb.com.tr/uploads/file/ece618e406ec1b452e0c7a9e3359ee18-1639386053562.pdf

TTGV. (2010). *Türkiye'de Temiz Üretim Uygulamalarının Yaygınlaştırılması için Çerçeve Koşulların ve Ar-Ge İhtiyacının Belirlenmesi Projesi Sonuç Raporu*. TTGV. https://www.ttgv.org.tr/tur/images/publications/612e1c28d6114.pdf

UNDP. (2021). *TEVMOT Project E-Bulletin is Online*. UNDP. https://www.undp.org/turkiye/news/tevmot-project-e-bulletin-online

UNEP. (1996). *Cleaner Production: A Training Resource Package, Industry and Environment*. UNEP Publications.

UNEP. (2017). *Green Industrial Policy: Concept, Policies, Country Experiences*. Geneva, Bonn: UN Environment, German Development Institute. https://wedocs.unep.org/bitstream/handle/20.500.11822/22277/Green_industrial_policy.pdf?sequence=1&isAllowed=y

UNIDO. (2008). *The CP Concept: What is Cleaner Production?* UNIDO Publications.

UNIDO. (2011). *Industrial Development Report 2011. Industrial Energy Efficiency for Sustainable Wealth Creation: Capturing Environmental*. Economic and Social Dividends UNIDO Publications.

UNIDO. (2016). *Overview: Industrial Development Report 2016: The Role of Technology and Innovation in Inclusive and Sustainable Industrial Development*. UNIDO Publications.

UNIDO-UNEP. (2010). *Taking Stock and Moving Forward. Sustainable production in practice in developing and transition countries*. The UNIDO-UNEP National Cleaner Production Centers.

World Economic Forum. (2022). *Reducing the carbon footprint of the manufacturing industry through data sharing*. World Economic Forum. https://www.weforum.org/impact/carbon-footprint-manufacturing-industry/

Yavuz, V. A. (2010). Sürdürülebilirlik Kavramı ve İşletmeler Açısından Sürdürülebilir Üretim Stratejileri/ Concept of Sustainability and Sustainable Production Strategies for Business Practices. *Mustafa Kemal Üniversitesi Sosyal Bilimler Enstitüsü Dergisi, 7*(14), 63–86.

Yiğit, S. (2014). İnovasyonun Çevreci Yüzü ve Türkiye. *Yönetim ve Ekonomi, 21*(1), 251–265.

Yıldız, H. (2016). Sürdürülebilirlik Bağlamında Sağlık Sektöründe İnovatif Uygulamalar: Yeşil Hastaneler. *Kafkas Üniversitesi İktisadi ve İdari Bilimler Fakültesi Dergisi, 7*(13), 323–340.

Yücel, M. (2011). Çeşitli Endüstrilerde Temiz Üretim Sistemi Uygulamalarının İşletme Ekonomilerine Sağladığı Faydalar. *Elektronik Sosyal Bilimler Dergisi*, *10*(35), 150–166.

Zahra, Z. G., Seyed Nematollah, M., & Bahaeddin, N. (2019). Economic Evaluation of the Effects of Exerting Green Tax on the Dispersion of Bioenvironmental Pollutants Based on Multi-Regional General Equilibrium Model (GTAP-E). *Energy Sources. Part A, Recovery, Utilization, and Environmental Effects*, 1–12. doi:10.1080/15567036.2019.1679912

Chapter 9
Artificial Intelligence Retrofitting for Smart City Strategies in the Context of India's Growing Population

Pushpam Singh
Indira Gandhi National Tribal University, India

Madhuri Yadav
Indira Gandhi National Tribal University, India

Sukanta Kumar Baral
Indira Gandhi National Tribal University, India

ABSTRACT

Artificial intelligence has gained momentum by assimilating into almost every aspect of the country's development, and smart city innovation is one aspect among them. It is a possible solution for issues related to rapid urban growth. This chapter addresses the top five smart city countries: Singapore, Zurich, Oslo, Taipei City, and Lausanne, implementing artificial intelligence in their smart city strategies. The study analyzed how those strategies can be applied to India's smart city by retrofitting artificial intelligence. The study used quantitative data from secondary sources such as government websites, journals, articles, and online books. R programming was applied to show the statistical performance of those five countries and area-based developmental projects of India. The study's findings will be beneficial for assisting decision-makers, professionals, and academicians in making more informed choices by providing insight into potential opportunities associated with the widespread implementation of artificial intelligence.

DOI: 10.4018/978-1-6684-8969-7.ch009

INTRODUCTION

With substantial developments in fields like the Internet of Things (IoT), automation, machine learning, robotics, and much other advanced analytics deployed for various purposes, the artificial intelligence (AI) explosion significantly impacts practically every part of our lives. It has transformed traditional systems into cognitive computing by merging information and communication technologies (Chawla et al., 2022). AI applications are increasingly being applied in a broad spectrum of industries contributing to advancements in instant information delivery, decision-making, research extension, and reliable data repositories (Shivaprakash et al., 2022). Over the past century, the global population has drastically expanded, and urbanization increased to 57% worldwide in 2022. Reportedly, India is the second largest metropolis after China, with extreme urbanization covering about 35% of the population, growing by 2.1% annually. By 2030, it is anticipated to rise to 40% and create 75% GDP of India through cities (Statista, 2023). Cities have transformed over the past few decades. They have become the driving force of social, environmental, and economic advancement through comprehensive and integrated strategy and the source of citizens' hope and opportunity (Mitra & Mehta, 2011). Many policymakers, professionals, and academicians believe that advanced urban innovations will usher in human evolution due to the current technological revolution (Tomitsch & Haeusler, 2015). Some of the wealthy countries have already surpassed this urbanization rate. For instance, over 80% of people in the UK live in metropolitan regions (Cowley et al., 2018). It needs the involvement of many organizations, incorporating sustainable growth, ICT infrastructure support, green economy, and multi-stakeholder alliances on diverse scales to successfully convert an urban area into a smart city (Kaluarachchi, 2022).

The inception of "smart cities" has gained popularity due to the constantly changing situation surrounding the administration and management of emerging technological powers as it is being challenged to reinvent itself and try out new perspectives concerning innovation and how it might be utilized to serve the general welfare since both technologies and societies change drastically (Angelidou, 2016). Developing "smart cities" involves initiatives and programs that encourage urban innovation and the thorough integration of ICT. The smart city concept incorporates basic infrastructure, ICT innovations, socialization, intellectual capital, and cultural connections to establish an eco-friendly environment. The "Smart Cities Mission" was enacted in 2015 by the Indian government to promote economic progression and raise living standards in 100 chosen cities. The "Ministry of Housing and Urban Affairs", responsible for the accountability of the "Smart Cities Mission", has received 61,905 crores from the national government. The program deliberately sought to initiate this by empowering the community's development and incorporating technology to offer innovative measures for residents (Praharaj et al., 2018).

Many nations, including Japan, the European Union, the United States, and others, have realized that a smart city project successfully solves the approaching difficulties because it encompasses human ecology (Harnal et al., 2022). This transformation is observed through the report of Philips lighting and SmartCitiesWorld, where the Barcelona government retained 378 crores by integrating IoT services and technologies into its smart city projects and achieved 324.64 crores through smart auto parking. According to the Smart City Index 2021, 118 cities listed worldwide adopt smart city strategies. In the drive towards pervasive computing, Singapore is viewed as a trendsetter. With the aid of sensing devices, robots, and other cyber-physical technologies, emerging IoT solutions are applied to create smart cities for resource management, environmental monitoring, smart logistics operations, and smart farming. The resultant output is utilized to create approaches for smart cities by transferring all the statistical data to the server for interpretation (Wang et al., 2021).

By 2050, 70% of the overall population will shift to towns and urban centers, as forecasted by the United Nations, which will culminate in skyrocketing emissions and energy consumption. The United Nations Population Fund reported that India is anticipated to exceed China as the heavily populated global nation in 2023. The graph of India's growing population indicates the need to structure renewable energy sources, efficient urban transportation networks, and eco-friendly waste disposal. The plan of establishing a smart city, potentially offering a solution to issues like overpopulation and pollution, has gained momentum as industry and population have expanded (Gupta & Gupta, 2023). It was observed that the Indian government's smart city guidelines lacked a proper framework or foundation regarding how these numerous projects will be integrated for the betterment of the nation (Praharaj et al., 2018).

Much research has been done on smart city strategies in India with different contexts but looking at and examining AI-based strategies in other developed countries and developing plans to incorporate those strategies is yet to be conducted. This study examines how AI adoption can lead to smart city enhancement by identifying the most widely used systems. It further studies plans to be laid for AI penetration into smart city strategies in India by selecting the top five countries (Singapore, Zurich, Oslo, Taipei City, Lausanne) with smart city strategies collected from worldwide, which was taken from the Smart City Index 2021 to identify and examine rising AI trends from those countries. This "Smart City Index" was announced by the "Institute for Management Development" in partnership with "Singapore University for Technology and Design (SUTD)", which includes important data concerning how high urban population growth has compelled city officials to undertake additional duties. This index assessed 118 cities' technological infrastructure about five essential sectors covering health & safety, mobility, opportunities, governance, and activities. Some smart cities have shown greater mobilization capacity and resource utilization, while other cities are lacking in those areas. The data of the top five countries adopting smart city strategies were analyzed. The study used R programming to show the statistical performance of those countries and area-based developmental projects in India. The study's findings will be beneficial for assisting decision-makers, professionals, and academicians make more informed choices by providing insight into potential opportunities and constraints associated with the widespread implementation of Artificial Intelligence.

LITERATURE REVIEW

Population Growth and Urbanization in India

Countries are being impacted by numerous interrelated factors that are also impacting their existence. Overpopulation and urbanization, which have a variety of repercussions on city transportation, global warming, excessive waste output, and a finite resource supply constitute some of them (Subramanian, 2007). As per the "Department of Economic and Social Affairs" report of the "United Nations" (UN), it is anticipated that India will overtake China by being the heavily populated country in 2023 and increase the number of urban residents by 40.4 crores by the year 2050.

For a country to be economically sustainable, it is crucial to effectively administer its urban population and provide for its fundamental requirements regarding infrastructure, environment protection, health, and energy resources (Santamouris & Vasilakopoulou, 2021). The Theory of Demographic Transition (DTT), which describes the impact of a change in birth and death rates on population growth, is the most fundamental theory employed to study the correlation between urbanization and population shifts. The

"Demographic Transition" model primarily depicts how populations fluctuate across periods. India's urbanization policies have been historically adverse and lacked management competency (Sarkar, 2020). Due to fast unplanned urbanization, modern urban living has evolved into a complex form. Urban life, which is fast-paced and extensively reliant on technology, has impacted individuals' lifestyles and behavior patterns, putting them more vulnerable to various diseases (Ali et al., 2022). India will face challenges because of its population boom, fast urbanization, and densely populated cities that will create skills and education disparity among younger generations, impacting India compared to other nations (Muttarak & Wilde, 2022). The development of major cities will serve as a counterpart to the small and medium cities progression. The expansion of industrial zones and the need to boost existing cities are the driving strengths behind the emergence of new major cities (Sahasranaman, 2012). In order to implement sustainable urban planning and administration in areas that are swiftly urbanizing in developing nations, it is crucial to have a comprehensive knowledge of how different sociodemographic populations view the economic, societal, and ecological consequences of uncontrolled urban population growth (Hatab et al., 2021).

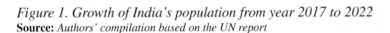

Figure 1. Growth of India's population from year 2017 to 2022
Source: *Authors' compilation based on the UN report*

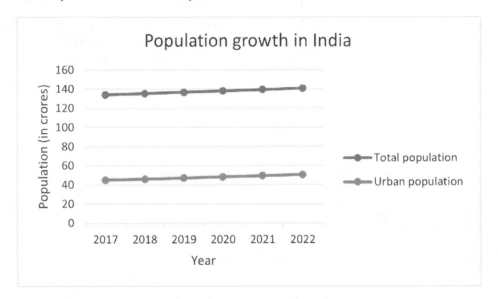

Conceptualizing Smart City

The "smart city" describes a society that makes use of "Internet-of-Things", data processing, and ICT to enhance the effectiveness of cities' infrastructure, services, and resources to deliver its residents an excellent living environment (Kuo et al., 2023). The technologically advanced city integrates data into the physical infrastructure but only introducing intelligence into each component area such as energy, transportation, education, etc., is not enough. Smart cities should be viewed as network connectivity (Nam & Pardo, 2011). Smart city applications containing big data analytics have a broad outlook to achieve sustainability, higher robustness, and quick resource management (Anjum et el., 2018). "Information and communication technology" is taken as a crucial factor for smart city implementation as it includes tools to raise the living standards of citizens and information management capabilities. Although it can monitor and communicate city activities like criminal control, environmental report, etc., the city is a complex entity with many different interests and objectives.

The smart city notion can be disseminated into fundamental dimensions and constituents through an ontology that enables graphic representation, articulating its parts using structured human Language and displaying the infinite richness of smart cities (Ramaprasad et al., 2017). The smart cities endeavor has two distinct consequences, which are internal forces and external forces. External forces such as individuals and societies, the global ecosystem, and infrastructure have a more massive impact than internal forces comprising technology, regulations, and organization. Considering that technology possesses the potential to affect other forces significantly, it may be regarded as a theme in efforts to create smart cities (Chourabi et al., 2012). Globally, the smart city revolution has drawn attention to many programs, yet practically all fail to construct sustainable urban visions. Existing smart city policies depict technologically driven and oversimplified perspectives of cities, which is the major cause of this shortcoming. These strategies neglect the social aspects, which creates a surge in social disparity and exclusion (Yigitcanlar, 2021). Chun et al. (2021) described a smart city as a strategic model framework involving various risk levels and decision-making processes related to complex issues.

Figure 2. Smart city dimensions
Source: *Author's compilation*

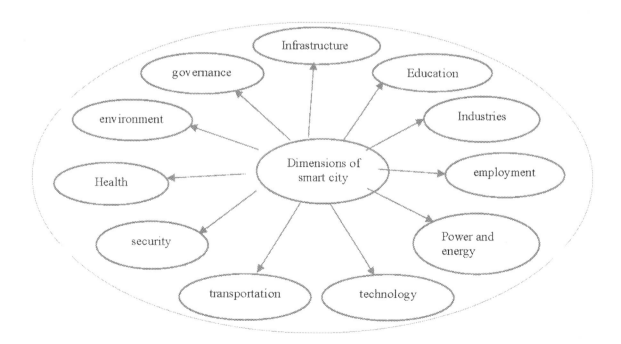

Trends of Smart Cities in Recent Decades

Although smart cities first appeared in 1974, a significant turning point occurred in smart cities' advancement when the digital city was formed for local citizens to encourage web usage in Amsterdam in 1994 (Alberts et al., 2017). The field of smart cities has seen several advancements over the past few years. These advances provided new possibilities for building smarter cities. Regarding healthcare, technology provides network-integrated medical diagnosis and ensures connection availability in remote operations for patient monitoring and treatment. Blockchain technology revolutionized smart city strategies that delegate authority among distinctive data storage and security networks. Smart energy city, the pillar of the smart city concept, offers its residents an affordable, eco-friendly environment that encourages a sustainable economy. The initial phase of a smart city formation focused on technological features that emphasized strengthening service and infrastructure. With the rising market volume and challenges in recent decades, a new iteration of smart cities has formed that concentrates on enriching the experience of citizens by engaging them in the administration and decision-making activities of smart cities (Bohloul, 2020). Numerous smart cities are projected to emerge in the years ahead, alongside developing new innovative technologies that reinforce the concept. Current and emerging smart cities are causing a spike in scholarly reviews that address the global debate on smart cities across a broad spectrum of topics (Sharifi et al., 2021). Many technological advancements over the recent decades have led to rising of human comfort. From the viewpoint of industrial growth, the advent of the smart city model is a solution to making an ideal future city that ensures communities' security and well-being (Singh et al., 2022).

Smart Cities and Artificial Intelligence

Enabling computers to imitate human thought processes and behaviour is described as artificial intelligence. In particular, it is a discipline in computer science specialized in imitating human intelligence functions and a computation system that permits software to perform actions or make decisions (Herath & Mittal, 2022). While forming a smart city, various challenges are encountered regarding administration, ecological sustainability, economic transformation, etc. which can be solved by artificial intelligence through the adoption of software applications and tech devices aiding in sustainable growth (Voda & Radu, 2018). Smart city applications are drastically advanced due to artificial intelligence innovation. It has become a vital element of smart cities that does smart analysis via sensors. The algorithms used in artificial intelligence make data processing and pattern identification easier than conventional methods (Luckey et al., 2021). Transportation networks such as e-route, e-location, travel security, etc. allow vehicles to share their current location in real time. The applications allow carbon monitoring, traffic enforcement, and payment supervision for effective traffic management (Agarwal et al., 2015). The incorporation of artificial intelligence in smart cities has helped to address enormous challenges such as data transparency, safety and security, putting strategic actions, and ensuring socialization (Bokhari & Myeong, 2022) Different fields of artificial intelligence have made conventional cities into highly advanced smart cities by integrating technology into individuals' everyday activities and aiding sustainable growth (Navarathna & Malagi, 2018).

OBJECTIVES

1. To identify AI-based smart city strategies of top ranked countries with smart city.
2. To examine how AI adoption can lead to smart city development in India.

METHODOLOGY

Smart city research is an incredibly important area that is perpetually advancing. Previous research works relating to smart city strategies have helped in getting a substantial knowledge base, enabling integrated analytical findings. The study employed quantitative data that were approached from a secondary source. The data were obtained from government websites such as the "Ministry of Housing and Urban Affairs" to derive "area-based development" of chosen smart cities under India's smart city mission. The ranking of the top five countries, i.e., Singapore, Zurich, Oslo, Taipei City, and Lausanne, based on mobility, governance, health and safety, activities, and opportunities, was derived from the smart city index published by IMD-SUTD. These five areas depict the technological advancement in specific countries and how it contributed to the country's progress. The study used R programming to statistically represent conclusive results. The R software was devised by Ross Ihaka and Robert Gentleman in 1993 as a solution for S. Users can use the software to perform data analysis, statistical and graphical visualization tools in an integrated windows-based interface (Ihaka & Gentleman, 1996). The data was first modified using tools called "tidyr" and "tidyverse" packages available in R language to make it uniformly dispersed over the grid. The coding was done on "ggplot2" of R studio to plot graphs and obtain ready-to-print visualizations.

RESULTS

Smart City Analysis of India

The Smart City Mission executed in India adopted an Area Based Development model covering 100 cities with substantial use of technology to transform some urban areas into smart cities. The framework was drafted that enclosed retrofitting, redevelopment, and extension for enhancement of habitability, infrastructure, and energy efficiency. Smart city projects engaged a certain percentage of the city population which showed a spatial disparity in infrastructural growth.

Figure 3 depicts a pattern where comparatively small cities such as Silvassa, Namchi, Kakinada, and Dharamshala reflect a more significant percentage of city and population extension for the project. Namchi with 73.8% covered the highest percentage of the population followed by Vellore (63.2%) and Silvassa (63%). When comparing the area-wise percentage, Silvassa with 50%, covers a greater area followed by Tiruppur (41%) and Kakinada (27%). Pune with 0.8%, has the lowest extension of city population followed by Ahmedabad (1.5%) and Ludhiana (2.2%). Likewise, the lowest extension of the city area is Ludhiana at 0.3% followed by Ahmedabad and Jaipur at 0.5%. The adopted strategies concentrated on only 5% of the urban areas and deprived 90% of residents of new opportunities and amenities. The investment in various projects resulted in the least impactful output due to the unequal area distribution by which citizens with small urban areas received negligible benefits from this program such as medical services, education, housing possession, and infrastructure facilities. Even after heavy investments, the number of primitive areas remains the same. Inadequate implementation of smart city projects indicates an absence of strategy and resource shortfall.

Figure 3. Population and area coverage for smart cities project in India
Source: *Authors' compilation based on the report of Housing and Land Rights Network 2018*

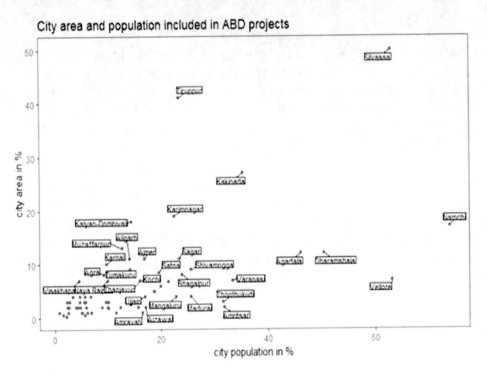

Smart City Analysis of Countries Based on AI

Health and Safety

It represents the constituents that include online filling of issues related to city maintenance, quick return of useless stuff using the website, enhancement of public utility accessibility due to open Wi-Fi networks, surveillance cameras for citizens' security, website accessibility for carbon emission monitoring, and online scheduling of medical visits. The ranking of all these activities employed in different countries was taken on an average basis.

Figure 4 depicts rating of health and safety related aspects in five countries where Singapore's sufficient amenities stands on top with 73%, followed by Taipei City (72.3%). Oslo holds 55.2%, Lausanne with 53.2% and Zurich having 52.8% holds fewer amnesties compared to other mentioned countries.

Figure 4. Ranking of smart city countries based on AI-driven health & safety
Source: *Authors' compilation*

Mobility

It represents the constituents that include traffic mitigation through car-sharing applications, reduced time-taking process for a parking spot, traffic mitigation through hiring bicycles, online sales of tickets, and traffic information through phones.

Figure 5 depicts the rating of mobility related aspects in five countries where Taipei City has high amenities related to mobility with 68%, followed by Singapore (61.5%). Oslo holds 55.8%, Zurich (55.1%), and Lausanne (50.8).

Activities

It represents constituent that include online booking availability for visiting events and exhibitions. The countries accessing AI for online booking have made it easier for citizens. Figure 6 depicts that Taipei City has a higher rating of 85% containing sufficient facilities for activities related aspects. Singapore holds the second rank with 83.5%, Lausanne and Zurich were rated 78.5%, and Oslo with 76.3%.

Opportunities (Work and School)

It represents the constituents that include online quick job searching, effective IT training in schools, simplified business establishment process, and internet connection requirements in school and work.

Figure 7 depicts that Singapore has the highest amenities for opportunities related aspects and stands on top at 76.4% rating followed by Zurich with 66.5%, Taipei City (66.4%), Lausanne (64.7%), and Oslo (62.7%).

Figure 5. Ranking of smart city countries based on AI-driven mobility
Source: *Authors' compilation*

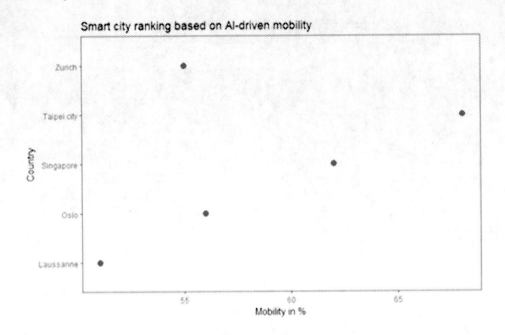

Figure 6. Ranking of smart city countries based on AI-driven activities
Source: *Authors' compilation*

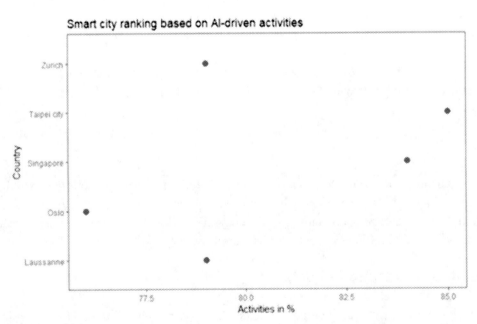

Figure 7. Ranking of smart city countries based on AI-driven opportunities
Source: *Authors' compilation*

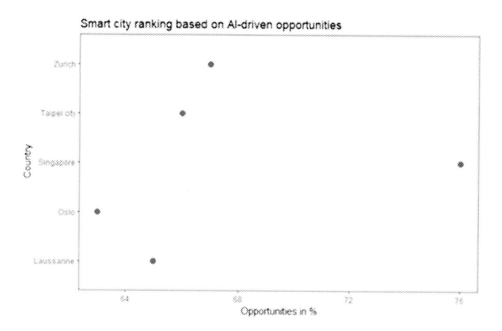

Governance

It represents the constituents that include minimized corruption rates due to the accessibility of online public finance, increased voting participation, citizens' participation in proposing ideas through the website, and decreased documentation processing time.

Figure 8 depicts that Taipei City has a maximum rating on Governance aspects that stands on top at 68.8% followed by Singapore with 61.6%, Zurich (50.8%), Lausanne (50.2%), and Oslo (49%).

From the graphs presented above, it can be inferred that Singapore is overall positioned highest across all sectors, encompassing mobility indicators, healthcare, safety, education, competitiveness, and administration.

DISCUSSION

AI Advancements of Top Smart City Countries

Singapore's Smart Nation plan, which aims to create a digital civilization, was introduced in November 2014. It is acknowledged with accelerating change in healthcare, training, mobility, urban initiatives, and financial services. It can be observed from the Mariana Barrage flood prevention system way in which the dam was built and positioned as the most secure city worldwide (Johnston, 2019). The installation of Smart Water Systems in households gives users information by relying on a person's actions regarding water usage, leakage information, and minimum consumption practices on their devices. Singapore uses drones to monitor rooftop drains, sewage, and other open sources to determine where mosquitoes

Figure 8. Ranking of smart city countries based on AI-driven governance
Source: *Authors' compilation*

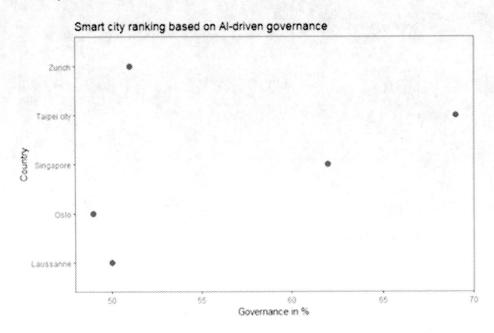

can mutate. Telehealth software was integrated to simplify providing and facilitating hospital and health-related amenities, such as nursing facilities, patient counseling, patient information, and self-care via information technology (Kumar et al., 2022). Singapore strongly emphasizes job creation, cutting commute time between the workplace and home to build a smart nation that is easily navigable. All the utilities are distributed strategically for a comfortable livelihood.

In Zurich, numerous sensors are already inbuilt to detect pedestrian and bike congestion of individuals without creating personal data discrepancy. Zurich is recognized as an economically robust city with 45 crores of citizens using the transit network annually. Zurich, being the first city to generate surplus energy worldwide, aims to achieve a carbon-neutral city by 2050. It covers 50% of the city's land area with green spaces labeling it the greenest city. The city intends to reduce waste volume and raise recyclability through a rigorous waste disposable system. It has allied with stakeholders to experiment and launch innovative technologies in its smart city laboratory (Menendez & Ambuhl, 2022).

Oslo proposes prohibiting the sales of automobiles with internal combustion engines to achieve rigorous sustainability objectives by 2025. The software that connects local representatives and new entrepreneurs has been built, letting business owners showcase innovative ideas that enrich citizens' lives across the spectrum. This city shows a real illustration of sustainable urban development because it aimed to build a resourceful community. It has the largest charging station housed within, with a parking lot that currently fits 102 electric cars and as many columns. In the years between 2008 and 2011, Oslo added more than 400 roadside charging stations. In the past four years, the availability of on-road charging stations and the acceptance of electric vehicles has grown (Ruggieri et al., 2021). The city uses technology to insert pipelines that are non-destructive and less detrimental to citizens and traffic congestion. In terms of energy efficiency and environmental sustainability, Oslo has advanced significantly over time.

It encourages the transformation to an energy grid exclusively generated by clean energy sources which adheres to the Paris Agreement (Julsrud & Krogstad, 2020).

Taipei City focuses on digitalizing education and has built smart classrooms using the HiTeach Smarter Teaching System. It incorporates artificial intelligence and big data to assist teachers and students in achieving the modern classroom goal and transform the conventional teaching environment without requiring a complicated operation. The city mandated configuring a GPS device on every bus to provide legit bus location to travelers on their portable devices by developing a flexible bus management system using the Sensor information (Chang et al., 2021). In order to address public issues and create a system where the government, people, and industry can coexist, the Taipei city government has utilized cutting-edge technology and information. For undertaking research projects and trials for smart healthcare," Taipei City hospital is the best option given the city's medical facilities and resources. By increasing the number of self-developed projects, clinical trials, business contracts, and field experiments, the hospital has taken the initiative to coordinate all resources (Iqbal, 2021).

Lausanne, being one of the top smart cities throughout the globe, its principal target is to boost its living standards while preserving resources and delivering services more effectively. It is renowned for being a pioneer in the development of eco-communities, which are residential structures that adhere to energy and environmental requirements from the beginning of construction (Calbimonte et al., 2017). The city has turned the information security sector into a digital economy. Taipei City is building a smart city that is focused on information security which includes encompassing smart applications such as smart education, public housing, manufacturing, transportation, and health care (Wu et al., 2020).

Plans for Retrofitting AI to India's Smart City

Smart cities are essential for controlling the number of materials and resources used. It is observed that comprehensive urban development is required to develop a more sustainable society and cities. With the global emerging trends of globalization, urbanization, population hike, climate change, and digitalization, the exchange of best practices on smart city initiatives is extremely valuable (Yadav et al., 2017). Although the use of data-driven models for smart cities is not new, there is still a significant gap to be filled in terms of AI integration (Golubchikov & Thornbush, 2020). Coordination between the national and state level government is, therefore, necessary for the successful implementation of smart city programs that are focused on the needs of citizens and social inclusion.

AI should be retrofitted in a way that people get easily acquainted with it. It should emphasize taking feedback from residents related to smart city adoption and encourage inclusive participation of citizens in the smart city. There are a number of problems with the way that traffic is now managed, including significant traffic congestion and steadily rising energy costs. Systems utilizing AI approaches may greatly improve this scenario by providing information on traffic congestion, air quality, and energy use (Putra & Warnars, 2018). Prior to using AI in the energy sector, the Indian government must first recognize its potential. As a result, such a comprehensive, strategy-driven approach would be beneficial for the wider implementation of AI in India. It will improve energy consumption by giving crucial knowledge to residents and encouraging them to be smart energy users. All the cities should be prioritized for meaningful participation and engagement when choosing and carrying out smart city programs.

Before choosing a project and moving forward with its development, it is important to get the open, prior, and informed permission of individuals who are likely to be influenced by smart city initiatives. All Indian cities and villages should receive enough funding, with a focus on balanced rural and urban development. AI can also increase the IoT's efficacy and stability, which will enhance network connectivity (Lv et al., 2021). In exchange, this would promote innovation and entrepreneurship and better knowledge sharing. AI-enabled wearable technology, often known as smart textiles will be able to identify changes in the human body and transmit information to medical professionals. AI-enabled monitoring devices can be utilized in the acute care section by using technological gadgets. It will help lower overall healthcare expenditures and enhance patient outcomes. By offering a useful database of medical knowledge and the capacity to acquire, evaluate, and use complex medical data more effectively, AI systems can significantly improve health diagnoses. Helping medical professionals with duties including the gathering and recording of information could free up more resources for health care (Chidambaram et al., 2022). Intelligent learning systems in the field of education can offer students highly personalized educational programs by simulating the one-on-one interaction between tutor and student. AI systems that monitor environmental changes, react to user needs, and increase energy efficiency can be used to create smarter houses. The objective of AI in the context of smart cities with regard to sustainable transportation is to determine the most effective ways to reduce the time taken to reach the locations. This results in a decrease in energy use, which therefore lowers air and noise pollution, traffic, and other externalities like the need for infrastructure in parking and transportation. By assessing real-time metrics, such as traffic signal regulation, AI can be utilized to optimize transportation by adjusting routes to balance user demands and improve parking. AI may also be utilized from the standpoint of transport planning to distinguish spatial structures in aerial photographs and gather vast amounts of data for the creation of more precise and responsive models that can be used to create a more environmentally friendly transportation system (Iyer, 2021). Drones and other autonomous devices, along with motion detection, predictive analytics, and advanced AI surveillance technologies, can be used to monitor metropolitan areas and identify dangers like crime (Jha et al., 2021). The government needs to incorporate multiple stakeholders to bring innovative solutions. As AI-enabled systems for smart cities deals with large databases having a range of data formats and integrity protection along with other essential security to ensure long-term growth, the systems' architecture for smart cities must be adaptable and scalable, allowing for simpler integration and implementation of new platforms. Data mining technology must be vigorously supported, and various data formats must be integrated in order to build a data-centric smart city. Data visualization technology bridges the knowledge gap between the technology and its users by providing complicated city data in a clear and organized format to them (Al Nuaimi et al., 2015). Before implementing hardcore technologies, cities need to ensure about security and privacy of citizens' data. Without this assurance, citizens will not be able to trust the government, and data collection will be challenging.

CONCLUSION

The enhancement of smart city strategies is always ongoing and molds according to the country's social and economic needs. This research has shown strategies undertaken by five countries in implementing artificial intelligence for the upgradation of smart cities. Those strategies were analyzed to help create a holistic view toward urban innovation through digital transformation in India for the sustainable progress of the country. Governance is a key pillar of smart city structure which helps citizens live a quality life, safeguards the ecosystem, and promotes a sustainable environment. The government requires to have strategic policies and frameworks related to smart city initiatives that support effective operations in a particular area. Rather than just prioritizing the areas and sectors, it should focus on overall inclusiveness to remove inequalities. AI is an approach towards achieving remarkable transformation in all dimensions of smart city strategies. However, India being in its inception stage of technology adoption, should restrain from adopting overvaluing strategies that are not sustainably effective. India's distinctive cultural diversity and economic position restrain to execution of smart city strategies in the same manner as in developed nations. There is a need to enact smart city programs in accordance with Indian standards by recognizing their capabilities and ensuring a competitive edge. The study opted for five major areas, namely mobility, governance, health and safety, opportunities, and activities that use innovative technologies for smart city strategies. This study can be extended in a more comprehensive way for future research that addresses the degree of retrofitting artificial intelligence for smart city innovation by considering its social impact and how individuals respond to its implementation.

REFERENCES

Agarwal, P. K., Gurjar, J., Agarwal, A. K., & Birla, R. (2015). Application of artificial intelligence for development of intelligent transport system in smart cities. *Journal of Traffic and Transportation Engineering*, *1*(1), 20–30.

Al Nuaimi, E., Al Neyadi, H., Mohamed, N., & Al-Jaroodi, J. (2015). Applications of big data to smart cities. *Journal of Internet Services and Applications*, *6*(1), 1–15. doi:10.118613174-015-0041-5

Alberts, G., Went, M., & Jansma, R. (2017). Archaeology of the Amsterdam digital city; why digital data are dynamic and should be treated accordingly. *Internet Histories*, *1*(1-2), 146–159. doi:10.1080/24701475.2017.1309852

Ali, M. J., Rahaman, M., & Hossain, S. I. (2022). Urban green spaces for elderly human health: A planning model for healthy city living. *Land Use Policy*, *114*, 105970. doi:10.1016/j.landusepol.2021.105970

Angelidou, M. (2016). Four European smart city strategies. *International Journal of Social Science Studies*, *4*(4), 18–30. doi:10.11114/ijsss.v4i4.1364

Anjum, A., Ahmed, T., Khan, A., Ahmad, N., Ahmad, M., Asif, M., Reddy, A. G., Saba, T., & Farooq, N. (2018). Privacy preserving data by conceptualizing smart cities using MIDR-Angelization. *Sustainable Cities and Society*, *40*, 326–334. doi:10.1016/j.scs.2018.04.014

Bohloul, S. M. (2020). Smart cities: A survey on new developments, trends, and opportunities. *Journal of Industrial Integration and Management*, *5*(3), 311–326. doi:10.1142/S2424862220500128

Bokhari, S. A. A., & Myeong, S. (2022). Use of artificial intelligence in smart cities for smart decision-making: A social innovation perspective. *Sustainability (Basel)*, *14*(2), 620. doi:10.3390u14020620

Calbimonte, J. P., Eberle, J., & Aberer, K. (2017). Toward self-monitoring smart cities: The opensense2 approach. *Informatik-Spektrum*, *40*(1), 75–87. doi:10.100700287-016-1009-y

Chang, I. C. C., Jou, S. C., & Chung, M. K. (2021). Provincialising smart urbanism in Taipei: The smart city as a strategy for urban regime transition. *Urban Studies (Edinburgh, Scotland)*, *58*(3), 559–580. doi:10.1177/0042098020947908

Chawla, Y., Shimpo, F., & Sokołowski, M. M. (2022). Artificial intelligence and information management in the energy transition of India: Lessons from the global IT heart. *Digital Policy. Regulation & Governance*, *24*(1), 17–29. doi:10.1108/DPRG-05-2021-0062

Chidambaram, S., Maheswaran, Y., Patel, K., Sounderajah, V., Hashimoto, D. A., Seastedt, K. P., McGregor, A. H., Markar, S. R., & Darzi, A. (2022). Using Artificial Intelligence-Enhanced Sensing and Wearable Technology in Sports Medicine and Performance Optimisation. *Sensors (Basel)*, *22*(18), 6920. doi:10.339022186920 PMID:36146263

Chourabi, H., Nam, T., Walker, S., Gil-Garcia, J. R., Mellouli, S., Nahon, K., Pardo, T. A., & Scholl, H. J. (2012). Understanding smart cities: An integrative framework. In *2012 45th Hawaii international conference on system sciences*, (pp. 2289-2297). IEEE.

Chun, S. A., Kim, D., Cho, J. S., Chuang, M., Shin, S., & Jun, D. (2021). Framework for smart city model composition: Choice of component design models and risks. *International Journal of E-Planning Research*, *10*(3), 50–69. doi:10.4018/IJEPR.20210701.oa4

Cowley, R., Joss, S., & Dayot, Y. (2018). The smart city and its publics: Insights from across six UK cities. *Urban Research & Practice*, *11*(1), 53–77. doi:10.1080/17535069.2017.1293150

Golubchikov, O., & Thornbush, M. (2020). Artificial intelligence and robotics in smart city strategies and planned smart development. *Smart Cities*, *3*(4), 1133–1144. doi:10.3390martcities3040056

Gupta, M., & Gupta, H. (2023). Sustainable Urban Development of Smart Cities in India-A Systematic Literature Review. *Sustainability, Agri. Food and Environmental Research*, *11*(10), 1–20.

Harnal, S., Sharma, G., Malik, S., Kaur, G., Khurana, S., Kaur, P., Simaiya, S., & Bagga, D. (2022). Bibliometric mapping of trends, applications and challenges of artificial intelligence in smart cities. *EAI Endorsed Transactions on Scalable Information Systems*, *9*(4), 1–21. doi:10.4108/eetsis.vi.489

Hatab, A. A., Ravula, P., Nedumaran, S., & Lagerkvist, C. J. (2021). Perceptions of the impacts of urban sprawl among urban and peri-urban dwellers of Hyderabad, India: A Latent class clustering analysis. *Environment, Development and Sustainability*, *24*(11), 12787–12812. doi:10.100710668-021-01964-2

Herath, H. M. K. K. M. B., & Mittal, M. (2022). Adoption of artificial intelligence in smart cities: A comprehensive review. *International Journal of Information Management Data Insights*, *2*(1), 1–21. doi:10.1016/j.jjimei.2022.100076

Housing and Land Rights Network. (2018). *India's Smart Cities Mission: Smart for whom? Cities for whom?* Housing and Land Rights Network. Smart_Cities_Report_2018.pdf (hlrn.org.in)

Ihaka, R., & Gentleman, R. (1996). R: a language for data analysis and graphics. *Journal of Computational and Graphical Statistics*, *5*(3), 299–314.

IMD Smart City Observatory. (2021). *Smart City Index 2021*. IMD. https://www.imd.org/smart-city-observatory/home/#_smartCity

Iqbal, M. (2021). Smart city in practice: Learn from Taipei City. *Journal of Governance and Public Policy*, *8*(1), 50–59. doi:10.18196/jgpp.811342

Iyer, L. S. (2021). AI enabled applications towards intelligent transportation. *Transportation Engineering*, 1-11. https://doi.org/ doi:10.1016/j.treng.2021.100083

Jha, A. K., Ghimire, A., Thapa, S., Jha, A. M., & Raj, R. (2021). A review of AI for urban planning: Towards building sustainable smart cities. In *Proceedings of the 6th International Conference on Inventive Computation Technologies*, (pp. 937-944). IEEE. 10.1109/ICICT50816.2021.9358548

Johnston, K. (2019). A comparison of two smart cities: Singapore and Atlanta. *Journal of Comparative Urban Law and Policy*, *3*, 191–206.

Julsrud, T. E., & Krogstad, J. R. (2020). Is there enough trust for the smart city? exploring acceptance for use of mobile phone data in oslo and tallinn. *Technological Forecasting and Social Change*, *161*, 1–11. doi:10.1016/j.techfore.2020.120314 PMID:32981976

Kaluarachchi, Y. (2022). Implementing data-driven smart city applications for future cities. *Smart Cities*, *5*(2), 455–474. doi:10.3390martcities5020025

Kumar, A., Kapoor, N. R., Arora, H. C., & Kumar, A. (2022). Smart cities: A step toward sustainable development. In Smart Cities, 1-43, CRC Press. https:// doi:10.1201/9781003287186-1

Kuo, Y. H., Leung, J. M., & Yan, Y. (2023). Public transport for smart cities: Recent innovations and future challenges. *European Journal of Operational Research*, *306*(3), 1001–1026. doi:10.1016/j.ejor.2022.06.057

Luckey, D., Fritz, H., Legatiuk, D., Dragos, K., & Smarsly, K. (2021). Artificial intelligence techniques for smart city applications. In *Proceedings of the 18th International Conference on Computing in Civil and Building Engineering*, (pp. 1-14). Springer International Publishing. 10.1007/978-3-030-51295-8_1

Lv, Z., Qiao, L., Kumar Singh, A., & Wang, Q. (2021). AI-empowered IoT security for smart cities. *ACM Transactions on Internet Technology*, *21*(4), 1–21.

Menendez, M., & Ambuhl, L. (2022). Implementing design and operational measures for sustainable mobility: Lessons from Zurich. *Sustainability (Basel)*, *14*(2), 625. doi:10.3390u14020625

Ministry of Housing and Urban Affairs. (2023). [Data set]. Ministry of Housing and Urban Affairs. https://smartcities.data.gov.in/cities

Mitra, A., & Mehta, B. (2011). Cities as the engine of growth: Evidence from India. *Journal of Urban Planning and Development*, *137*(2), 171–183. doi:10.1061/(ASCE)UP.1943-5444.0000056

Muttarak, R., & Wilde, J. (2022). *The World at 8 Billion*. Population Council. doi:10.31899/pdr2022.1000

Nam, T., & Pardo, T. A. (2011). Conceptualizing smart city with dimensions of technology, people, and institutions. In *Proceedings of the 12th Annual International Digital Government Research Conference: Digital Government Innovation in Challenging Times*, (pp. 282-291). 10.1145/2037556.2037602

Navarathna, P. J., & Malagi, V. P. (2018). Artificial intelligence in smart city analysis. In *Proceedings of the International Conference on Smart Systems and Inventive Technology*, (pp. 44-47). IEEE.

Praharaj, S., Han, J. H., & Hawken, S. (2018). Urban innovation through policy integration: Critical perspectives from 100 smart cities mission in India. *City, culture and society, 12*, 35-43.

Putra, A. S., & Warnars, H. L. H. S. (2018). Intelligent traffic monitoring system (ITMS) for smart city based on IoT monitoring. In *Proceedings of the Indonesian Association for Pattern Recognition International Conference*, (pp. 161-165). IEEE. 10.1109/INAPR.2018.8626855

Ramaprasad, A., Sánchez-Ortiz, A., & Syn, T. (2017). A unified definition of a smart city. In *Proceedings of the 16th International Conference, EGOV*, (pp. 13-24). Springer International Publishing. 10.1007/978-3-319-64677-0_2

Ruggieri, R., Ruggeri, M., Vinci, G., & Poponi, S. (2021). Electric mobility in a smart city: European overview. *Energies*, *14*(2), 315. doi:10.3390/en14020315

Sahasranaman, A. (2012). Financing the development of small and medium cities. *Economic and Political Weekly*, *47*(24), 59–66.

Santamouris, M., & Vasilakopoulou, K. (2021). *Present and future energy consumption of buildings: Challenges and opportunities towards decarbonisation. e-Prime-Advances in Electrical Engineering. Electronics and Energy.* doi:10.1016/j.prime.2021.100002

Sarkar, R. (2020). Association of urbanisation with demographic dynamics in India. *GeoJournal*, *85*(3), 779–803. doi:10.100710708-019-09988-y

Sharifi, A., Allam, Z., Feizizadeh, B., & Ghamari, H. (2021). Three decades of research on smart cities: Mapping knowledge structure and trends. *Sustainability (Basel)*, *13*(13), 1–23. doi:10.3390u13137140

Shivaprakash, K. N., Swami, N., Mysorekar, S., Arora, R., Gangadharan, A., Vohra, K., Jadeyegowda, M., & Kiesecker, J. M. (2022). Potential for Artificial Intelligence (AI) and Machine Learning (ML) applications in biodiversity conservation, managing forests, and related services in India. *Sustainability (Basel)*, *14*(12), 1–20. doi:10.3390u14127154

Singh, T., Solanki, A., Sharma, S. K., Nayyar, A., & Paul, A. (2022). A Decade Review on Smart Cities: Paradigms, Challenges and Opportunities. *IEEE Access : Practical Innovations, Open Solutions*, *10*, 68319–68364. doi:10.1109/ACCESS.2022.3184710

Statista (2023). *India: Degree of urbanization from 2011 to 2021*. Statista. https://www.statista.com/statistics/271312/urbanization-in-india/#:~:text=In%202021%2C%20approximately%20a%20third,a%20living%20in%20the%20cities

Subramanian, N. (2007). Sustainability-Challenges and solutions. *Indian Concrete Journal*, *81*(12), 39.

Tomitsch, M., & Haeusler, M. H. (2015). Infostructures: Towards a complementary approach for solving urban challenges through digital technologies. *Journal of Urban Technology*, *22*(3), 37–53. doi:10.1080/10630732.2015.1040296

United Nations World Population Prospects. (2022). *Development*. UN. https://www.un.org/development/desa/pd/sites/www.un.org.development.desa.pd/files/wpp2022_summary_of_results.pdf

Voda, A. I., & Radu, L. D. (2018). Artificial intelligence and the future of smart cities. *Broad Research in Artificial Intelligence and Neuroscience*, *9*(2), 110–127.

Wang, K., Zhao, Y., Gangadhari, R. K., & Li, Z. (2021). Analyzing the adoption challenges of the Internet of things (Iot) and artificial intelligence (ai) for smart cities in China. *Sustainability (Basel)*, *13*(19), 1–35. doi:10.3390u131910983

Wu, Y. C., Sun, R., & Wu, Y. J. (2020). Smart city development in Taiwan: From the perspective of the information security policy. *Sustainability (Basel)*, *12*(7), 2916. doi:10.3390u12072916

Yadav, P., Hasan, S., Ojo, A., & Curry, E. (2017). The role of open data in driving sustainable mobility in nine smart cities. In *Proceedings of the 25th European Conference on Information Systems*, (pp. 1248-1263). IEEE.

Yigitcanlar, T. (2021). Smart City Beyond Efficiency: Technology–Policy–Community at Play for Sustainable Urban Futures. *Housing Policy Debate*, *31*(1), 88–92. doi:10.1080/10511482.2020.1846885

Chapter 10
Green Bonds for Mobilising Environmental Finance:
A Conceptual Framework for a Greener Economy

G. Sreelekshmi
https://orcid.org/0000-0002-0114-1951
University of Kerala, India

A. V. Biju
https://orcid.org/0000-0001-5583-6495
University of Kerala, India

ABSTRACT

Sustainability in production and consumption requires infrastructure, pointing to the enormous financial prerequisite. Green bonds are an innovative means for channelling capital toward the environment and sustainability. Through a methodical evaluation of the literature, global green bond frameworks, and issuances to date, this chapter attempts to develop a comprehensive understanding of green bonds, as well as their importance in achieving sustainable development. The authors examine the potential of green bonds in unleashing sustainability focusing on the UN SDG 12, titled "responsible consumption and production." The results suggest that green bonds have huge potential in financing green infrastructure that enables responsible production and consumption. The interdependencies of the sustainability pillars result in overall sustainability with the benefits derived from green bond issuances.

1. INTRODUCTION

The development humankind has attained so far has drastically altered the environmental systems, as a consequence of which we are on the brink of an unprecedented crisis today- the threat to sustainability. This necessitates striking a balance between development and sustainability, which has led us to adopt the sustainable development agenda. The United Nations (UN) Brundtland Commission in its 1987

DOI: 10.4018/978-1-6684-8969-7.ch010

report defines sustainable development as "meeting the needs of the present without compromising the ability of future generations to meet their own needs" (Commission on Environment, 1987). It thereby underlines the responsibility in our hands to fine-tune the present development pathways toward sustainability, which is crucial for the survival of humankind. The 17 UN Sustainable Development Goals (SDGs) attempt at implementing a global transformative agenda on this behalf[1].

The triple global catastrophes of climate change, biodiversity loss, and pollution are all caused by unsustainable production and consumption, which coupled with environmental deterioration, endanger human welfare and the realisation of SDGs (United Nations, 2022). The climate crisis is extremely significant to counteract as it presents irreversible damage to survival on the planet. Global surface temperatures will continue to increase throughout the twenty-first century unless significant initiatives toward reduced carbon dioxide (CO_2) and other greenhouse gas emissions are made in the coming decades (IPCC, 2022). The probability of nations attaining the Paris 2°C goal is low. However, the probability of rapid climate change over the next century is high if no meaningful reforms are implemented (Nordhaus, 2018). To battle these adversities and attain global goals, the current machinery of conventional unsustainable developmental agendas should be revolutionised with sustainable developmental models, based on sustainable production and consumption.

The development and implementation of sustainable production and consumption models have become the need of the hour, which in turn, brings the circular economy and carbon neutrality a reality. Technologies in support of the circular economy and reduced carbon footprint of production and consumption are of utmost importance for sustainability. Such a transition to sustainability is tough, restraining the adoption of such development models. Funding this 'just transition' is even more complicated. Even though institutional support has been on the rise, fund allocation remains a bottleneck. Numerous innovations in the field of sustainable finance have emerged to bridge this enormous climate financing gap. In this respect, one of the greatest innovations in the sustainable debt market, that has been gaining mass acclaim is the rise of green bonds.

As per Flammer (2020), green bonds are those bonds the proceeds of which are pledged to finance low-carbon, environmentally beneficial projects. They are also referred to as climate bonds. The green bond market, though nascent, has shown exponential growth over the years. However, the developments in this current niche market, the 'green bond boom'[2], present immense potential for bridging the SDG-financing gap. The previously scanty literature on green bonds has been attracting wide academic interest with the rise in both issuers' and investors' interest in the green bond market. Certain studies have drawn their insights on green bonds from the primary market, whereas some have focused on the secondary market. Some of the studies followed a matching approach by comparing green bonds with similar non-green issues of the same issuer (Bachelet et al., 2019; Flammer, 2020; Flammer, 2021; Hachenberg & Schiereck, 2018). However, one of the significant areas yet to attract wide scholarly interest is the significance of green bonds in sustainability and climate action.

This chapter analyses the green bond landscape, its overall significance, and its potential in unleashing the capital for attaining the UN SDGs focusing on SDG 12, titled "responsible consumption and production". The potential of green bonds in financing projects that promote green consumption and production is noteworthy, and an interesting quest to find answers to. This study also presents a conceptual framework for the green bond market, which would aid researchers, issuers, investors, and regulatory authorities in gaining insights into the market and leveraging the green segment for sustainability. The suggestions and future research avenues are also proposed to encourage policymakers and researchers, and further lead to the comprehensive development of the market. Therefore, this chapter would help align our development pathways with the sustainable development models and the SDGs, which need to become the pressing priority for the well-being of all.

To provide a comprehensive view of these research objectives, the chapter is structured in the following way. Section 2 presents the green bond landscape and issuances. Section 3 outlines the significance of green bonds and Section 4 the regulatory framework of green bonds respectively. Section 5 discusses the potential of green bonds in sustainable development and SDG 12. The hindrances to market growth are briefed in Section 6 and the conclusion is presented in Section 7. Section 8 puts forward suggestions from the study and Section 9 provides an account of the future research directions.

2. GREEN DEBT FOR A GREENER ECONOMY

In general, there has been a greater emphasis on sustainability, and Environment, Social, and Governance (ESG) globally, and this is evident in the financial systems and markets across the world too. Companies with ESG ratings outperform others, with investors supporting their green and non-green ESG-focused issuances (Hachenberg & Schiereck, 2018). Although sustainable finance composes of a broad spectrum of stocks, loans, and guarantees, the debt market witnessed the rise of a revolutionary finance mechanism, with the ever-growing issue of sustainability-based thematic bond instruments. The Climate Bonds Initiative (CBI) categorises sustainable bonds, which are thematic bonds with varied purposes and use of proceeds, as GSS+ bonds, with G being green, S for social, and the following S for sustainability bonds. The plus symbol (+) signifies the other labelled bonds including transition bonds and sustainability-linked bonds.

Green bonds are basically a new class of fixed-income securities, to fund environmental and climate-friendly initiatives including recycling, renewable energy, and green infrastructure institutions (Gilchrist et al., 2021). The Climate Bonds Standard Version 3.0, a global green issuance standard by the CBI has defined a green bond as "a bond where the proceeds will be exclusively applied to finance or re-finance, in part or in full, new and/or existing eligible green projects, and which is aligned with the four core components of the Green Bond Principles. A green bond should not be considered fungible or interchangeable with bonds which are not aligned with those four core components"[3]. The four fundamental components for GBP alignment are as follows.

i. Use of Proceeds,
ii. Process for Project Evaluation and Selection,
iii. Management of Proceeds, and
iv. Reporting

The green bond segment has shown an excellent growth trajectory since its inception. The Climate Awareness Bond, issued by the European Investment Bank in 2007, was the initial green bond. The World Bank's first green bond, issued in 2008, was the first to determine project eligibility and served as the criterion for green bond assistance. It introduced impact reporting as an intrinsic component of the process and included CICERO Shades of Green as a second-opinion provider. It served as the foundation for the Green Bond Principles (GBP), currently managed by the International Capital Markets Association (ICMA). The following years witnessed the emergence of the green bonds market as a specialised debt market segment, actively attracting investors' and issuers' interest simultaneously, as evident from Figure 1.

Figure 1. Cumulative green bond issuances (in $ Billion) classified by markets
Note. Data sourced from www.climatebonds.net. Contains data only up to the first half of 2022.

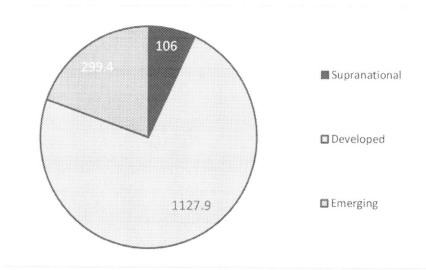

Figure 1 shows that the largest share in green bond issuances in aggregate i.e., 1,127.9 billion USD, is attributed to developed countries. As per the CBI report "Sustainable Debt Global State of The Market 2021", the green debt segment is rapidly growing, with volumes increasing by 75% year on year. In the first half of 2022, the cumulative total of green debt amounted to USD 1.9 trillion, as per the Sustainable Debt Market Summary released by the CBI. As per another of their market reports[4], the cumulative green bond issuance passed the USD 2 trillion milestone at the end of September 2022. Sovereign issuances in local currencies are on a growth trend. Many national governments and non-government entities have proposed frameworks and taxonomies- all these point out the possible opportunities before issuers in adopting sustainable approaches and funding their projects efficiently.

Following the indication of Figure 1, Figure 2 shows the US being the topmost green bond issuer followed by China. The rest of the top issuances are made by France, Germany, Supranational issuances, the Netherlands, and so on.

As shown by Figure 2, Figure 3 indicates that top issuances have come from the American and Chinese markets and the European markets.

Figure 4 shows that the EUR and USD occupy the top two positions. The share of CNY has been increasing over the years, which conforms with the insights from Figure 2 and Figure 3.

3. THE POWER OF GREEN BONDS

In this era of green innovation, the focus has been to promote economic and business growth while reducing negative environmental consequences with the help of several novel techniques, regulations, or tactics. The creation of sustainable green bonds is one of the most well-known financial developments in sustainable finance in recent years (Heydari et al., 2023). Green bonds are the result of green innovation that channelises funds towards the development of green infrastructure and thereby contributing to a greener economy.

Figure 2. Top green bond-issuing countries
Note. Data sourced from www.climatebonds.net. The data is in $ Billion.

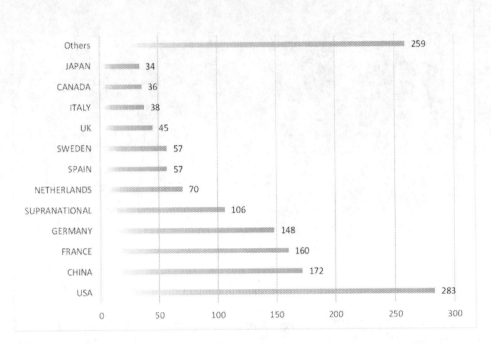

Figure 3. Top green bond-issuing countries- geographical
Note. Data sourced from www.climatebonds.net. The data is in $ Billion.

Green bonds have emerged as one of the most significant breakthroughs in the field of sustainable finance which help mobilise finances toward clean and sustainable investments (Gianfrate & Peri, 2019; Maltais & Nykvist, 2020). They are innovative bond instruments that have a bonus element of greenness in addition to the characteristics of conventional bonds. Its issuances also help corporates broaden their investor base post-issuance (Tang & Zhang, 2020) and unlike conventional bonds, they open dialogue between issuers and investors. Its issuance can be seen as a powerful signalling tool that firms are invest-

Figure 4. Currencies dominating the green bond issues
Note. Data sourced from www.climatebonds.net.

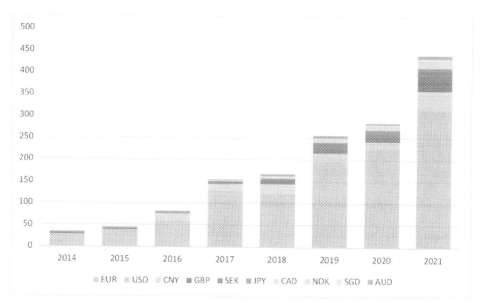

ing in environment-friendly initiatives and altering their ESG characteristics (Tang & Zhang, 2020). It allows corporations to demonstrate their environmental commitment (Flammer, 2021). This signalling effect can assist attract new investors who are more concerned with including a sustainability footprint in their portfolio investing decisions (Cortellini & Panetta, 2021).

Conventional bonds and green bonds differ in terms of their exposure to market situations and sentiments. As a consequence of this, green bonds have been widely seen as a hedging tool against the market. Dong et al. (2023) find that green bonds are preferred due to their pro-environmental qualities, which allow them to insure against tail risks, regardless of geopolitical, economic, and climate policy concerns. Thus, investors could diversify their portfolios with green bond inclusion and reduce overall losses as this would give them the best hedging. The study by Martiradonna et al. (2023) also found similar results. The diversification benefits were consistent for all strategies and periods, including the extreme Covid pandemic. The bonds displayed reduced losses in the bear period, while they had positive but lower returns during the bull sub-period. In a CBI market report on the pricing of green bonds in the primary market, it is known that numerous green bond issuers also emphasised that the green label for green bonds supported deal placement in volatile markets (Harrison, 2023). Taking regulatory and financial initiatives to de-risk and hedge will encourage investors to allocate resources to climate-resilient activities. Green bonds may protect against adverse price movements in low-carbon companies, allowing climate-conscious investors to hedge portfolio risk using exclusively green financial instruments consistent with their green goals (Reboredo et al., 2022).

Above all, the issuance of green bonds brings climate sustainability and circular economy into action, which is crucial for long-term sustainability, gaining great significance. These bonds reduce the environmental impact of anthropogenic intervention. In this respect, it is noteworthy that the issuance of green bonds has the potential to fund sustainable production and consumption, thus contributing to UN SDG 12, which calls for responsible consumption and production.

3.1. The Use of Proceeds

The proceeds from the issuances of green bonds enable firms to fund environmentally friendly initiatives and promote sustainable development (Bhutta et al., 2022). These might range from projects aiming at emission reduction to clean energy, energy efficiency, climate change adaptation, and so on[5].

Figure 5. Use of proceeds of green bonds
Note. Data sourced from www.climatebonds.net.

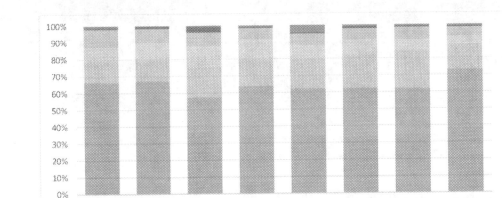

As per Figure 5, energy, buildings, and transport remain the top three use of proceeds areas in the green bond issuances, and they more or less remain the same over the years.

3.2. Green Bond Issuers

The exponential growth of the market can be attributed to the wide issuer support that it has gathered. The issuers' stock prices rise dramatically following the issue announcement. First-time issuers experience a more pronounced effect on the stock market reactions than repeat issuers, and corporate issuers experience stronger reactions than financial institution issuers (Tang & Zhang, 2020). Green bond issuances are evidenced to improve issuers' performance through positive stock reactions and improved environmental performance post-bond issue announcements (Flammer, 2020). Therefore, there have been improved subscriptions to corporate and sovereign green issuances, even in developing countries, especially emerging ones. Governments, governmental organisations, supranational agencies businesses, corporations, and municipalities, are the major green bond issuers (Flammer, 2020; Gilchrist et al., 2021). Figure 6 and Figure 7 shed light on the type of issuers dominating the green bond market.

The figure shows that corporate issuances both financial and non-financial corporates equally dominate the issuance statistics. This is followed by government-backed entities, development banks, and sovereign issuances.

Figure 6. Issuers' data on cumulative green bond issuances
Note. Data sourced from www.climatebonds.net. The cumulative issuance data up to the first half of 2022 have only been considered.

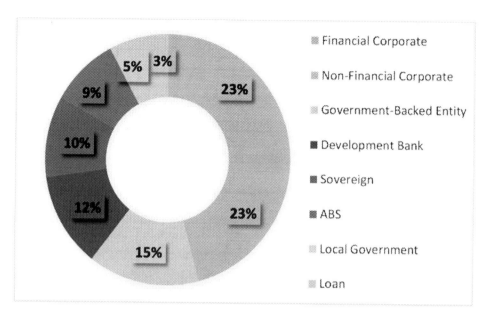

Figure 7. Green bond issuances (in $ billion) classified by issuer type
Note. Data sourced from www.climatebonds.net.

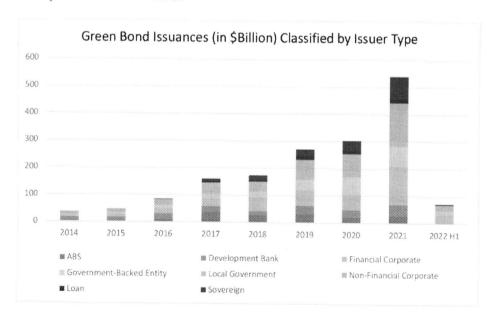

In the initial years, the development banks and non-financial corporates were the key players, as evident from Figure 7. Although they possess a relatively key position, financial corporates, and government-backed entities have occupied a major stake. It deserves attention as the figure shows that sovereign issuances have seen a rapid rise over the years.

3.3. Green Bond Premium

The issuers could raise funds at a lower cost of capital by issuing green bonds, as the bond investors would be willing to forego some portion of financial returns for the additional environmental and societal returns they gain from their subscription to green bonds. This green bond premium is often referred to as 'greenium'. Long before green bonds occupied a mainstream seat in the sustainable finance field, Chava (2014) validated the conventional concept that the cost of capital decreases when climate change apprehensions are alleviated. Compared to comparatively eco-friendly businesses, investors and lenders expected greater returns on stocks and loans from enterprises with environmental issues, demonstrating pricing for climate risks. However, studies on green bonds show mixed empirical shreds of evidence although the majority are on the positive side. Still, a consensus is yet to be reached.

The ownership of green bonds remains concentrated within a small group of investors prepared to forego economic profits in exchange for environmental benefits, as a result of which green bonds shall be issued with lower yields (Baker et al., 2018). Gianfrate and Peri (2019), also found green bonds as more financially convenient than comparable conventional bonds even after factoring in green certification costs. For corporate issuers, the advantage is larger and it persists in the secondary market. This points to the potential of green bonds in framing a greener economy without penalizing the issuers financially. In contrast, Fatica et al. (2021) find greenium in issuances by supranational institutions and corporates, but not in issuances by financial institutions. While financial institutions' green issuances remain higher, there is no indication of a greenium, which may be due to inherent difficulties in precisely linking the proceeds from the bond issue with specific green initiatives. Tang and Zhang (2020) find no evidence of greenium, indicating that cost-effective debt financing is not the primary benefit. Yet, following the issuance of green bonds, they observe enhanced institutional ownership and stock liquidity that may arise from a broadened investor base due to media attention along with increased impact investing opportunities. Flammer (2021) also found no pricing differences, consistent with the results of Larcker and Watts (2020) who found that investors consider green and non-green securities issued by the same issuer as nearly identical substitutes when risk and payoffs are constant and known to investors ex-ante. A systematic review of the greenium studies in the primary market by MacAskill et al. (2021) revealed a positive consensus, although marginal, existing in the literature. It is expected that more clarity and consensus would arrive once the market attains a certain momentum. Social, economic, and environmental factors drive the greenium. Although these determinants share synergies, still, environmental and social factors are projected to have a greater impact on market demand and prospects (MacAskill et al., 2021).

Green bonds may be issued with or without external verification by CBI or through a second-party opinion. If the green bonds are validated by external verifiers, both the price and ownership are found to have more pronounced effects, the understanding of which is critical for issuers and for the development of certifications and standards (Baker et al., 2018). Dorfleitner et al. (2022) also point to a statistically significant positive premium for green bonds with a rise in external greenness ratings. Investors reward green bonds with a premium in the form of lower yield and higher bond prices when the bonds are recognized as having genuine green objectives certified by independent examinations. Fatica et al. (2021) also stated that green bonds with external scrutiny receive a higher premium than self-labelled green securities. In essence, external assessment is necessary for this emerging sector. Besides, repeat issuers receive a higher premium than first-time green borrowers, evidencing a reputation effect.

4. REGULATORY FRAMEWORK FOR GREEN BONDS

A just transition necessitates the support of a transformative system. Based on a survey of European asset managers administered by the CBI, Sangiorgi and Schopohl (2021) provide insights into the factors affecting green bond investment. Competitive pricing and strong green credentials, both pre-and post-issuance, are most impactful in decision-making, whereas unclear and poor reporting on the allocation of proceeds hinders green bond investments. Thus, the issuances must align with a green bond framework. Increased market demand and momentum of green bond issuance have led to improved consensus on the concept, and taxonomies and frameworks have been developing worldwide at an improved pace.

A market-driven initiative has been made to provide a standardised method of evaluating the environmental effect and integrity of green bonds (MacAskill et al., 2021). The Green Bond Principles (GBP), by the International Capital Market Association (ICMA), a voluntary market-led effort, encourage openness in the disclosure of bond revenues. The GBP aids issuers in launching credible green bonds and investors in evaluating their green bond investments by ensuring guidance on bringing transparency to the market. The four fundamental components for GBP alignment are the Use of Proceeds, the Process for Project Evaluation and Selection, the Management of Proceeds, and Reporting. It encourages transparency making it easier to follow the capital invested into environmental initiatives while also attempting to increase insight into their anticipated effect by suggesting that issuers report on the usage of green bond revenues[6].

The Climate Bonds Standard run by the CBI is another critical initiative in the green bond market, which aids the certification process of green bonds[7]. It has helped build trust in the green label in the market, which is highly significant as the overall sustainable finance market is highly susceptible to greenwashing. This helps in reducing investor apprehensions and enhancing their participation in the issues. The Climate Bonds Taxonomy, which is another initiative by the CBI classifies projects and acts as a tool for the stakeholders to comprehend the areas financed under green bonds. The Green Bond Standards by the European Union High-Level Expert Group on Sustainable Finance, the Green Bond Standards of the Association of Southeast Asian Nations (ASEAN), the Green Bond Assessment and Verification Guidelines by the People's Bank of China and China Securities Regulatory Commission are the regional standards in the green bond segment. National-level frameworks have also been released by national governments.

5. UNLOCKING SUSTAINABLE DEVELOPMENT WITH GREEN BONDS

Sustainability is a broader theme that is viewed mainly from three dimensions- economic, environmental, and social, as reflected in the UN SDGs. Decision-makers should analyse the linkages, complementarities, and trade-offs among these pillars, and they must assure responsible behaviour and action at the international, national, community, and individual levels to work for the benefit of human development (Mensah, 2019). Financing sustainable development requires enormous finances, which attracts significance to sustainable finance. Thus, a sustainable financing model is necessary for the execution of the SDGs.

The SDGs are implemented to a greater extent when the financial model is more sustainable, with the environmental pillar of sustainable development seeing the most significant influence. The association between the sustainable finance model and SDG implementation is most pronounced in nations using the 3.0 version of the model, which consists of both public and private financial systems (Ziolo et al.,

2020). Migliorelli (2021) identifies SDG finance, which indicates meeting the financing requirements of the 17 UN SDGs, and green finance as subsets of sustainable finance. Green finance is a sect of sustainable finance, which directs funds toward green projects as per the environmental SDGs, which range from climate action to life on earth to water to biodiversity to a circular economy. The environmental SDGs include SDG 6 Clean Water and Sanitation, SDG 7 Renewable Energy, SDG 13 Climate Action, SDG 14 Life Below Water, and SDG 15 Life on Land. Climate finance may be considered as that part of green finance that is aimed at financing climate action (Migliorelli, 2021). Thus, the focus of climate finance is on SDG 13. The investors' attention to climate-friendly securities is crucial for just transition (Reboredo et al., 2022). This renders the growing attention gained by the green bond market an excellent fillip to sustainability.

Although plenty of financial instruments have been innovated, the role and adoption of green bonds as a sustainable finance instrument, most importantly green finance tool in facilitating the transition to sustainability is noteworthy. Ahmed et al. (2023) find the existence of positive significant cumulative abnormal returns post-issue announcement. It may be indicating that investors are understanding the need to address climate change, acting to do so, and motivating businesses by supporting these bonds. The shareholders' enthusiastic response to the news of the bond issue indicates that they have a favourable opinion of the ESG practices of the companies. As a result, green bonds serve as a link between current development objectives and potential funding methods for future green projects. Maltais and Nykvist (2020) opined that how investors and issuers interact in the capital markets is genuinely changing, and this development has a positive effect on sustainability at the operational level within organisations. The use of the proceeds clause which is a bonus element for green bonds as compared to other bonds makes this possible. Even though bond investors do not possess the same voting rights as equity investors, the green bond market fosters dialogues between the bond investors and issuers about sustainability expectations that would not have happened in the absence of green bonds. However, a concern is that green bonds may wrongly convey the impression of having a greater influence than they actually do (Maltais & Nykvist, 2020). Nevertheless, the significance of green bonds remains meaningful from the pace of growth of the market. The same is stated in Figure 8.

Figure 8. Green bonds contributing to sustainability
Note. Author's own illustration

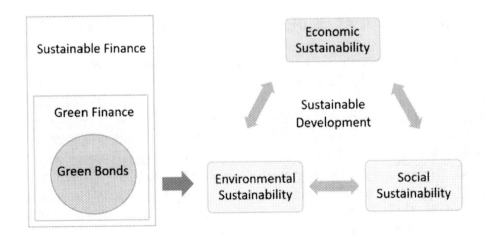

The basic objective behind green bonds is to contribute to environmental sustainability and they are evidenced to contribute to the same. The interlinkage of the pillars of sustainability contributes to overall sustainable development.

5.1. Green Bonds for Responsible Consumption and Production: Advancing SDG 12

A circular economy is a developmental model that incentivises efficient resource utilisation by reducing, repairing, reusing, and recycling waste, thereby returning the resources extracted back into the economy. This can assist to conserve the environment, make the best use of limited natural resources, establish new industries, create jobs, and develop new skills[8]. SDG 12 titled "responsible consumption and production" underlines this great aspect of ensuring sustainable development. Fu et al. (2019) categorises the 17 SDGs into three heads i.e., essential needs, expected objectives, and finally governance, which includes SDG 12. Effective governance is heavily reliant on interdisciplinary guidance, necessitating inputs from the natural sciences and social sciences for the implementation and achievement of the goals. The study found responsible production and consumption models to be crucial in reducing emissions from agriculture and energy usage. Transition in production and consumption patterns necessitates green investments, which mobilises capital for modifying the current production standards (Bachelet et al., 2019). Green bonds enter into significance at this critical perspective. At present, green bonds are considered a great avenue for green investments.

Green bonds can be a major boost in financing green projects like improved waste management mechanisms, greater resource efficiency, transition to renewable energy resources, waste-to-energy facilities, etc. The issuance can aid in mainstreaming responsible production as well as consumption. The contribution of green bonds to SDG 12 is both direct and indirect. First, it contributes to responsible production and consumption by financing those projects that ensure a transition to novel sustainable models from conventional unsustainable models. Second, it supports the environmental SDGs, and thereby indirectly contributes to responsible consumption. The nature of the SDG aids in reaping the benefits of green bonds.

It is worth noting that all other SDGs would be meaningful only if SDG 12 can be realised. Through responsible production and consumption and by improving resource efficiency and reducing wastage, the environmental burdens could be reduced and lead to the advancement of linked SDGs for water, biodiversity, climate change, and oceans. This will also free up resources for tackling poverty and striving for a fair distribution of material well-being (The World in 2050, 2018). It is widely believed that SDG 12 and SDG 17 will have a large influence on the remainder of Agenda 2030. To counteract stratification of the SDGs and more thoroughly integrate the network of SDGs, the interconnections between progress on SDGs 1 to 3 and other goals, particularly SDG 12, but also SDGs 4, 5, 9, 14, and 17 need to be enhanced, which is a major bottleneck before policy-makers (Dawes, 2022). Bengtsson et al. (2018) also identify the cross-cutting nature of the SDGs and sustainable consumption and production, which implies that several related goals may be achieved by properly executing SDG 12. The same is shown in the framework presented in Figure 9.

While most of the 2030 Agenda's aims are expected to complement one another, there is a goal conflict with Target 8.1 on economic (Gross Domestic Product (GDP)) growth. This poses a major concern to all stakeholders as the conventional developmental agenda has always focused on economic growth as an indicator of development. If countries concentrate their efforts solely on economic development driven by GDP growth, SDG12, and other related goals would be neglected (Bengtsson et al., 2018). Thus, innovation and collaboration across disciplines are vital.

Figure 9. Framework of green bonds and SDGs
Note. Authors own illustration using insights on the interdependencies between the UN SDGs derived from the literature study.

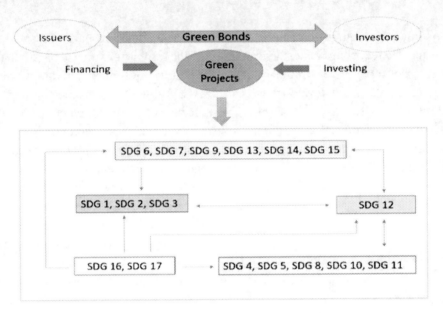

6. HINDRANCES TO MARKET GROWTH

Greenwashing is the most significant issue in the sustainable finance market. It is complex to ascertain and understand if the funds procured are applied to the right cause or not. In the case of green bond issuance, transparency is found to lower the green bond yields. In contrast, the yields were found to increase with lower credit ratings, longer maturity, and lower redemption price, and vice versa (Jankovic et al., 2022). Bhutta et al. (2022) suggest that investors are reluctant to purchase green bonds given the costs of issuance and the risky nature of the projects they aim to finance. Furthermore, many organizations have widely different ideas of what it means to be "green" (Gilchrist et al., 2021), adding to the problem. Another challenge is that the issuances by big corporates are given higher evaluations, whereas the contributions by smaller companies are overlooked.

7. CONCLUSION

Through a methodical evaluation of the global green bond frameworks and issuances to date, this study attempts to gain a comprehensive understanding of green bonds, which would help better understand the segment, its prospects, and policy demands. The literature review assisted in unveiling the field's theoretical underpinnings, comprehending the state-of-the-art, understanding how green bonds fit into UN SDG 12, and developing a conceptual framework. The understanding of the issuance and post-issuance consequences was furthered by an analysis of the issuances of green bonds, which also helped identify potential bottlenecks in the process. The role of issuers and investors in scaling up the green bond effects is remarkable, with the greenium argument opening doors for reduced transition costs. Although the market shows promising prospects, challenges like lack of trust, ambiguity in definition, harmonised standards, greenwashing, and biased and divergent ratings still need to be addressed, impeding the market's growth. These issues demand collaborative efforts from governments, central banks, and other market regulators and the market needs to transform into a broader investor-centric market.

8. SUGGESTIONS

The investment landscape should support the issue and utilisation of the green bond frameworks. The regulatory authorities and policymakers need to implement frameworks to confirmation of the latest developments in the global and national markets. To enhance the utility of ESG data, Kotsantonis and Serafeim (2019) suggest that ESG data suppliers should work together to codify best practices and bring transparency to data management. Similarly, green bond issuers need to ensure transparency in their issues, most importantly for the use of the proceeds. Agliardi and Agliardi (2019) state that transparency would improve the issuer's creditworthiness. They also recommend reducing the cost of obtaining and administering the green label, which would especially benefit developing economies where the debt markets have not matured enough to properly leverage green bonds. Improved disclosure and the readability of the issuance documentation, which would comprise green bond frameworks and annual reports, are seen to increase liquidity (Lebelle et al., 2022). An investor-led sustainability program encompassing investor empowerment, the development of coalitions comprised of significant institutional investors, investor campaigns, and cost-sharing of involvement would have a greater impact than a regulated transition to sustainability (Ringe, 2021). Thus, developing broader policy frameworks and adherence to them, and gathering investor engagement could be crucial for enhancing the utility of green bond instruments.

9. FUTURE RESEARCH DIRECTIONS

Zhang et al. (2019) opine that there is an urgent need to study green finance issues from finance perspectives and topics such as green bonds, green risk management, and green governance should be of interest in mainstream finance journals. Although the publications in green bonds have increased exponentially, there is a need for country-level research, with a primary focus on developing countries to better understand the overall state of the markets by exploring the key drivers and their greater impact on the green economy (Abhilash et al., 2022). Cortellini and Panetta (2021) also found that a large majority of the greenium literature places a global focus and not a regional or country basis. The impact of green bonds on carbon emission and energy transition is yet another area demanding scholarly exploration (Pham & Luu Duc Huynh, 2020). Additionally, understanding the far-reaching implication of green bond issuance can also be vital for market growth.

REFERENCES

Abhilash, S., Shenoy, S. S., & Shetty, D. K. (2022). A state-of-the-art overview of green bond markets: Evidence from technology empowered systematic literature review. *Cogent Economics & Finance*, *10*(1), 2135834. doi:10.1080/23322039.2022.2135834

Agliardi, E., & Agliardi, R. (2019). Financing environmentally-sustainable projects with green bonds. *Environment and Development Economics*, *24*(6), 608–623. doi:10.1017/S1355770X19000020

Ahmed, R., Yusuf, F., & Ishaque, M. (2023). Green bonds as a bridge to the UN sustainable development goals on environment: A climate change empirical investigation. *International Journal of Finance & Economics*, ijfe.2787. doi:10.1002/ijfe.2787

Bachelet, M. J., Becchetti, L., & Manfredonia, S. (2019). The Green Bonds Premium Puzzle: The Role of Issuer Characteristics and Third-Party Verification. *Sustainability (Basel)*, *11*(4), 1098. doi:10.3390u11041098

Baker, M., Bergstresser, D., Serafeim, G., & Wurgler, J. (2018). *Financing the Response to Climate Change: The Pricing and Ownership of U.S. Green Bonds*. NBER. doi:10.3386/w25194

Bengtsson, M., Alfredsson, E., Cohen, M., Lorek, S., & Schroeder, P. (2018). Transforming systems of consumption and production for achieving the sustainable development goals: Moving beyond efficiency. *Sustainability Science*, *13*(6), 1533–1547. Advance online publication. doi:10.100711625-018-0582-1 PMID:30546486

Bhutta, U. S., Tariq, A., Farrukh, M., Raza, A., & Iqbal, M. K. (2022). Green bonds for sustainable development: Review of literature on development and impact of green bonds. *Technological Forecasting and Social Change*, *175*, 121378. doi:10.1016/j.techfore.2021.121378

Chava, S. (2014). Environmental externalities and cost of capital. *Management Science*, *60*(9), 2223–2247. Advance online publication. doi:10.1287/mnsc.2013.1863

Commission on Environment. (1987). *Report of the World Commission on Environment and Development: Our Common Future Towards Sustainable Development 2. Part II. Common Challenges Population and Human Resources 4*. World Commission.

Cortellini, G., & Panetta, I. C. (2021). Green Bond: A Systematic Literature Review for Future Research Agendas. *Journal of Risk and Financial Management*, *14*(12), 589. doi:10.3390/jrfm14120589

Dawes, J. H. P. (2022). SDG interlinkage networks: Analysis, robustness, sensitivities, and hierarchies. *World Development*, *149*, 105693. doi:10.1016/j.worlddev.2021.105693

Dong, X., Xiong, Y., Nie, S., & Yoon, S. M. (2023). Can bonds hedge stock market risks? Green bonds vs conventional bonds. *Finance Research Letters*, *52*, 103367. doi:10.1016/j.frl.2022.103367

Dorfleitner, G., Utz, S., & Zhang, R. (2022). The pricing of green bonds: External reviews and the shades of green. *Review of Managerial Science*, *16*(3), 797–834. doi:10.100711846-021-00458-9

Fatica, S., Panzica, R., & Rancan, M. (2021). The pricing of green bonds: Are financial institutions special? *Journal of Financial Stability*, *54*, 100873. doi:10.1016/j.jfs.2021.100873

Flammer, C. (2020). Green Bonds: Effectiveness and Implications for Public Policy. *Environmental and Energy Policy and the Economy, 1*, 95–128. doi:10.1086/706794

Flammer, C. (2021). Corporate green bonds. *Journal of Financial Economics, 142*(2), 499–516. doi:10.1016/j.jfineco.2021.01.010

Fu, B., Wang, S., Zhang, J., Hou, Z., & Li, J. (2019). Unravelling the complexity in achieving the 17 sustainable-development goals. *National Science Review, 6*(3), 386–388. doi:10.1093/nsr/nwz038 PMID:34691883

Gianfrate, G., & Peri, M. (2019). The green advantage: Exploring the convenience of issuing green bonds. *Journal of Cleaner Production, 219*, 127–135. doi:10.1016/j.jclepro.2019.02.022

Gilchrist, D., Yu, J., & Zhong, R. (2021). The Limits of Green Finance: A Survey of Literature in the Context of Green Bonds and Green Loans. *Sustainability (Basel), 13*(2), 478. doi:10.3390u13020478

Hachenberg, B., & Schiereck, D. (2018). Are green bonds priced differently from conventional bonds? *Journal of Asset Management, 19*(6), 371–383. doi:10.105741260-018-0088-5

Harrison, C. (2023). [*Climate Bonds Initiative.*]. *Green Bond Pricing in the Primary Market, H2*, 2022.

Heydari, H., Taleizadeh, A. A., & Jolai, F. (2023). Financing a two-stage sustainable supply chain using green bonds: Preventing environmental pollution and waste generation. *Engineering Applications of Artificial Intelligence, 117*, 105583. doi:10.1016/j.engappai.2022.105583

IPCC. (2022). IPCC Sixth Assessment Report Impacts, Adaptation and Vulnerability. *IPCC Sixth Assessment Report*. IPCC.

Jankovic, I., Vasic, V., & Kovacevic, V. (2022). Does transparency matter? Evidence from panel analysis of the EU government green bonds. *Energy Economics, 114*, 106325. doi:10.1016/j.eneco.2022.106325

Kotsantonis, S., & Serafeim, G. (2019). Four Things No One Will Tell You About ESG Data. *The Bank of America Journal of Applied Corporate Finance, 31*(2), 50–58. Advance online publication. doi:10.1111/jacf.12346

Larcker, D. F., & Watts, E. M. (2020). Where's the greenium? *Journal of Accounting and Economics, 69*(2-3), 101312. doi:10.1016/j.jacceco.2020.101312

Lebelle, M., Lajili Jarjir, S., & Sassi, S. (2022). The effect of issuance documentation disclosure and readability on liquidity: Evidence from green bonds. *Global Finance Journal, 51*, 100678. doi:10.1016/j.gfj.2021.100678

MacAskill, S., Roca, E., Liu, B., Stewart, R. A., & Sahin, O. (2021). Is there a green premium in the green bond market? Systematic literature review revealing premium determinants. *Journal of Cleaner Production, 280*, 124491. doi:10.1016/j.jclepro.2020.124491

Maltais, A., & Nykvist, B. (2020). Understanding the role of green bonds in advancing sustainability. *Journal of Sustainable Finance & Investment*, 1–20. doi:10.1080/20430795.2020.1724864

Martiradonna, M., Romagnoli, S., & Santini, A. (2023). The beneficial role of green bonds as a new strategic asset class: Dynamic dependencies, allocation and diversification before and during the pandemic era. *Energy Economics*, *120*, 106587. doi:10.1016/j.eneco.2023.106587

Mensah, J. (2019). Sustainable development: Meaning, history, principles, pillars, and implications for human action: Literature review. *Editorial Manager*, *5*(1). doi:10.1080/23311886.2019.1653531

Migliorelli, M. (2021). What Do We Mean by Sustainable Finance? Assessing Existing Frameworks and Policy Risks. *Sustainability (Basel)*, *13*(2), 975. doi:10.3390u13020975

Nordhaus, W. (2018). Projections and Uncertainties about Climate Change in an Era of Minimal Climate Policies †. *American Economic Journal. Economic Policy*, *10*(3), 333–360. doi:10.1257/pol.20170046

Pham, L., & Luu Duc Huynh, T. (2020). How does investor attention influence the green bond market? *Finance Research Letters*, *35*, 101533. doi:10.1016/j.frl.2020.101533

Reboredo, J. C., Ugolini, A., & Ojea-Ferreiro, J. (2022). Do green bonds de-risk investment in low-carbon stocks? *Economic Modelling*, *108*, 105765. doi:10.1016/j.econmod.2022.105765

Ringe, W.-G. (2021). Investor-led Sustainability in Corporate Governance. SSRN *Electronic Journal*. https://doi.org/ doi:10.2139/ssrn.3958960

Sangiorgi, I., & Schopohl, L. (2021). Why do institutional investors buy green bonds: Evidence from a survey of European asset managers. *International Review of Financial Analysis*, *75*, 101738. doi:10.1016/j.irfa.2021.101738

Tang, D. Y., & Zhang, Y. (2020). Do shareholders benefit from green bonds? *Journal of Corporate Finance*, *61*, 101427. doi:10.1016/j.jcorpfin.2018.12.001

The World in 2050. (2018). *Transformations to Achieve the Sustainable Development Goals Report prepared by The World in 2050 initiative*. The World in 2050. www.twi2050.org

United Nations. (2022). *The Sustainable Development Goals Report*. UN.

Zhang, D., Zhang, Z., & Managi, S. (2019). A bibliometric analysis on green finance: Current status, development, and future directions. *Finance Research Letters*, *29*, 425–430. doi:10.1016/j.frl.2019.02.003

Ziolo, M., Bak, I., & Cheba, K. (2020). THE ROLE OF SUSTAINABLE FINANCE IN ACHIEVING SUSTAINABLE DEVELOPMENT GOALS: DOES IT WORK? *Technological and Economic Development of Economy*, *27*(1), 45–70. doi:10.3846/tede.2020.13863

ENDNOTES

1. Transforming Our World: The 2030 Agenda for Sustainable Development, 2015
2. www.morganstanley.com/ideas/green-bond-boom
3. www.climatebonds.net/climate-bonds-standard-v3
4. Sustainable Debt Market Summary Q3 2022, accessible from https://www.climatebonds.net/resources/reports/q3-2022-market-summary

5   www.climatebonds.net/resources/understanding
6   www.icmagroup.org/sustainable-finance/the-principles-guidelines-and-handbooks/green-bond-principles-gbp/
7   www.climatebonds.net/climate-bonds-standard-v3
8   www.unctad.org/topic/trade-and-environment/circular-economy

Chapter 11
Factors Affecting the Purchase Intention of Indian Youths:
Special Reference to the Textile and Clothing Industry

Akamsha Krishnan
Amity University, Noida, India

Shivani Mehta
Amity University, Noida, India

ABSTRACT

The objective of the study is to identify the factors affecting purchase intention of consumers while purchasing green clothes and textiles using theory of planned behavior (TPB) and theory of reasoned actions (TRA). Furthermore, the study intends to investigate gender disparities in green purchasing intentions. The study employs a quantitative and qualitative method, with sample size of 384 youths through a self-administer five-point Likert scale-based questionnaire. For data analysis, exploratory factor analysis, and multiple regression analysis, and a Mann-Whitney U test has been adopted. The empirical findings reveal that the female consumers are more likely than male consumers to purchase green items. The results of the study will provide better understanding of different factors that can influence purchase intention towards sustainable fashion and offer some useful insights to help the marketers and firms.

INTRODUCTION

One of the biggest markets in the world, India offers great potential for sustainable goods. However, there is so little information available about Indian consumer's sustainable purchasing habits, foreign green and sustainable marketers have difficulty reaching India consumers. To penetrate the Indian sustainable market, foreign green and sustainable marketers should invest in research to understand the sustainable purchasing behavior of Indian buyers. The current study examines the influence of crucial characteristics

DOI: 10.4018/978-1-6684-8969-7.ch011

on the long-term purchasing behavior of young consumers in Delhi, India's capital. This can aid in the construction of a sustainable market in India.

The textile industry is one sector that has a significant impact on the environment. The production of textiles requires vast amounts of water, and the treatment and dyeing process contributes to water contamination. Not every consumer understands that a solitary cotton shirt requires 2,700 liters of water and solitary sets of pants need 6,800 liters of water. Synthetic fiber utilizes less water to produce, yet coloring both cotton and manufactures textile requires 4,92,00000 liters of water every year. Apparel processing and coloring are answerable for 20 percent of worldwide water pollution (AEPC, 2022).

The traditional Indian family structure was a longstanding joint family model that propagated a collectivist ideology and housed several generations under one roof, albeit recent socio-economic transformations, such as liberalism, globalization, and urbanization, have led to the disintegration of collectivist cultures in India and ushered in nuclear family arrangements. However, a sizeable portion of Indian families still cling to collectivist tenets. Critics have chastised the fashion industry for their inhumane practices involving child labour, animal welfare violations, textile pollution stemming from production process, use of non-renewable resources, and excessive packaging, thereby infringing both socio-economic and environmental rights. As a result, a textile manufacturer would not only think about fashionable, aesthetically pleasing patterns but also more environmentally friendly production techniques, or to put it another way essentially an eco-life cycle analysis approach.

BACKGROUND

One of the most important problems is environmental deterioration, which leads to the overuse of natural resources, the use of inappropriate production techniques, and increased consumption. Modern civilization in environmental degradation also influences consumer's purchasing behaviour of consumers who choose environmentally friendly products. Rising social inequality, globalization processes and industrialization of economies have resulted in negative effects of social and economic growth on modern civilization in addition to growth.

Serious environmental problems including pollution, resource depletion, growing greenhouse gas emissions, and global warming are caused by today's unsustainable patterns of consumerism. Due to these difficulties, the "green" movement was sparked, which in turn increased consumer demand for green goods. Elkington (Elkington, J., 1994) drew attention to the fact that consumers avoid purchasing items that use excessive amounts of energy, cause waste, contain materials from threatened or endangered species, harm animals, or even constitute animal cruelty. The institutionalization of an open trade policy and the expansion of its financial system have contributed to India's phenomenal economic growth over the past 20 years (Agrawal, 2015). (Agrawal, 2015). However, India's rapid economic expansion has had a number of unwanted side effects.

In 2018, the domestic textile and clothing sector in India accounted for 14 percent of industrial production, roughly 2 percent of the country's GDP (Apparel Consumption Trends in India, 2018). However, this excessive use of natural resources to satisfy rising demand exerts great pressure on the environment and is responsible for negative externalities with a 20 percent of the industrial water pollution and 4 percent of greenhouse gas emissions worldwide (World Bank, 2020). Moreover, an estimated 50 percent of the fabric is lost during the production process, and fast fashion trends cause 81 percent of all manufactured garments to wind up in landfills (AEPC, 2022). Hence, the textile and clothing industry is considered ecologically one of the most polluting industries globally (A. K. Roy Choudhury, 2014).

Due to the challenges of global warming, nations and people are nowadays very concerned about environmental protection. The confluence of these challenges has engendered the advent of novel enterprises like green businesses, thereby enriching the entrepreneurial landscape and this has led to the emergence of a new kind of business: Green Business. The businesses that claim to be eco-friendly and care about society are called green businesses, their marketing philosophy is called green marketing and eco-friendly products are called green products. Given the growing significance of the Sustainable Development Goals (SDGs), this study dwells deepen into the concept of green innovation of clothing brands and green purchase intentions. The shift in consumer behaviour from egocentrism to ecocentrism is becoming more and more significant as concern for the environment and for people grows. This is connected to the development of a new awareness among consumers who are more sensitive of the environment, their health and safety, greater quality, and other people's needs while making purchases (Brya, P., 2019).

In order to protect the environment, green goods employ energy efficient resources and reduce the use of hazardous chemicals and waste. (Ottman, 1992). The concern that consumers have for their environment may have been articulated, but it is not necessarily translated into real acceptance of or purchases of green items. This explains why consumers don't engage in many sustainable purchase habits. It should come as no surprise that Dangelico and Vocalelli consider environmental sustainability to be the third goal, after customer satisfaction and earning profit for an organization. Companies recognised these pressures and began to remedy the situation by greening their business (Henion & Kinnear, 1976; Schaper, 2002). Therefore, there is an urgent need to identify factors that determine and limit its growth.

The market for green products is viewed as a sector with tremendous growth potential, generating benefits to the economy and new employment while also being crucial to moving economies towards a sustainable environment Despite the fact that consumers in both developed and developing nations are increasingly eager to make eco-friendly purchases, the fashion sector still generates over 53 million tonnes of fibre yearly, 70 percent of which is thrown away or burned.

According to Tan Booi Chen and Lau Teck Chai (2010), green shopping can be summed up as favoring environmentally friendly items while avoiding those that are harmful to the environment. The market for green products is now seen as a sector with strong growth in industrialized countries.

Young consumers are more receptive to new ideas, are better able to understand the value of sustainable consumption and are more concerned about social and environmental issues. Understanding young people's attitudes towards environmentally responsible behavior is important since they will be future customers and representatives of society. Youth consumers were chosen as the study's population due to their significance in bringing about the intended change in terms of sustainable consumption. (M. Kanchanapibul et al., 2014). As a result, the activities of all groups of stakeholders are being driven by an increasing awareness of shifting consumer preferences and urgency of acting to address ecological problems.

Research Gap

Among the various socio-demographic variables in environmental studies, gender has received relatively little attention, especially in the context of growing markets. Men and women have different interests and preferences when making purchase decisions. The gender of the buyer influences their intention to purchase green products. According to Fisher and Arnold (Fisher, E.; Arnold, S.J., 1994), women are more sensitive to environmental issues than men because they go through different socialisation processes that can explain their behavioral differences. Women are more compassionate, social, and empathetic about the environment than men. Hence, this study compares and assesses the inter gender differences of green purchasing of clothes.

Research Objective

1. To identify the variables that affect consumer's intention to buy in the textile and apparel sector.
2. To analyse the variations in green purchase intentions across genders.
3. To suggest measures to encourage youth to adopt green clothing purchase intentions.

Research Questions

The variables influencing Indian consumer's willingness to buy environmentally friendly items are the focus of this study project. The following questions were developed to extract the information required for our study.

1. Does gender have any influence on the intent to buy clothes that are environmentally friendly?
2. Which one out of environmental knowledge or environmental consciousness has a significant influence on the intention to buy green clothing?
3. How does consumer attitude affect intentions to buy eco-friendly clothing?
4. How do subjective norms affect the intentions to buy garments that are environmentally friendly?
5. What steps may be taken to raise consumer interest in and adoption of eco-friendly clothing in India?

By analysing the impact of sociodemographic factors on the strategy for green purchasing, businesses may improve in their marketing plan in terms of the effectiveness of their operations. Therefore, the suggested actions will also help the firms adopt the best business plan.

Significance of the Study

The goal of this study is to better understand the variables that affect consumer's willingness to pay for organic clothes in India, a rising industry. Gaining a holistic knowledge of the elements that impact purchase intention for organic apparel is the specific research challenge addressed in the study. Consumers around the world and in emerging economies have started to realise the value of sustainability and also appreciate the fact that organic clothing is better for the skin and human health. The educated youth showed great interest in green products, but there were still some barriers to greening, such as the availability of substitute products, counterfeit brands, process redesign and cost (Polonsky & Rosenberger, 2001). The changing trends and demands of consumers opened an arena for green marketers (Lin, Tan & Geng, 2013).

The textile and garment sector, one of India's most promising industries, provides 2.3 percent of the country's GDP and represents 7 percent of total industrial production in terms of value. India's exports of textiles and clothing have increase by 41 percent (Fashion Industry Statistics, India, 2022). A recent study has shown that buyers in India consider sustainable manufacturing process as the most important factor for consuming sustainable fashion products. Consumer's and researcher's interest in sustainable clothing is growing these days. In addition to expanding their own market potential businesses are also introducing sustainable garment items in an effort to jump on the promising bandwagon and expand India's organic apparel industry. There are so many alignments in the business community towards a call for environmental protection and corporate social responsibility. Consumers are aware of various government policies, environmental values, and environmental sustainability. They give preference to green brands and buy environmentally friendly products that carry a certified eco-label. Environmentally conscious consumers expect loyalty from the manufacturers when they buy green products. Therefore, it is important to research customer preferences and buying intentions.

The two most major generations of consumers of clothing are Generation Y and Z. Consumers from Generation Y, sometimes, known as "Millennials", who were born between 1980 and 1994, are particularly fond of fashion goods, especially apparel (hill & lee et al., 2012). According to Bakewell & Mitchell's 2003 citation, this generation spends 70 percents of its income on apparel and accessories. Generation Z sometimes referred to as the "internet generation" is made up of people who were born between 1995 and 2010. (Chaturvedi et al., 2011). People are more inclined to adopt new behaviors and utilize environmentally friendly goods. Younger consumers are more receptive to new ideas, aware of the value of sustainable consumption and concerned about social and environmental concerns (Singh, 2009). Additionally younger consumers are likely to live longer, which can contribute to the beneficial shift being maintained and handed on to future generations. The findings of the study will therefore improve understanding of many aspects that might affect consumer's attitudes and purchase intention towards sustainable fashion and related items utilizing the responses from our target demographic. To ensure that the good change is sustained and passed on to future generations. Hence, using the responses from our target population, the results of this study would provide better understanding of different factors that can influence consumer's attitude and purchase intention towards sustainable fashion and corresponding products.

Younger generations are more skeptical of corporate operations and have a greater understanding of environmental conservation. They also demonstrate a great capability of influencing other family members' purchasing decisions. Furthermore, they have knowledge of how to use modern media. This is a buyer segment with significant purchasing power in the future. Moreover, they have promising potential due to the early acquisition of ecological habits and ecological knowledge. These factors imply that young consumers comprise a large segment of customers who demand special attention, but this offers obstacles to green marketing. Young consumers are more likely than older generations to accept new and innovative products. Moreover, previous studies have indicated that there is still room for improvement in the level of awareness of green clothes among people in India, and practitioners and policymakers must work to increase this awareness (Witek L, Kuźniar W., 2021).

Companies are expected to advance in their marketing strategy in terms of efficiency of their operations by evaluating the effect of sociodemographic variables on the approach to green purchasing. Hence, the suggestive measures will also enable the businesses to implement the appropriate business strategy.

LITERATURE REVIEW

Green Purchase Intention

Choosing environmentally friendly items while avoiding those that are damaging to the environment is known as "green purchasing" (Chan, 2001). The two dimensions of green purchasing that are most frequently measured are intention and conduct. The willingness of customers to purchase environmentally friendly goods is referred to as "green purchase intention". The driving factors that influence consumer's green purchase decisions are captured by intentions (Ramayah, Lee, and Mohamad, 2010). These products are better in that they have a minimum detrimental influence on the environment. These products require minimal packaging, are recyclable, and are made of ecologically friendly materials (Chan and Chai, 2010). They include things like organic foods, energy saving lights, herbal remedies etc.

According to Ajzen (1991), in the theory of planned behavior, intention refers to a person's readiness to carry out a certain behavior, also know a purchase intention. Previous studies have focused on characterizing the underlying beliefs, attitude, and behavioral intentions towards environmentally friendly items in an effort to explain customer green purchase behavior. (Foxall and Pallister et al., 2007). Theory of reasoned action (TRA) by Ajzen and Fishbein (1980) and the theory of planned behaviour (TPB) by Ajzen (1985) were the two primary theoretical frameworks adopted by the bulk of the studies.

Theory of Reasoned Action (TRA)

Two key elements individual attitude and societal norms determine individual behavior, in accordance with TRA (Fishbein and Ajzen, 1980). Perceived behavioral control was introduced to TPB (Ajzen, 1988) as an additional factor influencing individual conduct. It is a sense of control over someone's beliefs they have over their purchasing choices.

They found that environmental consciousness, appearance consciousness, and prior exposure to organic goods all had an influence on consumer's views towards and intents to purchase organic products, an individual consumer's potential to affect environmental resource problems, and product knowledge were all significant factors in the purchase of organic clothing. Their ecologically conscious purchases could be explained by the Theory of Planned Behavior. Their beliefs, subjective norms, and perceived behavioral control indicated why they intended to buy fabrics and clothing made from sustainable materials.

The TRA (Fishbein and Ajzen, 1975) discovered two more components. First, a positive attitude toward a certain conduct may not be converted into actual behaviour due to a lack of social pressure from the person's close friends or, conversely, due to social pressure not to engage in the behaviour. Second, it is a thought that desire to conduct acts as a mediating cognitive link between attitude and subjective norms and action.

Theory of Planned Behavior (TPB)

Individual intention is a term that is intimately connected to attitude, subjective norms, and perceived behavioral control aspects, according to Ajzen's (1991). The choice to engage in a certain conduct throughout the planning and seeking stages is related to this intention construct. The TPB contends that perceived behavioral control, attitude, and subjective norms all predict an individual's purpose (Ajzen, 1991).

Subjective Norms

Normative beliefs, also known as subjective norms, are the extent to which other people's viewpoints influence our decision-making. According to Schlegelmilch et al. (1996), people who believe their buying habits have an adverse impact on the environment experience environmental guilt and are under societal pressure to behave sustainably. In fact, feeling guilty about the environment has become a social norm (Ellen et al., 1991). The influence of subjective norm on consumer's green attitudes was also found to have an indirect effect on consumer's green purchasing decision. (Gadenne et al., 2013). According to previous studies, peer groups and other nearby consumers, in particular, have a greater influence on consumer's decisions to make green purchases (Lee et al., 2013).

Attitude

According to Ajzen and Fishbein, a person's attitude directly influences their behavioral intention: as a result, on their behavioral intention; one important factor in determining a consumer's intention to buy green items is their attitude towards the environment. A previous study on green items and environmental activities has also verified the premise that attitude and intention to buy ecologically friendly products have a positive association. (Aman et al., 2013).

Recent study from India indicates that among all the TPB predictor factors that most directly affected buyer's propensity to buy environmentally friendly products were attitudes among others. Geetika et al. (2017).

Perceived Behavioral Control (PBC)

The external PBC explains how a person may overcome external limitations, such as the time and money required to complete a task (Kidwell and jewell, 2003). PBC measures examine a person's willingness to go above and beyond to obtain a green product, his perception of the product's quality, and his sense of control over his decision to purchase the product.

Environmental Consciousness

An individual's readiness to take action to improve his or her is referred to as having environmental consciousness. Environmental consciousness is the degree to which a person is aware of their activities affecting the environment, according to Kollmuss and Agyeman (2002). According to Lin and Huang, developing environmental consciousness requires time as well as a charge in attitudes and purchase behavior as result, it is important to monito the connection between environmental consciousness, attitude, and purchase intention.

Environmental Knowledge

According to (K. Maichum, S. Parichatnon, and K.-C. Peng, 2016). Environmental information, according to Stutzman and Green, is critical in developing the essential mindset towards green consumption. Environmental knowledge according to Pagiaslis and Krontalis (2014), is the understanding of one's surroundings as an environmentally interrelated system. Environmental knowledge may be defined by a person's understanding of environmental concerns. (Yadav & 2016a) and an attempt to participate in environmental knowledge refers to one's knowledge about his/her surroundings as an ecologically interconnected system and tries to get involved in environmental sustainability's development. In a narrow sense, environmental knowledge refers to one's knowledge about environmental issues (Yadav & Pathak, 2016a) and individual environmental responsibility, which can contribute to sustainable development.

Gender

Gender related concerns have gotten relatively little attention among the socio-demographic variables in environmental studies, particularly in the context of rising markets. Males and females have different interests and preference while buying purchases, men and women have interests and perspective. The gender of the buyer influences his or her decisions about green items. Women are more sensitive to environmentalist challenges. The purchaser's gender has a bearing on his or her purchasing decisions towards green products Fisher and Arnold (Fischer, E.; Arnold, S.J., 1994) demonstrated that women are more sensitive about environmental issues than men.

Men and women behave differently, and this difference can be explained because of the different socialization process that men and women undergo as far as the environment is concerned, women are more prosocial, altruistic, and empathetic than men. Fisher and Arnold.,. (1994) The general consensus is that more women than men are found to be enthusiasts of fashion (Parker et al., 2004), women may be explained by the distinct socialism Hence, they have a more positive attitude towards products that protect the environment.

RESEARCH METHODOLOGY

Research Design

Environmental attitude measurements are based on a scale developed by McCaty and Shrum in 1994. Th test measures an individual's preference for environmentally friendly products over conventional ones and his assessment of how important environmentally friendly products are to protecting the environment. A scale created by Armitage and Conner (1999) is used to adapt subjective norms, PBC and purchase intention assessments. Measures of subjective norms assist in determining the impact of social norms on your purchase behavior. PBC measures examine a person's willingness to go above and beyond to obtain a green product, his perception of the product's quality, and his sense of control over his decision to purchase the product.

Target Population

Indian youths are the study's target audience. According to earlier studies (Hedlund et al., 2011), individuals are more aware about green products and can thus understand the green context. As a result, graduates continue to be the minimum educational need for the target demographic. The young people in the Delhi region are the study's target audience. The changing trends and demands of consumers opened an arena for green markets (Lin,, Tan & Geng, 2013) (Polonsky & Rosenberger, 2001).

The changing trends and demands of consumers opened an arena for green marketers (Lin, Tan & Geng, 2013). Young consumers are more receptive to new ideas, aware of the value of sustainable consumption, and concerned about social and environmental concerns (Singh, 2009). However, it would be expensive and difficult to poll every consumer. Therefore, a sampling strategy was applied to get pertinent and insightful comments. As a result, a sampling approach was used to obtain relevant and meaningful responses. Because the population is so huge, the authors computed a sample size using the Krejcie and Morgan's sampling method and the sample size is calculated as 384.

Data Collection

In this study, a self-administered questionnaire was used to gather data from 384 respondents for the study's quantitative and qualitative components. The first section of the questionnaire is intended to gather information on the respondent's demographic traits. The second section is intended to gather information on the study's goal and is divided into six parts to make up this.

The above table shows the sample's demographics. A measuring instrument is created for data collection by using scale elements from previous investigations. Questions are then tweaked to remove any ambiguity and elicit suitable responses from responders. Table 1 contains a detailed breakdown of the respondent's profiles. The readings of the table show that, 212 responses for from female respondents and 172 responses from male respondents. The majority of responders (65.8 percent) were between the ages of 20 and 25, followed by 21.3 percent responses from the people aged between 20 and 29, and 12.7 percent responses from respondents aged between 15 and 20.

Table 1. Demographic profile of the respondents

Attribute	Category	Frequency	Percentage (percent)
Age	15-20	49	12.7
	20-25	253	65.8
	25-29	82	21.3
Gender	Female	212	55.2
	Male	172	44.7
Education	High School	38	9.8
	Graduation	297	77.3
	Post Graduation	45	11.7
	P.H. D	4	1.0
Employment Status	Student	282	73.4
	Employee	58	15.1
	Business/Self- Employed	44	11.4
Monthly Household Income	< Rs 25,000	69	17.9
	Rs 25000-Rs 50,000	22	5.7
	Rs 50,000- Rs 75,000	38	9.8
	Rs 75,000 – Rs 1,00,000	88	22.9
	>Rs 1,00,000	167	43.4

Note: Data compiled by author

In terms of education, the majority of respondents are highly educated, with 297 (77.3 percent) possessing a bachelor's degree, followed by 11.7 percent hold a master's degree which is further followed by 9.8 percent and 1 percent representing high school level of qualification and P.H.D degree. Furthermore, 282 of the 384 respondents (73.4 percent) were students, followed by 58 employees (15.1 percent) and 44 respondents who were entrepreneurs/self- employed (11.4 percent). Moreover, 167 respondents (43.4 percent) had a monthly household income more than Rs 1,00,000, followed by 22.9 percent between Rs 75,000 and Rs 1,00,00, 17.9 percent between till Rs 25,000, 9.8 percent between Rs 50,000 and Rs 75,000 and 5.7 percent of respondents having monthly household income between Rs 25,000 and Rs 50,000.

FINDINGS AND RESULTS

Data Analysis

SPSS version 24 software is used for exploratory factor analysis and multiple regression analysis to study the data. Multiple Regression Analysis was employed in data analysis to determine the correlation between several independent variables and dependent variables. In this study, the analysis has been applied to investigate the factors that impact the green purchasing intention of clothes among young people.

Measurement Model

The dependability of the item may be assessed using Cronbach's alpha value. A gauge of "internal consistency" reliability is Cronbach's alpha. Additionally, the reliability of the test items selected for each research variable may be evaluated using Cronbach's alpha (Hair et al., 2010). The value of alpha must lie in the range between 0 and 1 to maintain consistency. According to Tavakol and Dennick (2011), a score close to zero implies little consistency while a number closer to one show high consistency.

The Cronbach's alpha values for each variable utilized in the study are shown in Table 2. According to Nunnally (1967), each variable's alpha value needs to be higher than cut-off value of $\alpha > 0.6$. As a result, the reported values for each research item range from 0.651 to 0.906.

Table 2. Reliability analysis

Factor	No. of Cases	No. of Items	α
Environmental Consciousness	384	5	0.886
Environmental Knowledge	384	5	0.862
Subjective Norm	384	5	0.831
Attitude	384	5	0.651
Perceived Behavioral Control	384	5	0.833
Green Purchase Intention	384	5	0.906

Note: Data compiled by author

Correlation

The link between the study's components was evaluated using correlation. A statical method called correlation is used to look at the link between two or more variables. The observation and measurement of the relationship between two or more statistical series are central to the theory of correlation.

As per the results shown in Table 3 strong correlation (0.8006) was found between Green Purchase Intention (GPI) and Perceived Behavioral Control (PBC), followed by Environmental Consciousness (EC) and GPI (0.7521), Environmental Knowledge (0.7354) and Attitude (0.7044) whereas a weak correlation (0.4121) was found between Subjective Norms (SN) and GPI.

Table 3. Correlation

	EC	EK	SN	A	PBC	GPI
EC	1.0000					
EK	0.8157	1.0000				
SN	0.5128	0.6550	1.0000			
A	0.6885	0.6925	0.5132	1.0000		
PBC	0.7694	0.8509	0.5700	0.7289	1.0000	
GPI	0.7521	0.7354	0.4121	0.7044	0.8006	1.0000

Note: Data compiled by author

Exploratory Factor Analysis

The link between the variables selected for the study is frequently evaluated using the exploratory factor analysis (EFA) (Pallant, 2007). Since the test splits all the items into strongly correlated groups, the group set also referred to as the component set has a significant influence on the research analysis is commonly used to assess the relationship between the variables chosen for the study (Hair et al., 2012).

The variables correlation is an essential EFA requirement, but it must not be too high to prevent the development of the multi-collinearity issue (Pallant, 2010). The Bartlett's Test of Sphericity and the Kaiser-Meyer-Olkin (KMO) result must also fall between the range of 0 and 1. The best suitable value is one which is closest to 1. According to Hair et al. (2012), a figure greater than 0.6 qualifies as appropriate for the sampling's adequacy. Most KMO test results are shown in Table 4. KMO value of 0.838 in the findings, which is significant for the KMO test as it exceeded the necessary cut-off threshold.

Due to the satisfactory correlation between the variables, the study data were Qualified and suitable for principle component analysis. Additionally, Bartlett's method was used to check for variance equality. As a result, the research data were qualified and appropriate for principal component analysis by indicating an acceptable correlation between the variables. Furthermore, Bartlett's approach was employed to test variance equality.

With a recorded Chi-square value of around 1561.650 and a p-value less than 0.001, the Bartlett test findings for this study demonstrated statistical significance. Hence with a value achieved, which was about 0.000, this test was declared successful.

Table 4. KMO and Bartlett test of sphericity

KMO and Bartlett's Test	Value
Kaiser-Meyer-Olkin Measure of Sampling Adequacy	**0.838**
Bartlett test of sphericity	
Chi-square	**1561.650**
Degrees of freedom	**10**
p-value	**0.0000**

Note: Data compiled by author

Table 5. Exploratory factor analysis

	Factor	EC	EK	SN	A	PBC
Environmental Consciousness	EC_1					
	EC_2					
	EC_3	0.6209				
	EC_4	0.8352				
	EC_5	0.7539				
Environmental Knowledge	EK_1					
	EK_2		0.6664			
	EK_3		0.5702			
	EK_4		0.5617			
	EK_5					
Subjective Norm	SN_1			0.5563		
	SN_2					
	SN_3			0.6045		
	SN_4					
	SN_5					
Attitude	A_1					
	A_2				0.5007	
	A_3				0.7427	
	A_4					
	A_5				0.6161	
Perceived Behavioral Control	PBC_1					
	PBC_2					0.5179
	PBC_3					0.6286
	PBC_4					
	PBC_5					
Initial eigenvalues		11.654	2.359	1.177	1.076	1.014
percent Variance		23.778	19.941	16.136	4.890	4.373
Cumulative percent		23.778	43.718	59.854	64.744	69.117

Note: Data compiled by author

The Varimax rotation approach, which is a technique for removing essential components, was used for EFA (Malhotra & Birks, 2007). The analysis takes into account positive factor loadings that might be deemed significant. Since the commonality must be larger than 0.7 and the factor number is less than 30, the value must be greater than 0.5 with an eigenvalue with a cut-off point of 0.1. But a cut-off value between 0.7 and 0.8 is seen to be adequate (jolliffe, 2002). The EFA findings show that 10 of the 25 items were rejected because they did not fulfil the minimum requirements. The EFA results are shown in Table 5. The remaining factors were categorised into five categories (i.e., environmental consciousness, environmental knowledge, subjective norms, attitude, perceived behavioral control), account for 69.1 percent of the variation in the variables that were examined. Along with the five components, the variance percentage, cumulative variance, and factor loading were all provided.

Environmental consciousness is the most influential factor (with total variance 23.778 percent), followed by environmental knowledge (19.941 percent), and subjective norms (16.136 percent). Attitude and perceived behavioral control show least influence over green purchase intention which account for 4.890 percent and 4.373 percent respectively in the model. The five items i.e., environmental consciousness, environmental knowledge, subjective norms, attitude, and perceived behavioral control account for 69.117 percent of variation.

Regression Analysis

The regression between the dependent variable, Green Purchase Intention (GPI), and the independent variables, Environmental Consciousness (EC), Environmental Knowledge (EK), Subjective Norms (SN), Attitude (A) and Perceived Behavioral Control (PBC), was investigated using multiple regression analysis. This method, sometimes known as the research scoop, analysis of social science data (Shabbir et al., 2010). Regression analysis is also a method for figuring out the linear connection between predictors and criteria. According to Zikmund et al. (2009), this is the most typical style of analysis used in social science research.

Table 6. Multiple regression analysis

Variable	β_1	Standard Error	β_0	t	P
(Constant)	0.43988	0.212233	.	2.07	0.039
EC	0.28821910	0.534697	0.2778396	5.39	0.000
EK	0.2426482	0.617182	0.2519725	3.93	0.000
SN	-0.1343719	0.330314	-0.1421673	-4.07	0.000
A	0.206359	0.64118	0.1347444	3.22	0.001
PBC	0.3570421	0.605307	0.3460967	5.90	0.000

Note: Data compiled by author

The R square for the aforementioned model is 0.7393, while the adjusted R square is 0.7358 shown by . According to the data, the Perceived Behavioral Control predictor had the greatest Beta Coefficient value (β= 0.3460), followed by the Environment Consciousness predictor (β= 0.2778), Environment Knowledge (β = 0.2519) and Attitude of the buyer (β=0.1347). Subjective Norms, however, had the lowest Beta Coefficient value of β= - 0.1421 as shown in Table 6.

The Environmental Consciousness (EC), Environmental Knowledge (EK), Subjective Norms (SN) and Perceived Behavioral Control (PBC) predictor had the lowest p-value, with a significant p-value of 0.00, followed by the attitude of the consumer (A), with a p- value of 0.001. With p-values below 0.05, environmental knowledge, subjective norms, attitude, and perceived behavioral control are all significant and positively correlated with the intention to make green purchases. This suggests that any modifications to these parameters cause green purchasing intention to significantly increase.

Mann- Whitney U Test

Gender differences have been studied in a variety of fields, including marketing, psychology, and education, and play an essential part in the search and processing of product information (Kim and Lee, 2015). Riedl et al. (2010) used fMRI experiment research to demonstrate that men and women absorb information differently by showing that more brain regions are active in females than in males. Men and women differ greatly in terms of the aspects that affect how they make decisions, according to (Van Aswegen, 2015). Men and women each have different reasons for shopping, opinions, justifications, and factors to take into account while making selections (Van Aswegen, 2015). Fisher and Arnold (Fischer, E.; Arnold, S.J., 1994) investigated the relationship between gender and environmental attitudes and found that the women are more environmentally conscious than men. This difference in attitude can be attributed to the different socialization processes that men and women undergo regarding the environment. Women have been found to be more prosocial, altruistic, and empathetic towards environmental issues than men. Additionally, (Parker et al. 2004) found that more women than men are enthusiastic of fashion, making them more likely to have a positive attitude towards products that protect the environment.

The information gathered from the participants was examined using the Mann-Whitney U test. This test is regarded as the most effective of the non-parametric alternatives to t-test for independent samples of two samples. (Szwed et al. 2008)

Table 7. Mann-Whitney U test

Total N	384
Mann-Whitney U	15404.500
Wilcoxon W	30282.500
Test Statistic	15404.500
Standard Error	1076.204
Standardized Test Statistic	-2.627
Asymptotic Sig (2-sided test)	.009

Note: Data compiled by author

The rankings for tyre brands I and II differ from what we would anticipate if the null hypothesis were true by the amount represented by the value U. If the 2-tailed significance is less than 0.005, then we may rule out the null hypothesis at a 0.05 level of significance. The p-value, shown as $p = 0.009$ in Table 7, is less than 0.05 and is provided next to Asymp. Sig. (2-tailed).

Therefore, we have strong evidence to reject null hypothesis that the distribution of purchase intention is the same for male and female gender groups. null hypothesis that a collection of data is normal is tested using the Kolmogorov-Smirnov test. Together with a degree of freedom parameter, the Kolmogorov-Smirnov test produces test statistics that are used to test for normality.

Table 8. Test of normality

		Kolmogorov - Smirnov		
	Gender	Statistic	Df	Sig.
GPI	Female	0.168	212	<0.001
	Male	0.184	172	<0.001
		Shapiro-Wilk		
	Gender	Statistic	Df	Sig.
GPI	Female	0.918	212	< 0.001
	Male	0.926	172	< 0.001

Note: Data compiled by author

As the shown by Table 8, for females there are 212 data points, hence there are 212 degrees of freedom for the Kolmogorov-Smirnov test. The p value in this instance is 0.000, which is less than 0.05 (stated as $p < 0.001$). Thus, the null hypothesis that the variable has a normal distribution is strongly refuted. The degrees of freedom for the Kolmogorov-Smirnov test for men, however, are equal to the 172 data points. The p value in this case is 0.000 (stated as $p < 0.001$), which is less than 0.05 (provided under Sig. for Kolmogorov- Smirnov). Thus, the null hypothesis that the variable has a normal distribution is strongly refuted.

Table 9. Ranks

Gender	Observation	Rank Sum	Expected
Female	212	43756.5	40810
Male	172	30163.5	33110
Combined	384	73920	73920

Note: Data compiled by author

The first step in the Mann-Whitney test is to create a ranked list of the observations that have been divided into two groups. According to Table 9, there are 212 observations in the female category, adding up to a rank total of 4376.5. The resulting average rank is 40810 points. We have 172 observations with a total rank sum of 3163.5 for the male group. As a consequence, the average rank is 33110.

Comparing the rank and mean of the variable's distribution reveals that the female gender category has a higher mean rank (40810) than the male category of gender (33110). There was a statistically significant difference (15404.500, p = 0.009). The findings show that, compared to men, women tend to have higher purchase intentions for eco-friendly fabrics and clothes.

FINDINGS

The purpose of this study is to identify the variables that affect buyer's intent while purchasing green clothes. As a result, Ajzen's (1991) TPB was used to create the conceptual model. Environmental consciousness, environmental knowledge, subjective norms, attitude of the buyer, and perceived behavioral control were taken as the study's predictors.

While investigating the relationship between the subjective norm and the intention of the buyer, the results of the data analyses demonstrated that the hypothesis was backed by substantial results. The predictor and the criteria showed a positive correlation shown by the value of the Beta Coefficient was -0. 142. Additionally, the p-value was larger than 0.000 and the t-value was -4.07. These results demonstrated a substantial positive relationship between green buying intention and the Subjective Norms component. Previous studies on Taiwanese consumer's intents to buy green items, such as those conducted by, hman's (2011) study and Chen's (2007), provided support for these analyses.

The study's results showed a strong correlation between consumer's attitude and their propensity to buy green clothes. The predictor and criteria showed a strong correlation, as indicated by the beta coefficient's value of 0.134. Additionally, the p-value was higher than 0.0001 and the t value was 3.22. These results showed a strong positive relationship between the attitude and the intention to buy green clothes. The study's results also showed a strong positive relationship between the perceived behavioral component and green purchasing intention.

The positive correlation between the predictor and the criteria was confirmed by the beta coefficient value of 0.346. Additionally, the p-value was larger than 0.000 and the t-value was 5.90. Environmental consciousness was discovered to have a favorable impact on young people's intention to make green purchases. The positive correlation between the predictors

and the criteria was confirmed by the beta coefficient value of 0.277. Additionally, the p-value was larger than 0.000 and the t-value was 5.39. These results showed a strong positive relationship between the environmental consciousness and the buyer's intention to buy green clothes. The findings of the data analysis of the study also showed a positive and substantial relationship between customer's intentions to buy eco-friendly products and their environmental knowledge. Environmental Knowledge had a beta Coefficient value of 0.251, the t-value of 3.93 higher than the p-value of 0.000. These results show a strong and favorable relationship between environmental knowledge and the intent to buy green clothes.

These results were in line with other research on green purchasing intent, such as the green purchasing behavior in Penang (Rahabar and Wahid, 2011) Finally, on analyzing the association between gender of the buyer and their green purchase intention, p value of 0.006 was found to be less than the significant value of 0.50 which shows that green purchasing intention of buyer is influenced by the gender of the buyer.

CONCLUSION AND RECOMMENDATIONS

Conclusion

In a growing country like India, the aim of the study is to pinpoint the factors that influence young people's intents to purchase environmentally friendly products. The results of this study offer a deeper knowledge of the elements influencing young Indian consumer's purchase environmentally friendly products. The results of this study offer a deeper knowledge of the elements influencing Indian youth's purchase intention towards green items using the fundamentals of TPB. The examination of data collected revealed evidence in favor of each of the all the six hypotheses.

The study's findings demonstrate that young people's intention to buy sustainable products is significantly influenced by the degree of their knowledge related to environment, their consciousness towards environment, and their attitude, subjective norms along with perceived behavioral control. An overall variation of 69.1 percent in Indian youth's intentions to make green purchases is shown by the study of five components. The results of the study demonstrate that environmental consciousness, environmental knowledge, subjective norms, attitude of the buyer and their perceived behavioral control all significantly and favorably impact the intentions of Indian youth to make green purchases. The consumer subjective norms, component, however, showed to have a mildly favorable relationship with the desire to make green purchases. As a result, the subjective norm component has little impact on the Indian youth's intention to buy green items.

The environmental consciousness component is the strongest construct among the others, having the greatest meaningful influence on green purchasing intention. This suggests that consumer's understanding of environmental challenges and results influences their purchasing intentions for a product. The second biggest influence is the perceived behavioral control, showing that packaging and increased marketing with detailed information about the product can encourage purchase intention. Finally, the environment knowledge component is the final positive impactful predictor with a moderate impact on green purchasing intention.

The findings of this study provide sufficient support for the connections between the factors used in the study. This research study has shown that gender has a bearing on consumers purchasing decisions towards green products. Women are more likely to have a positive attitude towards environmental mindset by promoting the benefits of buying green clothes. Consumer's attitudes towards sustainable purchasing and perceived marketing impact are important predictors of their long-term purchasing behavior. This suggests that consumers are concerned about the environmental impact of their sustainable purchases.

By highlighting the benefits of wearing green clothing, marketers may promote a pro-environmental perspective. Additionally, as young consumers tend to consider more objectively, messages promoting sustainable consumption practices might be aired in a way that appeals to their reason. Through compelling message, sustainable marketers should convince young people to embrace sustainable buying practices. To inform and motivate young customers, the messaging could be designed to attract attention to certain ecological or societal issues. Hence as per the findings, knowledge and education are important influential background variables for developing positive attitudes among young consumers.

Recommendations And Future Research Direction

In India, green marketing remains an incipient concept, as skepticism about the authenticity and benefits of green products prevails. The government and marketers must endeavor to foster credibility by developing conscientious advertisements, while manufacturers need to commit to producing environmentally friendly products from the outset. This, in turn, will bolster positive attitudes and perceptions towards green products. To promote sustainable practices, the Indian government has undertaken initiatives such as Swachh Bharat Abhiyan and the Indian Eco-mark scheme, yet industry participation has been minimal. Despite this, there is an increasing demand for environmentally friendly products among Indian consumers. Therefore, investing in research to understand the sustainable purchasing behavior of Indian buyers can aid in overcoming these challenges and promoting sustainable products in India.

This study was conducted by focusing the youths of India the future research could be conducted on focusing on other age groups. Future research could be done focusing on examining the relationship between price sensitivity and the consumer's intent to make green purchases of clothes. Price has a significant impact on consumer decision making. Therefore, it is crucial to understand how price sensitivity affects Indian consumer's willingness to make green purchases. Analysisng the effectiveness of price strategies, such as discounts and promotions, in motivating eco-friendly consumer habits among budget conscious Indian consumers.

The analysis of how cultural values affect green purchase intentions is integral to comprehending consumer behavior. Subsequent research endeavors could examine the impact of specific cultural values, such as collectivism and environmentalism, and their connection with green purchase intentions among Indian consumers. The findings of such studies could ais clothing brands and retailers in crafting marketing tactics that are in line with the cultural values of their intended customer base.

Suggestions for Promoting More Sustainable Consumer Attitudes and Intentions

By emphasizing the following actions, the government and marketers must concentrate on encouraging collectivistic outlook in individualistic groups to further increase their willingness to purchase environmentally friendly products:

1. Attitude towards sustainable purchasing and recognized influence of marketing campaigns are significant indicators of consumer's sustained buying habits. This emphasizes the importance that the buyers place on the ecological impact of their sustainable purchases. Furthermore, since younger buyers tend to possess a more objective mindset, messaging that appeals to their logic could be disseminated to promote environmentally conscious consumption behaviours. Through compelling messaging, sustainable marketers should convince young people to adopt sustainable shopping practices. The messaging could be developed to draw attention to specific ecological or societal issues to inspire young consumers.
2. Sustainability behavior such as recycling helps eliminate waste and provides marketing opportunities as well (Ghose et al., 2006). Organizations and state-run administrations should urge reusing to decrease natural harm brought about by ecologically dangerous assembling and utilization of resources. Reusing motivators in the form of incentives could go quite far towards accomplishing the objective. Compensation for such behavior may include concessions on the next purchase if the consumer returns the product after use. Recycling could also be considered as a practice that benefits consumers. For instance, it is important to promote lucrative activities like reselling second-hand things such as apparel, shoes, and electronics. For these kinds of transactions, the internet is a brilliant medium.
3. Price is an essential factor. Even consumers who believe themselves to be environmentally sensitive may frequently choose a fast-fashion alternative from one of the industry's leading players. Sustainable apparel and fabrics are frequently more expensive, and consumers value obtaining a good deal. As long as sustainable garments and textiles are not offered at a low enough price point in the collections of fast-fashion brands, consumers will not modify their shopping habits.
4. The producer's sustainability approach should revolve around three E's: equity, environment, and economics (Invest India, 2021). They should be committed to preserving and enhancing the natural environment by reintroducing more nature into all business disciplines. This strategy reduces the loss of critical resources and will also help in reducing the health impact caused by the same.

REFERENCES

Abrar, M., Sibtain, M. M., & Shabbir, R. (2021). Understanding purchase intention towards eco-friendly clothing for generation Y & Z. *Cogent Business & Management*, 8(1), 1997247. Advance online publication. doi:10.1080/23311975.2021.1997247

Ajzen, I. (1991). The Theory of Planned Behavior. *Organizational Behavior and Human Decision Processes*, 50(2), 179–211. doi:10.1016/0749-5978(91)90020-T

Ajzen, I. (2002). Perceived behavioral control, self-efficacy, locus of control, and the theory of planned behavior. *Journal of Applied Social Psychology*, 32(4), 665–683. doi:10.1111/j.1559-1816.2002.tb00236.x

Armitage, C. J., Armitage, C. J., Conner, M., Loach, J., & Willetts, D. (1999). Different Perceptions of Control: Applying an Extended Theory of Planned Behavior to Legal and Illegal Drug Use. *Basic and Applied Social Psychology*, 21(4), 301–316. doi:10.1207/S15324834BASP2104_4

Lin, P.-H., & Chen, W.-H. (2022). Factors That Influence Consumers' Sustainable Apparel Purchase Intention: The Moderating Effect of Generational Cohorts. *Sustainability (Basel)*, 14(14), 8950. doi:10.3390u14148950

Momberg, D., Jacobs, B., & Sonnenberg, N. (2012). The role of environmental knowledge in young female consumers' evaluation and selection of apparel in South Africa. *International Journal of Consumer Studies*, 36(4), 408–415. doi:10.1111/j.1470-6431.2011.01061.x

Parzonko, A. J., Balińska, A., & Sieczko, A. (2021). Pro-Environmental Behaviors of Generation Z in the Context of the Concept of Homo Socio-Oeconomicus. *Energies*, 14(6), 1597. doi:10.3390/en14061597

Peña-García, N., Gil-Saura, I., Rodríguez-Orejuela, A., & Siqueira-Junior, J. R. (2020). Purchase intention and purchase behavior online: A cross-cultural approach. *Heliyon*, 6(6), e04284. doi:10.1016/j.heliyon.2020.e04284 PMID:32613132

Prakash, G., & Pathak, P. (2017). Intention to buy eco-friendly packaged products among young consumers of India: A study on developing nation. *Journal of Cleaner Production*, 141, 385–393. doi:10.1016/j.jclepro.2016.09.116

Tan, Z., Sadiq, B., Bashir, T., Mahmood, H., & Rasool, Y. (2022). Investigating the Impact of Green Marketing Components on Purchase Intention: The Mediating Role of Brand Image and Brand Trust. *Sustainability (Basel)*, 14(10), 5939. doi:10.3390u14105939

KEY TERMS AND DEFINITIONS

Attitude: "Attitude is defined as a neurological condition of preparedness" writes Allport (1935).

Environment Knowledge: Environment knowledge according to Pagiaslis and Krontalis (2014), is the awareness of one's surroundings as an ecologically interrelated system and efforts to contribute to the advancement of environmental sustainability. Environmental knowledge, in a narrow sense, refers to one's understanding of environmental issues, environmental knowledge is most narrowly defined as one's comprehension of environmental challenges, writes Yadav & Pathak, (2016a)

Environmental Consciousness: Environmental consciousness, as defined by Kollmuss and Agyeman (2002), is the degree to which an individual is aware of how their activities affect the environment.

Green Purchase Intention: Green purchasing intention is the tendency of a consumer to choose a green product above non-green options when making a purchase decision (Hasan, 2013).

Perceived Behavioral Control: "An individual's potential for behavior depends on the level of availability of relevant resources and existence of opportunities to positively assess these resources and behave appropriately." writes (Ajzen, 1991).

Purchase Intention: According to (Ajzen, 1991), "behaviour can be determined and derived with considerable accuracy from purpose."

Subjective Norms: Douglas (1977), defined a subjective norm as a "a kind of belied that people approve or disapprove of certain behavior when undertaking and performing the behavior."

Chapter 12
Can Asia Accomplish the Sustainable Development Goal for Water and Sanitation by 2030?

Madhuri Yadav
Indira Gandhi National Tribal University, India

Sukanta Kumar Baral
Indira Gandhi National Tribal University, India

ABSTRACT

The SDGs are a global call to action to eradicate poverty, protect the natural environment, and ensure everyone lives in prosperity and peace. Asian countries to achieve the United Nations SDGs, particularly SDG 6 are concerned with providing all sanitation and water systems that are addressed sustainably. To evaluate a composite index (CI) for SDG 6 in Asia, data has been taken for water stress, basic drinking water, and sanitation facilities for 41 of the 48 Asian countries. According to the findings, the countries that scored highest in the assessment, such as Kuwait, United Arab Emirates, Turkmenistan, Bahrain, Saudi Arabia, Qatar, and Israel, and might be achieved SDG 6. Whereas the three countries (Cambodia, Afghanistan, and Timor- Lee) that showed low scores in both indicators of SDG6 also had lower overall points in the water and sanitation and water stress-related SDG Composite index. The SDGs provide a framework for sustainable development and guide policies and programs at the global, nationwide, and regional levels.

INTRODUCTION

Water is a basic need for sustainable development and the foundation of life and livelihood (Guppy et al., 2019). Water is crucial to functioning ecosystems, economic growth, energy, food production, livelihoods, and environmental sustainability. All people have access to sustainable sanitation and water

DOI: 10.4018/978-1-6684-8969-7.ch012

management, according to UN SDG6 (Roy et al., 2019). Even though water is "essential to all life," which includes humans and the environment, it is frequently overlooked, at least for those with convenient access to a reliable supply of it reasonably priced. SDG6 aims to mark water resources' value and long-term availability for environmental and human survival, drinkable water, hygiene, and sanitation facilities. The SDGs are framed as a "blueprint for a better and more sustainable future for all" and address various issues. The SDGs 2015, the world development goal, significantly emphasizes sustainable development and aims to address world issues and challenges through cooperative partnerships across and among United Nations members to balance the aspects of sustainable progress: social integration and ecological sustainability (FAO, 2017). The UN framed 17 SDGs and 169 targets in 2015, covering three primary components: environmental (like weather change and life on land and life below water), social (including gender equality, poverty, and hunger eradication, good institutions, economic growth), and economic (including economic growth, decent work and reducing inequality) (Sachs, 2012). The UN developed an indicators list (Tiers 1-3) for monitoring growth toward achieving SDGs goals to confirm that no country remains. The goals are intended to be achieved by 2030 and are designed to be incorporated and undivided so that growth on one aim frequently relies on growth on other targets. The min-max method was previously used to calculate the SDG Indicator, an agriculture-related SDG indicator, and Afro-barometer focused on gender empowerment (Nhamo et al., 2019). The research provides a tentative benchmark for monitoring growth towards meeting SDG6 in Asia, using available data on three components: access to basic facilities for accessing drinkable water, sanitation, and water stress. For evaluating CI for SDG 6 in Asia, data has been taken for Water stress, basic drinking water, and sanitation components for 41 of the 48 Asian countries. However, due to the unavailability of data, seven countries have not been considered in the study. The raw data has been used to determine the composite indices, and data are normalized by applying the min-max method, in which each index was rescaled from 0 to 100. It is crucial to have accurate indicators to track progress toward the goal. The world needs a reliable and standard baseline and monitoring system to achieve this goal. Kyrgyzstan's performance on the economic SDG ranked lowest among the three indicators of SDGs, and it urgently needed to be improved. Besides that, it was clear that Kazakhstan surpassed Kyrgyzstan regarding social SDG performance (Huan et al., 2019). Due to competing needs for resources and severe environmental stress, South Asian countries face rising difficulties in encountering the region's increasing demand for water, food, and energy (Rasul, G. 2016). However, one study carried out at the behest of the World Bank gave WASH a new perspective. By 2030, blended financing must achieve universal sanitation and water access (Leigland et al., 2016). The lowest water availability per person worldwide is found in the Pacific and Asia, which accounts for 36% of the global water resources. While the urban population of the Pacific and Asia is more than twice that between 1950 to 2000, causing an enormous consumption of wastewater and water treatment, approximately 50% of the region's rural population does not have basic sanitation facilities (ADB, 2016). The World Economic Forum (WEF) in 2015 drew attention to the increasing world apprehension regarding water resources, reflected in the SDGs. Although SDG6, named the 'Water Goal', directly targets water resources, the SDGs acknowledge that water significantly affects the overall development agenda (Ait-Kadi, 2016). The WHO Southeast Asia Region has significantly improved in providing affordable drinking water, sanitation, and hygiene (WASH) facilities in the past 20 as part of the Millennium Development Goals (MDGs). Despite progress in WASH provision in the WHO Southeast Asia Region, arranging water quality and wastewater remains a significant task. It is due to the weak tracking initiatives in many regional countries (Hering, 2017). However, access to clean drinking water has improved across the region, despite some countries still struggling to provide adequate sanitation services to their population (Chakravarty et al., 2017). As per the UN (2018a), more than two billion people reside in countries where water stress is a significant concern, spanning all continents. Countries are considered to be under severe stress if their water stress levels are above 70%. Still, some nations, such as Libya, Egypt, Saudi Arabia, the UAE, and Kuwait, have water stress levels exceeding 100% and rely heavily on desalination to fulfill their water needs. While Singapore has become a leader in water resource management in Southeast Asia (McIntosh et al., 2014). The study examined the progress made in the 20 years regarding affordable drinking water and sanitation services. Data from the World Development Indicators has been gathered to evaluate the current status of Water and Sanitation-related SDGs in Asian countries. Firstly, it aimed to understand SDG 6 better, which focuses on safe water and sanitation facilities. Secondly, it aimed to identify trends in the availability of drinking water and sanitation facilities over 20 years and determine whether the countries examined in the study are on track to accomplish specific targets related to SDG 6 by the year 2030. The findings showed in the study offer a helpful understanding of the status quo development of Asian countries' Water & Sanitation-related SDGs.

Table 1. SDG6 ensure that everyone has access to and can sustainably manage water and sanitation

6.1	Ensure everyone has equal access to clean, affordable drinking water by the year 2030.
6.2	Every Individual has adequate sanitation and hygiene, with a special focus on the needs of women, girls, and those in difficult circumstances and ending open defecation by 2030
6.3	Reducing pollution, halting disposal, limiting the release of hazardous substances and chemicals, cutting the proportion of wastewater discharges in half, and significantly boosting reusing and clean reuse by 2030.
6.4	By 2030, Enhance the efficiency of water usage and help sustain freshwater drawdown and supply sustainability to confront water scarcity and, importantly, lessen the number of people affected by it.
6.5	Necessary to establish a comprehensive approach for managing water resources at all levels, which includes collaborating with neighboring countries when necessary to ensure the sustainable use of water by 2030
6.6	Safeguard and rebuild water-related environments, including lakes, rivers, aquifers, waterways, mountainous regions, and forests by 2030
6.a	Enhance global cooperation and capacity-building help for initiatives related to water and sanitation in developing countries, which include advanced technology for irrigation systems, desalination, water efficiency, treatment of wastewater, reusing by 2030
6.b	Promote and encourage community engagement in local water and sanitation management improvements.

Source: Compiled by the Researchers based on a United Nations

Literature Review

The 2030 Agenda indicates 17 Sustainable Development Goals (SDGs) encompassing various social, economic, and environmental issues, which all countries are expected to achieve by 2030. Additionally, the IAEG-SDGs has established a set of 17 goals and has identified 169 specific targets, along with 232 indicators, to track progress toward achieving these goals (Diaz-Sarachaga et al., 2018). The SDGs are framed as a "blueprint for a better and more sustainable future for all" and address various issues. Asia faces significant hurdles in accessing clean and sustainable water and sanitation facilities by 2030. The study indicated that over 500 million people in Asia are still insufficient in achieving essential sanitation services, and over 400 million are also not getting clean water facilities (ESCAP, 2018). Despite that, it is encouraging to see notable advancements in sanitation in some South Asian nations, particularly Pakistan, with 14% and Nepal, with 13%, but Bangladesh at 4%, and India at 3%; both continue to make slow progress (ADB, 2018). In the past century, the world has experienced a substantial decline in its natural wetlands, with approximately 70% disappearing. This loss has severely affected freshwater species that are essential for sustainable development. Water-related ecosystems are vital for achieving various sustainable development goals (SDGs), including food and energy production, biodiversity, and land and sea ecosystems. Therefore, the decline of these ecosystems poses a significant threat to achieving sustainable development (Ortigara, 2018). Asia has marked Development in increasing to obtain water and sanitation facilities, but significant challenges remain. Water management plays a fundamental role in achieving numerous SDGs and is specifically critical for realizing SDG 6. In essence, the sustainable administration of water resources forms the basis for attaining many of the 17 SDGs (Guppy et al., 2019). The depletion of groundwater, contamination of surface water, and ocean acidification have severely impacted water, a crucial natural resource, adversely affecting human health and biodiversity (Biswas et al., 2021). Therefore, there is a pressing need to address these issues through sustainable water management practices to ensure water security (Lutterodt et al., 2019). Achieving sustainable water management practices in Southeast Asia depends on developing water literacy among the countries. As such, there is an urgent need to enhance the water literacy levels in the area to encourage the sustainable usage and management of water resources (Maniam et al., 2021). The UN has announced that sanitation and safe drinking water are fundamental human rights. SDG 6 is intended to guarantee equitable access to water and sanitation for all individuals, as stated by the UN (2018). Moreover, access to clean and easily accessible water is a basic requirement for everyone to live in. It must be accessible globally for all individuals (Amezaga et al., 2019). Due to the fast-paced growth of the world's population, advancements in Economic Development, and the enhancement of living standards, humans' need for water resources has surged dramatically. However, this surge in demand has led to water shortages, becoming a significant challenge to human society's Sustainable Development (Huang et al., 2021). The 2015 SDG has prioritized sustainable Development as an important aspect of the global development agenda. For countries to evaluate their progress toward achieving these goals, it is essential to have dependable baseline indicators (Nhemachena et al., 2018). Vedachalam has expressed concerns regarding the potential negative impact of underreported high-risk WASH (Water, Sanitation, and hygiene) practices on achieving SDG 6. Approximately 25 million people regularly drink dirty water, according to a sample of 245,054 respondents from 14 cycles of smartphone household studies conducted in Asia and Africa. In contrast, 50 million people practice open defecation regularly, and these figures may not have been accurately reported (Vedachalam et al., 2017). Many developing countries, including Asia, continue to face a significant challenge with data gaps, as will be discussed in the methodology section. It was found that Kyrgyzstan's SDGs had performed poorly over the 18 years, particularly in the economic SDGs. Similarly, Kazakhstan's SDGs experienced inconsistent performance over the same period. The study suggests that the SDG accomplishment across Central Asia was not significantly promising (Huan et al., 2019). Besides that, In Cambodia, approximately 18.3% of study from "unimproved" open wells tested unsafe for drinking water according to Cambodian standards (Weststrate et al., 2018). Due to inadequate or nonexistent sanitation facilities, women in informal settlements frequently experienced harassment and violence. In Southeast Asia, adequate sanitation is still a major concern compared to water access because open defecation is still a problem in India. Because of a significant decrease in diarrhea cases from 1990 to 2012, poor WASH caused 1000 infant deaths per day worldwide (Kulkarni et al., 2017). However, 4.2 billion people do not have basic sanitation facilities, while 2.2 billion do not have safe drinking water worldwide (United Nations, 2021). The study uses the advanced Sustainability Analysis to show sustainability analyses of the SDGs' synergy in developing nations, including Bangladesh, Sri Lanka, Nepal from Southern Asia, and Ghana, Rwanda, and Ethiopia from Sub-Saharan Africa for 1990–2012. The analysis revealed significant overlap between several SDG targets. However, over time and between different countries, the synergies change. Among diverse goals related to energy and other purposes, Sri Lanka has relatively more potential synergy than Nepal in South Asia, while Ghana has a comparatively high potential synergy than Rwanda in Sub-Saharan Africa (Mainali et al., 2018). It was discovered that the level of water stress is almost twice as high as in 1975. In 2050, India will need 111 billion m3 of water for household use (Roy et al., 2019). In 2015, approximately 89% of the global population had drinkable water facilities, but around 663 million people did not have such access. Most of these individuals survived in sub-Saharan Africa, with around 408 million and 219 million from southern and central Asia. Availability of domestic water supplies and sanitation has enhanced in the area. However, some nations, such as Afghanistan, Cambodia, and Timor-Leste, exhibit a widening rural-urban disparity in the availability of enhanced and piped water (ADB, 2016). According to the data, just 27% of the people residing in the least developed nations have access to handwashing service within their homes that comprises water and soap (Bain et al., 2019). The study, which was carried out in Indonesia, discovered a connection between sanitation, health, and water (Hudaefi, 2020).

Table 2. Bird's eye view of SDG 6 indicators

Target	Indicator	Classification
6.1 Ensure everyone has equal access to clean, safe drinking water by 2030.	6.1.1 Proportion of people who use facilities to manage drinking water safely	2
6.2 Every Individual has adequate sanitation and hygiene, with a special focus on the needs of women, girls, and those in difficult circumstances and ending open defecation by 2030	6.2.1 Percentage of people who are using(a) Proper sanitation facilities and (b) Facilities of hand wash with soap	2
6.4 By 2030, Enhance the efficiency of water usage and help sustain freshwater drawdown and supply sustainability to confront water scarcity and, importantly lessen the number of people affected by it.	6.4.1 Utilization of water use has transformed over the period.	1

Source: Compiled by the Researcher

METHODOLOGY

The study had two goals: (1) To know more about SDG6 and to identify overall patterns available in drinking water and sanitation facilities over 20 years and (2) to determine whether the countries included in the study will likely achieve specific targets related to SDG 6 by 2030. The researchers used data from the World Development Indicators (WDI) 2020 set of data (2018 for water stress) and the CI, which was used by Sach et al. (2016) to rank countries on their performance related to essential drinkable water, sanitation facilities, and water stress. Only three out of the 12 components were taken from SDG6 goals due to data availability on world data indicators. These three indicators had data accessible for 41 of the 48 Asian countries, including water stress, basic drinking water, and sanitation facilities. The CI was computed using the min-max method to normalize the data (UNDP, 2016), followed by weighting and aggregation. The arithmetic mean aggregation method was used to determine the Asian water and sanitation-related SDG index. Significant factors to consider when weighing the effects of the CI results and ranking countries according to their development. It is crucial to remember that even though the SDG index computation justifies equal weighting, there is the potential to use different indexes on various bases. Each indicator carried a 33.33% weighting, and the arithmetic mean aggregation method was applied. Using the scale, the data were arranged for each index from bad to better (Saisana et al., 2002). A composite index for SDGs, zero denotes worst performance, and 100 indicates good performance, was calculated for the 41 Asian countries. The Composite Index (CI) relies on an approach of incorporating several variables or indicators. Each approach to integrating the element indicators generates a unique value for the CI and a different set of rankings for the data source (Chakrabartty, 2017). Governments failed to set thresholds during the Millennium Development Goals (MDGs) to gauge progress toward the objectives (Nhemachena et al., 2018). The method of min-max is broadly used in various composite indexes like the SDG index, human development index, Green Growth Index (Kararach et al., 2018), Global Innovation Index (WIPO, 2016), and gender development index (Sach, 2016). The arithmetic mean's convenience of application and communication is used to compare it to other methods (Nhemachena et al., 2018). A CI is a statistical construct involving a numerical aggregate of a set of indices used to evaluate multi-dimensional concepts. These indicators often need more standard units of measurement and may need a transparent weighting approach for the sub-indicators (Nardo et al., 2005). It is applied in various areas such as the economy, environment, and society to track performance, examine policies, benchmark, and communicate to the Public (Cherchye et al., 2008). The UN developed an indicators list (Tiers 1-3) for monitoring growth toward accessing SDGs target to sure no country remains. Indicator Tier 1 is found in the traditional data list, and most nations have access to them (Nhamo et al., 2019). The method of execution includes the duties of reporting, tracking, and checking through domestication and localization by nations. The study indicated information for three indicators, including Tier I and II from the IAEG-SDGs (2018), for 41 out of the 48 Asian countries. The indicators are related to water and sanitation. Tier 1 denotes that it is "conceptually clear, has an internationally established methodology and standards available, and countries regularly produce data for at least 50% of countries and the population in every region where the indicator is relevant". It is slightly different from a Tier II indicator, whose only significant difference is that countries do not consistently gather statistics (Nhamo et al., 2018). 6.1. Clean and accessible drinkable water (Tier 2), 6.2. The percent of people who utilize effectively maintained sanitation facilities, and 6.4. Improving water quality, wastewater treatment, and safe reusing (Tier 1). Based on the indicators used, Palestine, north Korea, and South Korea were excluded from the 48 Asian countries due to a lack of data. Moreover, four more Asian countries were not included due to data unavailability. The study to know the progress in sanitation facilities and basic drinking water for 20 years (2001-2020), determine the status of SDGs 6 on the composite index and know if countries can achieve the target. The data were normalized, and equal weights were given to each of the three indicators.

For each country, a linear weighted aggregate function was used to estimate the (CI) of the chosen SDG 6 indicators. This function considered N normalized indicators, denoted as y_{it}^t, with a weight w_i. The formula used for this estimation was applied for each country.

$$SDG6\,CI_c^t = \frac{\sum_{i=1}^{N} w_i \cdot y_{it}^t}{\sum_{i=1}^{N} w_i}, \text{ where } y_{it}^t = \frac{x_{it}^t - \min\left(x_i^t\right)}{range\left(x_{it}^t\right)}$$

Where x_{it}^{t} depicts indicator value i, c for country and t represents time, w_i indicates weight for indicators (i), x_i^t shows the lowest value of indices across all countries, $range\left(x_{it}^t\right)$ shows the difference of the highest and lowest value of each index among the countries in time t.

Results and Discussion of Findings

Fig. 1 denotes Asia's top 10 countries with basic drinking water facilities. These countries are ranked based on the 20-year (2001 to 2020) annual average. Singapore, Kuwait, and Israel maintained consistency from 2001 to 2020, with 100 scores in using basic drinkable water facilities for their population. It can be seen that Cyprus and the United Arab show little decline in water access. Qatar has reduced access to drinkable water in 20 years, and Saudi Arabia showed upward trends in access to drinking water facilities in 2000 with 97.46% and in 2020 with 100%. Generally, the top ten performing nations maintained their performance by providing basic drinking water facilities to their population (Nhamo et al., 2019). Fig. 2 denotes the bottom ten countries with basic drinking water facilities. The bottom countries are ranked based on the 20-year annual average from 2001 to 2020. Only Cambodia registered low progress, and Afghanistan reported a huge upward ranking of basic drinking water facilities for all people. Despite the growth, it still needs a higher-ranking score in accessing sanitation facilities. Moreover, Tajikistan, Timor Leste, Myanmar, Nepal, and India have noted good leaps. Other than that, Timor Leste 2001 data on the World development indicator was unavailable. Fig. 3 presents trends based on 20-year annual averages for the ten bottom countries of Asia. All other nations in the same group displayed an upward trend indicating their positive intentions. The annual averages per country cover the period from 2001 to 2020, ranging from Afghanistan at 35.19%, Cambodia at 38.36%, and Bangladesh at 38.96%. Jordan reported a noticeable downward trend. Unlike, Uzbekistan (93.29% in 2001 to 100% in 2020) has reported tremendous growth. Fig. 4 presents trends based on 20-year averages for the top ten countries. Kuwait, Qatar, and Singapore annual averages are 100. Most of the countries in the group either demonstrated an upward trend or maintained their standards of basic sanitation facilities. Nevertheless, some countries such as Jordon, Cyprus(reduced sanitation facilities from 99.73 to 99.39), and Israel(reduced from 100 to 99.94) displayed a declining trend. In Jordan, 98.58% of people having sanitation facilities in 2000; this figure reduced to 97.08% in 2020. In contrast, Uzbekistan, Saudi Arabia, and Kazakistan showed a positive trend for the same period, with growth in the proportion of the population accessing sanitation facilities, from 93.29 to 100% for Uzbekistan, 98.43 to 100% for Saudi Arabia, and 96.80 to 97.6% for Kazakistan.

The Y-axis in Fig. 5 represents the normalized scores for the three indicators (drinkable water, water stress, and sanitation) and the Composite Index (CI) scores. While the maximum score for each indicator is 33.33 points. The global water stress level stands at 11%, but significant disparities exist among nations and regions, and some areas have hidden stress levels. Western Asia and Northern Africa, with 79%, and Southern and Central Asia, with an average of 66%, suffer from severe water stress. However, Sub-Saharan Africa's water stress level is very low, at just 3% (United Nations, 2018a). There is a lot of pressure on the agencies of the UN contributing to the world tracking and assessment programs for SDG6 to develop effective, precise, and thorough tracking and assessment systems, methods and techniques, and documenting protocols (Guppy, 2019).

Figure 1. Top ten Asian countries' data to access basic drinking water supply services
Source: Compiled by the Researchers

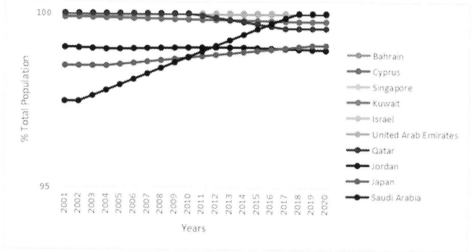

Figure 2. Bottom ten Asian countries to basic drinking water facilities
Source: Compiled by the Researchers

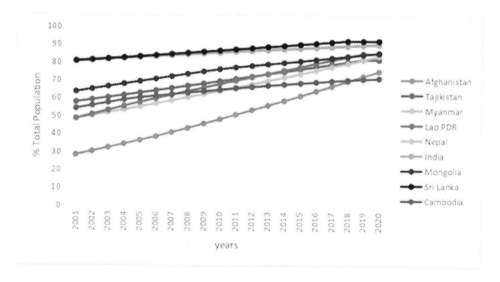

Composite Index (CI) SDG 6

The Composite Index (CI) displays the rankings of countries based on their performance, with the top ten countries like Qatar, Kuwait, UAE, Saudi Arabia, Thailand, Bahrain, Turkmenistan, Israel, Singapore, and Cyprus. The weighted scores vary from 66.89 out of 100 for Cyprus to 100 for Kuwait. While Afghanistan, Cambodia, Timor-Leste, Mongolia, Bangladesh, Myanmar, Pakistan, Lao PDR, Nepal, and India are the bottom countries. The data shows the countries ranking based on the Composite index SDG 6. The table depicts the baseline of Asia's water and sanitation-related SDG6 composite index. The index measures the country's development and indicates to accomplishment targets of SDG6.

Figure 3. Bottom ten Asian countries' data to access basic Sanitation
Source: Compiled by the Researchers

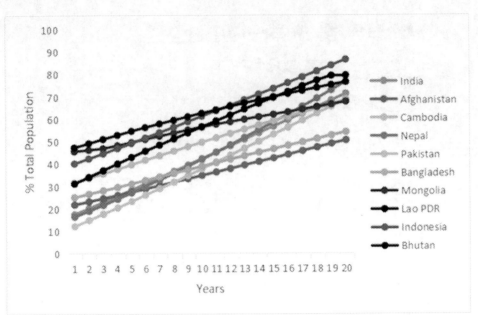

Figure 4. Top ten Asian countries' data to access basic Sanitation
Source: Compiled by the Researchers

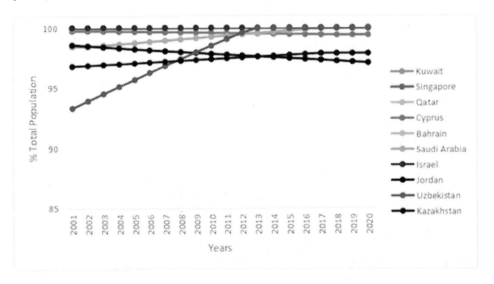

Table 3 depicts Kuwait, UAE, Saudi Arabia, Qatar, Thailand, and Bahrain are the top-performing countries among the 41 countries as per the Composite indices. Meanwhile, Afghanistan, Cambodia, Timor-Leste, Mongolia, Bangladesh, Myanmar, and Pakistan are the bottom countries, scoring less than 40. Kuwait scored the highest weighted score, which is 100. Fifteen countries have scored between 60 to 70 points, and one country, Saudi Arabia, with a weighted score of 75.08. Six countries scored between 30 to 40 points. Moreover, the top ten bottom countries scored less than 40. Three countries scored less than 20, Afghanistan with 4.94, Cambodia with 12.3, and Timor-Leste with 20.98. Consequently, it is hard to tell whether Asia will attain SDG6 because some nations, like Cambodia, Afghanistan, and Timor-Leste, have registered very low scores while others have marked good scores. Achieving SDG6 is critical for achieving sustainable development and other SDGs. Despite progress, there are still significant challenges that must be addressed.

Figure 5. Baseline SDG6 indicators in scatter plot
Source: compiled by the Researcher

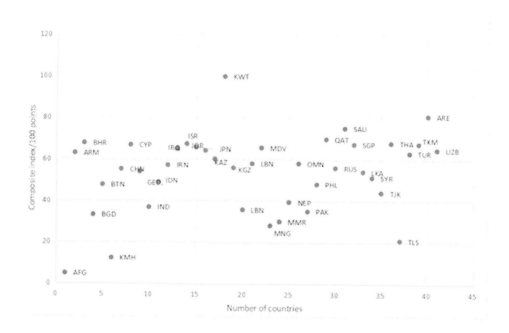

Table 3. Countries ranking on the base of composite index SDG 6

Rank	Code	Country	Score/100 points
1	KWT	Kuwait	100
2	ARE	United Arab Emirates	80.93
3	SAU	Saudi Arabia	75.08
4	QAT	Qatar	69.88
5	THA	Thailand	67.88
6	BHR	Bahrain	67.8
7	TKM	Turkmenistan	67.49
8	ISR	Israel	67.44
9	SGP	Singapore	67.35
10	CYP	Cyprus	66.89
11	JPN	Japan	65.83
12	MDV	Maldives	65.67

continues on following page

Table 3. Continued

Rank	Code	Country	Score/100 points
13	IRQ	Iraq	65.12
14	JOR	Jordan	64.63
15	UZB	Uzbekistan	64.33
16	TUR	Turkiye	63.04
17	ARM	Armenia	62.99
18	KAZ	Kazakhstan	60.19
19	OMN	Oman	58.13
20	LBN	Lebanon	58.05
21	IRN	Iran, Islamic Rep.	57.2
22	RUS	Russian Federation	56.04
23	KGZ	Kyrgyz Republic	56
24	CHN	China	55.23
25	LKA	Sri Lanka	54.15
26	GEO	Georgia	54.02
27	SYR	Syrian Arab Republic	51.38
28	IDN	Indonesia	49
29	PHL	Philippines	48.11
30	BTN	Bhutan	47.7
31	TJK	Tajikistan	44
32	NPL	Nepal	39.47
33	IND	India	36.85
34	LAO	Lao PDR	35.75
35	PAK	Pakistan	34.98
36	BGD	Bangladesh	33.16
37	MMR	Myanmar	30.09
38	MNG	Mongolia	28.15
39	TLS	Timor-Leste	20.98
40	KHM	Cambodia	12.3
41	AFG	Afghanistan	4.94

Source: Compiled by the Researchers

CONCLUSION

Despite progress, it is difficult to predict with certainty whether Asia as a whole will achieve SDG6 by 2030, as progress towards the goal varies across countries and regions. While some nations have achieved important strides in enhancing access to clean water and sanitation facilities, others still require assistance. Achieving SDG 6 by 2030 will require significant efforts from governments, communities, and other stakeholders to improve water management, increase investment in water and sanitation framework, and address the root causes of disparity in achieve to these facilities. While there is still a long way to go, many countries in Asia are working towards achieving SDG 6 and making progress in this area. Most Asian countries have shown upward trends in both indicators except for some regarding basic drinking water and sanitation facilities. Although progress is very slow in some countries such as Oman and Jordon, little downward trends in sanitation facilities have been noted. Same as Afghanistan, Bangladesh, and Timor Leste showed very slow progress in accessing clean water facilities, where 21.88% in 2001 to 50.49% in 2020 for Afghanistan, Bangladesh with 25.15% in 2001 to 54.16% in 2020 and Timor Leste 56.76% in 2020 having basic drinking water facilities. It can be seen that the CI of Afghanistan and Cambodia scored less than 15 points, which is an alarming situation. SDG6 has many indicators, but only three indicators are available and discussed in the study. However, many countries' data regarding SDG 6 for basic access to drinking and Sanitation facilities were unavailable. It makes it difficult to predict whether Asia will accomplish or not. In conclusion, it is critical to note that although the methods used are well-supported by academic works, the study was limited by the unavailability of data for some of the SDGs for some countries. Many Asian governments face water scarcity, poor sanitation infrastructure, and inadequate drinkable water, making it difficult whole to attain targets. To accomplish SDG6, Asian governments should take several steps, including improving water management and infrastructure, building more water purifier plants, expanding water supply networks, and strengthening management and regulatory frameworks to ensure that water resources are governed properly, the water sector should be transparent and accountable. Moreover, Governments should encourage water conservation and efficiency through public education campaigns and incentives for households and industries to reduce water consumption. Governments should collaborate with other countries and international institutions to share knowledge and resources and to address cross-border water-related challenges such as pollution and water scarcity. By taking these steps, Asian governments can work towards attaining SDG6 and assuring that every individual has drinkable water and adequate sanitation facilities. The SDGs provide a framework for sustainable development and guide schemes and programs at the global, national, and local levels. The study can provide valuable insights for policymakers to comprehend the interconnected and evolving nature of challenges and opportunities among countries. It can aid in assessing current development models and formulating sustainable development policies to accomplish SDG6. Future endeavors should prioritize collecting data for the remaining SDGs to expand the study's applicability.

REFERENCES

Ait-Kadi, M. (2016). Water for development and development for water: Realizing the sustainable development goals (SDGs) vision. *Aquatic Procedia*, 6, 106–110. doi:10.1016/j.aqpro.2016.06.013

Amezaga, J., Bathurst, J., Iroumé, A., Jones, J., Kotru, R., Bhatta, L. D., & de Jong, W. (2019). *SDG 6: clean water and sanitation–forest-related targets and their impacts on forests and people. Sustainable development goals: their impacts on forests and people*. Cambridge University Press.

Asian Development Bank. (2016). *Asian water development outlook 2016: Strengthening water security in Asia and the pacific*. ADB. https://www.adb.org/sites/default/files/publication/189411/awdo-2016.pdf

Asian Development Bank. (2018). *Asian Water Development Outlook 2018: Strengthening Water Security in Asia and the Pacific*. ADB. https://www.adb.org/sites/default/files/publication/455071/awdo-2018.pdf

Bain, R., Johnston, R., Mitis, F., Chatterley, C., & Slaymaker, T. (2018). Establishing sustainable development goal baselines for household drinking water, sanitation and hygiene services. *Water (Basel)*, *10*(12), 1711. doi:10.3390/w10121711

Biswas, J. K., Mondal, B., Priyadarshini, P., Abhilash, P. C., Biswas, S., & Bhatnagar, A. (2022). Formulation of Water Sustainability Index for India as a performance gauge for realizing the United Nations Sustainable Development Goal 6. *Ambio*, *51*(6), 1569–1587. doi:10.100713280-021-01680-1 PMID:34932186

Chakrabartty, S. N. (2017). Composite index: Methods and properties. *Journal of Applied Quantitative Methods*, *12*(2), 25–33.

Chakravarty, I., Bhattacharya, A., & Das, S. K. (2017). Water, sanitation, and hygiene: The unfinished agenda in the World Health Organization South-East Asia Region. *WHO South-East Asia Journal of Public Health*, *6*(2), 21–26. doi:10.4103/2224-3151.213787 PMID:28857059

Cherchye, L., Moesen, W., Rogge, N., Van Puyenbroeck, T., Saisana, M., Saltelli, A., Liska, R., & Tarantola, S. (2008). Creating composite indicators with DEA and robustness analysis: The case of the Technology Achievement Index. *The Journal of the Operational Research Society*, *59*(2), 239–251. doi:10.1057/palgrave.jors.2602445

Diaz-Sarachaga, J. M., Jato-Espino, D., & Castro-Fresno, D. (2018). Is the Sustainable Development Goals (SDG) index an adequate framework to measure the progress of the 2030 Agenda? *Sustainable Development (Bradford)*, *26*(6), 663–671. doi:10.1002d.1735

Dutta, S., Lanvin, B., & Wunsch-Vincent, S. (2019). Global innovation index, 1-39. Cornell University.

UNESCAP (2018). *SDG 6: Clean water and sanitation: ensure availability and sustainable management of water and sanitation for all*. UNESCAP. https://www.unescap.org/resources/sdg6-goal-profile

Food and Agriculture Organization (FAO). (2017). Fao and the sdgs. In *Indicators: Measuring Up to the 2030 Agenda for Sustainable Development*. Food and Agriculture Organisation of the United Nations.

Guppy, L., Mehta, P., & Qadir, M. (2019). Sustainable development goal 6: Two gaps in the race for indicators. *Sustainability Science*, *14*(2), 501–513. doi:10.100711625-018-0649-z

Hering, J. G. (2017). Managing the 'monitoring imperative' in the context of SDG Target 6.3 on water quality and wastewater. *Sustainability (Basel)*, *9*(9), 1572. doi:10.3390u9091572

Huan, Y., Li, H., & Liang, T. (2019). A new method for the quantitative assessment of Sustainable Development Goals (SDGs) and a case study on Central Asia. *Sustainability (Basel)*, *11*(13), 3504. doi:10.3390u11133504

Huang, Z., Liu, X., Sun, S., Tang, Y., Yuan, X., & Tang, Q. (2021). Global assessment of future sectoral water scarcity under adaptive inner-basin water allocation measures. *The Science of the Total Environment*, *783*, 146973. doi:10.1016/j.scitotenv.2021.146973 PMID:33866163

Hudaefi, F. A., Saoqi, A. A. Y., Farchatunnisa, H., & Junari, U. L. (2020). Zakat and SDG 6: A case study of Baznas, Indonesia. *Journal of Islamic Monetary Economics and Finance*, *6*(4), 919–934. doi:10.21098/jimf.v6i4.1144

Hutton, G., & Chase, C. (2016). The knowledge base for achieving the sustainable development goal targets on water supply, sanitation, and hygiene. *International Journal of Environmental Research and Public Health, 13*(6), 536. doi:10.3390/ijerph13060536 PMID:27240389

IAEG-SDGs (United Nations Inter-agency and Expert Group on SDG Indicators). (2018). *Tier Classification for Global SDG Indicators*. UN. https://unstats.un.org/sdgs/iaeg-sdgs/

Kararach, G., Nhamo, G., Mubila, M., Nhamo, S., Nhemachena, C., & Babu, S. (2018). Reflections on the Green Growth Index for developing countries: A focus of selected African countries. *Development Policy Review, 36*, O432–O454. doi:10.1111/dpr.12265

Kulkarni, S., O'Reilly, K., & Bhat, S. (2017). No relief: Lived experiences of inadequate sanitation access of poor urban women in India. *Gender and Development, 25*(2), 167–183. doi:10.1080/13552074.2017.1331531

Leigland, J., Trémolet, S., & Ikeda, J. (2016). *Achieving Universal Access to Water and Sanitation by 2030: The Role of Blended Finance*. World Bank. doi:10.1596/25111

Lutterodt, G., Akuffo, F. O., & Donkoh, S. A. (2019). Improving water security through sustainable water management practices. *Journal of Cleaner Production, 222*, 376–388.

Mainali, B., Luukkanen, J., Silveira, S., & Kaivo-oja, J. (2018). Evaluating synergies and trade-offs among Sustainable Development Goals (SDGs): Explorative analyses of development paths in South Asia and Sub-Saharan Africa. *Sustainability (Basel), 10*(3), 815. doi:10.3390u10030815

Maniam, G., Poh, P. E., Htar, T. T., Poon, W. C., & Chuah, L. H. (2021). Water Literacy in the Southeast Asian Context: Are We There Yet? *Water (Basel), 13*(16), 2311. doi:10.3390/w13162311

McIntosh, A. C., Makin, I., Paw, T. G., Dhamasiri, C., Thapan, A., Rivera, P., & White, M. (2014). *Urban water supply and sanitation in Southeast Asia: a guide to good practice*.

Nardo, M., Saisana, M., Saltelli, A., Tarantola, S., Hoffman, A., & Giovannini, E. (2005). Handbook on constructing composite indicators. In *OECD Statistics Working Paper 2005/3*. OECD Publishing.

Nhamo, G., Nhamo, S., & Nhemachena, C. (2018). What gets measured gets done! Towards an Afrobarometer for tracking progress in achieving Sustainable Development Goal 5. *Agenda (Durban, South Africa), 32*(1), 60–75. doi:10.1080/10130950.2018.1433365

Nhamo, G., Nhemachena, C., & Nhamo, S. (2019). Is 2030 too soon for Africa to achieve the water and sanitation sustainable development goal? *The Science of the Total Environment, 669*, 129–139. doi:10.1016/j.scitotenv.2019.03.109 PMID:30878921

Nhemachena, C., Matchaya, G., Nhemachena, C. R., Karuaihe, S., Muchara, B., & Nhlengethwa, S. (2018). Measuring baseline agriculture-related sustainable development goals index for Southern Africa. *Sustainability (Basel), 10*(3), 849. doi:10.3390u10030849

Nhemachena, C., Matchaya, G., Nhlengethwa, S., & Nhemachena, C. R. (2018). Exploring ways to increase public investments in agricultural water management and irrigation for improved agricultural productivity in Southern Africa. *Water S.A., 44*(3), 474–481.

Ortigara, A. R. C., Kay, M., & Uhlenbrook, S. (2018). A review of the SDG 6 synthesis report 2018 from an education, training, and research perspective. *Water (Basel)*, *10*(10), 1353. doi:10.3390/w10101353

Rasul, G. (2016). Managing the food, water, and energy nexus for achieving the Sustainable Development Goals in South Asia. *Environmental Development*, *18*, 14–25. doi:10.1016/j.envdev.2015.12.001

Roy, A., & Pramanick, K. (2019). Analyzing progress of sustainable development goal 6 in India: Past, present, and future. *Journal of Environmental Management*, *232*, 1049–1065. doi:10.1016/j.jenvman.2018.11.060 PMID:33395757

Roy, A., & Pramanick, K. (2019). Analyzing progress of sustainable development goal 6 in India: Past, present, and future. *Journal of Environmental Management*, *232*, 1049–1065. doi:10.1016/j.jenvman.2018.11.060 PMID:33395757

Sachs, D. J. (2012). From millennium development goals to sustainable development goals. *Lancet*, *379*(9832), 2206–2211. doi:10.1016/S0140-6736(12)60685-0 PMID:22682467

Sachs, J., Schmidt-Traub, G., Kroll, C., Durand-Delacre, D., & Teksoz, K. (2016). *SDG Index and Dashboards - Global Report. Bertelsmann Stiftung and Sustainable Development Solutions Network.* SDSN., https://www.sdgindex.org/reports/sdg-index-and-dashboards-2016/

Saisana, M., Saltelli, A., & Tarantola, S. (2005). Uncertainty and sensitivity analysis techniques as tools for the quality assessment of composite indicators. *Journal of the Royal Statistical Society. Series A, (Statistics in Society)*, *168*(2), 307–323. doi:10.1111/j.1467-985X.2005.00350.x

United Nations. (2015). *Transforming our World: The 2030 Agenda for Sustainable Development.* United Nations Secretariat, New York. https://sdgs.un.org/2030agenda

United Nations. (2018a). *Sustainable Development Goal 6 Synthesis Report 2018 on Water and Sanitation.* United Nations, New York https://www.unwater.org/publications/sdg-6-synthesis-report-2018-water-and-sanitation

United Nations Development Programme (UNDP). (2016). Human development report 2016. In *Human Development for Everyone*. United Nations Development Programme.

United Nations Economic and Social Commission for Asia and the Pacific. (2020). *Water Security in Asia and the Pacific: Progress, Challenges, and Prospects.* UNESCAP. https://www.unescap.org/sites/default/files/publications/Water-Security-in-Asia-and-the-Pacific-Progress-Challenges-and-Prospects.pdf

Vedachalam, S., MacDonald, L.H., Shiferaw, S., Seme, A., & Schwab, K.J. (2017). Underreporting of high-risk water and sanitation practices undermines progress on global targets. *PLoSOne*, *12*(5), e0176272. . doi:10.1371/journal.pone.0176272

Weststrate, J., Dijkstra, G., Eshuis, J., Gianoli, A., & Rusca, M. (2019). The sustainable development goal on water and sanitation: Learning from the millennium development goals. *Social Indicators Research*, *143*(2), 795–810. doi:10.100711205-018-1965-5

World Bank. (2018). *World Bank Development Indicators (WDI)*. World Bank, Washington DC https://datacatalog.worldbank.org/dataset/world-development-indicators

Chapter 13
Achieving a Picturesque Global Green Economy by Sustainable Consumption and Production (SCP):
Green Economy and Sustainable Development

Ayush Khandelwal
Mahatma Jyotiba Phule Rohilkhand University, India

Yukta Chawla
Mahatma Jyotiba Phule Rohilkhand University, India

Harshit Saxena
ICAR-IVRI University (Deemed), India

ABSTRACT

The necessity for investments or financing of sustainable consumption and production is highlighted by the green economy. However, unsustainable patterns of consumption and production are the root causes of the triple planetary crisis of climate change, biodiversity loss, and pollution. SCP system aims to build recovery plans and improve production and consumption patterns toward a sustainable future. Now, SCP is accelerating opportunities in green jobs, managing resources that are scarce and valuable, expanding the market for more sustainable products and increasing the contribution of economic activities, and also contributing substantially to poverty alleviation and the transition towards low-carbon and greener economies. Hence, this chapter gives insights into promoting eco-friendly resources, efficient energy utilization, and approaches for achieving global sustainable economic growth.

DOI: 10.4018/978-1-6684-8969-7.ch013

INTRODUCTION

The UNEP promoted the idea of "green stimulus packages" in the context of the financial crisis and worries about a global recession (Pearce, 1989), and it identified particular fields where significant public investment could jump-start a "green economy." It encouraged other governments to adopt large "green stimulus" programs as part of their efforts to boost the economy. The GGND outlined three goals and urged governments to devote a sizable portion of stimulus money to green industries. (i) a return to economic growth; (ii) the eradication of poverty; and (iii) a decrease in carbon emissions and ecosystem deterioration. (UNEMG, 2011)

Discussions about sustainability have risen to the top of the global agenda in recent years. This is due to the fact that it is obvious that the economic model needs to alter based on the most recent scientific research as well as our personal experiences with environmental destruction and climate change (Karl Burkart, 2009). The major United Nations conference on sustainable development (Rio+20), which was held in Rio in June 2012, had the green economy as its main focus.

The green economy is described by UNEP as "one that considerably reduces environmental dangers and ecological scarcities while enhancing human well-being and social fairness." "It is socially inclusive, resource-efficient, and low-carbon" (UNEP, 2011). Many more recent reports have cited this concept, including those from the UNEMG and the OECD. (UNEP, 2011)

Through targeted public spending, policy changes, and adjustments to tax and regulatory policies, it is necessary to enable and support these green investments. In especially for disadvantaged people whose livelihoods depend on natural resources, UN Environment promotes a development path that sees natural capital as a crucial economic asset and a source of public benefits. (Lesser J A., 2010). Instead of replacing sustainable development, the concept of a green economy places a new emphasis on the economies of the region, investments in capital and infrastructure, jobs and skills, and favorable social and environmental consequences. (Atkisson, 2012)

To hasten and consolidate sustainable changes in consumption and production patterns, multi-stakeholder collaborations for the promotion of a green economy are encouraged. UN Environment has extended its involvement with the corporate sector, which is a key player in promoting resource efficiency and the green economy, in addition to governments and non-profit organizations.

What is a Green Economy?

The idea of a green economy is connected to numerous economic theories, notions, real-world strategies, and evaluation techniques. The following definitions, which have been put out by numerous writers, scholars, organisations, and others, are provided to make these clear:

- UNEP (2011) defines a green economy is one that "improves human well-being and social fairness, while considerably lowering environmental dangers and ecological scarcities," according to the UN Environment Programme. A green economy can be defined as one that is low in carbon emissions, resource-efficient, and socially inclusive.
- The Green Economic Coalition (2012) is to hasten this inclusive and environmentally friendly change. In order to give people a voice, hold governments accountable, and promote genuine economic change, we collaborate with our partners all around the world. The green economy is fundamentally altering the current state of affairs in the world. The government's priorities will

need to change significantly. Although accepting this transition is difficult, it is essential if the sustainable development goals are to be met.
- The United Nation Conference Trade and Development (UNCTAD, 2010) defines green economy places a focus on manufacturing and consumption practices that are socially and environmentally responsible. It safeguards the global commons and enables present and future generations to meet their needs by preserving natural resources and ecosystem services.
- The International Chamber of Commerce (ICC) defines green economy in which environmental responsibility and economic growth coexist in a way that advances social development which represents international commerce. The political distinction of Green parties, which are formally constituted and claim the capitalized Green term as a unique and distinguishing mark, further muddies the term's application. So, it is preferable to speak of a broad group of "green economists," who typically support changes that would lead to a green economy, biomimicry, and a more thorough accounting of biodiversity.
- The Organization for Economic Co-operation and Development (OECD 2011) defines "green growth" as promoting economic growth and development while ensuring that natural resources and environmental services that are essential to human well-being continue to be provided. The definition makes it quite obvious that adopting green measures need not impede economic expansion.
- The United Nations Industrial Development Organization (UNIDO) is encouraging the development of industrial skills in emerging and developing countries, and it can be a key factor in accelerating the shift to a green economy expansion. Systematic adjustments are necessary for the transition to a low-carbon, resource-efficient economy, which will lead to new products and services as well as altered business structures and manufacturing procedures. The skills needed and the duties involved in many of the current occupations will alter as a result of the greening of the economy.

These different definitions highlight a long-term viewpoint and are concerned with how resources are used to benefit society. It's not just about using low-carbon fuels; it's also about how resource efficiency and sufficiency may be encouraged to provide wealth, resilience, and wellbeing for today's and tomorrow's populations while also respecting the ecological constraints of our world. A green economy has inclusive and non-discriminatory behaviors, from environmental activities to investments in well-being. It's a model that ensures a considerable decrease in environmental dangers and resource scarcity while simultaneously enhancing wellbeing.

What is Sustainable Development?

The concept of sustainable development can be interpreted in a variety of ways, but at its heart it refers to a growth strategy that aims to achieve a balance between many contradictory needs and a realisation of the social, economic, and environmental restrictions that our society is subject to. To clarify these, the definitions that have been published by a wide range of authors, academics, organisations, and others are listed below:

- Sustainable development Commission defines " Sustainable development means meeting current demands while conserving the ability of future generations to meet their own needs.."

- The United Nations <u>World Commission on Environment and Development</u> defines the development that is sustainable is one which satisfies existing demands without jeopardizing the capacity of future generations to satisfy their own needs. It includes two essential ideas:
  - The idea of "needs," especially the basic needs of the world's poor, to whom top attention should be given.
  - The notion that the environment is limited in its ability to supply present and future demands due to societal structures and technological advancements.
- <u>The World Health Organization</u> says that a broad term used to describe investments, projects, and policies that yield benefits today without compromising the environment, society, or individual health in the long run is sustainable development. Due to their emphasis on reducing the negative effects of development on the environment, these policies are frequently referred to as "green". Nevertheless, the advantages of sustainable development are also felt across a broad spectrum of human health and well-being, including declines in disease linked to pollution and the environment, enhanced health outcomes, and reduced stress.
- With the 1987 release of the UN-sponsored <u>World Commission on Environment and Development (WCED)</u> report, Our Common Future, the terms "sustainable development" and "sustainability" "rose to the prominence of mantra—or a shibboleth" (Daly 1996). The WCED definition of sustainable development has been extremely helpful in creating a "global picture" regarding the future of our planet, despite being widely praised for being imprecise and ambiguous.
- The phrase first appeared in use by <u>The Club of Rome "Donnella and Dennis Meadows'</u> team of scientists wrote the 1972 study "The Limits to Growth" and referred to it as "sustainable". According to the authors' description of the ideal "state of global equilibrium," We're looking for a model output that shows a world that can provide for everyone's basic material needs without experiencing an abrupt and uncontrollable collapse. "

These many definitions emphasize a long-term perspective and focus on the use of resources for the good of society. In order to create an effective legal system that is compatible with the unique legal, economic, scientific, and political circumstances in India, the conclusion discusses the best practices used globally to achieve the goals of sustainable development through recent advancements in interdisciplinary studies. By attempting to manage the paradoxes of growth and arriving at the prospect of achieving sustainable development, it ensures that natural resources, scientific advancement, and cultural resources serve as both the means and the goal of this intricately intertwined process.

CASE STUDIES ON GREEN ECONOMY AND SUSTAINABLE DEVELOPMENT

McDonald's

We are identifying novel approaches to lower emissions, keep trash out of the environment, and protect natural resources in collaboration with our Franchisees, suppliers, and producers.

The resilience of our food supply is significantly at danger due to climate change, as are all communities. By cutting emissions, we are protecting our shared planet, improving food systems, and adapting and securing our ability to feed communities both now and in the future.

Packaging plays a vital role in decreasing food waste. Our packaging and waste management methods, as well as our initiatives to eliminate plastics in Happy Meal toys, assist to keep communities clean, safeguard the environment for future generations, and support long-term business resilience. Notwithstanding systemic constraints, such as limited recycling infrastructure, we are committed to achieving a more circular economy, in which we help maintain resources in use rather than relying on new ones. We want to help protect and restore nature, maintain biodiversity, and work with local people and farmers to build resilience together. We can continue to reduce our effect while contributing to nature-positive supply chains and a more sustainable future by using natural resources in ways that help conserve the environment – and encouraging others to do the same. Learn how our ambitious aims are driving our responsible sourcing and how we are strengthening our company's resilience in a changing environment. Additionally, we are dedicated to upholding the human rights of all System employees.

Dell

For leaders in business and government around the world, talks on sustainability have taken centre stage. E-waste reduction and the effects it has on the environment have been hot topics. E-waste production on a global scale reached 53.6 million metric tones in 2019 and is projected to reach 74.7 million metric tones by 2030. The market for all kinds of electronics is expanding, but there is only a small amount of formal recycling and reuse programs. Simply put, the world continues to be too consumed and wasteful. Businesses have been reluctant to adopt sustainable IT equipment. Most don't have an environmentally appropriate way of getting rid of IT equipment. Making a difference and altering the course must be given more priority. There are still opportunities to manage the lifecycle of IT infrastructure and manage e-waste more effectively.

Regulations and regulatory constraints in various parts of the world control how end users are supposed to dispose of their equipment, helping to keep it out of landfills as the devices near the end of their useful lives. The question is: How can a client solve this e-waste issue while meeting their commercial and operational goals? The circular economy is one of the primary methods for encouraging change in the sustainability industry. The impact of sustainability measures must be taken into account by IT leadership. IT leadership will need to take future e-waste generated by their infrastructure environment into account as part of sustainability activities. It's not simply a fad; it's a requirement.

Honda

When one considers what automakers can do to help the environment, the first thing that comes to mind is "increase fuel efficiency" or "find alternatives to petroleum". Both are critical to lowering CO_2 emissions, which contribute to climate change. That is why, in order to address the challenge of lowering CO_2, we are creating zero-emission automobiles and enhanced hybrid technology. Yet, lowering the environmental impact of autos, especially CO_2, is more than merely improving fuel efficiency. The environmental consequences of designing, constructing, distributing, and marketing a car are also being addressed. Our all-encompassing strategy to decreasing environmental effect in all aspects of our organization is referred to as the "Green Way." The "Green Way" entails minimizing or eliminating the usage of hazardous substances (SOCs) and scarce resources.

MANUFACTURING TO REDUCE OVERALL IMPACT

Cars have the greatest environmental impact, other from driving them. Auto factories consume a lot of energy and natural resources, which we are aiming to reduce in all aspects of our operations. The usage of natural gas and electricity, both of which emit CO2, has the greatest impact. We can discover high energy consumption areas by monitoring energy use in real time. Equipment can be turned off between production shifts and while no production is taking place. Car body painting is one of the most energy-intensive procedures in our plants. We created a strategy to reduce energy consumption during the painting process, which has allowed us to dramatically lower the overall energy consumption of our operations. By implementing a variety of measures, we have lowered our energy use per vehicle by 14% over the last decade. It's not just about energy consumption. We're also lowering waste: less than half of our total garbage from our 12 North American manufacturing locations is disposed of in landfills. And we are now taking steps to generate our own clean energy in order to minimize our reliance on electricity even further. In our Ohio transmission facility, two on-site wind turbines produce 10,000 megawatt hours of electricity annually, which is equal to the typical annual energy demand of 1,000 residences.

Green Dealers

From bright lights in showrooms and parking lots to auto service bays and car washes, auto dealerships have a variety of energy requirements. It doesn't mean they can't also take the lead in being environmentally conscious enterprises. Honda has established a set of best practises to assist dealers in reducing their energy and water consumption. The Honda Environmental Leadership Program assists our dealers in developing plans to reduce CO2 emissions to zero.

Our "Green Dealers" programme encourages businesses to utilise more energy-efficient lighting and to install solar panels that generate all of the power they require to operate. Ron Rossi Honda in Vineland, New Jersey, became the country's first auto dealer to reach "electric-grid neutral status," which means that it generates as much or more electricity from on-site renewable energy as it consumes from the electric utility each year. We are continually challenging ourselves to find innovative ways to lessen our environmental effect throughout the life of our cars. At the end of the day, it's a win for Honda, a win for our consumers, and a win for the environment.

Energly

Energly is a startup in the **Bangalore founder institute's portfolio** that **Dayal Nathan** founded.

The startup specializes in energy analytics, assisting niche markets, companies, and homes to lower their energy expenses. By integrating compelling graphics and context-rich real-time data, they developed an innovative visualization engine that gives end users real-time energy monitoring to drive savings. This encourages customers to actively participate in reducing their energy consumption.

According to the UN, 13 percent of the world's population lacks access to modern power. Another 3 billion people cook and heat their homes with materials like wood and coal, which release dangerous airborne pollutants. Our climate is already changing as a result of greenhouse gas emissions from human activities, and in a few decades those changes will become significantly more severe.

The goal of clean, dependable, inexpensive energy aims to increase access to these types of sources of energy.

JetBlue

In order to attain net zero carbon emissions for its airline operations by 2040, boost the use of renewable energy, and increase the use of sustainable fuel, among other objectives, JetBlue has published a series of short- and medium-term ESG targets.

Since 2006, JetBlue has made its operations more transparent by publishing in-depth sustainability reports. Jetblue and carbongund.org have teamed to allow passengers to donate to programs that reduce carbon emissions, JetBlue takes part in tree-planting activities, has contributed to seven programs aimed at reducing carbon emissions and renewable energy costs, and has offset more than 1.5 billion pounds of CO_2 emissions.

JetBlue is evaluating several technologies, materials, and feedstocks over the long term. JetBlue intends to purchase more than 33 million gallons of mixed jet fuel annually for at least 10 years in order to begin the strategic partnership with SG Preston. The fuel will be a blend of 70% conventional Jet-A gasoline and 30% renewable jet fuel. Based on a life-cycle analysis, the fraction of renewable jet fuel made from particular plant oils is intended to deliver a decrease in greenhouse gas emissions per gallon of at least 50%. The fuel is anticipated to pass both the Roundtable on Sustainable Biomaterials certification standard for sustainable biofuel production and the Environmental Protection Agency's (EPA) qualification for renewable fuel regulations.

Physical Manifestation

As a result of their GHG emissions, airlines contribute to the physical effects of climate change, which are also having an increasing impact on air travel.

First, climate change is probably to blame for the faster jet streams that result from higher temperatures and stronger winds. Jet stream speeds that are higher may make certain trips faster and slower, but overall they are likely to lengthen round-trip travel times[i]. For example, a delay of just 1 minute and 18 seconds every day on transatlantic flights results in an additional $22 million in fuel costs and an additional 70 million kg of CO_2 emissions annually.

The second effect is that flying in exceptionally hot weather will become more difficult as temperatures rise. Less dense hot air has an impact on both the plane's aerodynamics and engine performance. Aircraft weight reduction is a "hot" topic in light of climate change because taking off in hot weather necessitates more energy and runway area.

JetBlue's Focus on the Environment

JetBlue's carbon reduction initiatives center on reducing emissions through aircraft, operations, and the use of environmentally friendly aviation fuels. New targets for JetBlue include:

- By 2040, reach net zero carbon emissions, taking into account carbon offsets.
- Reduction of 25% per available seat mile (ASM) of aviation emissions from 2015 levels by 2030, excluding offsets
- By 2030, incorporate sustainable aviation fuel (SAF) into 10% of all aircraft fuel.
- Between 2025 and 2030, electrify 40%, 50%, and 60% of the three primary types of ground service equipment vehicles, respectively.

- Where practical, eliminate single-use plastics from service ware. Make sure plastic is recyclable if at all possible.
- Keep the domestic audited flight recycle rate at least at 80#.

Nike

Even the most powerful and well-known companies need to take a stand. This is acknowledged by Nike, a pioneer in international sportswear. To protect the future of sports, they want to "Move to Zero," which stands for lowering waste and carbon emissions. Nike's increased use of recycled materials in their products strongly connects to SDG 12: Responsible Consumption and Production.

In addition to "Nike Grind," which is linked with three UN SDGs, Industrial Innovation and Infrastructure (9), Responsible Consumption and Production (12), and Partnerships for the Goal, Nike is implementing "Reuse-a-Shoe" in all of its retail locations (17). Through this invention, resources and products that would typically be wasted can now be used.

Nike's Sustainability Program

Nike continues to make significant progress in promoting their environmental sustainability programs as they are aware that "there is no planet, there is no sport" if there isn't one.

Nike makes sure that its manufacturers and suppliers are committed to their objective of becoming carbon neutral by 2025 through the Supplier Climate Action Program. According to the company's announcements thus far, 48% of its global operations, all of its North American facilities, and 99.9% of its tier 1 suppliers' production waste have been kept out of landfills. In 2020, the amount of fresh water utilized to manufacture textiles and materials was decreased by 30% as a result of this new initiative.

Nike is utilizing reusable and recyclable products as well as more sustainable materials in its product lines in an effort to further reduce waste. The percentage of sustainable materials used in their apparel lines climbed from 41% to 59% in 2020. The company is concentrating on sustainable materials like Fly leather, a material created with at least 50% recycled leather scraps, even though [EE1] [MH2] the utilization of sustainable materials in their footwear stayed unchanged in 2020. Almost 4 billion plastic bottles have already been recycled and turned into polyester and other textiles that are utilized in their goods. Nike is also testing substitute packaging strategies that use reusable shipping totes in place of corrugated cardboard.

2025 Targets

- Reduced GHG emissions by 0.5M tones by using 50% of all major materials that are environmentally friendly.
- Through increased design and operating efficiency, production, distribution, headquarters, and packing waste can be reduced by 10% per unit.
- 100% of garbage in our extended supply chain is diverted from landfill, and at least 80% of that waste is recycled back into NIKE products and other products.
- 25% less fresh water is used per kg during the finishing of textiles, which results in 10 times as much finished product waste being given, repurposed, or reconditioned.

- Replacement of our top 10 chemistries with clean chemical alternatives throughout our supply chain.

COCA-COLA

Packaging

Continuing to design recyclable packaging. Collecting and recovering the fellow of 100 of our barrels and bottles by 2030. Reducing the quantum of new plastic, we use – including all our bottles under one litre being made from recycled plastic across our range of potables, similar as Coke, Fanta, Sprite, Mt Franklin and Pump. Our caps and markers aren't presently made from recycled content, but we're exploring technology options to help us address this. By using recycled plastic we avoid using around,1000tones of new plastic each time. This was the largest commitment to use recycled plastic in the Australian potables assiduity. We're strong sympathizers of vessel deposit schemes across Australia. Not only do they reduce waste, they also give our bottles and barrels the stylish chance of another life. Our bottling mate Coca- Cola Euro pacific mates, formerly Coca- Cola Amatil, has a 40- time history of operating the collection scheme in South Australia, and also helps operate the schemes in Queensland, NSW and the ACT. Partnering with organizations that can help us gauge results. Since 2017, together with the Coca- Cola Foundation, we've invested over$ 6 million in environmental hookups concentrated on reducing the impact of plastic pollution, recycling, collecting marine waste and water loss. This includes our support for The Seabin Project to collect and track the impact of ocean pollution, and EcoBarge on the Great hedge Reef, who collect and upcycle marine plastic and Earth watch.

Water

Water is also at the heart of our business, yet we know there isn't enough freshwater to support our earth. This is why further than a decade agone, we set a pioneering thing to replenish – or ' give back '- the water we use in our drinks. Not only did we meet this thing but we met it five times beforehand. In Australia we give back further than doubly as important water as we use each time. We support water cooperation across the world, furnishing communities with access to safe drinking water and guarding original ecosystems, including the Great hedge Reef. In Australia, we're proud to mate with WWF to support Project Catalyst that works to save the Great hedge Reef through innovative club sugar farming ecycling, collecting marine waste and water loss. This includes our support for The Seabin Project to collect and track the impact of ocean pollution, and EcoBarge on the Great hedge Reef, who collect and upcycle marine plastic and Earthwatch.

Need of the Study

- To understand the importance of green economy and sustainable development among different countries.
- To focus on the green GDP and sustainable development goals to eradicate poverty, unemployment and many more.

- By adopting this SCP system, we can achieve environmentally sound management and benefit the societal goals.

Data and Methodology

Primary data – Data that has been generated by the researcher by himself/herself such as questionnaire, surveys, personal interview, observation, etc.

Secondary data – Data collected by someone else earlier such as websites, journals, articles, books.

Methodology – A way of doing something based on particular principles and methods.

The data for the study is based on secondary data which was collected from websites, books, journals, and articles.

LITERATURE REVIEW

The shift to cleaner manufacturing for a fully sustainable growth of industrialized countries is attracting more and more attention to the research topic regarding the impact of green economy advances on employment. In addition, these economic regions have high unemployment rates as a result of the financial and economic crisis that began in 2006. To examine the advantages and disadvantages of the transition process in terms of costs and benefits, further empirical research on these structural changes is needed.

The phrase "sustainable development" was first used in the Brundtland Commission's in 1987, report on the state of the world's environment and development. The panel defined sustainable development as "growth that meets present needs without compromising the capacity of future generations to fulfil their own needs." Beyond this justification, Michael Needham states that sustainable development is "the capacity to meet the requirements of the present while... assisting in [meeting] the needs of future generations." According to Wikipedia, sustainable development strives to satisfy human needs while protecting the environment so that these needs can be satisfied not only now but also in the future generations to come."

In order to carry out the recommendations made in the report, the Brundtland Report also urged the UN to create the UN Plans of Action on Sustainable Development. The 1992 Rio Summit, which took place in Rio de Janeiro, set the groundwork for the UN Commission on Sustainable Development to be established later that year.

It was proposed at the inaugural Global Public Conference on Culture, which took place in Porto Alegre, Brazil, in 2002, to create principles for regional cultural policy, similar to what Agenda 21 did for the environment. These will be implemented through a variety of sub-programs, starting with the G8 nations, and will be incorporated in various Agenda 21 subsections.

According to a report Joy Hecht wrote for the U.S. "Sustainability has become the customary phrase for summarising the goals of public policy throughout the world," the Environmental Protection Agency stated in 2007. At the same time, sustainability indicators have emerged as the go-to instrument for monitoring public agencies' operations, which include monitoring how much progress has been made towards sustainability.

According to Helen Clark, head of the United Nations Development Program, "If the way that both rich and poor nations develop is destructive of the very ecosystems on which life on this planet depends, then the burden will fall disproportionately on the poorest and most vulnerable people who depend on healthy ecosystems for their survival and have the least means to address it."

The Sustainable Development Goals, often known as Agenda 2030, were chosen during the UN Sustainable Development Conference in 2015. "We reaffirm all the principles of the Rio Declaration on Environment and Development," it declares, taking all of Agenda 21's objectives and using them as the cornerstone for sustainable development. There are now a total of 17 goals that have been agreed upon, all of which revolve around the same ideas as Agenda 21: people, planet, prosperity, peace, and collaboration. (Ramirez et al., 2019; Gue et al., 2020; Niestroy, 2016).

The SDGs are now a widely accepted development plan for the world until 2030 that is utilised by business, industry, governmental, non-governmental, and regional groups (Hametner and Kostetckaia, 2020).

Three conceptual frameworks for sustainable development—the circular economy (CE), degrowth (DG), and green growth (GG) outlined by the SDGs—stand out because they specifically address the interplay between the environment, development, plus society (Millar et al., 2019). Several models have been put forth in prior literature to categorise and identify academic contributions to the SDGs (Engelmann et al., 2019; UN, 2017; Wu et al., 2018).

According to Fulai (2010), the term "green economy" refers to an economic system that is harmonious with the environment, ecologically sound, environmentally benign, and, for many organisations, also socially just. Others, like the Economic and Social Commission of the United Nations,

Green growth is a focus of policy that emphasises "environmentally sustainable economic success to support low-carbon, socially inclusive development," according to the Economic and Social Commission for Asia and the Pacific (ESCAP) (Greening the Economy, 2011, p. 3).

Due to the complimentary and synergistic nature of the correlations between these notions, Kazstelan (2017) came to the logical conclusion that the trinity of "green economy, green growth, and sustainable development" may coexist. The author contends that the economic reform aimed at the so-called "green" solutions. The first requirement for starting down the road to sustainable development is to implement "green" solutions (green economy), which are founded on the tenets of the green growth strategy.

Last but not least, Kazstelan (2017) offers the following definition of "green growth": economic growth that promotes the wise use of natural resources, prevents and decreases pollution, and generates opportunities to enhance overall social welfare by constructing green infrastructure. This allows for the beginning of the journey towards sustainable growth. The author may emphasize the coherence of the trio of green growth, green economy, and sustainable development thanks to this treatment.

CONCLUSION

The categories "green economy," "green technologies," "eco-innovation," "green innovation," and "and green growth" all contain content that attests to the growing interest in the green economy and offers potential directions for future development in the direction of the creation of a set of indicators that are consistent across the board. Their lack of homogeneity at this point is a major issue. Each organization uses a unique set of metrics, frequently with quite different definitions.

We were able to pinpoint the distinctive traits of the green economy and its connection to the idea of sustainable development through the analysis of scientific material used in this study. In accordance with it, the following was stated as the authors' meaning of the term "green economy".

An economic framework for sustainable development (SD) built on sustainable development principles. It guarantees economic growth while being environmentally benign and in harmony with the environment. Several social groups find it difficult to understand how certain environmental policy instruments are implemented and how their views are spread through the educational system. The newly created concept was also used to analyse several models and indexes related to the green economy.

The developers of the indices claim that as a tool for sustainable development, the green economy indicators highlight some of the most crucial components of sustainability. As a result, the structure of these indexes varies and is dependent upon the authors' chosen definition of sustainable development.

A few indices solely take into account the natural environment, some the economy, others the social, political, and so on. As a result, the indexes' structure is determined by how the writers view sustainable development.

Advantages

For the financial industry as well as the environment as a whole, green economies and sustainable development can work wonders. These are the benefits:

1. **Encourages more sustainable development**:

Setting and accomplishing sustainable development goals is prioritized in green economics. Economic entities must responsibly use natural resources while keeping in mind how to reuse and recycle them if they are to be sustainable. This guarantees that natural resources can benefit both the present and future generations while ensuring that they are responsible stewards of the planet.

2. **Helps fight climate change**:

Governments and the corporate sector collaborate to effectively mitigate climate change by directing the economy in a more environmentally friendly path. There is hope that the population of the planet may avert many of the worst consequences of global warming by reducing carbon emissions from both production and transportation.

3. **Improves the ecosystem**:

You contribute to the preservation of biodiversity in all of the world's ecologies when you insist that environmental protections be incorporated into all commercial operations. In equal measure, effective ecosystem services support human, animal, and plant life—all of which are essential to maintaining the economy.

4. **Increases equity**:

The goal of green finance and economic growth is to guarantee fair outcomes for every member of the global society. Green economists argue that industrial countries should bear the majority of the burden for the economic and energy transition to greener technologies rather than largely placing it on underdeveloped nations. This enables the global community to pursue both traditional environmental activities and the eradication of poverty at the same time.

5. **Lower environmental impact:**

The primary tenet on which everything rests and the place where concepts for advancing the economy without endangering nature are developed. It entails cutting back on the emissions of gases that contribute to environmental issues like acid rain and global warming, which directly fuels the hunt for more sustainable and efficient forms of energy. Following this philosophy calls for taking steps to lessen pollution because a significant amount of human activities is to blame for the deterioration of the environment. As a result, the planet's biodiversity can be preserved, more species can survive, the air quality can be improved, there will be more green space, etc.

6. **Future improvement is assured:**

The fact that actions are being done to decrease the effects of global warming and other occurrences like the melting of the poles or changes in such an unnatural climate ensures that future generations will be able to live peacefully given the status of the environment as it stands today. This includes ensuring that the planet's natural resources are not exhausted and that there is an adequate supply for renewal or, in the absence of that, that they last for a long period, as is the situation with oil and natural gas.

7. **Ensure growth and progress:**

Using waste reduction techniques, modern technology that runs on clean energy, and building materials with lower carbon footprints are just a few easy ways to start. The benefits of going against traditional development and choosing to build in a more mindful way for the environment and business operations are perhaps the most clear.

8. **A rising productivity:**

Our performance is improved when we live in a sustainable community, especially in this day and age when we spend most of our time at home or in one place. When we are in a better setting, whether that be working from home or remaining active, we can concentrate better and finish jobs more quickly. As a result, our attention shifts from the environment to our accomplishments, which leads to an improvement in our overall health and interpersonal connections.

Disadvantages

The concept faces some challenges. These are the disadvantages:

1. **Going green takes some effort:**

    Becoming green offers many significant benefits, but it also has certain drawbacks. The drawback of going green is that it takes work to implement eco-friendly jobs and lifestyle changes. The more effort you put into reducing your ecological footprint, the harder it may be, especially if your job is demanding and you frequently arrive home exhausted. Thus, don't anticipate it to be too simple. While some green initiatives could be quite easy to implement, others might require more work.

2. **Initial cost can be high:**

    Although going green is not a new concept, much of the technology associated with it is relatively new and undoubtedly more expensive than traditional technology. As a result, taking steps to become more environmentally friendly can be costly at first. Consider the installation of solar power. This is an expensive investment, particularly if big systems are required. Once implemented, there will undoubtedly be significant savings, but the upfront expenditures may be rather substantial.

3. **High cost of product:**

    Choosing green items over conventional ones often means spending more money. This is passed on to the consumer in the form of higher prices for the organization's products or services.

4. **You may need to do some research and educate yourself:**

    Being green also means becoming aware of how your actions impact the environment and what steps you may take to reduce your ecological imprint. Even if you can obtain this material online for free, it will still require some time and a significant amount of self-reliance on your part to accomplish it. As a result, you must educate yourself and truly act upon this information; many people may find it difficult to do so.

5. **Social isolation:**

    Becoming green could also be very challenging socially, depending on the area. Living sustainably may be difficult if you are in a region where people are extremely resistant to change and where many stores do not provide environmentally friendly products. Furthermore, if you don't follow regional traditions that in some places suggest an eco-unfriendly behaviour, you could even experience social isolation.

6. **Confined variety of products:**

    Although the selection of environmentally friendly products has grown dramatically over the past ten years, it is still somewhat limited, and going green may be challenging in some places. This can mean that you'll need to spend a lot of time browsing at numerous different stores to find everything you want. It could be challenging to locate subject matter experts. Since turning green has gained popularity in recent years, there are still not many industry professionals in this field, and it may be challenging to find qualified technicians that can repair your equipment.

7. **Companies may misuse the term green for their purposes:**

Customers like the sound of the word "green," thus businesses may exploit it improperly to their advantage. For instance, some businesses might assert that their products adhere to the idea of going green, even though they may not be at all eco-friendly. So, be sure to educate oneself so you can spot false advertising before purchasing particular products.

8. **Level of motivation to stay green:**

Starting a green lifestyle is comparatively simple. Yet, maintaining a green lifestyle for an extended period of time can be challenging and requires strong motivation. Many people could lack this drive and eventually give up living sustainably.

FUTURE SCOPE

In a green economy, infrastructure and assets that enable decreased carbon emissions and pollution, improved energy and resource efficiency, and the prevention of the loss of biodiversity and ecosystem services are what generate growth in employment and income.

By targeted public spending, policy changes, and adjustments to tax and regulatory policies, it is necessary to enable and support these green investments. In particular for poor people whose livelihoods depend on natural resources, UN Environment advocates for a development path that views natural capital as a crucial economic asset and a source of public benefits. Instead of replacing sustainable development, the concept of a green economy places a new emphasis on the economies of the region, investments in capital and infrastructure, jobs and skills, and favourable social and environmental consequences.

You might be thinking of Greta Thunberg statements from Twitter and rainforest tree collapses. Yes, these are components of the movement towards a responsible future, but environmental efforts sometimes dominate discussions about sustainability as a whole. In actuality, this movement encompasses much more than just "reuse and recycle," "rescue our world," etc. Sustainability is actually defined as "filling the requirements of the present without compromising the potential of future generations to meet their own needs" in the Brundtland Commission report for the United Nations from 1987. Be aware that evangelical environmentalists are not the only ones who care about "the demands of the present." Instead, it is a modest yet ardent call for reformation in all areas and focuses.

Cultural, social, technical, economic, political, and, last but not least, environmental considerations are all part of sustainability. All businesses may identify activities to support John Elkington's triple bottom line: Profit, People, and Planet. This is true whether they are high-end fashion houses or overvalued internet startups. Although profit has dominated the triad throughout the majority of this planet's illustrious history, earlier civilizations did not view sustainability and profit as mutually exclusive. You should visit Rome, Paris, or Ephesus to behold once-profitable economies that were designed to last forever.

You'll be reminded that, in reality, profit was never the bad guy—makeshift swiftness done just for financial gain is. Hurricanes' devastating effects on affordable housing, quick "solutions" like redlining, and how "fast food" has led to many people fighting protracted health battles are just a few examples. We not only misunderstand the extent of sustainability and the effects it has on many societal aspects, but we also believe that quick and "tokenized" greenwashing is an almost humorous method to get around the issue. Change is urgently needed in our environment, schools, infrastructure, energy, transportation, culture, etc., but any solution must be long-lasting.

These kinds of initiatives help the world satisfy its immediate needs while also empowering future generations to better meet their own needs. The emphasis changes from creating the regenerative legacy of "do more good" to challenging the sustainability myth of "do no harm."

REFERENCES

Aldieri, L., & Vinci, C. P. (2018, October 2). *Green Economy and Sustainable Development: The Economic Impact of Innovation on Employment.* MDPI. doi:10.3390/su10103541

Brand, U. (2012). Green economy–the next oxymoron? No lessons learned from failures of implementing sustainable development. *Gaia (Heidelberg), 21*(1), 28–32. doi:10.14512/gaia.21.1.9

World Commission on Environment and Development. (n.d.). *Brundtland Report.* Encyclopedia Britannica. https://www.britannica.com/topic/Brundtland-Report

Yakovleva, N. & Vazquez-Brust, D. (2021, April 2). *Circular Economy, Degrowth and Green Growth as Pathways for Research on Sustainable Development Goals: A Global Analysis and Future Agenda.* ScienceDirect. doi:10.1016/j.ecolecon.2021.107050

Zazzini, P. & Grifa, G. (2018, October 29). *Energy Performance Improvements in Historic Buildings by Application of Green Walls: Numerical Analysis of an Italian Case Study.* ScienceDirect. doi:10.1016/j.egypro.2018.08.028

Founder Institute Portfolio Companies Helping Meet the 17 UN Sustainable Development Goals. (2021, July 15). The Founder Institute. https://FI.co/insight/17-companies-helping-meet-the-17-un-sustainable-development-goals

Georgeson, L., Maslin, M., & Poessinouw, M. (2017). The global green economy: A review of concepts, definitions, measurement methodologies and their interactions. *Geo : Geography and Environment, 4*(1), e00036. doi:10.1002/geo2.36

Holbrook, E. (2021, April 2). *JetBlue to Aim for Emission, Recycling, and Sustainable Aviation.* Environment + Energy Leader. https://www.environmentalleader.com/2021/04/jetblue-sets-big-goals-for-emissions-recycling-and-sustainable-aviation-fuel-usage/

Sustainable Development. (2023, March 23). *Home.* Sustainable Development. https://sdgs.un.org/

Introduction to the green economy. (2013, March 5). Why Green Economy? https://whygreeneconomy.org/introduction-to-the-green-economy/

Kahle, L. R., & Gurel-Atay, E. (Eds.). (2013). *Communicating sustainability for the green economy.* ME Sharpe.

Lavrinenko, O., Rybalkin, O., Danileviča, A., & Sprūde, M. (2022). Green economy: Content and methodological approaches. *Entrepreneurship and Sustainability Issues, 10*(2), 635–652. doi:10.9770/jesi.2022.10.2(40)

Nike Corporate Social Responsibility (CSR) and Sustainability. (n.d.). *Nike Corporate Social Responsibility (CSR) and Sustainability*. Nike. https://www.thomasnet.com/articles/other/nike-csr/

Pradhan, P., Costa, L., Rybski, D., Lucht, W., & Kropp, J. P. (2017). A systematic study of sustainable development goal (SDG) interactions. *Earth's Future, 5*(11), 1169–1179. doi:10.1002/2017EF000632

The Scope of Sustainability. (n.d.). Net Impact. https://netimpact.org/blog/scope-sustainability

Tseng, M. L., Tan, K. H., Geng, Y., & Govindan, K. (2016). Sustainable consumption and production in emerging markets. *International Journal of Production Economics, 181*, 257–261. doi:10.1016/j.ijpe.2016.09.016

Chapter 14
Constructing New Greener Infrastructures, Retrofitting, and Exploiting the Potential of Smart Technologies

Tarun Madan Kanade
Vishwakarma University, India

Radhakrishna Batule
Vishwakarma University, India

ABSTRACT

Humans made a common habit and became dependent on others, the main dependency is on mother nature and making the most of its benefits which are provided in the forms of food, clean water, clean air, climate regulation, materials, etc. The known fact that all these commodities are free of cost and in unlimited supply available, humans are using them in abundant quantity without giving anything in return for retaining it, and this is not at all appreciated by intellectual humans. This is giving rise to humans who are nature lovers creating some alternative or substitute for such nature. This can be termed as natural building or rebuilding the green environment. Day-to-day innovations in science gave rise to smart technologies which can be used in building and maintaining green infrastructure. As known to all that the GI can be implemented in multiple sectors at various locations, the authors will be highlighting the sites where it can be implemented, which related technology will be used in deploying such GI, and what will be their benefits to humans.

WHAT IS GREEN INFRASTRUCTURE?

The term Green Infrastructure (GI) is as per the word itself the environment or surrounding to be green as mother nature. It is a humanmade nature which is built after getting benefits from natural one. To elaborate more in detail, it is termed as a subset of "Sustainable and Resilient Infrastructure", which is

DOI: 10.4018/978-1-6684-8969-7.ch014

defined in standards such as SuRe, the Standard for Sustainable and Resilient Infrastructure. In simpler terms, researchers have mentioned infrastructure that has low carbon emissions like renewable energy infrastructures, public transportation systems, etc.

GI denotes any fruitful infrastructure which magnifies the natural environment by its direct or indirect contribution. It gives and associates the attachment with the important services of the ecosystem which gives or magnifies urban sustainability and the natural environment. It is also termed as a well-designed matrix of natural and semi-natural zones with other areas featuring systems and a well-connected to manage and provide an outcome which is a broader range of environmental services provided to humans. It includes the green spaces when compared to the forest environment, blue if aquatic territory, and other physical specifications of terrain including the sealine coastal area and marine lives. On earth, GI is present in urban and rural areas like roofs, rain gardens, parks, living walls, canopy cover, urban forests, community gardens, and parklands.

GI is progressing toward aqua management that safeguards and reinstates the natural cycle of water generation and maintaining the ecosystem. It is successful, inexpensive, and magnifies community well-being and quality of human life.

Due to its multifunctional character, every nation has given its definition of Green Infrastructure. Listing a few explanations below.

European Union (2013): Green Infrastructure can be broadly defined as a strategically planned network of high-quality natural and semi-natural areas with other environmental features, which is designed and managed to deliver a wide range of ecosystem services and protect biodiversity in both rural and urban settings. More specifically GI, being a spatial structure providing benefits from nature to people, aims to enhance nature's ability to deliver multiple valuable ecosystem goods and services, such as clean air or water.

US Environmental Protection Agency (2008): Green Infrastructure is an approach to wet weather management that uses soils and vegetation to utilize, enhance and/or mimic the natural hydrological cycle processes of infiltration, evapotranspiration, and reuse.

Natural England (2009): Green Infrastructure includes established green spaces and new sites and should thread through, surround the built environment, and connect the urban area to its wider rural hinterland. Consequently, it needs to be delivered at all spatial scales from sub-regional to local neighborhood levels, accommodating both accessible natural green spaces within local communities and often much larger sites in the urban fringe and wider countryside.

In simpler words the researcher can quote it as Green Infrastructure (GI) is experimented application that provides economic, ecological, and social benefits through natural solutions. Preparing for investments to sustain and increase the alternate source for human society. It assists in alternate dependable solutions on infrastructure that is much costlier to build up and when nature can provide the same at a cheaper cost, which is more long-lasting returns for human society. GI is based on the concept that it shields and increases nature and natural processes, and many other advantages which are received by human society from mother nature. It is a building of a human-made nature.

Developing this GI into a site or in a nearby already developed structure is termed a green retrofit. It is assumed to be impossible in most cases, because the site or the area is already developed a long time ago, and again re-inserting the green infrastructure into this developed area is a bit complicated process. Its inclusions might be major or minor renovation and equipping of the products in a trial that will lower the emission of carbon of the building and in future operations.

This is not a set parameter that mentions what all to be included and not included when going for green retrofitting as it varies on the actual factors of the location such as the makeup of the constructed building, challenges faced by this, and the outcomes of the project. There are a few considerable points to keep in mind that will be covered looking ahead in this chapter.

Keeping a track of this GI is very important and it helps in regulating the efficiency. But doing this is not that easy, as most of the GI is not even checked once they are implemented. Keeping continuous track includes practices like placing various types of sensors at multiple locations within the green infrastructure. These sensors are connected by the cables to the record loggers and then it is redeemed using the internet. And this is not at all easy as loopholes are all where, so from time-to-time monitoring, servicing, and maintaining things have vital importance.

The drastic change in the era of the 21st century was observed by society with new creative technology like Augmented Reality, Virtual Reality, the Internet of Things, Big Data, Artificial Intelligence, etc. By making the most use of these things most of the benefits can be consumed from the implemented GI.

Green infrastructure retrofitting can give society most of the useful products which will result in minimal damage to mother nature. This gives a rise to new terms like 'Green City' or 'Future City.' Things to keep in consideration while building this GI using smart technologies will give humans most of a sustainable environment, healthy transport climate, long lifespan living people, and safe nature which will be possible only by getting the required efficiency from the deployed GI.

A few retrofitting structures which can be easily done in already deployed areas are green and blue roofing over the buildings, Green Buildings, Green Parking, Green Streets, and Rain Gardens, this are general infrastructures that cost less pricing in buildings and can be easily deployed in already settled areas. And humans can explore new smart technologies like Embracing digital innovation, Sustainable transport systems, geothermal heating, and cooling, etc.

The main crux of this chapter is to understand how the retrofitting of green infrastructure and the use of potential smart technologies is used to build a better place for the human society which will be a more secure, sustainable and pollution free, eco-friendly, and reliable place for living communities so as dreamed future city thought by every citizen or the researcher.

CONSTRUCTION OF GREEN INFRASTRUCTURE

Construction of green infrastructure can be termed as choosing the technological escapes that support the development of environmentally and technologically advanced eco-friendly surroundings which will be resulting more durable surroundings for, us humans.

Construction of these structures generates multiple job openings in many fields, inclusive of landing, engineering, building, technology, plumbing, and design. It also associates and helps in maintaining the balance in generating jobs and supply chains which are linked to the manufacturing sectors of various materials which are used in building green infrastructure.

It began in the 19th century with the landscape's designs, as it helps in improving the lives of urban citizens and it is provided with the help of GI which is optimized in assisting and providing sustainable goals. Its initial constructions were building green parks and gardens, green trail systems, and at other natural landscape places.

While building any new site or area developing from the initial stage, is not that hard effort, as most of the things are pre-planned and well accordingly designed too before starting construction. So, in newly constructed sites and large-scale projects, such GI is given more importance so that the area is more eco-friendly and even it stays pollution free by less emission of carbons and proper water management to avoid wastage.

If society is implementing this in predeveloped areas, then it is termed retrofitting. In these cases, the designs are hard to be implemented as we are modifying the constructions and fitting some new designs into them. This is mostly done in areas after checking all the parameters of what emissions and amount of carbon in that area are or what benefits it would provide by implementing GI for that area.

CONCEPT OF RETROFITTING

This concept can be explained in a way that, when the addition of some new technology is done to the older constructed system, it can then be termed as a retrofitted infrastructure. It is also very important from the view of climate maintaining and adapting its changes because when the initial construction was done, the magnitude of the environment was considered, but after a few decades it changed. So, considering these changes and estimating for future decades changes this redevelopment or retrofitting of modern technologies is designed to maintain the balance of the ecosystem.

Retrofits are used to magnify construction efficiency. Considering the scenario, it lowers the gross negative impacts which are caused due to climate change by lowering the carbon or other harmful emissions for the environment and lowers the adverse inputs which were earlier given due to outdated building structure. It also allows the building for being a more friendly and healthy environment for residing or living in a particular area.

Green and Blue Roofing of Buildings

Green roofs of the buildings are mostly covered, or half covered with the plantation and growing medium or small plants on the terrace level or even on the balconies. This results in reducing the hot waves or the emissions of gases which helps in healing the ecosystem.

A Blue roof of the building is due to its structure. Small structures of ponds or tanks are made on the roofs for the storage of naturally received rainwater. This proper storage lasts for months. Once the rainy season is over, this structure slowly releases water for the use of the owners in the building. In short, depending on the hydrological site of the building such a structure is constructed. short

Viewing the modern version of these technologies, Blue-green roofs are combined giving rise to the more advanced versions for getting benefits to form them which will help in maintaining ecosystem balance. Traditional green roofs are used as plantations or vegetation of small or medium size plants on the roofs of buildings. Traditional blue roofs are used for storing rainwater and later using it during the post-rain season. Combining both can increase the way that much water is stored at lower levels which will be used post-rain season and over its plantation to be done. This will give double advantages to a single roof structure. The initial setup cost will be higher, but the benefits will be higher and for long-term purposes. Thus, blending both infrastructures will be more beneficial for human societies.

Considering an example: Watermill Residence, Water Mill, New York:: Famous architect Andre Berman designed and came up with the innovative home design which was a weekend home for summer duration for the three generations of a family. This was named Watermill Residence located on Long Island an Island in New York states. The design was made in such a way that each living roof was done plantation with wildflowers and local grasses for the home which is a single story with garage and guest rooms. This tree plantation was designed by the Goode Green organization.

Considering an example: Stadel Museum, Frankfurt, Germany:: In 1815 a Stadel Museum was constructed which displays a surprising collection of European art. In 2012 a sub-terrain expansion was given by the architectural firms Schneider and Schumacher. The modern place is the home to a 20th-century art collection and the roof is topped with a domed garden, and an airy ceiling created with circular roof lights this makes the base for the outstanding grassy above and the museum below.

Considering an example: Noltemeyer Hoefe, Braunschweig, Germany has an area particularly designed for the blue roofs covering an area of 5,780m^2. This is a residential development. It also has an intensive green roof of an area covering 2,500 m^2.

Considering an example: Shanghai Tower, Shanghai, China:: It is the world's second tallest building i.e., a 632-meter-high skyscraper in Pudong the financial district of China. It is a sustainable green structure. It is designed in such a way as to collect rainwater and recycles some of the wastewater for internal purpose of usage.

Green Building

Green Building can be termed as a structure that reflects the features like, improving and maintaining the quality of life for the environmental changes and maintaining the balance with the ecosystem.

This building lowers water and energy consumption and is vitally important as its part of durable urban development which helps in combatting environmental changes. From vast structures of skyscrapers to heritage museums, all the constructions can be converted to green buildings to make the environment more balanced and sustainable for human society.

Considering an example: World Trade Centre, Manama, Bahrain:: Manama, the capital of Bahrain, has an eye-catching construction of 240-meter-high twin towers. It is the first in the world to have an integrated wind turbine in its design. Both buildings inclusively cover around 15% of the tower's total energy consumption. Both towers are identically constructed and shaped like sails which are to direct the wind direction. These towers are connected by three bridges, and each has a diameter of the 29-meter turbine.

Considering an example: Pixel Building, Melbourne, Australia:: This building is Australia's first carbon-neutral infrastructure. Materializing an example set how the offices should be in future it should have a green blue roof with the solar panels fitted on it to generate own energy and to store all the water and make its usage as and when required. It has an eye-catching facade of multicolor which gives the advantage of having enough ventilation and natural lighting to reduce energy usage.

Green Parking

Green parking lots are specifically designed for more environmentally friendly and sustainable. A few things which can be kept or thought to retrofit or constructed when building a parking lot on land instead of the building are that it can have more rain gardens, bioretention areas, infiltration trenches permeable pavements, etc. The trees used for shading the lots are also used for the reduction of stormwater running off by volumes and evaporating the rainfall.

Implementation costs for green parking lots are generally on the higher end when compared to the earlier surfaces. It varies depending on the surface site climate, soil type, topography, etc., and as per the usage, it also varies. In past three to four decades parking lots are the fastest-growing land use.

Considering an example: H. B. Fuller Company Parking Lot, Minneapolis, USA:: It is a parking lot that was constructed in an eco-friendly manner. It was retrofitted infrastructure. It gives implementation of helping the sustainable environment in such a way that it reduces stormwater discharge by 73%, reduces sediment discharge by 94%, and reduces phosphorus loading by 70%.

Green Streets

Green streets can be defined as streets that have environmental features like rain gardens, infiltration planters, and permeable paving to catch and slow down the flowing waterways.

These are mainly constructed to collect the rainwater at its origination where the rain falls. Whereas earlier the streets were designed to show the direction for running water from the surface area to the sewer systems, this discharges the direction of surface water.

Considering an example: Seattle Street, Washington State, USA:: Thousands of trees and bushes were planted across the streets in the city giving a newer retrofitted look. The gross temperature of the city came around 2 degrees Celsius down and also controlled around 99% reduction of total runoff water.

Considering an example: Green Alleys, Chicago, USA:: It is one of the most successful projects of CDOT. A penetrable layer of asphalt or concrete is layered on streets that are made in such a way that it filters through the stormwater and drains it into the ground. This flowing water is collected into the sewer system. These surfaces are lighter in color, which helps in reflecting the sunlight rather than absorbing light. Due to such construction, the urban heat effect which is increasing the surface temperature is reduced.

Rain Gardens

Rain Gardens are also termed bioretention facilities which are one of the varieties of the practice which was designed to increase the reabsorption of running water into the soil. They are also treated to conserve the runoff of stormwater. It is a small-scale vegetated garden that is used for storing and infiltration of water.

Rain gardens are mostly implemented on private property close to the buildings. When roof-collected water reaches the drainage system pipelines, this is redirected and rerouted to the rain garden. These are mostly built upon the landscape areas. More beautiful and cost-effective by planting flowering perennials, and grasses on it. It helps in providing food and shelter to butterflies, and songbirds and somewhere helps in conserving wildlife habitation to a small extent.

Considering an example: Michigan Avenue Engineered Rain Gardens, USA:: An initiative was taken to bring together and promote all local environmental and nature-related projects for the well-being of an eco-friendly environment. The first project was in Michigan, USA and it was implemented in the city of Lansing the capital of the state. This was planned to implement in the downtown area and then named an engineered rain garden which was used to show how green infrastructure can function smoothly in an urban environment. This planting helped in improving the water quality of the Grand River.

It was completed successfully building the whole project in conjunction area with the sewer separation for work and rain garden and streetscape enhancements. Rain gardens were built on the overall streetscape which was designed to address the stormwater and to make a highlight point for the city and state that the low impact can make greener the city with positive impacts.

Considering an example: Rain Garden at Uppsala, Sweden:: When building this rain garden the main purpose was to treat the stormwater rather than to retain it. These rain gardens also serve the urban settings which serve biodiversity purposes and importantly they add value to the highway design.

Considering an example: Rain garden at bottom of swale at Hobert, Tasmania, Australia:: A rain garden was constructed on the highways and city roads. Running of the flowing water was designed to infiltrate through the rain garden which was part of the runoff system of water and the surplus with the lead along the swale.

CHARACTERISTICS OF BUILDING A GREEN INFRASTRUCTURE

When going for sustainable green infrastructure, a few parameters are to be taken into consideration for more economic and beneficial advantages for humankind. An internationally accepted official recognition was confirmed for checking if the infrastructures are meeting the minimum requirements to be certified as green infrastructure.

To meet these requirements, it is mandatory to have a high level of efficiency, minimizing pollution and reducing the consumption of energy, water, and other natural resources. To evaluate this LEED certification is required. LEED: Leadership in Energy and Environmental Design; is an internationally recognized body that checks whether the building or infrastructure is meeting the considerable sustainable requirements to be certified as green infrastructure.

i. Design and innovation: Providing a world-class design for the infrastructure which will easily accommodating the sustainability strategies and can be easily implemented during its construction
ii. Efficient use of water: Minimizing the usage and recycling of most natural resources is the prime motive of green infrastructure. Water has been one of them, so minimizing it for construction purposes and some alternative mechanisms to reduce the water footprint of water.
iii. Energy and atmosphere: For the atmosphere reducing the output of harmful energy gases and increasing the consumption of renewable energy sources and increasing efficiency which will result in lowering pollution.
iv. Indoor environmental quality: Providing a quality area and space for the residents and giving them clean air, a thermally controlled environment, and a noise-free ambiance.
v. Location and transport: Not to build the setups in sensitive areas which are near or in the vicinity of the environment. Providing public transport which will reduce the pollution and other impacts caused due to increasing vehicle populations.
vi. Materials and resources: During construction save as many as possible resources. Recycling most of the systems and using sustainable materials in building the infrastructure.
vii. Regional priority: Providing the improvements for the place where it is located easily reachable for people considering other terms such as environment, social equity, and public health.
viii. Sustainable sites: Reducing all types of pollution which are impacting the environment and minimizing the use of natural resources and increasing the use of renewable energy resources. Protecting and maintaining the natural habitat and making it easy for interaction with nature.

REASONS TO CHOOSE AND INVEST IN SMART GREEN INFRASTRUCTURE

Magnifying the smart and green infrastructure combined with the technology can give a modern face to the enlarged energy grid's reliability. The input of some renewable or clean energy in urban areas lowers the power outages for humankind. This infrastructure can be implemented on all levels starting from small houses, buildings, or large constructures or even for the broader landscape areas.

On the local level, green infrastructures can be implemented like rain gardens, permeable pavements, blue and green roofing, rainwater harvesting systems, etc. Green infrastructure is the combination of both engineered systems and the natural environment which implements providing clean water, maintaining the thermal atmosphere of earth, conserving ecosystem values and functions, and providing a wider scope of the array to the humankind. Below are a few explained by city planners that the community should invest in using smart green technology for building some sustainable green infrastructure.

Improving Security

Using the cloud and IoT which gets information about whatever happening on the streets or any corner of the city by viewing it through the connected camera and other identification collection devices. This can help society to identify and track illegal activity with drones. By identifying the concerns of safety on the streets, the responsible authorities can respond immediately and efficiently which provides improving security.

Smartly designed monitors can additionally refine public safety by keeping track of indoor emissions in public spaces.

Decreasing Urban Heat Islands

Green infrastructure is dependent on renewable energy and efficiency-magnifying technologies. Reducing the outflow of gases prevents the accumulation of pollutants on the surface. When the surface level gets in touch with the ozone layer and sunlight it increases the local temperature.

In the summer season, urban islands' heat can cause heatstroke and other heat concerned issues. Due to the implementation of green infrastructure the greenhouse gas outflow will be lowered and making use of solar energy can effectively prevent the localized temperature increase which helps in protecting human health and biodiversity.

Minimizing Energy costs

Giving the inputs by using renewable systems along with embedded IoT technology can help in lowering utility costs. Solar power is always the least cost-effective power source and is easily available on the earth's surface. Making full use of energy-efficient devices can reduce energy bills, and further increase the cost of sustainable smart cities.

Reducing Atmospheric Degradation

Lower emissions and magnifying the sustainability levels is the major reason why most cities are opting for smart green infrastructure. Modern things used in new constructions for urban areas are solar and wind power implementation into their infrastructure. Renewable energy sources can give additional help to the builders which will effectively implement and be an easy way to maintain green infrastructure. Also, electric heavy machinery is in use to reduce tailpipe emissions into the atmosphere. In the future reduction efforts can reduce atmospheric degradation and can enhance the greenhouse effect.

Network Works Best

Available sources of clean water are streams, wetlands, floodplains, rivers, and forests which are critical to be kept under protection. We shall build an essential and effective infrastructure that will preserve the component of water.

Purchasing land around Catskills reservoirs by New York City makes it ensure that the polluted runoff water from roads and lawn does not enter the main water supply and maintains the great quality of tap water which is been supplied to the city.

Not Wasting Money

Wisely, investment of money means getting multi-purpose solutions that are obtained by lower cost investment and multiples of benefits from it. Recently in 2019, a saving of $300 million was done by the City of Indianapolis, USA. By using the trees, wetlands, and downspouts it has disconnected to reduce the flow of storm waters into the sewer systems. This helped in reducing the pipe from 33' to 26'.

Enhancing Community Safety and Enjoyment

Long years ago, when the construction was done, it was not built with the capacity to handle huge floods or droughts that would come in the future due to global warming. So now, as in the 3rd decade of the 21st century, society needs to build up a modern approach to protect the public health, safety, and betterment quality of humankind. Green infrastructure gives the communities security and flexibility as and when required to them.

EXPLOITING THE POTENTIAL SMART TECHNOLOGIES

Green infrastructure uses advanced use of smart technologies to develop and construct more sustainable buildings with the lowest adverse effect on the environment while its total tenure of work considering from designing, construction, operation, maintenance, renovation till the end demolition of the site.

As there is a huge number of benefits which are resulted from green building technology, builder engineers, facility managers, and architecture firms are magnifying the concepts to build up more and more efficient buildings, construction, and operation costs.

The main motive of green infrastructure is to reduce the impacts caused due to buildings on the ozone and environment. This includes the reduction of the emissions of harmful greenhouse gases, carbon dioxide, various carbon gases, and toxic gases as well which are the result of the usage or irresponsible harvesting of construction materials.

Below are a few of the potential examples of the newly invented technologies which can be used for upscaling the green infrastructure.

Electrochromic Glass

This glass is also termed the smart glasses. These are made in a very special way such that the glass uses a tiny gust of electricity to charge the ions on the layer of the windows and alter the amount of light reflected.

Currently, available glasses are not that smart and cannot be controlled by the systems. Whereas this new electrochromic glass allows the user to make the selection using the control system as that what amount of light to be allowed to enter through the glass. This was not possible with the earlier present glasses, there were low-emittance windows that could not block the solar radiations.

This smart glass is better suitable for urban, huge, constructed buildings or skyscrapers, which like to have some modern glassy look for their infrastructure. Mostly on sunny days or noon when heat is in abundant quality, it can be controlled automatically to allow what amount of heat to be allowed to enter inside by controlling the tint level of the glass.

Proponents of electrochromic glass state that 25% of the thermal heating in the building can be reduced using this technology or smart glass and can lower around 40% of the cost of ventilation and air conditioning.

Smart Appliances

As society is already living in the modern world, with voice-controlled devices all over houses and office places. Same way increasing and updating the modern available home appliances provisioned with innovative technology helps save energy and make life easier and more cost-friendly for humankind.

For example, we can bring up more usage of newly invented intelligent washing machines, refrigerators, and dishwaters to be connected to the smart meters which are made to make and track the usage and be more energy efficient. These are advanced electric meters that in real-time collect the data using their intelligent systems and then pass messages to the devices to output the valuable power usage data. With this data, the devices or the appliances can transmit it for using the optimal power. By analyzing this data, the appliances can determine the power rates and then automatically lower the level and keep it operating the same.

Zero Energy Buildings

This type of green infrastructure is designed and constructed in such a way that it produces electricity using the renewable resources built up on it. Thus, it eliminates the need of getting connected to the standard available electrical connection.

As per the name, the zero-energy building consumes zero of the net energy per year from other available resources. Zero or minimal emission of carbon gases and other harmful gases are emitted out of the building into the atmosphere. As own energy producing and zero emission of carbon, this is dependent on the renewable energy generators or the solar and wind energy creators.

This may sound more advanced, but the future of the green building is already started. Construction of zero-energy buildings is already going on across various developed nations with the government offerings them subsidies to incentivize zero-emission constructions.

For example, In the USA, the government is offering green buildings that are zero-energy buildings the solar investment tax credit of 30% off on the total system cost. And on the other side, the California government is offering an additional money-back policy for the builders or the consumers who are going with the addition of renewable energy sources into their existing construction plan.

Embracing Digital Innovation

Digital innovation is trending the variety of offerings to humankind, which is making a more easy lifestyle for living. It is also providing various ways which help the construction team to reduce its impact which is caused to the natural environment during the building. Using the advanced sensors in the infrastructure, society can track the amount of carbon and gases emitted from the building and try new ways to reduce and maintain the same outflow and preserve biodiversity as the built environment changes and expands.

Few areas are there where digital innovation is required and using this track, we can control the emissions and make a sustainable environment.

a. Buildings: Various electronically developed sensors can be implemented at the time of constructing the infrastructure into the building. This will help to detect the amount of natural heat, light, and gases if they are emitting out of the building. Depending on the threshold point, it can be controlled using the systems what further action to be taken to reduce the emissions. Mostly to lower the temperature by using renewable energy sources to reduce the outflow of carbon emissions.
b. Traffic: Usage of private vehicles makes the most generation of carbon emissions and pollution like air and sound pollution. This is the major harm for humans. Government should build up more public transport and keep some limitations when using private vehicles. Public transport vehicles like metro trains or electrically operated buses are to be increased so that those will also reduce the minimum amount of emissions and fast routing will be done for the public.
c. Electricity Production: The major and only barrier to renewable energy sources is that those are less reliable compared to non-renewable fossil fuels. Considering the usage of solar and wind energy sources, this is also not available across the year, this is majorly dependent on the weather outside. Thus, the usage of digital sensors arranged in a smart network grid is useful in getting time-to-time information and then regulating the amount of electricity that will trigger the switch and flow of the renewable source will be provided for the usage purpose. We can also start implementing solar panels or windows which can capture the heat and convert it to electricity on high-rise buildings or skyscrapers. And install the windmills on the same so that it would be helpful to get electricity and if more than usage of the building then can be passed on to the nearby vicinity infrastructures for usage.

Sustainable Transport System

The key element for having a smart and green environment by eliminating or reducing the major source of carbon emissions is by having a sustainable transport system present in the area or the city. It means that there will be low or minimum emissions from the vehicles and affordable modes of transport which can include electric, biofuel, or any alternative fuel vehicles.

Transportation has become the centre of many economic and social development of the major nations. Government should continue the expansion of bike lanes, and walkable cities, and increase the electric micro-mobility by multiplying the number of electric vehicles like bicycles, mopeds, scooters, bikes, cars, and even buses for public or private transportation, this shall be increased in the urban area because those are the main generators of carbon emissions compared to rural cities.

Government subsidies should go take some initiatives for using the sustainable transport system and checking the alternatives to fossil fuels. Transportation is the single major source of air pollution on the planet and its greenhouse gas emissions as well If any way to help to reduce this the only way is to have a sustainable transportation system.

Considering that if we opt for the sustainable mode of transportation on daily basis, we will be benefitted from multiple things for humankind, the city, and the environment as well. Few as noted below.

a. A vibrant economy is supported by the local businesses
b. Healthier lifestyle and a better quality of human life
c. Increased physical activity is done by humans
d. Increased social interaction while traveling by public modes
e. Lowered the dependency on fossil fuels and non-renewable energy sources
f. Minimized emissions of carbon and greenhouse gases
g. Reduction in air pollution by not using personal vehicles
h. Reduced traffic congestion on roads
i. Reduction in transportation cost

Geothermal Heating and Cooling

Geothermal Heating and Cooling technology have been harnessed below the ground level within the earth's crust. Just a few feet below the surface, which is used to keep or maintain the constant temperature of the building or small residential area. Maintaining the temperature is dependent on the outside temperature of the building as per season might be summer or winter. This is one of the available renewable energies. The fact known by all is that temperature when higher goes down with time, this shows the study that temperature moves from a higher magnitude towards a lower magnitude. This model also behaves in the same flow of heat and further can be explained more easily as done ahead.

Heating Mode: The pumps kept above the surface level move the water inside it towards another fluid which is buried below the surface level with the help of pre-arranged pipes.

As the water or fluid passes through the surface to the earth, it absorbs the heat from the warmer soil or rocks or groundwater by which it is surrounded.

This heated fluid in the pump is returned to the building. The system uses a heat exchange that emits the heat of the pumps and absorbs the cooler temperature inside it.

This cooler temperature is again sent down to the ground through pipes, which absorb there the warmer heat from nearby sources, and after some time again received up in the building.

Thus, this system or setup is used as the heating mode, which consumes, natural free cost available renewable warm energy from the surroundings and same has been utilized by the building residents.

Cooling Mode: Water or other present fluid in the pipes, absorbs the heat from the building using the heat exchanger as which a cooler or air conditioner does.

This heat is moved down with the help of the pump pipes below the surface of the earth, and while going down heat is removed, and cooler air or temperature is gathered by the fluid or water as heat flows from higher to lower temperature as we know.

This makes the fluid with the cooler temperature now and as it passed down in the earth it absorbs the heat from the surrounding rocks, soil, groundwater, etc.

This when going up again gives out cooler air to the building, and the same circulation is maintained.

This system or setup is used as the cooling mode, which does not utilize any fossil fuel for making the surroundings cool. This is the naturally available abundant quality renewable energy source.

FUTURE SCOPE AND MODEL

In the above chapter, researcher have showcased and explained a few examples of Green infrastructure and a few retrofits. These retrofits can be termed the Grey infrastructure, as with the modern era, the upgrade of the system of infrastructure was done to earlier existing structures.

Combining all the concepts and rearranging them on a single platform and range, the researcher is trying to put all the sets into a fit outline for smart secure future cities. This will give society as required design and flow for the dream world which everyone has often thought of living in.

Below is the illustration for the same.

Figure 1. Tarun & Radhakrishna's Model for Embedded infrastructure and Technology which contributes to achieving the dream future cities

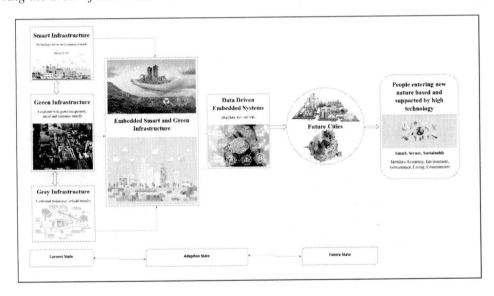

Many nations are now moving towards the building of future cities as human existing communities have already entered the third decade of the 21st century. Above is the suggested small model or the flow researcher had shown how the infrastructures are connected in building or achieving the most suitable future cities for us or our upcoming generations.

Let's discuss a few of the blocks of the figure for a better understanding of how easy it is to achieve living in the most dreamed future cities.

Smart Infrastructure: This infrastructure includes the smart grid of modern technology and implementing it with sensors and other modern equipment so that it would make living easier and in the comfort zone for humans. It provided fast and speedy smart services for day-to-day working routines might be at home or workplace or in public places.

Every component or device is connected to the network which can be handled by voice command or on a remote at the fingertips. This gives the extreme implementation of the technology at every point in living connected to high-speed internet services and over a network easy for humans to manage from any remote location.

This brings more use of fossil fuels or other energy resources which are used for giving energy to smart devices and networks. This brings up more danger for the coming generations as it makes fast use and early exhaustion of fossil fuel or energy sources.

Green Infrastructure: This infrastructure includes the strategically planned green environment and the living of humans. Here the usage minimum of natural fossil fuels or exhausting energy sources. Most of the time renewable energy sources are used for day-to-day energy sources. It gives a greener environment and produced minimum carbon emissions which do not damage the ozone layer by the gases and keeps the temperature of the earth to a maintained level and makes the surroundings more sustainable for living.

This living saves the naturally available things like drinkable water, oxygen for breathing, and normal temperature earth, etc. Every component is combined or designed in such a way that it gives more benefit to social living towards humankind.

Grey Infrastructure: This is the type of cement infrastructure that builds huge buildings for human development and modernizes humankind. It was also termed as it was built for helping to save the environment from natural calamities and save the lives of humans. In this construction nature was not thought of, only humankind's well-being was constructed. A few examples were dams, seawalls, roads, pipes, wastewater treatment plants, etc.

These structures are in the fashion of buildings from long decades or centuries ago. Demolition and rebuilding the new green structure at the same place are not feasible, so modification or we can term the addition of the new component was done to this existing structure. Which was termed Retrofitting.

Current State: These three blocks are the different infrastructures in our current state. Where all are built as per human purpose and requirements for the day to day living. We do not have any structure which is a combined nature of all three. So, each infrastructure has its advantages along with a few drawbacks, which are not good for humankind.

Embedded Smart and Green Infrastructure: This infrastructure is the optimal output or the combination of all currently available infrastructures. Researcher have discussed Smart infrastructure, Green infrastructure, and Grey infrastructure. As highlighted earlier its benefits and drawbacks which are not good for the global environment and humankind. Thus, an optimal solution is there, that is constructing such a structure that will emit minimal adverse or drawbacks and provide the combined multiplied benefits towards economic growth, social life increasing, added green components, and advanced technology-driven systems.

This will give society a secure place for human living with more advantages in the arms of nature. This will reduce the usage of non-renewable energy sources and they will not exhaust so early and even future generations can take benefits from them. More usage of renewable or naturally free abundantly availed sources like solar energy or wind energy and more greenery will produce more oxygen on planet earth which will eventually help in reducing carbon emissions. Even the increase in temperature will be at a very slow rate, which will help in reducing or stopping global warming.

Data-Driven Embedded Systems: The new embedded infrastructure will be connected over a network for smart accessing the equipment or the services available. This will give the touch or easy access to the modern world to the humans who are residing in the embedded smart and green infrastructure. This data will be connected to the cloud at a remote location and can be accessed from any remote location with just by few clicks. It will reduce human labour and increase the automation process, which will help minimize error and have a hassle-free process for any system. It might even use robots. This technology update will be going ahead and taking care of maintaining the environmental parameters for reducing carbon emissions or lowering the temperature, etc.

These embedded systems will be based on newly designed technologies likes, Virtual Reality, Augmented Reality, Bid Data, Data Analytics, the Internet of Things, Artificial Intelligence, etc. This will give a boost to the technology using each other and then make a more sustainable and secure environment with no damage to nature for humans.

Future Cities: This is the most dreamed destination of the current generation. Current generations are having all the facilities but, on another side, this is causing damaging effects on nature, this is mostly due to carbon emissions. This is all minimized and reduced in the concept of the future city. Here humans get all things just at their fingertips when they require them. These are all technically advanced things, which are using topmost technologies and connected databases on the cloud which can be accessed from any remote location as and when required as per requirement.

This will eventually give a better place for living and mainly it will save not even damaging the environment. People will be entering the new living hood where they will be surrounded by nature all over which will be supported by high-end technical gadgets.

This layman's language can be termed as a safe, secure, sustainable place for human living. Which will provide benefits for human lives in terms of ease of mobility, economic balance, safe and healthy environment, transparent governance, healthy living, and mainly happily living communities.

CONCLUSION

Researcher have highlighted the concept of green infrastructure and how it is obtained by retrofitting the existing infrastructure. It is a network that is connected to multifunctional green spaces and other features which are eco-friendly and for the usage of urban and rural residences. This will be the optimal solution for delivering the best quality life deliverables for human life and environmental benefits to the living communities.

It is not just the alternative description for the conventional living space. It also has some additional things like open parks, open spaces, woodlands, playgrounds, and with the tree streets allotments of green and blue roofs and walls, sustainable drainage, and water storing systems for preventing soil erosions.

Some of the key features which give an output for the building green infrastructure are integrated into the network spaces and features are not for any individual purpose but are developed for the environment and on large scale for public well-being. Some benefits can be noted as down.

- Attractive investment
- Carbon reduction
- Cool urban and rural areas during the summer seasons
- Encouraged active travel

- Provided sustainable drainage system
- Reduced runoff water during flash floodings
- Supports people's mental and physical health

Looking in more depth the benefits that are absorbed from green infrastructure are the way how society is dependent on it and the quality of its design and post-implementation how the maintenance is carried out throughout the maturity period and how is the health of the elements which were used in building the same.

REFERENCES

Better Buildings Partnership. (2022, February 21). *British Land's 1 Triton Square Shows the Commercial Value of Circular Economy Leadership*. Better Buildings Partnership.

Crossley, H. (2021, June 22). *Rain gardens: 10 stunning ideas and designs that soak up rain run-off*. Gardeningetc.

Fenlon, W. (2011, March 21). *10 Technologies Used in Green Construction*. HowStuffWorks.

US EPA. (2014, October 28). *Geothermal Heating and Cooling Technologies*. US EPA.

City of Chicago. (2018, June 15). *Green Alleys*. Chicago.gov.

EPA. (2016). Green Infrastructure and Climate Change Collaborating to Improve Community Resiliency. EPA.

Pennington's Law. (2021). *Green retrofit: what is it and what does it mean for the development industry?* Penningtonslaw.com.

Handley, E. (2022, January 6). *How do we define green infrastructure?* Open Access Government.

Iberdrola. (2021, April 22). *Green Or Sustainable Buildings*. Iberdrola; Iberdrola.

Intellis. (2021, July 31). *What is Green Building Technology? Plus: The Top 5 Green Tech Trends Transforming Facility Management Right Now!* Intellis.

Kaluarachchi, Y. (2021). Potential advantages in combining smart and green infrastructure over silo approaches for future cities. *Front. Eng. Manag.*, *8*(1), 98–108. doi:10.100742524-020-0136-y

NASA. (2021). *Lessons from 50 years of UN sustainable development policy The Road to Sustainable Transport Key Messages and Recommendations*. International Institute for Sustainable Development.

Robinson, T., Schulte-Herbrüggen, H., Mácsik, J., & Andersson, J. (2019). *Raingardens for stormwater management: Potential of raingardens in a Nordic climate. DIVA*. Trafikverket.

Senseware. (2022). *Top 10 Retrofit Methods for Sustainable Buildings*. Attuneiot.com.

Smartcity. (2021, November 15). 4 Reasons to Invest in Smart and Green Infrastructure. *Smartcity press*.

StateUp. (2021, April 22). *Why digital innovation in the built environment is integral to a Green Recovery*. StateUp.

Dreamstime. (2023). Vectors, Video & Audio - Dreamstime. Dreamstime.

City of Vaughan. (2022). *Sustainable Transportation*. Vaughan.ca.

Types of Green Infrastructure - DEP. (2023). Nyc.gov.

Unsplash. (2023). *Beautiful Free Images & Pictures*. Unsplash.

Venter, Z. S., Barton, D. N., Martinez-Izquierdo, L., Langemeyer, J., Baró, F., & McPhearson, T. (2021). Interactive spatial planning of urban green infrastructure – Retrofitting green roofs where ecosystem services are most needed in Oslo. *Ecosystem Services*, *50*, 101314. doi:10.1016/j.ecoser.2021.101314

WGIN-mockup. (2021, April 12). *Key Definition: Green Infrastructure - World Green Infrastructure Network*. World Green Infrastructure Network.

Chapter 15
Green Manufacturing:
Opening Doors to Greener Economy

Arpita Nayak
KIIT School of Management, KIIT University, India

Ipseeta Satpathy
KIIT School of Management, KIIT University, India

B. C. M. Patnaik
KIIT School of Management, KIIT University, India

Sukanta Kumar Baral
Indira Gandhi National Tribal University, India

Atmika Patnaik
King's College, UK

ABSTRACT

The goal of this work is to provide an overview of the different advantages of green manufacturing to society, it is a step taken towards a greener economy. This analysis comprises approximately 47+ published research articles on this topic. The evaluation covers papers from prominent publications as well as general management journals with significant links to the topic. This chapter makes a significant contribution to theory by giving insights into the advantages of green manufacturing and its impact on a greener economy, and it draws on various works of literature and numerous theoretical perspectives to get a more thorough understanding of green manufacturing's influence on society, the environment, and the economy. The chapter also addresses the integrated perspective's consequences for philosophy and practice. This study states the advantages of green manufacturing adoption by some of the organizations in our society.

DOI: 10.4018/978-1-6684-8969-7.ch015

INTRODUCTION

Green manufacturing also referred to as green production, refers to the use of ecologically friendly industrial processes to reduce the environmental effect. Green production aims to eliminate waste, protect the environment, and minimize pollution. Consumers and companies alike are getting more worried about the environment. And in order to thrive in the years to come, we must follow the trend of green manufacturing. Additionally, green manufacturing typically concentrates on environmentally friendly production practices, which can result in much-improved market stability over time. Green manufacturing (GM) has several synonyms, including cleaner production and green practices. This issue has grown substantially during the previous decade. The term "green" has become a significant and intrigu3ing topic of discussion for a variety of reasons, including increased pollution and waste, natural resource scarcity and depletion, and the influence of global warming. Green manufacturing refers to the act of updating manufacturing processes and implementing ecologically responsible operations in the manufacturing business. It is essentially "greening" manufacturing, in which employees utilize less natural resources, reduce waste and pollution, recycle or reuse materials, and reduce carbon emissions in their processes. Apart from the ecological advantages of green manufacturing, an increasing number of businesses throughout the country are discovering that a focus on recycling and waste reduction can help their whole company. Businesses' bottom lines are improving, while employees' motivation, productivity, and public relations are upgrading. Going green in the production process in business is the approach that stresses the use of environmentally friendly techniques, resources, and technology to lessen the environmental effect of industrial operations. It has a number of potential advantages, including lower environmental impact, greater public health, and economic opportunity. By fostering innovation, job creation, and investment in innovative green technology, businesses may lower their carbon footprint, conserve natural resources, minimize the risk of environmental disasters, and generate economic possibilities (Setyaningsih,2019).

Green manufacturing has also emerged as a long-term employment growth driver in the United States. Green manufacturing presently employs 26% of all renewable energy employees, per a recent piece in Quality Magazine. Additionally, between 2003 and 2010, clean and green manufacturing created 35,382 employments while the rest of the industry shed jobs. Workers in the clean economy earn 13% more than other workers in the US economy because of their unique skill set. Given the critical importance of achieving net-zero emissions for climate a better understanding of the factors influencing the eco-friendly industry, as well as a growing manufacturing corporate strategy for constructing net-zero economies thru eco-friendly production and consumption, is becoming extremely relevant (Nyangchak,2022). Green manufacturing practices have the potential to boost economic growth by spurring innovation, increasing efficiency, and lowering prices. Organizations may boost their competitiveness, enter new markets, and generate employment by incorporating sustainable concepts into their operations. This article investigates how green manufacturing helps promote economic development and builds the groundwork for a more resilient and sustainable economy. Green manufacturing seeks to minimize the number of natural resources required to manufacture final items by implementing more energy- and material-efficient manufacturing methods. This will include paying attention to the product's lifespan and integrating, especially, supply chain corporations and small and medium-sized businesses. Resource efficiency and decoupling can contribute to competitive advantages and long-term growth (Urena,2021). According to the US Energy Administration, emissions from the manufacturing process would grow by 26% by 2050, while other high-producing industries will drop or stabilize at current levels. Given that a growing number of prominent firms are pursuing a sustainability goal — such as McDonald's, which plans to source 100% of their

Figure 1. Three pillars of green manufacturing

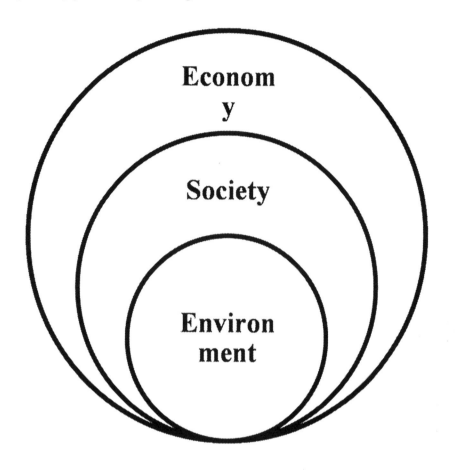

guest wraps from sustainable, reused, or approved sources by 2025 —, we must continue to see this trend shifting through the supply chain. (Moktadir,2018; Thomas,2022). Green Manufacturing, commonly referred to as Lean & Green, is a method of examining and optimizing the manufacturing process. It's built on Lean manufacturing concepts, so it's a dynamic, tried-and-true way to turning green. The Green Manufacturing structure is based on the seven Green Value streams and provides a clear objective for each of them, such as achieving 100% renewable energy-driven operations or waste minimization sent to landfill. Going green (and lean) provides huge economic benefits, and any organization that has yet to go on this path has an opportunity to find it for themselves. Those who have previously made efforts in this manner have reported several benefits. Companies that improve their ESG (environmental, social, and governance) performance do better financially. This is confirmed by a meta-study of nearly 2000 individual studies of ESG performance across investment businesses between 1970 and 2014. Companies with high ESG performance provided superior financial returns in nearly half of the situations. Only 11% of the correlations were negative (Bag,2022; Wojnarowska,2021). A green economy improves human well enough and social fairness while lowering environmental dangers and shortages dramatically. Pearce 1989 advocated the green economy in response to the current price system's undervaluation of social and environmental costs. It is well-known for its low-carbon footprint, resource efficiency, and social equity.

The United Nations Environment Program (UNEP) supports natural capital protection, which includes ecosystems and natural services. The green economy is quantitative growth that is cheap in terms of natural resource consumption, clean in terms of reducing pollution and other environmental harm, and robust in terms of explaining natural hazards. These potentially contradicting consequences necessitate confirmation of a green economy implementation's ability to facilitate a transition to sustainability (Loiseau,2016; Mealy,2022). International environmental regulations such as the Montreal Convention, the Kyoto Protocol, the Restriction of the Use of Particularly Hazardous Substances in Electronic and Electrical Equipment (RoHS), and Waste Electronics and Electric Devices (WEEE), as well as consumer environmental protection, have emerged would result in a more environmentally conscious society big global business consequence. Sustainability has kept promoting company growth and development. For example, BMW's automotive recycling policy was a preventative measure to avoid government restrictions. BMW has initiated development on a dismantling design that might result in the world's largest first 100% recyclable vehicle. Eco-innovation has the potential to be a substantial economic development engine. Several businesses have begun to work on the next generation of sustainable solutions to power future economic growth. BP and Shell are boosting their investment in solar, wind, and other forms of renewable energy in the belief that these new energy sources would someday supplant their big petroleum businesses (Huang,2022; Sezen,2013). Manufacturing is a necessary and essential business in practically every country. It is vital to create jobs, eliminate poverty, improve living conditions, and accomplish other economic and social goals. Going green is a long-term manufacturing pathfinder at reducing the environmental impact of manufacturing processes and products. It encompasses a variety of techniques and technology aimed at reducing waste, lowering greenhouse gas emissions, conserving resources, and improving energy efficiency. Green manufacturing may have a huge influence on the green economy. A green economy is one built on sustainable, low-carbon, and resource-efficient companies and goods. Green manufacturing is an integral component of the green economy since it promotes the creation of sustainable goods and services while decreasing manufacturing's environmental effects (Yuan,2020; Cheng,2019). Green manufacturing involves employing sustainable manufacturing techniques and materials to lessen the environmental effect of industrial production. It strives to eliminate waste, minimize the use of natural resources, and lower the amount of pollution and greenhouse gas emissions related to industrial activities. A green economy is an economic system that promotes long-term development by balancing economic growth, environmental conservation, and social well-being. It has the potential to create jobs, increase energy security, and improve people's and communities' quality of life (Ji,2022; Mendonça,2009). Green manufacturing may contribute to a green economy in a number of different manners which are described below:

- Green manufacturing lessens the environmental effect of industrial production by consuming less energy, water, and natural resources, as well as creating less pollution and waste products.
- It encourages sustainable practices across the supply chain, from raw material procurement through product design and production
- Green manufacturing would stimulate innovation in sustainable technology and processes, resulting in new efficient and environmentally friendly goods and services.
- It would support economic growth and social well-being by creating jobs in sectors such as renewable energy, fuel efficiency, and waste reduction.
- Green manufacturing helps boost a company's competitiveness by lowering costs, increasing efficiency, and adapting to changing consumer demands for ecologically friendly products.

Figure 2. Contribution of green manufacturing in green economy in different manners

These Emissions of greenhouse gases not only pollute the natural world but are also hazardous to employees and society's health. This problem urges the industrial industry to implement sustainable efforts such as green manufacturing practices (GMPs). GMP assists businesses in complying with environmental regulations and laws by revamping operational processes to adhere to the 6Rs: rebuild, recycle, reuse, remanufacture, reduce, and recover (Afum,2020). Green manufacturing is gaining popularity because of the considerable influence it has on the economy, society, and the environment. According to the United Nations Industrial Development Organisation (UNIDO), its economic advantages are significant, with possible productivity gains of 15-20% and energy and material cost savings of 30-50%. By 2025, the worldwide market for green technology and goods is expected to exceed $2.5 trillion, propelling economic development and opening up new commercial opportunities. According to the World Bank, nations that embrace green manufacturing have achieved greater GDP growth rates than those that use standard industrial practices. Green manufacturing has the potential to stimulate economic growth, improve social well-being, reduce environmental impact, and contribute to global sustainability initiatives. It helps to create long-term jobs, promotes better working conditions and community development, and decreases carbon emissions. Governments are enacting legislation and regulations to encourage green manufacturing, while international programs such as the United Nations Sustainable Development Goals emphasize the relevance of green manufacturing in meeting global sustainability standards.

Research Questions

The following research question has been formulated based on the scope of the study;

- How does green manufacturing help with environmental growth and industry development?
- How can green manufacturing benefit and assist society?
- How does green manufacturing benefits economic development?

Research Methodology

The study incorporates a comprehensive literature evaluation conducted utilizing three main databases: Science Direct, Web of Science, and Google Scholar. These databases were chosen for their comprehensive coverage of academic publications from a wide range of subjects. The goal of the literature review is to collect current and relevant information on the influence of green manufacturing on the economy, society, and the environment. The first step is to search the proper databases for terms linked to green manufacturing, sustainability, and their influence on the economy, society, and the environment. Search criteria might include "green manufacturing," "sustainable manufacturing," "economy," "environment," and "economy." The search results are then filtered based on relevancy, publication date, and the study's inclusion requirements. Relevance to the study topic, publication date, and availability of full-text articles are included as inclusion criteria for article selection. The articles that do not directly answer the study topics have been excluded. The goal is to pick papers that give thorough insights into the economic, social, and environmental impacts of green manufacturing. Following the application of the inclusion and exclusion criteria, a final set of 53 relevant articles is chosen for in-depth study. These publications are reviewed and analyzed carefully in order to extract key results, techniques, and theoretical views on the influence of green manufacturing on the three priority areas. The findings of the evaluated publications are synthesized to highlight common themes, trends, and insights about the economic, social, and environmental implications of green manufacturing. The synthesis process entails categorizing and organizing the gathered material in order to build a complete grasp of the issue.

Green Manufacturing: Sustainable Approaches to Reduce Environmental Footprints

Green manufacturers conduct studies and develop, or use technologies and practices to lessen their environmental impact. "Green" is expounded as "interested with or supporting environmentalism and striving to preserve environmental quality (as by being recyclable, biodegradable, or nonpolluting)". Green manufacturing is referred to as a method or structure that employs as few resources as possible with, nonexistent, or detrimental impact on the environment when used to produce. Green signifies ecological sustainability and covers a wide range of subjects such as waste generation and reuse, air, water, and soil contamination, energy consumption, and efficiency (Khan,2022; Bhattacharya et al. 2011). According to the European Commission, extending green usage into other critical areas, such as green economics, will deliver more value with fewer resources by using far more ecologically friendly products whenever feasible (Leong,2019; Dronfeld,2012). Employees in green businesses must get particular manufacturing training in green technology and practices such as renewable energy, pollution reduction and elimination, GHG reduction, and recycling. These technologies and techniques are used to decrease or eliminate pollutants, lower greenhouse gas emissions, reduce waste, gather, reuse, recycle, or compost garbage, and preserve the environment. Green manufacturing has an environmental impact by lowering greenhouse gas emissions. Manufacturers may considerably minimize their carbon footprint by using the beginning of renewable energy such as solar or wind energy to generate electricity. Manufacturers can also reduce energy use by using energy-efficient technologies and methods, such as LED lighting or upgraded HVAC system (Angelo,2022; Rusinko,2007). Green manufacturing may also be beneficial to water resources. Manufacturers may drastically reduce water use by introducing water conservation methods such as reusing water or installing low-flow fixtures. This not only saves water but also helps to avoid water pollution by minimizing the quantity of wastewater created during the manufacturing process. Green manufacturing may also contribute to the growth of a green economy by providing new jobs in companies that focus on environmentally friendly practices and technology. As people grow more conscious of the significance of environmental sustainability, there is a booming market for goods and services that are environmentally friendly. Companies may supply this demand while simultaneously lowering their environmental effect by implementing green manufacturing processes. Here are some illustrations of how green manufacturing may benefit the environment: (He,2019; Mao,2019).

Figure 3. Illustration of benefits of green manufacturing on the environment

- Minimize Carbon Emissions - Green manufacturing may help decrease carbon emissions by utilizing renewable energy sources, improving energy efficiency, and reducing waste as well as emissions from industrial operations.
- Optimize Resource - By employing sustainable production processes and technology, green manufacturing help save natural resources such as water, energy, and raw materials.
- Reduction of Waste - Green manufacturing may assist to reduce the amount of trash that goes into landfills by establishing reducing waste and recycling programs, lowering the demand for new landfills, and avoiding toxic materials and pollutants from seeping into the ecosystem.
- Enhanced air and water quality - green manufacturing techniques can aid in the reduction of air and water pollution by reducing emissions and limiting the discharge of hazardous chemicals and contaminants.

In a CBS poll, 70% of Americans think that humans monitor activities to climate change and 56% say that we should take action immediately to combat it. Being green is therefore not only good for the environment but also excellent for your business since consumers are increasingly exclusively purchasing with companies who practice responsible production. As according to existing production trends and projections, it's a rising practice among manufacturing organizations and consumers, with business associates and consumers abandoning enterprises that do not improve their operations for the benefit of the environment (Agarwal,2020). Green manufacturing is the process of producing items in an ecologically beneficial and sustainable manner. It benefits the environment by lowering carbon footprint, conserving water, reducing waste, improving air quality, and increasing energy efficiency. Green manufacturing procedures make use of renewable energy, decrease waste, and enhance air quality. It also minimizes energy use, prices, and greenhouse gas emissions (Setyaningsih,2019; Rehman,2016). CO_2 emissions must be cut in half by 2030, according to a new United Nations assessment. As India embarks on an ambitious development program, green and sustainable manufacturing will be critical to its success. Green manufacturing employs green energy alternatives such as renewable or non-fossil fuel energy, lowers waste, promotes safe production, and decreases environmental impact. Organizations can not only alter their energy source, but they can also optimize their processes using technology to lower the amount of energy required to generate products. Due to rising environmental strain, eco-innovation is an important strategic instrument for achieving sustainable growth in industrial businesses. It is defined as the development, implementation, or use of a novel product, manufacturing method, service, management, or corporate strategy that decreases environmental risk, contamination, and other negative repercussions. The three major categories are eco-product development, environmental innovation, and sustainable environmental innovation. Eco-product implementation improves the environmental performance of current eco-products or contributes to the creation of the implementation of eco-products. Green products not only benefit the environment but also give leverage to an organization making them competitively more aggressive. One of the first things you'll notice is that there is substantially less garbage created, which might result in massive savings over time. Garbage affects every aspect of your business. Turning off laptops every evening, for example, will result in monthly electricity reductions. Waste reduction can improve several areas of your office. Anything from energy saving (turning off workplace lights at night) to basic paper recycling benefits both the environment and your pocketbook line (Tarraço,2021; Sezen,2013).

Role of Green Manufacturing on the Economy

A green economy is one that is low-carbon, a source of energy, and social inclusion. In a green economy, community and business investments in commercial operations, infrastructure, and investments that minimize carbon emissions and environmental harm generate employment and income growth, managed to improve resource and power effectiveness, and the retention of ecosystem services and biodiversity, as described by the United Nations Programme on Climate Change. Environmentally friendly manufacturing practices can also assist firms in obtaining tax incentives and deductions. Local and federal programs can give significant tax advantages to businesses that minimize their carbon impact. Attempts to expand more sustainably may benefit any business. It contributes to the brand's image, cleaner, safer work conditions, and increased profitability. Environmental protection has never been simpler or more productive. Making the switch to more environmentally friendly production practices is a guaranteed way to save money. Changing traditional incandescent lightbulbs with LED and CFL bulbs may significantly reduce energy expenses. Appliances can also be replaced with EnergyStar equipment to help buildings run more effectively. Lowering energy use benefits both the environment and the firm financially (Hjemdahl,2020; Afum,2020). Sustainability is a difficult endeavor that necessitates an organizational change in order to implement sustainable practices in the production chain. Green manufacturing and green logistics have received a lot of attention as part of the circular economy concept, which encompasses reuse and recycling. Implementing green manufacturing processes guarantees optimum functioning by enhancing characteristics such as longevity, maintenance, reusing, refurbishing, and recycling (Umar,2022).

Productivity rises as a result of innovation, allowing businesses to concentrate more on GM practices such as protocols and eco-design. Management is more likely to embrace GM techniques if they are prepared to participate in conventional and advanced supplier expansion rather than risk avoidance and reputation preservation (Wang, 2019). Attempts to build GM practices inside the organization are effective when all levels of business are considered; this may be accomplished through the creation of sustainability measures, guidelines, and focus groups. Employing green manufacturing practices may help the economy in several ways, as shown below (Ghadim,2019):

- Cost Savings - Green manufacturing may help organizations save money on production expenses by decreasing waste, energy usage, and other resource inputs, which can increase their competitiveness and profitability.
- Employment creation: The transition to green manufacturing may result in the development of new jobs in areas such as renewable power, waste disposal, and sustainable agriculture, in addition to existing manufacturing sectors that embrace sustainable methods.
- Market demand: As customer awareness and concern for the environment grows, they prefer items created in a sustainable manner. Globalization creates a consumer need for environmentally friendly items, which can encourage economic development and innovation.
- International competitiveness: Companies may improve their international competitiveness by implementing sustainable practices that fulfill global environmental standards and laws.
- Minimized Environmental Effects - Green manufacturing may assist to decrease the negative environmental effect of production by reducing emissions of greenhouse gases, pollution, and generation of waste. This can aid in the preservation of natural resources and habitats, which can support sectors such as recreation and tourism.

In accordance with research done in 2014 at Indiana University, one form of sustainable manufacturing earned $7 billion, whereas the other saved $80 million per year by reducing energy use. Customers want companies that are not just great at what they do but also good again for the causes they promote. Branding your company as an environmental champion may increase the perception of your manufacturing brand, which is crucial to your company's overall performance (Thomas,2022). Green manufacturing encompasses more than just the use of high-tech materials and the promotion of energy-efficient procedures. It needs a major transformation in product transportation. In contrast, the green production process is circular. It expands on the 3R concept of "reduce, reuse, recycle" to a 5R strategy of "repair, reuse, refurbish, re-manufacture, and recycle," which leads to reduced resource usage and products with longer life. It is practically possible to attain "zero rubbish to landfill" status. Schneider has committed to collecting 100% of industrial wastewater at its 200 manufacturing sites by 2030. Apart from environmental benefits, our circular business strategies have resulted in a 12% increase in circular revenue and sustainable growth. Whirlpool, a multinational appliance maker, has likewise embraced improved recycling processes and is on track to save $1 million over the next three years. (Tricoire,2019). Becoming green is profitable, as research has shown for years, but it is dependent on the company's capacity to implement best-practice sustainability techniques. In his book "The New Sustainability Advantage," Bob Willard (an internationally recognized pioneer in the field of sustainability) believes that by implementing best-practice sustainability measures, a typical company's earnings may increase by 51% to 81% over three to five years. Among other things, the business potential is connected to improved income, reduced energy, waste management, water, and material expenditures (Hans,2021). Several state and federal governments provide tax breaks to businesses that adopt green manufacturing practices. Becoming green might involve large upfront expenditures, but there are various incentives to get you started. Because governments do not want huge polluters on their soil, encouraging firms to use green manufacturing practices is vital. It's something your firm may use to make the transition go more smoothly. Examine your options and discover what monetary incentives are available to your organization (Bag,2020). Sustainability may be achieved in a variety of ways, including the Green Economy, Environmental Manufacturing and Consumption, and proficiency. Sustainable production and use aims to enhance manufacturing and consumption practises in order to reduce resource consumption, waste generation, and emissions during the life of a product or technique. Adaptive reuse, on the other hand, is concerned with lowering the quantity of resources used as well as the amount of waste and emissions produced per unit of item or service. Conversely, the Green Economy is a comprehensive economic growth plan that promotes long-term sustainable growth through investment, employment, and developing skills. Advocating for a macroeconomic approach to long-term economic growth, demonstrating Green Economy techniques, gaining access to green financing, technology, and investments, and assisting nations in transitioning to a Green Economy. The UN Environment Programme is assisting Mongolia in the execution of its National Green Development Strategy, the incorporation of a green economy into local-level expansion plans, SDG indicators, and the greening of important sectors. Green manufacturing is the application of environmentally friendly and sustainable techniques in the manufacturing process. This might include lowering waste, employing renewable energy, and avoiding the usage of dangerous products. Manufacturing businesses may lower their environmental effect and generate more sustainable goods by using these techniques. In consequence, this can help the economy move toward a green economy in a few aspects as manufacturing organizations may become more effective and save money on materials and energy expenses by minimizing waste and adopting renewable energy sources. This can assist to lower overall manufacturing costs and make green products more accessible to customers (AI,2021; Yuan,2020). Moreover, green manufacturing may aid in the promotion of innovation and competitiveness. Companies may differentia themselves from the market and get a competitive edge by inventing new and sustainable goods. This can spur innovation and open up new avenues for development and expansion Several countries provide tax breaks, grants, and subsidies to businesses that embrace sustainable practices. It also encourages collaboration among enterprises, communities, and other stakeholders in pursuit of a common objective of sustainability. This can lead to new collaborations and initiatives that support long-term economic prosperity. These incentives can assist to offset the expenses of implementing green industrial techniques, speeding up the shift to a more environmentally friendly economy (Khan,2019).

The Green Manufacturing Ripple Effect: Creating a Sustainable Society

Manufacturing contributes significantly to the ever-increasing emissions of greenhouse gases. Green manufacturing has grown in popularity over the years as a result of its sustainable methods and contribution to pollution reduction. Changing the industrial industry is no easy task, but it is essential for reducing society's carbon impact. Manufacturers who set "sustainability" as a goal in their company operations will gain the long-term rewards of making eco-friendly innovations. The most important advantage of this list is life. The acts of a firm have an influence on the social welfare of its community and the globe. Businesses steadily reduce the number of toxic pollutants discharged into the atmosphere through developing sustainable efforts. Overall, the purpose of green manufacturing is to reduce the global carbon footprint and create a healthier environment for society (Li,2020; Tran,2022). In today's competitive market, pursuing sustainability in all company activities is a significant issue for organizations. Consumers are crucial stakeholders who are growing more conscious of firms' societal and environmentally friendly efforts. In today's competitive market, pursuing sustainability in all company activities is a significant issue for organizations. Consumers are crucial stakeholders who are growing more conscious of firms' eco-friendly efforts such as described below; (Waheed,2020; Singh,2022).

- Green manufacturing techniques can assist to minimise air and water pollution, which can benefit public health significantly. This can reduce the occurrence of respiratory ailments, malignancies, and other pollution-related health concerns. Green manufacturing can assist to cut healthcare expenses and enhance the quality of life by encouraging a healthier society.
- The shift to green manufacturing has the potential to produce new opportunities in a variety of disciplines, including engineering, technology, and management. This employment can contribute to economic growth while also providing new chances for employees. Moreover, green manufacturing may help regenerate towns by fostering long-term economic growth.
- Green manufacturing may assist address the rising demand for environmentally friendly products and services. Customers are increasingly looking for items made using environmentally friendly procedures and materials, and firms that can match this need are more likely to succeed in the marketplace. This can assist to fuel economic growth and open up new business prospects.

It assists to lower manufacturing activities' carbon footprint by reducing energy usage and utilizing clean energy sources. This can assist to minimise our reliance on fossil fuels and the potential impact of climate disruption. Thinking about the sustainability benefits us all by saving money, time, and resources, allowing us to live life more completely while also ensuring subsequent generations have access to clean air and water (Salazaar,2022). The larger the customer demand for green products and the environmental benefits of green manufacturing, the higher the influence of social welfare. To promote social well-being, businesses should involve in the change in green production, and governments should consider consumer interests as well as environmental advantages (Zhang,2019). Manufacturing's centrality in society today makes it a crucial focus in the larger picture of sustainability. Green manufacturing is distinguished by a dedication to social responsibility, which includes encouraging, upholding human rights, and mitigating harmful effects on local communities. This can serve to increase fairness and social justice while also improving the reputation of enterprises that practice sustainable manufacturing. It helps businesses and communities become more resilient by lowering their reliance on nonrenewable resources and boosting their ability to resist environmental and economic shocks. Over time, this can contribute to more secure and environmentally friendly economies and civilizations (Pang,2019). Constructing a green manufacturing system is essential to achieving ecologically responsible production and the long-term development of living things, and attempting to evaluate its sustainable development can validate its role as a foundation for political decisions, creating a cycle between such foreign financial and innate green production strategies. Users may lessen their environmental impact and the number of toxins discharged into the atmosphere by making changes. Future generations will benefit from cleaner air and water, fewer landfills, and more sustainable energy sources. (Lagas,2019). In a research done by United Nations Industrial Development Organization (UNIDO) Green Industry relates to economies pursuing a more sustainable growth path through green investment projects and public policy actions that support eco friendly capital activity. It makes excellent commercial sense to take care of materials, energy, water, trash, and emissions. RECP is the method for accomplishing this. RECP encompasses the use of preventative management measures to maximize the efficient use of natural resources, reduce waste and emissions, and promote safe and responsible manufacturing. Economic expansion and economic energy usage have gained increased attention in recent decades due to their impact on global CO2 emissions. Green manufacturing promotes innovation by encouraging the creation of novel technologies, materials, and techniques that are more environmentally friendly and sustainable. This could result in new commercial prospects as well as economic growth. It increases transparency in the supply chain by encouraging the adoption of environmentally and socially responsible sourcing techniques, which can assist to decrease social and environmental hazards in global value chains. (Dauda,2019). Since the nineteenth century, the constant development in globalization and industrialization has reinforced the need for sustainable methods that ensure environmental preservation. It assists to strengthen communities by encouraging local manufacturing and consumption, minimizing reliance on international supply chains, and helping small companies and employment (Baah,2021). Pollution and scarcity of resources place a growing strain on the global ecology, resulting in higher commodity prices and unpredictability. GM helps to promote social justice by encouraging fair labor standards, minimizing environmental injustices, and advocating for the rights of vulnerable populations. This can contribute to a more egalitarian and just society. It does help policymakers innovate by demonstrating effective sustainability practices and the economic advantages of sustainability. This can result in new rules and regulations that encourage the green economy (Ciliberto,2021). GM could be regarded as a company that manufactures green products. GM may be characterized as the "greening of manufacturing" from the standpoint of the board. GM is a branch of conventional manufacturing that generates environmentally friendly goods (output) by utilizing raw materials and energy more effectively (input), with safe and waste-reducing techniques (process). GM is a combination of manufacturing practices (input, process, and output) designed to reduce the environmental impact of production. GM is supposed to be able to handle environmental issues that develop throughout an industry's manufacturing process, such as waste and carbon dioxide emissions. Implementing green manufacturing techniques may help a company's brand recognition and entice environmentally concerned customers prepared to pay a premium for environmentally friendly items (Giri,2019; Setyaningsih,2021). GM also allows us to be less reliant on fossil fuels; it helps to reduce geopolitical tensions and improve energy independence by employing renewable energy sources and reducing reliance on fossil fuels. Help to enhance resource usage and decrease waste, which can have a positive impact on natural resource availability and cost. It contributes to biodiversity conservation by reducing the negative effects of industrial activities on ecosystems and habitats. Green manufacturing might assist to reduce habitat loss, pollution, and the usage of dangerous chemicals that can harm animals by promoting environmentally friendly practices. By providing jobs and economic possibilities in previously neglected or afflicted communities, GM can help to promote social equity. It can also close socioeconomic gaps in access to safe drinking water, clean air, and other resources, improve disaster resilience, reduce the negative environmental impact of industrial operations, and encourage cultural values such as environmental stewardship, sustainable development, and social responsibility. Finally, it may be used to raise environmental awareness and motivate individuals and corporations to take action to protect the environment. It allows for collaboration among Organizations and communities to embrace green practices that support sustainable development and raise societal awareness (Green,2019).

Global Green Manufacturing Initiatives: Nations From Across the Globe

Several nations have legislation and programs in place to support environmental manufacturing and ecologically sustainable techniques. Implementation of these initiatives and policies helps contribute to the creation of a more equitable and environmentally friendly global economy, as well as to the battle against the effects of climate change and other ecological concerns. Here are a couple of such examples:

- Germany - The German government has put in place a comprehensive policy framework to encourage sustainable manufacturing and resource efficiency, which includes the National Program for Sustainable Consumption and Production as well as the Resource Efficiency Program.
- China - Many measures have been established by the Chinese government to encourage sustainable manufacturing, including the Circular Economy Promotion Law and the Made in China 2025 policy, which prioritizes green manufacturing as well as the development of sustainable technology.
- United States - The US government has put in place a number of measures to encourage green manufacturing, such as tax breaks for renewable energy and energy-efficient technology, as well as the Sustainable Manufacturing Initiative, which seeks to encourage sustainable manufacturing practices.
- Japan - Many efforts, like the Eco-Action 21 program and the Green Procurement Program, have been adopted by the Japanese government to encourage sustainable production and resource economy.
- European Union - The European Union has put in place a number of laws and programs to encourage sustainable manufacturing and resource efficiency, such as the Circular Economy Action Plan and the EU Eco-Management and Audit System.
- Brazil - The Brazilian government has implemented the National Solid Waste Policy, which seeks to encourage sustainable waste management and decrease the environmental effect of industry and consumerism.

FINDINGS AND CONCLUSION

Green manufacturing has a substantial economic, social, and environmental effect. It has the potential to boost efficiency, cut waste and expenses, and provide new job possibilities. It can also improve worker health and safety, minimize environmental impact, and encourage a circular economy. Green manufacturing is a viable path for a greener, more sustainable economy. Companies may decrease their environmental effect and promote sustainable growth by implementing eco-friendly production methods, materials, and technology. This, in turn, may benefit the economy by encouraging innovation, creating jobs, and lowering the risk of natural catastrophes and economic disruptions. Furthermore, green manufacturing may have a wide range of good societal effects, such as better public health, higher social fairness, improved catastrophe resilience, and the advancement of cultural values. Green manufacturing benefits the green economy by creating new employment, enhancing competitiveness, lowering resource consumption, lowering environmental impact, and fostering innovation. It also improves sustainability by decreasing waste and pollution while also opening up new business opportunities. By eliminating waste, enhancing efficiency, and supporting environmental preservation, green manufacturing may assist to develop a more sustainable and resilient economy. Finally, green manufacturing is a step forward toward a more ecological and fair future

ACKNOWLEDGMENT

I would like to thank all my co-authors, Dr.Ipseeta Satpathy, Dr. B.C.M. Patnaik, Dr. Sukanta Kumar Baral, and Atmika Patnaik for their valuable contribution to this study.

REFERENCES

Afum, E., Agyabeng-Mensah, Y., Sun, Z., Frimpong, B., Kusi, L. Y., & Acquah, I. S. K. (2020). Exploring the link between green manufacturing, operational competitiveness, firm reputation and sustainable performance dimensions: A mediated approach. *Journal of Manufacturing Technology Management*, *31*(7), 1417–1438. doi:10.1108/JMTM-02-2020-0036

Agarwal, S., Agrawal, V., & Dixit, J. K. (2020). Green manufacturing: A MCDM approach. *Materials Today: Proceedings*, *26*, 2869–2874. doi:10.1016/j.matpr.2020.02.595

Ai, O., Chioma, E., Okenwa, G. O., Samuel, I., & Abiodun Ademola, A. (2021). *Green Manufacturing: Rethinking the Sustainability of Nigerian Manufacturing Firms*.

Baah, C., Opoku-Agyeman, D., Acquah, I. S. K., Agyabeng-Mensah, Y., Afum, E., Faibil, D., & Abdoulaye, F. A. M. (2021). Examining the correlations between stakeholder pressures, green production practices, firm reputation, environmental and financial performance: Evidence from manufacturing SMEs. *Sustainable Production and Consumption*, *27*, 100–114. doi:10.1016/j.spc.2020.10.015

Bag, S., & Pretorius, J. H. C. (2022). Relationships between industry 4.0, sustainable manufacturing and circular economy: Proposal of a research framework. *The International Journal of Organizational Analysis*, *30*(4), 864–898. doi:10.1108/IJOA-04-2020-2120

Bag, S., Yadav, G., Wood, L. C., Dhamija, P., & Joshi, S. (2020). Industry 4.0 and the circular economy: Resource melioration in logistics. *Resources Policy*, *68*, 101776. doi:10.1016/j.resourpol.2020.101776

Cheng, J., Yi, J., Dai, S., & Xiong, Y. (2019). Can low-carbon city construction facilitate green growth? Evidence from China's pilot low-carbon city initiative. *Journal of Cleaner Production*, *231*, 1158–1170. doi:10.1016/j.jclepro.2019.05.327

Ciliberto, C., Szopik-Depczyńska, K., Tarczyńska-Łuniewska, M., Ruggieri, A., & Ioppolo, G. (2021). Enabling the Circular Economy transition: A sustainable lean manufacturing recipe for Industry 4.0. *Business Strategy and the Environment*, *30*(7), 3255–3272. doi:10.1002/bse.2801

D'Angelo, V., Cappa, F., & Peruffo, E. (2022). Green manufacturing for sustainable development: The positive effects of green activities, green investments, and non-green products on economic performance. *Business Strategy and the Environment*.

Dauda, L., Long, X., Mensah, C. N., & Salman, M. (2019). The effects of economic growth and innovation on CO 2 emissions in different regions. *Environmental Science and Pollution Research International*, *26*(15), 15028–15038. doi:10.100711356-019-04891-y PMID:30919181

Dornfeld, D., Yuan, C., Diaz, N., Zhang, T., & Vijayaraghavan, A. (2012). Introduction to green manufacturing. In *Green manufacturing: fundamentals and applications* (pp. 1–23). Springer US.

Eslami, Y., Dassisti, M., Lezoche, M., & Panetto, H. (2019). A survey on sustainability in manufacturing organisations: Dimensions and future insights. *International Journal of Production Research*, *57*(15-16), 5194–5214. doi:10.1080/00207543.2018.1544723

Ghadimi, P., O'Neill, S., Wang, C., & Sutherland, J. W. (2021). Analysis of enablers on the successful implementation of green manufacturing for Irish SMEs. *Journal of Manufacturing Technology Management*, *32*(1), 85–109. doi:10.1108/JMTM-10-2019-0382

Giri, R. N., Mondal, S. K., & Maiti, M. (2019). Government intervention on a competing supply chain with two green manufacturers and a retailer. *Computers & Industrial Engineering*, *128*, 104–121. doi:10.1016/j.cie.2018.12.030

Green, J. M., Croft, S. A., Durán, A. P., Balmford, A. P., Burgess, N. D., Fick, S., Gardner, T. A., Godar, J., Suavet, C., Virah-Sawmy, M., Young, L. E., & West, C. D. (2019). Linking global drivers of agricultural trade to on-the-ground impacts on biodiversity. *Proceedings of the National Academy of Sciences of the United States of America*, *116*(46), 23202–23208. doi:10.1073/pnas.1905618116 PMID:31659031

Green Economy. (n.d.). UNEP - UN Environment Programme. https://www.unep.org/regions/asia-and-pacific/regional-initiatives/supporting-resource-efficiency/green-economy#:~:text=In%20a%20green%20economy%2C%20growth,of%20biodiversity%20and%20ecosystem%20services

Hans, R. (2022). Complete Guide to Green Manufacturing. *Deskera Blog*. https://www.deskera.com/blog/green-manufacturing/

He, X., Huang, S. Z., Chau, K. Y., Shen, H. W., & Zhu, Y. L. (2019). A study on the effect of environmental regulation on green innovation performance: A case of green manufacturing enterprises in pearl river delta in China. *Ekoloji*, *28*(107), 727–736.

WEF. (2022b, May 20). *Here's why green manufacturing is crucial for a low-carbon future*. World Economic Forum. https://www.weforum.org/agenda/2019/01/here-s-why-green-manufacturing-is-crucial-for-a-low-carbon-future/

Hjemdahl, P. W. (2020, March 17). Green Manufacturing: The Business Benefits of Sustainability. *rePurpose Global*. https://repurpose.global/blog/post/green-manufacturing-the-business-benefits-of-sustainability#:~:text=Taking%20steps%20to%20become%20more,the%20company%20become%20more%20profitable.

Huang, L., & Zhao, W. (2022). The impact of green trade and green growth on natural resources. *Resources Policy*, *77*, 102749. doi:10.1016/j.resourpol.2022.102749

Ji, J., Xie, Z., Li, C., & Ji, F. (2022). The influence of the manufacturing agglomeration heterogeneity on the green economic efficiency in China. *Electronic Commerce Research*, 1–25. doi:10.100710660-022-09641-w

Khan, S. A. R., Sharif, A., Golpîra, H., & Kumar, A. (2019). A green ideology in Asian emerging economies: From environmental policy and sustainable development. *Sustainable Development (Bradford)*, 27(6), 1063–1075. doi:10.1002d.1958

Khan, S. A. R., Yu, Z., & Umar, M. (2022). A road map for environmental sustainability and green economic development: An empirical study. *Environmental Science and Pollution Research International*, 29(11), 1–9. doi:10.100711356-021-16961-1 PMID:34643866

Lagas, B. (2019). *Five Benefits of Embracing Sustainability and Green Manufacturing*. NIST. https://www.nist.gov/blogs/manufacturing-innovation-blog/five-benefits-embracing-sustainability-and-green-manufacturing

Leong, W. D., Lam, H. L., Ng, W. P. Q., Lim, C. H., Tan, C. P., & Ponnambalam, S. G. (2019). Lean and green manufacturing—a review on its applications and impacts. *Process integration and optimization for sustainability, 3*, 5-23.

Li, G., Lim, M. K., & Wang, Z. (2020). Stakeholders, green manufacturing, and practice performance: Empirical evidence from Chinese fashion businesses. *Annals of Operations Research, 290*(1-2), 961–982. doi:10.100710479-019-03157-7

Mao, Y., & Wang, J. (2019). Is green manufacturing expensive? Empirical evidence from China. *International Journal of Production Research*, 57(23), 7235–7247. doi:10.1080/00207543.2018.1480842

Mealy, P., & Teytelboym, A. (2022). Economic complexity and the green economy. *Research Policy*, 51(8), 103948. doi:10.1016/j.respol.2020.103948

Mendonca, M., Jacobs, D., & Sovacool, B. K. (2009). Powering the green economy: *The feed-in tariff handbook*. Earthscan.

Moktadir, M. A., Rahman, T., Rahman, M. H., Ali, S. M., & Paul, S. K. (2018). Drivers to sustainable manufacturing practices and circular economy: A perspective of leather industries in Bangladesh. *Journal of Cleaner Production*, 174, 1366–1380. doi:10.1016/j.jclepro.2017.11.063

Pang, R., & Zhang, X. (2019). Achieving environmental sustainability in manufacture: A 28-year bibliometric cartography of green manufacturing research. *Journal of Cleaner Production*, 233, 84–99. doi:10.1016/j.jclepro.2019.05.303

Rehman, M. A., Seth, D., & Shrivastava, R. L. (2016). Impact of green manufacturing practices on organisational performance in Indian context: An empirical study. *Journal of Cleaner Production*, 137, 427–448. doi:10.1016/j.jclepro.2016.07.106

Rusinko, C. (2007). Green manufacturing: An evaluation of environmentally sustainable manufacturing practices and their impact on competitive outcomes. *IEEE Transactions on Engineering Management*, 54(3), 445–454. doi:10.1109/TEM.2007.900806

Seow, C. N., & Hamid, N. A. A. (2017, June). Green manufacturing performance measure for automobile manufacturers. In *2017 International Conference on Industrial Engineering, Management Science and Application (ICIMSA)* (pp. 1-5). IEEE. 10.1109/ICIMSA.2017.7985589

Setyaningsih, I., Ciptono, W. S., Indarti, N., & Kemal, N. I. V. (2019). What is green manufacturing? A quantitative literature review. In *E3S Web of Conferences* (Vol. 120, p. 01001). EDP Sciences.

Setyaningsih, I., & Indarti, N., & Ciptono, W. S. (2018). Green Manufacturing's adoption by Indonesian smes: A conceptual model. *2018 IEEE International Conference on Industrial Engineering and Engineering Management (IEEM)*. IEEE. https://doi.org/10.1109/IEEM.2018.8607389

Sezen, B., & Cankaya, S. Y. (2013). Effects of green manufacturing and eco-innovation on sustainability performance. *Procedia: Social and Behavioral Sciences*, 99, 154–163. doi:10.1016/j.sbspro.2013.10.481

Singh, J., Singh, C. D., & Deepak, D. (2022). Impact of green manufacturing parameters on strategic success in Indian manufacturing industries. *International Journal of Competitiveness*, 2(2), 91–111. doi:10.1504/IJC.2022.125747

Tarraço, E. L., Borini, F. M., Bernardes, R. C., & Della Santa Navarrete, S. (2021). The differentiated impact of the institutional environment on eco-innovation and green manufacturing strategies: A comparative analysis between emerging and developed countries. *IEEE Transactions on Engineering Management*.

Thomas. (n.d.). Green Manufacturing: The Business Benefits Of Sustainability. *Thomas Blog*. https://blog.thomasnet.com/green-manufacturing-sustainability-benefits

Tran, Q. H. (2022). The impact of green finance, economic growth and energy usage on CO2 emission in Vietnam–a multivariate time series analysis. *China Finance Review International*, 12(2), 280–296. doi:10.1108/CFRI-03-2021-0049

Umar, M., Khan, S. A. R., Zia-ul-haq, H. M., Yusliza, M. Y., & Farooq, K. (2022). The role of emerging technologies in implementing green practices to achieve sustainable operations. *The TQM Journal*, 34(2), 232–249. doi:10.1108/TQM-06-2021-0172

Waheed, A., Zhang, Q., Rashid, Y., Tahir, M. S., & Zafar, M. W. (2020). Impact of green manufacturing on consumer ecological behavior: Stakeholder engagement through green production and innovation. *Sustainable Development (Bradford)*, 28(5), 1395–1403. doi:10.1002d.2093

Wang, C. H. (2019). How organizational green culture influences green performance and competitive advantage: The mediating role of green innovation. *Journal of Manufacturing Technology Management*, 30(4), 666–683. doi:10.1108/JMTM-09-2018-0314

Wojnarowska, M., Sołtysik, M., & Prusak, A. (2021). Impact of eco-labelling on the implementation of sustainable production and consumption. *Environmental Impact Assessment Review*, 86, 106505. doi:10.1016/j.eiar.2020.106505

Yuan, H., Feng, Y., Lee, C. C., & Cen, Y. (2020). How does manufacturing agglomeration affect green economic efficiency? *Energy Economics*, 92, 104944. doi:10.1016/j.eneco.2020.104944

Zameer, H., Wang, Y., Yasmeen, H., & Mubarak, S. (2022). Green innovation as a mediator in the impact of business analytics and environmental orientation on green competitive advantage. *Management Decision*, *60*(2), 488–507. doi:10.1108/MD-01-2020-0065

Zhang, Z., Wang, Y., Meng, Q., & Luan, X. (2019). Impacts of green production decision on social welfare. *Sustainability (Basel)*, *11*(2), 453. doi:10.3390u11020453

Chapter 16
Factors Influencing Green Purchase Intention Among Food Retail Consumers:
An Empirical Study on Uttar Pradesh

Nikita Sharma

Amity University, Noida, India

Shivani Mehta

https://orcid.org/0000-0003-3979-1324

Amity University, Noida, India

ABSTRACT

The main objective of the study is to investigate the factors influencing the green purchase intention of Indian food retail consumers using the theory of planned behavior (TPB). Additionally, the study also aims to determine the effect of green consciousness and health consciousness over green purchase intention among Indian food retail consumers and give suggestive measures for effective implementation of green policies and green practices of the consumers. The study is conducted based on the quantitative as well as qualitative approach, with data collected from 384 Indian consumers of Uttar Pradesh through a self-administered five-point rating questionnaire. Exploratory factor analysis, and regression analysis are adopted for the data analysis to identify the predictors of green purchase intention of the consumers, highlighting the importance of subjective norms, environmental knowledge, green consciousness, and health consciousness, which are positively and significantly influenced the green purchase intention with consumer attitude being least significant variable in the study.

DOI: 10.4018/978-1-6684-8969-7.ch016

INTRODUCTION

Background

Environment issues such as global warming, climate change, extinction of animals and plant species, and depletion of limited natural resources are the major concern of all the societies for the last two-three decades. The "environment" more specifically the green environment plays a significant role in influencing human roles and their activities, making it one of the marketing issues (Moisander,2007). Today, marketers' primary concern is the environment and SDGs are at the heart of policy makers globally due to which green consumerism became one of seventeen sustainable development goals based on consumers' belief in the consequences of their actions. One cannot side-line the importance of sustainable and green consumption.

Green Consumption refers to environmentally conscious consumption. Environmentally conscious purchasing, as well as the utilization and correct disposal of various products and services, must be carried out correctly, and environmentally responsible strategies must be followed both by consumers and producers. Through adopting green eco-friendly consumption practices and only purchasing green products, goods and services, consumers can lessen the negative impact that they have on the environment as well as to avert environmental degradation. With the increased environment awareness and green demand trends of products, only 3 percent of the total market share is represented by eco-friendly products (Bray et al., 2011). These findings suggest that consumers of today continue to ignore the environmental impacts of product acquisitions (Mohr et al., 2001).

The authorities in India have therefore changed their activities to be more eco-friendly because of global environmental awareness. By launching environmentally responsible initiatives and measures since start of 21st century, the higher authorities demonstrated significant support for environment friendly projects. By diversifying the responsible economy and increasing productivity in the face of environmental challenges, the nation is now regarded as one of those striving for a green economy (Jain & Kaur, 2006). Over the last few years in India, the market specifically for green food products has been growing at a quick pace from the fact that many organic food stores are opening in India. Due to increasing health concern among Indian consumers in major cities have been the major important factor contributing to rapid growth in the market. The market of green food in India is likely to grow at a CAGR of over 25 percent. (Indian Organic Food Market Forecast & Opportunities, 2020). Despite all these efforts and initiatives that have been taken by Indian government, the knowledge about behavioural trends and consumers intention to buy green food products is still restricted among Indians.

Food retail stores are amongst the key stakeholders of natural resources through sustainable production, which could help to transform routine corporate operations into more environmentally friendly ones (Claro, Neto, and Claro, 2013). Thus, with varied degrees of success, majority of merchants are incorporating green practices into their daily operations. To achieve this, a detailed understanding of green production and consumption is required by both food retailers and food retail consumers for implementation of green practices and green purchase intentions respectively. Therefore, it is important to understand the food retail consumers purchase intentions of food products as well to get a thorough grasp of the elements influencing consumers' decision to buy green products.

Environmental responsible purchasing is essential since impulsive purchases of products and services can seriously harm the planet and the environment. 40 percent of the environmental harm was caused by consumer-related household purchases (Grunert, 1995). Consumer intention to purchase is a crucial topic, irrespective of consumerism (Chen, Chen, and Tung, 2018). Green purchasing refers to the purchasing of environmentally responsible goods and is most responsible to measure intention to make green purchases and behaviour. There is a segment of society that is really interested and supportive of the environment. It is also impossible to overlook the fact that a sizable portion of society continues to be either unconcerned or uninformed of their environment. However, a lot of factors influence a consumers' decision to buy organic food goods.

This study contributes to enrich the theoretical consumer behaviour using Theory of Planned Behavior (TPB) in Indian literature review. In addition, the study's findings will assist organizations, marketers, and policy makers in comprehending the behavioural dimensions of customers and putting the orientation procedures into action. With a better understanding of these factors, more businesses and marketers will be attracted, leading to the creation and improvement of green marketing strategies to draw in more green clients and put methods in place to encourage green buying.

Research Problem Statement

Using TPB as the theoretical base/frame, there is a vast literature that analyses the factors that influence consumers' intention to make green purchases to provide suggestive measures that promote appropriate environmental behavior effectively. However, the literature suggests a variety of determinants, and some studies have contradictory results regarding overall effects, effective size, and the relative importance of factors, probably because of differences in the context of the studies. According to Liobikien and Bernatonien (2017), these distinctions are the result of distinct cultures from various nations. To comprehend these differences, additional research is required. In response to this call, empirical studies on TPB have been carried out in a variety of regions in both Western and Eastern nations. However, most of these studies have focused only on variables that were selected based on a literature review and have not investigated variables that are related to specific cultural contexts. Among all study regions, very few have examined Eastern nations. Only a few studies were conducted on India, and several authors have recognized the need for additional, theoretically sound research to explain green purchasing decisions (Abdul, 2007). There has been a disparity or "gap" between positive sentiments that consumers have expressed, their awareness of the environment, and their actual purchasing behaviours in numerous studies examining green purchase behaviour (Tanner et al., 2008). According to Hughner (2007), even though 67 percent of consumers expressed a favourable sentiment toward purchasing organic food products, only four percent did so. Even though empirical studies on a variety of aspects of green consumption were found, the numerous elements influencing customers' desire to make green purchases are still not fully understood. In addition, these factors and barriers may assist in elucidating the different causes of the present inconsistency in attitude, behaviour, and knowledge. As a result, the various content-specific factors that influence Indian food retail consumers' green purchase intentions are sufficiently explored and investigated in this paper with special reference to Uttar Pradesh state.

The Overall Aim of the Study

This study analyses the available literature on purchase intention of green food products and attempts is to investigate factors influencing the green purchase intention using the Theory of Planned Behaviour (TPB) to obtain a structured explanation of Indian retail buyers' intention to make green purchases. In addition, this study also aims to determine the impact of green consciousness and health consciousness over green purchasing intention among Indian food retail consumers and give suggestive measures for effective implementation of green policies and green practices of food retail consumers. In this study, three constructs—attitude, subjective norms, and perceived behavioural control—are combined using the TPB model. The TPB Model's subjective norms and consumer attitude variables were directly used. Based on a review of the literature, environmental awareness and green label variables were also introduced.

Numerous elements influencing consumers' desire to make green purchases are found after a thorough literature analysis. Based on these variables, plausible recommendations are provided for bridging the attitude-behavior-knowledge gap in green purchasing behaviour and for converting the favourable attitude towards green purchasing into actual purchasing actions.

Research Gaps

Research Gap 1

The factors influencing green purchase intention in India are insufficiently understood.

Research Gap 2

Existing research on consumer behaviour in different countries and regions, including middle east and eastern regions, largely depends on the TPB, and insufficiently explores context-specific variables.

These gaps lead to the research objective of this work.

Research Objectives

The research objectives of this study are-

1. To determine and explain the factors influencing green purchasing intention among Indian food retail consumers.
2. To identify the effect of green consciousness and health consciousness over green purchasing intention among Indian food retail consumers.
3. To outline the suggestive measures for effective implementation of green policies and green practices of food retail consumers.

Research Questions

The following are the research questions for this study:

1. What are the factors that predict the green purchasing intentions of Indian food retail consumers?
2. Which of the two i.e., Health or green consciousness has greater influence on the purchase intentions of the Indian food retail consumers?
3. What can be different measures for effective implementation of green policies and green practices of food retail consumers?
4. What impact does consumer attitude has on the purchase intention of Indian retail food consumers?
5. What impact does subjective norms has on the purchase intention of Indian retail food consumers?

6. What impact does environmental knowledge has on the purchase intention of Indian food retail consumers?
7. What impact does eco-label products has on the purchase intention of Indian retail food consumers?

Significance of the Study

The study's goals must be met for Indian food retail customers to change many areas of their green practises. By developing more sustainable practices and encouraging the consumers to opt for environmentally friendly food products, it is possible influence their purchasing intentions to some extent. It is hoped that this study will significantly advance the work of academics and marketers in several ways. First off, unlike past research that have largely focused on the development of environmentally friendly food goods, this empirical study focuses on consumers' intentions to purchase such products. One of the earliest initiatives to investigate how green goods are used in the food sector is the current study. This study expands previous research on green marketing using real data from the food business.

Second, the TPB used in this study has specific indirect antecedents to purchase intention. By putting the proposed model to the test, the study illustrates the steps leading to the intention to buy environmentally friendly food products. Few research has incorporated numerous antecedents into TPB, even though many prior marketing studies have explored the effects of each antecedent and outcome separately. As a result, this study assists academically in understanding the interactions between the variables that affect intention to purchase green/organic food goods.

Finally, this research adds to our understanding of how Indian consumers shop for eco-friendly food products. Although consumers' cultural values and consumption patterns in India have been the subject of several studies. Marketers of eco-friendly food items now have access to more precise information about Indian customers' intentions to buy eco-friendly food items. The requirements that Indian consumers have in terms of green food products can be better understood by Indian Food retail companies that intend to expand their brands.

REVIEW OF LITERATURE

Due to ongoing use of natural resources and the discharge of dangerous chemicals, our planet has experienced risks to the environment as well as a lack of resources. Because of this, experts came up with a "green" idea that can be used as a tool to encourage individuals and businesses to preserve natural resources and protect the environment. The term "green" had been defined by various researchers. You can also use "organic," "eco-friendly," or "sustainable" for "green." Green products, systems, and services are those that consume less energy, utilise renewable resources, are recyclable, all-natural, environmentally friendly, long-lasting, low-maintenance, reusable, biodegradable, and free of ozone damaging chemicals.

A natural operation that minimizes harmful gas emissions, eliminates waste, and conserves natural resources is referred to as "green.". The "environment" more specifically the "green environment," has a significant role in influencing human roles and activities, making it one of the marketing issues. Today, marketers' primary concern is the environment. Before the late 1980s, environmentalism and going green weren't as popular ideas. Britain was where the green movement began; The "Greening" movement's initial contributors were British consumers.

Fortes referred to the situation as a won for both the organization and the nature when green practices are implemented. It is possible to explain that an organization is achieving economically efficient production methods if it can produce products using recyclable materials and renewable energy. To put it another way, using renewable energy and recyclable materials lessens the exploitation of natural resources and protects the environment from dangerous chemicals. Green production also helps to improve product design and quality because it starts with designing the product and ensures the product's cycle of life. Therefore, effective, and efficient design of the product and longer seven-life cycles are further measures of environmental sustainability through reducing waste and reprocessing. Avoiding the wasteful use of natural resources and the emission of harmful gases into the atmosphere, both of which endanger society, is another aspect of being environmentally responsible.

Due to the company's involvement in environmental harm and degradation, consumers supported the greening movement. As a result, green marketing strategies were adopted outside of Great Britain. A few realists also spoke out in favour of sustainable and environmentally beneficial consumption.

Green practises are ethical business methods that avoid resource waste, inefficient use of resources, and environmental harm. Smith and Friend define "green practises" as actions geared towards protecting the environment. Using natural and organic resources to construct factories, tightening emission controls, and finding environmentally friendly materials are a few examples of green practises. Green practice, according to Gupta and Kumar, starts with the efficient use of natural resources, which leads to wise management of costs and waste. The company's financial capacity benefits from this. Managers learn how to use technology, research, and information systems to advance sustainability through green practice. Finding areas where a store can improve its efficiency is helpful.

Green practices can improve a food retail business's image, efficiency, financial profits, and market share, employee commitment, customer satisfaction, and business performance by reducing unwanted organizational idiosyncratic risk (Gleim et al., 2013). However, several researchers have described the difficulties and obstacles that may arise because of adopting environment friendly business practices. A manager's mindset, the cost of sustainability investments, customer loyalty, and inadequate human resource capability are all potential obstacles. As a result, an effort must be made to build a formal and informal strategy and set of tactics at both the top-down and bottom-up levels of a commercial organisation.

The typical methods for measuring green purchasing include green purchase intention and behaviour. The willingness of consumers to buy environmentally friendly products is known as green buying intention. The motivational elements that affect consumers' green purchase behaviour are captured by intentions. Because it involves a complicated form of ethical decision-making, green purchasing is seen as a type of socially responsible activity. As a socially conscious consumer, the green consumer "considers the public consequences of his or her private consumption and attempts to use his or her purchasing power to bring about social change." A green product is one that satisfies customers' requirements without endangering the environment and helps create a more sustainable world (Shamdasami et al., 1993). These goods are less harmful to the environment and better for the environment. Green products use components that are better for the environment, recyclable, and require less packaging (Chan and Chai, 2010). Organic products, energy-efficient lightbulbs, herbal treatments, and other items fall under the category of green products.

To understand consumer green purchase behaviour, prior research has mostly described the underlying beliefs, attitudes, and behavioural intentions towards environmentally friendly products. Most of the research used TRA and TPB, which were the two most popular theoretical techniques. (Ajzen, 1985).

The individual's purpose is a construct that is closely tied to attitude, subjective norms, and perceived behavioural control elements. This intention construct pertains to the assessment of carrying out a given behaviour at the planning and seeking stage. However, TPB is one of the theories that is utilized the most frequently when analysing and evaluating consumer green intention confirmed that this theory could evaluate consumer intention using behavioral control, subjective norms, and attitude factors (Ajzen, 1991).

The individual's intention is envisioned by the perceived behavioral control, attitude, and subjective norms, according to the TPB (Ajzen, 1991). As a result, two other factors—environmental knowledge and the green label—were used in place of perceived behavioral control in this study (Joshi et al., 2018). This theory takes as its two main variables attitude and subjective norms.

Green Purchase Intention

One connotation that is shared by these definitions is the willingness of an individual to think about and show a preference for green items over traditional or conventional products (Ali et al., 2011). This intention, however, represents a person's behaviour towards a certain thing, which is strongly connected with how that object is perceived and how eager a person is to pay for it. A study on Algerian consumers was conducted to determine the variables that affect customers' willingness to buy green products. However, the research has shown that environmental concern and purchasing intention are significantly correlated (Troudi & Bouyoucef, 2020).

Consumer Attitude

Consumer attitudes are defined as consumers' preferences for a product and are often represented as their liking or disliking Ajzen (2001), This phrase refers to a person's propensity to behave a certain manner towards advantageous or disadvantageous circumstances or objects. The significant connection between consumer attitudes and behavioral intentions has been confirmed by numerous researchers. According to Fishbein & Ajzen (1975), additional events or factors can also alter the relationship. In addition, a quantitative study on purchase intention of green product revealed consumers' attitudes positively influences their intention to purchase green products (Mohd Suki, 2016). A study was done on people's intentions to buy environmentally friendly food items. The results showed that, with environmental concerns acting as a moderator, there was a positive correlation between consumers' attitudes and their intentions to buy green food (Troudi & Bouyoucef, 2020).

Subjective Norms

The idea of subjective norms refers to the consumer's impression of the external social pressure that could affect the performance of a specific behaviour. The notion reflects social pressure and perception, which can influence people's opinions and perspectives and consequently have a big impact on their intention to make green purchases. This indicates that the consumer purchase intention and, as a outcome, behavior is reflected in the surrounding people's persuasive or unconvincing actions (DeLamater & Myers, 2010).

According to hman (2011), several researchers have reported that subjective norms has a significant role in influencing green purchase intention. However, Taylor & Cosenza (2002) found that the subjective norms predictor was effective in determining consumers' intentions to purchase green products. Subjective norms have been the subject of these studies, which investigated how they affected consumer intentions toward green products and played a role in this. Subjective norms have a significant impact on organic food purchase intention in a Vienna high school student study (Gotschi et al., 2007).

Environmental Knowledge

According to Mostafa (2009), environmental knowledge is the collection, organization, and appraisal of a wide range of information by persons regarding the environment, its problems (such imbalanced human consumption), and the precautions needed to preserve and safeguard the ecosystem. Green knowledge is a substantial predictor of the intention to make green purchases because it has a significant impact on all phases of the green decision-making process (Ukenna et al., 2012). This finding was supported by several studies, all of which agreed that consumers' purchase intention is affected by environmental knowledge (Diamantopoulos et al., 2003; Laroche and group, 2001). The importance of the connection between environmental awareness and green product purchase intention was demonstrated via study (Aman et al., 2012). According to these findings (Chan & Lau, 2000), consumers with an increased level of green knowledge are more likely to make environmentally conscious purchases.

Green Label / Eco-label

According to Yücel & Ekmekçiler (2008), the idea behind eco-labelling was to inform customers about the product's commitment to environmental protection. Despite the concept's many names, green labelling, eco-labelling, and eco-friendly labelling all refer to the product or service certification of eco-characteristics. According to Can Kirgiz (2014) claims that the eco-labelling certificate is granted by a recognised organisation known for its dependability, transparency, and concern for the environment. Eco-labelling is regarded as a persuasive method for alerting clients about how their purchases affect the environment, according to Nik & Rashid (2009). Numerous studies have found that eco-labelling is an important factor in the growth of green consumption and is recognised as a credible indicator of environmentally sound items (D'Souza et al., 2006).

This study applies the theory of planned behaviour (TPB) to obtain a structured clarification regarding the green purchase intention of Indians because previous reviews and studies with the Indian context have not included research on factors influencing the green purchase intention using the TPB model. Furthermore, the research is incomplete and inconsistent in its genuine green purchase intentions. The purpose of this study is to close the gaps and propose and examine a conceptual model that considers the numerous background variables that may affect Indian consumers' inclinations to purchase green products.

The study's primary contribution is to enrich the theoretical consumer behavior in Indian context literature review. In addition, the study's findings will assist organizations and marketers in comprehending the behavioral dimensions of customers and putting the orientation procedures into action. Knowing these factors will bring in more businesses and marketers to enhance their marketing strategies to attract more green customers.

RESEARCH METHODOLOGY

Research Design

Using the TPB that was suggested by Ajzen (1991), the purpose of this study is to empirically assess the factors that impact the purchase intention of Indian food retail consumers toward green/organic food products. The four important variables involved in the conception served as the basis for the basis of the study; the intention to buy eco-friendly products, which includes a positive attitude toward eco-friendly food products, subjective norms for buying eco-friendly food products, environmental expertise related to using an eco-label and purchasing environmentally friendly food goods. However, this study's suggested research model is derived from a comprehensive analysis of previous studies. The model of this study includes four independent variables and one dependent variable based on the TPB variables and the literature review. Attitude, subjective norms, environmental knowledge, eco-label (green label), and intention to buy are these variables.

Sampling Technique and Target Population

According to Sekaran and Bougie (2009), " A subset of the intended population is the sampling." The process of selecting the informant size through a variety of methods is called sampling. The target population's elements and objects that are available for selection during sampling are referred to as sampling units, and the target population's available elements and objects are referred to as the "Sample Frame" (Hair et al., 2007). The example ought to address the testing outline. When determining the appropriate sampling size, (Sekaran and Bougie, 2009) state that numerous factors must be taken into consideration.

The population size of this study are food retail consumers of the state Uttar Pradesh which accounted for 19,98,12,341 crores. The sample size for the presented study is calculated using the Krejcie and Morgan's sampling method and the sample size is calculated as 384.

Data Collection Methods

A survey designed in accordance with the TPB is developed using the quantitative method to explore the determining factors that have influenced green purchase intention of Indian food retail consumers. The things in the study are changed and embraced by the exploration targets. Closed-ended and scale response questions are used in the design of the questionnaire. The shut finished questions are carried out in the initial segment of the study that zeroed in on the respondent's qualities profile. Importantly, the first section used demographic and specialized screening questions to gather information about the respondents' profiles. In the first section of the survey, eight items are presented. In the meantime, the second section is made to get information about the goals of the presented study. This part is divided into seven sections. Through the evaluation of variables like 'consumer attitude',' subjective norms', 'green label', and 'environmental knowledge', each section is designed to check the impact of these variables on the purchase intention. While fifth and sixth sections of health consciousness and green consciousness is designed to find the effect of these consciousness over purchase intention. A five-point likert scale was used to assess each response, with 5 representing Strongly Disagree to 1 representing Strongly Agree.

Data Collection

The information is gathered using google forms from 384 respondents from Uttar Pradesh, India. Additionally, the questionnaire was distributed to customers who have been identified as "Green Consumers," i.e., those who have bought or plan to buy green products. From the selected respondents, 384 questionnaires were collected. Notably, the study's target respondents were consumers who have expressed green demand, while the study's population consisted of consumers in Uttar Pradesh who have a green purchase intention.

Demographic details collected, such as age, gender, educational qualification, occupation, marital status, monthly household income, monthly spending on food products, area of living, and purchasing partner for food products, are presented in the Table 1.

Table 1. Demographic profile of the respondents

Attributes	Category	Frequencies	Percentage
Gender	Male	99	25.85
	Female	285	74.2
Age Group	<25	202	71.12
	25-35	35	9.11
	35-45	88	22.91
	45-55	49	12.7
	>55	10	2.60
Educational Qualifications	Undergraduate	209	54.4
	Postgraduate	100	19.5
	Others	75	26.0
Occupation	Student	294	76.6
	Employee	66	17.2
	Business/self-employed	7	1.8
	Retired	4	1.0
	Housewife	2	0.5
	Others	11	2.9
Marital Status	Single	282	73.4
	Married	91	23.7
	Divorced	4	1.0
	Widow	7	1.8
Monthly Household Income	<Rs20000	152	39.65
	Rs20000-30000	52	13.5
	Rs30000-40000	34	8.9
	Rs40000-50000	22	5.7
	>Rs50000	124	32.3
Monthly Spending on Food Products	<Rs5000	41	10.6
	Rs5000-10000	118	30.7
	Rs10000-20000	153	39.8
	>Rs20000	72	18.7
Area of Living	Rural	45	11.7
	Urban	339	88.3
Purchasing Partner of Consumers for Food Products	Alone	94	24.5
	Spouse	57	14.8
	Parent	202	52.6
	Siblings	12	3.1
	Friends	19	4.9

Note: Data compiled by author

To get the characteristics of the sample respondents, the statistics were calculated using frequencies and percentages. The profile of respondents is examined in detail in Table 1. There are 285 females as respondents and 99 males as respondents. 71.12 percent of respondents fall into the <25year-old age range. However, only 91 of the 384 respondents are married, with a rate of 23.7 percent; and 282 respondents are single, with a rate of 73.4 percent. Most respondents have a high level of education, with 100 of them holding a master's degree (26 percent), followed by 54.4 percent with a bachelor's degree. In addition, 76.6 percent of the 340 respondents are students, followed by 66 employees (17.2 percent). Majority respondents resided in urban area with the rate of 88.3 percent among which the majority respondents (52.6 percent) have their parents as their purchasing partner for food products.

Data Analysis

The data is analysed using SPSS version 24 data analysis software, using exploratory factor analysis and multiple regression analysis. It is used to present data in tables and graphs and to interpret it numerically. Additionally, Quantitative data is analysed and presented using two methods. The questionnaire data is summarized using descriptive statistics (Parumasur, 2014).

Reliability analysis is conducted to confirm the consistency of the selected items. The Cronbach's alpha value can be used to evaluate the item's reliability. In addition, the alpha value can be utilized to evaluate the degree of consistency among the measured items chosen for each research variable (Hair et al., 2010). To verify consistency, alpha must have a value in the range of zero to one. According to Vavakol & Dennick (2011), a value close to one indicates perfect consistency, while a value close to zero indicates that there is no consistency. The alpha values for each of the study's selected variables are presented in Table 4. For each variable, Nunnally states that the alpha value must be greater than the cut-off value of >.6. Subsequently, all the items in this study have recorded values between 0.6-0.9 which confirms the reliability of the questionnaire.

Table 2. Reliability analysis

Factor	No. of Cases	No. of Items	Cronbach's Alpha
Consumer Attitude	384	5	0.68%
Subjective Norms	384	5	0.79%
Environmental Knowledge	384	5	0.73%
Eco-Labelling	384	5	0.73%
Purchase Intention	384	5	0.65%
Green Consciousness	384	5	0.79%
Health Consciousness	384	5	0.87%

Note: Data compiled by author

Exploratory Factor Analysis

The EFA relies heavily on the correlation between the variables; however, to avoid multi-collinearity, this correlation must not be too high (Pallant, 2010).

Before proceeding with the EFA, KMO test must also be performed. In addition, the accepted value for the test must range from 0 to 1. The ideal value is the one that is closest to one. However, a value greater than .6 qualifies for the sampling's adequacy to be appropriate (Hair et al., 2012). The KMO test results are shown in Table 3. The KMO value came out to be 0.803, which is thought to be significant for the KMO test because it was higher than the required cut-off point. By showing that there is an acceptable correlation between the parameters, the research data qualified and is suitable for the principal components analysis. The variance equality was also tested using the Bartley method. The results of the Bartley test showed statistical significance for this study, with a p-value of less than .001 and a Chi-square value of approximately 862.038. As a result, this test was deemed successful because the result, as shown in Table 3, was approximately 0.

Table 3. KMO and Bartlett's test

Kaiser-Meyer-Olkin Measure of Sampling Adequacy		0.803
Bartlett's Test of Sphericity	Approx. Chi-Square	862.038
	df	10
	p-value:	0.000

Note: Data compiled by author

The Varimax rotation method, which is a technique for extracting principal components, which is used in EFA (Malhotra et al, 2007). The evaluation considers the potentially significant useful factor loadings. As a result, the value needs to be greater than .5 and have an eigenvalue with a cut-off point of 1. This is especially true if the commonalities are greater than .7 and the factor number is less than 30. However, according to Jolliffe (2002), the cut-off value of 0.7 to 0.8 is considered acceptable.

According to results, 10 out of 20 items were excluded, as these items did not meet the minimum requirements. The Exploratory Factor Analysis's findings are presented in Table 4. The four items' accounts for 71.666 percent of the variation in the measured variables. The environmental knowledge factor showed the highest total variance value of 24.965 percent, followed by the total variance value of the subjective norm factor (19.068 percent). Consumer attitude came out to have least influence over purchase intention of Indian food retail consumers.

Multiple Regression Analysis

According to the results, in table 5 the p-values of all the factors are less than 0.05 (p<0.05). Thus, these predictors have positive and significant influences on the green purchase intention. The highest Beta Coefficient value is for environmental knowledge predictor(β=0.4180038), followed by subjective norms (β=0.4100879). On the other hand, the consumer attitude predictor recorded the lower Beta Coefficients value of 0.2236242), followed by the Eco-labelling predictor (β=0.1378071).

In table 6 the Beta value of green consciousness(β=0.6556419) is found to be greater than Beta Coefficient value of health consciousness(β=0.277166), therefore green consciousness has more influence than health consciousness over green purchase intention of Indian food retail consumers.

Table 4. Exploratory factor analysis

Factor		Consumer Attitude	Subjective Norms	Environmental Knowledge	Eco-Labelling
Consumer Attitude	CA1 CA2 CA3 CA4 CA5	0.534 0.73			
Subjective Norms	SN1 SN2 SN3 SN4 SN5		0.603 0.501 0.597		
Environmental Knowledge	EK1 EK2 EK3 EK4 EK5			0.504 0.554	
Eco-Labelling	EL1 EL2 EL3 EL4 EL5				0.683 0.512 0.765
Initial Eigenvalues		9.343	2.611	1.367	1.013
% of variance		10.683	19.068	24.965	16.950
Cumulative%		10.683	29.751	54.716	71.666

Note: Data compiled by author

Table 5. Multiple regression analysis

Variable	Coefficient	S.E.	t	p
Constant	0.1659021	0.880535	1.88	0.050
Consumer Attitude	0.2236242	0.356587	6.27	0.000
Subjective Norms	0.4100879	0.448267	9.15	0.000
Environmental Knowledge	0.4180038	0.474094	3.12	0.002
Eco-Labelling	0.137871	0.476874	2.89	0.004

Note: Data compiled by author

Table 6. Multiple regression analysis

Variable	Coefficient	S.E.	t	p
Constant	0.1455413	0.733592	1.98	0.048
Health Consciousness	0.277166	0.0402192	6.89	0.000
Green Consciousness	0.6556419	0.0431701	15.19	0.000

Note: Data compiled by author

Table 7. ANOVA for multiple regression analysis

Model		Sum of Squares	df	Mean Square	f	p
1	Regression	239.612	4	59.903	126.824	0.000
	Residual	179.013	379	0.472		
	Total	418.625	383			

Note: Data compiled by author

ANOVA variance analysis is presented in Table 7. The values of the F-ratio are 26.824 with a significant value of less than 0.05(p<0.000). Therefore F-ratio revealed that 26.825 percent variance in green purchase intention is significantly resulted from the four factors, namely consumer attitude, environmental knowledge, subjective norms, Eco-labelling.

FINDINGS

This study aims to ascertain the factors that influence Indian food consumers' green purchase intentions. As a result, Ajzen's (1991) TPB was used to create the conceptual model. The consumer's green purchase intention is significantly influenced by the subjective norms factor (beta=0.4100879, p<0.000). This indicates that consumers may consider the opinions and judgments of others in their immediate environment, such as family and friends. The social environment's favorable opinions of products have a significant impact on purchasing intentions of consumers to purchase green products (hman, 2011; 2002 (Taylor & Cosenza). As a result, Indian food retail consumers' purchase intentions of green products can be significantly predicted by the subjective norms factor.

The intention of Indian food retail consumers to purchase eco-friendly products is significantly influenced by the consumer attitude factor (β=0.2236242, p<0.000). As a result, customers' actions reflect a green attitude. This indicates that a consumer's green attitude influences their decision to buy a green product when they are exposed to one (Chen & Chai, 2010). However, there are other important factors, such as price, availability, and quality, that may influence the intention to purchase green products (Nik & Rashid, 2009), so this preconceived knowledge about the environment is not essential.

The discoveries of the review uncovered that the natural information factor is a significant indicator for green buy aim (beta=0.1480038, p<0.002). This indicates that purchasing decisions are significantly influenced by environmental awareness. The level of knowledge consumers possesses a significant impact on their decision to purchase a product as well as the consequences of doing so (Moisander, 2007; Ukenna and other, 2012; Vantomme and other, 2005).

Customers who are careful about the environment are more likely to buy a product with an eco-labelling, just like the green label factor. This indicates that customers trust the presence of a green label to indicate that the products were produced using environmentally friendly methods (β=0.1378071, p<0.004). Because the eco-label demonstrates that the product purchased was produced in environmentally friendly ways, it provides customers with a source of trust and dependability.

34.1 percent of respondents fall into the 18- to 29-year-old age range and 76.6 percent of the 340 respondents are students. Therefore, these respondents consider the green consciousness (β=0.6556419, p<0.000) more than health consciousness (β=0.277166, p<0.000) while making a purchase decision regarding the food products.

CONCLUSION

Majority of the respondents of this study are female (74.2 percent) lying under the age group of <20 years (71.12 percent) with the educational qualification of bachelor's degree. Most of the respondents (almost 39.8 percent) have their monthly expenditure of 10000-20000 rupees on the food products with majority having parents as their purchasing partner of the food products.

The analysis of the four constructs reveals a variance of 71.66 percent in Indian food retail consumers' green purchase intentions. The presented study shows that Indian food retail consumers' green purchase intentions are positively and significantly influenced by environmental awareness, green labels, subjective norms, and consumer attitude. In the meantime, the consumer attitude and Eco-labelling factor analysis also showed a positive but weak relationship with the intention to buy green products.

Since it has the most significant impact on green purchase intention, the environmental knowledge factor is the strongest construct among the others. This suggests that consumers' intentions to purchase a product will be most influenced by their awareness of environmental issues and outcomes. The fact that subjective norms is the second most important factor shows that comments or suggestions from friends, co-workers, and even salespeople have a substantial impact on consumers' intentions to make green purchases. Finally, the eco-label component, the second-to-last positive impactful predictor, had a marginally positive influence on Indian customers' intentions to make green purchases. This suggests that the green label can inspire a buyer to make a purchase for green food products.

In addition, Indian consumers' intentions to buy environmentally friendly food products are more affected by the green consciousness. This means that large part of the respondents lying in the age of 20-30 years in the study are satisfied with green consciousness about the food products.

RECOMMENDATIONS FOR FUTURE RESEARCH

There are many kinds of green activities, like using green products, recycling, and reusing. The presented study focused on consumption among the many green persuit. To examine and generalize consumers' green behaviors, additional studies are recommended to investigate additional green activities.

This study is primarily focused on purchase intention. Although other outcomes, such as genuine purchase, contentment, trust, and willingness to pay more, are suggested for future studies.

The study had restrictions on survey participants (Food retail consumers of Uttar Pradesh only) and survey locations, which may have limited the findings' generalizability.

Subsequently, the discoveries of this study could vary assuming information were gathered in various regions of the Uttar Pradesh. Furthermore, to obtain more accurate and comprehensive results, future studies might collect data in various locations with various demographic groups.

Findings of this study show that environmental knowledge is the major factor that influences Indian food retail consumers for organic food purchase. A more detailed and comprehensive study can be focused on environmental knowledge, for improving awareness regarding environment issues would be more insightful. The study may help policymakers, practitioners, and marketers to have better understanding on sustainable development of consumers' health and well-being.

The presented study concentrated on consumers of green food products, further study can be focused on non-users of organic food products to find the reason for not using the green food products and perception of the non-users towards food products.

Suggestive Strategies to Promote More Sustainable Consumer Attitude and Intention

According to the findings of the study, to promote a green lifestyle, several bodies, including consumers, businesses, and non-governmental organizations, need to work together. To achieve a cleaner and greener environment, it is everyone's duty to contribute in some way.

The major recommendations as given by the respondents and the researcher are enlisted as-

Suggestions to Marketers

1. Since most of the Uttar Pradesh population was found to be concerned about the environment and conservation, there exists a significant untapped market for green products that can be targeted by Fast Moving Consumer Goods manufacturers.
2. Marketers ought to oversee ensuring that products are readily available, according to the past studies. Green products shouldn't just be available in some places; consumers should also always have the option of choosing between a green product and a conventional product.
3. To bait the sane purchasers, eco-accommodating options ought to be sensibly evaluated, for guaranteeing positive buy goal. Marketers can also use promotional tactics like discounts, free gifts, and free services to get the segment of people who aren't interested in their products or services.

Suggestions to Consumers

1. The consumer must lead by explaining to others the advantages of eco-friendly products and highlighting the advantages of eco-friendly products.
2. By cultivating a pro-environmental mindset and a positive outlook on green products, every citizen of the nation is obligated to save the planet and contribute to sustainability.
3. Recycling recyclable waste should be prioritized by customers to make the most of available resources.
4. Planet most importantly belongs to future generation, it is time that development of a proactive strategy should be made to protect the environment. Humans will have to go green sooner or later, the sooner the better! As a result, let's begin with FMCG Green Products, a market that is perfectly viable due to the overwhelming and unavoidable demand from consumers.

Suggestions to Government and Other Bodies

1. It is recommended to further enrich the environmental education syllabus and to encourage educational institutions to develop a strong commitment to sustainability, even though environmental study is included in our school and university curriculums.

2. Consumers will become more receptive to the FMCG brands of green products if there is increased government support and promotion for those brands.
3. The scientist emphatically suggests that administration ought to keep a severe beware of the green cases made by FMCG area. Companies would develop a sense of responsibility and sincerity through regular inspections of the production and distribution of green goods.
4. NGOs ought to speak up and emphasize the significance of sustainability, recycling waste, minimizing chemical use, and, in a nutshell, environmental protection.

REFERENCES

Ajzen, I. (1991). The theory of planned behavior. *Organizational Behavior and Human Decision Processes*, *50*(2), 179–211. doi:10.1016/0749-5978(91)90020-T

Alalei, A., & Jan, M. T. (2023). Factors influencing the green purchase intention among consumers: An empirical study in Algeria. *Journal of Global Business Insights*, *8*(1), 49–65.

Alam, S. S., & Sayuti, N. M. (2011). Applying the theory of planned behavior (TPB) in halal food purchasing. *International Journal of Commerce and Management*, *21*(1), 8–20. doi:10.1108/10569211111111676

Arvola, M., Vassallo, M., Dean, P., Lampila, A., Saba, L., Lähteenmäki, R., & Shepherd, R. (2008). Predicting intentions to purchase organic food: The role of affective and moral attitudes in the theory of planned behaviour. *Appetite*, *50*(2–3), 443–454. doi:10.1016/j.appet.2007.09.010 PMID:18036702

Chen, T. B., & Chai, L. T. (2010). Attitude towards the environment and green products: Consumers' perspective. *Management Science and Engineering*, *4*(2), 27–39.

Joshi, Y., & Rahman, Z. (2015). *Factors affecting green purchase behaviour and future research directions*. International. *Strategic Management Review*, *3*(1-2), 128–143.

Nguyen-Viet, B. (2022). Understanding the influence of eco-label, and green advertising on green purchase intention: The mediating role of green brand equity. *Journal of Food Products Marketing*, *28*(2), 87–103. doi:10.1080/10454446.2022.2043212

Reysen, S., Chadborn, D., & Plante, C. N. (2018). Theory of planned behavior and intention to attend a fan convention. []. Routledge.]. *Journal of Convention & Event Tourism*, *19*(3), 204–218. doi:10.1080/15470148.2017.1419153

Teng, C.-C., & Wang, Y.-M. (2015). Decisional factors driving organic food consumption Generation of consumer purchase intentions. *British Food Journal*, *117*(3), 1066–1081. doi:10.1108/BFJ-12-2013-0361

Xincheng, M. (2022). *Research on Influencing Factors of Chinese Public Renewable Energy Acceptance Intention: Based on Theory of Planned Behavior Approach* [Doctoral dissertation, Pukyong National University].

KEY TERMS AND DEFINITIONS

Consumer Attitude: It reflects either favourable and unfavourable evaluations of an "attitude towards and object". Attitudes are often consistent with behaviors, then can be situational as well.

Environmental Knowledge: Environmental knowledge is a broad understanding of the facts, ideas, and connections relating to the natural world.

Green Consciousness: A mindset that is conscious of harm to ecosystems or the environment being decreased, minimal, or non-existent.

Green Consumerism: Green consumerism refers to a consumer's preference for goods and services that are not only environmentally friendly but also beneficial to the environment. The marketing industry adopted a green consumerism approach in response to the growing demand for green products.

Green Products: The performance of green products is enhanced for both society and the environment. When compared to standard product options on the market, green products are vastly superior in terms of their creation, use, and disposal. (Peattie, 1995). For example, green cars, recycled products, energy efficient electronics, organic tea, etc.

Health Consciousness: A mindset that is conscious of how healthy one's diet and lifestyle are.

Intention: An individual's intention is a sign that they are prepared to engage in a particular behaviour.

Organic Food Knowledge: An attitude in which one has awareness of its features, nutrition values, benefits, etc.

Perceived Behavioral Control: The apparent ease or difficulty of carrying out a behaviour is known as perceived behavioural control, and it is thought to reflect experience as well as anticipated obstacles and effects.

Subjective Norm: A person's view of the attitudes of important persons towards the adoption of a behaviour is known as a subjective norm.

Sustainable Development: The fulfilling of human needs without endangering the environment for both the present and future generations is referred to as sustainable development. To protect environmental deterioration and improve people's quality of life, sustainable development must consider the demands of future generations, social justice regardless of racial prejudice, and future generations' needs.

Chapter 17
Conversion of Cellulosic Raw Feed Stock Into Cellulose Nanocrystals (CNC):
Methods, Characterization, and Novel Applications

Sunil Jayant Kulkarni
Gharda Institute of Technology, India

ABSTRACT

Over the period, cellulosic biomass and wood were used as a source of energy, clothing, construction material. Cellulose can be modified into microcrystalline and nanocrystalline form for better mechanical and antimicrobial properties. Wood contains 40 to 60% cellulose whereas cotton, 90%. In nanotechnology, the material is disintegrated to have at least one dimension in nanoscale (1 to 100 nanometre). Nanosized particles have unique properties. Nanocellulose can be isolated from cellulosic materials that are abundantly available in nature. Cellulose nanocrystals can be obtained by alkaline treatment, bleaching, hydrolysis, and dewatering route. The crystallinity index of derived CNC varies from 52 to 99%. Sugarcane peel fiber was reported to have a maximum of 99.2% crystallinity. Combination of CNC with other materials, this can yield better and desired properties. Water sensibility and permeability can be minimized for their application in films by adding citric acid in the structure.

1. INTRODUCTION

Agricultural sector is the backbone of economy of developing nations like India. Strengthening farmers by increasing value of their product can boost agricultural economy. Waste generated in agroindustry in upstream and downstream processing can be converted into useful product (Ilyas et al., 2020). Cellulose is abundantly available component in the agricultural biomass (Huang et al., 2019; Martínez-Luévanos, 2021). Over the period of time, the cellulosic biomass, wood was used as a source of energy, clothing,

DOI: 10.4018/978-1-6684-8969-7.ch017

construction material for supporting the structures (Aziz et al., 2020). Modern applications of cellulose include cellophane films, dietary fibers, and advanced chemicals (Shojaeiarani et al., 2021). Sustainable synthesis of products from raw feedstocks to yield high value products can serve the purpose of waste minimization (Trache et al., 2020). Within cellulose fibrils, there are crystalline and amorphous regions (Alves et al., 2015). Cellulose was known to human being from ancient times (Ioelovich, 2017). Cellulose can be modified by chemical and mechanical methods to get customised properties (Abitbol et al., 2016). Materials, when broken into nano scale exhibits special properties. Cellulose, synthesized as nanocellulose, thus has some unique properties (Moon et al., 2013). Important drawbacks of cellulose are its hygroscopic nature and lack of melting properties(Composites et al., 2017). The modification of cellulose into nanocellulose brings about better surface and mechanical properties (Composites et al., 2017; Saastamoinen et al., 2012). Apart from plants, cellulose is present in algae, fungi and bacteria (George & Sabapathi, 2015). One third of plants anatomy consists of cellulose (Camacho et al., 2017). Cellulose with an at least one of its dimensions equal to or less than 100 nm is termed as nanocellulose (Ullah et al., 2021). Cellulose also finds application in biosensors, membranes, polymers, etc. (Jasim et al., 2017; Shoukat et al., 2019; Yan et al., 2014). It can be modified into microcrystalline and nanocrystalline form for better mechanical and antimicrobial properties. Also it can be combined with other polymers to yield customized properties (Battista, 1950; Battista & Smith, 1962).

Wood contains 40 to 60% cellulose whereas cotton, 90% (Yang, 2016). Cellulose has two anhydro glucose units coupled by β-1,4 glycosidic linkage between anomeric carbon C1 and an oxygen atom, C4. In nanotechnology, the material is disintegrated to have at least one dimension in nanoscale (1 to 100 nanometre). Nanosized particles have unique properties. Nanocellulose can be isolated from cellulosic materials that are available abundantly in nature (Yang, 2016). Cellulose nanocrystals (CNC) and cellulose fibers(CNF) are two forms of nano-cellulose (NC).

2. MATERIALS

Softwood kraft pulp sheets were used as starting material for CNC by Yang et al. (2016). Pineapple leaf (PL) waste was used for nanocellulose by Nguyen et al. (2021). Pineapple is one of the most abundant crops across the world. The waste leaves of pineapple are generally burnt, emitting carbonaceous gases. Rich in cellulose content, the waste can be used for cellulose synthesis.28 metric ton of pineapple was cultivated as per 2019 data (Nguyen et al., 2021; Shahbandeh, 2021). The cellulosic crops contains 30 to 40% cellulose (Saha, 2003; Santos et al., 2013). Bio hydrogel synthesis from dried palm oil empty fruit bunch fiber and Filled Polyvinyl Alcohol-Polyacrylic Acid combination is also reported (Wirjosentono, 2021). Nanocomposites derived from Horseshoe Crab have excellent antimicrobial properties (Agusnar et al., 2021). Loelovich reported zero discharge technology for CNC synthesis from bleached kraft pulp (Ioelovich, 2017). Kenaf pulp for CNC synthesis with acid hydrolysis was also investigated by Suleiman et al. (2015). Agricultural crop waste of sugar cane, bagasse was reported as raw material for CNC by Evans et al. (2019). Shanmugarajah et al. reported Malesia Palm Oil Empty Fruit Bunch (EFB) as raw material for CNC (Shanmugarajah et al., 2015). According to Abiaziem et al., the nuisance caused by sugar cane peels can be reduced by using it for synthesis of cellulose products (Abiaziem et al., 2020). Sugarcane peel as a raw material for CNC is attracting many investigators (Abiaziem et al., 2020; Barakat & Fahmy, 2021; Evans et al., 2019). Conventional scanning electron microscopy (SEM) was used for characterization of CNC obtained from Kernal and sisal fibers with usual route of alkaline treatment, hydrogen peroxide bleaching, hydrolysis and dewatering (Sosiati & Muhaimin, 2014). Liu et al. used wheat straw and corn stalk for synthesis of CNC (Liu et al., 2019). They compared the CNC obtained from these two materials. Brewery factory waste, Brewery spent grain (BSG) was employed for CNC synthesis by Matebie et al. (2021).They optimized the hydrolysis parameters namely time, temperature, liquid to solid ratio, acid strength. Beltramino et al. investigated use of cotton linters for CNC synthesis (Beltramino et al., 2015).They used fungal biproducts obtained from fungus for cellulose treatment to increase yield of CNC. CNC modification from insulating material to conducting material with combination of conducting polymers and carbonizing CNC into carbon nanorods can provide novel application of CNC (Wu, 2016). Nanocrystalline cellulose was studied for its application in Pickering emulsion by Foo et al. (2017). Also papers can be used by synthesis of CNC. Mariano et al., in their investigation used papers for CNC (Marcos et al., 2018). Date palm (Phoenix Dactylifera L.) sheath fibers were used for synthesis of Sulphated and Phosphorylated Nanocrystalline Cellulose (SNCC & PNCC) by Adel et al. (2019). They used the nanocellulose for increasing the mechanical and vapour barrier properties of the chitosan films used in food packaging (Adel et al., 2019). Frost and Foster, in their investigation to form thermally stable CNC, used spent coffee grounds as raw material (Frost & Foster, 2019). The coffee grounds have enough cellulosic composition for its use as a raw material for CNC (Ballesteros et al., 2014; Mussatto, Carneiro, Silva et al, 2011; Mussatto, Machado, Martins et al, 2011). Soxhlet apparatus for CNC from oil palm trunk waste was used with usual methodology involving hydrolysis and bleaching by Mazlita et al. (2016). Various raw materials suitable for CNC synthesis are selected based on availability in the region (Costa et al., 2015; Herawati, 2019; Kumar et al., 2014; Mariano et al., 2018; Musa et al., 2017; Oliveira et al., 2020; Song et al., 2019; Taiwo, 2017; Wijaya et al., 2019; Zhang et al., 2014; Zuliat et al., 2020). These include bamboo materials, sugarcane bagasse waste, papers, rice straw, corn stover, southern pine, bamboo shoots, oil palm fronds biomass, calotropis procera biomass, pineapple peel residues and wheat straw (Costa et al., 2015; Herawati, 2019; Kumar et al., 2014; Mariano et al., 2018; Musa et al., 2017; Oliveira et al., 2020; Song et al., 2019; Taiwo, 2017; Wijaya et al., 2019; Zhang et al., 2014; Zuliat et al., 2020). Raw materials used for CNC are summarized in figure 1. Table 1 depicts composition of various raw materials.

3. SYNTHESIS METHODOLOGIES

In his methodology, Yang soaked the softwood kraft pulp sheets in water (Yang, 2016). The dispersion of the sheets was done by using disintegrator. After removing extra water from the pulp, it was treated with a solution of sodium periodate, Grignard's reagent (GT) and sodium chloride in water. The beaker was shielded from sunlight using Aluminium foils (Yang, 2016). After 24 hours of stirring, drops of ethylene glycol were added to stop the reaction. The hydroxylamine hydrochloride was used to determine aldehyde contain of the fibers that were washed with water and filtered. The fibers then were added to water and pH was adjusted to 4.5 to get cationic dialdehyde modified cellulose(CDAMC). This suspension after stirring at 60 ^{0}C for half an hour was centrifuged. Addition of propanol to these yields cationized Nano crystalline cellulose (CNCC).

For pineapple, leaves are treated with acid for hydrolysis (Nguyen et al., 2021). The alkaline treatment is used to remove lignin and hemicellulose. The oxidant pre-treatments can be used but it may result in decrease in cellulose content (Nguyen et al., 2021). Three types of extraction methods namely acid hydrolysis, enzymatic hydrolysis, mechanical methods can be employed for nanocellulose from pineapple leaves. For isolation, steam explosion or alkaline treatment can be used. Sodium hydroxide treatment in autoclave degrades lignin. Sodium hypochlorite and acetate treatment is used to improve cellulose content. Finally oxalic acid extraction followed by steam treatment yields CNC. After acid hydrolysis the crystallinity index of 92 is reported for pineapple leave CNC (Santos et al., 2013; Zulnazri et al., 2021).

Figure 1. Raw materials for CNC

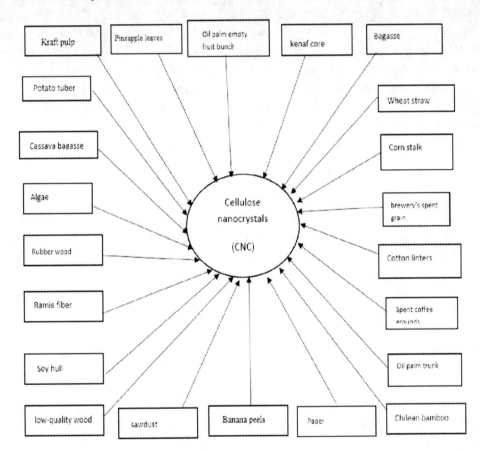

The acid hydrolysis, enzymatic hydrolysis, stream treatment methods are reported to be effective with crystallinity ranging from 70 to 96% (Cerqueira et al., 2017; Saha, 2003; Santos et al., 2013; Shahbandeh, 2021; Zulnazri et al., 2021). In a methodology involving oil palm empty fruit bunch (OEFB), Alkaline treatment and sodium hypochlorite bleaching were initial steps (Zulnazri et al., 2021). The resulting mixture was treated in ultrasonic bath with 28 kHz frequency followed by hydrolysis in hydrothermal reactor. In the method involving synthesis of bio hydrogel, the dried palm oil empty fruit bunches were treated with nitric acid and sodium nitrate for 120 minutes (Wirjosentono, 2021). After that, the hydrogen peroxide treatment was followed by hydrolysis with hydrogen chloride. In a method involving craft pulp, the microcrystalline cellulose was obtained first, and then it was soaked in water and treated with concentrated sulphuric acid. The suspension then kept in ice bath followed by stirring and acidic treatment yields CNC, which is further concentrated by centrifugation and dialysis (Ioelovich, 2017). For

Table 1. Raw material composition

Sr no	Raw Material	Reference no.	Cellulose%	Hemicellulose%	Lignin%	Ash%/Other
1	Wheat straw	22	30	50	20	-
2	Pineapple leaves	22	36	23	28	3
3	Coconut fiber	22	32	-	38	-
4	Bleached Kraft pulp	30	92(alpha Cellulose)			
5	Alkaline-treated kenaf core	31			4.855	
6	sugarcane baggase	32				19.6
7	Palm Oil Empty Fruit Bunch (EFB)	33				
8	sugarcane peel fiber	34	7-8	27-28	47-48	17-18
9	Bleached wheat straw pulp	37	66.3	17.1	4.3	
10	Bleached corn stalk pulp	37	67.2	18.3	3.5	
11	Date palm Sheath FIbers	43	43			6.7
12	Spent coffee grounds	44	8-10	36-39	23	5-15
13	Corn stover	55	45.5	27.6	6.8	20

Kenaf core MCC, the raw material was cooked at 170 °C to produce pulp (Sulaiman et al., 2015). The pulp was dried and again sodium hydroxide treatment was carried out. Then it was bleached in acetate buffer with sodium hypochlorite. The fibers, grinded and sieved were treated for hydrolysis. Product thus obtained, was washed, distilled and centrifuged to obtain CNC. The methodology involving sugarcane bagasse involved chemical treatment using HNO_3, NaOH and a bleaching agent. This was followed by usual acid hydrolysis and washing by water and acetone (Evans et al., 2019). Similar method with slight modification was used by Abiaziem et al. for sugarcane peel. To obtain the CNC from wheat straw and corn stalk, Liu et al., carried out methodology involving pulverization, sieving, Sodium hydroxide-Anthraquinone pulping, chlorine dioxide-hydrogen peroxide pulping, dewatering and hydrolysis (Liu et al., 2019).To improve yield of CNC from cotton linters use of biochemical pathway is reported (Beltramino et al., 2015). Enzymatic reaction with fungal bioproduct for cellulose was found to be effective in increasing the CNC yield. Controlled acid hydrolysis was employed to convert cellulose into CNC. The yield increased by 12% due to cellulose pre-treatment. The cellulose which occurs in nature is Cellulose I that has parallel strands. There is no inter sheet bonding in cellulose I. In cellulose II, there is inter sheet bonding and has antiparallel strands. These are thermally more stable. Mercerization process converts cellulose I to cellulose II. In their investigation, Adel et al. used sulphuric and phosphoric acid for Sulphated and Phosphorylated Nanocrystalline Cellulose (SNCC & PNCC) modification of CNC (Adel et al., 2019). A methodology involving Phosphoric acid hydrolysis was used for CNC synthesis from spend coffee grounds (Frost & Foster, 2019). Investigations suggest that milder acids can be used for obtaining the CNC of desired quality by using intensification methods such as sonication (Mazlita et al., 2016). Many agricultural raw materials are used for CNC synthesis with more or less modification of the usual method including alkaline treatment, bleaching, hydrolysis and dewatering/washing (Costa et al., 2015; Herawati, 2019; Kumar et al., 2014; Mariano et al., 2018; Musa et al., 2017; Oliveira et al., 2020; Song et al., 2019; Taiwo, 2017; Wijaya et al., 2019; Zhang et al., 2014; Zuliat et al., 2020).

4. CHARACTERIZATIONS

The optical images of periodate modified DAMC don't differ much from original fibers (Yang, 2016). The DAMC fibers were doubled in size after reaction with GT. The positive charge induces electrostatic forces which becomes cause of repulsion among the nanocellulose structures resulting into nanosized structures (Yang, 2016). The zeta potential was indication of positive charge. In FTIR studies, carbonyl group stretches and dialdehyde induced hemiacetal linkages cause a peak around 1700 cm^{-1} and 880 cm^{-1}. At, 1700 cm^{-1} it is due to carbonyl in GT. Nuclear magnetic resonance(NMR) spectroscopy was used for detail analysis and confirmation of imine bonds. Carbon nitrogen double bond is characteristic of imine. Hemiacetal linkages formation was confirmed by the absence of a carbonyl signal expected at 175-172 ppm for the aldehyde groups of solid DAMC fibers (Yang, 2016). Elemental compositions and oxidation status can be confirmed by X-ray photoelectron spectroscopy (XPS). In this analysis for DMAC and CNC fibers, in addition to signals for oxygen and carbon, two more peaks for chlorine and nitrogen were observed which is proof of presence of grafted GT. Decreased ratio of peaks for CNCC compared to DMAC indicates consumption of aldehyde. X-ray Powder Diffraction (XRD) analysis indicated that the crystallinity index of initial cellulose was 75, 49 for DAMC and 67 for CNCC. The XRD confirms the retention of initial crystalline structure of cellulose fibers.

For oil palm empty fruit bunch(OEFB), hydrolysis of 2 to 3 hours yielded 48 to 52% yield and 70 to 73% crystallinity (Zulnazri et al., 2021). Removal of hemi celluloid and lignin in the amorphous region results in high crystallinity. The peaks obtained for 2800 cm^{-1} to 2900 cm^{-1} were due to the group –CH_2. C-H vibration deformation and pyranose C-O-C resulted in peaks at 1000 to 1100 cm^{-1}. The crystallinity of dry oil palm empty fruit CNC was 78.59% with hydrogen peroxide treatment and membrane dialysis purification in bidistilled water (Wirjosentono, 2021).

For alkaline treated kenaf core pulp, FTIR indicated lignin peaks at 1734 cm^{-1} (Sulaiman et al., 2015). Usual peaks for stretching of aromatic ring in lignin, O-H bond from water adsorption, C-O-C from pyranose ring stretching, vibration of functional groups C-H and stretching of C-O group were observed for kenaf pulp CNC at various levels of synthesis (Sulaiman et al., 2015).

Infrared absorption peaks for EFB studies includes peaks for A. O-H stretching(3300-3350 cm^{-1}), B. C-H stretching(2917 cm-1), C. C=O of ketone and carboxyl(1724-1725 cm^{-1}), D. O-H bending of absorbed water(1641-1642 cm^{-1}), E. C-H bending(1422-1426 cm^{-1}), F. C=C stretching vibration of aromatic ring(1235-1240 cm^{-1}), G. C-O stretching(1029-1032 cm^{-1}), H. B-glycosidic linkages between the sugar units(896-897 cm^{-1}) (Shanmugarajah et al., 2015). Peaks C and D were absent for alkali treated fiber. Peaks C,D,E and F were absent for bleached fiber. For CNC, only A and D type peaks were present indicating removed of lignin and other residues.

For sugar cane peel CNC, the moisture content was reported to be 6% (Abiaziem et al., 2020). High crystallinity value, 99.2%, indicates good mechanical and thermal stability. FTIR spectra indicated effective removal of amorphous domain. The synthesis yield for brewer's yeast CNC was obtained 34.42-43.02% (Matebie et al., 2021). The investigation on temperature and concentration of acid indicated

3 to 5% increase in yield for 5°C increase in temperature and 4% rise in acid concentration (Matebie et al., 2021). The optimum parameters for hydrolysis were found to be contact time of 41 min, 50° C temperature, 51 wt.% acid concentration, and liquid-solid ratio of 19 ml/g. CNC from oil palm empty fruit bunch exhibited zeta potential of -48.7 mV, making it a candidate for its application in Pickering emulsion study (Foo et al., 2017). For Date palm sheath CNC, the CNC from cellulose II was thermally and mechanically more stable (Adel et al., 2019). Phosphoric acid treated CNC (p CNC) was dispersible in multiple organic solvents (Frost & Foster, 2019). Also tensile modulus can be increased threefold by adding 10% each of p CNC and commercial CNC in thermoplastic polyurethane (PU). Sugarcanes bagasse MCC has crystallinity index of 72.5%, more than twice of the bagasse (Kumar et al., 2014). Tensile strength of polymers can be increased with addition of CNC. 38 to 40% increases in tensile strength is reported by adding 5% CNC in rubber (Zhang et al., 2014). Characteristics CNCs obtained from various raw materials are tabulated in Table 2.

CNCs find application in medical industry due to chemical and mechanical stability and nontoxic nature. They can be used for implants in nanocomposite forms (Chawalitsakunchai et al., 2019). Also light weight aerogels can be formed from CNCs (Thomas et al., 2019; Gumrah Dumanli, 2017). The CNCs can be used to hydrogel for application in medical sector (Wirjosentono, 2021). The combination of Nanocellulose (NC), polyvinyl alcohol (PVA), acrylic acid (AA), N'N-Methylene bisacrylamide (MBA), and ammonium persulfate (AP) was developed by Wirjosentono et al. (2021). Nanocomposites derived from Horseshoe Crab have excellent antimicrobial properties for their application in coatings (Agusnar et al., 2021). Glycidyl methacrylate (GM) was used for improving physicochemical properties and biological activity of sugarcane bagasse CNC by Barakat and Fahmy (2021). GM grafted CNC was observed to have better compatibility and antimicrobial behaviour. CNC can be combined with conducting polymer or can be converted into carbon rods for its application as highly conducting material as supercapacitor (SP), catalyst, metal-free catalyst, and sensor (Wu, 2016). Surface modification of the paper derived CNC can exhibit better surface properties compared to CNC (Marcos et al., 2018). Oxidation enhances the coating phenomenon of internal cellulose chains (Marcos et al., 2018). Biocompatibility, cell adhesion and growth can be increased by introducing high phosphate content in CNC (Frost & Foster, 2019). Emulsion stability index of emulsion(cyclic natural rubber) can be increased with addition of CNC (Mahendra & Wirjosentono, 2019). CNCs can also be modified with Hydroxyazetidinium salts to improve thermal properties and mechanical properties (Forsgren et al., 2019). CNCs can reinforced into composite materials (Bhat et al., 2017). Nanocarbon and nano cellulosic materials are also being explored in medical and pharmaceutical application dur to their biocompatible, antifungal and to some extent antitumor nature (Bacakova et al., 2020; Xie, Zhang, Walcott, & Lin, 2018). For improving adhesion properties, it can be modified by using coupling agent (Aziz et al., 2021). Various novel applications of CNCs such as edible films, electrical conductive agents and as hydrogel have increased investigations for their applications (Mariano et al., 2014). Nanocellulose applications in healable polymeric materials, in supporting matrix for catalyst, in the release pattern of drugs, bio-based food packaging applications and in electronics applications is attracting the scientist community to explore more modifications in CNC for novel applications (Azeredo et al., 2016; Peng et al., 2011; Soeiro et al., 2021; Tahir et al., 2022; Xie, Zhang, Walcott, & Lin, 2018). Investigations on cellulosic biomass focused on specific applications are reported in past decade. These include research for properties of the complex materials on addition of CNC, crosslinking of cellulose with other compound, bioactivity studies, melting and blending properties, etc. (Favier et al., 1995; Moon et al., 2005; Ojagh et al., 2010; Shi et al., 2008; Shi et al., 2007; Thomsen, 2005). Combination of CNC with other materials can yield better and desired properties (Badri et al., 2001; Bertran & Dale, 1986; Das et al., 2009; Natterodt et al., 2017; Nikje et al., 2012; Pardo-Alonso et al., 2013; Pereira et al., 2017; Septevani et al., 2017). Water sensibility and permeability can be minimized for their application in films aby adding citric acid in the structure (Pereira et al., 2017). Various applications of CNC are depicted in Figure 2.

Table 2. CNC characterization

Sr no	Raw Material	Reference no	Dimensions/Yield	Zeta Potential	Crystallinity Index %
1	Softwood kraft pulp sheets CNC	21	120 nm x 5 nm	27 ± 0.7 mV at pH 6.3	67
2	Pineapple leaves CNC	22	130 to 117 nm		92
3	oil palm empty fruit bunch(OEFB) CNC	27			70 to 73
4	Dry oil palm empty fruit bunch(OEFB) CNC with H_2O_2 treatment	28			78.59
5	bleached kraft pulp	30	120 x 15 nm, Yield 60-64%		73-75
6	kenaf core CNC	31	131x13.76 nm		81.2
7	sugarcane bagasse CNC	32	38 nm		76.89
8	Palm Oil Empty Fruit Bunch (EFB) CNC	33	499.2 nm		
9	sugarcane peel fiber	34	20.57±9.47 nm in width and 153.05±70.8 nm in length		99.2
10	The natural fibers of kenaf (hibiscus cannabinus) and (sisal (agave sisalana) fibers	36	300-600 nm and 40-60 nm		
11	Wheat straw CNC	37	840 nm		52.1
12	Corn stalk CNC	37	630 nm		65.2
13	brewery's spent grain (BSG) CNC	38	an average particle size of 309.4 nm		76.3
14	Cotton linters CNC	39	2 mm x 22 micrometre, Average size 90 to 150 nm		
15	Oil palm empty fruit bunch (EFB) fibers	41	15 – 25 nm in width and 200 – 500 nm in length	-48.7 mV	
16	Sulphated CNC from Cellulose I	43	30.3 x 8.8 d.nm	-35.6 mV	
17	Sulphated CNC from Cellulose II	43	25.7 x 7.7 d.nm	-36.7 mV	
18	Phosphorus modified CNC from Cellulose I	43	94x16 d.nm	-12.7 mV	
19	Phosphorus modified CNC from Cellulose I	43	74x14 d.nm	-16.9 mV	
20	Spent coffee grounds	44	Length 199-225 nm, dia 17-21 nm		74.2
21	Oil palm trunk CNC	48	95-100nm (L) × 25-27 nm (d)		54-59
22	Chilean bamboo, Chusquea quila CNC	49			88
23	Sugarcane Bagasse CNC	50	250-480 nm (length) and 20-60 nm (diameter)		72.5
24	Paper CNC	51	145nm length, 8-9 nm diameter		88
25	Corn stover MCC	55	an average diameter and length of 6.9 nm and 356 nm,		45
26	Southern pine pulp	56	Length 77-97 nm, diameter 9 to11 nm		

Figure 2. Applications of CNC

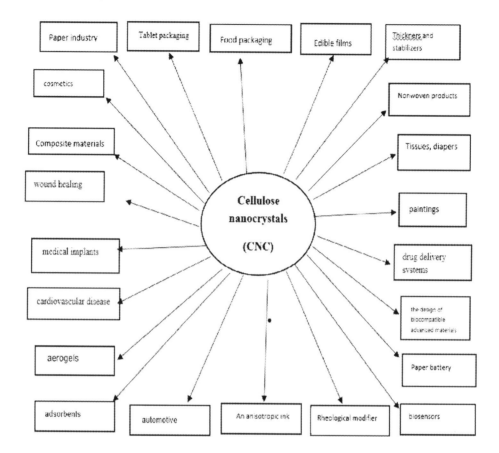

5. CONCLUSION

Cellulosic materials can provide sustainable and viable solution to many material selection problems in pharmaceutical and cosmetic industries (Albers et al., 2006; Cameron, 2000; Seddiqi et al., 2021; de Ven et al., 2013). Sustainable synthesis of ethanol like compounds is also possible from cellulosic materials (Kulkarni, 2016; Sedlak & Nancy, 2004). Pristine cellulose can be modified for improvement in mechanical, chemical and antimicrobial properties. Microcrystalline cellulose (MCC) is form of cellulose modified by removing lignin and other residues and improved bacterial, chemical and mechanical properties (Azubuike & Okhamafe, 2012; Debnath et al., 2021; Shlieout et al., 2002; Thoorens et al., 2014). MCC and CNC differ in morphology and size. CNC was reported to have better mechanical properties than MCC (Ramires et al., 2020; Santos et al., 2017).

Various raw materials for CNC include bamboo materials, sugarcane bagasse waste, papers, rice straw, corn stover, southern pine, bamboo shoots, Oil Palm Fronds Biomass, Calotropis procera biomass, Pineapple Peel Residues and Wheat straw. Cellulose nanocrystals can be obtained by alkaline treatment, bleaching, hydrolysis and dewatering route. This article contains review of investigations on materials, methods and characterization studies in recent past. Also characterization studies and investigations for modern applications of CNC are also reported. The crystallinity index of derived CNC varies from 52 to 99%. Sugarcane peel fiber was reported to have maximum 99.2% crystallinity. Oil palm empty fruit bunch (EFB) fibers CNC had maximum negative zeta potential(-48.7 mV) while Phosphorus modified CNC from Cellulose I had minimum, -12.7 mV.

Investigations on cellulosic biomass focused on specific applications are reported in past decade. These include research for properties of the complex materials on addition of CNC, crosslinking of cellulose with other compound, bioactivity studies, melting and blending properties etc. Combination of CNC with other materials can yield better and desired properties. Water sensibility and permeability can be minimized for their application in films aby adding citric acid in the structure.

ACKNOWLEDGMENT

The author is thankful to Gharda Institute of Technology, Maharashtra, India.

Availability of Data and Materials: No additional data and materials are associated with this article to support the findings of the article.

Author's Contributions: All authors contributed to the study conception and design. All authors also read and approved the final manuscript.

Funding: Not applicable

Declarations Ethics Approval and Consent to Participate: Not applicable.

Consent for Publication: Not applicable.

Competing Interests: The authors declare no competing interests.

REFERENCES

Abiaziem. C.V., Williams, A.B., Inegbenebor, A.I., Onwordi, C.T., Ehi-Eromosele, C.O. & Petrik, L.F. (2020). Isolation And Characterisation Of Cellulose Nanocrystal Obtained From Sugarcane Peel. *Rasayan J. Chem., 13*(1), 177-187. http://dx.doi.org/ C.2020.1315328 doi:10.31788/RJ

Abitbol, T., Rivkin, A., Cao, Y., Nevo, Y., Abraham, E., Ben-Shalom, T., Lapidot, S., & Shoseyov, O. (2016). Nanocellulose, a tiny fiber with huge applications. *Current Opinion in Biotechnology, 39*, 76–88. doi:10.1016/j.copbio.2016.01.002 PMID:26930621

Adel, A. M., El-Shafei, A. M., Ibrahim, A. A., & Al-Shemy, M. T. (2019). Chitosan/Nanocrystalline Cellulose Biocomposites Based on Date Palm (Phoenix Dactylifera L.) Sheath Fibers. *Journal of Renewable Materials, 7*(6), 567–582. doi:10.32604/jrm.2019.00034

Agusnar, H., Zaidar, E., & Lenny, S. (2021). Synthesis and characterization of nanocomposite chitosan from Horseshoe Crab to improve antibacterial properties. *AIP Conference Proceedings, 2342*, 020009. doi:10.1063/5.0046157

Albers, J., Knop, K., & Kleinebudde, P. (2006). Brand-to-brand and batch-to-batch uniformity of microcrystalline cellulose in direct tableting with a pneumo-hydraulic tablet press. *Die Pharmazeutische Industrie, 68*, 1420–1428.

Alves, L., Medronho, B., Antunes, F.E., Fernández-García, M.P., Ventura, J., Araújo, J.P., Romano, A., Lindman, B. (2015). Unusual extraction and characterization of nanocrystalline cellulose from cellulose derivatives. *Journal of Molecular Liquids, 210,* 106-112. . doi:10.1016/j.molliq.2014.12.010

Azeredo, H.M.C., Rosa, M.F., & Mattoso, L.H.C. (2016). Nanocellulose in bio-based food packaging applications. *Ind. Crops Prod., 97,* 664-671. http://dx.doi.org/. 2016.03.013 doi:10.1016/j.indcrop

Aziz, T., Fan, H., Zhang, X., Haq, F., Ullah, A., Ullah, R., Khan, F. U., & Iqbal, M. (2020). Advance Study of Cellulose Nanocrystals Properties and Applications. *Journal of Polymers and the Environment, 28*(4), 1117–1128. doi:10.100710924-020-01674-2

Aziz, T., Iqbal, M., Ullah, R., Jamil, M.I., & Raheel, M. (2021). Improving Adhesive Properties of Cellulose Nanocrystals Modifying by 3-Glycidoxypropyltrimethoxy Silane (KH-560) Coupling Agents. *Biomed J Sci & Tech Res., 34*(1), 26402-26407.

Azubuike, C. P., & Okhamafe, A. O. (2012). Physicochemical, spectroscopic and thermal properties of microcrystalline cellulose derived from corn cobs. *International Journal of Recycling of Organic Waste in Agriculture, 1*(9), 1–7. doi:10.1186/2251-7715-1-9

Bacakova, L., Pajorova, J., Tomkova, M., Matejka, R., Broz, A., Stepanovska, J., Prazak, S., Skogberg, A., Siljander, S., & Kallio, P. (2020). Applications of Nanocellulose/Nanocarbon Composites: Focus on Biotechnology and Medicine. *Nanomaterials (Basel, Switzerland), 10*(2), 196. doi:10.3390/nano10020196 PMID:31979245

Badri, K. H., Ahmad, S. H., & Zakaria, S. (2001). Production of a High-Functionality RBD Palm Kernel Oil-Based Polyester Polyol. *Journal of Applied Polymer Science, 81*(2), 384–389. doi:10.1002/app.1449

Ballesteros, L. F., Teixeira, J. A., & Mussatto, S. I. (2014). Chemical, functional, and structural properties of spent coffee grounds and coffee silverskin. *Food and Bioprocess Technology, 7*(12), 3493–3503. doi:10.100711947-014-1349-z

Barakat, A., & Fahmy, A. (2021). Cellulose nanocrystals from sugarcane bagasse and its graft with GMA: Synthesis, characterization, and biocompatibility assessment. *Journal of Applied Pharmaceutical Science, 11*(02), 114–125. doi:10.7324/JAPS.2021.110215

Battista, O. A. (1950). Hydrolysis and crystallization of cellulose. *Industrial & Engineering Chemistry, 42*(3), 502–507. doi:10.1021/ie50483a029

Battista, O. A., & Smith, P. A. (1962). Microcrystalline cellulose. *Industrial & Engineering Chemistry, 54*(9), 20–29. doi:10.1021/ie50633a003

Beltramino, F., Roncero, M. B., Vidal, T., Torres, A. L., & Valls, C. (2015). Increasing yield of nanocrystalline cellulose preparation process by a cellulase pretreatment. *Bioresource Technology, 192,* 574–581. doi:10.1016/j.biortech.2015.06.007 PMID:26092069

Bertran, M. S., & Dale, B. E. (1986). Determination of Cellulose Accessibility by Differential Scanning Calorimetry. *Journal of Applied Polymer Science, 32*(3), 4241–4253. doi:10.1002/app.1986.070320335

Bhat, A.H. & Dasan, Y. & Khan, I., Soleimani, H., Usmani, M. (2017). Application of nanocrystalline cellulose: Processing and biomedical applications. *Application of nanocrystalline cellulose.* . doi:10.1016/B978-0-08-100957-4.00009-7

Camacho, M., Regina, Y., Lopretti, M., Carballo, L. B., & Moreno, G. (2017). Synthesis and Characterization of Nanocrystalline Cellulose Derived from Pineapple Peel Residues. *Journal of Renewable Materials, 5*(5), 271–279. doi:10.7569/JRM.2017.634117

Cameron, J. S. (2000). Practical haemodialysis began with cellophane and heparin: The crucial role of William Thalhimer (1884–1961). *Nephrology, Dialysis, Transplantation, 15*(7), 1086–1091. doi:10.1093/ndt/15.7.1086 PMID:10862657

Cerqueira, J. C., Penha, J. S., Oliveira, R. S., Guarieiro, L. L. N., Melo, P. D. S., Viana, J. D., & Machado, B. A. S. (2017). Production of biodegradable starch nanocomposites using cellulose nanocrystals extracted from coconut fibers. *Polímeros, 27*(4), 320–329. doi:10.1590/0104-1428.05316

Chawalitsakunchai, W., Dittanet, P., Loykulnunt, S., Tanpichai, S., & Prapainainar, P. (2019). Extraction of nanocellulose from pineapple leaves by acid-hydrolysis and pressurized acid hydrolysis for reinforcement in natural rubber composites. *IOP Conference Series. Materials Science and Engineering, 526*(1), 012019–012019. doi:10.1088/1757-899X/526/1/012019

Costa, L. A. S., Assis, D. J., Gomes, G. V. P., da Silva, J. B. A., Fonseca, A. F., & Druzian, J. I. (2015). Extraction and Characterization of Nanocellulose from Corn Stover. *Materials Today: Proceedings, 2*(1), 287–294. doi:10.1016/j.matpr.2015.04.045

Das, S., Dave, M., & Wilkes, G. L. (2009). Characterization of flexible polyurethane foams based on soybean-based polyols. *Journal of Applied Polymer Science, 112*(1), 299–308. doi:10.1002/app.29402

Debnath, B., Haldar, D., & Purkait, M. (2021). A critical review on the techniques used for the synthesis and applications of crystalline cellulose derived from agricultural wastes and forest residues. *Carbohydrate Polymers, 273*, 118537. doi:10.1016/j.carbpol.2021.118537 PMID:34560949

Evans, S. K., Wesley, O. N., Nathan, O., & Moloto, M. J. (2019). Chemically purified cellulose and its nanocrystals from sugarcane baggase: Isolation and characterization. *Heliyon, 5*(10), e02635. doi:10.1016/j.heliyon.2019.e02635 PMID:31687498

Favier, V., Canova, G. R., Cavaillé, J. Y., Chanzy, H., Dufresne, A., & Gauthier, C. (1995). Nanocomposite materials from latex and cellulose whiskers. *Polymers for Advanced Technologies, 6*(5), 351–355. doi:10.1002/pat.1995.220060514

Foo, M., Tan, K., Wu, T., Chan, E., & Chew, I. (2017). A Characteristic Study of Nanocrystalline Cellulose and its Potential in Forming Pickering Emulsion. *Chemical Engineering Transactions, 60*, 97–102.

Forsgren, L., Sahlin-Sjövold, K., Venkatesh, A., Thunberg, J., Kádár, R., Boldizar, A., Westman, G., & Rigdahl, M. (2019). Composites with surface-grafted cellulose nanocrystals (CNC). *Journal of Materials Science, 54*(4), 3009–3022. doi:10.100710853-018-3029-2

Frost, B., & Foster, E. J. (2019). Isolation of Thermally Stable Cellulose Nanocrystals from Spent Coffee Grounds via Phosphoric Acid Hydrolysis. *Journal of Renewable Materials, 7*, 187–203. doi:10.32604/jrm.2020.07940

George, J. & Sabapathi, S.N.(2015). Cellulose nanocrystals: synthesis, functional properties, and applications. *Nanotech.Sci.Appl., 8*, 45-54.

Gopakumar, D. A., Pottathara, Y. B., Sabu, K., Khalil, H. A., Grohens, Y., & Thomas, S. (2019). Nanocellulose-based aerogels for industrial applications. Chapter. In S. Thomas, N. Kalarikkal, & A. Abraham (Eds.), *Industrial Applications of Nanomaterials* (pp. 403–421). doi:10.1016/B978-0-12-815749-7.00014-1

Gumrah Dumanli, A. (2017). Nanocellulose and its composites for biomedical applications. *Current Medicinal Chemistry, 24*(5), 512–528. doi:10.2174/0929867323666161014124008 PMID:27758719

Herawati, H. (2019). Production Technology and Utilization of Nano Cellulose. *IOP Conf. Series: Journal of Physics: Conf. Series 1295*. IOP Publishing 10.1088/1742-6596/1295/1/012051

Huang, J., Ma, X., Yang, G., & Alain, D. (2019). Introduction to Nanocellulose. In J. Huang, A. Dufresne, & N. Lin (Eds.), *Nanocellulose*. doi:10.1002/9783527807437.ch1

Ilyas, R. A., Sapuan, S. M., Ibrahim, R., Atikah, M. S. N., Atiqah, A., Ansari, M. N. M., & Norrrahim, M. N. F. (2020). Production, Processes and Modification of Nanocrystalline Cellulose from Agro-Waste: A Review. *Nanocrystalline Materials*. doi:10.5772/intechopen.87001

Ioelovich, M. (2017). Characterization of Various Kinds of Nanocellulose. In Handbook of Nanocellulose and Cellulose Nanocomposites. John Wiley & Sons.

Ioelovich, M. (2017). Zero-discharge Technology for Production of Nanocrystalline Cellulose. *Research Journal of Nanoscience and Engineering, 1*(1), 29–33.

Jasim, A., Ullah, M. W., Shi, Z., Lin, X., & Yang, G. (2017). Fabrication of bacterial cellulose/polyaniline/single-walled carbon nanotubes membrane for potential application as biosensor. *Carbohydrate Polymers, 163*, 62–69. doi:10.1016/j.carbpol.2017.01.056 PMID:28267519

Kulkarni, S. J. (2016). Downstream processing in biotechnology: Research and studies. *International Journal of Science and Healthcare Research, 1*(3), 8–10.

Kumar, A., Negi, Y. S., Choudhary, V., & Bhardwaj, N. K. (2014). Characterization of Cellulose Nanocrystals Produced by Acid-Hydrolysis from Sugarcane Bagasse as Agro Waste. *Journal of Materials Physics and Chemistry, 2*(1), 1–8. doi:10.12691/jmpc-2-1-1

Liu, Z., He, M., Ma, G., Yang, G., & Chen, J. (2019). Preparation and Characterization of Cellulose Nanocrystals from Wheat Straw and Corn Stalk. *Korean Society of Pulp and Paper Engineers Pulp & Paper Technology Academic Journals Pulp and Paper Technology, 51*(2), 40–48. doi:10.7584/JKTAPPI.2019.04.51.2.40

Mahendra, I.P., & Wirjosentono, B., Tamrin, I. H., & Mendez, J.A. (2019). Oil Palm-Based Nanocrystalline Cellulose In The Emulsion System Of Cyclic Natural Rubber. *Rasayan Journal of Chemistry, 12*(2), 635–640. doi:10.31788/RJC.2019.1225089

Marcos, M., Nadia, E. K., & Dufresne, A. (2018). Cellulose nanomaterials: Size and surface influence on the thermal and rheological behavior. *Polímeros*, *28*(2), 93–102. doi:10.1590/0104-1428.2413

Mariano, M., Kissi, N., & Dufresne, A. (2014). Cellulose Nanocrystals and Related Nanocomposites: Review of some Properties and Challenges. *Journal of Polymer Science. Part B, Polymer Physics*, *52*(12), 791–706. doi:10.1002/polb.23490

Mariano, M., Kissi, N. E., & Dufresne, A. (2018). Cellulose nanomaterials: Size and surface influence on the thermal and rheological behavior. *Polímeros*, *28*(2), 93–102. Advance online publication. doi:10.1590/0104-1428.2413

Martínez-Luévanos, A., Perez Berumen, C., Ceniceros, A., Owoyokun, T., & Sifuentes, L. (2021). Cellulose Nanocrystals: Obtaining and Sources of a Promising Bionanomaterial for Advanced Applications Taiwo. *Biointerface Research in Applied Chemistry*, *11*, 11797–11816.

Matebie, B.Y., Tizazu, B.Z., Kadhem, A.A., & Prabhu, S.V. (2021). Synthesis of Cellulose Nanocrystals (CNCs) from Brewer's Spent Grain Using Acid Hydrolysis: Characterization and Optimization. *Journal of Nanomaterials*. doi:10.1155/2021/7133154

Mazlita, Y., Lee, H. V., & Hamid, S. B. A. (2016). Preparation of Cellulose Nanocrystals Bio-Polymer from Agro-Industrial Wastes: Separation and Characterization. *Polymers & Polymer Composites*, *24*(9), 719–728. doi:10.1177/096739111602400907

Mohammed, N., Rokiah, H., Othman, S., & Mohammad, A. (2017). Nanocellulose: Preparation methods and applications. In C.-R. N. Composites (Ed.), *In Woodhead Publishing Series in Composites Science and Engineering* (pp. 261–276). Mohammad Jawaid, Sami Boufi, Abdul Khalil H.P.S. doi:10.1016/B978-0-08-100957-4.00011-5

Moon, J. S., Park, J. H., Lee, T. Y., Kim, Y. W., Yoo, J. B., Park, C. Y., Kim, J. M., & Jin, K. W. (2005). Transparent conductive film based on carbon nanotubes and PEDOT composites. *Diamond and Related Materials*, *14*(11-12), 1882–1887. doi:10.1016/j.diamond.2005.07.015

Moon, R., Beck, S., & Rudie, A. (2013). Cellulose Nanocrystals – A Material with Unique Properties and Many Potential Applications. In *Production and Applications of Cellulose Nanomaterials* (pp. 9–13). Ed. Robert Moon, Stephanie Beck and Alan Rudie Michael T. Postek Robert J. Moon Alan W. Rudie and Michael A. Bilodeau. TAPPI PRESS.

Musa, A., Ahmad, M.B., Hussein, M.Z., Izham, S.M. (2017). Acid Hydrolysis-Mediated preparation of Nanocrystalline Cellulose from Rice Straw. *Int J Nanomater Nanotechnol Nanomed*, *3*(2), 51-56. doi:10.17352/2455-3492.000021

Mussatto, S. I., Carneiro, L. M., Silva, J. P. A., Roberto, I. C., & Teixeira, J. A. (2011). A study on chemical constituents and sugars extraction from spent coffee grounds. *Carbohydrate Polymers*, *83*(2), 368–374. doi:10.1016/j.carbpol.2010.07.063

Mussatto, S. I., Machado, E. M. S., Martins, S., Teixeira, J. A. (2011). Production, composition, and application of coffee and its industrial residues. *Food and Bioprocess Technology, 4*(5), 661–672. . 32. doi:10.1007/s11947-011-0565-z

Natterodt, J. C., Petri-Fink, A., Weder, C., & Zoppe, J. O. (2017). Cellulose Nanocrystals: Surface Modification, Applications and Opportunities at Interfaces. *Chimia*, *71*(6), 376–383. doi:10.2533/chimia.2017.376 PMID:28662741

Nguyen, C. T. X., Bui, K. H., Truong, B. Y., Do, N. H. N., & Le, P. T. K. (2021). Nanocellulose from Pineapple Leaf and Its Applications towards High-value Engineering Materials. *Chemical Engineering Transactions*, *89*, 19–24.

Nikje, M. M. A., Diarjani, E., & Haghshenas, M. (2012). Nanoclay-Flexible Polyurethane Nanocomposites Formulated by Recycled Polyether Polyols. *Cellular Polymers*, *31*(5), 257–267. doi:10.1177/026248931203100502

Ojagh, S. M., Rezaei, M., Razavi, S. H., & Hosseini, S. M. H. (2010). Development and evaluation of a novel biodegradable film made from chitosan and cinnamon essential oil with low affinity toward water. *Food Chemistry*, *122*(1), 161–166. doi:10.1016/j.foodchem.2010.02.033

Oliveira, P. E., Petit-Breuilh, X., Rojas, O. J., & Gracitua, W. (2020). Production of cellulose nanostructures from Chilean bamboo, Chusquea quila. *Agronomy Research (Tartu)*, *18*(4), 2520–2534. doi:10.15159/AR.20.193

Pardo-Alonso, S., Solórzano, E., Brabant, L., Vanderniepen, P., Dierick, M., Van Hoorebeke, L., & RodríguezPérez, M. A. (2013). 3D Analysis of the progressive modification of the cellular architecture in polyurethane nanocomposite foams via X-ray microtomography. *European Polymer Journal*, *49*, 999-1006, doi:10.1016/j.eurpolymj.2013.01.005

Peng, B. L., Dhar, N., Liu, H. L., & Tam, K. C. (2011). Chemistry and Applications of Nanocrystalline Cellulose and its Derivatives: A Nanotechnology Perspective. *Canadian Journal of Chemical Engineering*, *9999*(5), 1–16. doi:10.1002/cjce.20554

Pereira, P. H. F., Waldron, K. W., Wilson, D. R., Cunha, A. P., de Brito, E. S., Rodrigues, T. H. S., Rosa, M. F., & Azeredo, H. M. C. (2017). Wheat straw hemicelluloses added with cellulose nanocrystals and citric acid. Effect on film physical properties. *Carbohydrate Polymers*, *164*, 317–324. doi:10.1016/j.carbpol.2017.02.019 PMID:28325332

Ramires, E. C., Megiatto, J. D. Jr, Dufresne, A., & Frollini, E. (2020). Cellulose Nanocrystals versus Microcrystalline Cellulose as Reinforcement of Lignopolyurethane Matrix. *Fibers (Basel, Switzerland)*, *8*(4), 21. doi:10.3390/fib8040021

Saastamoinen, P., Mattinen, M.-L., Hippi, U., Nousiainen, P., Sipilä, J., Lille, M., Suurnäkki, A., & Pere, J. (2012). Laccase aided modification of nano fibrillated cellulose with dodecyl gallate. *BioResources*, *7*(4), 5749–5770. doi:10.15376/biores.7.4.5749-5770

Saha, B. C. (2003). Hemicellulose bioconversion. *Journal of Industrial Microbiology & Biotechnology*, *30*(5), 279–291. doi:10.100710295-003-0049-x PMID:12698321

Santos, F. A., Lulianelli, G. C. V., & Tavares, M. I. B. (2017). Effect of microcrystalline and nanocrystals cellulose fillers in materials based on PLA matrix. *Polymer Testing*, *61*, 280–288. doi:10.1016/j.polymertesting.2017.05.028

Santos, R. M., Flauzino Neto, W. P., Silvério, H. A., Martins, D. F., Dantas, N. O., & Pasquini, D. (2013). Cellulose nanocrystals from pineapple leaf, a new approach for the reuse of this agro-waste. *Industrial Crops and Products*, *50*, 707–714. doi:10.1016/j.indcrop.2013.08.049

Seddiqi, H., Oliaei, E., Honarkar, H., Jin, J., Geonzon, L. C., Bacabac, R. G., & Klein-Nulend, J. (2021). Cellulose and its derivatives: Towards biomedical applications. *Cellulose (London, England)*, *28*(4), 1893–1931. doi:10.100710570-020-03674-w

Sedlak, M., & Nancy, W. Y. H. (2004). Production of Ethanol from Cellulosic Biomass Hydrolysates Using Genetically Engineered Saccharomyces Yeast Capable of Cofermenting Glucose and Xylose. *Applied Biochemistry and Biotechnology*, *113–116*(1-3), 403–416. doi:10.1385/ABAB:114:1-3:403 PMID:15054267

Septevani, A. A., Annamalai, P. K., & Martin, D. J. (2017). Synthesis and characterization of cellulose nanocrystals as reinforcing agent in solely palm based polyurethane foam. In *Proceedings of the 3rd International Symposium on Applied Chemistry 2017*. AIP Publishing. 10.1063/1.5011899

Shahbandeh, M. (2021). *Global pineapple production 2002-2019*. Statista. https://www.statista.com/statistics/298517/global-pineapple-production-by-leading-countries/

Shanmugarajah, B., Kiew, P. L., Chew, I. M. L., Choong, T. S. Y., & Tan, K. W. (2015). Isolation of nanocrystalline cellulose (NCC) from palm oil empty fruit bunch (EFB): Preliminary result on ftir and dls analysis. *Chemical Engineering Transactions*, *45*, 1705–1710. doi:10.3303/CET1545285

Shi, R., Bi, J., Zhang, Z., Zhu, A., Chen, D., Zhou, X., Zhang, L., & Tian, W. (2008). The effect of citric acid on the structural properties and cytotoxicity of the polyvinyl alcohol/starch films when molding at high temperature. *Carbohydrate Polymers*, *74*(4), 763–770. doi:10.1016/j.carbpol.2008.04.045

Shi, R., Zhang, Z., Liu, Q., Han, Y., Zhang, L., Chen, D., & Tian, W. (2007). Characterization of citric acid/glycerol co-plasticized thermoplastic starch prepared by melt blending. *Carbohydrate Polymers*, *69*(4), 748–755. doi:10.1016/j.carbpol.2007.02.010

Shlieout, G., Arnold, K., & Muller, G. (2002). Powder and mechanical properties of microcrystalline cellulose with different degrees of polymerization. *AAPS PharmSciTech*, *3*(2), 45–84. doi:10.1208/pt030211 PMID:12916948

Shojaeiarani, J., Bajwa, D., & Chanda, S. (2021). Cellulose nanocrystal based composites: A review. *Composites Part C: Open Access*, *5*, 100164. https://doi.org/.2021.100164 doi:10.1016/j.jcomc

Shokri, J., & Adibkia, K. (2013). Application of Cellulose and Cellulose Derivatives in Pharmaceutical Industries. In T. a. de Ven & L. Godbout (Eds.), *Cellulose - Medical, Pharmaceutical and Electronic Applications*. IntechOpen. doi:10.5772/55178

Shoukat, A., Wahid, F., Khan, T., Siddique, M., Nasreen, S., Yang, G., Ullah, M. W., & Khan, R. (2019). Titanium oxide-bacterial cellulose bioadsorbent for the removal of lead ions from aqueous solution. *International Journal of Biological Macromolecules*, *129*, 965–971. doi:10.1016/j.ijbiomac.2019.02.032 PMID:30738165

Soeiro, V. S., Tundisi, L. L., Novaes, L. C. L., Mazzola, P. G., Aranha, N., Grotto, D., Junior, J. M. O., Komatsu, D., Gama, F. M. P., Chaud, M. V., & Jozala, A. F. (2021). Production of bacterial cellulose nanocrystals via enzymatic hydrolysis and evaluation of their coating on alginate particles formed by ionotropic gelation. *Carbohydrate Polymer Technologies and Applications, 2*, 100155. doi:10.1016/j.carpta.2021.100155

Song, K., Zhu, X., Zhu, W., & Li, X. (2019). Preparation and characterization of cellulose nanocrystal extracted from *Calotropis procera* biomass. *Bioresources and Bioprocessing, 6*(1), 45. doi:10.118640643-019-0279-z

Sosiati, H., Muhaimin, M., Purwanto, Wijayanti, D.A., & Triyana, K. (2014). Nanocrystalline Cellulose Studied with a Conventional SEM. In *2014 International Conference on Physics (ICP 2014)*. Atlantis Press. 10.2991/icp-14.2014.3

Sulaiman, H. S., Chan, C. H., Chia, C. H., Zakaria, S., & Sharifah Nabihah Syed Jaafar, S. N. S. (2015). Isolation and Fractionation of Cellulose Nanocrystals from Kenaf Core. *Sains Malaysiana, 44*(11), 1635–1642.

Tahir, D., Karim, M. R. A., Hu, H., Naseem, S., Rehan, M., Ahmad, M., & Zhang, M. (2022). Sources, Chemical Functionalization, and Commercial Applications of Nanocellulose and Nanocellulose Based Composites: A Review. *Polymers, 14*(21), 4468. doi:10.3390/polym14214468 PMID:36365462

Taiwo, F. A. T. (2017). Preparation and Fundamental Characterization of Cellulose Nanocrystal from Oil Palm Fronds Biomass. *Journal of Polymers and the Environment, 25*(3), 1–9. doi:10.100710924-016-0854-8

Thomsen, M. (2005). Complex media from processing of agricultural crops for microbial fermentation. *Applied Microbiology and Biotechnology, 68*(5), 598–606. doi:10.100700253-005-0056-0 PMID:16082554

Thoorens, G., Fabrice, K., Bruno, L., Brian, C., & Brigitte, E. (2014). Microcrystalline cellulose, a direct compression binder in a quality by design environment-A review. *International Journal of Pharmaceutics, 473*(1), 64–72. doi:10.1016/j.ijpharm.2014.06.055 PMID:24993785

Trache, D., Tarchoun, A. F., Derradji, M., Hamidon, T. S., Masruchin, N., Brosse, N., & Hussin, M. H. (2020). Nanocellulose: From Fundamentals to Advanced Applications. *Frontiers in Chemistry, 8*, 392. doi:10.3389/fchem.2020.00392 PMID:32435633

Ullah, M. W., Manan, S., Ul-Islam, M., Revin, V. V., Thomas, S., & Yang, G. (2021) Introduction to Nanocellulose. Nanocellulose: Synthesis, Structure, Properties and Applications, 1-50. doi:10.1142/9781786349477_0001

Wijaya, C. J., Ismadji, S., Aparamarta, H. W., & Gunawan, S. (2019). Optimization of cellulose nanocrystals from bamboo shoots using Response Surface Methodology. *Heliyon, 5*(11), e02807. doi:10.1016/j.heliyon.2019.e02807 PMID:31844732

Wirjosentono, B., Zulnazri, Tarigan, A.S., Naomi, T., & Nasution, D.A. (2021). Preparation of palm oil empty fruit bunches nanocellulose-filled polyvinyl alcohol-polyacrylic acid biohydrogel. AIP Conference Proceedings, 2342. doi:10.1063/5.0046399

Wu, X. (2016). *Conductive Cellulose Nanocrystals for Electrochemical Applications* [Thesis]. University of Waterloo. https://core.ac.uk/download/pdf/144149343.pdf

Xie, S., Zhang, X., Walcott, M., & Lin, H. (2018). Cellulose Nanocrystals (CNCs) Applications: A Review. *Engineering and Science*, 2, 4–16. doi:10.30919/es.1803302

Xie, S., Zhang, X., Walcott, M. P., & Lin, H. (2018). Applications of Cellulose Nanocrystals: A Review. *Engineering and Science*, 2, 4–16.

Yan, C., Wang, J., Kang, W., Cui, M., Wang, X., Foo, C. Y., Chee, K. J., & Lee, P. S. (2014). Highly stretchable piezoresistive graphene-nanocellulose nanopaper for strain sensors. *Advanced Materials*, 26(13), 2022–2027. doi:10.1002/adma.201304742 PMID:24343930

Yang, H. (2016). *Multifunctional hairy nanocrystalline cellulose* [Thesis]. McGill University. https://escholarship.mcgill.ca/concern/theses/2n49t4752

Zhang, C., Dan, Y., Peng, J., Turng, L., Sabo, R., & Clemons, C. (2014). Thermal and Mechanical Properties of Natural Rubber Composites Reinforced with Cellulosic Nanocrystals from Southern Pine. *Advances in Polymerv Tech.*, 1-7. doi:10.1002/adv.21448

Zuliat, F. A., Suardi, M., & Djamaan, A. (2020). CNC (Cellulose Nanocrystals) Isolationfrom Various Agriculture and Industrial Waste Using Acid Hydrolysis Methods. *IOSR Journal of Pharmacy and Biological Sciences*, 15(6), 42–58.

Zulnazri, Z., Daud, M., & Sylvia, N. (2021). Synthesis of cellulose nanocrystals (CNCS) from oil palm empty fruit bunch by hydrothermal with pre-treatment sonication. *AIP Conference Proceedings*, 2342, 030003. doi:10.1063/5.0046000

Chapter 18
Inching Towards Sustainability in Developing Countries:
An Analysis of the Food Industry – A Case Study of India

Anahita Sawhney
Amity University, Noida, India

Pooja Mehra
Amity University, Noida, India

ABSTRACT

Sustainable development stands on three core elements: environment, economy, and social equity. The environment is under constant pressure from a long list of hazards. Even though there have been various innovations and developments of new practices to reduce the pressure and tackle the negative externalities, there still seems to be a long way to go. This chapter lays its entire focus on the sustainable consumption and production patterns of the food industry in the developing countries, while paying special attention to India and the impacts it has on the human habitat. The current state of the environment calls for the innovation of methods which lead to an efficient future. To understand more of this, a study was run on the people of Delhi, NCR so as to understand their current degree of awareness about sustainability, their consumption behaviours, and the importance laid on sustainability. The impact of factors like price, nutrition, taste, availability, convenience, sustainability, brand reputation, and packaging were also highlighted.

INTRODUCTION

The Brundtland Commission defined sustainability as "meeting the needs of the present without compromising the ability of the future generations to meet their own needs" in the year 1987. As a concept, sustainability is gaining a lot of importance as the world is increasingly threatened by issues such as climate change, global warming, resource depletion, hunger, poverty, and other social inequalities.

DOI: 10.4018/978-1-6684-8969-7.ch018

Under the 2030 Agenda of Sustainable Development, the United Nations laid down seventeen Sustainable Development Goals (SDGs), which try to tackle the complications of poverty, hunger, inequality, education, etc while trying to establish responsible consumption and production and spreading peace, justice, and strong institutions. Brought to force on Jan 1, 2016, these seventeen goals have been adopted by all 193 UN Member Nations (Dpicampaigns, 2020).

Since the beginning of the 21st century, the demands of humans have grown ten times (European Commission, 2018), leading to a rise that is faster than nature's capacity to produce, let alone replenish its resources. Every year we observe Earth Overshoot Day in July which marks the date when humanity has exhausted the earth's budget for the year. This basically suggests that the natural resources only last us till the month of July. The coming of the pandemic momentarily reduced the ecological footprint, however, the struggle against long-term unsustainability, remains a perpetual issue.

Reports suggest that the global food industry is responsible for about 21% of anthropogenic greenhouse gas (GHG) emissions, and total GHG emissions of about 42% (Langen et al., 2022). This, therefore, makes it important to push this industry towards sustainability.

Consumer preferences and behaviours are affected by a lot of factors. While consumers believe that their choices are based on individual likes, they tend to overlook the susceptibility of these choices by external and environmental stimuli. Producers hold the power to nudge consumers towards a more sustainable livelihood, aided by eating better. This works at both, the demand and supply, sides. Organisations involved in digitally dealing with their consumers hold an abundance of consumer data. This is what is termed as a behavioural surplus. This behavioural surplus can be used to shape and structure consumer behaviour, to generate what is known as a societal surplus (Zuboff, 2018). Zuboff goes ahead to explain that a societal surplus is *"the sum of the benefits that accrue to society by advancing economic vitality; environmental sustainability; lifetime well-being; access, equity, and inclusion; ethical capacity; and social progress."* This suggests that societal surplus is generative and so, benefits everyone. Using the behavioural surplus to nudge consumers towards sustainable consumption practices is a very important step in this road towards attaining sustainability. An example of a company nudge could be a food delivery application that has the ability to promote restaurants on the basis of their sustainability rating. Every small or big marketing action, too, is a nudge towards changing consumer behaviour (DaSilva et al., 2023).

Researches have mentioned the need for a sustainable consumption and production system (SCP), which creates a sustainable balance between consumers and producers. While it influences the producers to try and bring out a greater variety of green products and wider consumption options, it also mentions that this rise in price should drive down prices, making green products more affordable. Thus, creating a closed system (Staniškis, 2011).

Rationale of the Study

This study has been conducted for the sole purpose of learning more about the concept of sustainability. It is done so as to understand the threats to sustainability, their consequences, and ways to avert them, while particularly focusing of the food industry. The fact that sustainability is the need of the hour is not an unpopular opinion. Growing population and growing demands have been key factors in boosting production processes. Various social, economic, and environmental aspects are being hindered due to the same. This study shall provide insights to all of this, while laying a special focus on the food industry of India.

To know more, the study also inculcates a primary survey which has been conducted to understand consumer preferences and behaviours along the lines of sustainable consumption patterns, specifically in the food industry. This shall give a better look into the effects that demographic variables have on the topic at hand.

To sum up, the study tries to explore various factors that hinder sustainable consumption and how they can be effectively avoided. It focuses on the food industry and tries to surround the findings around developing countries, specifically India.

Research Questions

1. What are the environmental issues that hinder the movement towards a sustainable future and the practices that help fight these issues?
2. What is the current situation of the global food industry and what challenges does it face along the lines of sustainability?
3. What are the various demographic variables that may affect sustainable consumption practices and how do these affect the awareness, behaviour, and importance of sustainability?

Research Objectives

1. To understand the meaning and issues around sustainability and track down the prevalent practices to fight these issues.
2. To decipher the economic scenario of the global food industry and the problems around sustainability that are faced by the developing nations in this industry, with a case study of India.
3. To research various demographic variables and understand their impact on awareness, importance, and behaviour around sustainable consumption practices and unearth the factors responsible for the same.

Type of Research

In this paper, a literature review has been conducted through secondary research to understand the prevalent sustainable consumption and production practices in the food industry with a special case study of India. It covers the ins and outs of the basic environmental problems that call for the need for sustainability and the solutions to the same. The primary focus has been laid on the food industry and its allied sectors.

The second part of the paper contains a primary survey conducted in the National Capital of India and the territories surrounding it. It aims to analyse the sustainable consumption practices of the population and run a comparison along various demographics like age. It also tries to explore the factors that play an important role in the behaviour of people with regard to consumption practices.

It, however, is important to note that the study is limited by the available data on sustainable consumption practices and the data collected through the primary survey is subject to the interpretations of each individual.

LITERATURE REVIEW

An Overview

The environmental issues that are growing at a fast rate call for the need of sustainable consumption and production practices. Some problems that are hindering sustainable development have been discussed below:

1. **Resource Scarcity:** As the world population reached 8 billion in 2022 (United Nations, n.d.), the demands are also rising. As mentioned above, the human needs outstrip the earth's capacity to provide. Basic essentials like water, energy, and raw materials are going scarce. As per the International Energy Agency, with a robust economic growth of countries like China and India, that rely heavily on coal, the global coal demand crossed 8 billion tonnes in 2022, reaching an all-time high **(IEA, 2022)**. Depletion of resources and their in-equitable distribution is a major constraint in the path of growth and development.
2. **Climate Change:** The Intergovernmental Panel on Climate Change, in its recent reports, has mentioned that the global temperature has seen a rise of $1.1°$ C above the pre-industrial levels. The sea levels are rising, and the ice caps are melting. All this has made room for floods, heatwaves, and droughts, causing immense devastation around the globe with millions of people losing their lives (***AR6 Synthesis Report: Climate Change 2023 — IPCC, n.d.***). The United Nations Environment Programme suggests that if the situation is not tackled, the rise in temperature would be between $2.4°$ C – $2.6°$ C by the end of the century (United Nations, n.d.-a).
3. **Waste Generation:** The generation of all sorts of waste materials (food waste, e-waste, plastic waste, etc) is a global concern. Lack of proper disposal of such waste materials is an environmental as well as a health hazard.

Reports by World Bank suggest that by 2050, global waste production is set to rise to 3.4 billion metric tons (World Bank Group, 2018). A very insignificant part of this waste is segregated and recycled in low-income countries, while their contribution to generating the same seems to be rising continuously.

4. **Biodiversity Loss:** Many species, over the decades, have gone extinct or have become endangered. Biodiversity is being deprived of basic necessities such as clean air, water, and proper food, affecting the well-being of the planet and its inhabitants.

However, it would be unfair to recognize the methods that have been taken up and the techniques that have been introduced to tackle these issues and ensure a sustainable livelihood. Some prevalent practices include:

1. **Renewable Energy:** Talking about the growing demand for coal, it is important to shift to renewable energy resources. Examples of this are resorting to hydropower, wind power, and solar-power techniques. As per the International Energy Agency, power generation from solar energy increased by 22% in 2022 as compared to 2021. It accounted for 3.6% of global electricity generation. Hydropower and wind power are extremely popular and account for a greater share. These

inexhaustible resources can prove to be extremely beneficial in providing for the global population (***Solar PV – Analysis - IEA, n.d.***).
2. **Circular Economy:** A relatively new and interesting method is the adoption of a circular economy. It is a market system that incentivizes reusing products instead of extracting new ones. All sorts of waste materials are put back into the economy and leakages in the form of waste disposal are minimized to every possible extent (***Circular Economy, 2023***). Old clothes, obsolete electronics, scrap metals, etc are reused, recycled, and/or replenished. This optimizes the utilization of resources, minimizes waste, and promotes sustainability.
3. **Sustainable Transportation:** The transport sector is one of the most crucial contributors to global greenhouse gas emissions. This, therefore, makes it essential to resort to more sustainable practices. People have started moving towards low-emission cars, electric vehicles, and even public transport. Countries like the Netherlands promote the utilization of cycles and trams. To keep a better check on emissions, the Indian Government introduced the BS6 Emission Norms, which require the carmakers to equip their vehicles with. Portable Emission Measurement System (PEMS), that will test and measure the pollutants emitted by the vehicle in real-time (*applicable from April 2023*).
4. **Sustainable Agriculture:** A major cause of emissions, biodiversity loss, and deforestation, agriculture is now being pushed towards adopting sustainable practices. Encouraging organic farming and reducing the use of pesticides is a common method (Lai, 2023). Along with all of this, sustainable tourism, sustainable fisheries, sustainable building, waste reduction, etc are other practices that are being promoted. Sustainable agriculture is closely linked to the practices of the food industry, which is the heart of this research.

The Food Industry

As the planet tries to make room for the growing population, providing for their basic necessities like food, clothing, and housing is becoming challenging. With the demand outstripping the available resources, pressure on the environment is immense.

According to the Food and beverages market size, trends, and Global Forecast to 2032 (published by The Business Research Company), the global food industry is a constantly growing industry. It grew from $6729.54 billion in 2022 to $7221.73 billion in 2023. This resulted in a compounded annual growth (CAGR) of 7.3%. The value is expected to reach $9225.37 by 2027, a CAGR of 6.3%.

Reports suggest that 50% of the global habitable land is used for food production, and agriculture takes up 70% of global freshwater. 78% of freshwater and ocean water eutrophication is also a result of agriculture (***How Are Food and the Environment Related? | Taking Charge of Your Health & Wellbeing, n.d.***). The contribution of the food industry to the emissions of greenhouse gases (GHG) is also huge. **As per the reports of United Nations Organisation (UNO),** this industry is responsible for one third of global greenhouse gas emissions (United Nations. (n.d.). Food and climate change: Healthy diets for a healthier planet. United Nations).

Reports have suggested that one-third of the food produced is wasted. This waste generation occurs at every stage of the food supply chain. The food waste is sent to landfills. On decomposition, this waste generates Methane, which is a potent greenhouse gas (Morone et al., 2019). Overcapacity has also been witnessed in cases of a lot of crops. Even though this has reduced the prices of the crop, it has challenged the capability of the land.

The food industry across the world is huge, as evidence suggests. It is divided into various sub-parts like agriculture, production, processing, packaging, food transportation, restaurants, and cloud kitchens, etc. Since it has many parts to it, each of these individually impacts the environment. Even before production begins, the fields need to be cleared out for the produce to grow. This not only affects the plant life but also impacts the wildlife as their natural habitat gets destroyed. To understand the various parts of this industry and the impact they lay on the environment, while highlighting the solutions to tackle the same is crucial for this paper. The corresponding section has been specifically designed to focus on the developing countries.

Agriculture, Meat, and Poultry

Agriculture and the environment have always been interconnected. While agriculture contributes to an unsustainable world, it is also a victim of the same. The creation of farmland requires the clearing of the forests. This causes deforestation as well as loss of biodiversity. Reports suggest that South-East Asia is losing 1.2% of forests every year. Intensive farming and overgrazing are responsible for soil erosion, thus reducing the fertility of the soil. **According to the United Nations Food and Agriculture** Organization (FAO), one-third of the world's soil is degraded, with the majority being in Africa and Asia (*Key Messages | Global Symposium on Soil Erosion | Food and Agriculture Organization of the United Nations*, n.d.). The agriculture sector holds multiple allied areas under its umbrella. Some of these include livestock, fisheries, poultry, animal husbandry, and but not limited to dairy farming. The growth is agriculture is significantly influenced by the individual growth of all its sub-sectors. Along with this, the environmental impacts resulting from agriculture are also a culmination of individual activities of these sectors.

The meat and poultry sector are sub-sectors of agriculture that have shown a beautiful growth trajectory over the years and are regarded as the fastest-growing sub-sectors. This is very evident in developing countries. **The Food and Agriculture Organization (FAO)** reports that global meat production stood at 337 million tonnes in 2020, with poultry meat representing 40% of it. Asia holds a 67% share of global egg production, with China being responsible for most of it. In the past few decades, the reported rise in egg production lies at 150%. The growth in Asian produce, in itself, was fourfold. (*Gateway to Poultry Production and Products | Food and Agriculture Organization of the United Nations*, n.d.) These two industries, meat and poultry, hold a strong impact on the environment and the economy, particularly in developing countries. The major reason behind this is the prevalence of inadequate infrastructure, a lesser number of regulations, and poor waste management.

Greenpeace comments that the industrial meat system consumes a large number of resources, particularly land, in order to sustain itself. Deforestation and forest fires are among the first negative effects of the agriculture sector and the meat and poultry industry, as forests get cleared to make room for grazing land and farmland. This deforestation causes a loss of biodiversity and also leads to global warming due to increased greenhouse gas emissions. Greenpeace also reports that this deforestation can push the Amazon Rainforests to a "tipping point", where it will no longer be able to maintain its lush greenery and would fail to sustain itself. (Chadwick, 2023) Due to the digestion and decomposition processes of livestock, methane, and other greenhouse gases are emitted into the atmosphere, contributing to climate change. If this animal waste reaches the water, it contributes to water pollution along with the already existing pollutants resulting from the fertilizers and pesticides that have been used to grow crops and fodder. (Thornton, 2010)

Meat is an excellent source of protein and can be a benefit for nations suffering from malnutrition, a problem prevalent in underdeveloped and developing countries, particularly in Africa and Asia. But its impact on the environment cannot be ignored (Marinova & Bogueva, 2019). To ensure sustainability, waste management needs to be practiced, deforestation needs to be restricted, and investing in alternative food sources can be taken into consideration.

A lot of people have shifted to plant-based and vegan diets. Lentils and legumes also offer a great amount of protein and so, can be easily included in a balanced diet without harming the environment to uncontrollable levels. These days, alternatives like plant-based meat are also gaining popularity due to their innovative existence, animal-meat-like taste, vegan properties, and health benefits. Researchers suggest that plant-based meat might even be healthier than conventional meat. Its ecological footprint is also lower than real meat and has the potential to transmogrify the entire meat and poultry industry into something healthier, sustainable, and more eco-friendly (Santo et al., 2020).

Food Packaging Industry and the Environment

Food packaging is another important part of the food industry. The growth of processed food, drive-throughs and takeaways, packaged foods, etc. have boosted the demand for food packaging. It has led to a rise in the usage of plastic wrappers, parchment papers, aluminum foils, etc. The packaging industry is also a big contributor to the production of GHGs. This includes all greenhouse gases that are generated in the manufacturing of raw materials to the transportation of the finished product to the consumer. It also includes the emissions, if any, at the end of the packaging material's life.

The packaging industry also produces 146 metric tonnes of plastic packaging waste every year and this is set to double by 2050, as per a report by the Ellen MacArthur Foundation. (*Plastics and the Circular Economy*, n.d.). Most of the waste produced by the food industry is single use plastic which, upon disposal, ends up in landfills or even water. Aluminum foils also end up in the same place. These materials take centuries to degrade. The demand for resources such as paper, aluminum, and plastic require an immense amount of energy to be produced. From the extraction of raw materials to their processing and transportation, a lot of resources are utilized. With their increasing demand, resource depletion is a common problem.

The companies involved in various sectors of the food industry (restaurants, cafes, processed, packaged and frozen food industry, etc.) try to make their products look more and more attractive using various techniques. The metal used in cans, the glass used in bottles, the single-use plastic used for beverages and water bottles, and the big packets of chips that contain very little material to eat are a few examples of how diverse food packaging is. The excellent packaging of food products can be a contributing factor to consumer buying behavior, acting as a nudge to influencing consumers into buying the company's products. However, its harm to the environment cannot be neglected. There are various ways to promote sustainability in this industry.

Sustainable packaging is a relatively new concept, but it promotes ecological balance by reducing the impact the industry has on the environment. **According to the Sustainable Packaging Coalition (2011),** "*Sustainable packaging is beneficial, safe and healthy for individuals and communities throughout its life cycle; meets market criteria for performance and cost; is sourced, manufactured, transported, and recycled using renewable energy; maximises the use of renewable or recycled source materials; is manufactured using clean production technologies and best practices; is made from materials healthy* *in all probable end of life scenarios; is physically designed to optimise materials and energy; and is effectively recovered and utilised in biological and/or industrial cradle-to-cradle cycles."*

Sustainable packaging suggests reducing the use of packaging material, wherever needed. Consumers are often suggested to carry purchase bigger containers, rather than buying multiple smaller ones as it cuts down the packaging of the products. Plant-based plastics or other natural materials are often used to replace normal plastic packaging. Resorting to alternatives to aluminum foil like parchment paper is also becoming a popular practice. Companies try to endure eco-friendly packaging by using tapes, stickers, or tissue papers made of recycled or Forest Stewardship Council (FSC) paper.

While sustainable packaging is being adopted by many sectors, it is still limited in practice. Banning single-use plastic in countries like India has caused a shift to buying paper bags from stores, rather than people carrying their own bags. While it is a step in the right direction, it is not enough. Waste is still a matter of concern (Moshood et al., 2022).

Cloud Kitchens and Take-Outs and the Environment

A very interesting concept that has surfaced over the past few years is that of cloud kitchens. These kitchens are also called ghost kitchens or virtual kitchens and exclusively provide take-outs and deliveries rather than a dine-out service. Needless to say, they have gained a lot of popularity too from both a consumer's as well as a producer's point of view, particularly in developing countries. The pandemic played a really important role in their rise. These kitchens are flexible and have a lower overhead cost as compared to a normal restaurant. Reports have suggested that the market share of cloud kitchens is growing and is expected to reach 1 billion USD in India by 2023 (Chatterjee et al., 2022).

The environmental implications of cloud kitchens, however, are not something that one can overlook. Like other kitchens, these require high energy for food production, lighting, running kitchen equipment, etc. Since they are working in the sector for deliveries and takeouts, they have a significant amount of waste generation, adding to the already existing problems around sustainability in developing countries. For their venture to become popular, they use a lot of printed takeout menus to distribute them over their delivery area. Most of these kitchens hand out a menu with each order they deliver. This not only leads to immense waste but also unnecessary utilization of paper and printing material They use disposable packaging materials, often involving plastic containers, spoons, glasses, etc. The transportation of this food also contributes to greenhouse gas emissions as these kitchens focus on speed over sustainability.

Cloud kitchens, while negatively impacting the environment, also have several benefits. A major benefit is that they do not require indoor heating or cooling for their customers to get a dine-in experience. They function in a small area, and so require fewer resources to power their air conditioners and heaters.

They also use up less water as the aspect of washing cutlery and other serving utensils are out of the question. With the restaurant industry being huge, cloud kitchens are often regarded as a boon to this sector. It is often suggested that cloud kitchens shift to renewable energy resources and bio-degradable packaging. They are also suggested to print fewer menus and resort to e-menus as much as possible.

Their gaining popularity and several benefits are not enough to work towards a sustainable future. It is, therefore, needed to reduce the pollution caused by transportation, it is important to optimize delivery routes and take up the smallest distance possible, while covering maximum delivery stops and shifting to electrically powered scooters and vehicles (Choudhary, 2019). Providing vegan and plant-based products helps protect biodiversity and thus, protects the environment. With vegan food becoming very popular among the masses, it attracts a new segment of the population to the kitchen. Purchasing locally sourced and avoiding off-season fruits and vegetables is also a helpful mechanism. While local sourcing cuts down the transportation impact, the fruits and vegetables in season are also beneficial and more sustainable.

Coming up with food delivery applications like Zomato and Swiggy has also contributed to the popularity of takeouts. While this affects the environment, these apps try and ensure sustainable consumption and production by optimizing delivery routes, minimizing cutleries, saying no to plastic, prioritizing sustainable restaurants etc. (Frederick, 2021).

Sustainability has also become prevalent in the catering industry, making room for sustainable weddings. Couples try to provide individual portions of food rather than setting an elaborate buffet. These individual portions are from a menu, and so are according to the guest's preference. This reduces the wastage of food (Flood et al., 2014).

A Case Study of India

Indian food is very sustainable, from the roots of it. While the world inches towards sustainable food consumption, India has been into this since ancient times. Every Indian household knowingly or unknowingly knows how to consume food in a sustainably viable manner. From the seeds of fruits like melons and watermelons being used to make refreshing summer drinks to the skins of many vegetables turning into pickles, and the leftovers from last night being turned into an innovative dish the next morning, Indians try to use every part of the product to its full potential. Ignoring the complexities of words such as green kitchens, zero-wastes, etc, many households have simplified their practice.

The food industry not only significantly contributes to the country's economy, but also acts as a threat to the environment. Most of these threats fall in line with the challenges witnessed globally.

Food Waste

Food wastage is a key issue that is faced across the world. **As per the Food Safety and Standards Authority of India (FSSAI)**, one-third of the food produced in India gets spoilt or is wasted, and not eaten. India's annual food wastage is about 68 million tons. 40% of the food produced is wasted, leading to a daily wastage of 7.5 tons of food (*UNEP Food Waste Index Report 2021*, **n.d.**). Hunger, poverty, and malnutrition are among key national issues for the country and the food wasted can actually feed an entire hunger-struck state, like that of Bihar. Lost resources, improper waste management, and severe environmental impacts are not the only problems that India faces due to the wastage of food. Millions of children are suffering from stunted growth or are underweight. Women and children are also prone to energy deficiencies and anaemia (*Deaths Due to Malnutrition*, **n.d.**).

The wasted food is not just a threat to the environment, but also affects the social and economic aspects of the society. The food that is wasted can be used to feed millions. This would increase the human capital of the country. The resources used up in the production of this food can be employed elsewhere, becoming economically beneficial for India.

To solve this, initiatives like Feeding India by Zomato have really come in handy. They collect excess food from restaurants and hotels and redistribute it among those who need it **(Panigrahi et al., 2020)**. Robin Hood Army is also involved in a similar practice and is doing a good job at the same. The food wasted can be used as compost or can be turned into animal feed. A lot of Indian households make it a daily practice to save used tea leaves and use them to fertilize their plants.

Use of Pesticides and Fertilizers

We already know that chemically replenishing soil nutrients as per the crop's need affects the soil's health and causes it to erode. With a growing demand for agricultural produce, the use of pesticides and fertilizers is growing too.

Despite the banning of several pesticides in India, their use continues to be there. Reports suggest that the size of the Indian Pesticide Market is 229.4 billion INR and is expected to grow to 342.3 billion INR by 2028, showing a CAGR of 6.6% between the two years (*Indian Pesticides Market Size, Share, Trends & Forecast 2023-2028*, n.d.). **The Indian market, however, is gradually shifting toward the demand for organic produce. These products, being free from chemicals, are not only a step ahead for the environment but also act as a boon for the health of consumers. In 2019, Sikkim was declared a 100% organic state, the first Indian state to attain this certification. Not too far behind are the states of Kerala, Mizoram, and Nagaland** (Sherpa et al., 2021).

Processed Food

While talking about availability and convenience when it comes to food items, processed food is the first option people look at. As and when the industry booms, it leaves certain environmental impacts. The turmoil is particularly evident in developing countries. This industry emits various greenhouse gases like carbon dioxide and methane. It is resource intensive and takes up a lot of water, unabashed by the scarcity of the same in many developing countries. The processed food industry is a key contributor to waste. It requires heavy packaging, which comes in a variety of forms. From vacuum-sealing cheese and other products to boxing breakfast cereals, all these residual packaging materials end up in landfills. The waste of tinned food products is also a major environmental hazard. Along with affecting the environment, they also affect the consumer directly. They are a leading cause of chronic obesity and many heart problems. The lack of nutrients and the introduction of a lot of chemicals cause more harm than this food can fix (*Processed Foods and Health*, 2023).

One benefit of processed food, however, is that they increase the shelf-life of otherwise short-lived products. This reduces the waste generated by fruits and vegetables going stale. Owing to this thought, the Indian government is trying to work on schemes that created cold chains and preservation infrastructure. These chains and infrastructural developments will work towards grading sorting, weighing, packing, etc, as well as quick freezing. As per the official website of Make in India, till March 2019, 299 approved cold chain projects were starting to be implemented. (*6 Schemes That Would Reduce Food Waste, Benefit Farmers | Make in India*, n.d.)

Apart from all of this, it is important that India resorts to locally sourced produce and moves towards more plant-based and vegan options to ensure a more sustainable livelihood. While price can be a factor of concern, there are inexpensive options available to attain the same as well. The practice of sustainability has been going on for ages in India. With the majority of the population being vegetarian, this is a deep-rooted culinary skill present widely across the country. A vegetarian diet demands less water and resources and also protects biodiversity and the demand for plant-based proteins like soybean and lentils rises. Vegetable and fruit seeds and peels are excellent ingredients for broths and condiments. The traditional methods of cooking on tandoors and clay pots over a low flame also reduce the demand for energy. These practices that have been entrenched in India's cooking culture can act as an example of sustainably efficient and eco-friendly cooking practices around the world.

However, there is yet a long way to go for India to become more efficient and create a rather sustainable environment for its population. The country continues to hold a proactive approach towards doing full justice to the twelfth sustainable development goal (sustainable production and consumption) and reducing the negative externalities it is creating for the environment.

The population of India is culturally and demographically diverse. This leads to an assortment of consumption practices and a mixture of perceptions. Each household has its set consumption behaviors, which further branch out as we try and look at these behaviors through age groups, gender, or income groups. With this aim taken under consideration, primary research was conducted to take a better look at these practices along the lines of various demographic variables. The authors believe that to nudge the consumers towards a sustainable livelihood, what needs to be understood is the existing practices. For this, a study of Delhi, NCR has been undertaken.

METHODOLOGY

This part of the paper has been taken to analyse the extent of sustainable food consumption in the people of the National Capital Region of India (Delhi, NCR). The research was aimed at running a comparative study on the basis of age. An online questionnaire was created using Google Forms, and both hard copies and soft copies of the same were circulated among people.

The questionnaire primarily aims to study the behaviour, attitude, and perception of people about sustainability and sustainable consumption practices, particularly in the food industry.

Upon taking the total population of Delhi, NCR the sample size came out to 384. On floating the questionnaire, 250 responses were received ranging between ages 18 and 75. These responses were then divided into three age groups and a number was allotted to them:

Group 1: Under 25 (0)
Group 2: 25-45 (1)
Group 3: Equal to or over 45 (2)

To analyse equal respondents of all three groups, these 250 responses were randomly reduced to 225, leading to 75 responses in each. These responses have been compared to obtain desired results.

The questionnaire was divided into three broad areas: Awareness, Behaviour, Factors, and the respondents were asked to rate on a four-point Likert scale, with 4 being highly agree to 1 being highly disagree. The reason behind choosing this scale was to provide a point-to-point result without creating ambiguity.

Eight factors were considered, namely: price, nutritional value, sustainability, availability, taste, convenience, packaging, and brand reputation. This has then been compared with behaviour to understand the impact these factors hold.

To analyse the data so attained, the first step was to run descriptive statistics on the demographic variables to get a clearer picture of the sample that has been studied. After that, Cronbach's Alpha Reliability Test has been applied to understand the reliability of the factors.

Various hypotheses were formulated, and to test them, non-parametric tests were to be applied. Kruskal-Wallis Test was used to check the same since there were three age groups that were taken under consideration. To provide more evidence and information to the hypotheses testing, Spearman Correlation was also applied.

All analyses have been performed on SPSS, a statistical software, and certain frequency diagrams have been obtained through google form responses and Microsoft Excel.

The questionnaire was easy to comprehend and included only those questions which were relevant to the study. All the questions were framed in such a way that their responses fit in with the Likert scale. The questionnaires were completely anonymous, and the results have also been held confidential. The questionnaire, in no way, tries to influence or entice the respondents into answering in a particular way to attain the results needed. Along with all of this, certain subjective questions were also included in the questionnaire. The results of the same have also been discussed below.

Results

To understand the results of the data obtained, let us first look at the demographics. Distributed across Delhi, NCR the responses were spread over different demographic variables:

Demographics

- **Age**

As mentioned above, 250 forms were collected. These respondents belonged to ages between 18 and 75. For ease of research and comparison, these ages were divided into three groups.

Group 1: Under 25 (0)
Group 2: 25-45 (1)
Group 3: Equal to or over 45 (2)

Table 1. Frequency distribution across age groups

	AGE			
	Frequency	Percent	Valid Percent	Cumulative Frequency
0	75	33.3	33.3	33.3
1	75	33.3	33.3	66.7
2	75	33.3	33.3	100.0
Total	225	100.0	100.0	

- **Gender**

The 225 responses had 102 (45.8%) female respondents and 122 (54.2%) male respondents. The objective was to see the gender distribution of the respondents. Gender distribution can be seen from Table 3.

Inching Towards Sustainability in Developing Countries

Table 2. Frequency distribution across gender

	GENDER			
	Frequency	Percent	Valid Percent	Cumulative Frequency
0	103	45.8	45.8	45.8
1	122	54.2	54.2	100
Total	225	100.0	100.0	

- **Education**

The education distribution suggests that the entire sample is educated, with the majority being post graduate. Roughly half the sample has completed their post-graduation while 30% of the respondents have only finished their high school education. 16% are graduates and only 2.2% hold a doctorate in their respective fields. This demographic was taken into consideration because the researchers believed that education plays an important role in people's attitude, behaviour, and perception of role. Table 4 highlights the same.

Table 3. Frequency distribution across Education

	EDUCATION			
	Frequency	Percent	Valid Percent	Cumulative Frequency
BLIS	1	0.4	0.4	0.4
Graduate	36	16.0	16.0	16.4
High school	68	30.2	30.2	46.7
M. Phil.	1	0.4	0.4	47.1
PhD	5	2.2	2.2	49.3
Post Graduate	115	49.8	49.8	99.1
Primary Education	2	0.9	0.9	100.0
Total	225	100.0	100.0	

- **Employment**

The employment distribution falls in line with the education of people. Majority of respondents are full-time employed, with students being second in line. About 45.5% of the sample is employed, 31% represents students, 12.5% of the sample is unemployed. The employment status, too, affects the attitude of people around sustainability as it affects their income as well as impacts their behaviour. Table 5 showcases this distribution.

Table 4. Frequency distribution across employment

EMPLOYMENT				
	Frequency	Percent	Valid Percent	Cumulative Frequency
Full-time employed	93	41.3	41.3	41.3
Home Maker	1	0.4	0.4	41.8
Part-time employed	3	1.3	1.3	43.1
Retired	24	10.7	10.7	53.8
Self-Employed	7	3.1	3.1	56.9
Student	70	31.1	31.1	88.0
Unemployed and not seeking work	25	11.1	11.1	99.1
Unemployed but actively seeking work	2	0.9	0.9	100.0
Total	225	100.0	100.0	

- **Income**

Income is a very important demographic variable as the buying behaviour of people, their lifestyle, their affordability, etc is all governed by it. For this very reason, this demographic was considered. Four income groups were created, and responses were collected according to them. Each income group was allotted a dummy. The income groups are as-follows:

Group 1: <Rs. 5 Lakhs per annum (0)
Group 2: Rs. 5- Rs. 15 Lakhs per annum (1)
Group 3: Rs. 15- Rs. 25 Lakhs per annum (2)
Group 4: >Rs. 25 Lakhs per annum (3)

An attempt to broadly keep the responses equal along the income groups was considered. Maximum respondents belonged to the second group, making up roughly 40% of the population, followed by group 2, constituting 29%. Only 13% of the population belonged to the last group. Table 6 highlights this distribution.

Table 5. Frequency distribution across income

INCOME				
	Frequency	Percent	Valid Percent	Cumulative Frequency
0	45	20.0	20.0	20.0
1	87	38.7	38.7	58.7
2	64	38.4	38.4	87.1
3	29	12.9	12.9	100.0
Total	225	100.0	100.0	

Reliability Test

Cronbach's Alpha Test was run on the factors taken under consideration. This test is used to measure the reliability of the data by taking into account the shared variance of the items. It measures the internal consistency of the data.

The categories of the questionnaire were awareness, behaviour, and factors affecting the sustainable consumption behaviour of people, while also looking at the importance of the same. Eight factors were considered, as already mentioned, namely price, taste, nutritional value, convenience, availability, sustainability, packaging, and brand reputation.

The test was run on all of them, and the results obtained can be seen in Table 7:

Table 6. Cronbach's alpha reliability test

RELIABILITY STATISTICS	
CRONBACH'S ALPHA	**NUMBER OF ITEMS**
0.748	11

Since the value of the test statistic lies between the acceptable range of 0.6-0.8, the factors can be considered reliable for conducting further analysis.

On the basis of this, hypothesis testing could be conducted.

Hypotheses

The main parameter for comparison is taken as age in this study. To understand the impact that age has on various factors, several conditions have been hypothesized.

Since the data is non-parametric, Kruskal Wallis test was applied to test these hypotheses.

Let us look at the study in a more detailed way.

- **Hypothesis 1:** Age and Awareness

This aims to study the effect of age on awareness. For this, the following null and alternative hypotheses have been considered:

H_0 (Null Hypothesis): The distribution of awareness is the same across all categories of age.

H_1 (Alternative Hypothesis): The distribution of awareness is not the same across all categories of age.

Table 7. Kruskal-Wallis test (age and awareness)

HYPOTHESIS TEST SUMMARY			
Null Hypothesis	**Test**	**Test Statistic**	**Decision**
The distribution of Awareness is the same across categories of Age	Independent-Samples Kruskal-Wallis Test	<0.001	Reject Null Hypothesis

The level of significance taken in consideration is 0.01 and on the basis of the same, the null hypothesis has been **rejected.** This means that there exists a variation in the distribution of awareness across the categories of age.

To get a better look at the variation, Spearman Correlation has been analysed. The results of the same are as follows:

Table 8. Spearman's non-parametric correlation (age and awareness)

CORRELATIONS			
		Age	Awareness
Spearman's rho	Correlation Coefficient	1.00	-0.315
	Sig. (2-tailed)		<0.01
	N	225	225
CORRELATION IS SIGNIFICANT AT THE 0.01 LEVEL			

The result suggests a weak, yet significant, negative correlation between age and awareness, which primarily suggests that as age increases, the awareness among people tends to fall.

- **Hypothesis 2:** Age and Importance

This aims to study the effect of age on the importance of sustainability. For this, the following null and alternative hypotheses have been considered:

H_0 (Null Hypothesis): The distribution of importance is the same across all categories of age.
H_1 (Alternative Hypothesis): The distribution of importance is not the same across all categories of age.

Table 9. Kruskal-Wallis test (age and importance)

HYPOTHESIS TEST SUMMARY			
Null Hypothesis	Test	Test Statistic	Decision
The distribution of Importance is the same across categories of Age	Independent-Samples Kruskal-Wallis Test	0.291	Retain Null Hypothesis

The level of significance taken in consideration is 0.01 and on the basis of the same, the null hypothesis has been **retained.** This means that there exists no variation in the distribution of importance across the categories of age.

Even though age and awareness show a relationship, importance and age do not. To get a better idea of importance of sustainable consumption, this sections prior to this provided instances of sustainability to provide an idea to people regarding the real essence of this concept.

- **Hypothesis 3:** Age and Behaviour

This aims to study the effect of age on the importance of sustainability. For this, the following null and alternative hypotheses have been considered:

H_0 (Null Hypothesis): The distribution of behaviour is the same across all categories of age.
H_1 (Alternative Hypothesis): The distribution of behaviour is not the same across all categories of age.

Table 10. Kruskal-Wallis test (age and behaviour)

HYPOTHESIS TEST SUMMARY			
Null Hypothesis	Test	Test Statistic	Decision
The distribution of Behaviour is the same across categories of Age	Independent-Samples Kruskal-Wallis Test	<0.001	Reject Null Hypothesis

The level of significance taken in consideration is 0.01 and on the basis of the same, the null hypothesis has been **rejected.** This means that there exists a variation in the distribution of behaviour across the categories of age.

The Spearman Correlation has been applied to this as well and the results are as follows:

Table 11. Spearman's non-parametric correlation (age and behaviour)

CORRELATIONS			
		Age	Behaviour
Spearman's rho	Correlation Coefficient	1.00	-0.68
	Sig. (2-tailed)		0.311
	N	225	225
CORRELATION IS INSIGNIFICANT AT THE 0.01 LEVEL			

The correlation between the two comes out to be insignificant on the basis of the data obtained and so, no confirmed conclusion can be stated. However, through the negative sign, one can deduce that there exists an inverse relationship between the two factors.

- **Hypothesis 4:** Age and Factors

On the basis of literature, several factors were deduced, and analysis was run to see whether the importance of these factors changes with age. The Kruskal-Wallis Test was applied, and correlation was studied.

The null and alternative hypothesis for the factors were taken as:

H_0 (Null Hypothesis): The distribution of factor is the same across all categories of age.
H_1 (Alternative Hypothesis): The distribution of factor is not the same across all categories of age.

The results of the tests and their interpretations are as follows:

Table 12. Kruskal-Wallis test (age and factors)

HYPOTHESIS TEST SUMMARY			
Null Hypothesis	**Test**	**Test Statistic**	**Decision**
The distribution of Price is the same across categories of Age	Independent-Samples Kruskal-Wallis Test	0.006	Reject Null Hypothesis
The distribution of Nutrition is the same across categories of Age	Independent-Samples Kruskal-Wallis Test	<0.001	Reject Null Hypothesis
The distribution of Convenience is the same across categories of Age	Independent-Samples Kruskal-Wallis Test	<0.001	Reject Null Hypothesis
The distribution of Taste is the same across categories of Age	Independent-Samples Kruskal-Wallis Test	<0.001	Reject Null Hypothesis
The distribution of Sustainability is the same across categories of Age	Independent-Samples Kruskal-Wallis Test	<0.001	Reject Null Hypothesis
The distribution of Availability is the same across categories of Age	Independent-Samples Kruskal-Wallis Test	0.003	Reject Null Hypothesis
The distribution of Packaging is the same across categories of Age	Independent-Samples Kruskal-Wallis Test	<0.001	Reject Null Hypothesis
The distribution of Brand Reputation is the same across categories of Age	Independent-Samples Kruskal-Wallis Test	<0.001	Reject Null Hypothesis

From the above table, it can be concluded that the importance given to all the factors is affected by age. The correlation can be analysed individually.

a). Price and Age
   The correlation is significant and positive. This means that the importance given to price rises with age.

Table 13. Spearman's non-parametric correlation (age and price)

CORRELATIONS			
		Age	**Price**
Spearman's rho	**Correlation Coefficient**	1	0.212
	Sig. (2-tailed)		0.001
	N	225	225
CORRELATION IS SIGNIFICANT AT THE 0.01 LEVEL			

b). Nutritional Value and Age

The relationship is similar to what was seen in the previous case. The correlation is significant and positive. This means that the importance given to nutritional value also rises with age.

Table 14. Spearman's non-parametric correlation (age and nutritional value)

CORRELATIONS			
		Age	Nutrition
Spearman's rho	Correlation Coefficient	1	0.212
	Sig. (2-tailed)		<0.001
	N	225	225
CORRELATION IS SIGNIFICANT AT THE 0.01 LEVEL			

c). Convenience and Age

The correlation is significant and positive. This means that the importance given to convenience rises with age.

Table 15. Spearman's non-parametric correlation (age and convenience)

CORRELATIONS			
		Age	Convenience
Spearman's rho	Correlation Coefficient	1	0.212
	Sig. (2-tailed)		0.022
	N	225	225
CORRELATION IS INSIGNIFICANT AT THE 0.01 LEVEL (But significant at 0.05 level)			

d). Taste and Age

The correlation is significant and negative. This suggests that as age rises, the importance given to age begins to fall.

Table 16. Spearman's non-parametric correlation (age and taste)

CORRELATIONS			
		Age	Taste
Spearman's rho	Correlation Coefficient	1	-.0381
	Sig. (2-tailed)		<0.001
	N	225	225
CORRELATION IS SIGNIFICANT AT THE 0.01 LEVEL			

e). Sustainability and Age
A significant and positive correlation is exhibited, suggesting that the importance given to sustainability rises as the age rises.

Table 17. Spearman's non-parametric correlation (age and sustainability)

CORRELATIONS			
		Age	Sustainability
Spearman's rho	Correlation Coefficient	1	-0.142
	Sig. (2-tailed)		0.034
	N	225	225
CORRELATION IS INSIGNIFICANT AT THE 0.01 LEVEL (But significant at 0.05 level)			

f). Availability and Age
The relationship between the factors is positive. The importance of availability rises with rise in age.

Table 18. Spearman's non-parametric correlation (age and availability)

CORRELATIONS			
		Age	Availability
Spearman's rho	Correlation Coefficient	1	-0.154
	Sig. (2-tailed)		0.021
	N	225	225
CORRELATION IS INSIGNIFICANT AT THE 0.01 LEVEL (But significant at 0.05 level)			

g). Packaging and Age
A negative correlation suggests that as the age rises, the importance given to product packaging tends to fall.

Table 19. Spearman's non-parametric correlation (age and packaging)

CORRELATIONS			
		Age	Packaging
Spearman's rho	Correlation Coefficient	1	-0.364
	Sig. (2-tailed)		<0.001
	N	225	225
CORRELATION IS SIGNIFICANT AT THE 0.01 LEVEL			

h) Brand Reputation and Age
Just like packaging, brand reputation and age also show a negative correlation, suggesting the falling importance of brand reputation with rising age.

Table 20. Spearman's non-parametric correlation (age and packaging)

CORRELATIONS			
		Age	Brand Reputation
Spearman's rho	Correlation Coefficient	1	-0.266
	Sig. (2-tailed)		<0.001
	N	225	225
CORRELATION IS SIGNIFICANT AT THE 0.01 LEVEL			

On the basis of the above analysis, we conclude that **Age** affects the awareness of people about sustainability and their consumption behaviours around the same. It does not, however, affect the importance given by people to sustainable consumption and production. The consumption for the food industry depends on several factors. Some of these factors, too, are affected by age. Such factors include: Price, Nutritional Value, Convenience, Taste, Sustainability, Availability, Packaging, and Brand Reputation.

CONCLUSION

Sustainability, as we know, is important and holds the key to a future where people can maintain a decent living standard and avoid dying due to lack of resources. It is the need of the hour and is the only way that ensures a better life for years to come. Various environmental factors such as resource scarcity, biodiversity loss, excess waste generation, and climate change, are few of the many threats that hinder this sustainable lifestyle. As threats surface so does the need of methods to tackle these threats. Some of the methods which have gained a lot of popularity include renewable energy resources, movement towards a circular economy, and adopting practices such as sustainable agriculture and sustainable transportation. Each industry across the globe contributes to the negative as well as positive externalities that the environment faces, while also affecting the social and economic standings. This paper focuses on the effects caused by the food industry.

The food industry, across the globe, is immense and so are its contributions to the environmental damages that persist. It alone is responsible for about 30% of the total greenhouse gas emissions. The food industry is troubled with issues in the field of agriculture, packaging, transportation, the meat and poultry industry, and the processed food industry, etc. The growth of various allied sectors has impacted the overall standing of the food industry in the sustainability index. The heaviest hit is taken by the developing countries, but the maximum benefit may or may not accrue to them.

The coming up of cloud kitchens has acted as both boon and bane for the developing countries as while it provides an avenue for a more sustainable livelihood, it also contributes to the struggles. A shift to organic produce and locally sourced products is being witnessed along with the coming up of programs like Feeding India. All of this nudges the environment towards a better tomorrow.

However, the world still seeks proper regulations, infrastructural developments, monitoring, and coming up of initiatives at not only a global level but also a personal level. It would be incorrect to state that change comes in overnight. It is a slow and gradual process, but it is achievable. In a world that has people who are powered by trends, sustainability, as a practice, in youth is becoming popular. The market provides what the consumers demand and so, a shift is on its way.

People often resort to sustainable consumption practices without realising or without any intention. This can be due to the intriguing nature of the concept, the fancy and appealing packaging of the product, or simple peer influence. Nowadays, people have also started to carry their own bags to the market. This can be due to low requirements of paper bags, the rising prices of these bags, or simply the convenience of handling one's own bag. With the ban of plastic straws, paper straws came into being. However, since they start dissolving in the beverage, a lot of people have started carrying metal straws with them. What now appears to be a simple want or a luxury, will slowly turn into a necessity. Metal straws should reduce the amount of waste that is generated and due to their strength and non-dissolving properties, they hold the potential of becoming a star among the masses. Various biodegradable disposable utensils have also surfaced. Such innovations try and reduce harm to the environment as far as possible, while ensuring minimum adjustment problems among the consumers. The looks, marketing, pricing, and uniqueness of these products often act as the basic factors influencing their position among the population.

The delivery apps in India such as Zepto, BlinkIt, Swiggy Instamart have also changed their packaging. They have reduced the amount of tape as compared to the earlier bags that were delivered and have also started using either recycled bags, jute bags, or paper bags. These small initiatives have big contributions.

To come up with policies and methods which can have a long-lasting effect on sustainability, it is important to look at the existing practices and perceptions. To get a first-hand view of sustainable consumption practices, a primary survey was conducted and the data obtained was analysed.

To summarise,

Table 21. Summary of methodology used for primary research

	Method	Tool
Demographics	Descriptive Statistics	Frequency Distribution
Factors and Variables under study	Reliability Test	Cronbach's Alpha
Understanding the distribution of variables across age	Hypothesis Testing	Kruskal-Wallis Test
Understanding the relationship between the variables and age	Correlation	Spearman's Non-Parametric Correlation

The results to the analysis done to compare age and the variables in summarized below:

The above results conclude that age is also a significant factor that influences the consumption patterns of people (sample from Delhi, NCR) by affecting their awareness, behaviour, and importance given towards the same.

The same analysis was also run on the basis of gender, only to conclude that gender has no effect on consumption behaviour. This practice is a state of mind and attitude. It is not an overnight behaviour change, rather it comes with learning.

Table 22. Summary of results (age)

	Variables	Acceptance/Rejection	Correlation
Hypothesis 1	Age and Awareness	Reject Null	Significant, negative
Hypothesis 2	Age and Importance	Reject Null	Significant, negative
Hypothesis 3	Age and Behaviour	Accept Null	-
Hypothesis 4	Age and Price	Accept Null	-
	Age and Nutritional Value	Reject Null	Significant, positive
	Age and Convenience	Reject Null	Insignificant
	Age and Taste	Reject Null	Significant, negative
	Age and Sustainability	Accept Null	-
	Age and Availability	Reject Null	Insignificant
	Age and Packaging	Accept Null	-
	Age and Brand Reputation	Reject Null	Insignificant

Slowly, sustainability is becoming a daily habit in people and sooner or later, its hold on people's behaviour will grow resulting in a better livelihood for all. This will contribute to achieving the sustainable development goals and standing tall in front of 2030 Agenda of Sustainable Development.

Various nudging practices have been taken up and companies continue to adopt more of them. Over the past few years, people have become more conscious towards the idea of sustainability and this has been due to various reasons. These reasons revolve around the growing importance of education and changes associated with cognitive behaviours such as compassion, empathy, mindfulness, etc. All of this has collectively altered the way people perceive sustainability and so, has leveraged changes **(Wamsler, 2020)**. Sustainability is an interdisciplinary concept and so, involves various theoretical and practical frameworks that together influence its applicability at the global level.

With the evolution of the humanity, comes the urgency for a habitat that is socially, economically, and environmentally inhabitable for mankind.

REFERENCES

AR6 Synthesis Report: Climate Change. (n.d.). IPCC. https://www.ipcc.ch/report/sixth-assessment-report-cycle/

Abdullah, M. A., Kedah, Z., & Anwar, M. A. (2016). The Impact of Millionaires' Secret Strategy on Entrepreneurial Performance through Entrepreneurial Motivation. *ResearchGate*. https://www.researchgate.net/publication/317714795_The_Impact_of_Millionaires'_Secret_Strategy_on_Entrepreneurial_Performance_through_Entrepreneurial_Motivation

American Association for the Advancement of Science. (2017, November 6). Plastic waste inputs from land into the ocean. *Science*. https://www.science.org/doi/10.1126/science.1260352

Arora, N. K. (2018). Environmental Sustainability—Necessary for survival. *Environmental Sustainability*, *1*(1), 1–2. doi:10.100742398-018-0013-3

Chadwick, M. (2023). 7 reasons why meat is bad for the environment. *Greenpeace UK*. https://www.greenpeace.org.uk/news/why-meat-is-bad-for-the-environment/

Chatterjee, R., Singh, A., & Singh, V. (2022). Ethical and Sustainable Perceptions on Cloud Kitchen Business-A Study of Consumers and Stakeholders during the Covid-19 Pandemic. Inter*national Journal of Hospitality and Tourism Systems, Special Issue on COVID-19*, 76-87.

Chowdhury, S., Khan, S., Sarker, M. F. H., Islam, K., Tamal, M. A., & Khan, N. A. (2022). Does agricultural ecology cause environmental degradation? Empirical evidence from Bangladesh. *Heliyon*, *8*(6), e09750. doi:10.1016/j.heliyon.2022.e09750 PMID:35785220

Circular Economy. (2023, May 16). UNCTAD. https://unctad.org/topic/trade-and-environment/circular-economy

Climate Change 2023: Synthesis Report. (n.d.). UNEP - UN Environment Programme. https://www.unep.org/resources/report/climate-change-2023-synthesis-report

DaSilva, B., Dhar, J., Rafiq, S., & Young, D. (2023). *Nudging Consumers Toward Sustainability*. BCG Global. https://www.bcg.com/publications/2022/nudging-consumers-to-make-sustainable-choices

Deaths due to Malnutrition. (n.d.). PIB. https://pib.gov.in/Pressreleaseshare.aspx?PRID=1580452

Flood, E., Kapoor, S., & De Villa-Lopez, B. (2014). The Sustainability of Food Served at Wedding Banquets. *Journal of Culinary Science & Technology*, *12*(2), 137–152. doi:10.1080/15428052.2013.846882

Global Energy Review 2021 – Analysis - IEA. (n.d.). IEA. https://www.iea.org/reports/global-energy-review-2021

Govindan, K. (2018). Sustainable consumption and production in the food supply chain: A conceptual framework. *International Journal of Production Economics*, *195*, 419–431. doi:10.1016/j.ijpe.2017.03.003

How we feed the world today. (n.d.). OECD. https://www.oecd.org/agriculture/understanding-the-global-food-system/how-we-feed-the-world-today/

IMARC Group. (n.d.). *Indian Pesticides Market Size, Share, Trends & Forecast 2023-2028*. IMARK Gorup. https://www.imarcgroup.com/indian-pesticides-market

Key messages. (n.d.). Food and Agriculture Organization of the United Nations. https://www.fao.org/about/meetings/soil-erosion-symposium/key-messages/en/

Kroyer, G. (1995). *Impact of food processing on the environment--an overview*. AGRIS: International Information System for the Agricultural Science and Technology. https://agris.fao.org/agris-search/search.do?recordID=US201301513547

Lai, O. (2023). Deforestation in Southeast Asia: Causes and Solutions. *Earth.Org*. https://earth.org/deforestation-in-southeast-asia/

Lattimore, B., Smith, C., Titus, B. D., Stupak, I., & Egnell, G. (2009). Environmental factors in woodfuel production: Opportunities, risks, and criteria and indicators for sustainable practices. *Biomass and Bioenergy*, *33*(10), 1321–1342. doi:10.1016/j.biombioe.2009.06.005

Liu, L., Zhang, M., & Ye, W. (2019). The adoption of sustainable practices: A supplier's perspective. *Journal of Environmental Management*, *232*, 692–701. doi:10.1016/j.jenvman.2018.11.067 PMID:30522074

Marinova, D., & Bogueva, D. (2019). Planetary health and reduction in meat consumption. *Sustainable Earth*, *2*(1), 3. doi:10.118642055-019-0010-0

Morone, P. (2019). *Food waste: Challenges and opportunities for enhancing the emerging bio-economy.* AGRIS: International Information System for the Agricultural Science and Technology. https://agris.fao.org/agris-search/search.do?recordID=US201900212695

Moshood, T. D., Nawanir, G., Mahmud, F., Mohamad, F. B., Ahmad, M. S., & AbdulGhani, A. (2022). Biodegradable plastic applications towards sustainability: A recent innovations in the green product. *Cleaner Engineering and Technology*, *6*, 100404. doi:10.1016/j.clet.2022.100404

Panigrahi, A. K., Saha, A., Shrinet, A., Nauityal, M., & Gaur, V. (2020). A case study on Zomato – The online Foodking of India. *Journal of Management Research and Analysis*, *7*(1), 25–33. doi:10.18231/j.jmra.2020.007

Santo, R., Kim, B. F., Goldman, S. E., Dutkiewicz, J., Biehl, E., Bloem, M. W., Neff, R. A., & Nachman, K. E. (2020). Considering Plant-Based Meat Substitutes and Cell-Based Meats: A Public Health and Food Systems Perspective. *Frontiers in Sustainable Food Systems*, *4*, 134. doi:10.3389/fsufs.2020.00134

Make in Inida. (n.d.). *Schemes that would reduce food waste, benefit farmers.* Make In India. https://www.makeinindia.com/6-schemes-would-reduce-food-waste-benefit-farmers

Sherpa, M. L., Sharma, L., Bag, N., & Das, S. (2021). Isolation, Characterization, and Evaluation of Native Rhizobacterial Consortia Developed From the Rhizosphere of Rice Grown in Organic State Sikkim, India, and Their Effect on Plant Growth. *Frontiers in Microbiology*, *12*, 713660. doi:10.3389/fmicb.2021.713660 PMID:34552571

Single-use plastics: A roadmap for sustainability. (n.d.). UNEP - UN Environment Programme. https://www.unep.org/resources/report/single-use-plastics-roadmap-sustainability

Solar PV – Analysis - IEA. (n.d.). IEA. https://www.iea.org/reports/solar-pv

Staniškis, J. K. (2012). Sustainable consumption and production. *Clean Technologies and Environmental Policy*, *14*(6), 1013–1014. doi:10.100710098-012-0517-y

Sustainable lifestyles. (n.d.). UNEP - UN Environment Programme. https://www.unep.org/explore-topics/resource-efficiency/what-we-do/sustainable-lifestyles

Thornton, P. K. (2010). Livestock production: Recent trends, future prospects. *Philosophical Transactions of the Royal Society of London. Series B, Biological Sciences*, *365*(1554), 2853–2867. doi:10.1098/rstb.2010.0134 PMID:20713389

Tukker, A., Emmert, S., Charter, M., Vezzoli, C., Stø, E., Andersen, M. M., Geerken, T., Tischner, U., & Lahlou, S. (2008). Fostering change to sustainable consumption and production: An evidence based view. *Journal of Cleaner Production*, *16*(11), 1218–1225. doi:10.1016/j.jclepro.2007.08.015

United Nations. (n.d.). *Climate Reports.* United Nations. https://www.un.org/en/climatechange/reports

Visual feature: The Emissions Gap Report 2022. (n.d.). UNEP. https://www.unep.org/interactive/emissions-gap-report/2022/

Wang, C., Ghadimi, P., Lim, M. K., & Tseng, M. (2019). A literature review of sustainable consumption and production: A comparative analysis in developed and developing economies. *Journal of Cleaner Production, 206,* 741–754. doi:10.1016/j.jclepro.2018.09.172

World Bank Group. (2018, September 24). *Global Waste to Grow by 70 Percent by 2050 Unless Urgent Action is Taken: World Bank Report.* World Bank. https://www.worldbank.org/en/news/press-release/2018/09/20/global-waste-to-grow-by-70-percent-by-2050-unless-urgent-action-is-taken-world-bank-report

Chapter 19
Greener Economy for Sustainable Development Through AI Intervention:
Demystifying Critical Factors

Prajnya Paramita Pradhan
KIIT School of Management, KIIT University, Bhubaneswar, India

Biswajit Das
KIIT School of Management, KIIT University, India

Abhiraj Malia
KIIT School of Management, KIIT University, India

Bhubaneswari Bisoyi
Sri Sri University, Cuttack, India

Ipseeta Satpathy
KIIT School of Management, KIIT University, India

ABSTRACT

This research chapter deals with understanding the concept of the sustainable ecosystem through the development of a greener economy, and managing the environment for socio-eco environmental growth. The chapter introspects to understand the implication of AI intervention for an eco-friendly economy. It's an exploration into the faces of inclusive growth and equitable equality in life betting natural disasters and environmental degradation towards a greener economy. It explores the cause and effect of climate change for promoting sustainable consumption and production growth and exploration of the potential of AI. The research essentially reviews, analysis, and explores qualitatively and quantitatively the concern of ensuring the consumption of sustainable order through a pattern of production under the ambit of SDG 17. Eventually, it will identify the essential critical factors that can combat the obstacle to greener economy for sustainable consumption by eradicating the restraining forces and measuring barriers that the producer and the consumer encounter towards sustainable peace.

DOI: 10.4018/978-1-6684-8969-7.ch019

INTRODUCTION

The Millennium Goals for Development (MDGs) are an important and effective global mobilization approach for a number of key socioeconomic priorities worldwide. As artificial intelligence (AI) develops, a growing variety of sectors are being shaped by it. The world economy, social integration and equal opportunity, the environment, and a variety of other areas are all expected to be impacted by AI both now and in the future. According to the claimed possible implications of AI, there can be both good and bad effects on sustainable development. Developing nations have made significant strides towards achieving the MDGs, though the rates of progress vary greatly between objectives, nations, and areas.

Between 1990 and 2010, the poverty rate in developing nations as a whole was cut in half, largely due to China's startling economic development. While some nations will accomplish many or all of the MDGs, others will only accomplish a very small number. The majority of nations will have significantly advanced towards the majority of the objectives by 2015. Additionally, for more than ten years, national and international policymaking has continued to center on the MDGs. They are made available to students from all educational backgrounds and have been included in the undertakings of non-governmental organizations and civic societies more broadly. The MDGs were vital in striving to achieve that development, and it is generally recognized by decision-makers and civil society organizations that the internationally accepted targets to tackle poverty must continue past 2015. There is also a common understanding that, in a world facing dangerous global warming and other serious ecological evils, worldwide ecological ambitions need to be given more prominence alongside the goals of reducing poverty. The governments of the world appear prepared to approve a new set of international objectives to follow the MDG period of 15 years. In June 2012, Ban Ki-Moon, the UN Secretary-General created an effective panel for global sustainability in the run-up to the Rio+20 summit. The globe should implement the Sustainable Development Goals, according to the panel's report (SDGs). During the Rio+20 summit, Secretary-General Ban said he intended to organize a high-level panel with UK Prime Minister David Cameron, Indonesian President Susilo Bambang Yudhoyono, and Liberian President Ellen Johnson Sirleaf serving as co-chairs to explore the specifics of the post-2015 targets.

Currently, there is no proper study available for the systematically assesses of the extenuation of AI implications on all aspects of sustainable development. In this document, sustainable development is defined as the 17 sustainable development Goals (SDGs) and 169 targets that have been universally accepted in the 2030 agenda. The study was summed up as a prevailing opinion expert elicitation process, which was used to describe relationships. These methods were informed by earlier studies targeted at mapping the interlinkage of the SDGs. The importance of the triple bottom line is created for a new understanding that has come to light thanks to geoscience and the seasonal changes in our surroundings. A geological age has begun where human activity has a large and harmful impact on fundamental earth dynamics. The world's ecosystems are under tremendous pressure from a population that reached 7 billion the year before (and is projected to surpass 8 billion by 2024) and from emerging nations, which are currently leading global GDP growth per person. The simultaneous impact of multiple different key earth systems, such as the cycle of carbon, and nitrogen into the air, and water cycles, on these pressures, which are global as well as local, distinguishes the current period. Climate change is brought on by greenhouse gas emissions from human activity, severe environmental pollution (such as the poisoning of coastal areas and other ecosystems due to the excess use of fertilizer which reduces nitrogen), and the oceans' acidification, which is primarily brought on by the increased concentration of greenhouse gases in the atmosphere, which is the main cause, are just a few of the crises of environmental sustainability that humanity is currently facing. the enormous loss of species brought on by unsustainable forest use. The circular and green economies provide particularly targeted strategies for putting the sustainable development idea into practice. A conceptual image of the ideal future for humanity is a sustainable development aim. In the Republic of Belarus, the key drivers of the shift to a green economy and the major avenues for its growth are described.

The difficulty of growing grain output is rising, and it poses risks such as the continuation of habitat destruction, changes in the climate, water stress, expanded fertilizer pollution, loss of biodiversity, and others. Due to the threat that sharp rising food costs will cause thousands of millions of individuals to experience chronic hunger, social consequences could be extremely destabilizing. Hence, sustainable development must set goals and challenges for every country, and the wealthy should help the poor, and all countries should jointly help for the well-being of the next generation as well. Middle-income developing markets (Brazil, China, Russia, and India), and other markets will be the SDG front-runners, but they also must overcome their internal obstacles, such as balancing growth with environmental protection, being vulnerable to undesirable trends like global warming, and playing larger geopolitical roles on a regional and global level. The SDGs may have three goals, but achieving even one of them will probably require concerted worldwide efforts to accomplish the other two. Additionally, the fourth requirement—decent administration at all levels i.e. local, national, regional, and global—will be necessary for all three of the primary objectives to be met.

The economic component should be built upon the MDGs, which support the advanced global agenda for battle compared to poverty, starvation, and disease. The MDGs should be achieved between 2015 and 2030, along with securing everyone's fundamental human rights and meeting their basic material requirements if they haven't already. The Universal Declaration of Human Rights, which was adopted by the UN at its inception, embodies this objective. The prediction of extreme deficiency for hunger, financial poverty, preventable sickness, and deaths might be eradicated by 2030 both plausible and meaningful.

Energy consumption, agribusiness, urbanization accompanied by pollution and dangers, and population expansion are the main factors causing human-induced worldwide changes in the environment that I have highlighted. For instance, the production of food has a big impact on greenhouse gas emissions, the decline in biodiversity, and the increased stress on freshwater resources. These difficulties will be significant but solvable by humanity which can be changed by the causing factors with considerate, civilized, reasonable, and indication-based by effective economic institutions. If these problems are not addressed, they will ultimately become catastrophic. The third overarching SDG is social integration, which entails a dedication to future technological and economic development under the premise of justice and egalitarian access to public services, as well as a pledge from the government to combat social discrimination based on gender, ethnic origin, religion, and race. Traditional indicators of economic success, such as the country's economic output and household income, only adequately reflect the factors that affect people's well-being. In addition to meeting basic requirements, many other factors affect how happy and satisfied people are in life. These factors include social trust, an honest government, workplace empowerment, access to mental health products and services, and high levels of civic engagement. In addition to the government sector and civic society, sustainability necessitates the private sector's leadership and accountability. The private sector, which makes up the majority of the global economy's productive sectors, is also where most of the cutting-edge management and technological innovations that are essential to the achievement of the SDGs are found. In their regulations, production procedures, and interaction with stakeholders, private sector businesses ought to encourage the SDGs in real-world and quantifiable ways. To protect the SDGs, they should abstain from political and lobbying activity.

And last, for the SDGs to succeed, societies around the world must spend enough in achieving them. Sustainable growth is the only path forward that humanity can take, but this won't happen until some of our current consumption expenditures are becoming investments for long-term existence. Funding for long-term growth (such as switching to renewable energy systems) won't be expensive, especially compared to the enormous costs of doing nothing. Compared to the MDGs, the SDGs are supposed to be more concentrated and financially feasible. Instead of depending on assistance charity, for which the nations release their own aid capacities, nations should acknowledge clear and particular guidelines of funding, such as quota systems and assessment procedures associated with incomes and imposed by nationwide emissions of greenhouse gases (e.g., dollars per ton of CO_2 discharged per year and then fail to honor them in most cases). The amounts are modest, controllable, and necessary for achievement. Identification of novel, essential routes to sustainability is necessary for the SDGs. For example, switching to energy with a low-carbon system will require complex global development and research, infrastructure investments, investment from the private sector in energy production from renewable sources, and new regulatory and urban planning strategies. Mostly because of modern technology and communication channels, the world today has been becoming a place with opportunities for open, issue-solving with the primary concerns affecting sustainable development. Researchers, engineers, activists of civil society, and others with increasing use of online networks collaboration, crowdfunding, collaborative issue, and the creation of accessible software and its applications. The paths to sustainable development won't determine by a top-down method, with a highly revitalized period with solving of networked problem that involves governments, businesses, nongovernmental organizations, academic institutions, and particularly young individuals who should become the experts and leaders of a new and significantly challenging era.

We conclude that the ability to achieve all SDGs may be impacted by AI, indicating a crucial research gap.

REVIEW OF LITERATURE

Sustainable Development

The 2030 Agenda for Sustainable Development is a strategy for economics, lawmakers, and the world that undergo sustainable development in all three areas: financial, social, and environmental. The robust sustainability of the environmental score is based on the paradigm gap of environmental sustainability (Usubiaga and Ekins, 2021). There are 21 indicators to index the gap and every indicator link to the different aspects of natural resources. The possible disconnect between addressing climate change and accomplishing the other SDGs is a major critique of the SDGs. A growing corpus of research in particular fields examines the connections between moral and factual promises made under the Paris Agreement and the 2030 Agenda. To achieve the UN SDGs, significant steps must be taken in all spheres of life, making full use of technical innovation of them (Cancino et al., 2018). Even though the connection between climate change and sustainable development is genuinely accepted by everyone, only a few organizations are working hard to fulfill the SDG target. According to a part of the IPCC special report, the global warming of 1.5^0 c looks at the connection between specific climate measurements and the 17 goals of SDG. Vulnerable nations like Africa, the Minimum Developed Countries, Landlocked Developing Countries, and Small Developing States, had special challenges that were taken into account when the United Nations and other stakeholders set goals and targets. The difficulties faced by middle-income nations and faced by middle-income nations along with the environment surrounding those hosting armed conflicts were taken into account when the objectives were developed. The general absence of baseline information on many goals is one of the main obstacles to effective tracking and assessment of the progress and performance of member nations following the SDGs. The advancements brought about by the 4th industrial revolution with present opportunities for effective information to certify that national and international reference points are made present and make it possible for evaluating the member states' advancement, especially when it comes to goals lacking specific, measurable numbers. With a shift to highly efficient growth in the economy that relies on expertise and innovation, the latter national strategy's strategic objective of sustainable development aims to ensure a high standard of living for the populace and favorable conditions for the individual's development while preserving the environment's favorable conditions for both the present and future generations. The very specific approaches i.e., the practical implementation of the sustainable development idea are offered by the green and circular economies. The idea of a sustainable development goal is a conceptual representation of the anticipated future of humanity. In the Republic of Belarus, the key drivers of the shift to a green economy and the major avenues for its growth are described (Shimova, 2019). Mangla et al.,(2017) and Girella et al., (2019) their study demonstrated that SMEs are becoming more conscious of sustainable practices. It demonstrated that even small enterprises are making efforts to enhance their sustainability performance. However, the fact that many companies lack the necessary technology, such as EMS tools and resources, means that they are unable to fully appreciate its advantages or gauge the extent to which their performance in terms of sustainability and carbon emissions has improved. This may also be related to their hesitation to spend money on EMS and carbon emission control equipment.

The term "VUCA" has become more and more popular as a shorthand for the current situation of the globe. The United States Army War College has been using the VUCA acronym since it was originally proposed in 1987 to denote the volatility, uncertainty, complexity, and ambiguity connected with emerging developments. VUCA demands proper foresight and comprehension in the context of international business (IB), as well as the planning of strategic responses and efficient implementation of management or policy initiatives. To reduce risks without compromising the welfare of people and ecosystems, a comprehensive and equitable management approach for socio-ecological systems is necessary to achieve true sustainability: a more extreme approach to the ecology (Ibisch et al., 2010).it should be " as simple as it can be but no simpler" than necessary to comprehend and express the goal of comprehending and expressing the issue while attempting to describe complicated systems. It is necessary to explain to stakeholders the complex connections between all recognized elements that make up an ecosystem since oversimplified explanations of issues faced in conservation sites are likely to result in oversimplified plans and remedies. It is crucial to have a complete understanding of a scenario in the current climate change environment (Holling, 2001). Situational awareness is highly valued in integrative organizations because it fosters a sense of collective consciousness. The military defines this as being aware of circumstances, including threats, possibilities, and socioeconomic and cultural background, that may influence operations both inside and outside of an organization. Environmentally responsible businesses have systems in place that continuously watch for trailing signals, market dynamics, and emerging patterns. All managers regularly scan their surroundings to notice what is happening and take necessary action (Krawchuk, 2017).

Green Economy

An inclusive green economy is a substitute for today's ubiquitous economic paradigm, which intensifies inequalities, promotes waste, causes resource scarcity, and creates pervasive environmental and human health threats. The idea of the green economy has emerged as a strategic goal for many governments over the last decade. According to a UNEP and World Bank report, about 60% of ecosystem products and services degraded at the cost of massively increasing global economic growth in the last 5 decades. With the worsening of climate change, the green economy plays an essential part in economic and environmental growth, and it has garnered widespread attention from researchers and governments worldwide. The idea of a green economy was first introduced in 1989 with a Framework for Green Economy study produced by the United Kingdom Government by an assembly of green economic experts (Pearce, 1992). Ali et al., 2021 used the SWOT analytical method to investigate the strengths, weaknesses, opportunities, and dangers of Ghana's greening efforts. The findings indicate that, despite the implementation of various green economy policies and strategies, Ghana continues to suffer from insufficient long-term policies, insufficient financing for technological innovation, and weak institutions. Other variables that can endanger the ecosystem and impede progress toward a green economy include the rigorous use of capital and unable to control the use of natural capital. Meadows et al., (1972) and Colombo (2001) predict how society might advance while taking into consideration the need for technological advancements like resource efficiency and recycling as well as the possibility of population increase. The circular economy now offers a new business model to the state and business to improve resource efficiency, minimize the environmental effects of production activities, and achieve social effects in the consumption of goods, particularly through increased producer responsibility. Further development of the conceptual frameworks allowed expanding the window of opportunities for the circular economy. D'Amato et al., (2017), Ghisellini et al., (2016), Mol (2002), and Zink and Geyer (2017) showed that within the context of the green economy, special attention is given to the issues of green investment, tourism, education, and employment, the growth of renewable energy sources, the conservation of land resources, and a decrease of emissions. Additionally, it was demonstrated that within the context of the circular - features of sustainable development in the area of industrialization and urbanization, it was shortening the life cycle of products, recycling and reuse of waste, etc. By comparing these ideas, it was possible to see how closely related they are and how the circular economy—which employs business strategies that arrange a different, circular movement of materials—is a step towards a green economy. According to Bisoyi & Das (2023), owing to a many factors like regulatory requirements from government, industrial growth and effect on the habit of other enterprises to ensure that they are developing green products. Being environmentally friendly gives the company for a unique selling proposition which competitors may use to challenge it. Therefore, being environmentally responsible makes a business more cost effective and customer focused.

Another study shows that environmental efforts benefit from technological advancements that raise their standard (Li et al., 2022). Technology can be used to support green economics. The desire to lessen greenhouse gas emissions, combat climate change and rely less on foreign energy sources initially drove the acceptance of possible sustainable technologies (Lee et al., 2022). Due to a lack of budgetary room to boost demand and the possibility of a protracted pandemic, many fragile nations are at risk of losing a decade to the pandemic. In 2022 and 2023, it's anticipated that the economic production in several emerging countries will reach pre-pandemic levels. According to the United Nations Department of Economic and Social Affairs, the COVID-19 epidemic brought about severe poverty for roughly 114.4

million people, of which 57.8 million were women and girls. Because of the demands of caring for kids at the worst time of the pandemic, it is claimed that women lost more jobs and money than males. The pandemic presents a turning point for health disaster preparation and investment in crucial public services for the twenty-first century, according to the United Nations. There is substantial proof that, if correctly harnessed, AI can aid in achieving the majority of the SDGs, from one up to seventeen, with relation to the AI implication and machine learning. A current application of AI is to find secure exit paths for people who have been stranded by rising waters in Houston following Hurricane Harvey. This was done by combining satellite images with AI applications. The latest apps that are helping to provide relief to numerous visually disabled people, many of whom live in poor countries, are also based on AI-powered object recognition. The program, which syncs with a smartphone, uses AI to identify acquaintances and characterize individuals as well as particular items, like bills of currency. This serves as evidence that, when used properly, AI can contribute to the advancement of social objectives. According to Gunay et al., (2022) Compared to regions in Europe and Asia, the green economy of the US and worldwide relationship with sustainability show larger diversity. Volatility modeling shows that environmentally friendly economies are important factors for each area in determining how sustainability changes globally. In this relationship, Europe and Asia possess the greatest and least significant impacts, respectively. The findings were in line with the areas' carbon emission data and the government's initiatives to support sustainable growth. This research also associates with the European Union's initiatives to address environmental change and environmental concerns to build an efficient resources economy and a genuinely prosperous society. According to the experts, adverse environmental trends could result in a 30–50% increase in global food costs and a rise in price volatility for all-natural ingredients in the future decades, significantly worsening the impoverisher's condition would significantly worsen the condition of the impoverished. The 1.3 billion people who work in agriculture, logging, fishing, hunting, and other environmental management activities are anticipated to face the greatest dangers. There is now a greater understanding of the need for a new "green" economic growth path as environmental threats and limitations have grown. The term "green" is now more frequently used in international papers to refer to green jobs, green marketplaces, and green inventions (such as renewable energy, electric vehicles, and biofuels).

Sustainability Through AI Intervention

Nowadays, AI is the trending aspect of everyone's life. Even though it is a popular subject right now, many people seem to be aware of how long ago the first event in its past. A large area of computer science called artificial intelligence (AI) produces intelligent, autonomous, or imitation-capable systems. Otherwise, artificial intelligence (AI) is a collection of connected technologies that enable computers to perceive, understand, act, and acquire knowledge with a degree of intellect comparable to that of individuals. There are two types of artificial intelligence: broad AI, also known as powerful AI, and limited AI, also known as weak AI. What we commonly refer to as "narrow AI" is AI that only conducts a single job or a set of associated operations, such as digital assistants and weather apps, among other things. Although these technologies and programs are strong, the small pool of competitors makes them appear small and feeble. Weak or limited AI has enormous transformative potential, particularly when used effectively, and has the potential to affect the operation and reside on a worldwide scale. Weak AI is primarily concerned with maximizing benefits in different contexts. The digital computer is an electronic device that was created in the early 1900s, with the collection of the abstract core of mathematical logic. A few scientists were motivated to begin truly debating the notion of creating an electronic brain with this device and the concepts it represented. Here, AI is taken into account in its context rather than as an impartial and decoupled tool. Instead of conducting an isolationist study of this technology, this involves considering AI as a component of a socio-technical system that is made up of various structures and economic and political systems (Barley, 2020). According to the 2015 publication Changing our world: the 2030 Plan for sustainable development, the UN laid out sustainable development goals. The Millennium Development Goals (MDG), a set of eight objectives created in 2000 with the intention of being achieved by 2015, were continued with the 17 goals (Halisçelik and Soytas, 2019). Although the SDG framework is linked to many different types of human rights, it is still very different from them because it places a focus on people, the earth, wealth, peace, and collaboration. Speech identification relies heavily on statistics, which is why it is also known as statistical learning. Since the philosophy of sustainable development is, in reality, the state ideology of Belarus and is reflected in all of its official programs and projection papers for socioeconomic development, the similarity of the content of the global goals and tasks of NSDS-2030 is reasonable. However, the upcoming NSDS for a time frame up to 2035, those developing countries is now getting considerable focus from the leadership, academia, and the public at large, should already purposefully ensure the process of "nationalization" of the worldwide SDGs in Belarus following the nation's international obligations. We can draw the conclusion that there are concrete preconditions for the execution of the global SDGs in the upcoming National Strategy for Sustainable Socio-Economic Development of the Republic of Belarus thanks to the existing institutional framework for guaranteeing sustainable development. Bisoyi et al., (2021) analyzed with innovative ideation, the elements of the urban environment that are pertinent to the policies and innovations have been envisioned. It was critically analyzed from the standpoint of ecological sustainability, which is essential for urban habitation in growth-driven of urban ecology. Better urban governance has been claimed to result from cities making strategic transformative investments in sustainable development that result in a planned urbanization process.

A machine can compose and comprehend a document in a language in the area of natural language processing. Machine language can detect and analyze valuable information in the area of computerization. The subject of computer vision falls under the umbrella of how computers handle information symbolically. The second area with AI pattern detection, where computers can identify designs like collections of related items. The area of machine learning needs more data and data in more dimensions. Then, in the area of robotics, robots can comprehend their surroundings and move about freely. The synapses in the network that make up the human brain are employed for learning. The same structure and function, or "area of neural networks," is therefore used by robots to develop cognitive abilities. When complex networks are used to understand a difficult concept, this is known as deep learning. Typically, a neural network based on con is used to identify items in an image. This is where computer vision comes in, and AI is used to recognize objects. Recurrent neural networks are the most well-known type of neural network because they can remember only a small portion of the past. There are two methods by that neural networks can operate: symbolically and dramatically. computer learning, which involves feeding the computer a lot of data before it can learn, is another name for the database. As opposed to this, symbolic learning enables developers to clearly describe relationships between various items and ideas by using symbols to represent them. All of these machine learning methods can be used to perform categorization or forecast. Machines can use a variety of deep learning methods, which are ways to mimic the capability of the human brain. When a network can analyze pictures from every bit and every corner, it is said to have a convolution neural network. Typically, a neural network based on con is used to identify items in an image. This is where computer vision comes in, and AI is used to recognize objects. Recurrent neural networks are the most well-known type of neural network because they can remember only a small portion of the past. There are two methods by that neural networks can operate: symbolically. computer learning, which involves feeding the computer a lot of data beforehand it can learn, is another name for the database. As opposed to this, symbolic learning enables developers to clearly describe relationships between various items and ideas by using symbols to represent them. These machine learning methods can be used to perform categorization or forecast.

According to Gabriel and Gouri (2019), sustainable development goals are mainly based on 3 motivational factors i.e. concreteness, prioritization, and moral message. According to Fauré et al., (2019) examination of the items and services used in Sweden that have the biggest impacts on emissions and resource consumption, and the identification of the nations or regions where these impacts occur. A hybrid model created for the PRINCE project was used to determine the results by fusing information with data from the multi-regional database EXIOBASE from the Department of Economic and environmental statements of Swedish. According to the Swedish economic accounts, product groupings are those products and services purchased for capital investments as well as for individual or public consumption. The findings indicate that, except for land usage and material use, all embodied environmental constraints are imported by Sweden on a net basis. Construction, food items, and residential direct emissions are the most significant product categories in terms of environmental pressures (except for sulfur dioxide emissions). Craig and Petterson (2005) claimed that online healthcare has been used in emergency situations where there is no other option, particularly in distant settings. It can use in circumstances where the superior to traditional services, such as teleradiology for clinics in rural areas. Telemedicine is thought to have improved access to healthcare for all people, the standard of treatment, and even the efficacy and efficiency of service delivery. Vinuesa et al., (2016) analyzed the massive, interconnected information to create combined activities to target protecting the ecosystem with the help of AI. When it comes to SDG 13 on climate achievement, advances in AI will be improving our knowledge of its potential effects. Additionally, AI is promoting low-carbon energy systems that integrate renewable energy and energy conservation, which is essential for addressing climate change. With the potential to handle a large number of areas in a relatively brief passé of time, neural networks and goal-achieving methods can be used to develop the identification of satellite-based images. In order to prevent further desertification, these AI interventions can help to identify patterns in desertification across vast geographic regions and provide information that is pertinent for planning for the environment, decision-making, and management. They can also promote reversing trends by finding the main causes (Mohamadi et al., 2016).

Problem Identification

The UN General Assembly's adoption of the 2030 Agenda for Sustainable Development in 2015 lays out a bold plan for the global pursuit of institutional, economic, social, and environmental goals. The agenda is comprised of 17 SDGs and 169 related targets. The 2030 Agenda works with other international accords to make sure that development patterns promote well-being and social inclusion while preserving the Earth's biophysical life support stability systems. There is no in-depth study about sustainable development with ai intervention and its impact on the green economy. In this article, we investigate whether ai adaptation helps to achieve the SDGs and which will help further in the green economy.

Research Gap

This specific introspective pertains to knowing how Artificial intelligence helps to achieve sustainable development goals which lead to improving the green economy.

Research Objective

1. To demonstrate how ai helps to achieve sustainable development goals.
2. To support the green economy by achieving the SDGs per the agenda.

Achieving the SDGs With the Help of AI

It is simply amazing how quickly digital technology is advancing today. Massive data sets will enable humans to leverage AI innovation and make revolutionary advancements in industries including the health sector, educational sector, food industries, etc. Furthermore, we are seeing how AI-enhanced computing helps doctors find researchers, increase grower yields, personalizes student teaching, and decreases medical blunders. Interest in the connection between artificial intelligence and climate change has recently increased significantly. AI may be employed in a range of economic applications and settings, such as managing environmental implications and changes. These are only a few examples of potential applications; others include improved supply chains, environmental management, and forecasting of the weather.

AI METHODS FOR REACHING SDGS OBJECTIVES

AI in Environment

Even though AI for Sustainability is receiving more attention, the sustainability of developing and using AI systems has to be considered. (Such as reaching the SDGs). According to my definition, sustainable AI is a measure that seeks to promote change across the whole lifetime with AI inventions (i.e., concept development, fine-tuning, implementation, and authority) in the direction of better ecological integrity and equitable society. The recent wave has concentrated on sustainable development. Although there is a growing movement to direct AI usage towards "good" objectives (such as the SDGs, or "AI4Good"), Beyond that, it is important to think about how sustainable it is to develop and use AI systems on its own. The process of developing a single machine learning (ML) NLP (natural language processing) model (GPU) can result in over 600,000 lb of carbon dioxide emissions, according to Strubell et al., 2019. I also think it's important to concentrate on AI's sustainability. This shift in perspective is crucial because it makes it impossible to discuss AI for Climate Change or AI for Good without also discussing the effects that create a particular AI model's impact on environmental sustainability. Nayak et al., (2023) analyzed to make wise policy selections in order to maximize system efficiency. Service broker policy helps to pick the right data center and decreases data center overload. When they are compared on the based on the factors like the time for respondent and the data center for processing, and the cost for virtual machine, it is discovered that the nearest service broker leads the other policies. Strubell et al., 2019 demonstrated that 'tuning' an AI model costs more than developing a model. The policymakers must comprehend this type of research in order to decide if particular AI techniques are proportionate to their intended use. In other words, it's time for policymakers to regulate AI more precisely and propose that some techniques, like fine-tuning an advanced NLP model, shouldn't be allowed for morally contentious tasks like hiring new employees or predicting when workers might leave their jobs. The justification is that it would be too expensive to maintain environmental sustainability with such a basic (not to mention ethically unbiased) use. Sustainable AI put its development with the principle of its definition due to three concurrent conflicts among innovation on AI approach and impartial resource distribution, intergenerational and intragenerational justice, and the interaction between the environment, society, and economy. It also demonstrates how each of the three sustainability pillars—social, economic, and environmental—engages with sustainable AI (Van Wynsberghe, 2021). By putting into practice techniques that make efficient and environmentally friendly use of computer resources, green computing seeks to achieve a sustainable future. Recycling of outdated goods and manufacturing waste is promoted by green computing. Companies that use information technology through time have come to understand the benefits of turning green in terms of maintaining good public relations and cutting costs (Bisoyi & Das, 2018).

AI in Transforming Agriculture

Recent improvements in the availability of appropriate data, and its processing, and algorithms have empowered artificial intelligence (AI) to start distributing on the promise of providing genuine value. Automation and robotics technology will boost agricultural output and well-being while decreasing the quantity of human decision-making that is necessary. Artificial intelligence will also be necessary for businesses to maximize the worth of data scattered during supply, including agricultural data. The creation of digital matchings will be a significant paradigm for improving the organization of data regarding agricultural enterprises to improve decision-making. It is also conceivable that AI will have negative effects, such as altering the responsibilities and abilities required of agricultural employees. This shows to think about the social and proper implications of AI every time a new capacity is announced (Smith, 2018). A workforce shortage is not unexpected given that agriculture is a manpower-intensive business. Automation, though, may be able to assist in finding a solution. Tractors with automatic driving capabilities, intelligent irrigation, spraying, and fertilizing systems, and AI-based harvester robots are a few examples. For software companies, explaining the complete AI system to farmers may be challenging. Field the harvesting process, surveillance of health, pest management, and deficiency diagnosis are all areas in which AI is employed in agriculture. In the agriculture industry, ML and AI are replacing antiquated forecasting and intelligence techniques (Wongchai et al., 2022). By swiftly recognizing plant ailments and effectively dispensing agrochemicals, AI in agriculture may be utilized to enhance crop management and productivity. Fluent plant phenotyping, used for farming monitoring, evaluation of soil composition, climate forecasting, and prediction of yield may all be aided by machine learning. To improve the production of their land, more farmers are adopting AI, IoT, and other technology advancements (V. Lešić et al., 2021).

According to this framework, ai has a huge application in the agriculture sector. According to the figure agricultural robotics help to Identify the state of the crop and apply the appropriate chemicals, spraying, or harvesting as needed by the fruit or plant. Mobile manipulation using team-based arms. By functioning autonomously on four separate levels, the BACCHUS AI robotic system claims to mimic human harvesting activities while removing manual labor: Through its integrated sensor system, the robot automatically navigates to check crops and gather information from the agricultural region. The robot efficiently completes bi-manual harvesting tasks with the dexterity demanded by the surroundings. The robot gripper is modified using additive fabrication to fit the geometry of various crops. superior cognitive and decision-making abilities are demonstrated. By recognizing, detecting, and tracking herds, intelligent agricultural sensors make it simple to recognize animals, sense heat, and keep an eye on their health. This aids in the isolation and recovery of ill cows. Farmers are able to record their crops, monitor their efficacy from a distance, deal with agricultural pests, and respond quickly to safeguard their crops from environmental risks thanks to the use of smart sensors in agriculture. Many things might go wrong while crops develop and ripen: illnesses, insect infestations, or unfavorable weather circumstances could possibly result in permanent damage before farmers even realize it. Smart sensing technology is used in crop monitoring to gather data on the condition of the crops (temperature, moisture, health indicators, etc.) and allows farmers to respond quickly if something goes wrong. Forecasting the future market to make more profit with the use of AI and also help the farmer to know about the weather status for their desired crops. One of the most demanding challenges in agriculture is predicting crop yields. It is crucial to decision-making at the international, regional, and local levels. Crop yield is predicted using soil, climatic, environmental, and crop characteristics.

Figure 1. Agricultural robotics help to Identify the state of the crop and apply the appropriate chemicals, spraying, or harvesting as needed by the fruit or plant
Source: Dara et al., (2022)

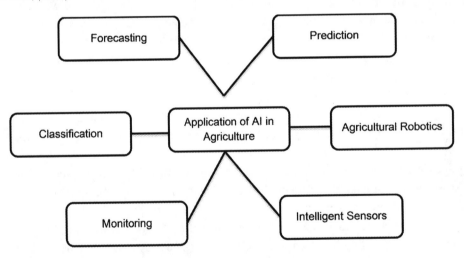

AI for Energy Solutions Revolutionization

Although using AI in the energy business isn't straightforward, the potential advantages exceed the drawbacks. Smart grids, data digitization, forecasting, and more sophisticated resource management are just a few examples of the potential uses of artificial intelligence in the energy sector. By using the two-way flow of data and electricity, a smart grid offers a novel approach to reducing energy consumption networks. The use of AI and other technological innovations that assist control and self-regulation is the primary distinction between this network and the standard ones. The collaboration between IBM's cloud-based analytics and London's National Grid is one of the most notable instances of the smart grid. The smart grid provides preventive and predictive maintenance, which are essential components of the grid's operation. As a whole, the AI-powered smart grid contributes to more accurate forecasting while also enhancing the grid's security and resilience. Major energy suppliers must strike a balance between conventional and renewable energy sources. The optimal conditions for the accurate integration of renewables may now be forecasted and predicted through the use of energy and machine learning. In other words, it aids in the management of the integration of energy from renewable sources into the established electrical grid. Predicting wind and solar farms and distributing the energy outputs to balance the current system may be involved. To create predictions or suggestions, it can extract patterns from the data. Each company is moving towards adopting AI in the energy industry because of the growth it has brought about and the need to properly balance energy demand and supply. AI algorithms assist in managing energy supply and demand, forecasting customer energy requirements through the SM deployed at each consumer's side, and advising consumers on energy consumption habits that might lower their energy costs. The market for artificial intelligence in energy management reached $4439.1 million, and by 2024, it is expected to reach $12,200.9 million. Cooperation between the manufacturing and logistics industries, environmental regulations, and technical input significantly influence GTFP (Green Total factor Productivity). This suggests that improving manufacturing and logistics sector collaboration, implementing environmental legislation effectively, and adopting technology infrastructure may all lessen the negative effects of manufacturing and logistics operations, which can ultimately increase a nation's gross domestic product (GDP). By establishing green standards in logistics and manufacturing processes, improvements in technical input in both the manufacturing and logistics industries contribute to a green economy.

Figure 2. Conventional power systems must add additional generation capacity to keep up with the twenty-first century's continuously rising demand for electricity
Source: Som (2021).

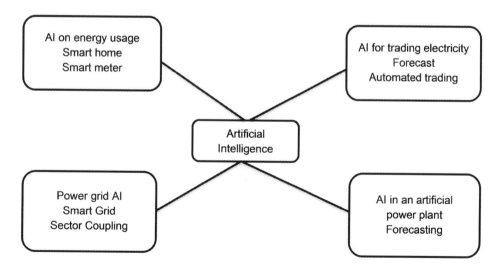

According to the figure conventional power systems must add additional generation capacity to keep up with the twenty-first century's continuously rising demand for electricity. To do this, transmission and distribution networks must be upgraded over utility infrastructure in a way that is ecologically friendly and expanded to new remote and rural regions. Decentralized power distribution systems have therefore emerged as a new option to maintain technological, economic, and environmental sustainability. Artificial intelligence approaches with qualities like limited reality, unpredictability, inaccurate specification, and calculation, which frequently exist in issues of real-world importance of energy economics, will be investigated in an effort to produce better and more accurate answers.

CONCLUSION

To offer a consistent analytical framework for a study of the necessary transitions toward sustainable development, the goal space formulation discussed above is crucial. It offers a starting point for the analysis of how to accomplish the SDGs concurrently. The scientific community may collaborate on this project and begin with a set of comparable and internally consistent assumptions by using a common, clear, and science-based specification of the goals. The evaluation of the indicators and goal values, the handling of non-linearities and interdependences within the target area as it develops through 2050 and beyond and the consistent application of indicators at various geographic scales are other crucial challenges that require further refining. The fourth industrial revolution's advances offer prospects for efficient data mining to make a baseline for both national and international which is available for all for the measurement of member state progress, particularly with regard to goals lacking specific, measurable numbers. The lessons we learn from this are that governments must increase their trust in AI and machine learning in order to address future health issues and ensure that the sustainable development goals concerning well-being are met, despite the disruptions and rise in the number of unintended implications of technology in the industrial revolution. The findings of this study are crucial for raising public understanding of how AI when used correctly, may significantly advance the achievement of the SDGs.

REFERENCES

Ali, E. B., Anufriev, V. P., & Amfo, B. (2021). Green economy implementation in Ghana as a road map for a sustainable development drive: A review. *Scientific African*, *12*, e00756. doi:10.1016/j.sciaf.2021.e00756

Barley, S. R. (2020). *Work and technological change*. Oxford University Press. doi:10.1093/oso/9780198795209.001.0001

Bisoyi, B., & Das, B. (2018). An approach to en route environmentally sustainable future through green computing. In *Smart Computing and Informatics: Proceedings of the First International Conference on SCI 2016,* (pp. 621-629). Springer Singapore. 10.1007/978-981-10-5544-7_61

Bisoyi, B., & Das, B. (2023). A paradigm shift: Nano-sensory nudges stimulating consumer's purchase behaviour for green products driving towards environmental sustainability. *Materials Today: Proceedings*, *80*, 3887–3892. doi:10.1016/j.matpr.2021.07.407

Bisoyi, B., Nayak, B., Das, B., & Pasumarti, S. S. (2021). Urban Resilience and Inclusion of Smart Cities in the Transformation Process for Sustainable Development: Critical Deflections on the Smart City of Bhubaneswar in India. In *Advances in Power Systems and Energy Management: Select Proceedings of ETAEERE 2020* (pp. 149-160). Springer Singapore.

Cancino, C. A., La Paz, A. I., Ramaprasad, A., & Syn, T. (2018). Technological innovation for sustainable growth: An ontological perspective. *Journal of Cleaner Production*, *179*, 31–41. doi:10.1016/j.jclepro.2018.01.059

Colombo, U. (2001). The Club of Rome and sustainable development. *Futures*, *33*(1), 7–11. doi:10.1016/S0016-3287(00)00048-3

Craig, J., & Petterson, V. (2005). Introduction to the practice of telemedicine. *Journal of Telemedicine and Telecare*, *11*(1), 3–9. doi:10.1177/1357633X0501100102 PMID:15829036

D'Amato, D., Droste, N., Allen, B., Kettunen, M., Lähtinen, K., Korhonen, J., Leskinen, P., Matthies, B. D., & Toppinen, A. (2017). Green, circular, bio economy: A comparative analysis of sustainability avenues. *Journal of Cleaner Production*, *168*, 716–734. doi:10.1016/j.jclepro.2017.09.053

Dara, R., Hazrati Fard, S. M., & Kaur, J. (2022). Recommendations for ethical and responsible use of artificial intelligence in digital agriculture. *Frontiers in Artificial Intelligence*, *5*, 884192. doi:10.3389/frai.2022.884192 PMID:35968036

Fauré, E., Dawkins, E., Wood, R., Finnveden, G., Palm, V., Persson, L., & Schmidt, S. (2019). Environmental pressure from Swedish consumption–The largest contributing producer countries, products and services. *Journal of Cleaner Production*, *231*, 698–713. doi:10.1016/j.jclepro.2019.05.148

Gabriel, I., & Gauri, V. (2019). Towards a new global narrative for the sustainable development goals. *Sustainable Development Goals: Harnessing Business to Achieve the SDGs through Finance, Technology, and Law Reform*, 53-70.

Ghisellini, P., Cialani, C., & Ulgiati, S. (2016). A review on circular economy: The expected transition to a balanced interplay of environmental and economic systems. *Journal of Cleaner Production*, *114*, 11–32. doi:10.1016/j.jclepro.2015.09.007

Girella, L., Zambon, S., & Rossi, P. (2019). Reporting on sustainable development: A comparison of three Italian small and medium-sized enterprises. *Corporate Social Responsibility and Environmental Management*, *26*(4), 981–996. doi:10.1002/csr.1738

Gunay, S., Kurtishi-Kastrati, S., & Krsteska, K. (2022). Regional green economy and community impact on global sustainability. *Journal of Enterprising Communities: People and Places in the Global Economy*.

Halisçelik, E., & Soytas, M. A. (2019). Sustainable development from millennium 2015 to Sustainable Development Goals 2030. *Sustainable Development (Bradford)*, *27*(4), 545–572. doi:10.1002d.1921

Holling, C. S. (2001). Understanding the complexity of economic, ecological, and social systems. *Ecosystems (New York, N.Y.)*, *4*(5), 390–405. doi:10.100710021-001-0101-5

Ibisch, P. L., Hobson, P., & Vega, A. E. (2010). Mutual mainstreaming of biodiversity conservation and human development: towards a more radical ecosystem approach. In *Interdependence of biodiversity and development under global change* (pp. 15–34). Secretariat of the Convention on Biological Diversity.

Khoshnava, S. M., Rostami, R., Zin, R. M., Štreimikienė, D., Yousefpour, A., Strielkowski, W., & Mardani, A. (2019). Aligning the criteria of green economy (GE) and sustainable development goals (SDGs) to implement sustainable development. *Sustainability (Basel)*, *11*(17), 4615. doi:10.3390u11174615

Krawchuk, F. T. (2017). Collaboration in a VUCA environment. In *Visionary Leadership in a Turbulent World* (pp. 133–154). Emerald Publishing Limited. doi:10.1108/978-1-78714-242-820171007

Lee, C. C., Wang, C. W., & Ho, S. J. (2022). The dimension of green economy: Culture viewpoint. *Economic Analysis and Policy*, *74*, 122–138. doi:10.1016/j.eap.2022.01.015

Lešić, V. (2021). *Rapid Plant Development Modelling System for Predictive Agriculture Based on Artificial Intelligence*. 2021 16th International Conference on Telecommunications (ConTEL), Zagreb, Croatia. 10.23919/ConTEL52528.2021.9495972

Li, X., Ozturk, I., Majeed, M. T., Hafeez, M., & Ullah, S. (2022). Considering the asymmetric effect of financial deepening on environmental quality in BRICS economies: Policy options for the green economy. *Journal of Cleaner Production*, *331*, 129909. doi:10.1016/j.jclepro.2021.129909

Mangla, S. K., Govindan, K., & Luthra, S. (2017). Prioritizing the barriers to achieve sustainable consumption and production trends in supply chains using fuzzy Analytical Hierarchy Process. *Journal of Cleaner Production*, *151*, 509–525. doi:10.1016/j.jclepro.2017.02.099

Meadows, D. H., Meadows, D. H., Randers, J., & Behrens, W. W. III. (1972). The limits to growth: A report to the club of Rome (1972). *Google Scholar*, *91*, 2.

Mohamadi, A., Heidarizadi, Z., & Nourollahi, H. (2016). Assessing the desertification trend using neural network classification and object-oriented techniques (Case study: Changouleh watershed-Ilam Province of Iran). *Istanbul Üniversitesi Orman Fakültesi Dergisi*, *66*(2), 683–690.

Mol, A. P. (2002). Ecological modernization and the global economy. *Global Environmental Politics*, *2*(2), 92–115. doi:10.1162/15263800260047844

Nayak, B., Bisoyi, B., & Pattnaik, P. K. (2023). Data center selection through service broker policy in cloud computing environment. *Materials Today: Proceedings*, *80*, 2218–2223. doi:10.1016/j.matpr.2021.06.185

Pearce, D. (1992). Green economics. *Environmental Values*, *1*(1), 3–13. doi:10.3197/096327192776680179

Shimova, O. (2019). Belarus on the way to sustainable development: circular economy and green technologies. In *Modeling economic growth in contemporary Belarus* (pp. 89–106). Emerald Publishing Limited. doi:10.1108/978-1-83867-695-720191007

Smith, M. J. (2018). Getting value from artificial intelligence in agriculture. *Animal Production Science*, *60*(1), 46–54. doi:10.1071/AN18522

Som, T. (2021). Sustainability in Energy Economy and Environment: Role of AI Based Techniques. In *Computational Management: Applications of Computational Intelligence in Business Management* (pp. 647–682). Springer International Publishing. doi:10.1007/978-3-030-72929-5_31

Strubell, E., Ganesh, A., & McCallum, A. (2019). Energy and policy considerations for deep learning in NLP. *arXiv preprint arXiv:1906.02243*. doi:10.18653/v1/P19-1355

Usubiaga-Liano, A., & Ekins, P. (2021). Monitoring the environmental sustainability of countries through the strong environmental sustainability index. *Ecological Indicators*, *132*, 108281. doi:10.1016/j.ecolind.2021.108281

Van Wynsberghe, A. (2021). Sustainable AI: AI for sustainability and the sustainability of AI. *AI and Ethics*, *1*(3), 213–218. doi:10.100743681-021-00043-6

Vinuesa, R., Fdez. de Arévalo, L., Luna, M., & Cachafeiro, H. (2016). Simulations and experiments of heat loss from a parabolic trough absorber tube over a range of pressures and gas compositions in the vacuum chamber. *Journal of Renewable and Sustainable Energy*, *8*(2), 023701. doi:10.1063/1.4944975

Wongchai, A., Shukla, S. K., Ahmed, M. A., Sakthi, U., Jagdish, M., & kumar, R. (2022). Artificial intelligence-enabled soft sensor and internet of things for sustainable agriculture using ensemble deep learning architecture. *Computers & Electrical Engineering*, *102*, 108128. doi:10.1016/j.compeleceng.2022.108128

Zink, T., & Geyer, R. (2017). Circular economy rebound. *Journal of Industrial Ecology*, *21*(3), 593–602. doi:10.1111/jiec.12545

Chapter 20
Green Finance Products and Investments in the Changing Business World

Rajeev Sengupta
https://orcid.org/0000-0001-7451-239X
Dr. Vishwanath Karad MIT World Peace University, India

Ameya Patil
Dr. Vishwanath Karad MIT World Peace University, India

ABSTRACT

There is a promulgation in the 21st century that those projects which are green should be given preference for financing, amid growing climate change concerns. As a result, green finance, which deals with financing sustainable projects, is in vogue. This study seeks to understand various investments in green finance as well as the green finance products such as green bonds and green insurance, along with vouching the use of weather derivatives for sustainable finance projects. The factors determining green finance are also incorporated, along with green fintech. The study finds that though investments in green finance are increasing, it is not enough. Government policy and support, innovativeness, and further awareness will determine the further investments in sustainable projects. The combination of fintech and green finance can help society to transition to near zero emissions, and protect the planet.

INTRODUCTION

The world is growing at a CAGR of 3-4% annually. However, when considered over a century, this expansion has been harmful to the ecosystem and could be considered life-threatening (Sun et al.,2020). The greatest environmental threat is climate change. Finance lies at the centre of the business parlance, providing the funds necessary for the business and he economic growth. The major sources of finance include debt, especially bonds and loans form banks, equity capital, venture capital financing and the funds by the Government or the public sector. Infrastructure development is driven by finance, notably

DOI: 10.4018/978-1-6684-8969-7.ch020

the development of energy projects. Renewable energy projects are associated with risks due to new technologies (Sun et al.,2020), and lower returns. As a result, financial institutions are often more interested in fossil fuel endeavours than environmentally friendly ones. Now, given the deteriorating environmental conditions globally, the time has come for the finance sector to provide financing for emerging businesses that provide environmental remedies and innovations that speed the transition to sustainable societies. To accomplish the Sustainable Development Goals (SDGs), a new file for green projects must be created, and funding for initiatives with a beneficial environmental impact must be increased. The related term 'Green financing' ought to encompass innovative financial instruments and regulations, including green bonds, green banks, fintech, and community-based green funds.

Green finance is a broad term that covers investments in activities and projects that promote sustainable development, environmental well-being, and policies that lead to a more sustainable economy. In recent years, there has been a lot of focus on green finance because of the need to combat climate change and promote sustainable development. This strategy recognises the critical role of finance in accomplishing environmental goals and promoting long-term economic growth. Green finance is founded on the idea that environmental protection and economic growth do not have to be mutually exclusive, but may be linked to achieve long-term sustainability. It is important to remember that climate finance is only one facet of green finance. Furthermore, green financing encompasses a broader variety of environmental goals, such as biodiversity preservation and industrial pollution reduction. Money for climate change mitigation and adaptation is very important. Investments in low-carbon technology and practises, renewable energy projects, and other measures targeted at lowering greenhouse gas emissions constitute mitigation funding. Adaptation funding, on the other hand, helps communities and ecosystems become more robust to the effects of climate change, such as rising sea levels, extreme weather events, and droughts. Green finance is a concept that seeks to ensure that economic growth, environmental protection, and environmental integrity all coexist (Kumar et al.,2022). Green finance is thus a blend of environmental conservation with finance. Green finance investments are driven by the need for renewable energy (Madaleno et al.,2022). Green finance refers to financial goods and services that incorporate environmental considerations while making lending decisions, monitoring post-investment, and managing risks in the banking business. These financial services are provided to stimulate environmentally responsible investments as well as the promotion of low-carbon technologies, industries, projects, and businesses.

The need for clean energy is one of the main drivers of green finance. As countries around the world seek to transition to a low-carbon economy, investments in renewable energy and energy efficiency have increased significantly. Green finance plays a vital role in supporting these efforts by providing the necessary funding for clean energy projects and initiatives.

INVESTMENTS IN GREEN FINANCE

Green finance can help mobilize private capital to finance green technologies and projects, and can also provide incentives for companies to adopt sustainable practices. Green finance certainly has dominant policy importance, as evidenced by the intense debates that have occurred among international organizations and national governments since its initiation(Zhang et al.,2019). Policymakers and researchers have recently concentrated on green finance as interest in environmental preservation, climate change, and sustainable development grows on a worldwide scale. Green finance arose to address climatic change by providing ecologically good investment opportunities without supporting environmentally harmful firms

(Chen et al., 2021). Given the requirement of capital, green finance is crucial for supporting renewable and green energy projects (Steffen, 2018). Investing in green finance is a way to support sustainable development and mitigate the effects of climate change. Green finance encompasses a wide range of investments, including renewable energy, energy efficiency, sustainable agriculture, clean transportation, and green buildings, among others. Increased money flow is required for the success of innovative green ventures (Hsu et al., 2014). The financial flows into this sector can be accelerated through innovative financial tools such as tax incentives and carbon tax (Mazzucato & Semieniuk,2018). Green quantitative easing from central banks can encourage green bond market investment and green stock market investment (Aloui et al.,2023). These initiatives have the potential to lower carbon emissions, construct climate-resilient infrastructure for cities, and ensure environmental sustainability. Infrastructure financing for renewable energy projects is urgently needed. The transition of energy projects from fossil fuel dependent to renewable energy require sufficient financing (Mazzucatoa & Semieniuk, 2017). Green financing, in particular the issuance of green bonds, is a crucial driver of the development of renewable energy (Alharbi et al.,2023).

In the first half of 2022, global investment in the renewable energy sector increased 11% to $226 billion (Source: BNEF). New large- and small-scale solar projects received $120 billion in major investments, and wind project funding received $84 billion. There is growing evidence that investments in green finance can generate competitive financial returns. A meta-analysis of 2,200 studies by Friede et al.(2015) found that in 90% of the cases, companies with high ESG ratings had equal or higher financial performance compared to companies with lower ESG ratings.

Figure 1. Climate finance flows over the last decade
Compiled by author (Source: Climate Policy Initiative)

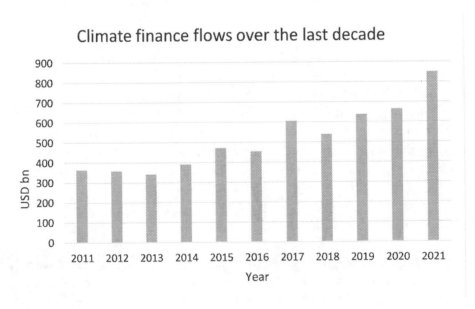

In the last decade, green finance flows have grown at a CAGR of nearly 7%, increasing from USD 364 bn in 2011 to USD 850 bn in 2021 (Figure 1). However, more finance flows are required for climate change initiatives in order to achieve the Sustainable Development Goals (SDGs) and protect the planet.

GREEN FINANCE PRODUCTS/INSTRUMENTS

Green finance products refer to financial instruments that aim to encourage sustainable development and combat climate change. Their popularity is on the rise as both businesses and governments search for innovative ways to tackle environmental issues. Given the amount of money needed to combat climate change, green financing has grown in importance. According to bankers (Zheng et al.,2021), green finance is critical for the development of banking strategy. Green finance products are becoming more popular in the financial industry as the need for sustainable investments grows. Green finance products allow investors to support ecologically sustainable initiatives while earning a reasonable return on their investment. They can assist to speed up the transition to a more sustainable economy by funding the development of new technologies and programmes that cut carbon emissions and mitigate climate change. Green finance products are a variety of financial instruments that aim to fund ecologically beneficial projects and efforts, such as green bonds, green loans, green insurance, and green funds. Green insurance, green credit, and green infrastructure bonds have been the most popular green finance products offered by banks (Akomea-Frimpong et al.,2022). Green banks and green bonds are two novel funding solutions for environmentally friendly enterprises that have emerged in recent years.

Green bonds and green banks could help with renewable energy finance to a large extent. Green banks have several benefits, including improved credit terms for clean energy projects, the amalgamation of smaller projects into larger ones that are more commercially viable, and the development of innovative financial products. Green bonds and green funds have been found to deliver returns comparable to conventional investments, indicating that environmentally sustainable investments can be profitable. Additionally, green investments can provide diversification benefits to investors, reducing their overall portfolio risk. Different green finance products are discussed subsequently.

Green Bonds

The rise of green bonds has been one of the most significant financial advancements in sustainable finance in the last decade. The market for green bonds has grown substantially over the years. In contrast to regular bonds that fund the issuer's overall working capital, green bonds should solely finance or refinance environmentally-friendly projects or assets. Green bonds were initially used by Nordic countries to finance sustainable infrastructure and related businesses. Amongst the most dynamic tools in green finance is green bonds, which are fixed-income products . Its proceeds are utilized towards environmental projects by the issuer. In order to entice more people to buy green bonds, Governments may offer tax breaks. Concerns about climate change and the need to reallocate capital have increased investor interest for these securities during the past decade. Green bonds are occasionally emphasized as a means of increasing sustainable infrastructure investments from institutional investors by enhancing the liquidity of infrastructure assets

The primary objective of issuing green bonds is to ensure use of renewable energy rather than dirty energy, maximize the efficiency of their material consumption, and develop effective waste management strategies(Karim et al.,2022). Green bonds provide an innovative approach to the generation of funding for sustainable energy projects, allowing for the pursuit of both efficacy and optimization (Zhao et al.,2022).Green bonds have a huge potential to attract substantial amounts of funding from the private sector for financing for renewable energy initiatives (Ng & Tao, 2016). However, transparency is a vital element for investors investing in green bonds and it is this particular factor that will majorly determine the future growth of these instruments(Kyriakou, 2017). The environment is directly and tangibly impacted by green bonds. Many buyers of green bonds are curious about the precise nature of that impact. Companies can currently report on a variety of indicators, which causes confusion. The inclusion of KPIs, such as the actual levels of water waste reduction or the amount of waste that has been recycled, can be done by corporations who issue green bonds in their annual reports.

The rise in the issuing of green bonds can be attributed to several incentive policies (Day et al., 2016). Many times, financial incentives in the form of grants for renewable energy or energy efficiency were utilized to encourage decarburization .For increasing popularity of green bonds, they should be made tax- exempt, and also attempts towards environmentally responsible education should be made (Agliardi & Agliardi,2019). Green bond proponents contend that once a project has completed the building phase and is working properly, it can be refinanced with long-term, reasonably priced capital. Green bonds investment has increased as public awareness regarding implications of climate change has grown(Bagnoli and Watts, 2020) . Investors place a higher value on corporations that issue green bonds(Sisodia et al., 2022). Greenness of the portfolio reduces the risk of green portfolio, which shows that green finance instruments, especially green bonds act as hedging instruments (Akhtaruzzaman et al.,2022).

Governments of some countries have also issued green bonds, referred to as 'Sovereign green bonds". The first sovereign green bond was issued in 2016.Since then, the global sovereign green bond market has expanded at a rapid pace. The issue of sovereign green bonds can be thought of as a sort of industrial policy that is intended to assist in the development of the sustainable finance industry. Investors view the issue of a green bond as reflecting a value-enhancing and risk-reducing behavior of the issuing nation(Dell'Atti et al.,2022) .This viewpoint is confirmed by the fact that these environmentally friendly bonds have gained more and more popularity in recent years. By boosting the social and reputational benefits, the issue of a sovereign green bond sends a powerful signal regarding the nation's commitment to making the move toward an economy with lower levels of carbon emissions. Thus, green bond market has grown rapidly in recent years, but there is still room for improvement in terms of standardization, transparency, and the alignment of green bonds with environmental goals.

Green Loans and Concessional Finance

Green loans are another popular green finance product. They are loans provided by banks or other financial institutions for environmentally-friendly projects. Green loans can be used for a variety of purposes, such as energy-efficient upgrades for buildings or the purchase of electric vehicles. Like green bonds, the funds raised through green loans are earmarked for specific green projects. In the decade of 2011-20, Concessional finance represented 16% of total climate finance. Debt has continuously been the primary method for climate finance. In order to manage the risks and uncertainties associated with developing markets and technologies, concessional financing is essential. Grant funding is increasing and will nearly triple between 2011 and 2020. Less than 5% of their funding goes towards combating climate change, which is still a minimal fraction. The vast majority of the money came from governments in the form of subsidies or international climate support. While the private sector relied on investments made from its own resources or balance sheet, the public sector provided loans at preferential or market rates. Due to the growth of renewable energy in those regions, North America and Western Europe raised the most debt, followed by East Asia Pacific.

Green Insurance

A more recent type of green financial product that is gaining popularity is green insurance. It provides insurance coverage for environmentally-friendly projects, such as renewable energy projects, sustainable agriculture, and other green initiatives. Green insurance can help reduce the financial risks associated with these projects, making them more attractive to investors. Green insurance was developed due to the increasing awareness of the impact of climate change on both the economy and the environment. With the rising prominence of climate-related risks, there is a growing demand among businesses and individuals for insurance products that offer coverage for these specific risks.

Sustainability is included into insurance through green insurance. Insurance businesses have the potential to hasten the change of the global economy and assist governments in achieving their sustainability objectives. The insurance sector plays a key role in ensuring the long-term health of economies, communities, and ecosystems around the world through its risk management and investment practices (Nobanee et al.,2021). . Businesses that employ alternative materials and energies in their structures and surroundings should have access to insurance that rewards and encourages them to continue improving an environmentally friendly environment. Reduced premiums for the green sector or electric vehicles (EVs), the establishment of incentives and tax policies for sustainable/green insurance, the promotion of new sustainable/green products, and the acceptance of investments in projects that satisfy the sustainability/green criteria are all examples of sustainability in the insurance sector. A new product designed to combat climate change or a product that promotes clients' sustainability and green behaviors could also be considered sustainable/green insurance. Green insurance is a tool that can be used to encourage the development of emission-cutting innovations that can adjust to the ever-shifting climates of the planet (Wang et al. 2017).

Products that cover the creation, usage, and liability associated with these sustainable products are considered sustainable and green insurance products.. This notion of sustainable/green products would also generally include regulations where specific characteristics encourage sustainable or green behavior. Consequently, a wide range of insurance products are included in sustainable and green insurance products. Green innovation risk can be dealt through a risk transfer via insurance (Sun et al.,2020)

Technical companies and individuals may be covered by renewable energy insurance policies that cover engineering and construction risks throughout the project development stage and offer aid with income loss and business interruption support. Sustainable insurance can also include green home insurance, in which insurers provide homeowners with insurance discounts or add-ons that help them save money and motivate them to build using eco-friendly materials and use less energy . 'Global weather insurance' and 'green car insurance' can be considered as products of green insurance.The world's central banks and regulators acknowledge the crucial role that environmentally friendly insurance plans play in reducing the effects of climate change. Green insurance is becoming increasingly significant in influencing company decisions regarding overseas investments (Chen et al.,2021) .

Weather Derivatives

Industries that rely on renewable energy sources are inherently tied to weather variables, which can impact their operational and financial performance. For instance, the solar industry is highly dependent on incident radiation, which can vary depending on weather conditions such as cloud cover and precipitation. Wind turbulence and speed, which might differ by location and season, have an effect on the wind business. For investors in green finance, these meteorological factors might present both opportunities and difficulties. On the one hand, variations in the generation of renewable energy can lead to price volatility and uncertain supplies, making it challenging for investors to forecast future profits. However, improvements in weather forecasting and data analytics can aid investors in understanding the risks and opportunities related to weather variability. Weather derivatives, as financial products, can efficiently control monetary losses brought on by changes in climatic circumstances.

Businesses which have entered into weather derivative contracts may seek a specific amount of compensation if the climate change exceeds the predetermined level. To mitigate the risks related to weather variability, investors in the renewable energy sector are increasingly employing weather derivatives.

These financial instruments help investors hedge against weather-related risks such as temperature or precipitation deviations from historical averages. Weather derivatives are commonly structured as over-the-counter contracts between the investor and the counterparty, specifying a weather variable and a settlement mechanism. If the weather variable deviates from a predetermined threshold, the investor receives compensation from the counterparty in the form of a payout, which helps offset any losses in revenue caused by the weather variability.

The capital investment for corporates involved in renewable energy can be considerably enhanced through managing key risk concerns for renewable generation arising from uncertain weather variations via suitable financial instruments (Bhattacharya et al.,2015). This is because climate change and other weather events represent a significant threat to renewable energy initiatives. In this regard, hedging through weather derivatives to reduce weather-related risks can be investigated. To protect against weather-based risks in the power markets, weather derivatives can be effectively used (Yang et al.,2009; Mori & Fujita,2015)

DETERMINANTS OF GREEN FINANCE INVESTMENTS

The factors that influence green finance investments are multifaceted and involve a combination of environmental, economic, and regulatory elements. To make well-informed investment decisions that support sustainable projects, investors take these factors into careful consideration. Based on different research studies and the reports of different international agencies, the authors identify the different determinants of green finance.

Firstly, awareness regarding green finance and its importance plays a crucial role in green finance investments. Lack of awareness has been affecting the very investments in sustainable ventures(Ozili,2022). Investors who are not aware of the potential benefits of green finance may be hesitant to invest their money in environmentally responsible projects. Therefore, creating awareness about the importance of green finance and its potential benefits is crucial to increase investments in sustainable ventures. This can be achieved through education and outreach programs, campaigns, and incentives that promote environmentally responsible investments. Lack of awareness has been identified as a significant barrier

Green Finance Products, Investments in the Changing Business World

to green finance investments, and addressing this issue can help unlock more funding for sustainable initiatives. Secondly, the upsurge of new technologies and harnessing them is a crucial factor in justifying feasibility of these investments. With the rise of new technologies, it is becoming increasingly feasible to invest in renewable energy projects, which can help reduce greenhouse gas emissions and promote sustainability. Innovative technologies can help reduce the cost and improve the efficiency of renewable energy production, storage, and distribution. Innovation is a vital link between green finance and renewable energy(Alharbi et al.,2023). Thirdly, cost of capital plays a pivotal role in electricity generation, and the finite amount of capital restraints investments to capital intensive technologies that produce zero emissions(Ekholm et al.,2013), especially in the developing nations of Asia and Africa, where capital is limited, and financing can be challenging to obtain. Addressing the cost of capital issue can help unlock more funding for sustainable initiatives, making it more feasible to invest in renewable energy and other green technologies

Continued fossil fuel support acts as a barrier in moving towards sustainability.The total amount of subsidies for fossil fuels in only 51 large nations was 40% larger than the whole amount of money invested globally in climate finance between 2011 and 2020. This is concerning because support for high emitting activities overall only includes a small portion of fossil fuel subsidies. In addition to improving consumer price stability and boosting energy independence, immediate action to decrease dependency on fossil fuels, including subsidies, will free up resources for more environmentally friendly initiatives. Changing from dirty to clean manufacturing technologies requires significant changes to our economic and energy systems (Lööf et al., 2017).

Even policy changes towards favourable impact on green projects should be speedier, since Policy uncertainty in the form of detrimental changes to a subsidy program has a significant impact on investment decisions. (Dalby et al.,2018).The investment choice is significantly impacted by policy uncertainty in the form of unfavorable changes to a subsidy program (Dalby et al.,2018).Green credit policy, which should put penalties for polluting companies(Lv et al. 2021), and incentivize those investing in green projects, or take efforts towards lower carbon emissions in terms of their production or sales, should be clearly stated and implemented.

Due to high transaction costs, a small market, excessive government interference or lack of support, financial limitations, and a lack of institutional arrangements, the potential of green finance in developing countries is still limited. For instance, people in remote areas cannot afford to use fossil fuels or solar energy, even though this presents an opportunity to integrate alternative energy sources into the economy (Hyun et al., 2021). Still, larger investmets are garnered by energy projects that are environmentally harmful, given the low investment returns on green finance projects(Sachs et al., 2019; Yoshino & Taghizadeh-Hesary, 2019). Hence, green finance initiatives can be accelerated if, incentives to invest in green finance are provided to investors and corporations(Ekholm et al.,2013). India's environmentally friendly financing policies led to a significant reduction in industrial carbon dioxide emissions during the last 15 years(Nenavath,2022). Technology is another important determinant of green financing. Green finance investments can be impacted by the availability and scalability of sustainable technologies, since the integration of innovative technologies can improve both the environmental and financial outcomes of projects. The use of technology can make sustainable projects more economically feasible for investors by lowering costs. Energy efficiency technologies, for example, can reduce energy usage and operating costs for businesses. Additionally, technology can minimize environmental and financial risks associated with sustainable projects. For instance, remote sensing technologies can manage environmental risks, and blockchain can improve transparency and accountability in sustainable supply chains. The expansion of financial technology (Fintech) is helpful in reducing sulphur dioxide emissions and has a positive impact on environmental sustainability and investment businesses.

Renewable energy initiatives will prove to be a real boon for several developing countries in Asia and Africa, due to two reasons. Firstly, the natural endowments such as enough sunlight, by which these countries are blessed with, it will make them self-sufficient in energy, as well as reduce any import bills related to the same. Oil price increases hinder economic expansion and cause inflation in the majority of oil-importing nations. By investing in renewable energy projects, these countries can reduce their dependence on oil and other fossil fuels, leading to greater energy security and economic stability. Secondly, renewable energy initiatives can help reduce pollution in these countries, particularly given their high population density. These initiatives can help reduce the use of fossil fuels and lower emissions of harmful pollutants, leading to better air quality and improved public health. This can have a positive impact on the economy by reducing healthcare costs and improving the overall quality of life. Owing to the apprehensions of investors regarding region's high risk due to policy uncertainty (Fabrizio,2013), these nations should concentrate on lowering financial obstacles to sustainable projects ((Ng & Tao, 2016). This can include providing incentives for renewable energy projects, streamlining regulatory processes, and improving access to financing. By doing so, they can attract more investment and promote sustainable development while also addressing the urgent need to reduce greenhouse gas emissions.

FINTECH AND GREEN FINANCE

The development of markets for eco-friendly products and services, which are being driven by urgent environmental and social concerns, can be facilitated by technology. This, in turn, can help establish a foundation for a more sustainable and equitable future. Thanks to digitization, the financial system is now able to play a pivotal role in other sectors. Fintech is a wider expansion of the financial ecosystem that includes advances in payment systems (such as cryptocurrencies), credit markets (like peer-to-peer lending) and insurance. Blockchain technology and smart contracts are also becoming increasingly important in facilitating these innovations . One can also view fintech as businesses or their representatives that integrate contemporary and innovative technologies with financial services. The progress of ICT has brought about a significant transformation in the financial sector over time, resulting in more efficient service delivery and improved environmental performance. New forms of capital and risk management strategies can be offered by the FinTech sector. With the emergence of technologies such as cloud computing, analytics, and big data, the FinTech industry can also provide valuable insights into the probability, intensity, and early detection of risks. The renewable energy industry's consumption, savings, and investment decisions are impacted by FinTech. In case of OECD countries, the correlation between the advancement of FinTech and the adoption of renewable energy is strong and favorable (Croutzet & Dabbous,2021). Hence, the governments and policymakers should support the growth of eco-friendly energy industries by promoting and incentivizing the application of FinTech. In India, the expansion of financial technology has been helpful in reducing sulphur dioxide emissions and has a positive impact on environmental sustainability and investment businesses(Nenavath,2022). In the Euro zone, investments in financial technology have led to an increase in green lending, which can be attributed to the improved efficiency of new technologies in searching, conducting due diligence, and monitoring green projects (Mirza et al.,2023).

Green FinTech is a relatively new concept that aims to reduce carbon emissions and promote environmental sustainability through the use of financial technology. The fintech industry is positioned to play a major role in delivering green finance by utilizing advanced technologies such as big data analytics and artificial intelligence. These technologies may encourage people and businesses to adopt more ecologically responsible behaviors. According to the "Green FinTech" theory, financial technology may be able to reduce carbon emissions, which would result in environmental sustainability (Tamasiga et al., 2022).The fintech industry has the ability to realise the potential of green finance and assure its mobilization by relying on its inherent organizational agility and inventive nature. Through IOT and big data technology, fintech has the potential to advance green financing (Nassiry, 2019).

By offering information on energy use and carbon emissions that can be utilised to make wise investment decisions, the IoT has the potential to support green financing. Big data can be used to analyse environmental concerns and find areas where green technology investments are possible. Among other things, blockchain technology can be used to track the proceeds from green bonds, trade carbon credits, and expedite international climate finance transfers (Marke, 2018).

Innovation in technology and the creation of new financial instruments are required to cut expenses and generate funds in a timely and efficient manner.

The combination of green finance and fintech is of particular interest to policy makers, especially in developing nations, as they strive to implement the Paris Agreement and achieve the Sustainable Development Goals (SDGs). Fintech enhances green finance's positive influence in terms of the ecological environment and economic structure (Yang et al.,2021).For instance, fintech has been recognized as a factor in driving the adoption of sustainable agricultural practices in China by ensuring access to credit, reducing information disparities, and improving trust levels among farming communities(Yu et al.,2020). Combination of Fintech and green finance can aid in achieving a high quality economic development (Steffen, 2018).There exists a considerable causal relationship between green economy and financial technologies(Fu & Mishra,2022). Fintech hastens the growth of green finance by minimizing information asymmetry for investors, increasing efficiency, placing a higher value on natural assets, and encouraging sustainable lifestyles, all of which contribute to robust economic expansion. Digital technology and financial development can make a substantial contribution to long-term development(Sun et al.,2023). Digital finance, defined by the use of digital media such as the Internet, mobile phones, and applications, has the potential to address traditional finance's limitations such as high financial service costs and asymmetric information. For people and businesses, digital finance offers a simple and an effective way to fund environmental projects that promote sustainability(Ozili,2021). This can be achieved through crowdfunding platforms or digital investment platforms that specialize in green investments. Digital finance can also help to promote sustainable practices by providing incentives for environmentally-friendly behaviors, such as reducing energy consumption or using public transport.

CONCLUSION AND SUGGESTIONS

Green investing is environmentally responsible and takes into account the worth of the planet and the natural capital it contains. It also aims to boost human welfare and social eauity while simultaneously lowering environmental hazards and enhancing ecological integrity.. Thanks to increasing awareness about climate change, the green investments are increasing. However, the pace of investments is still not enough to meet sustainable development goals. At the same time, the investments into fossil fuel projects are growing faster than the renewable energy initiatives. This is a matter of concern for the environment. The emergence of green finance instruments has the potential to lessen society's reliance on fossil fuels and ease the globe's journey toward a world with negative carbon emissions. Green bonds, including sovereign green bonds, which are debt instruments of finance, are the largest source of green finance, and have been used widely across the globe. Given the risky nature of new technology renewable projects, there exists a place for green insurance and weather derivatives in the arena of sustainable development(Mori & Fujita,2015;Sun et al.,2020). Concessional financing makes up a considerable part of green finance.The Government should create a healthy market for green bonds. .There is a need of a comprehensive policy for enhancing environmental stewardship and green financing by supporting green technologies to achieve effective energy transition and sustainable development (Madaleno et al.,2022). It is necessary to enact essential supportive policies for renewable generation, with the goal of lowering the capital market bias toward conventional power production technologies(Ng & Tao, 2016) .Investments in green finance shall are determined by several factors such as the awareness regarding climate change(Ozili,2022), innovation(Alharbi et al.,2023), incentives and Government policy(Fabrizio,2013). .A wide usage of digital finance tools or fintech can help in accentuating the pace of green finance(Yang et al.,2021; Tamasiga et al.,2022).

REFERENCES

Agliardi, E., & Agliardi, R. (2019). Financing environmentally-sustainable projects with green bonds. *Environment and Development Economics*, *24*(6), 608–623. doi:10.1017/S1355770X19000020

Akhtaruzzaman, M., Banerjee, A. K., Ghardallou, W., & Umar, Z. (2022). Is greenness an optimal hedge for sectoral stock indices? *Economic Modelling*, *117*, 106030. doi:10.1016/j.econmod.2022.106030

Akomea-Frimpong, I., Adeabah, D., Ofosu, D., & Tenakwah, E. J. (2022). A review of studies on green finance of banks, research gaps and future directions. *Journal of Sustainable Finance & Investment*, *12*(4), 1241–1264. doi:10.1080/20430795.2020.1870202

Alharbi, S. S., Al Mamun, M., Boubaker, S., & Rizvi, S. K. A. (2023). Green finance and renewable energy: A worldwide evidence. *Energy Economics*, *106499*, 106499. Advance online publication. doi:10.1016/j.eneco.2022.106499

Aloui, D., Benkraiem, R., Guesmi, K., & Vigne, S. (2023). The European Central Bank and green finance: How would the green quantitative easing affect the investors' behavior during times of crisis? *International Review of Financial Analysis*, *85*, 102464. doi:10.1016/j.irfa.2022.102464

Bhattacharya, S., Gupta, A., Kar, K., & Owusu, A. (2015, November). Hedging strategies for risk reduction through weather derivatives in renewable energy markets. In *2015 International Conference on Renewable Energy Research and Applications (ICRERA)* (pp. 1190-1195). IEEE. 10.1109/ICRERA.2015.7418597

Chen, Q., Ning, B., Pan, Y., & Xiao, J. (2021). Green finance and outward foreign direct investment: Evidence from a quasi-natural experiment of green insurance in China. *Asia Pacific Journal of Management*, 1–26. doi:10.100710490-020-09750-w

Croutzet, A., & Dabbous, A. (2021). Do FinTech trigger renewable energy use? Evidence from OECD countries. *Renewable Energy, 179*, 1608–1617. doi:10.1016/j.renene.2021.07.144

Dalby, P. A., Gillerhaugen, G. R., Hagspiel, V., Leth-Olsen, T., & Thijssen, J. J. (2018). Green investment under policy uncertainty and Bayesian learning. *Energy, 161*, 1262–1281. doi:10.1016/j.energy.2018.07.137

Day, R., Walker, G., & Simcock, N. (2016). Conceptualising energy use and energy poverty using a capabilities framework. *Energy Policy, 93*, 255–264. doi:10.1016/j.enpol.2016.03.019

Dell'Atti, S., Di Tommaso, C., & Pacelli, V. (2022). Sovereign green bond and country value and risk: Evidence from European Union countries. *Journal of International Financial Management & Accounting, 33*(3), 505–521. doi:10.1111/jifm.12155

Ekholm, T., Ghoddusi, H., Krey, V., & Riahi, K. (2013). The effect of financial constraints on energy-climate scenarios. *Energy Policy, 59*, 562–572. doi:10.1016/j.enpol.2013.04.001

Fabrizio, K. R. (2013). The effect of regulatory uncertainty on investment: Evidence from renewable energy generation. *Journal of Law Economics and Organization, 29*(4), 765–798. doi:10.1093/jleo/ews007

Friede, G., Busch, T., & Bassen, A. (2015). ESG and financial performance: Aggregated evidence from more than 2000 empirical studies. *Journal of Sustainable Finance & Investment, 5*(4), 210–233. doi:10.1080/20430795.2015.1118917

Fu, J., & Mishra, M. (2022). Fintech in the time of COVID– 19: Technological adoption during crises. *Journal of Financial Intermediation, 50*, 100945. doi:10.1016/j.jfi.2021.100945

Hsu, P. H., Tian, X., & Xu, Y. (2014). Financial development and innovation: Cross-country evidence. *Journal of Financial Economics, 112*(1), 116–135. doi:10.1016/j.jfineco.2013.12.002

Karim, S., Naeem, M. A., Hu, M., Zhang, D., & Taghizadeh–Hesary, F. (2022). Determining dependence, centrality, and dynamic networks between green bonds and financial markets. *Journal of Environmental Management, 318*, 115618. doi:10.1016/j.jenvman.2022.115618 PMID:35949085

Kumar, L., Nadeem, F., Sloan, M., Restle-Steinert, J., Deitch, M. J., Ali Naqvi, S., Kumar, A., & Sassanelli, C. (2022). Fostering green finance for sustainable development: A focus on textile and leather small medium enterprises in Pakistan. *Sustainability (Basel), 14*(19), 11908. doi:10.3390u141911908

Kyriakou, S. (2017) Green bond investors demand transparency. *Financial Times*. https://www.ftadviser.com/investments/2017/06/14/green-bond-investors-demand-transparency/.

Lööf, H., Martinsson, G., & Mohammadi, A. (2017). *Finance and Innovative Investment in Environmental Technology: The Case of Sweden (No. 445)*. Royal Institute of Technology, CESIS-Centre of Excellence for Science and Innovation Studies.

Lv, C., Bian, B., Lee, C. C., & He, Z. (2021). Regional gap and the trend of green finance development in China. *Energy Economics, 102*, 105476. doi:10.1016/j.eneco.2021.105476

Madaleno, M., Dogan, E., & Taskin, D. (2022). A step forward on sustainability: The nexus of environmental responsibility, green technology, clean energy and green finance. *Energy Economics, 109*, 105945. doi:10.1016/j.eneco.2022.105945

Marke, A. (Ed.). (2018). *Transforming climate finance and green investment with blockchains* (1st ed.). Elsevier., doi:10.1016/C2017-0-01389-7

Mazzucato, M., & Semieniuk, G. (2018). Financing renewable energy: Who is financing what and why it matters. *Technological Forecasting and Social Change, 127*, 8–22. doi:10.1016/j.techfore.2017.05.021

Mirza, N., Umar, M., Afzal, A., & Firdousi, S. F. (2023). The role of fintech in promoting green finance, and profitability: Evidence from the banking sector in the euro zone. *Economic Analysis and Policy, 78*, 33–40. doi:10.1016/j.eap.2023.02.001

Mori, H., & Fujita, H. (2015). *Application of EPSO to designing a contract model of weather derivatives in smart grid. In 2015 IEEE Congress on Evolutionary Computation (CEC)*. IEEE. https://www.climate-policyinitiative.org/publication/global-landscape-of-climate-finance-a-decade-of-data/, doi:10.1109/CEC.2015.7256909

Mutezo, G., & Mulopo, J. (2021). A review of Africa's transition from fossil fuels to renewable energy using circular economy principles. *Renewable & Sustainable Energy Reviews, 137*, 110609. doi:10.1016/j.rser.2020.110609

Nassiry, D. (2019). The role of fintech in unlocking green finance. In *Handbook of Green Finance* (pp. 315–336). Springer. doi:10.1007/978-981-13-0227-5_27

Nenavath, S. (2022). Impact of fintech and green finance on environmental quality protection in India: By applying the semi-parametric difference-in-differences (SDID). *Renewable Energy, 193*, 913–919. doi:10.1016/j.renene.2022.05.020

Ng, T. H., & Tao, J. Y. (2016). Bond financing for renewable energy in Asia. *Energy Policy, 95*, 509–517. doi:10.1016/j.enpol.2016.03.015

Nobanee, H., Alqubaisi, G. B., Alhameli, A., Alqubaisi, H., Alhammadi, N., Almasahli, S. A., & Wazir, N. (2021). Green and sustainable life insurance: A bibliometric review. *Journal of Risk and Financial Management, 14*(11), 563. doi:10.3390/jrfm14110563

Ozili, P. K. (2021). Digital finance, green finance and social finance: Is there a link? *Financial Internet Quarterly, 17*(1), 1–7. doi:10.2478/fiqf-2021-0001

Ozili, P. K. (2022). Green finance research around the world: A review of literature. *International Journal of Green Economics, 16*(1), 56–75. doi:10.1504/IJGE.2022.125554

Repinski, C. (2017). *Unlocking the potential of green fintech.* Stockholm Green Digital Finance. https://static1.squarespace.com/static/59b29215c027d84ada066d3b/t/5a4f73e6e4966b7a764114ba/1515156458061/stockholm-green-digital-finance-insight-brief-no1-2017.pdf.

Sachs, J. D., Woo, W. T., Yoshino, N., & Taghizadeh-Hesary, F. (2019). Importance of green finance for achieving sustainable development goals and energy security. In *Handbook of Green Finance* (pp. 3–12). Springer., doi:10.1007/978-981-13-0227-5_13

Sisodia, G., Joseph, A., & Dominic, J. (2022). Whether corporate green bonds act as armour during crises? Evidence from a natural experiment. *International Journal of Managerial Finance.*

Steffen, B. (2018). The importance of project finance for renewable energy projects. *Energy Economics*, *69*, 280–294. doi:10.1016/j.eneco.2017.11.006

Sun, B., Li, J., Zhong, S., & Liang, T. (2023). Impact of digital finance on energy-based carbon intensity: Evidence from mediating effects perspective. *Journal of Environmental Management*, *327*, 116832. doi:10.1016/j.jenvman.2022.116832 PMID:36462482

Sun, Y., Bi, K., & Yin, S. (2020). Measuring and integrating risk management into green innovation practices for green manufacturing under the global value chain. *Sustainability (Basel)*, *12*(2), 545. doi:10.3390u12020545

Tamasiga, P., Onyeaka, H., & Ouassou, E. H. (2022). Unlocking the Green Economy in African Countries: An Integrated Framework of FinTech as an Enabler of the Transition to Sustainability. *Energies*, *15*(22), 8658. doi:10.3390/en15228658

Wang, C., Nie, P. Y., Peng, D. H., & Li, Z. H. (2017). Green insurance subsidy for promoting clean production innovation. *Journal of Cleaner Production*, *148*, 111–117. doi:10.1016/j.jclepro.2017.01.145

Yang, C. C., Brockett, P. L., & Wen, M. M. (2009). Basis risk and hedging efficiency of weather derivatives. *The Journal of Risk Finance*, *10*(5), 517–536. doi:10.1108/15265940911001411

Yang, Y., Su, X., & Yao, S. (2021). Nexus between green finance, fintech, and high-quality economic development: Empirical evidence from China. *Resources Policy*, *74*, 102445. doi:10.1016/j.resourpol.2021.102445

Yoshino, N., & Taghizadeh-Hesary, F. (2019). Optimal credit guarantee ratio for small and medium-sized enterprises' financing: Evidence from Asia. *Economic Analysis and Policy*, *62*, 342–356. doi:10.1016/j.eap.2018.09.011

Yu, L., Zhao, D., Xue, Z., & Gao, Y. (2020). Research on the use of digital finance and the adoption of green control techniques by family farms in China. *Technology in Society*, *62*, 101323. doi:10.1016/j.techsoc.2020.101323

Zhang, D., Zhang, Z., & Managi, S. (2019). A bibliometric analysis on green finance: Current status, development, and future directions. *Finance Research Letters*, *29*, 425–430. doi:10.1016/j.frl.2019.02.003

Zhao, L., Chau, K. Y., Tran, T. K., Sadiq, M., Xuyen, N. T. M., & Phan, T. T. H. (2022). Enhancing green economic recovery through green bonds financing and energy efficiency investments. *Economic Analysis and Policy*, *76*, 488–501. doi:10.1016/j.eap.2022.08.019

Zheng, G. W., Siddik, A. B., Masukujjaman, M., & Fatema, N. (2021). Factors affecting the sustainability performance of financial institutions in Bangladesh: The role of green finance. *Sustainability (Basel)*, *13*(18), 10165. doi:10.3390u131810165

Chapter 21
Scaling Up of Wood Waste Utilization for Sustainable Green Future

C. Shibu
Kerala Agricultural University, India

Sunandani Chandel
Kerala Agricultural University, India

Preeti Vats
Kerala Agricultural University, India

ABSTRACT

Utilization of wood waste for sustainable production is becoming increasingly important in the current environmental and economic scenario. Various types of wood waste are generated by different industries. The current practices of wood waste recycling and reuse exhibit several benefits and limitations. The various technological innovations include the production of biofuels, engineered wood products, nanomaterials, animal bedding, and other potential applications. The importance of using wood waste for sustainable production includes various technological, environmental, economic, and social implications. Thus, the scaling of wood waste utilization for sustainable green production is a new age tool that offers immense potential for achieving sustainable development goals.

INTRODUCTION

Utilization of wood waste for sustainable production is becoming increasingly important in the current environmental and economic scenario. The production of wood waste is a significant challenge for many industries, but it also offers opportunities for sustainable production practices. The term "wood waste" refers to discarded wood products from a variety of sources, such as wood packaging, construction and demolition sites, the wood processing industry, private households, and railway construction (Van et

DOI: 10.4018/978-1-6684-8969-7.ch021

al., 2007). However, the wood waste derived from diverse sources can be technologically utilized for producing various value-added products, such as lignocellulosic materials (Packalen et al., 2017). renewable and clean energy sources (biofuels) (Mendieta et al., 2021), engineered wood products (Yadav and Kumar, 2021), wood plastic composites (Carus et al., 2014), activated carbon and biochar (Yan et al., 2020)., nanomaterials (such as nanocellulose, carbon quantum dots, and 3D printing) (Han et al., 2022), as well as construction and pharmaceutical chemicals. In addition to this ever-increasing climate instability all over the worldwide has reinforced the need to transform it into more environmentally friendly value-added products (Corona et al., 2020).

Regarding sustainability, waste-to-energy (WTE) is a promising concept that holds great potential for establishing more sustainable matrices and generating energy. Wood waste is a significant by-product of the lumber industry and other wood processing activities, produced during the production and processing of timber, as well as at the end of the lifecycle of wood products, such as old furniture or construction debris. Mismanagement of this waste can result in environmental pollution and the loss of valuable resources. Fortunately, advancements in technology have been made to utilize this waste in a sustainable and economically feasible manner. Thus, this chapter aims to provide an overview of the utilization of wood waste for sustainable production and economic considerations and several challenges associated with it.

PRODUCTION OF WOOD WASTE

More than half of harvested wood is turned into wood waste (Figure 1) during production and processing of wood in industries during its life cycle *viz.* construction, furniture, packaging, and paper. However, the extent and characteristics of wood waste generated can be influenced by several factors such as size, quality (physical and mechanical properties), and contamination. Forestry operations and sawmills typically generate maximum amount of wastage in the form of logging residues, including treetops and stumps, as well as sawmills residues such as sawdust, wood chips, and bark. Wood waste from forestry sector is categorized as primary residues (by-products from forest management activities aimed at roundwood production), secondary residues (by-products from the industrial processing of roundwood), and tertiary residues (post-consumer wood) (FAO, 2023). The construction industry generates wood waste from a variety of sources, including framing lumber, plywood, particleboard, and other wood-based materials. Similarly, the furniture industry contributes to the issue by producing sawdust, wood chips, and scraps during manufacturing. The packaging industry also contributes to wood waste in the form of pallets, crates, and other wooden containers used to transport goods. Finally, the paper industry generates wood waste during the production of paper and paper products, in the form of pulpwood, wood chips, and sawdust. Effective waste management strategies such as recycling, repurposing, and conversion of wood waste into usable products, along with the implementation of closed-loop production systems, can mitigate the environmental impact of wood waste and maximize the utilization of raw materials. These strategies have significant potential to promote sustainability in various industries and contribute to the development of a circular economy (Pandey, 2020).

Figure 1. Wood waste production and woody biomass streams from forest land base and trees outside of forests

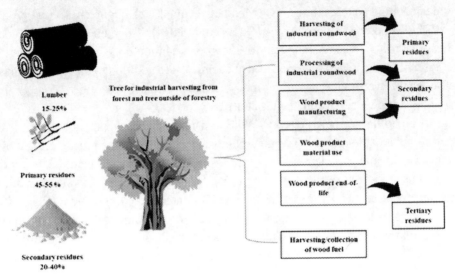

WOOD WASTE CLASSIFICATION

However, a standard definition for this type of waste has yet to be established (Vis et al., 2016). Therefore, different countries and sectors have created their own standards to define and classify it and despite of this, wood waste serve as a valuable secondary source of raw material. Broadly, wood waste can be classified into two categories, namely virgin and non-virgin wood waste, as illustrated in Figure 2.

Virgin wood waste is derived from areas where trees have been felled or log processing operations that are not harmful to the environment or human health. This type of wood may not be considered waste if it is reused for the same purpose as virgin timber. For example, in the production of fuel wood, both logs and residues can be used for fuel or composite production, such as particle board and fiberboard (MDF). However, the residues of structural logs are considered wood waste, which have lower economic value than virgin logs. Non-virgin wood waste is derived from construction, demolition, composite production, and other wood product manufacturing operations.

Figure 2. General classification of wood waste

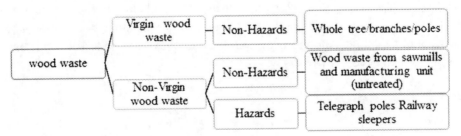

Hazardous wood waste may have encountered toxic substances during its life cycle, which can harm humans or the environment. This type of wood waste cannot be easily distinguished from non-hazardous wood waste and requires laboratory analysis for classification. Non-hazardous wood waste may or may not have been chemically treated, and its disposal does not have any adverse impacts on human health or the environment. Waste can be defined as "any substance or object that the holder discards, intends to discard, or is required to discard" (Besserer et al., 2021).

Faraca et al. (2019) tried to classify the wood waste according to origin and its types and level of contamination (Table 1). Initially wood waste classified based on its origin and followed to types based on presence or absence of MDF and finally "type" classified into various classes based on level of impurities in wood waste.

Table 1. Classification of wood waste based on its origin

Origin	Type	Level
Off-cuts	Off-cuts, left-over or large wood chips (solid wood/untreated)	Class 1 and 2
	Off-cuts, with MDF a and/or treated wood	Class 3
Packaging	Pallets, (untreated, no MDF)	Class 1 and 2
	Pallets, with MDF and/or treated wood	Class 3
	Other wood packaging, clean wood (crates, boxes, etc.)	Class 1 and 2
Construction and demolition	Wood from Construction and demolition and rebuilding, solid wood or with engineered wood construction (no MDF) a indoor use	Class 1 and 2
	Old wood from demolition and rebuilding, with MDF and/or treated wood, indoor use	Class 3
Furniture	Furniture, solid wood or with engineered wood construction (no MDF)	Class 1 and 2
	Furniture, with MDF and/or treated wood	Class 3
	Furniture, upholstered	Class 3
Others	Impregnated wood treated with creosote/ CCA/PCP	Class 4
	Composite building materials from C&D	Class 3
	Wood, rotten or covered by plants	Class 3
	Miscellaneous (items made out of glass, plastic, cardboard metal)	Class 3

CURRENT PRACTICES AND TECHNOLOGICAL INNOVATIONS FOR WOOD WASTE UTILISATION

Adoption of more defensible matrices and energy generation (waste-to-energy (WTE) concept) has significant potential for various industries and provides enormous potential for sustainable wood waste management. This potential can be realised in the effective management of wood waste, which is a significant byproduct of the lumber industry and other wood processing activities. Technological advances have paved the way for innovative solutions that enable the sustainable and economically viable utilisation of wood waste. Companies can develop efficient systems and processes for handling wood waste responsibly by using more defensible matrices. Adopting these practises not only contributes to the circular economy but also aids in the transition to a greener and more sustainable future. These technological innovations have the potential to significantly reduce the amount of wood waste generated by the lumber industry and other wood processing activities while also creating new economic opportunities. In recent years, there has been an increasing interest in advanced conversion technologies that can transform wood into value-added products and reduce waste. These technologies offer several advantages over traditional conversion methods, including higher efficiency, lower environmental impact, and improved product quality (Demirbas, 2011).

Traditional Technologies

Direct Combustion

The primary approach to producing energy from wood waste is by directly burning it, creating heat which is then converted into electricity by turbines (Corona et al., 2020). This method has benefits like decreased reliance on fossil fuels and the establishment of a market for wood waste. However, older technology used in direct combustion can lead to air pollution.

Palletization

It involves compressing wood waste into small and consistent pellets for use as fuel, has become increasingly popular, particularly in Europe for domestic heating. Wood pellets have a high energy density and low moisture content, making them a useful and efficient fuel source. Nevertheless, this process has some limitations, including the necessity for specialised equipment and high transportation costs (Hoefnagels et al., 2014).

Pyrolysis

Pyrolysis is a thermal decomposition at 400-600°C in the absence of oxygen that converts biomass, including wood, into a liquid bio-oil, a solid biochar, and a gaseous mixture of carbon dioxide, carbon monoxide, and hydrogen. The resulting bio-oil can be upgraded into a range of biofuels, like gasoline, diesel, and jet fuel, while the biochar can be used as a soil amendment and a carbon sequestration material. Pyrolysis has several advantages over traditional conversion methods, including higher efficiency and lower emissions. Other technologies available are palletization, pyro-plasma, and flash pyrolysis (Kumar, 2000).

To counter the disadvantages of pyrolysis, torrefaction, a mild pyrolysis, converts biomass, including wood, into a more stable and energy-dense material *viz.* heating the wood to a temperature of 200-300°C in the absence of oxygen (Wang et al., 2020). Removal of moisture and volatile compounds leaves behind a dry and carbon-rich material. Torrefied wood has several advantages over raw wood, including higher energy density, improved grind ability, and better combustion properties. It is proven to be used as a feedstock for producing bio-based chemicals (Chen et al., 2018).

Hydrothermal Carbonization

Hydrothermal carbonization (HTC) is a process that converts biomass, including wood, into a solid hydro char through a combination of temperatures of 180-250°C and a pressure of 20-30 bar in an aqueous medium. The resulting hydro char has higher energy density, improved stability, and better combustion properties similar to lignite. Gao et al. (2016) showed HTC from Eucalyptus bark with high HHV (High Heating Value) as compared to raw material.

Liquefaction

Liquefaction is another process that converts wood into a liquid product using solvents or catalysts by breaking down the wood into its constituent lignocellulosic components, such as cellulose, hemicellulose, and lignin, using a solvent or catalyst. The resulting liquid product can be used as a feedstock to produce chemicals and materials, such as adhesives, coatings, and plastics (Kim and Pal, 2010; Olszewski et al., 2021).

Biorefinery is a process that integrates various conversion technologies (thermo-chemical, biochemical, and physical conversion methods) to produce a range of products from wood, including fuels, chemicals, and materials. For example (Liu et al., 2022; Wang et al., 2022), wood can be first converted into a liquid bio-oil through pyrolysis or liquefaction, which can then be upgraded into different biofuels and chemicals.

Heat exchangers are a critical component of waste heat recovery systems, as they transfer heat from the waste stream to the working fluid. For example, a study by Chai and Tassou (2020) found that a new type of heat exchanger made from aluminium had a higher thermal conductivity than traditional copper heat exchangers, leading to improved heat transfer and overall system efficiency. Advancements in Organic Rankine Cycle Technology (ORC) is a widely used technology for converting waste heat into electricity. In recent years, there have been significant advancements in ORC technology that have improved its efficiency and reliability. For example, a study by Feng et al. (2020) found that using a regenerative organic Rankine cycle (RORC) system could improve the efficiency of waste heat recovery systems by up to 10%, compared to traditional ORC systems. RORC systems use a heat regenerator to increase the temperature of the working fluid before it enters the evaporator, improving the overall efficiency of the system.

Integration with Renewable Energy Sources is another innovation in waste heat recovery systems is their integration with renewable energy sources, such as solar and wind power. By combining waste heat recovery systems with renewable energy sources, it is possible to create a more sustainable and reliable energy system. For example, a study by Wang et al. (2021) found that combining a waste heat recovery system with a solar power plant could increase overall energy efficiency by up to 25%, compared to using the systems separately. There are many examples of waste heat recovery systems being successfully implemented in a variety of industries. For example, a study by Verma et al. (2021) found that a waste heat recovery system in a cement plant was able to generate 5.5 MW of electricity, reducing the plant's energy costs and carbon emissions. Another study by Wu et al. (2020) found that a waste heat recovery system in a steel mill was able to recover over 70% of the waste heat generated by the mill, improving the mill's energy efficiency and reducing its environmental impact.

Advanced Technologies

Thus, advanced conversion technologies offer several advantages over traditional conversion methods, including higher efficiency, lower environmental impact, and improved product quality. These technologies can help reduce waste and increase the value of wood as a renewable and sustainable resource. In the context of wood waste utilization, to optimize these operations digitization (use of technology to streamline processes) tools can help to track waste, identify opportunities for recycling, and reduce waste generation. Below are some of the digitalization tools that can be used to manage wood waste *viz.*

Waste Management Software

These can be used to track and manage wood waste generated by a company. The software can be customized to track waste at different stages of the process, from initial production to final disposal. This tool can help to identify areas where waste is being generated and allow companies to take corrective action to reduce waste production (Pinho and Calmon, 2023).

Internet of Things (IoT)

Maksimovic (2018) highlighted the efficiency of IoT sensors that can be potentially used to monitor the flow of wood waste throughout the production process. These sensors can be installed at various stages of the production process to measure factors such as moisture content, temperature, and humidity. By monitoring these factors, companies can optimize the production process to reduce waste generation. One of the primary benefits of IoT sensors is their ability to provide real-time data. By collecting data in real time, companies can quickly identify issues and take corrective action to reduce waste generation. For example, if an IoT sensor detects that the moisture content of a batch of wood waste is too high, the company can take corrective action to reduce the moisture content and prevent waste generation. IoT sensors can also be used to track the flow of wood waste through the production process. By installing sensors at various stages of the production process, companies can track the movement of waste and identify areas where waste is being generated. This information can then be used to optimize the production process and reduce waste generation. Another benefit of IoT sensors is their ability to communicate with other systems. For example, IoT sensors can be integrated with waste management software to provide a more comprehensive view of waste generation. This integration can help companies to identify patterns and trends in waste generation and develop strategies to reduce waste. In addition to their use in waste management, IoT sensors can also be used to monitor environmental conditions such as air quality and water quality. By monitoring these conditions, companies can take corrective action to reduce environmental impact and improve sustainability.

Data Analytics Tools

These can be used to analyze data collected by waste management software and IoT sensors. By analyzing this data, companies can identify patterns and trends in waste generation and develop strategies to reduce waste. For example, data analytics tools can be used to identify products that generate the most waste and develop strategies to reduce waste production.

Recycling Technologies

There are various digital recycling technologies available that can help to convert wood waste into usable products. For example, pyrolysis technology can be used to convert wood waste into biochar, which can be used as a soil amendment. Similarly, gasification technology can be used to convert wood waste into energy.

Artificial intelligence, data analytics, and automation also, in the context of wood waste utilization, can be categorised as Industry 4.0 and be used to optimize the production process, reduce waste generation, and improve environmental sustainability.

One of the primary benefits of Industry 4.0 in wood waste utilization is its ability to provide real-time data. By collecting data in real time, companies can quickly identify issues and take corrective action to reduce waste generation. Robotic technologies are increasingly being used in various industries, including waste management, to automate processes that are traditionally done by human workers. In the context of wood waste utilization, robotics can be used for sorting and processing wood waste. Sorting is an essential step in wood waste utilization. It involves separating the wood waste into different categories based on its properties such as size, type, and quality. Traditionally, this task is done by human workers, but it can be time-consuming and physically demanding. With the advent of robotic technologies, sorting wood waste can now be automated. Robotic sorting systems use sensors (Grigorev et al., 2021) and cameras to detect and analyse different types of wood waste. Once the wood waste is identified, the robotic arm sorts it into different categories based on its properties. Robotic sorting systems can sort wood waste more quickly and accurately than human workers, reducing errors and improving efficiency. Processing is another important step in wood waste utilization. Processing involves converting wood waste into different products, such as wood pellets or biofuels. Traditionally, this task is done using heavy machinery, which can be expensive and time-consuming. With the advent of robotic technologies, wood waste processing can now be automated.

APPLICATIONS OF WOOD WASTE FOR SUSTAINABLE PRODUCTION

The increasing climate instability all around the world has laid more emphasis on its conversion into more eco-friendly value-added products. Wood waste substantially contributes towards sustainable productivity. The waste coming from different sources can be technological used for generation of several value-added products *viz.* renewable and clean energy sources (bio-fuels), engineered wood products, wood plastic composites, activated carbon and biochar, nano-materials (nanocellulose, carbon quantum dots and 3D printing), construction, pharmaceutical chemicals, etc.

Energy Generation

In the last few decades, a drastic shift has been recorded in waste wood utilization as a feedstock for energy generation owing to its cost effectiveness and reduced emission of greenhouse gases (GHG) (Corona et al., 2020). In several European countries, the demand for waste wood for energy generation has become a substantial process in meeting the increasing demands for renewable energy (Kupeic, 2021). In India, many policy makers are efficiently promoting the sustainable utilization of waste wood for energy generation. Late back in November 2010, Renewable Energy Certificate (REC) commission was laid down by the government of India under India's National Action Plan on Climate Change (NAPCC). The government has also rationalized the Biomass Pellets for Power Generation (BPPG) (Purohit and Chaturvedi, 2018). Several types of wood waste, such as chips, unwanted logs and sawdust, generated from wood working mills can be potentially used for the production of second-generation biofuels *viz.* Bioethanol and Bio-ethylene using sustainable value addition technologies such as thermochemical and biochemical conversions (Lee et al., 2019; Mendietà et al., 2021).

Mulch Production

Mulches are layers of soil used for weed control, protecting roots from temperature changes, reducing water loss, and enhancing aesthetics. Wood chips, with high levels of lignin, tannins, and complex compounds, slowly absorb water and provide nutrients, making them environmentally sustainable for developed countries' gardens and green spaces. Chalker (2007) states that producing mulch from wood waste has several advantages, including reducing the demand for virgin wood fibre, creating a market for wood waste, and reducing greenhouse gas emissions. However, this process requires specialised equipment.

Animal Bedding

Animal bedding involves using wood waste as a raw material for producing bedding for livestock, such as dairy cows and horses. This process has several benefits, including reducing the need for virgin wood fibre, creating a market for wood waste, and improving animal welfare. However, this process also has some limitations, including the potential for contamination from paint, chemicals, and other contaminants. Panivivat et al. (2004) state that using wood waste to produce animal bedding has several benefits, including improving animal welfare, reducing the need for virgin wood fibre, and creating a market for wood waste.

Engineered Wood Products

Several engineered wood products such as Medium Density Fibreboard (MDF), Oriented Strand Board (OSB), Particle Board (PB) and Wooden I Beam are effectively manufactured from various forms of waste wood (Yadav and Kumar, 2021). The engineered wood products produced using waste wood is considered as a valuable sustainable technology. The wood/ timber waste generated from the forests, industries and wooden construction are being potentially used to prepare the cement-bonded particleboards in Hong Kong. These are often regarded as new age engineered wood products. The cement-bonded wood/ timber waste particleboards are a sustainable construction material owing to its light weight, enhanced structure and durability, thermal and noise insulating properties. Thus, cement-based particleboards offer great advantage in comparison to tradition particleboards *viz*. eco-friendly, cost-effective, and nontoxic in nature. However, this area needs to be further explored for better enhancements of strength and durability for use in constructional purposes (Wang et al., 2016; Pandey, 2020).

Wood Plastic Composites (WPC)

In recent years, the wood plastic composites have gained immense importance in different sectors, *viz*. automotive industry, decking, fencing, printed circuit boards, siding, and furniture industry all over the globe. The major producers of WPC are North America, China and Europe (Carus et al., 2014). WPC are often constructed using wood fibres and plastics. Thus, inclusion of the waste wood in WPC is a crucial step towards the sustainable and cost-effective utilization of waste wood for diversifying the composite constitution (Keskisaari and Karki, 2018). Nowadays, researchers are effectively using wood waste (wood flour, shavings and broken pieces and old furniture), recycled plastics (Polyesterene, PVC, etc.) in association with the cross-linkers to develop WPC. Then, again, at the end of product life, these are being crushed and potentially used as raw material for WPC (Khare et al., 2023).

Activated Carbon and Biochar

The sustainable utilization of waste wood includes efficient conversion to activated carbon and charcoal. The activated carbon produced from the waste woods in Domtar provided excellent properties over the traditional raw material, *viz.* Increased surface area and volumes of pores through CO_2 pyrolysis/ gasification (Yan et al., 2020). The waste wood-based bio-chars and activated carbons act as a potential absorbent for heavy metal and toxic dyes. The wood waste-based absorbent is cost-effective and is substantially a significant step towards the reduction of emissions *i.e.,* "*Zero Emission Concept*". Thus, value addition of waste wood using carbonization techniques is the need of the hour for production of sustainable bio-absorbents.

In the past few years, huge documentation has been done regarding lab scale production of activated carbon and biochar from wood waste. However, production on a large scale is still lacking due to variation in consistent production parameters, which ultimately affects the quality of end product (Samsudin et al., 2022).

Nano-Materials

Increased wood usage in the past decade has lead to the production of huge waste, which is growing concern for the sustainability of our planet. With the advancements in technology nowadays, nanotechnology has the potential to develop advanced value-added products from waste wood. Zikeli et al. (2019) laid down the emphasis on sustainable utilization of Iroko (*Milicia excelsa* (Welw.) C.C. Berg) and Norway spruce (*Picea abies* (L.) H. Karst.) waste wood in Italy. They demonstrated the proper circular economy of wood by employing the nanotechnology to develop lignin-based nanoparticles as a potential surface protectant owing to presence of "*chlorophorin* and *alfafuran*" (aromatic compounds) than enhanced the wood protection against harmful UV radiations. Further, the 3D anisotropic wood structure composed of amorphous and crystalline complex of cellulose, hemi-cellulose and lignin offers the opportunity to develop aerogel. The wood-based aerogels are gaining immense popularity as a sustainable construction material owing to high thermal and fire resistance properties as well as a potential step towards the carbon neutrality (Han et al., 2022). Gao et al. (2019) laid down the emphasis on the advanced techniques to utilize waste larch wood powder to produce carbon quantum dots and their application as a photo-catalyst. The carbon quantum dots are used as an eco-friendly photoluminescent particles having applications in wide range of fields *viz.* bioimaging, 3D printing, drug delivery and heavy metals.

Despite the benefits of wood waste recycling and reuse, there are also several challenges and limitations associated with these practices. One of the main challenges is the quality and consistency of wood waste feedstocks, which can vary significantly depending on the source and processing method. This variability can make it difficult to use wood waste in some applications, such as composite panel production, which requires consistent raw materials. Another challenge is the logistics of collecting and transporting wood waste, which can be complex and costly, particularly in rural areas where there may be limited infrastructure.

SUSTAINABLE WOOD UTILIZATION ASSESSMENT TECHNIQUES

Circular Economy

The well-developed nations *viz.* "European Union" lays an emphasis towards the sustainable utilization of bio-waste through the concept of *"circular economy"* (Figure 3). The idea was first popularized in late 1966 by Boulding (Boulding, 1966). Nowadays, the concept of circular economy is successfully implemented as a policy procedure in many countries, including Europe, China and Japan (Ghisellini et al., 2016). The waste management framework is composed of 3R's *viz.* Reduce, Reuse and Recycle. However, often when these frameworks and policies are implemented, the relationship dynamics co-exist between the various factors, dealing with sustainability should be taken into account, *viz. economic, social* and *environmental* (Geissdoerfer et al., 2017).

Figure 3. Cascading use of wood
(Source: https://mobil.wwf.de/fileadmin/fm-wwf/PublikationenPDF/Infographic_One_simple_example_of_cascading_use_of_wood.pdf.)

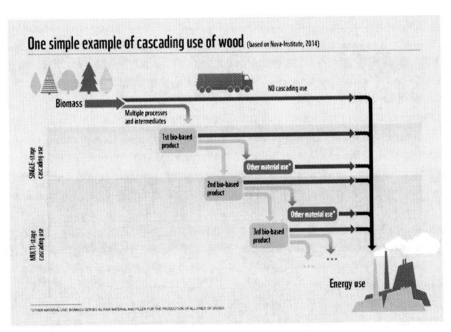

Wood Cascading

In addition to circular economy, *"Wood cascading"* is another important term relevant to sustainable waste wood utilization. The latter term gives more importance to the enhanced biomass utilization among the forest and other biomass related industries. Nowadays, cascading wood is a more sustainable and green option to reduce the pressure on natural forests in order to meet growing demand and supply of wood in different industries. There are various considerations which need to addressed while implementing it (Figure 4) as well their interrelationship with each other (Figure 5).

Thus, WWF in conjunction with Mondi (Global packaging and paper group) carried out a study to evaluate the effect of wood cascading in different countries under the European Commission (Finland, Germany, Poland, Spain, UK) and US (WWF, 2016). Odegard et al. (2012) suggested following approaches for wood cascading:

a) **Cascading in time:** This deals with the sustainable utilization of biomass is sequential order with respect to time. These include energy production (at end-of-life cycle), particle boards, etc.
b) **Cascading in value:** This deals with the sustainable utilization of waste wood by enhancing the maximum utilization during the whole life cycle of that product.
c) **Cascading in function:** This deals with the sustainable utilization of waste wood by optimizing the principle of co-production.

Figure 4. Factors affecting wood cascading implementation
(Jarre et al., 2020)

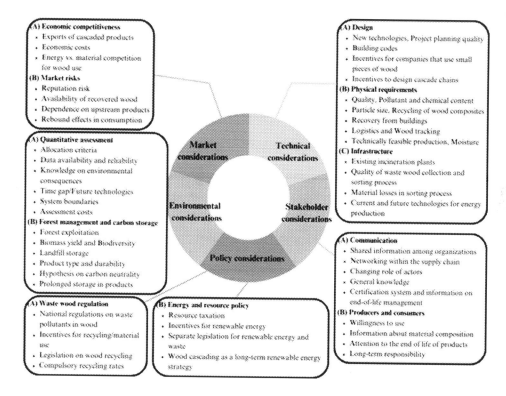

Life Cycle Assessment (LCA)

Wood is a versatile raw material and is extensively used in many industries. However, in respect to sustainability, there is a growing need to maintain an equilibrium co-existing between the growing need and supply of wood. Wood has a huge potential to store carbon dioxide and act as a carbon sink. Thus, during the research projects planning the valuation of the negative impact of wood on the environment needs to be studied judiciously. Thus, the International Standards Organization (ISO14044:2006) recognizes

Life Cycle Assessment (LCA) (Figure 6) and Life Cycle Inventory (LCI) consisting of different phases as an important technique to evaluate the sustainability assessment of any project *viz.* evaluating the impact of a project on the environmental conditions (Finkbeiner et al., 2006). The previous literature highlights the effectiveness of LCA in woody waste biomass recovery studies in different countries such as China, US and France from successful conversion of fresh and dry waste wood for energy production (Hossain & Poon, 2018).

Figure 5. Interrelationship between different factors affecting wood cascading (Jarre et al., 2020)

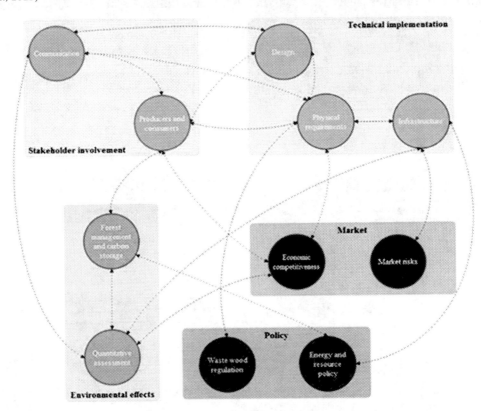

CHALLENGES ASSOCIATED WITH WOOD WASTE USAGE FOR SUSTAINABLE PRODUCTION

The use of wood waste for sustainable production offers a number of potential benefits, including reduced waste, reduced carbon footprint, and increased efficiency. However, there are several challenges associated with using wood waste, including technological (Charis et. al., 2019), economic, environmental, and regulatory factors. The various challenges and opportunities associated with wood waste usage for sustainable production.

Figure 6. Phases of life cycle assessment (LCA)
(Finkbeiner et al., 2006)

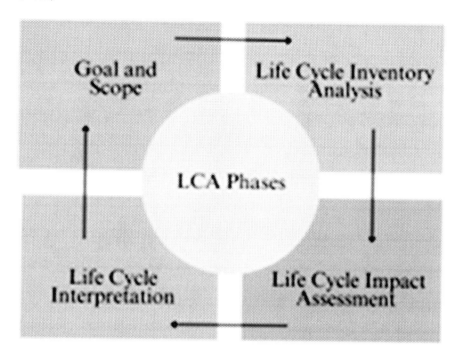

Technological Challenges

Addressing these technological challenges will be essential to maximizing the benefits of using wood waste for sustainable production. These includes:

1. *Size and shape of wood waste:* Wood waste is often irregular in size and shape, which can make it difficult to handle and process efficiently. For example, some wood waste may be too large to fit into equipment designed for smaller materials, or too small to be efficiently processed by larger equipment.
2. *Moisture content:* The moisture content of wood waste can vary widely depending on the source and the storage conditions. High moisture content can make wood waste difficult to process, as it can clog machinery and increase processing time.
3. *Contaminants:* Wood waste may contain contaminants such as dirt, rocks, or metal debris that can damage processing equipment or contaminate the final product.
4. *Storage and transportation:* Wood waste can be bulky and heavy, which can make it challenging to store and transport. Additionally, the storage and transportation of wood waste can result in additional costs and environmental impacts.
5. *Availability and consistency of supply:* The availability and consistency of wood waste supply can vary depending on the location, season, and other factors. This can make it difficult to plan and implement sustainable production processes that rely on wood waste.

6. *Compatibility with existing equipment and processes:* Wood waste usage for sustainable production may require modifications to existing equipment and processes, which can increase costs and require additional expertise.

Economic Challenges

Along with these technological challenges, some potential economic challenges could also be associated with the sustainable utilization of wood (Wang et. al.,2014; Jarre et. al.,2019; Bhattacharyya et. al.,2021):

1. *Reduced supply:* Sustainable utilization of wood often involves harvesting only a portion of the available wood in a forest to maintain its health and biodiversity. This can result in reduced supply and increased costs for wood products, as well as potentially reducing the income of forest-dependent communities and businesses.
2. *High certification costs:* Certification schemes such as the Forest Stewardship Council (FSC) can help ensure that wood is sustainably harvested, but the cost of certification can be high for small-scale producers. This can create a barrier to entry for these producers and limit their ability to compete in the marketplace.
3. *Lack of market demand:* Even if wood is sustainably harvested, there may not be enough market demand for sustainably sourced wood products to make it economically viable for producers. This could be due to factors such as consumer preference for cheaper, non-sustainably sourced products, or a lack of awareness about the benefits of sustainable wood products.
4. *Inconsistent enforcement:* In some cases, regulations and laws aimed at promoting sustainable utilization of wood may not be consistently enforced, leading to unfair competition and potentially incentivizing unsustainable practices.
5. *Limited access to finance:* Sustainable forestry practices often require significant investment in equipment, training, and infrastructure, which can be a barrier for small-scale producers and forest-dependent communities who may have limited access to finance.
6. *Competition with other land uses:* In some cases, land may be more valuable for other uses such as agriculture, mining, or real estate development, leading to pressure to convert forests to these alternative uses instead of sustainably utilizing the wood.

These are just a few potential economic challenges associated with the sustainable utilization of wood. It's important to note, however, that there are also economic benefits to sustainable forestry practices, such as promoting long-term economic viability, generating jobs and income for forest-dependent communities, and reducing costs associated with environmental degradation.

Environmental Challenges

Here are some potential environmental challenges associated with the sustainable utilization of wood (Demirbas, 2005; Buonocore et. al., 2019; Fort et. al., 2020):

1. *Deforestation and habitat loss:* Although sustainable utilization of wood is intended to be less damaging to forests than other practices, it still involves the removal of trees. Depending on the scale and intensity of the harvesting, this can result in deforestation and habitat loss for wildlife.

2. *Soil erosion:* Removing trees can leave soil exposed and vulnerable to erosion, which can harm the health of the forest ecosystem and surrounding waterways.
3. *Degradation of ecosystem services:* Forests provide a range of ecosystem services, such as carbon sequestration, water regulation, and biodiversity conservation. If these services are not taken into account in sustainable forest management practices, there is a risk of degradation and loss of these services over time.
4. *Forest fragmentation:* Sustainable utilization of wood often involves selective harvesting of trees, which can result in the fragmentation of forested areas. This can disrupt wildlife movement and genetic exchange and can also make forests more vulnerable to invasive species and other threats.
5. *Carbon emissions:* Although wood is a renewable resource, harvesting and processing it can result in carbon emissions if done unsustainably. For example, if harvesting is done at too high a rate or in a way that damages the forest floor, the soil may release carbon dioxide and other greenhouse gases.
6. *Social and cultural impacts:* Forests are often home to indigenous and local communities who rely on them for food, medicine, and cultural practices. Unsustainable utilization of wood can disrupt these communities and their traditional ways of life.

Regulatory Challenges

Potential regulatory challenges associated with the sustainable utilization of wood are important to recognize and work to address them in order to promote truly sustainable forest management practices. These include:

1. *Inadequate enforcement:* Regulations and laws aimed at promoting sustainable utilization of wood may not be consistently enforced, which can create a barrier to the development of a sustainable wood industry. This can also result in unfair competition and incentivize unsustainable practices.
2. *Complex regulatory frameworks:* The regulatory frameworks surrounding the sustainable utilization of wood can be complex and difficult to navigate, particularly for small-scale producers. This can create a barrier to entry and limit the ability of small-scale producers to participate in the sustainable wood industry.
3. *Inconsistent regulations:* Regulations related to the sustainable utilization of wood can vary widely between different regions and countries, which can create confusion and uncertainty for producers and consumers. This can also lead to inconsistencies in enforcement and a lack of coherence in the global wood market.
4. *Lack of coordination:* There may be a lack of coordination between different regulatory bodies and stakeholders involved in the sustainable wood industry. This can result in duplication of efforts, conflicting regulations, and inefficiencies.
5. *Limited resources for monitoring and enforcement:* Monitoring and enforcing sustainable wood regulations can require significant resources, which may not always be available, particularly in developing countries. This can limit the effectiveness of these regulations and make it more difficult to ensure sustainable wood production (Salmi *et.al.*, 2022).

6. ***Difficulty in measuring and verifying sustainability:*** It can be challenging to accurately measure and verify sustainability in the wood industry. Certification schemes such as the Forest Stewardship Council (FSC) can help to address this challenge, but they can be expensive and difficult to implement, particularly for small-scale producers (Proskurina *et. al.*, 2016).

Addressing all these challenges will require collaboration and coordination between different stakeholders, as well as ongoing efforts to develop an effective and efficient regulatory framework.

OPPORTUNITIES AND RECOMMENDATIONS FOR INCREASING WOOD WASTE USAGE FOR SUSTAINABLE PRODUCTION

On the other hand, the wood waste utilization industry offers several opportunities for innovation and growth. These include:

1. ***Development of new products:*** Wood waste can be used to create a variety of new products, such as composite materials, biofuels, and chemicals. Innovations in processing technologies can enable the development of these new products, creating opportunities for growth in the industry.
2. ***Advanced circular economy:*** Wood waste utilization can play an important role in advancing the circular economy, where waste is transformed into new products and materials. Innovations in recycling and reusing wood waste can reduce the environmental impact of the industry and create opportunities for growth.
3. ***Improved energy efficiency:*** Wood waste can be used as a source of renewable energy, such as biomass for power generation. Innovations in energy conversion technologies can improve the efficiency of these processes (Siciliano *et. al.*, 2023), creating new opportunities for growth in the renewable energy sector.
4. ***Enhanced sustainable forest management:*** The utilization of wood waste can contribute to sustainable forest management by reducing waste and increasing resource efficiency. Innovations in forest management practices, such as improved harvesting techniques and better monitoring systems, can create opportunities for growth in the sustainable forest management sector.
5. ***Developing new markets:*** The utilization of wood waste can open up new markets, such as for sustainable packaging materials or for construction materials. Innovations in product design and marketing can help to develop these new markets, creating opportunities for growth in the industry (Ihnat et. al., 2017; 2018).

These are just a few potential opportunities for innovation and growth in the wood waste utilization industry. By embracing these opportunities, the industry can become more sustainable and contribute to the development of a circular and low-carbon economy. The wood waste utilization industry can create new green jobs, particularly in rural areas where forestry and logging are important industries. Innovations in wood waste utilization can help to create new jobs in processing, manufacturing, and research and development. It can support local communities by providing economic opportunities and contributing to sustainable development. Innovations in wood waste utilization can help to create new economic opportunities for local communities, particularly in regions with abundant wood waste resources also to promote sustainable supply chains by reducing waste and promoting resource efficiency. This can improve the sustainability of the industry as a whole, creating opportunities for growth in the sustainable supply chain sector. Collaboration and partnerships between different stakeholders in the industry can create new opportunities for innovation and growth (Otoo and Drechsel, 2018). For example, partnerships between forestry companies, government agencies, and research institutions can help to develop new technologies and business models for the sustainable utilization of wood waste.

There are several strategies and recommendations that stakeholders can implement to increase the utilization of wood waste for sustainable production:

Stakeholder Implications

There are several strategies and recommendations that stakeholders can implement to increase the utilization of wood waste for sustainable production. By implementing these strategies and recommendations, stakeholders can increase the utilization of wood waste for sustainable production. This can help to create economic opportunities, promote sustainable forest management, and contribute to the development of a circular and low-carbon economy.

1. *Encourage policy and regulatory support:* Governments can incentivize the sustainable utilization of wood waste by implementing policies and regulations that support the development of the industry. For example, tax incentives, subsidies, and grants can encourage investments in wood waste utilization technologies and businesses. The Oxley–Sarbanes Act is a prime example of a regulation that came about as a result of some companies not being able to meet stakeholders' needs in so far as financial reporting is concerned (Sharma and Henriques, 2005).
2. *Develop partnerships and collaborations:* Collaboration between stakeholders can help to overcome barriers and foster innovation in wood waste utilization. Partnerships between industry, government, and research institutions can promote knowledge sharing, investment, and market development.
3. *Increase awareness and education:* Raising awareness among consumers, businesses, and governments about the benefits of wood waste utilization can help to create demand for wood waste products and promote sustainable production. Education and outreach campaigns can help to promote the importance of sustainable production and the role of wood waste utilization in achieving sustainability goals.
4. *Invest in research and development:* Investment in research and development can help to improve wood waste utilization technologies, increase efficiency, and develop new products and markets. Research can also help to identify new opportunities for wood waste utilization and support sustainable forest management practices. Companies can invest in research and development to develop new technologies and products that use wood waste. This can include technologies for recycling, energy production, and material development.
5. *Enhance supply chain management:* Improving supply chain management can help to increase the efficiency of wood waste utilization and reduce waste. This can include strategies such as optimizing logistics, reducing transportation costs, and implementing traceability systems.
6. *Promote circular economy principles:* Embracing circular economy principles (Unal et al., 2019), such as reducing waste and promoting reuse and recycling, can help to create a more sustainable and efficient wood waste utilization industry. This can include strategies such as incorporating recycled wood waste into new products, promoting the reuse of wood waste, and designing products for recyclability.

Policy Initiative Implications

The following policy recommendations and incentives that can support the sustainable utilization of wood waste include:

1. *Tax incentives and grants:* Governments can provide tax incentives or grants to businesses and individuals who invest in wood waste utilization technologies or businesses. Biomass Research and Development Act of 2000 addressed the utilization of wood, wood wastes and residues and grants were awarded to improve cellulosic biomass conversion technologies to biobased products. This can help to promote the adoption of sustainable wood waste practices and encourage innovation in the industry.
2. *Subsidies for sustainable practices:* Wood Building Programme 2016–2022 was launched by the Ministry of the Environment supporting the use of wood in construction and other products (Ministry of the Environment 2020a). It focuses on promoting the use of recycled wood and products in public buildings, and related activities with the provision of subsidies and information services to municipalities. This can encourage companies to reduce their waste and promote sustainable production.
3. *Mandatory wood waste diversion targets:* Governments can set mandatory targets for wood waste diversion, which would require companies to divert a certain percentage of their wood waste from landfill or burning. Three potential co-generation projects in Manicaland, by the Department of Energy (DoE) through the National Biomass Strategy are mind-blowing steps towards augmenting the electricity outlet of the state. It also encourages the development of wood waste utilization technologies and businesses.
4. *Product standards and labelling:* Governments can establish product standards and labelling requirements for wood products that incorporate recycled wood waste. This can increase the demand for wood waste products and promote sustainable production.
5. *Extended producer responsibility:* Governments can implement extended producer responsibility policies, which would require manufacturers to take responsibility for the disposal or recycling of their products, including wood waste. This can encourage companies to design products for recyclability and promote the development of wood waste utilization technologies.
6. *Certification programs:* Certification programs, such as the Forest Stewardship Council (FSC) or Sustainable Forestry Initiative (SFI), can provide incentives for companies to adopt sustainable wood waste practices. Companies that obtain certification can access new markets and demonstrate their commitment to sustainability.

Social Implications

1. *Collaborative research and development:* Collaboration between government, industry, and research institutions can help to promote research and development in wood waste utilization. This can lead to the development of new products, technologies, and markets that support sustainable production.

2. ***Public-private partnerships:*** Governments can establish public-private partnerships to promote the development of wood waste utilization technologies and businesses. These partnerships can leverage the resources and expertise of both the public and private sectors to create sustainable economic growth.
3. ***Innovation challenges:*** Governments and industry associations can sponsor innovation challenges to promote the development of new wood waste utilization technologies and products. These challenges can incentivize entrepreneurs, startups, and researchers to develop innovative solutions to wood waste utilization. Companies can also participate in industry associations that promote the sustainable utilization of wood waste, such as the National Wood Waste Recycling Association or the European Panel Federation.
4. ***Awareness campaigns:*** Governments, industry associations, and non-governmental organizations can launch awareness campaigns to promote the benefits of wood waste utilization and sustainable production. A noteworthy example of a large-scale sustainability project targeted to municipalities, in particular, is the Carbon Neutral Municipalities network (called "Hinku"). These campaigns can educate consumers and businesses about the environmental and economic benefits of wood waste utilization and encourage them to adopt sustainable practices.
5. ***Developing new markets for wood waste products:*** Companies can explore new markets for wood waste products, such as composite materials, biofuels, and bioplastics. This can help to create new revenue streams and reduce waste.
6. ***Sustainable forest management practices:*** Sustainable Forest management practices can help to promote the sustainable utilization of wood waste by ensuring the responsible management of forest resources. This can include strategies such as reducing waste, promoting biodiversity, and protecting ecosystem services.Top of Form Companies can also adopt sustainable practices, such as reducing waste, recycling, and sourcing materials from sustainably managed forests. This can help to reduce the environmental impact of their operations and promote sustainable production.

WASTE WOOD UTILIZATION: SUCCESS STORIES

Fatouma Otoke, a well-known female entrepreneur residing in the Democratic Republic of the Congo, is successfully running a small business which involves sustainable conversion of waste wood generated by industrial sawmill *viz.* CFT (Compagnie Forestiere et de Transformation) into alternative wood fuel *i.e.,* charcoal. This sustainable wood fuel is a boon for forest dwellers residing in Kisangani. Later on in the year 2020, their small business started receiving monetary fund for enhancing their share in local wood fuel market by ***AFEVADES (Association des femmes valorisatrices des déchets de scierie)*** which is jointly run by **Center for International Forestry Research (CIFOR)** and the **European Union.** However, a tremendous increase in women's contribution towards the charcoal value chain has been witnessed in sub-Saharan Africa (Gonzalez, 2021).

The European Commission has always been pioneers in upscaling wood waste utilization. "**Rilegno**" is among the leading Italian National Consortium established in 1997. It deals with sustainable utilization of waste packaging wood and enhancing its value through development of advanced wood products, *viz. Pannels in furniture industry by a* leading producer such as Mauro Saviola Group (Annual turnover - 552 million) and Frati Group. According to the annual budget report of 2022, a total of 1,985,251 tons of waste wood was recycled. However, the consortium categorizes wood recycling and cascading activities into the following groups (Gasperoni, 2019):

a) Producers
b) Suppliers of materials
c) Importers of packaging
d) Wooden packaging recyclers.

CONCLUSION

The utilization of wood waste for sustainable production presents significant opportunities for industries to reduce their environmental impact, lower their production costs, and create new revenue streams. However, it also presents various challenges associated with it at technological, economic and stakeholder's level. In consideration to this the wood utilization offers immense opportunities by considering the stakeholder, policy, and social implications. Thus, the scaling of wood waste utilization for sustainable green production is a new age tool that offers immense potential for achieving the sustainable development goals.

REFERENCES

Besserer, A., Troilo, S., Girods, P., Rogaume, Y., & Brosse, N. (2021). Cascading recycling of wood waste: A review. *Polymers, 13*(11), 1752. doi:10.3390/polym13111752 PMID:34071945

Bhattacharyya, P., Bisen, J., Bhaduri, D., Priyadarsini, S., Munda, S., Chakraborti, M., Adak, T., Panneerselvam, P., Mukherjee, A. K., Swain, S. L., Dash, P. K., Padhy, S. R., Nayak, A. K., Pathak, H., Arora, S., & Nimbrayan, P. (2021). Turn the wheel from waste to wealth: Economic and environmental gain of sustainable rice straw management practices over field burning in reference to India. *The Science of the Total Environment, 775*, 14589. doi:10.1016/j.scitotenv.2021.145896

Boulding, K. (1966). The economy of the coming spaceship earth. In H. Jarret (Ed.), *Environmental quality in a growing economy*. Johns Hopkins Press.

Buonocore, E., Paletto, A., Russo, G. F., & Franzese, P. P. (2019). Indicators of environmental performance to assess wood-based bioenergy production: A case study in Northern Italy. *Journal of Cleaner Production, 221*, 242–248. doi:10.1016/j.jclepro.2019.02.272

Butnaru, E., Stoleru, E., & Brebu, M. (2022). Valorization of forestry residues by thermal methods. The effect of temperature on gradual degradation of structural components in bark from silver fir (Abies alba Mill.). *Industrial Crops and Products, 187*, 115376. doi:10.1016/j.indcrop.2022.115376

Carus, M., Eder, A., Dammer, L., Korte, H., Scholz, L., Essel, R., Breitmayer, E., & Barth, M. (2015). *Wood-plastic composites (WPC) and natural fibre composites (NFC)*. Nova-Institute.

Chai, L., & Tassou, S. A. (2020). A review of printed circuit heat exchangers for helium and supercritical CO_2 Brayton cycles. Thermal Science and Engineering Progress, 18, 100543.Chalker Scott, L., 2007. Impact of mulches on landscape plants and the environment - A review. *Journal of Environmental Horticulture*, 25(4), 239–249.

Charis, G., Danha, G., & Muzenda, E. (2019). A review of timber waste utilization: Challenges and opportunities in Zimbabwe. *Procedia Manufacturing*, 35, 419–429. doi:10.1016/j.promfg.2019.07.005

Chen, W. H., Wang, C. W., Kumar, G., Rousset, P., & Hsieh, T. H. (2018). Effect of torrefaction pretreatment on the pyrolysis of rubber wood sawdust analyzed by Py-GC/MS. *Bioresource Technology*, 259, 469–473. doi:10.1016/j.biortech.2018.03.033 PMID:29580728

Cheng, H., Chen, C., Wu, S., Mirza, Z. A., & Liu, Z. (2017). Emergy evaluation of cropping, poultry rearing, and fish raising systems in the drawdown zone of Three Gorges Reservoir of China. *Journal of Cleaner Production*, 144, 559–571. doi:10.1016/j.jclepro.2016.12.053

Corona, B., Shen, L., Sommersacher, P., & Junginger, M. (2020). Consequential Life Cycle Assessment of energy generation from waste wood and forest residues: The effect of resource-efficient additives. *Journal of Cleaner Production*, 259, 120948. doi:10.1016/j.jclepro.2020.120948

Demirbas, A. (2005). Potential applications of renewable energy sources, biomass combustion problems in boiler power systems and combustion related environmental issues. *Progress in Energy and Combustion Science*, 31(2), 171–192. doi:10.1016/j.pecs.2005.02.002

Demirbas, A. (2011). Waste management, waste resource facilities and waste conversion processes. *Energy Conversion and Management*, 52(2), 1280–1287. doi:10.1016/j.enconman.2010.09.025

FAO. (2023). *The role of wood residues in the transition to sustainable bioenergy*. Food and Agriculture Organization.

Faraca, G., Boldrin, A., & Astrup, T. (2019). Resource quality of wood waste: The importance of physical and chemical impurities in wood waste for recycling. *Waste Management (New York, N.Y.)*, 87, 135–147. doi:10.1016/j.wasman.2019.02.005 PMID:31109513

Feng, Y., Zhang, W., Niaz, H., He, Z., Wang, S., Wang, X., & Liu, Y. (2020). Parametric analysis and thermo-economical optimization of a Supercritical-Subcritical organic Rankine cycle for waste heat utilization. *Energy Conversion and Management*, 212, 112773. doi:10.1016/j.enconman.2020.112773

Finkbeiner, M., Inaba, A., Tan, R., Christiansen, K., & Klüppel, H. J. (2006). The new international standards for life cycle assessment: ISO 14040 and ISO 14044. *The International Journal of Life Cycle Assessment*, 11(2), 80–85. doi:10.1065/lca2006.02.002

Fort, J., Sal, J., Zak, J., & Cerny, R. (2020). Assessment of wood-based fly ash as alternative cement replacement. *Sustainability*, 12(22), 1–16. doi:10.3390u12229580 PMID:35136666

Gao, P., Zhou, Y., Meng, F., Zhang, Y., Liu, Z., Zhang, W., & Xue, G. (2016). Preparation and characterization of hydrochar from waste eucalyptus bark by hydrothermal carbonization. *Energy*, 97, 238–245. doi:10.1016/j.energy.2015.12.123

Gao, X., Gong, X., Nguyen, T. T., Du, W., Chen, X., Song, Z., Chai, R., & Guo, M. (2019). Luminescent materials comprised of wood-based carbon quantum dots adsorbed on a $Ce_{0.7}Zr_{0.3}O_2$ solid solution: Synthesis, photoluminescence properties, and applications in light-emitting diode devices. *Journal of Materials Science, 54*(23), 14469–14482. doi:10.100710853-019-03912-y

Gasperoni, M. (2019, June 6). The cascading use of wood: Best pratices in the wood recycling sector. *Circular Business.* https://www.rilegno.org/rapporto-2022-rilegno/

Ghisellini, P., Cialani, C., & Ulgiati, S. (2016). A review on circular economy: The expected transition to a balanced interplay of environmental and economic systems. *Journal of Cleaner Production, 114,* 11–32. doi:10.1016/j.jclepro.2015.09.007

Gonzalez, A. (2021, May 24). Women entrepreneurs in DRC recover waste wood to produce clean cooking. *Forest News CIFOR.* https://forestsnews.cifor.org/72712/drc-women-entrepreneurs-recover-waste-wood-to-produce-clean-cooking-fuel?fnl=en

Grigorev, I., Shadrin, A., Katkov, S., Borisov, V., Druzyanova, V., Gnatovskaya, I., Diev, R., Kaznacheeva, N., Levushkin, D., & Akinin, D. (2021). Improving the quality of sorting wood chips by scanning and machine vision technology. *Journal of Forest Science, 67*(5), 212–218. doi:10.17221/10/2020-JFS

Han, Z. M., Sun, W. B., Yang, K. P., Yang, H. B., Liu, Z. X., Li, D. H., Yin, C. H., Liu, H. C., Zhao, Y. X., Ling, Z. C., Guan, Q. F., & Yu, S. H. (2023). An All-Natural Wood-Inspired Aerogel. *Angewandte Chemie, 135*(6), e202211099. PMID:36416072

Hoefnagels, R., Junginger, M., & Faaij, A. (2014). The economic potential of wood pellet production from alternative, low-value wood sources in the southeast of the US. *Biomass and Bioenergy, 71,* 443–454. doi:10.1016/j.biombioe.2014.09.006

Hossain, M. U., & Poon, C. S. (2018). Comparative LCA of wood waste management strategies generated from building construction activities. *Journal of Cleaner Production, 177,* 387–397. doi:10.1016/j.jclepro.2017.12.233

Hussain, A., Ali, M., Ali, H. M., Sabir, M. S., & Mehboob, M. (2020). An Experimental Analysis of Waste Heat Recovery Potential from A Rotary Kiln of Cement Industry. *The Nucleus, 57*(1), 33–38.

Ihnat, V., Lubke, H., Russ, A., Pazitny, A., & Boruvka, V. (2018). Waste agglomerated wood materials as a secondary raw material for chipboards and fibreboards part II. Preparation and characterisation of wood fibres in terms of their reuse. *Wood Research, 63*(3), 431–442.

Jarre, M., Petit-Boix, A., Priefer, C., Meyer, R., & Leipold, S. (2020). Transforming the bio-based sector towards a circular economy-What can we learn from wood cascading? *Forest Policy and Economics, 110,* 101872. doi:10.1016/j.forpol.2019.01.017

Keskisaari, A., & Karki, T. (2018). The use of waste materials in wood-plastic composites and their impact on the profitability of the product. *Resources, Conservation and Recycling, 134,* 257–261. doi:10.1016/j.resconrec.2018.03.023

Khare, A. P., Dwivedi, N., & Haq, S. (2023). Potential, Challenges, and Application for Wood–Plastic Composite Fabricated with Several Additives. In G. Du & X. Zhou (Eds.), Wood Industry - Past, Present and Future Outlook (pp. 1 -18). IntechOpen, UK.

Kim, J. K., & Pal, K. (2010). *Recent advances in the processing of wood-plastic composites*. Springer.

Kumar, S. (2000). Technology Options for Municipal Solid Waste-to-energy Project. *TERI Information Monitor on Environmental Science*, 5(1), 1–11.

Kupiec, B. (2021). *Legal status of a renewables self-consumer under Polish law in light of Directive (EU) 2018/2001* European Parliament.

Lee, S. Y., Sankaran, R., Chew, K. W., Tan, C. H., Krishnamoorthy, R., Chu, D. T., & Show, P. L. (2019). Waste to bioenergy: A review on the recent conversion technologies. *Bmc Energy*, 1(1), 1–22. doi:10.118642500-019-0004-7

Liu, S., Wu, G., Syed-Hassan, S. S. A., Li, B., Hu, X., Zhou, J., Huang, Y., Zhang, S., & Zhang, H. (2022). Catalytic pyrolysis of pine wood over char-supported Fe: Bio-oil upgrading and catalyst regeneration by CO_2/H_2O. *Fuel*, 307, 121778. doi:10.1016/j.fuel.2021.121778

Maksimovic, M. (2018). Greening the Future: Green Internet of Things (G-IoT) as a Key Technological Enabler of Sustainable Development. In N. Dey, A.E. Hassanien, C. Bhatt, A. S. Ashour & S.C. Satapathy. (Eds.), *Internet of Things and Big Data Analytics Toward Next-Generation Intelligence* (pp 238-313). Springer Cham Ministry of the Environment. https://ym.fi/en/wood-building

Monica Mendieta, C., Elizabet Cardozo, R., Esteban Felissia, F., Martin Clauser, N., Vallejos, M. E., & Area, M. C. (2021). Bioconversion of Wood Waste to Bio-ethylene: A Review. *BioResources*, 16(2), 4411–4437. doi:10.15376/biores.16.2.Mendieta

Odegard, I., Croezen, H., & Bergsma, G. (2012). *Cascading of Biomass. 13 Solutions for a Sustainable Bio-based Economy. Making Better Choices for Use of Biomass Residues, By-products and Wastes* (Report No. CE-12266552). CE Delft, Netherlands.

Olszewski, A., Kosmela, P., & Piszczyk, Ł. (2022). Synthesis and characterization of biopolyols through biomass liquefaction of wood shavings and their application in the preparation of polyurethane wood composites. *Holz als Roh- und Werkstoff*, 80(1), 57–74. doi:10.100700107-021-01755-6

Otoo, M., & Drechsel, P. (Eds.). (2018). *Resource recovery from waste: business models for energy, nutrient and water reuse in low-and middle-income countries*. Routledge. doi:10.4324/9781315780863

Packalen, T., Karkkainen, L., & Toppinen, A. (2017). The future operating environment of the Finnish sawmill industry in an era of climate change mitigation policies. *Forest Policy and Economics*, 82, 30–40. doi:10.1016/j.forpol.2016.09.017

Pandey, S. (2022). Wood waste utilization and associated product development from under-utilized low-quality wood and its prospects in Nepal. *SN Applied Sciences*, 4(6), 168. doi:10.100742452-022-05061-5

Panivivat, R., Kegley, E. B., Pennington, J. A., Kellogg, D. W., & Krumpelman, S. L. (2004). Growth performance and health of dairy calves bedded with different types of materials. *Journal of Dairy Science*, 87(11), 3736–3745. doi:10.3168/jds.S0022-0302(04)73512-2 PMID:15483157

Pinho, G. C., & Calmon, J. L. (2023). LCA of Wood Waste Management Systems: Guiding Proposal for the Standardization of Studies Based on a Critical Review. *Sustainability (Basel), 15*(3), 1854. doi:10.3390u15031854

Proskurina, S., Rimppi, H., Heinimo, J., Hansson, J., Orlov, A., Raghu, K., & Vakkilainen, E. (2016). Logistical, economic, environmental and regulatory conditions for future wood pellet transportation by sea to Europe: The case of Northwest Russian seaports. *Renewable & Sustainable Energy Reviews, 56*, 38–50. doi:10.1016/j.rser.2015.11.030

Purohit, P., & Chaturvedi, V. (2018). Biomass pellets for power generation in India: A techno-economic evaluation. *Environmental Science and Pollution Research International, 25*(29), 29614–29632. doi:10.100711356-018-2960-8 PMID:30141169

Routa, J., Brannstrom, H., Anttila, P., Makinen, M., Janis, J. and Asikainen, A. (2017). Wood extractives of Finnish pine, spruce and birch–availability and optimal sources of compounds. *Natural resources and bioeconomy studies, 73*, 55.

Salmi, A., Jussila, J., & Hamalainen, M. (2022). The role of municipalities in the transformation towards more sustainable construction: The case of wood construction in Finland. *Construction Management and Economics, 40*(11–12), 934–954. doi:10.1080/01446193.2022.2037145

Samsudin, M. H., Hassan, M. A., Yusoff, M. Z. M., Idris, J., Farid, M. A. A., Lawal, A. B. A., Norrrahim, M. N. F., & Shirai, Y. (2022). Production of nanopore structure bio-adsorbent from wood waste through a self-sustained carbonization process for landfill leachate treatment. *Biochemical Engineering Journal, 189*, 108740. doi:10.1016/j.bej.2022.108740

Sharma, S., & Henriques, I. (2005). Stakeholder influences on sustainability practices in the Canadian forest products industry. *Strategic Management Journal, 26*(2), 159–180. doi:10.1002mj.439

Unal, E., Urbinati, A., Chiaroni, D., & Manzini, R. (2019). Value Creation in Circular Business Models: The case of a US small medium enterprise in the building sector. *Resources, Conservation and Recycling, 146*, 291–307. doi:10.1016/j.resconrec.2018.12.034

Van Benthem, M., Leek, N., Mantau, U., & Weimar, H. (2007). Markets for recovered wood in Europe; case studies for the Netherlands and Germany based on the BioXchange project. In *Proc. of the 3rd European COST E31 Conf*. IEEE.

Verma, Y. K., Mazumdar, B., & Ghosh, P. (2021). Thermal energy consumption and its conservation for a cement production unit. *Environmental Engineering Research, 26*(3).

Vis, M., Mantau, U., & Allen, B. (Eds.). 2016. Study on the optimized cascading use of wood. No 394/PP/ENT/RCH/14/7689. Final report. Brussel.

Wang, K., Gao, S., Lai, C., Xie, Y., Sun, Y., Wang, J., Wang, C., Yong, Q., Chu, F., & Zhang, D. (2022). Upgrading wood biorefinery: An integration strategy for sugar production and reactive lignin preparation. *Industrial Crops and Products, 187*, 115366. doi:10.1016/j.indcrop.2022.115366

Wang, L., Chen, S. S., Tsang, D. C., Poon, C. S., & Shih, K. (2016). Value-added recycling of construction waste wood into noise and thermal insulating cement-bonded particleboards. *Construction & Building Materials*, *125*, 316–325. doi:10.1016/j.conbuildmat.2016.08.053

Wang, L., Toppinen, A., & Juslin, H. (2014). Use of wood in green building: A study of expert perspectives from the UK. *Journal of Cleaner Production*, *65*, 350–361. doi:10.1016/j.jclepro.2013.08.023

Wang, N., Zhan, H., Zhuang, X., Xu, B., Yin, X., Wang, X., & Wu, C. (2020). Torrefaction of waste wood-based panels: More understanding from the combination of upgrading and denitrogenation properties. *Fuel Processing Technology*, *206*(511), 106462. doi:10.1016/j.fuproc.2020.106462

Wang, S., Zhang, L., Liu, C., Liu, Z., Lan, S., Li, Q., & Wang, X. (2021). Techno-economic-environmental evaluation of a combined cooling heating and power system for gas turbine waste heat recovery. *Energy*, *231*, 120956. doi:10.1016/j.energy.2021.120956

Wu, Z., Zhu, P., Yao, J., Zhang, S., Ren, J., Yang, F., & Zhang, Z. (2020). Combined biomass gasification, SOFC, IC engine, and waste heat recovery system for power and heat generation: Energy, exergy, exergoeconomic, environmental (4E) evaluations. *Applied Energy*, *279*, 115794. doi:10.1016/j.apenergy.2020.115794

WWF. (2016). *Mapping Study on Cascading Use of Wood Products*. World Wildlife Fund.

Yadav, R., & Kumar, J. (2021). Engineered wood products as a sustainable construction material: A review. In M. Gong (Ed.), *Engineered Wood Products for Construction* (pp. 25–38).

Yan, Q., Li, J., & Cai, Z. (2021). Preparation and characterization of chars and activated carbons from wood wastes. *Carbon Letters*, *31*(5), 941–956. doi:10.100742823-020-00205-2

Zikeli, F., Vinciguerra, V., Annibale, A. D., Capitani, D., Romagnoli, M., & Scarascia Mugnozza, G. (2019). Preparation of lignin nanoparticles from wood waste for wood surface treatment. *Nanomaterials (Basel, Switzerland)*, *9*(2), 281. doi:10.3390/nano9020281 PMID:30781574

Chapter 22
Preparation and Extraction of Alpha Cellulose and Synthesis of Microcrystalline Cellulose From Agro-Waste (Pineapple Leaves)

Sunil Jayant Kulkarni

https://orcid.org/0000-0002-5988-3448

Gharda Institute of Technology, India

Burhan Abdur Rasheed Kalshekar

Gharda Institute of Technology, India

ABSTRACT

Microcrystalline cellulose ($C_6H_{10}O_5$) is purified, white free-flowing powder partially depolymerized cellulose prepared by treating alpha cellulose, obtained as a pulp from fibrous plant material. There are various fibrous materials such as rice husk, wheat husk, coconut husk, and cotton yarn, which contain cellulose can be used as a raw material. The chemical composition of these materials detects 65-70% cellulose content. The motive of our project is to highlight the significance of 3R's: Reduce, Reuse, and Recycle. There are many agricultural waste materials in our environment which can be recycled and transformed into new products. This project admitted this policy and chose the agricultural waste material of pineapple leaves. First pretreatment was done of the raw materials. Then they were given various chemical treatment such as acid hydrolysis, bleaching, etc. After successful extraction of alpha cellulose and microcrystalline cellulose, samples were sent for analysis which was FTIR the results showed the good quality of product was successfully extracted.

DOI: 10.4018/978-1-6684-8969-7.ch022

Preparation and Extraction of Alpha Cellulose and Synthesis of Microcrystalline Cellulose

INTRODUCTION

Today the major crisis our world is facing is the depleting natural resources. With every passing second resources are tending to exhaustion. Reduce, Recycle and Reuse has become the only way to survival. Just like food, clothing and shelter are our necessities, the three Rs have become the necessities of Earth. Waste disposal is another impending issue that must be tackled. Waste is generally a byproduct of a process. It is only a matter of thinking that can turn this undesired waste into a pretreated raw material. The process that generates waste serves as a pretreatment if the waste is further utilized. Thus, we can not only reduce the amount of waste but also save the energy required for its disposal. This also prevents the spending of extra energy on pretreatment to get this raw material. Cellulose is abundantly available in nature, but only in the form of highly cross-linked lignocellulose biomass. Lignin prevents the attack of reagents on cellulose while hemicellulose easily breaks down to form byproducts. As a result, various pretreatment methods are used to increase the reactivity of cellulose in the raw material by eliminating both components. Once the raw material is pretreated it is ready to be partially depolymerized to give our final product. Wood and cotton crops are important raw materials for MCCP production, but the difficulty of reducing raw material costs and the need to manage agricultural waste makes it necessary to explore other potential sources. Agricultural waste is finding wider interest among investigators for MCC synthesis (Asim et al., 2015; Kargarzadeh, et al., 2012; Sainorudin, et al., 2018; Tan & Supachok, 2017). The data show that MCCP can be extracted from peanuts, rice husks, cereal straws, pulp and maize, and Indian bamboo. Also, soybeans, oats, rice husks, beet pulp; Loofah and sawdust have been studied as potential sources of MCCP. Post-consumer (or waste) printing at different levels: paper, soil/newspaper and cardboard as cellulosic biomass can also be used as other raw materials for MCCP production. Alkali and bleach treatment are carried are widely used aspects of MCC synthesis (Boonmahitthisud et al., 2023; Grumo et al., 2017; Kumar et al., 2013). Millions of tons of paper are produced and used every year all over the world. For this reason, the problem of waste in the production and use of printed materials should be solved by using waste paper. However, when the material is recycled it often turns into low-quality paper; for example, recycled paper can be turned into newspapers, while recycled cardboard can be turned into toilet paper. This is because recycling in paper products leads to fiber reduction, which lowers the quality of the paper. Maximum efficiency in paper-to-paper recycling is around 65%. This results in a large amount of fiber material unsuitable for recycling. Mineral fillers (finely dispersed, relatively insoluble inorganic materials or minerals) are added to the fibers before paper is made to improve smoothness, opacity, and color. They also reduce transparency when the ink penetrates the paper and is visible on the outside. Fillers can also improve the ink absorption of offset paper. Literature indicates that has been resized but not filled will not accept printing fast enough for a good start, especially when printing at high speed. Fillers also reduce point distortion due to improved surface smoothness. Also, the filler reduces the transparency that occurs when images printed on one side of the paper can be seen from the other side due to lack of transparency. Fillers increase the gloss (whiteness) of the paper, making the printed images more "pop". Clay (from refined natural kaolin), titanium dioxide and calcium carbonate are the most used materials. Advanced methods for analysis and characterization enable investigators to study detailed morphology and structure to analyze the results (Ahmad et al., 2016; Shukla et al., 2013).

RAW MATERIAL SELECTION

The first step of every project planning is the selection of raw material. Unless the raw material is finalized further process cannot be decided. It also enables us to select a suitable site for our project. Raw material is selected on the basis of the following points:

- Composition
- Waste minimization
- Availability
- Alternative application
- Toxicity
- Cost
- Socio-economic considerations

Composition

It is one of the most important criteria for selection of raw material. A substance having higher cellulose content and lower hemicellulose and lignin content is preferred. The lower the hemicelluloses and lignin content lesser will be the amount of pretreatment required. As a result, there is a saving in resources like overhead power. There is also quite a saving in capital required for buying chemicals required for pretreatment.

Based on these criteria and composition stated in Table 2, we conclude that hard wood stem (40–55%), soft wood stem (45–50%), corn cobs (45%), cotton seed hairs (80–95%), sugarcane bagasse (45–55%), paper (85-95%) and waste papers from chemical pulps (60–70%) can be used. But for our project we choose pineapple leaves as the chemical composition of pineapple leaf detected 65-70% cellulose content.

Waste Minimization

Following on the lines of reduce, recycle and reuse, the raw material should be a waste generated due to some other process. Waste minimization is not only healthy for our environment, but also economical. Wastes are much cheaper than unused materials. In most of the cases waste disposal is a nuisance and unnecessary responsibility. It is expensive to dispose waste without causing damage to the surrounding. Among the 7 products that had been selected in earlier step wood and cotton seed hair are not waste. Hence it is not preferable to use this as raw material. While corn cob, sugarcane bagasse, paper and pineapple leaves are farm or agricultural waste from farm.

Alternative Application

If a raw material has better application in some other process, it should not be preferred. Such is the case with paper. It is readily recycled. Recycled paper or cardboards have a well-established market. Hence there is no need to find alternative uses of waste paper. But this is not the case with sugarcane bagasse. A huge proportion of bagasse generated is used as boiler fuel. This leads to pollution. Sugarcane under goes rigorous physical stress and as a result the bagasse generated has very small staple length cellulose and hence cannot be used in textile industries.

Toxicity

As MCC is used in food and pharmaceutical industries toxicity is a serious issue. MCC on its own is not toxic, but some impurities present in raw material may get carried all the way to the final product. As this is not desirable, we need to select a raw material which is least toxic. Pineapple leaves may contain impurities in the form of organic matters from soil or other natural organic impurities. These impurities are not highly toxic and can be easily eliminated. But waste paper from chemical pulp may contain traces of toxic material like heavy metals and hence should be avoided as expensive purification methods may be needed to be employed.

Cost

Pineapple leaves is a farm waste and is cheaply available.

Socio-Economic Considerations

India is agriculture-based country. Any growth or promotion of agricultural byproduct is very beneficial for our growth. Thus, Pineapple leaves waste utilization will be beneficial from socio-economic point of view. Hence, based on the above points we conclude that Pineapple leaves is the most suited raw material for this process.

EXPERIMENTAL WORK AND METHODOLOGY

Stages involved in Project:

1. **STAGE I-** Reagent Preparation
2. **STAGE II-** Processing of Raw Material
3. **STAGE III-** Pre-Treatment and Preparation of Alpha Cellulose
4. **STAGE IV-** Manufacturing Microcrystalline cellulose (MCC)

Materials

Analytical Balance, Hot Water bath, Domestic Blender, Hot air oven, Domestic Sieve, Whatman filter papers, PH meter, Hand gloves, Beakers, Conical Flasks, Petri dish, Magnetic Stirrer, Heater, Spatula, and other Glassware's. Pineapple Leaves, Nitric acid (HNO_3), sodium nitrite ($NaNO_2$), sodium hydroxide (NaOH), sodium sulphite ($NaSO_3$), sodium hypochlorite (NaOCl), 37% hydrochloric acid (HCl) and Distilled water.

Stage I: Reagent Preparation
Reagents of required strength were prepared.

Stage II: Processing of Raw material:
Fig. 1 shows stepwise raw material processing.

Preparation and Extraction of Alpha Cellulose and Synthesis of Microcrystalline Cellulose

Figure 1. Raw material processing

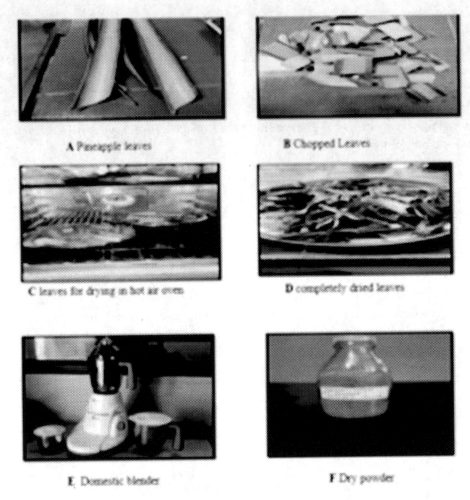

1. Pineapple Leaves which were collected from the local garden were first washed thoroughly with tap water to remove dirt.
2. Approximately 5kgs of pineapple leaves were collected.
3. These leaves were the chopped into pieces using scissors/knife.
4. After chopping the leaves, they were given hot water bath.
5. The leaves were distributed equally in each beaker containing distilled water.
6. This beaker was then given hot water bath for 100°c for half hour to kill bacteria's and germs present on the surface of the leaves.
7. After hot water bath these leaves were dried in hot air oven for 100°c initially and then it was raised to 180°c afterwards.
8. Drying of leaves was done for at least 24hrs until it was completely dried and became crispy.
9. After removing the moisture completely, it was then blended into fine powder by using domestic blender.
10. The powder was then sieved to separate saw dust and other particles and stored in bottle for further use.

11. Drying operation was carried out in 3 batches:
    - 1st batch- 173.5gms of fresh leaves were dried and moisture loss was 152.5gm (21gms of material were obtained)
    - 2nd batch- 478.5gms of fresh leaves were dried and moisture loss was of 422.5gms (56gms of material were obtained)
    - 3rd batch- 770gms of fresh leaves were dried and moisture loss was 682.5gms (88gms of material were obtained)

Stage III: Pretreatment and Synthesis of Alpha Cellulose

Figure 2 depicts pre-treatment for pineapple powder.

1. 100 gm pineapple powder was mixed with 1.4-liter nitric acid solution (3.5%) containing 15mg of sodium nitrite.
2. The mixture was then stirred with mechanical stirrer in a beaker.
3. This mixture was then given a hot water bath at 90°c for 2 hours until it forms a brownish colored cake like porous material.
4. After heating the mixture was cooled.
5. After cooling the pulp from the top was removed and kept aside in petri dishes.
6. The yellowish colored water was then filtered by using Whatman filter paper leaving a yellow-colored filtrate at the bottom of the flask.
7. The residue/pulp was collected and stored for further process.
8. The obtained yellow coloured pulp was then mixed with 1 lit of sodium hydroxide and 1 lit of sodium sulphite solution each of 2%. It turns into red oxide color.
9. After mixing it was the heated at 60°c for approximately 1hr by using laboratory heater.
10. It was then cooled and then filtered by using domestic sieve. The pulp obtained was again treated with 17.5% sodium hydroxide.
11. It was mixed with 680ml of 75% sodium hydroxide and then heated at 80þc for 30mins. The result was washed and filtered using domestic filtration sieve.
12. Separation of Alpha Cellulose:
    - After filtering the liquid obtained pulp/cake (as shown in figure 2) was the again bleached using sodium hypochlorite and distilled water.
    - 1:1 ratio was taken of sodium hypochlorite and distilled water i.e. (1 lit of sodium hypochlorite solution and 1 lit of distilled water)
    - Mix 60 ml of sodium hypochlorite in 1lit distilled water for preparing 1lit of solution
    - The pulp was then mixed in this sodium hypochlorite and distilled water solution and heated using laboratory heater at 100°c for 10-15 mins.
    - After heating the mixture, it was then cooled and filtered using the same domestic sieve.
    - The mixture was washed continuously with water until clear filtrate was obtained.
    - Then the obtained alpha cellulose was spread evenly in steel plate and sent to the hot air oven at 100°c for 2 hours until it was completely dried.

Figure 2. Pulping

A. mixing of pineapple powder
B. Hot water bath to the mixture
C. brownish porous cake
D. Separated cake in petri dish
E. Filtration
F. Yellow filtrate

Stage IV: Preparation of Microcrystalline Cellulose

This stage is depicted in Figure 5.

1. After alpha cellulose was obtained 15 gm was taken as a sample
2. The sample was then treated with hydrochloric acid 17.5%.
3. The mixture was stirred for 10 mins and then boiled at 100°c for 15-20 mins.

4. Then it was cooled and filtered by using What man filter paper.
5. After filtration was completed, the obtained material was washed until neutral PH was obtained.
6. After obtaining neutral ph. mcc was sent to the oven and dried completely at 60þc for 3 hours.
7. The mcc was obtained 10gms which was then stored at cool and dry place which has to be sent for analysis.
8. After drying mcc was subsequently crushed and stored in plastic bag as shown in fig 27.
9. All the samples i.e., pineapple powder, Alpha cellulose and MCC was stored in glass sample bottles as shown in fig 28. Which is sent for further analysis.

Figure 3. Pulp processing

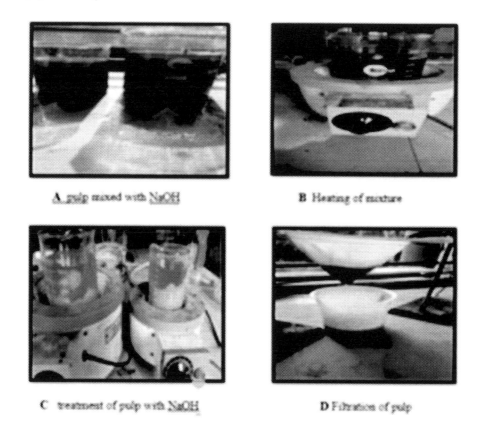

A. pulp mixed with NaOH   B. Heating of mixture
C. treatment of pulp with NaOH   D. Filtration of pulp

FTIR ANALYSIS

The main idea gained from the FTIR analysis is to understand what the meaning of the FTIR spectrum. The spectrum can result "absorption versus wavenumber" or "transmission versus wavenumber" data. We discuss only the "absorption versus wavenumber" curves. In short, the IR spectrum is divided into three wavenumber regions: far-IR spectrum, mid-IR spectrum (400-4000 cm1), and near-IR spectrum (4000-13000 cm-1). The mid-IR spectrum is the most widely used in the sample analysis, but far- and near-IR spectrum also contribute in providing information about the samples analyzed. This study focused on the analysis of FTIR in the mid-IR spectrum.

Figure 4. Pulp to alpha cellulose

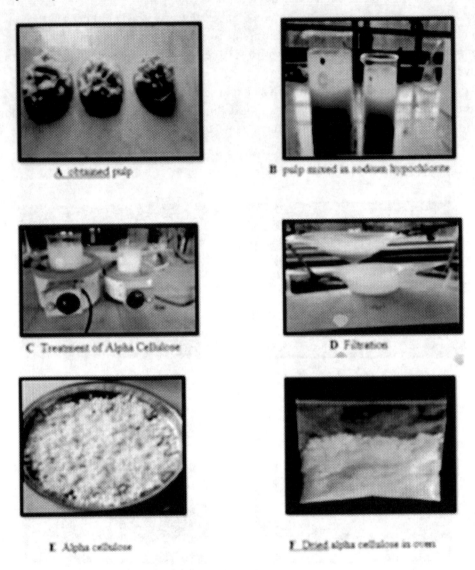

The mid-IR spectrum is divided into four regions:

(i) the single bond region (2500-4000 cm-1)
(ii) the triple bond region (2000-2500 cm-1)
(iii) the double bond region (1500-2000 cm-1)
(iv) The fingerprint region (600-1500 cm-1).

Figure 5. MCC from alpha cellulose

FTIR Results of MCC of Pineapple Leaves

From the figures (Figure 6) above results obtained Fourier transform infrared spectrum of microcrystalline cellulose from pineapple leaves

1] Wave number 3334 cm^{-1} shows the OH stretching vibration.
2] Absorption band at wavenumber 2887 cm^{-1} showed the presence of C-H aliphatic stretching vibration supported by an absorption band
3] At wavenumber 1919 cm^{-1} and 1364 cm^{-1}, which showed the presence of C-H aliphatic bending vibration.
4] In wavenumber 2262 cm^{-1} and 2128 cm^{-1} indicate the presence of O-H vibration.
5] Absorption band 1048 cm^{-1} shows the C = O bending vibration.
6] The highest peak i.e., wave number 1048 cm^{-1} shows the purity of microcrystalline cellulose.
7] Comparing the graph from the literature the resulted graph shows similar properties and quality of MCC

Figure 6. Fourier transform infrared spectrum of microcrystalline cellulose
(From Actual Expt. Results)

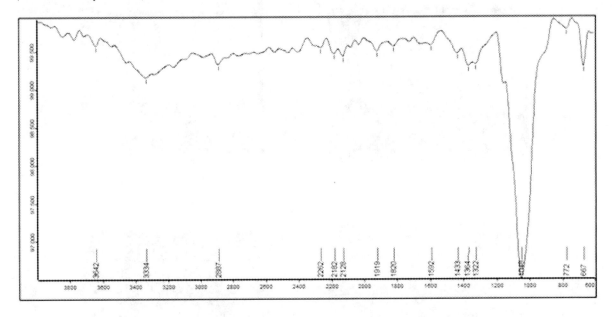

FTIR Analysis Results for Alpha Cellulose

From the figure (figure 7) above results obtained Fourier transform infrared spectrum of Alpha cellulose from pineapple leaves

1] Wave number 3234 cm^{-1} shows the OH stretching vibration.
2] Absorption band at wavenumber 2687 cm^{-1} showed the presence of C-H aliphatic stretching vibration supported by an absorption band
3] At wavenumber 1267 cm^{-1} and 1654 cm^{-1}, which showed the presence of C-H aliphatic bending vibration.
4] In wavenumber 2162 cm^{-1} and 2128 cm^{-1} indicate the presence of O-H vibration. 5] Absorption band 1045 cm^{-1} shows the C = O bending vibration.

6] The highest peak i.e., wave number 1043 cm⁻¹ shows the purity of microcrystalline cellulose.

7] Comparing the graph from the literature the resulted graph shows similar properties and quality of alpha cellulose.

Figure 7. Fourier transform infrared spectrum of alpha cellulose
(From Actual Expt. Results)

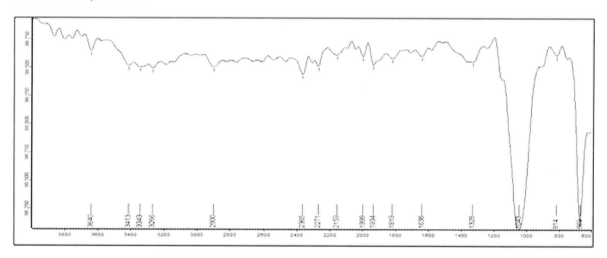

Comparison Table From the Above Results (Table 1 and Table 2)

Table 1. Results of data comparison from literature

Sr No.	Wave number of MCC from literature	Wave number of MCC from experimental work	Interpretation
1	3344.57 cm⁻¹	3996.22 cm⁻¹	O-H Stretching
2	2897.08 cm⁻¹	3990.04 cm⁻¹	C-H Aliphatic stretching
3	1431.18 cm⁻¹	2584.46 cm⁻¹	C-H Aliphatic Bending
4	2133.27 cm⁻¹	2580.54 cm⁻¹	O-H Stretching
5	2056.12 cm⁻¹	1438.22 cm⁻¹	C=O Bending
6	1635.64 cm⁻¹	1251.77 cm⁻¹	O-H Stretching

CONCLUSION

Pineapple leaves are the waste material that should be utilized for a valuable product such as alpha cellulose and microcrystalline cellulose. It can be further used in pharmaceutical and food industry. The investigation gives details about utilization of natural resources to give a valuable outcome for better environment. Our idea gives detail insight about utilization of natural resources and methodology for synthesis of a valuable product for better environment as well Human health. By utilizing this tree waste, farmers will also get financial support. Giving an alternative by using natural resources for synthesis of

MCC also results in health benefits for upcoming Generations as well as human beings. We conclude that the Pineapple leaves are good starting material for microcrystalline cellulose and alpha cellulose.

Table 2. Comparison of examination results of experiment and literature

Sr no.	Parameters	Results from Experiment	Specifications from literature
1.	Appearance	Fine powder	Fine powder
2.	Colour	White	White
3.	Smell	Odourless	Odourless
4.	Taste	Tasteless	Tasteless
5.	PH	6.4	5.0-7.5
6.	Colour Reagent	Violet	Violet Blue

ACKNOWLEDGMENT

The authors are thankful to Gharda Institute of Technology and its chemical engineering department for providing laboratory facilities for the work.

REFERENCES

Ahmad, Z., Roziaizan, N., Rozyanty, A.R., Mohamad, A., & Nawawi, W.I. (2016). *Isolation and Characterization of Microcrystalline Cellulose (MCC) from Rice Husk (RH)*. Semantic Scholar.

Asim, M., Khalina Abdan, M., Jawaid, M. Nasir, M., Dashtizadeh, Z., Ishak, M., & Hoque, M. (2015). A Review on Pineapple Leaves Fibre and Its Composites. Hindawi.

Boonmahitthisud, A., Booranapunpong, Cc., Pattaradechakul, & Tanpichai, S. (2023). Development of water-resistant paper using chitosan and plant-based wax extracted from banana leaves. *International Journal of Biological Macromolecules.* doi: 2023.124412. doi:10.1016/j.ijbiomac.vol

Grumo, J., Jabber, J., Patricio, J., Magdadaro, M., Lubguban, A., & Alguno, A. (2017). Alkali and bleach treatment of the extracted cellulose from pineapple (Ananas comosus) leaves. *Journal of Applied and Fundamental Sciences, 9,* 124-133. doi:. doi:10.4314/jfas.v9i7s.13

Kargarzadeh, H., Ahmad, I., Abdullah, I., Dufresne, A., Zainudin, S.Y., Sheltami, R.M. (2012). Effects of hydrolysis conditions on the morphology, crystallinity, and thermal stability of cellulose nanocrystals extracted from kenaf bast fibers. *Cellulose, 19*(3), 855-660. doi:10.1007/s10570-012-9684-6

Kumar, R., Hu, F., Hubbell, C. A., Ragauskas, A. J., & Wayman, C. E. (2013). Comparison of laboratory delignification methods, their selectivity, and impacts on physiochemical characteristic cellulosic biomass. Bioresour 130, 372-381.

Sainorudin, M.H., Mohammad, M., Kadir, N.H.A., Abdullah, N.A., Yaakob, Z. (2018). *Characterization of several microcrystalline cellulose (MCC)-based agricultural wastes via x-ray diffraction method.* Trans Tech Publications Ltd.

Shukla, S.K., Nidhi, S., Pooja, N., Charu, A., Silvi, M., Bharadvaja, A., & Dubey, G. C. (2013). Preparation and Characterization of Cellulose Derived from Rice Husk for Drug Delivery. *Adv. Mat. Lett, 4* (9), 714-719.

Tan, PSupachok, W. (2017, April 26). All-cellulose composite laminates prepared from pineapple leaf fibers treated with steam explosion and alkaline treatment. *Journal of Reinforced Plastics and Composites.*

Chapter 23
Industry 4.0, Sustainable Manufacturing, Circular Economy, and Sustainable Business Models for Sustainable Development

Saurabh Tiwari
https://orcid.org/0000-0002-4278-0389
University of Petroleum and Energy Studies, India

Richa Goel
SCMS Noida, Symbiosis International University (Deemed), Pune, India

ABSTRACT

Current international issues include the emergence and application of Industry 4.0 (I4.0), a cutting-edge manufacturing system powered by information technology (IT), as well as the development of a sustainable society. The implications for sustainable development (SD) from the perspectives of sustainable manufacturing (SM), sustainable business models (SBM), and the circular economy (CE) have received a lot of attention. I4.0 adoption and implementation, sustainable supply chains, and smart factories are frequently the subjects of studies on sustainable manufacturing. Two recently developed research areas that concentrate on I4.0 adoption and implementation as well as sustainable supply chains are the circular economy and sustainable business models. This chapter combines recent research developments in the disciplines of I4.0 and sustainability with the aid of the literature on the CE, SM, and SBM.

DOI: 10.4018/978-1-6684-8969-7.ch023

1. INTRODUCTION

In the modern world, there are many concerns that must be tackled, including the enhancement of a sustainable society and the rise and use of I4.0, an innovative manufacturing process driven by information technology (IT). New technologies that optimise outputs while effectively using resources have been brought by I4.0 to the manufacturing industry (Kamble et al., 2018). Cyber-physical systems (CPSs), the Internet of Things (IoT), and other modern technologies open up opportunities for technological advancement that allow for higher efficiency and productivity in a range of businesses. I4.0 combines big data (BD), IoT, with artificial intelligence (AI) to leverage production operations. I4.0 has a great deal of promise to enable the development of environmentally friendly manufacturing value in the economic, social, and environmental sectors by improving resource efficiency. The concept of sustainability within I4.0 raises concerns conventional methods to emerge handling and imposes more systemic attitudes to allocate with change (Trivedi et al., 2023). This indicates that for sustainability and green economies to advance, systems of "doing things better" must go from homogenous to comprehensive (Sterling, 2004; McKibben & McKibben, 2007; Bahuguna et al., 2022).

For manufacturers to succeed in achieving the objectives of sustainable development, they should accept a new viewpoint recognized as the CE (Blunck and Werthmann, 2017). However, there are some obstacles preventing the adoption and development of CE. Some of the main problems include higher initial installation costs, supply chain complexity, an absence of corporate teamwork, knowledge gaps for goods development and manufacturing procedures, insufficient expertise, quality modifications, lengthy turnaround periods for dismantling, and extraordinary costs associated with such operations. These problems can be solved with I4.0 technology. Making use of a CPS be able to assist with efficient job organizing and completing, saving time, money, and resources (Tiwari et al., 2022a; Kusiak, 2018), which increases the availability of environmental sources and lowers ecological budget. Less significant collections can result in reduced manufacturing waste and a additional accurate reaction to client requirement turns. I4.0 principles include service orientation, actual time capabilities, decentralisation, virtualization, and connectivity. A sustained equipment life cycle and a decrease in industrial waste output can be attributed to interoperability, and improved local resource and asset utilisation can be attributed to decentralisation. Real-time capabilities lead to enhanced demand curve adaptation, better utilisation of resources, and a faster reaction to alterations in the energy supply. Virtualisation can reduce waste from industries, make it simpler to encourage innovative ecological practises, and increase recycling possibilities. Modularity results in greater industrial resource utilisation and longer machine life cycles; and service orientation can boost options for recycling and reuse, as well as the use of final products.

The definition of SD comprehends a extensive extent of ideas, such as source utilisation, economic relationships, and human advancement. The three fundamental elements of sustainability, according to Elkington (1998), are social, economic, and the preservation of the environment. These pillars make up the triple bottom line, whose objective is to satisfy the source needs of generations to come without endangering the environment. I4.0 has a lot of promise for collecting sustainable economic generation that results in SM. SBMs take into consideration all parties involved in addition to the environment and the community at large. They are crucial in guiding and implementing into practise new company procedures for sustainability by adopting CE methods including enlargement, decreasing, and closing the asset loop, resulting in important factors of business competitiveness and complete SD.

Despite I4.0's significant significance as an SD enabler, there aren't many reviews that have examined it from the perspective of sustainability of view. This indicates that there is still room for development at the intersections of the sustainability and I4.0 paradigms. In respect to circular manufacturing and sustainable manufacturing, for instance, several scholars have deliberated I4.0 and connected knowledges (Asiimwe and de Kock, 2019) others have highlighted the development of sustainable industrial value by demonstrating how SBMs (Machado et al., 2020) can be used to interact among society, businesses, and environments. I4.0, SM, CE, and SBMs are merely a few of the four themes where they interact, according to a closer examination of these studies. This demonstrates that current literature assessments do not offer an improved comprehension of I4.0 for SD because of the crucial links among numerous associated subject areas and their size, which calls for more consideration. I4.0 for SD consists of the make from SM, CE, and SBMs due to the broadness of the topics; most studies fail to offer a thorough examination of the ideas that shape SD and do not search for literature to find ongoing and new interrelated themes, or important fields of study in which either I4.0 and SD are provide. The absence of studies on the combination of different concepts (I4.0, CE, SM, and SBM) for SD served as the inspiration for the current work. The next thing is the study's research question.

RQ1. *How far the field of I4.0, SM, the CE, and SBM has come in the literature.*
RQ2. *To develop a theoretical model using I4.0, SM, the CE, and SBM for sustainable development.*

The introduction to the subject is covered in the first section of the paper. Following is the breakdown of the final three portions. Section 2 discusses literature reviews. A summary of I4.0, SM, and the CE is provided in this section. The theoretical framework integrating I4.0, SM, and CE in the larger context of SD is reflected in Section 3. Conclusion and the plan for future research are covered in Section 4.

2. LITERATURE REVIEW

Any type of sustainability can assist provide the best conditions for addressing difficulties facing business and the environment in the twenty-first century. Rendering to the Brundtland Report, which was published in 1987, "the thought of environmentally friendly expansion implies boundaries, not complete restricts but constraints forced by the current state of technological development and social structure on the resources of the environment and by the capability that the environment to take in the effects caused by human activities." SD is commonly defined as "growth which meets the requirements of the present while safeguarding the capability of groups to come to meet their own needs" in The Brundtland Report (1987). This shows that SD deals with a wide range of complex difficulties that arise along with a host of environmental problems, human societies and ecosystems in nature around the world alter. Due to its suggested solutions for issues relating to the surroundings, energy, warming temperatures, and agricultural growth, among other things, the concepts of long-lasting development and SD have sparked attention on a global scale (Olawumi and Chan, 2018). Many people believed that the terms "sustainability" and "SD" were interchangeable and could be used interchangeably, however some believe they refer to two distinct concepts. To limit the depletion of natural resources, the second research stream focuses on conservation, biodiversity, and ecological integrity. It defines sustainable as simultaneously an idea and a vision for policy (Ekins et al., 2003). On the other hand, SD is a dense group social development that implies a range of interested parties. Both definitions of "societal education and steering processes" refer to sustainability as a discussion or method for doing SD goals.

The greatest relevant and current understanding of SD is the triple bottom line (Elkington, 1998). SM is supported by three pillars: the economy, society, and the environment. The environmental component refers to the use of resources that may be replicated form life to nothing, while the economic pillar seeks to protect liquidity and ensure profit. The social pillar encourages the expansion of individual and societal capital (Hubbard, 2009). Additionally, research into the use of CE as a macro-level SD tool for addressing societal concerns is expanding (Sauve et al., 2016). A new way of thinking called CE aims to use resources responsibly. The circular framework of "reduce, recycle, reuse, recover, remanufacture, and redesign" must be adopted to accomplish CE. The linear approach of "take, make, use, and dispose/waste" must be abandoned.

Although the idea of a conventional organisation model is restricted to the value flow within an organisation as an abstract representation, the sudden technology changes and sustainability ideologies influencing people and societies have highlighted SBMs. Following Machado et al. (2020), in the study, we describe SBMs as tools that maintain an equilibrium among environmental, social, and financial requirements while still upholding their selling point in relations of generating fresh employment possibilities, saving money, and decreasing opposing environmental effects. According to Smith et al. (2012), a CE, SBMs, and SM all have to be included in an integrated SD system since the SD process involves universal innovation and change in goods, regimes, ecosystems, procedures, and configurations (Dubey et al., 2012). Along with global issues related to society, the economy, and the environment, sudden technological advancement, digitization, and automation provide problems for the entire world. I4.0, an information driven by technology production system, was developed in answer to these challenges. I4.0 influences organisational economic factors like efficiency, effectiveness, and competitiveness as well as the environment and social goals. To assist define the future of the German economy, German academics Kagerman et al. (2011) developed the phrase "I4.0." I4.0 links people, machines, other resources, and goods and services in the real world using foundational technologies like CPSs and IoT. According to Beier et al. (2017), sustainability is also seen as one of I4.0's main motivators. By actively collecting and sending data, I4.0 technology may be included into value chains to give real-time information about equipment, manufacturing facilities, activities, and component movements. Managers can now watch, track, and manage natural choices on post-consumer item rescues. These retrieval-based methods restore the conventional sequential narrative of "take, make, use, and dispose" and benefit businesses and the supply chain in the areas of society, economy, and the environment. (Geissdoerfer et al., 2017). I4.0 scenarios, CE-based models of business would be the most practical operating equipment for expanding SBMs. IoT connectivity, which enables "businesses' yields and procedures to be connected and amalgamated to realise higher estimate for both consumers and the businesses' internal practices," is often the foundation of I4.0-based business models. I4.0 provides businesses with sustainable durability, effectiveness, and recovery by supporting their social, financial, and ecological values, compared with numerous sectors that have been buried for many years in unsustainable but economically successful business models. More precisely, if organisations concentrate on their ability for absorbing new technical breakthroughs and their individual innovation strategies, SMEs can allow I4.0-based business models.

2.1 Industry 4.0

Operations and supply chain management have new opportunities because to I4.0 (Bag et al., 2020). I4.0 has the power to change current systems, procedures, and competitive agendas. New technologies including CPS, IoT, and visual computing for SM have all been made possible by the development of I4.0

(Ardanza et al., 2019; Tiwari et al., 2022b). Adoption of I4.0 necessitates accurate knowledge, financial resources, talent enhancement, and the development of an open-minded and adaptable organisational culture. A flexible organisational structure, data management, data security, and collaboration with external stakeholders are also essential.

Advanced, versatile, and adaptable interfaces between humans and machines will increase output without compromising worker safety. SM systems can increase productivity and diagnose system health on their own. The objective of SM is to improve the capacity for both humans and machines to make decision-making as well as the efficiency of production operations. Manufacturing plant performance may be impacted by smart maintenance. The relationship among supply chain leadership and advertising activities can be handled using digital technologies. IoT can also be used to organise maintenance and warranty duties for remanufactured products. Designing business processes that are supported by mobile cyber-physical resources, incorporating a variety of stakeholders, and addressing team, task, and control are all ways that mobility organisation in procedure businesses can be performed (Barata et al., 2019). Implementing I4.0 is fraught with issues. It has been demonstrated that the resources and capabilities of medium-sized organisations are insufficient for projecting firm value (Bordeleau et al., 2020). Latin American businesses are concerned about the use of I4.0 technology to boost production. According to Brixner et al. (2020), this is mostly caused by a lack of technological, organisational, and communication abilities. Data analysis, mixing new skills with existing technology, and manpower, and overcoming computer constraints are some of the most challenging problems in I4.0 technologies. Overcoming these problems will create new opportunities for improved productivity, security, flexibility, and efficiency (Dalmarco et al., 2019). Small businesses have better prospects to perform when they work with companies that have a broad and deep dedication to I4.0 technology. Many manufacturers haven't been able to make use of the revolutionary prospects provided by I4.0, though, up to this point. Brazil has not been able to take use of I4.0 technology owed to an deficiency of skills that correspond to the knowledge needs of the I4.0 process. The use of I4.0 technology can give businesses a competitive edge. But businesses are quite concerned about the uncertainty and complexity surrounding technology investment decisions. Shop floor level technologies are prioritised by businesses with fewer than twenty employees and constrained resources. Companies with over twenty staff members and access to financing, as reported by Bosman et al. (2020), often concentrate on technology that supports operations. I4.0 technology are applied to achieve certain manufacturing goals. Lean tactics, design-to-cost, integrating the supply chain, service delivery, and tools incorporation might all be supported by I4.0 technology. While I4.0 raises the worth of manufacturing processes, servitization significantly increases the value of the consumer. By progressing with servitization, manufacturers can become data-driven (Kohtamäki et al., 2020). Dynamic skills are developed because of the coordination of all management team members' responsibilities towards I4.0 (Garbellano and Da Veiga, 2019). Technology connected to smart manufacturing is being adopted due to anticipated advantages and support from senior management. When factors like popularity and collection investment are connected to socially significant environmentally friendly goods, it is critical to focus on operational aspects along with costs.

The digital conversion cycle depends on design and manufacturing characteristics, which are operations-related needs. To improve design and manufacturing-related choices, manufacturers must collect and interpret immediate information via shop floor equipment. An architecture for gathering information from the factory floor was suggested by Farooqui et al. in 2020. Future supply chains are predicted to face new challenges and opportunities because of I4.0. An internet-based supply chain concept that targets to lower some I4.0 obstacles. The model has four basic components: both physical and digital environments, the virtual value chain, and I4.0 technology, concepts, facilitators, and features. Additionally, the model has the following dimensions: Cyber-physical systems as a platform for adoption of technology and digitalization; both physical and digital supply chain elements and operations inside cloud computing and robotics; and a system assembly for the supply chain of digital goods that links these elements. The I4.0 transition necessitates both a digital transformation of the complete value chain and the integration of numerous cutting-edge information technologies. The development of a lean-based digital manufacturing system is crucial in the I4.0 era for sustainability. If organisational competencies and approaches are in sync with the digitization of processes, higher productivity can be obtained. Thus, the digitization of the supply chain advances lean manufacturing methods. Supply chain performance will likely improve because of I4.0 technology' improved sharing of data and openness. The enhancement of purchasing, manufacturing, logistics, and other tasks is made possible by I4.0 technology, which enable procedure incorporation, robotics, and digitalization. Some of the front end I4.0 technologies consists of smart products, working, supply chain and manufacturing(Tiwari, 2023b). Base technologies include the IoT, cloud services, BDA. Smart manufacturing is a vital component of I4.0's front-end technologies, which must be adopted (Frank et al., 2019). Companies face difficulties adopting base technologies because BDA are still in their infancy from an application standpoint. I4.0-empowered supply chain development will, according to published studies, increase focus on efficiency in supply chains improvement, notably scalability and adaptability. Set-up enterprises are radically altering their operational strategies while depending on statistical analysis and the programme reduction. I4.0 is primarily driven by management goals to enhance real-time performance assessment and control. Worker and upper management opposition to I4.0 technology has been found to be a barrier to execution. Greater driving forces for the adoption of I4.0 can be produced by big international companies than by small and medium-sized firms. It is crucial to concentrate on the instrument and process quality while adopting I4.0 technologies into the organisation (Martinez, 2019). The production process can be redesigned, and new models can be put into use, thanks to I4.0. I4.0 technology help procedure re-engineering. These technologies can enable job execution, improve data gathering and exchange, and improve process performance (Patrucco et al., 2020). Studying contemporary digital technologies to lay a foundation and deepen awareness of their responsibilities within a data-oriented paradigm is another fascinating aspect of I4.0 research. 111 digital technologies were discovered through content analysis to perform the four data-related functions of data production and extraction, delivery, conditioned behaviour, processing and storage, and application. Technology relevant to value generation are found in the fourth group, which follows the first three divisions. While allowing technology are repeatedly explored in the sources, value-enhancing and creating technology are very rare. Data is one among the most valued resources in the modern world. Finding production-related information within the organisation is the first step in implementing SM. The next phases include determining preparedness, increasing awareness of smart manufacturing, creating a vision that is consistent to, and choosing methods and tools to actualize the vision. Today's digital era is significantly dependent on data for decision-making, communication, and information sharing. One of the most significant allowing technologies in the current digital era is cloud computing. Being able to analyse data and change data is necessary for the effective running of clouds-based organisations, as data has been designated as the main source of power for cloud computing. An efficient and flexible hybrid cloud supply chain model for integrating the supply chain network. Human challenges make up the I4.0 study second dimension. I4.0 technology advancements such and the IoT have drastically changed the workforce requirements by automating several high-skilled and medium-skilled vocations. Individuals in the age of technology now frequently fear losing their work because of this. During the digital revolution, businesses must take their workers' and employees' welfare into account pursuing a proactive strategy for I4.0 technology adoption (Nam, 2019). As a result of digital transformation, the human component of the system will need to change. The new skills and abilities required for various job profiles will vary according to the industry sector. Among the technology abilities needed are programming, robotics, BDA, and smart system maintenance. Continuous learning, original ideas, and critical analysis are examples of soft skills. From an operational standpoint, communication between the operator and their workstation is essential in the SM environment. From a sustainability standpoint, significant variables including operators safety and health and job satisfaction must be considered (Golan et al., 2020). The success of the I4.0 project depends on training, according to the literature. Without adequate I4.0 training, project managers are more likely to make mistakes. Additionally, it is crucial to have assistance and direction from outside advisors while putting the I4.0 project into practise. The sources claims that a major mediator in reaching a extreme intensity of operational effectiveness is one's capacity for learning. Thus, in the era of the internet, companies that prioritise knowledge transfer and information sharing stand to benefit tremendously (Tortorella et al., 2020). Small and medium-sized businesses must use data analytics to build expertise and systems for decision-support before making investments in staff members for education and training if they want to be ready for the digital age (Bahuguna et al., 2023). The infrastructure required for gathering data, storing it, analysis, interpretation, and contact with important supply chain participants must be provided by organisations. Ralston and Blackhurst (2020) claim that the improvement of fresh talent and the enhancement create flexible of skills in I4.0 smart systems may increase the resilience of the supply chain. Using CPS on the shop floor to plan critical jobs and manage a volatile and demanding market, savvy manufacturers may do so, according to research. Intelligent scheduling to establish variable and effective manufacturing plans. Smart systems can anticipate unforeseen and disruptive occurrences and react accordingly. Smart manufacturing approaches that produce goods when needed can aid in reducing inventory issues. The field of SM has also undergone a revolution because to advanced manufacturing technologies, which have also enhanced research and development capabilities and made it easier for teams to collaborate on new ideas (Szalavetz, 2019). From the standpoint of a sustainable supply chain, design issues, sensor technologies, and CPS standards and specifications are the biggest I4.0 roadblocks to creating a CE. According to I4.0, lean practises have a limited impact on improving operational performance. Low preparation procedures have a undesirable influence on performance that I4.0 innovations related to processes may help to reduce, whereas flow processes have a positive influence on performance that I4.0 technology related to goods and services can help to mitigate. Lean automation may help businesses obtain a competitive edge (Tiwari et al., 2011). Sustainability accounting and reporting are essential as the organisation approaches I4.0 maturity. The I4.0-based company structure exhibits three significant patterns, per the research, integrating, service delivery, and expertization are these. During integration, several supply chain components are joined together with the creation of an entirely novel company structure with distinct procedures. Expertization combines new products and services, whereas service delivery is hybrid in nature and combines goods and process-oriented business models. I4.0 has brought about a surge of radical breakthroughs that will have a significant influence on the nation's economy and lead to significant changes in the technology sector. This will require changes to policies, infrastructure, sociocultural norms, and the environment. Investigation into Industry 4.0 has shown a range of obstacles, motivators, difficulties, and opportunities. The importance of BDA for the adoption of foundational technologies has also been noted, even though it is still relatively new.

The significance of assets and capacities for deploying I4.0 technology has also been emphasized by the research. The part that follows offers an analysis of SM.

2.2 Sustainable Manufacturing

Production companies are rapidly benefiting economically and environmentally from sustainable business practises, according to an EPA study from 2020. Business plans that include themes from the circular economy go hand in hand with sustainable operational strategies. Industrial approaches are also arose to achieve the environmental advancement objectives. In their evaluation of the research on sustainable operations management, Atasu et al. (2020) divided the research into the following categories: closed-loop supply chains, environmentally friendly economies, management of the environment and efficiency, creativity, and social responsibility. Functional concentration, internal integration, and outside integration are the stages of the evolution of environmental management. Businesses in the function specialisation phase, who have limited knowledge and information consumption, frequently skip using a wider range of cleaner manufacturing processes. The knowledge about the utilisation and attributes of cleaner production are expanded to increase efficiency when the company approaches the mature phase of management of the environment growth stage. By increasing utilisation, information profusion connected to cost, inner memos on environmental issues, and external cooperation, cleaner manufacturing practises for sustainable can be strengthened. According to a centralised governance structure can result in sustainable operations, and key stakeholders' power to make decisions is positively connected with the organization's sustainability. This may help commercial globalisation. Sustainable manufacturing strategies are fundamental to a long-term operations plan. The technique of making products without harming the environment is known as sustainable manufacturing. The use of data and attributes of cleaner manufacturing is expanded to increase efficiency as the organisation moves closer to the matured stage of environmentally conscious growth. Improved price-related information availability, internal environmental reporting, and external partnerships can all help to enhance cleaner manufacturing practises for sustainability. A centralised system of governance can lead to sustainable operations, and the ability of important stakeholders to influence choices is positively correlated with the sustainability of the organisation. Global commerce might benefit from this. An operations plan for the long run must include SM techniques. SM is the process of producing goods without causing environmental damage. New authority processes can alleviate the sustainability issues encountered in transnational production networks. Each company approaches SM differently depending on the type of business. Each firm function, according to Macchi et al. (2020), has a substantial influence on sustainability. Knowledge of the production system's material and energy fluxes provides information on costs, efficiency, and environmental influence. There are numerous approaches for analysing flows, and including industrial schedules to reduce waste at the operational level is a good idea. Proper scheduling, according to Le Hesran et al. (2020), can reduce waste output by up to 10%. Chen and Bidanda (2019) investigated sustainable manufacturing approaches centred on resource recycling and emissions reduction to address the manufacturing-stock issue. The findings show that each sustainable manufacturing strategy has a distinct influence on how decisions are made. To reduce emissions and expenses, the volume of recovered item returns might be raised. The cap-and-trade technique has been shown to be more successful that the carbon tax approach at reducing emissions. Remanufacturing was investigated as a solution for SM. Remanufacturing subsidies, according to Zhu et al. (2019), can stimulate consumer demand for remanufactured items. However, it has been established that carbon regulation works best when refurbished goods emit less CO2. Subsidies for remanufacturing will boost a company's profitability, however carbon legislation may have an influence on profit margins. Dunuwila et al. (2020) also evaluated Sri Lanka's sustainable dipping rubber product production in terms of enhancing economic and environmental issues. Several process adjustment parameters were proposed to increase performance, including the installation of inverters and solar panels, the installation of modern trap tanks, and the extension of the sedimentation period. They suggested a clean strategy that tries to cut back on the use of cooling agents and lubricants as well as the right choice of materials. As a result, to succeed in this cutthroat market, manufacturing enterprises must attain monetary, ecological, and social stability. SM is one strategy of achieving this stability. Manufacturing processes that consume a lot of energy emit a lot of CO2. As a result, reducing negative environmental effects during the manufacturing process leads to improved energy efficiency, which may be seen as a critical accomplishment reason for SM. Energy sustainability is another benefit of improving industrial process energy efficiency. Techniques and methods such as energy analysis, energy assessment, and energy-saving strategies must be employed for better energy management. According to the literature, companies are currently concentrating on energy-effective machining for long-term production. The establishment of a model for the interchange of manufactured goods model data-numerical control has been learned to assist drive order management in machining conduct. Another strategy for reducing emissions and saving energy in SM is to lower the rate at which defective items are produced during the manufacturing process. Concentrating on quality can reduce failure rates while also increasing production viability (Goyal et al., 2019). Faults can be removed, particularly in the castings industry, by selecting the appropriate technique and changing the design. Three manufacturing approaches, lean (Tiwari & Tripathi, 2012), green, and six sigma, can be used to reduce errors, costs, and improve delivery performance. Innovation-lean practises in manufacturing can boost long-term performance (Tiwari, 2022). The major impediment to long-term economic success in developing countries is the excessive production of harmful gases such as carbon dioxide. Savings analysis and energy performance review can be used to determine the status of the business in relationship of energy usage and greenhouse gas emissions. Energy can be saved significantly by carefully planning plant shutdowns and scheduling non-production hours. Maintenance functions have a substantial influence on SM due to their role in sustaining the effectiveness of the production system. Inadequate repairs scheduling and performance not only harms production by increasing energy utilization and costs, but it also threatens worker health and safety. In addition to metal processing businesses, the building industry has a considerable detrimental influence on the environment. This industry, according to Giama and Papadopoulos (2020), utilizes a lot of energy and substantially promotes to global warming. A cement alternative with higher accomplishment and lower environmental influence could be favorable to the construction sector. Fly ash-based low-impact geopolymer-based hybrid foams have the potential to be an environmentally friendly building industry choice. Another cutting-edge substance in the building business is rubbing dust waste/polystyrene shoving insulating composite. It can be used as an alternative material because it has been shown to outperform pure polystyrene insulation boards in terms of thermal performance. Political and authoritarian obstacles restrict developing countries from utilising renewable energy. The study is supported by the discoveries that the use of non-renewable energy has increased unfairly in contrast to the use of renewable energy. Policy reforms are required to promote the usage of renewable energy sources and achieve the goals of SD. Making difficult decisions is required for long-term manufacturing in all three financial, environmental, and social dimensions. Customer needs, environmental constraints, and resource conservation are the driving factors behind SM practises. Procedure optimization directed by right decision support system is essential for efficient SM practises. According to the study, current DSSs put minimal attention on the operational level, instead integrating all three sustainability aspects at the tactical preparation level. Hartini et al. (2020) discovered that social planning objectives lacked concentration. The riskiest principles for the positive implementation of sustainable practises in the lean-agile corporate organisation are IT-enabled network support, supply chain members' reactivity and expertise, social concerns, and environmental resource shortage.

2.3 Circular Economy

Natural resources are strained by the growing world population. Use of energy, water, and food is rising alarmingly quickly. In addition, inappropriate consumption, and production harm the community and the natural world. By switching from an economy that is linear to a CE and integrating environmental research with the socioeconomic system, it is possible to prevent these negative consequences. Long-term city sustainability would be improved by population management, the creation of smart cities, and the growth of industrial parks. By creating an environmentally friendly supply chain that can balance everything, ecological issues in CE-based systems can be solved. A CE lengthens the useful lives of resources while lowering emissions and waste production. The triple bottom line has been negatively damaged by linear economies built on "take-make-dispose" ideas, according to the research. As a result, society is now looking for sustainable alternatives and, eventually, considering CE principles. Due to its favourable connotation with sustainability, CE has recently grown in popularity throughout the world. Due to their capacity to guarantee resource sustainability, promote economic growth, and safeguard the environment, CE-based business models are attracting the attention of more industries. According to business executives, policy makers, and academics, CE is a topic that is now and always will be of utmost importance. The core ideas of CE are renewal and repair. While restoration can offer a multitude of possibilities for cyclical procedures (Morseletto, 2020). Environmentally conscious businesses can simply migrate to a CE. Companies must overcome several obstacles to install CE. Jaeger and Upadhyay (2020) cite high beginning costs, complexity of supply chains, lack of business-to-business collaboration, an absence of information regarding the development and production of products procedures, talent gaps, excellence concerns, long wait periods for dismantling, as well as elevated costs related to such processes as the main challenges. Ex ante, an absence of technological and information structures, a lack of stakeholder's assistance, a lack of economic backing, and a lack of authorised guidelines are the main obstacles to the expansion of the CE textile and garment business. Other difficulties (post ante) include the absence of a strategy plan, training, performance evaluation systems, and infrastructure. However, the circular economy is propelled by pressure from rival businesses, customers, and the community as well as the obligation of top management. Although consumer purchases of remanufactured goods are not particularly common, municipal organisations and enterprises can work together to increase the value of the goods and enforce price restrictions to draw in more clients. The implementation of diverse environmentally friendly practises and small-scale elements of CE have received a big deal of study attention. It has been noticed that the organisation promotes CE practises gradually, starting with just a handful of activities and subsequently growing to a big number of activities. On the other hand, they don't react when resource loops are eventually closed by the system. Applying CE in towns, local governments, and districts requires a technique. Contextual evaluation, deciding on the adoption's scope, recognising opportunities, and lastly developing a roadmap are just a few of the several implementation stages that may be involved. Recovery, recycling, repurposing, remanufacturing, refurbishing, repair, reusing, reducing, rethinking, and discarding alternatives are some of the more popular CE projects. It has been discovered that CE procedures depend on both products and resources. Closing a loop makes sense when the substance can be used for a longer amount of time, but expanding the circle is suitable when the materials can be utilised heavily. While strengthening loop techniques are preferable for goods that will be worked more intensely, long life loop approaches are good if the manufacturer wants the product to live longer. Collaborative innovation is required for the adoption of diverse CE techniques. Because they promote conservation of resources, reuse, and recycling, environmental legislation and regulations are crucial drivers of innovation (Tiwari & Raju 2022). The use of CE may be required by eco-design guidelines that address design issues, firmware accessibility, accessibility of data, and the accessibility of crucial inputs (Peiro et al., 2020).

It is advisable to spot problems early on if there are no answers and convert them into cyclical business opportunities because moving to a CE is a drawn-out process. Status reviews can be carried out using analytical approaches like qualitative questionnaires and quantitative material flow analyses. Because the transformation from a traditional to a CE company structure entails a substantial adjustment in the organization's worth offering and capability development, top management is required. Assessing each solution as it comes accessible during Stage 2 and choosing the most suitable one to develop a business plan is the major goal. Using life cycle costs could help you get rid of inferior options. The decision on the solution is influenced by inside as well as outside corporate concerns. Enterprise risk evaluation is a useful technique that develops a low-risk solution by taking into consideration all the variables & the change goals of every horizon. The implementation of the ideal approach is the last action, and performance evaluation comes next. At this stage, the life cycles analysis method may be applied. The realization of the cyclical business model depends heavily on top management support. According to another investigation, the CE tactic can be identified by considering the produce level. Numerous factors and their effects on ecology must be taken into consideration. Sharing durable, little used items, for instance, can be acceptable. On the contrary hand, the cost of obtaining the shared commodities could go up due to transportation. The type of good (consumable or resilient, either passive or active, able to be continuously utilised throughout the duration of a technological advances lifelong or abandoned before it's worn out, how frequently it is use, and whether the function remains functional following use) can also affect the strategy that is selected (Böckin et al., 2020).

To enhance CE practises and build ecological capabilities, organisations utilise a variety of environmental competences (environmental management techniques, corporate social responsibility, transparency and accountability, and other ecological accounting practises). Circularity is dependent on capacity levels and affects the surroundings and the financial health of the company (Scarpellini et al., 2020; Tiwari, 2023aF). Businesses must change their organisational structures in order to migrate to a cyclical product system. According to Mura et al. (2020), businesses view CE as an opportunity to create value for itself and promote sustainability. For instance, the ability of I4.0 to support SM was highlighted in one of the few illustrative studies that connected I4.0 and manufacturing. Additionally, this has been bolstered on creating a framework connecting I4.0 with sustainable manufacturing. One of several prominent studies relating I4.0 to CE is the work, who highlighted how I4.0 may aid CE attempts while also demonstrating how the two can be merged. I4.0 may be helpful for the circularity of reusable scrap electrical equipment. Additionally, AI, service and regulatory frameworks, and CE are the important components connecting I4.0 and CE.

Thus, the study suggests that CE as well as I4.0 are associated with one another as well as that there is a recognised relationship between I4.0 and environmentally friendly production. There is, however, a paucity of research on how to integrate I4.0, sustainable production, and CE in the background of sustainable development.

3. FRAMEWORK

I4.0 for SD demonstrates a diversity of potential within, across, and within the SM, CE, and SBM structures both individually and together (Figure 1). They are said to increase resource effectiveness, improve organisational arrangements generally, employee well-being, and increase firm value, according to the sustainable I4.0 paradigm. The core elements of sustainable manufacturing are intelligent design, intelligent procurement, intelligent distribution, and intelligent quality control. CE adds tools like the 3Rs and 6Rs to help companies achieve these objectives. Geissdoerfer et al. (2017) assert that these notions have various views on what defines accountability. Sustainable manufacturing literature lays greater emphasis on gaining environmental advantages than CE does, even though CE seems to favour financial incentives over environmental benefits (Birkel et al., 2019). Better decision-making, energy efficiency, equitable cost distribution, and eco-design are only a few benefits of combining efforts to achieve circular manufacturing goals and sustainable manufacturing goals at the same time (Ghobakhloo, 2020). These coordinated efforts form the basis for the advancement of SBM that are unique and built on ecosystem innovation (Ejsmont et al., 2020). The I4.0 and CE concepts of connection and resource integration ultimately directed to noticeable and apparent product service schemes that give information for value development through their production of triple-layered, networked, and information-driven business models. By removing wastes, ineffectiveness, and non-value-added processes, this creative approach for business model transition towards sustainability offers lifetime value to customers (Tiwari, 2015), business profitability and attractiveness, and virtual twin schemes for precision. SD should be assessed as a policy-based universal strategy to develop environmentally friendly worth through source optimisation and co-optimizing economic and social outcomes, that helps the natural world, and society in equal proportion. A thoughtful approach to implementation for I4.0 should be given more thought, and this ought to be accompanied by innovative policies that consider the quadruple bottom line (social, financial, ecological, technical, and organisational) as well as the quadruple helix (industry, administration, higher education, environment, as well as society) in a scattered social and organisational environment.

4. CONCLUSION

In an I4.0 setting, this study provided existing patterns and cutting-edge SD research projects. Three main topics—the SM, SBMs, and CE—were used to categorise and evaluate the available SD literature. The original research showed that SD promotes CE aims in an I4.0 context by developing SBMs to ensure economic, social, and ecological advantages. Given that the SM is frequently the focus of sustainability research, CE and SBMs and their relationships should be given more consideration. Based on the scientific fields in which they have received extensive study, these interconnected topics were further divided into categories. This categorization served to both highlight research gaps to help related fields pursue further study as well as to unite various research efforts under the umbrella of SD. We discovered that many academics have investigated ethical adoption and usage of I4.0 technologies, particularly IoT, using conceptual analysis. Additionally, they have employed it to advance discussions of economic development,

Figure 1. Integrating industry 4.0, sustainable manufacturing, circular economy, and sustainable business models for sustainable development

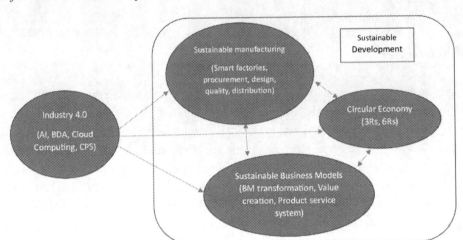

social equity, and environmental sustainability in well-established study fields like supply chains and smart factories (Tiwari, 2020). Our analysis showed a lack of studies in areas like waste from electronic products structures, water extraction structures, agri-food, protecting forests, accounting and reports, and agri-food and waste, even though I4.0 as sustainability research is being extensively conducted in the industrial sector. In contrast, investigating I4.0 technologies employing principles of CE for creating long-term value and SM as seen in other industries, including agriculture, could find a lot of hidden elements for modernisation and productivity. Just with other organised assessments, our study contains several drawbacks. Two more concepts that are connected to CE in the literature which also contribute to SD are lean manufacturing (such as waste reduction with higher efficient) and ecoefficiency (doing greater with less). To improve the quality of goods, distribution, environmentally friendly production, and organisational performance, the research shows that ecological efficiency, the notion of I4.0, and lean manufacturing all work better when coupled (Varela et al., 2019). Because our study's scope was too broad to address them, future research should investigate these problems. Our research included a mapping study that used theoretical and conceptual constructions rather than identifying causes and effects to establish facts and answer "what" and "how" queries. But because it will make it easier to identify the high-impact variables that should be the focus of I4.0 sustainability study, future research must also incorporate quantification.

REFERENCES

Ardanza, A., Moreno, A., Segura, Á., de la Cruz, M., & Aguinaga, D. (2019). Sustainable and flexible industrial human machine interfaces to support adaptable applications in the Industry 4.0 paradigm. *International Journal of Production Research*, 57(12), 4045–4059. doi:10.1080/00207543.2019.1572932

Atasu, A., Corbett, C. J., Huang, X., & Toktay, L. B. (2020). Sustainable operations management through the perspective of manufacturing & service operations management. *Manufacturing & Service Operations Management, 22*(1), 146–157. doi:10.1287/msom.2019.0804

Bag, S., Wood, L. C., Mangla, S. K., & Luthra, S. (2020). Procurement 4.0 and its implications on business process performance in a circular economy. *Resources, Conservation and Recycling, 152,* 104502. doi:10.1016/j.resconrec.2019.104502

Bahuguna, P. C., Srivastava, R., & Tiwari, S. (2022). Two-decade journey of green human resource management research: A bibliometric analysis. *Benchmarking.*

Bahuguna, P. C., Srivastava, R., & Tiwari, S. (2023). Human resources analytics: Where do we go from here? *Benchmarking.* doi:10.1108/BIJ-06-2022-0401

Barata, J., Rupino Cunha, P., & Coyle, S. (2020). Evolving manufacturing mobility in Industry 4.0: The case of process industries. *Journal of Manufacturing Technology Management, 31*(1), 52–71. doi:10.1108/JMTM-10-2018-0361

Beier, G., Niehoff, S., Ziems, T., & Xue, B. (2017). Sustainability aspects of a digitalized industry–A comparative study from China and Germany. *International journal of precision engineering and manufacturing-green technology, 4,* 227-234.

Birkel, H. S., Veile, J. W., Müller, J. M., Hartmann, E., & Voigt, K. I. (2019). Development of a risk framework for Industry 4.0 in the context of sustainability for established manufacturers. *Sustainability (Basel), 11*(2), 384. doi:10.3390u11020384

Böckin, D., Willskytt, S., André, H., Tillman, A. M., & Söderman, M. L. (2020). How product characteristics can guide measures for resource efficiency—A synthesis of assessment studies. *Resources, Conservation and Recycling, 154,* 104582. doi:10.1016/j.resconrec.2019.104582

Bordeleau, F. E., Mosconi, E., & de Santa-Eulalia, L. A. (2020). Business intelligence and analytics value creation in Industry 4.0: A multiple case study in manufacturing medium enterprises. *Production Planning and Control, 31*(2-3), 173–185. doi:10.1080/09537287.2019.1631458

Bosman, L., Hartman, N., & Sutherland, J. (2020). How manufacturing firm characteristics can influence decision making for investing in Industry 4.0 technologies. *Journal of Manufacturing Technology Management, 31*(5), 1117–1141. doi:10.1108/JMTM-09-2018-0283

Brixner, C., Isaak, P., Mochi, S., Ozono, M., Suárez, D., & Yoguel, G. (2020). Back to the future. Is industry 4.0 a new tecno-organizational paradigm? Implications for Latin American countries. *Economics of Innovation and New Technology, 29*(7), 705–719. doi:10.1080/10438599.2020.1719642

Brundtland, G. H. (1987). *Report of the World Commission on environment and development:" our common future."* UN.

Chen, Z., & Bidanda, B. (2019). Sustainable manufacturing production-inventory decision of multiple factories with JIT logistics, component recovery and emission control. *Transportation Research Part E, Logistics and Transportation Review, 128,* 356–383. doi:10.1016/j.tre.2019.06.013

Dalmarco, G., Ramalho, F. R., Barros, A. C., & Soares, A. L. (2019). Providing industry 4.0 technologies: The case of a production technology cluster. *The Journal of High Technology Management Research, 30*(2), 100355. doi:10.1016/j.hitech.2019.100355

Dev, N. K., Shankar, R., & Swami, S. (2020). Diffusion of green products in industry 4.0: Reverse logistics issues during design of inventory and production planning system. *International Journal of Production Economics, 223*, 107519. doi:10.1016/j.ijpe.2019.107519

Dubey, R., Singh, T., & Tiwari, S. (2012). Supply chain innovation is a key to superior firm performance an insight from Indian cement manufacturing. *International Journal of Innovation Science, 4*(4), 217–230. doi:10.1260/1757-2223.4.4.217

Dunuwila, P., Rodrigo, V. H. L., & Goto, N. (2020). Improving financial and environmental sustainability in concentrated latex manufacture. *Journal of Cleaner Production, 255*, 120202. doi:10.1016/j.jclepro.2020.120202

Ejsmont, K., Gladysz, B., & Kluczek, A. (2020). Impact of industry 4.0 on sustainability—Bibliometric literature review. *Sustainability (Basel), 12*(14), 5650. doi:10.3390u12145650

Elkington, J. (1998). Partnerships from cannibals with forks: The triple bottom line of 21st-century business. *Environmental Quality Management, 8*(1), 37–51. doi:10.1002/tqem.3310080106

Frank, A. G., Mendes, G. H., Ayala, N. F., & Ghezzi, A. (2019). Servitization and Industry 4.0 convergence in the digital transformation of product firms: A business model innovation perspective. *Technological Forecasting and Social Change, 141*, 341–351. doi:10.1016/j.techfore.2019.01.014

Garbellano, S., & Da Veiga, M. D. R. (2019). Dynamic capabilities in Italian leading SMEs adopting industry 4.0. *Measuring Business Excellence, 23*(4), 472–483. doi:10.1108/MBE-06-2019-0058

Geissdoerfer, M., Savaget, P., Bocken, N. M., & Hultink, E. J. (2017). The Circular Economy–A new sustainability paradigm? *Journal of Cleaner Production, 143*, 757–768. doi:10.1016/j.jclepro.2016.12.048

Ghobakhloo, M. (2020). Industry 4.0, digitization, and opportunities for sustainability. *Journal of Cleaner Production, 252*, 119869. doi:10.1016/j.jclepro.2019.119869

Giama, E., & Papadopoulos, A. M. (2020). Benchmarking carbon footprint and circularity in production processes: The case of stonewool and extruded polysterene. *Journal of Cleaner Production, 257*, 120559. doi:10.1016/j.jclepro.2020.120559

Golan, M., Cohen, Y., & Singer, G. (2020). A framework for operator–workstation interaction in Industry 4.0. *International Journal of Production Research, 58*(8), 2421–2432. doi:10.1080/00207543.2019.1639842

Goyal, A., Agrawal, R., & Saha, C. R. (2019). Quality management for sustainable manufacturing: Moving from number to impact of defects. *Journal of Cleaner Production, 241*, 118348. doi:10.1016/j.jclepro.2019.118348

Hartini, S., Ciptomulyono, U., Anityasari, M., & Sriyanto. (2020). Manufacturing sustainability assessment using a lean manufacturing tool: A case study in the Indonesian wooden furniture industry. *International Journal of Lean Six Sigma, 11*(5), 943–971. doi:10.1108/IJLSS-12-2017-0150

Hubbard, G. (2009). Measuring organizational performance: Beyond the triple bottom line. *Business Strategy and the Environment, 18*(3), 177–191. doi:10.1002/bse.564

Jaeger, B., & Upadhyay, A. (2020). Understanding barriers to circular economy: Cases from the manufacturing industry. *Journal of Enterprise Information Management, 33*(4), 729–745. doi:10.1108/JEIM-02-2019-0047

Kagermann, H., Lukas, W. D., & Wahlster, W. (2011). Industrie 4.0: Mit dem Internet der Dinge auf dem Weg zur 4. industriellen Revolution. *VDI nachrichten, 13*(1), 2-3.

Kamble, S. S., Gunasekaran, A., & Gawankar, S. A. (2018). Sustainable Industry 4.0 framework: A systematic literature review identifying the current trends and future perspectives. *Process Safety and Environmental Protection, 117*, 408–425. doi:10.1016/j.psep.2018.05.009

Kohtamäki, M., Parida, V., Patel, P. C., & Gebauer, H. (2020). The relationship between digitalization and servitization: The role of servitization in capturing the financial potential of digitalization. *Technological Forecasting and Social Change, 151*, 119804. doi:10.1016/j.techfore.2019.119804

Kusiak, A. (2018). Smart manufacturing. *International Journal of Production Research, 56*(1-2), 508–517. doi:10.1080/00207543.2017.1351644

Le Hesran, C., Ladier, A. L., Botta-Genoulaz, V., & Laforest, V. (2020). A methodology for the identification of waste-minimizing scheduling problems. *Journal of Cleaner Production, 246*, 119023. doi:10.1016/j.jclepro.2019.119023

Macchi, M., Savino, M., & Roda, I. (2020). Analysing the support of sustainability within the manufacturing strategy through multiple perspectives of different business functions. *Journal of Cleaner Production, 258*, 120771. doi:10.1016/j.jclepro.2020.120771

Machado, C. G., Winroth, M. P., & Ribeiro da Silva, E. H. D. (2020). Sustainable manufacturing in Industry 4.0: An emerging research agenda. *International Journal of Production Research, 58*(5), 1462–1484. doi:10.1080/00207543.2019.1652777

Martinez, F. (2019). Process excellence the key for digitalisation. *Business Process Management Journal, 25*(7), 1716–1733. doi:10.1108/BPMJ-08-2018-0237

McKibben, B., & McKibben, S. D. S. B. (2007). *Deep economy: The wealth of communities and the durable future.* Macmillan.

Morseletto, P. (2020). Restorative and regenerative: Exploring the concepts in the circular economy. *Journal of Industrial Ecology, 24*(4), 763–773. doi:10.1111/jiec.12987

Mura, M., Longo, M., & Zanni, S. (2020). Circular economy in Italian SMEs: A multi-method study. *Journal of Cleaner Production, 245*, 118821. doi:10.1016/j.jclepro.2019.118821

Nam, T. (2019). Technology usage, expected job sustainability, and perceived job insecurity. *Technological Forecasting and Social Change, 138*, 155–165. doi:10.1016/j.techfore.2018.08.017

Nascimento, D. L. M., Alencastro, V., Quelhas, O. L. G., Caiado, R. G. G., Garza-Reyes, J. A., Rocha-Lona, L., & Tortorella, G. (2019). Exploring Industry 4.0 technologies to enable circular economy practices in a manufacturing context: A business model proposal. *Journal of Manufacturing Technology Management*, *30*(3), 607–627. doi:10.1108/JMTM-03-2018-0071

Olawumi, T. O., & Chan, D. W. (2018). A scientometric review of global research on sustainability and sustainable development. *Journal of Cleaner Production*, *183*, 231–250. doi:10.1016/j.jclepro.2018.02.162

Peiró, L. T., Polverini, D., Ardente, F., & Mathieux, F. (2020). Advances towards circular economy policies in the EU: The new Ecodesign regulation of enterprise servers. *Resources, Conservation and Recycling*, *154*, 104426. doi:10.1016/j.resconrec.2019.104426 PMID:32127729

Ralston, P., & Blackhurst, J. (2020). Industry 4.0 and resilience in the supply chain: A driver of capability enhancement or capability loss? *International Journal of Production Research*, *58*(16), 5006–5019. doi:10.1080/00207543.2020.1736724

Sauvé, S., Bernard, S., & Sloan, P. (2016). Environmental sciences, sustainable development and circular economy: Alternative concepts for trans-disciplinary research. *Environmental Development*, *17*, 48–56. doi:10.1016/j.envdev.2015.09.002

Scarpellini, S., Marín-Vinuesa, L. M., Aranda-Usón, A., & Portillo-Tarragona, P. (2020). Dynamic capabilities and environmental accounting for the circular economy in businesses. *Sustainability Accounting. Management and Policy Journal*, *11*(7), 1129–1158.

Sterling, S. (2004). Higher education, sustainability, and the role of systemic learning. *Higher education and the challenge of sustainability: Problematics, promise, and practice*, 49-70.

Tiwari, S. (2015). Framework for adopting sustainability in the supply chain. *International Journal of Automation and Logistics*, *1*(3), 256–272. doi:10.1504/IJAL.2015.071724

Tiwari, S. (2020). Supply chain integration and Industry 4.0: A systematic literature review. *Benchmarking*, *28*(3), 990–1030. doi:10.1108/BIJ-08-2020-0428

Tiwari, S. (2022). Supply Chain Innovation in the Era of Industry 4.0. In Handbook of Research on Supply Chain Resiliency, Efficiency, and Visibility in the Post-Pandemic Era (pp. 40-60). IGI Global.

Tiwari, S. (2023a). Industry 4.0: Managing the Circular Supply Chain. In Handbook of Research on Designing Sustainable Supply Chains to Achieve a Circular Economy (pp. 164-185). IGI Global.

Tiwari, S. (2023b). Smart warehouse: A bibliometric analysis and future research direction. *Sustainable Manufacturing and Service Economics*, *2*, 100014. doi:10.1016/j.smse.2023.100014

Tiwari, S., Bahuguna, P. C., & Srivastava, R. (2022a). Smart manufacturing and sustainability: a bibliometric analysis. Benchmarking: An International Journal. doi:10.1108/BIJ-04-2022-0238

Tiwari, S., Dubey, R., & Tripathi, N. (2011). The journey of lean. *Indian Journal of Commerce and Management Studies*, *2*(2), 200–210.

Tiwari, S., & Raju, T. B. (2022). Management of Digital Innovation. In *Promoting Inclusivity and Diversity Through Internet of Things in Organizational Settings* (pp. 128–149). IGI Global. doi:10.4018/978-1-6684-5575-3.ch007

Tiwari, S., & Tripathi, N. (2012). Lean Manufacturing Practices and Firms Performance Measurement—A Review Paper. *Journal of Supply Chain Management Systems*, *1*(1), 44.

Tortorella, G. L., Vergara, A. M. C., Garza-Reyes, J. A., & Sawhney, R. (2020). Organizational learning paths based upon industry 4.0 adoption: An empirical study with Brazilian manufacturers. *International Journal of Production Economics*, *219*, 284–294. doi:10.1016/j.ijpe.2019.06.023

Trivedi, S., Negi, S., & Tiwari, S. (2023). Sustainability in the Aviation Industry in the Post-COVID-19 Era. In Challenges and Opportunities for Aviation Stakeholders in a Post-Pandemic World (pp. 235-244). IGI Global. doi:10.4018/978-1-6684-6835-7.ch012

Varela, L., Araújo, A., Ávila, P., Castro, H., & Putnik, G. (2019). Evaluation of the relation between lean manufacturing, industry 4.0, and sustainability. *Sustainability (Basel)*, *11*(5), 1439. doi:10.3390u11051439

Zhu, X., Ren, M., Chu, W., & Chiong, R. (2019). Remanufacturing subsidy or carbon regulation? An alternative toward sustainable production. *Journal of Cleaner Production*, *239*, 117988. doi:10.1016/j.jclepro.2019.117988

Compilation of References

Abada, Z., & Bouharkat, M. (2018). Study of management strategy of energy resources in Algeria. *Energy Reports*, *4*, 1–7. doi:10.1016/j.egyr.2017.09.004

Abdullah, M. A., Kedah, Z., & Anwar, M. A. (2016). The Impact of Millionaires' Secret Strategy on Entrepreneurial Performance through Entrepreneurial Motivation. *ResearchGate*. https://www.researchgate.net/publication/317714795_The_Impact_of_Millionaires'_Secret_Strategy_on_Entrepreneurial_Performance_through_Entrepreneurial_Motivation

Abhilash, S., Shenoy, S. S., & Shetty, D. K. (2022). A state-of-the-art overview of green bond markets: Evidence from technology empowered systematic literature review. *Cogent Economics & Finance*, *10*(1), 2135834. doi:10.1080/23322039.2022.2135834

Abiaziem. C.V., Williams, A.B., Inegbenebor, A.I., Onwordi, C.T., Ehi-Eromosele, C.O. & Petrik, L.F. (2020). Isolation And Characterisation Of Cellulose Nanocrystal Obtained From Sugarcane Peel. *Rasayan J. Chem.*, *13*(1), 177-187. http://dx.doi.org/ C.2020.1315328 doi:10.31788/RJ

Abisuga, A. O., Wang, C. C., & Sunindijo, R. Y. (2019). A holistic framework with user-centered facilities performance attributes for evaluating higher education buildings. *Facilities*, *38*(1/2), 132–160. doi:10.1108/F-07-2018-0083

Abitbol, T., Rivkin, A., Cao, Y., Nevo, Y., Abraham, E., Ben-Shalom, T., Lapidot, S., & Shoseyov, O. (2016). Nanocellulose, a tiny fiber with huge applications. *Current Opinion in Biotechnology*, *39*, 76–88. doi:10.1016/j.copbio.2016.01.002 PMID:26930621

Abrar, M., Sibtain, M. M., & Shabbir, R. (2021). Understanding purchase intention towards eco-friendly clothing for generation Y & Z. *Cogent Business & Management*, *8*(1), 1997247. Advance online publication. doi:10.1080/23311975.2021.1997247

Abu-Elsamen, A. A., Akroush, M. N., Asfour, N. A., & Al Jabali, H. (2019). Understanding contextual factors affecting the adoption of energy-efficient household products in Jordan. *Sustainability Accounting. Management and Policy Journal*, *10*(2), 314–332. doi:10.1108/SAMPJ-05-2018-0144

Acciaro, M., Vanelslander, T., Sys, C., Ferrari, C., Roumboutsos, A., Giuliano, G., Lam, J. S. L., & Kapros, S. (2014). Environmental sustainability in seaports: A framework for successful innovation. *Maritime Policy & Management*, *41*(5), 480–500. doi:10.1080/03088839.2014.932926

Achillas, C. (2019). *Green supply chain management*. Routledge, Taylor & Francis Group.

Adams, R., Jeanrenaud, S., Bessant, J., Denyer, D., & Overy, P. (2016). Sustainability-oriented Innovation: A Systematic Review: Sustainability-oriented Innovation. *International Journal of Management Reviews*, *18*(2), 180–205. doi:10.1111/ijmr.12068

Compilation of References

Adel, A. M., El-Shafei, A. M., Ibrahim, A. A., & Al-Shemy, M. T. (2019). Chitosan/Nanocrystalline Cellulose Biocomposites Based on Date Palm (Phoenix Dactylifera L.) Sheath Fibers. *Journal of Renewable Materials*, *7*(6), 567–582. doi:10.32604/jrm.2019.00034

Afum, E., Agyabeng-Mensah, Y., Sun, Z., Frimpong, B., Kusi, L. Y., & Acquah, I. S. K. (2020). Exploring the link between green manufacturing, operational competitiveness, firm reputation and sustainable performance dimensions: A mediated approach. *Journal of Manufacturing Technology Management*, *31*(7), 1417–1438. doi:10.1108/JMTM-02-2020-0036

Agarwal, P. K., Gurjar, J., Agarwal, A. K., & Birla, R. (2015). Application of artificial intelligence for development of intelligent transport system in smart cities. *Journal of Traffic and Transportation Engineering*, *1*(1), 20–30.

Agarwal, S., Agrawal, V., & Dixit, J. K. (2020). Green manufacturing: A MCDM approach. *Materials Today: Proceedings*, *26*, 2869–2874. doi:10.1016/j.matpr.2020.02.595

Ageron, B., Gunasekaran, A., & Spalanzani, A. (2012). Sustainable supply management: An empirical study. *International Journal of Production Economics*, *140*(1), 168–182. doi:10.1016/j.ijpe.2011.04.007

Aggarwal, A., Choudhary, C., & Mehrotra, D. (2018). Evaluation of smartphones in Indian market using EDAS, *International Conference on Computational Intelligence and Data Science (ICCIDS 2018), ScienceDirect*, (vol. *132*, pp. 236-243). Science Direct. 10.1016/j.procs.2018.05.193

Agliardi, E., & Agliardi, R. (2019). Financing environmentally-sustainable projects with green bonds. *Environment and Development Economics*, *24*(6), 608–623. doi:10.1017/S1355770X19000020

Agusnar, H., Zaidar, E., & Lenny, S. (2021). Synthesis and characterization of nanocomposite chitosan from Horseshoe Crab to improve antibacterial properties. *AIP Conference Proceedings*, *2342*, 020009. doi:10.1063/5.0046157

Ahi, P., & Searcy, C. (2013). A comparative literature analysis of definitions for green and sustainable supply chain management. *Journal of Cleaner Production*, *52*, 329–341. doi:10.1016/j.jclepro.2013.02.018

Ahmad, Z., Roziaizan, N., Rozyanty, A.R., Mohamad, A., & Nawawi, W.I. (2016). *Isolation and Characterization of Microcrystalline Cellulose (MCC) from Rice Husk (RH)*. Semantic Scholar.

Ahmed, R., Yusuf, F., & Ishaque, M. (2023). Green bonds as a bridge to the UN sustainable development goals on environment: A climate change empirical investigation. *International Journal of Finance & Economics*, ijfe.2787. doi:10.1002/ijfe.2787

Ai, O., Chioma, E., Okenwa, G. O., Samuel, I., & Abiodun Ademola, A. (2021). *Green Manufacturing: Rethinking the Sustainability of Nigerian Manufacturing Firms*.

Ait-Kadi, M. (2016). Water for development and development for water: Realizing the sustainable development goals (SDGs) vision. *Aquatic Procedia*, *6*, 106–110. doi:10.1016/j.aqpro.2016.06.013

Ajzen, I. (1991). The theory of planned behavior. *Organizational Behavior and Human Decision Processes*, *50*(2), 179–211. doi:10.1016/0749-5978(91)90020-T

Ajzen, I. (2002). Perceived behavioral control, self-efficacy, locus of control, and the theory of planned behavior. *Journal of Applied Social Psychology*, *32*(4), 665–683. doi:10.1111/j.1559-1816.2002.tb00236.x

Ajzen, I. (2020). The theory of planned behavior: Frequently asked questions. *Human Behavior and Emerging Technologies*, *2*(4), 314–324. doi:10.1002/hbe2.195

Akhtaruzzaman, M., Banerjee, A. K., Ghardallou, W., & Umar, Z. (2022). Is greenness an optimal hedge for sectoral stock indices? *Economic Modelling*, *117*, 106030. doi:10.1016/j.econmod.2022.106030

Akomea-Frimpong, I., Adeabah, D., Ofosu, D., & Tenakwah, E. J. (2022). A review of studies on green finance of banks, research gaps and future directions. *Journal of Sustainable Finance & Investment*, *12*(4), 1241–1264. doi:10.1080/20430795.2020.1870202

Akpınar, E. (2014). The use of interactive computer animations based on POE as a presentation tool in primary science teaching. *Journal of Science Education and Technology*, *23*(4), 527–537. doi:10.100710956-013-9482-4

Akroush, M. N., Zuriekat, M. I., Al Jabali, H. I., & Asfour, N. A. (2019). Determinants of purchasing intentions of energy-efficient products: The roles of energy awareness and perceived benefits. *International Journal of Energy Sector Management*, *13*(1), 128–148. doi:10.1108/IJESM-05-2018-0009

Al Nuaimi, E., Al Neyadi, H., Mohamed, N., & Al-Jaroodi, J. (2015). Applications of big data to smart cities. *Journal of Internet Services and Applications*, *6*(1), 1–15. doi:10.118613174-015-0041-5

Alalei, A., & Jan, M. T. (2023). Factors influencing the green purchase intention among consumers: An empirical study in Algeria. *Journal of Global Business Insights*, *8*(1), 49–65.

Alam, S. S., & Sayuti, N. M. (2011). Applying the theory of planned behavior (TPB) in halal food purchasing. *International Journal of Commerce and Management*, *21*(1), 8–20. doi:10.1108/10569211111111676

Albers, J., Knop, K., & Kleinebudde, P. (2006). Brand-to-brand and batch-to-batch uniformity of microcrystalline cellulose in direct tableting with a pneumo-hydraulic tablet press. *Die Pharmazeutische Industrie*, *68*, 1420–1428.

Alberts, G., Went, M., & Jansma, R. (2017). Archaeology of the Amsterdam digital city; why digital data are dynamic and should be treated accordingly. *Internet Histories*, *1*(1-2), 146–159. doi:10.1080/24701475.2017.1309852

Aldieri, L., & Vinci, C. P. (2018, October 2). *Green Economy and Sustainable Development: The Economic Impact of Innovation on Employment*. MDPI. doi:10.3390/su10103541

Alharbi, S. S., Al Mamun, M., Boubaker, S., & Rizvi, S. K. A. (2023). Green finance and renewable energy: A worldwide evidence. *Energy Economics*, *106499*, 106499. Advance online publication. doi:10.1016/j.eneco.2022.106499

Ali, E. B., Anufriev, V. P., & Amfo, B. (2021). Green economy implementation in Ghana as a road map for a sustainable development drive: A review. *Scientific African*, *12*, e00756. doi:10.1016/j.sciaf.2021.e00756

Ali, M. A. M., & Kim, J. G. (2021). Selection mining methods via multiple criteria decision analysis using TOPSIS and modification of the UBC method. *Journal of Sustainable Mining*, *20*(2), 49–55. doi:10.46873/2300-3960.1054

Ali, M. J., Rahaman, M., & Hossain, S. I. (2022). Urban green spaces for elderly human health: A planning model for healthy city living. *Land Use Policy*, *114*, 105970. doi:10.1016/j.landusepol.2021.105970

Ali, M. R., Shafiq, M., & Andejany, M. (2021). Determinants of consumers' intentions towards the purchase of energy-efficient appliances in Pakistan: An extended model of the theory of planned behavior. *Sustainability*, *13*(2), 1–17. doi:10.3390u13020565 PMID:34123411

Ali, S., Ullah, H., Akbar, M., Akhtar, W., & Zahid, H. (2019). Determinants of consumer intentions to purchase energy-saving household products in Pakistan. *Sustainability (Basel)*, *11*(5), 1–20. doi:10.3390u11051462

Aloui, D., Benkraiem, R., Guesmi, K., & Vigne, S. (2023). The European Central Bank and green finance: How would the green quantitative easing affect the investors' behavior during times of crisis? *International Review of Financial Analysis*, *85*, 102464. doi:10.1016/j.irfa.2022.102464

Compilation of References

Altomonte, S., Allen, J., Bluyssen, P. M., Brager, G., Heschong, L., Loder, A., Schiavon, S., Veitch, J. A., Wang, L., & Wargocki, P. (2020). Ten questions concerning well-being in the built environment. *Building and Environment*, *180*, 106949. doi:10.1016/j.buildenv.2020.106949

Aluko, O. A., Osei Opoku, E. E., & Ibrahim, M. (2021). Investigating the environmental effect of globalization: Insights from selected industrialized countries. *Journal of Environmental Management*, *281*, 111892. doi:10.1016/j.jenvman.2020.111892 PMID:33433368

Alves, L., Medronho, B., Antunes, F.E., Fernández-García, M.P., Ventura, J., Araújo, J.P., Romano, A., Lindman, B. (2015). Unusual extraction and characterization of nanocrystalline cellulose from cellulose derivatives. *Journal of Molecular Liquids, 210*, 106-112. . doi:10.1016/j.molliq.2014.12.010

American Association for the Advancement of Science. (2017, November 6). Plastic waste inputs from land into the ocean. *Science*. https://www.science.org/doi/10.1126/science.1260352

Amezaga, J., Bathurst, J., Iroumé, A., Jones, J., Kotru, R., Bhatta, L. D., & de Jong, W. (2019). *SDG 6: clean water and sanitation–forest-related targets and their impacts on forests and people. Sustainable development goals: their impacts on forests and people*. Cambridge University Press.

Amirazar, A. (2021). *Evidence-Based Human-Centric Lighting Assist Tool towards a Healthier Lit Environment* [Doctoral dissertation]. The University of North Carolina at Charlotte.

Ang, B. W., Choong, W. L., & Ng, T. S. (2015). Energy security: Definitions, dimensions and indexes. In *Renewable and Sustainable Energy Reviews* (Vol. 42, pp. 1077–1093). Elsevier Ltd. doi:10.1016/j.rser.2014.10.064

Angelidou, M. (2016). Four European smart city strategies. *International Journal of Social Science Studies*, *4*(4), 18–30. doi:10.11114/ijsss.v4i4.1364

Anjum, A., Ahmed, T., Khan, A., Ahmad, N., Ahmad, M., Asif, M., Reddy, A. G., Saba, T., & Farooq, N. (2018). Privacy preserving data by conceptualizing smart cities using MIDR-Angelization. *Sustainable Cities and Society*, *40*, 326–334. doi:10.1016/j.scs.2018.04.014

Anon. (2014). *4Country Analysis Brief: Algeria*. U.S. Energy Information Administration, Washington.

AR6 Synthesis Report: Climate Change. (n.d.). IPCC. https://www.ipcc.ch/report/sixth-assessment-report-cycle/

Ardanza, A., Moreno, A., Segura, Á., de la Cruz, M., & Aguinaga, D. (2019). Sustainable and flexible industrial human machine interfaces to support adaptable applications in the Industry 4.0 paradigm. *International Journal of Production Research*, *57*(12), 4045–4059. doi:10.1080/00207543.2019.1572932

Arifin, Z., & Frmanzah. (2015). The Effect of Dynamic Capability to Technology Adoption and its Determinant Factors for Improving Firm's Performance; Toward a Conceptual Model. *Procedia: Social and Behavioral Sciences*, *207*, 786–796. doi:10.1016/j.sbspro.2015.10.168

Arisal, I., & Atalar, T. (2016). The exploring relationships between environmental concern, collectivism, and ecological purchase intention. *Procedia: Social and Behavioral Sciences*, *235*, 514–521. doi:10.1016/j.sbspro.2016.11.063

Armitage, C. J., Armitage, C. J., Conner, M., Loach, J., & Willetts, D. (1999). Different Perceptions of Control: Applying an Extended Theory of Planned Behavior to Legal and Illegal Drug Use. *Basic and Applied Social Psychology*, *21*(4), 301–316. doi:10.1207/S15324834BASP2104_4

Arora, N. K. (2018). Environmental Sustainability—Necessary for survival. *Environmental Sustainability*, *1*(1), 1–2. doi:10.100742398-018-0013-3

Arvola, M., Vassallo, M., Dean, P., Lampila, A., Saba, L., Lähteenmäki, R., & Shepherd, R. (2008). Predicting intentions to purchase organic food: The role of affective and moral attitudes in the theory of planned behaviour. *Appetite*, *50*(2–3), 443–454. doi:10.1016/j.appet.2007.09.010 PMID:18036702

Asian Development Bank. (2016). *Asian water development outlook 2016: Strengthening water security in Asia and the pacific*. ADB. https://www.adb.org/sites/default/files/publication/189411/awdo-2016.pdf

Asian Development Bank. (2018). *Asian Water Development Outlook 2018: Strengthening Water Security in Asia and the Pacific*. ADB. https://www.adb.org/sites/default/files/publication/455071/awdo-2018.pdf

Aşıcı, M. A. (2021). *Avrupa Birliği'nin Sınırda Karbon Uyarlaması Mekanizması ve Türkiye Ekonomisi*. IPM-Mercator.

Asif, M. H., Zhongfu, T., Irfan, M., & Işık, C. (2023). Do environmental knowledge and green trust matter for purchase intention of eco-friendly home appliances? An application of extended theory of planned behavior. *Environmental Science and Pollution Research International*, *30*(13), 37762–37774. doi:10.100711356-022-24899-1 PMID:36574131

Asim, M., Khalina Abdan, M., Jawaid, M. Nasir, M., Dashtizadeh, Z., Ishak, M., & Hoque, M. (2015). A Review on Pineapple Leaves Fibre and Its Composites. Hindawi.

Atasu, A., Corbett, C. J., Huang, X., & Toktay, L. B. (2020). Sustainable operations management through the perspective of manufacturing & service operations management. *Manufacturing & Service Operations Management*, *22*(1), 146–157. doi:10.1287/msom.2019.0804

Ateş, S. A., & Ateş, M. (2015). Sosyo-Ekolojik Dönüşüm Karşısında Türkiye: Bir Alternatif Olarak Yeşil Büyüme. *Siyaset Ekonomi ve Yönetim Araştırmaları Dergisi*, *3*(4), 69–94.

Avunduk, Z. B. (2021). Üretim Yönetiminde Yeşil İnovasyon:(S) SCI Dergilerinde Yayımlanan Makalelerin İçerik Analizi. *Yönetim Bilimleri Dergisi*, *19*(Özel Sayı), 187–210. doi:10.35408/comuybd.974854

Azam, A., Rafiq, M., Shafique, M., Zhang, H., Ateeq, M., & Yuan, J. (2021). Analyzing the relationship between economic growth and electricity consumption from renewable and non-renewable sources: Fresh evidence from newly industrialized countries. *Sustainable Energy Technologies and Assessments*, *44*, 100991. doi:10.1016/j.seta.2021.100991

Azeredo, H.M.C., Rosa, M.F., & Mattoso, L.H.C. (2016). Nanocellulose in bio-based food packaging applications. *Ind. Crops Prod.*, *97*, 664-671. http://dx.doi.org/. 2016.03.013 doi:10.1016/j.indcrop

Aziz, T., Iqbal, M., Ullah, R., Jamil, M.I., & Raheel, M. (2021). Improving Adhesive Properties of Cellulose Nanocrystals Modifying by 3-Glycidoxypropyltrimethoxy Silane (KH-560) Coupling Agents. *Biomed J Sci & Tech Res.*, *34*(1), 26402-26407.

Aziz, T., Fan, H., Zhang, X., Haq, F., Ullah, A., Ullah, R., Khan, F. U., & Iqbal, M. (2020). Advance Study of Cellulose Nanocrystals Properties and Applications. *Journal of Polymers and the Environment*, *28*(4), 1117–1128. doi:10.100710924-020-01674-2

Azubuike, C. P., & Okhamafe, A. O. (2012). Physicochemical, spectroscopic and thermal properties of microcrystalline cellulose derived from corn cobs. *International Journal of Recycling of Organic Waste in Agriculture*, *1*(9), 1–7. doi:10.1186/2251-7715-1-9

B. (2023, March 23). *What is Azure Digital Twins? Azure Digital Twins*. Microsoft Learn. https://learn.microsoft.com/en-us/azure/digital-twins/overview

Compilation of References

Baah, C., Opoku-Agyeman, D., Acquah, I. S. K., Agyabeng-Mensah, Y., Afum, E., Faibil, D., & Abdoulaye, F. A. M. (2021). Examining the correlations between stakeholder pressures, green production practices, firm reputation, environmental and financial performance: Evidence from manufacturing SMEs. *Sustainable Production and Consumption*, *27*, 100–114. doi:10.1016/j.spc.2020.10.015

Bacakova, L., Pajorova, J., Tomkova, M., Matejka, R., Broz, A., Stepanovska, J., Prazak, S., Skogberg, A., Siljander, S., & Kallio, P. (2020). Applications of Nanocellulose/Nanocarbon Composites: Focus on Biotechnology and Medicine. *Nanomaterials (Basel, Switzerland)*, *10*(2), 196. doi:10.3390/nano10020196 PMID:31979245

Bachelet, M. J., Becchetti, L., & Manfredonia, S. (2019). The Green Bonds Premium Puzzle: The Role of Issuer Characteristics and Third-Party Verification. *Sustainability (Basel)*, *11*(4), 1098. doi:10.3390u11041098

Badri, K. H., Ahmad, S. H., & Zakaria, S. (2001). Production of a High-Functionality RBD Palm Kernel Oil-Based Polyester Polyol. *Journal of Applied Polymer Science*, *81*(2), 384–389. doi:10.1002/app.1449

Bag, S., & Pretorius, J. H. C. (2022). Relationships between industry 4.0, sustainable manufacturing and circular economy: Proposal of a research framework. *The International Journal of Organizational Analysis*, *30*(4), 864–898. doi:10.1108/IJOA-04-2020-2120

Bag, S., Wood, L. C., Mangla, S. K., & Luthra, S. (2020). Procurement 4.0 and its implications on business process performance in a circular economy. *Resources, Conservation and Recycling*, *152*, 104502. doi:10.1016/j.resconrec.2019.104502

Bag, S., Yadav, G., Wood, L. C., Dhamija, P., & Joshi, S. (2020). Industry 4.0 and the circular economy: Resource melioration in logistics. *Resources Policy*, *68*, 101776. doi:10.1016/j.resourpol.2020.101776

Bahuguna, P. C., Srivastava, R., & Tiwari, S. (2022). Two-decade journey of green human resource management research: A bibliometric analysis. *Benchmarking*.

Bahuguna, P. C., Srivastava, R., & Tiwari, S. (2023). Human resources analytics: Where do we go from here? *Benchmarking*. doi:10.1108/BIJ-06-2022-0401

Bain, R., Johnston, R., Mitis, F., Chatterley, C., & Slaymaker, T. (2018). Establishing sustainable development goal baselines for household drinking water, sanitation and hygiene services. *Water (Basel)*, *10*(12), 1711. doi:10.3390/w10121711

Baker, M., Bergstresser, D., Serafeim, G., & Wurgler, J. (2018). *Financing the Response to Climate Change: The Pricing and Ownership of U.S. Green Bonds*. NBER. doi:10.3386/w25194

Ballesteros, L. F., Teixeira, J. A., & Mussatto, S. I. (2014). Chemical, functional, and structural properties of spent coffee grounds and coffee silverskin. *Food and Bioprocess Technology*, *7*(12), 3493–3503. doi:10.100711947-014-1349-z

Barakat, A., & Fahmy, A. (2021). Cellulose nanocrystals from sugarcane bagasse and its graft with GMA: Synthesis, characterization, and biocompatibility assessment. *Journal of Applied Pharmaceutical Science*, *11*(02), 114–125. doi:10.7324/JAPS.2021.110215

Barata, J., Rupino Cunha, P., & Coyle, S. (2020). Evolving manufacturing mobility in Industry 4.0: The case of process industries. *Journal of Manufacturing Technology Management*, *31*(1), 52–71. doi:10.1108/JMTM-10-2018-0361

Barley, S. R. (2020). *Work and technological change*. Oxford University Press. doi:10.1093/oso/9780198795209.001.0001

Battista, O. A. (1950). Hydrolysis and crystallization of cellulose. *Industrial & Engineering Chemistry*, *42*(3), 502–507. doi:10.1021/ie50483a029

Battista, O. A., & Smith, P. A. (1962). Microcrystalline cellulose. *Industrial & Engineering Chemistry*, *54*(9), 20–29. doi:10.1021/ie50633a003

Battisti, G. (2008). Innovations and the Economics of New Technology Spreading within and across Users: Gaps and Way Forward. *Journal of Cleaner Production, 16*(1), 22–31. doi:10.1016/j.jclepro.2007.10.018

Beier, G., Niehoff, S., Ziems, T., & Xue, B. (2017). Sustainability aspects of a digitalized industry–A comparative study from China and Germany. *International journal of precision engineering and manufacturing-green technology, 4*, 227-234.

Bellucci, M., Simoni, L., Acuti, D., & Manetti, G. (2019). Stakeholder engagement and dialogic accounting: Empirical evidence in sustainability reporting. *Accounting, Auditing & Accountability Journal, 32*(5), 1467–1499. doi:10.1108/AAAJ-09-2017-3158

Beltramino, F., Roncero, M. B., Vidal, T., Torres, A. L., & Valls, C. (2015). Increasing yield of nanocrystalline cellulose preparation process by a cellulase pretreatment. *Bioresource Technology, 192*, 574–581. doi:10.1016/j.biortech.2015.06.007 PMID:26092069

Bengtsson, M., Alfredsson, E., Cohen, M., Lorek, S., & Schroeder, P. (2018). Transforming systems of consumption and production for achieving the sustainable development goals: Moving beyond efficiency. *Sustainability Science, 13*(6), 1533–1547. Advance online publication. doi:10.100711625-018-0582-1 PMID:30546486

Benitez-Amado, J., Llorens-Montes, F. J., & Fernandez-Perez, V. (2015). IT impact on talent management and operational environmental sustainability. *Information Technology and Management, 16*(3), 207–220. doi:10.100710799-015-0226-4

Berlin from Siemens Mobility GmbH and Niederbarnimer Eisenbahn (NEB). (2022). *Press Joint press release from Siemens Mobility GmbH and Niederbarnimer Eisenbahn*. NEB.

Bertran, M. S., & Dale, B. E. (1986). Determination of Cellulose Accessibility by Differential Scanning Calorimetry. *Journal of Applied Polymer Science, 32*(3), 4241–4253. doi:10.1002/app.1986.070320335

Besserer, A., Troilo, S., Girods, P., Rogaume, Y., & Brosse, N. (2021). Cascading recycling of wood waste: A review. *Polymers, 13*(11), 1752. doi:10.3390/polym13111752 PMID:34071945

Better Buildings Partnership. (2022, February 21). *British Land's 1 Triton Square Shows the Commercial Value of Circular Economy Leadership*. Better Buildings Partnership.

Bhat, A.H. & Dasan, Y. & Khan, I., Soleimani, H., Usmani, M. (2017). Application of nanocrystalline cellulose: Processing and biomedical applications. *Application of nanocrystalline cellulose.* . doi:10.1016/B978-0-08-100957-4.00009-7

Bhattacharya, S., Gupta, A., Kar, K., & Owusu, A. (2015, November). Hedging strategies for risk reduction through weather derivatives in renewable energy markets. In *2015 International Conference on Renewable Energy Research and Applications (ICRERA)* (pp. 1190-1195). IEEE. 10.1109/ICRERA.2015.7418597

Bhattacharyya, P., Bisen, J., Bhaduri, D., Priyadarsini, S., Munda, S., Chakraborti, M., Adak, T., Panneerselvam, P., Mukherjee, A. K., Swain, S. L., Dash, P. K., Padhy, S. R., Nayak, A. K., Pathak, H., Arora, S., & Nimbrayan, P. (2021). Turn the wheel from waste to wealth: Economic and environmental gain of sustainable rice straw management practices over field burning in reference to India. *The Science of the Total Environment, 775*, 14589. doi:10.1016/j.scitotenv.2021.145896

Bhutta, U. S., Tariq, A., Farrukh, M., Raza, A., & Iqbal, M. K. (2022). Green bonds for sustainable development: Review of literature on development and impact of green bonds. *Technological Forecasting and Social Change, 175*, 121378. doi:10.1016/j.techfore.2021.121378

Bhutto, M. Y., Liu, X., Soomro, Y. A., Ertz, M., & Baeshen, Y. (2021). Adoption of energy-efficient home appliances: Extending the theory of planned behavior. *Sustainability (Basel), 13*(1), 250. doi:10.3390u13010250

Bini, L., & Bellucci, M. (2020). Accounting for Sustainability. In L. Bini & M. Bellucci, Integrated Sustainability Reporting (pp. 9–51). Springer International Publishing. doi:10.1007/978-3-030-24954-0_2

Compilation of References

Birkel, H. S., Veile, J. W., Müller, J. M., Hartmann, E., & Voigt, K. I. (2019). Development of a risk framework for Industry 4.0 in the context of sustainability for established manufacturers. *Sustainability (Basel)*, *11*(2), 384. doi:10.3390u11020384

Bisoyi, B., & Das, B. (2018). An approach to en route environmentally sustainable future through green computing. In *Smart Computing and Informatics: Proceedings of the First International Conference on SCI 2016*, (pp. 621-629). Springer Singapore. 10.1007/978-981-10-5544-7_61

Bisoyi, B., Nayak, B., Das, B., & Pasumarti, S. S. (2021). Urban Resilience and Inclusion of Smart Cities in the Transformation Process for Sustainable Development: Critical Deflections on the Smart City of Bhubaneswar in India. In *Advances in Power Systems and Energy Management: Select Proceedings of ETAEERE 2020* (pp. 149-160). Springer Singapore.

Bisoyi, B., & Das, B. (2023). A paradigm shift: Nano-sensory nudges stimulating consumer's purchase behaviour for green products driving towards environmental sustainability. *Materials Today: Proceedings*, *80*, 3887–3892. doi:10.1016/j.matpr.2021.07.407

Biswas, J. K., Mondal, B., Priyadarshini, P., Abhilash, P. C., Biswas, S., & Bhatnagar, A. (2022). Formulation of Water Sustainability Index for India as a performance gauge for realizing the United Nations Sustainable Development Goal 6. *Ambio*, *51*(6), 1569–1587. doi:10.100713280-021-01680-1 PMID:34932186

Böckin, D., Willskytt, S., André, H., Tillman, A. M., & Söderman, M. L. (2020). How product characteristics can guide measures for resource efficiency—A synthesis of assessment studies. *Resources, Conservation and Recycling*, *154*, 104582. doi:10.1016/j.resconrec.2019.104582

Bogdanovic, D., Nikolic, D., & Ilic, I. (2012). Mining method selection by integrated AHP and PROMETHEE method. *Anais da Academia Brasileira de Ciências*, *84*(1), 219–233. doi:10.1590/S0001-37652012005000013 PMID:22441612

Bohloul, S. M. (2020). Smart cities: A survey on new developments, trends, and opportunities. *Journal of Industrial Integration and Management*, *5*(3), 311–326. doi:10.1142/S2424862220500128

Bokhari, S. A. A., & Myeong, S. (2022). Use of artificial intelligence in smart cities for smart decision-making: A social innovation perspective. *Sustainability (Basel)*, *14*(2), 620. doi:10.3390u14020620

Boonmahitthisud, A., Booranapunpong, Cc., Pattaradechakul, & Tanpichai, S. (2023). Development of water-resistant paper using chitosan and plant-based wax extracted from banana leaves. *International Journal of Biological Macromolecules*. doi: 2023.124412. doi:10.1016/j.ijbiomac.vol

Bordeleau, F. E., Mosconi, E., & de Santa-Eulalia, L. A. (2020). Business intelligence and analytics value creation in Industry 4.0: A multiple case study in manufacturing medium enterprises. *Production Planning and Control*, *31*(2-3), 173–185. doi:10.1080/09537287.2019.1631458

Bosman, L., Hartman, N., & Sutherland, J. (2020). How manufacturing firm characteristics can influence decision making for investing in Industry 4.0 technologies. *Journal of Manufacturing Technology Management*, *31*(5), 1117–1141. doi:10.1108/JMTM-09-2018-0283

Bouarar, A. C., Mouloudj, S., & Mouloudj, K. (2021). Extending the theory of planned behavior to explain intention to use online food delivery services in the context of COVID-19 pandemic. In C. Cobanoglu, & V. Della Corte (Eds.), Advances in global services and retail management (pp. 1–16). USF M3 Publishing.

Bouarar, A. C., Mouloudj, S., Makhlouf, A., & Mouloudj, K. (2022). Predicting students' intentions to create green start-ups: A theory of planned behaviour approach. In *SHS Web of Conferences* (Vol. 135). EDP Sciences. 10.1051hsconf/202213501002

Bouarar, A. C., & Mouloudj, K. (2021). Using the theory of planned behavior to explore employee's intentions to implement green practices. *Dirassat Journal Economic Issue*, *12*(1), 641–659. doi:10.34118/djei.v12i1.1118

Boulding, K. (1966). The economy of the coming spaceship earth. In H. Jarret (Ed.), *Environmental quality in a growing economy*. Johns Hopkins Press.

Bouznit, M., Pablo-Romero, M. P., & Sánchez-Braza, A. (2020). Measures to promote renewable energy for electricity generation in Algeria. *Sustainability (Basel)*, *12*(4), 1–14. doi:10.3390u12041468

Božić, L. (2021). Attitudes towards climate change and electric car purchase–The case of European consumers. *Market-Tržište*, *33*(SI), 81-94. doi:10.22598/mt/2021.33.spec-issue.81

Brand, U. (2012). Green economy–the next oxymoron? No lessons learned from failures of implementing sustainable development. *Gaia (Heidelberg)*, *21*(1), 28–32. doi:10.14512/gaia.21.1.9

Bretschger, T. (2005). Economics of Technological Change and the Natural Environment: How Effective Are Innovations as a Remedy for Resource Scarcity? *Ecological Economics*, *54*(2-3), 148–163. doi:10.1016/j.ecolecon.2004.12.026

Brinkmann, R. (2020a). Connections in Environmental Sustainability: Living in a Time of Rapid Environmental Change. In R. Brinkmann, Environmental Sustainability in a Time of Change (pp. 1–8). Springer International Publishing. doi:10.1007/978-3-030-28203-5_1

Brinkmann, R. (2020b). *Environmental Sustainability in a Time of Change*. Springer International Publishing. doi:10.1007/978-3-030-28203-5

Brixner, C., Isaak, P., Mochi, S., Ozono, M., Suárez, D., & Yoguel, G. (2020). Back to the future. Is industry 4.0 a new tecno-organizational paradigm? Implications for Latin American countries. *Economics of Innovation and New Technology*, *29*(7), 705–719. doi:10.1080/10438599.2020.1719642

Brundtland, G. H. (1987). *Report of the World Commission on environment and development:" our common future."* UN.

Buonocore, E., Paletto, A., Russo, G. F., & Franzese, P. P. (2019). Indicators of environmental performance to assess wood-based bioenergy production: A case study in Northern Italy. *Journal of Cleaner Production*, *221*, 242–248. doi:10.1016/j.jclepro.2019.02.272

Busch, T., & Friede, G. (2018). The robustness of the corporate social and financial performance relation: A second-order meta-analysis. *Corporate Social Responsibility and Environmental Management*, *25*(4), 583–608. doi:10.1002/csr.1480

Butnaru, E., Stoleru, E., & Brebu, M. (2022). Valorization of forestry residues by thermal methods. The effect of temperature on gradual degradation of structural components in bark from silver fir (Abies alba Mill.). *Industrial Crops and Products*, *187*, 115376. doi:10.1016/j.indcrop.2022.115376

Byrne, B. M. (2016). *Structural Equation Modeling with AMOS: Basic Concepts Applications, and Programming*. Routledge. doi:10.4324/9781315757421

Calbimonte, J. P., Eberle, J., & Aberer, K. (2017). Toward self-monitoring smart cities: The opensense2 approach. *Informatik-Spektrum*, *40*(1), 75–87. doi:10.100700287-016-1009-y

California Fuel Cell Partnership. (2022). *California Fuel Cell Partnership Envisions 70,000 Heavy-Duty Fuel Cell Electric Trucks Supported by 200 Hydrogen Stations in-State by 2035*. CA Fuel Cell Partnership.

Camacho, M., Regina, Y., Lopretti, M., Carballo, L. B., & Moreno, G. (2017). Synthesis and Characterization of Nanocrystalline Cellulose Derived from Pineapple Peel Residues. *Journal of Renewable Materials*, *5*(5), 271–279. doi:10.7569/JRM.2017.634117

Cameron, J. S. (2000). Practical haemodialysis began with cellophane and heparin: The crucial role of William Thalhimer (1884–1961). *Nephrology, Dialysis, Transplantation*, *15*(7), 1086–1091. doi:10.1093/ndt/15.7.1086 PMID:10862657

Cancino, C. A., La Paz, A. I., Ramaprasad, A., & Syn, T. (2018). Technological innovation for sustainable growth: An ontological perspective. *Journal of Cleaner Production*, *179*, 31–41. doi:10.1016/j.jclepro.2018.01.059

Carbon Brief. (2022). *Climate loss and damage in Africa: Massive costs on the Horizon.* Carbon Brief. https://www.carbonbrief.org/analysis-africas-unreported-extreme-weather-in-2022-and-climate-change

Carus, M., Eder, A., Dammer, L., Korte, H., Scholz, L., Essel, R., Breitmayer, E., & Barth, M. (2015). *Wood-plastic composites (WPC) and natural fibre composites (NFC)*. Nova-Institute.

Cattaneo, C. (2019). Internal and external barriers to energy efficiency: Which role for policy interventions? *Energy Efficiency*, *12*(5), 1293–1311. doi:10.100712053-019-09775-1

Ceres.org. (2022). *Major companies and investors call on the federal government to strengthen proposed truck emissions standards.* Ceres.

Cerqueira, J. C., Penha, J. S., Oliveira, R. S., Guarieiro, L. L. N., Melo, P. D. S., Viana, J. D., & Machado, B. A. S. (2017). Production of biodegradable starch nanocomposites using cellulose nanocrystals extracted from coconut fibers. *Polímeros*, *27*(4), 320–329. doi:10.1590/0104-1428.05316

Chadwick, M. (2023). 7 reasons why meat is bad for the environment. *Greenpeace UK*. https://www.greenpeace.org.uk/news/why-meat-is-bad-for-the-environment/

Chai, L., & Tassou, S. A. (2020). A review of printed circuit heat exchangers for helium and supercritical CO_2 Brayton cycles. Thermal Science and Engineering Progress, 18, 100543.Chalker Scott, L., 2007. Impact of mulches on landscape plants and the environment - A review. *Journal of Environmental Horticulture*, *25*(4), 239–249.

Chakrabartty, S. N. (2017). Composite index: Methods and properties. *Journal of Applied Quantitative Methods*, *12*(2), 25–33.

Chakravarty, I., Bhattacharya, A., & Das, S. K. (2017). Water, sanitation, and hygiene: The unfinished agenda in the World Health Organization South-East Asia Region. *WHO South-East Asia Journal of Public Health*, *6*(2), 21–26. doi:10.4103/2224-3151.213787 PMID:28857059

Chang, C., & Chen, Y. (2013). Green organizational identity and green innovation. *Management Decision*, *51*(5), 1056–1070. doi:10.1108/MD-09-2011-0314

Chang, I. C. C., Jou, S. C., & Chung, M. K. (2021). Provincialising smart urbanism in Taipei: The smart city as a strategy for urban regime transition. *Urban Studies (Edinburgh, Scotland)*, *58*(3), 559–580. doi:10.1177/0042098020947908

Chang, R.-D., Zuo, J., Zhao, Z.-Y., Zillante, G., Gan, X.-L., & Soebarto, V. (2017). Evolving theories of sustainability and firms: History, future directions and implications for renewable energy research. *Renewable & Sustainable Energy Reviews*, *72*, 48–56. doi:10.1016/j.rser.2017.01.029

Charis, G., Danha, G., & Muzenda, E. (2019). A review of timber waste utilization: Challenges and opportunities in Zimbabwe. *Procedia Manufacturing*, *35*, 419–429. doi:10.1016/j.promfg.2019.07.005

Charlton, C., & Howell, B. (2007). Life cycle assessment:A tool for solving environmental problems? *European Environment*, *2*(2), 2–5. doi:10.1002/eet.3320020203

Chatterjee, R., Singh, A., & Singh, V. (2022). Ethical and Sustainable Perceptions on Cloud Kitchen Business-A Study of Consumers and Stakeholders during the Covid-19 Pandemic. International *Journal of Hospitality and Tourism Systems*, *Special Issue on COVID-19*, 76-87.

Chava, S. (2014). Environmental externalities and cost of capital. *Management Science*, *60*(9), 2223–2247. Advance online publication. doi:10.1287/mnsc.2013.1863

Chawalitsakunchai, W., Dittanet, P., Loykulnunt, S., Tanpichai, S., & Prapainainar, P. (2019). Extraction of nanocellulose from pineapple leaves by acid-hydrolysis and pressurized acid hydrolysis for reinforcement in natural rubber composites. *IOP Conference Series. Materials Science and Engineering*, *526*(1), 012019–012019. doi:10.1088/1757-899X/526/1/012019

Chawla, Y., Shimpo, F., & Sokołowski, M. M. (2022). Artificial intelligence and information management in the energy transition of India: Lessons from the global IT heart. *Digital Policy. Regulation & Governance*, *24*(1), 17–29. doi:10.1108/DPRG-05-2021-0062

Chen, C., Chen, Y., & Jayaraman, V. (Eds.). (2021). *Pursuing Sustainability: OR/MS Applications in Sustainable Design, Manufacturing, Logistics, and Resource Management* (Vol. 301). Springer International Publishing. doi:10.1007/978-3-030-58023-0

Cheng, H., Chen, C., Wu, S., Mirza, Z. A., & Liu, Z. (2017). Emergy evaluation of cropping, poultry rearing, and fish raising systems in the drawdown zone of Three Gorges Reservoir of China. *Journal of Cleaner Production*, *144*, 559–571. doi:10.1016/j.jclepro.2016.12.053

Cheng, J., Yi, J., Dai, S., & Xiong, Y. (2019). Can low-carbon city construction facilitate green growth? Evidence from China's pilot low-carbon city initiative. *Journal of Cleaner Production*, *231*, 1158–1170. doi:10.1016/j.jclepro.2019.05.327

Chen, H., Meifang, Y., & Dazhi, C. (2019). Research on Institutional Innovation of China's Green Insurance Investment. *Journal of Industrial Integration and Management*, *4*(1), 1–17. doi:10.1142/S2424862219500039

Chen, Q., Ning, B., Pan, Y., & Xiao, J. (2021). Green finance and outward foreign direct investment: Evidence from a quasi-natural experiment of green insurance in China. *Asia Pacific Journal of Management*, 1–26. doi:10.100710490-020-09750-w

Chen, T. B., & Chai, L. T. (2010). Attitude towards the environment and green products: Consumers' perspective. *Management Science and Engineering*, *4*(2), 27–39.

Chen, W. H., Wang, C. W., Kumar, G., Rousset, P., & Hsieh, T. H. (2018). Effect of torrefaction pretreatment on the pyrolysis of rubber wood sawdust analyzed by Py-GC/MS. *Bioresource Technology*, *259*, 469–473. doi:10.1016/j.biortech.2018.03.033 PMID:29580728

Chen, Z., & Bidanda, B. (2019). Sustainable manufacturing production-inventory decision of multiple factories with JIT logistics, component recovery and emission control. *Transportation Research Part E, Logistics and Transportation Review*, *128*, 356–383. doi:10.1016/j.tre.2019.06.013

Cherchye, L., Moesen, W., Rogge, N., Van Puyenbroeck, T., Saisana, M., Saltelli, A., Liska, R., & Tarantola, S. (2008). Creating composite indicators with DEA and robustness analysis: The case of the Technology Achievement Index. *The Journal of the Operational Research Society*, *59*(2), 239–251. doi:10.1057/palgrave.jors.2602445

Chidambaram, S., Maheswaran, Y., Patel, K., Sounderajah, V., Hashimoto, D. A., Seastedt, K. P., McGregor, A. H., Markar, S. R., & Darzi, A. (2022). Using Artificial Intelligence-Enhanced Sensing and Wearable Technology in Sports Medicine and Performance Optimisation. *Sensors (Basel)*, *22*(18), 6920. doi:10.339022186920 PMID:36146263

Chien, F., Chau, K. Y., & Sadiq, M. (2023). Impact of climate mitigation technology and natural resource management on climate change in China. *Resources Policy*, *81*, 103367. doi:10.1016/j.resourpol.2023.103367

Choi, S. D. (2012). The Green Growth Movement in the Republic of Korea Options or Necessity. Sustainable Development Network. World Bank.

Chourabi, H., Nam, T., Walker, S., Gil-Garcia, J. R., Mellouli, S., Nahon, K., Pardo, T. A., & Scholl, H. J. (2012). Understanding smart cities: An integrative framework. In *2012 45th Hawaii international conference on system sciences*, (pp. 2289-2297). IEEE.

Chowdhury, S., Khan, S., Sarker, M. F. H., Islam, K., Tamal, M. A., & Khan, N. A. (2022). Does agricultural ecology cause environmental degradation? Empirical evidence from Bangladesh. *Heliyon*, *8*(6), e09750. doi:10.1016/j.heliyon.2022.e09750 PMID:35785220

Choy, Y. K. (2015). From Stockholm to Rio+20. *The International Journal of Environmental Sustainability*, *11*(1), 1–25. doi:10.18848/2325-1077/CGP/v12i01/55037

Chummun, B. Z. (2012). *Evaluating business success in the Microinsurance industry of South Africa* [Doctoral dissertation, North-West University].

Chummun, B. Z., & Bisschoff, C. A. (2014). A theoretical model to measure the business success of Microinsurance in South Africa. [KRE]. *Journal of Economics*, *5*(1), 87–96. doi:10.1080/09765239.2014.11884987

Chummun, B. Z., & Singh, A. (2019). Factors Influencing the Quality of Decision-Making Using Business Intelligence in a Metal Rolling Plant in KwaZulu-Natal. *Journal of Reviews on Global Economics*, *8*, 1108–1120. doi:10.6000/1929-7092.2019.08.96

Chun, S. A., Kim, D., Cho, J. S., Chuang, M., Shin, S., & Jun, D. (2021). Framework for smart city model composition: Choice of component design models and risks. *International Journal of E-Planning Research*, *10*(3), 50–69. doi:10.4018/IJEPR.20210701.oa4

Ciliberto, C., Szopik-Depczyńska, K., Tarczyńska-Łuniewska, M., Ruggieri, A., & Ioppolo, G. (2021). Enabling the Circular Economy transition: A sustainable lean manufacturing recipe for Industry 4.0. *Business Strategy and the Environment*, *30*(7), 3255–3272. doi:10.1002/bse.2801

Circular Economy. (2023, May 16). UNCTAD. https://unctad.org/topic/trade-and-environment/circular-economy

City of Chicago. (2018, June 15). *Green Alleys*. Chicago.gov.

City of Vaughan. (2022). *Sustainable Transportation*. Vaughan.ca.

Climate Change 2023: Synthesis Report. (n.d.). UNEP - UN Environment Programme. https://www.unep.org/resources/report/climate-change-2023-synthesis-report

Cochran Hameen, E., Ken-Opurum, B., & Son, Y. J. (2020). Protocol for post-occupancy evaluation in schools to improve indoor environmental quality and energy efficiency. *Sustainability (Basel)*, *12*(9), 3712. doi:10.3390u12093712

Collier, S. J., Elliott, R., & Lehtonen, T. K. (2021). Climate change and insurance. *Economy and Society*, *50*(2), 158–172. doi:10.1080/03085147.2021.1903771

Colombo, U. (2001). The Club of Rome and sustainable development. *Futures*, *33*(1), 7–11. doi:10.1016/S0016-3287(00)00048-3

Commission on Environment. (1987). *Report of the World Commission on Environment and Development: Our Common Future Towards Sustainable Development 2. Part II. Common Challenges Population and Human Resources 4*. World Commission.

Connolly, D., Lund, H., Mathiesen, B., & Leahy, M. (2010). A review of computer tools for analysing the integration of renewable energy into various energy systems. *Applied Energy*, *87*(4), 1059–1082. doi:10.1016/j.apenergy.2009.09.026

Cook, D. J., Augusto, J. C., & Jakkula, V. R. (2009). Ambient intelligence: Technologies, applications, and opportunities. *Pervasive and Mobile Computing*, *5*(4), 277–298. doi:10.1016/j.pmcj.2009.04.001

Corona, B., Shen, L., Sommersacher, P., & Junginger, M. (2020). Consequential Life Cycle Assessment of energy generation from waste wood and forest residues: The effect of resource-efficient additives. *Journal of Cleaner Production*, *259*, 120948. doi:10.1016/j.jclepro.2020.120948

Cortellini, G., & Panetta, I. C. (2021). Green Bond: A Systematic Literature Review for Future Research Agendas. *Journal of Risk and Financial Management*, *14*(12), 589. doi:10.3390/jrfm14120589

Costa, L. A. S., Assis, D. J., Gomes, G. V. P., da Silva, J. B. A., Fonseca, A. F., & Druzian, J. I. (2015). Extraction and Characterization of Nanocellulose from Corn Stover. *Materials Today: Proceedings*, *2*(1), 287–294. doi:10.1016/j.matpr.2015.04.045

Cowley, R., Joss, S., & Dayot, Y. (2018). The smart city and its publics: Insights from across six UK cities. *Urban Research & Practice*, *11*(1), 53–77. doi:10.1080/17535069.2017.1293150

Craig, J., & Petterson, V. (2005). Introduction to the practice of telemedicine. *Journal of Telemedicine and Telecare*, *11*(1), 3–9. doi:10.1177/1357633X0501100102 PMID:15829036

Crossley, H. (2021, June 22). *Rain gardens: 10 stunning ideas and designs that soak up rain run-off*. Gardeningetc.

Croutzet, A., & Dabbous, A. (2021). Do FinTech trigger renewable energy use? Evidence from OECD countries. *Renewable Energy*, *179*, 1608–1617. doi:10.1016/j.renene.2021.07.144

D'Amato, D., Droste, N., Allen, B., Kettunen, M., Lähtinen, K., Korhonen, J., Leskinen, P., Matthies, B. D., & Toppinen, A. (2017). Green, circular, bio economy: A comparative analysis of sustainability avenues. *Journal of Cleaner Production*, *168*, 716–734. doi:10.1016/j.jclepro.2017.09.053

D'Angelo, V., Cappa, F., & Peruffo, E. (2022). Green manufacturing for sustainable development: The positive effects of green activities, green investments, and non-green products on economic performance. *Business Strategy and the Environment*.

Dalby, P. A., Gillerhaugen, G. R., Hagspiel, V., Leth-Olsen, T., & Thijssen, J. J. (2018). Green investment under policy uncertainty and Bayesian learning. *Energy*, *161*, 1262–1281. doi:10.1016/j.energy.2018.07.137

Dalmarco, G., Ramalho, F. R., Barros, A. C., & Soares, A. L. (2019). Providing industry 4.0 technologies: The case of a production technology cluster. *The Journal of High Technology Management Research*, *30*(2), 100355. doi:10.1016/j.hitech.2019.100355

Dara, R., Hazrati Fard, S. M., & Kaur, J. (2022). Recommendations for ethical and responsible use of artificial intelligence in digital agriculture. *Frontiers in Artificial Intelligence*, *5*, 884192. doi:10.3389/frai.2022.884192 PMID:35968036

DaSilva, B., Dhar, J., Rafiq, S., & Young, D. (2023). *Nudging Consumers Toward Sustainability*. BCG Global. https://www.bcg.com/publications/2022/nudging-consumers-to-make-sustainable-choices

Das, S., Dave, M., & Wilkes, G. L. (2009). Characterization of flexible polyurethane foams based on soybean-based polyols. *Journal of Applied Polymer Science*, *112*(1), 299–308. doi:10.1002/app.29402

Dauda, L., Long, X., Mensah, C. N., & Salman, M. (2019). The effects of economic growth and innovation on CO_2 emissions in different regions. *Environmental Science and Pollution Research International*, *26*(15), 15028–15038. doi:10.100711356-019-04891-y PMID:30919181

David Wyatt. (2022). *Electric Truck Deployment Ready for Acceleration in 2023*. Idtechex.

Dawes, J. H. P. (2022). SDG interlinkage networks: Analysis, robustness, sensitivities, and hierarchies. *World Development*, *149*, 105693. doi:10.1016/j.worlddev.2021.105693

Day, R., Walker, G., & Simcock, N. (2016). Conceptualising energy use and energy poverty using a capabilities framework. *Energy Policy*, *93*, 255–264. doi:10.1016/j.enpol.2016.03.019

DCED. (2012). *Green Industries for Green Growth*. Enterprise. https://www.enterprise-development.org/wp-content/uploads/Green_Industries_for_Green_Growth.pdf

de Moura, G. N. P., Legey, L. F. L., & Howells, M. (2018). A Brazilian perspective of power systems integration using OSeMOSYS SAMBA – South America Model Base – and the bargaining power of neighbouring countries: A cooperative games approach. *Energy Policy*, *115*, 470–485. doi:10.1016/j.enpol.2018.01.045

Deaths due to Malnutrition. (n.d.). PIB. https://pib.gov.in/Pressreleaseshare.aspx?PRID=1580452

Debnath, B., Haldar, D., & Purkait, M. (2021). A critical review on the techniques used for the synthesis and applications of crystalline cellulose derived from agricultural wastes and forest residues. *Carbohydrate Polymers*, *273*, 118537. doi:10.1016/j.carbpol.2021.118537 PMID:34560949

Deif, A. (2011). A system model for green manufacturing. *Advances in Production Engineering & Management*, *6*(1), 27–36.

Dell'Atti, S., Di Tommaso, C., & Pacelli, V. (2022). Sovereign green bond and country value and risk: Evidence from European Union countries. *Journal of International Financial Management & Accounting*, *33*(3), 505–521. doi:10.1111/jifm.12155

Demirbas, A. (2005). Potential applications of renewable energy sources, biomass combustion problems in boiler power systems and combustion related environmental issues. *Progress in Energy and Combustion Science*, *31*(2), 171–192. doi:10.1016/j.pecs.2005.02.002

Demirbas, A. (2011). Waste management, waste resource facilities and waste conversion processes. *Energy Conversion and Management*, *52*(2), 1280–1287. doi:10.1016/j.enconman.2010.09.025

Dev, N. K., Shankar, R., & Swami, S. (2020). Diffusion of green products in industry 4.0: Reverse logistics issues during design of inventory and production planning system. *International Journal of Production Economics*, *223*, 107519. doi:10.1016/j.ijpe.2019.107519

Diab, S. M., AL-Bourini, F. A., & Abu-Rumman, A. H. (2015). The Impact of Green Supply Chain Management Practices on Organizational Performance: A Study of Jordanian Food Industries. *Journal of Management and Sustainability*, *5*(1), 149. doi:10.5539/jms.v5n1p149

Dianshu, F., Sovacool, B. K., & Vu, K. (2010). The barriers to energy efficiency in China: Assessing household electricity savings and consumer behavior in Liaoning province. *Energy Policy*, *38*(2), 1202–1209. doi:10.1016/j.enpol.2009.11.012

Diaz-Sarachaga, J. M., Jato-Espino, D., & Castro-Fresno, D. (2018). Is the Sustainable Development Goals (SDG) index an adequate framework to measure the progress of the 2030 Agenda? *Sustainable Development (Bradford)*, *26*(6), 663–671. doi:10.1002d.1735

Doherty, B., Haugh, H., & Lyon, F. (2014). Social Enterprises as Hybrid Organizations: A Review and Research Agenda: Social Enterprises as Hybrid Organizations. *International Journal of Management Reviews*, *16*(4), 417–436. doi:10.1111/ijmr.12028

Dong, F., Wang, Y., Su, B., Hua, Y., & Zhang, Y. (2019). The process of peak CO2 emissions in developed economies: A perspective of industrialization and urbanization. *Resources, Conservation and Recycling*, *141*, 61–75. doi:10.1016/j.resconrec.2018.10.010

Dong, X., Xiong, Y., Nie, S., & Yoon, S. M. (2023). Can bonds hedge stock market risks? Green bonds vs conventional bonds. *Finance Research Letters*, *52*, 103367. doi:10.1016/j.frl.2022.103367

Dorfleitner, G., Utz, S., & Zhang, R. (2022). The pricing of green bonds: External reviews and the shades of green. *Review of Managerial Science*, *16*(3), 797–834. doi:10.100711846-021-00458-9

Dornfeld, D., Yuan, C., Diaz, N., Zhang, T., & Vijayaraghavan, A. (2012). Introduction to green manufacturing. In *Green manufacturing: fundamentals and applications* (pp. 1–23). Springer US.

Dragulanescu, I.-V., & Dragulanescu, N. (2013). Some Theories Of Environmental Sustainability. *Romanian Statistical Review*, *61*(12), 14–23.

Dreamstime. (2023). Vectors, Video & Audio - Dreamstime. Dreamstime.

Dubey, R., Singh, T., & Tiwari, S. (2012). Supply chain innovation is a key to superior firm performance an insight from Indian cement manufacturing. *International Journal of Innovation Science*, *4*(4), 217–230. doi:10.1260/1757-2223.4.4.217

Dunuwila, P., Rodrigo, V. H. L., & Goto, N. (2020). Improving financial and environmental sustainability in concentrated latex manufacture. *Journal of Cleaner Production*, *255*, 120202. doi:10.1016/j.jclepro.2020.120202

Dutta, S., Lanvin, B., & Wunsch-Vincent, S. (2019). Global innovation index, 1-39. Cornell University.

Edirisinghe, R., & Woo, J. (2019). Drive towards real-time reasoning of building performance: Development of a live, cloud-based system. In *Advances in Informatics and Computing in Civil and Construction Engineering: Proceedings of the 35th CIB W78 2018 Conference: IT in Design, Construction, and Management* (pp. 661-668). Springer International Publishing.

Edwards, M., Benn, S., & Dunphy, D. (2023). Leadership for Sustainable Futures. In R. T. By, B. Burnes, & M. Hughes, Organizational Change, Leadership and Ethics (2nd ed., pp. 215–232). Routledge. doi:10.4324/9781003036395-15

Ejsmont, K., Gladysz, B., & Kluczek, A. (2020). Impact of industry 4.0 on sustainability—Bibliometric literature review. *Sustainability (Basel)*, *12*(14), 5650. doi:10.3390u12145650

Ekholm, T., Ghoddusi, H., Krey, V., & Riahi, K. (2013). The effect of financial constraints on energy-climate scenarios. *Energy Policy*, *59*, 562–572. doi:10.1016/j.enpol.2013.04.001

Elkington, J. (1998). Partnerships from cannibals with forks: The triple bottom line of 21st-century business. *Environmental Quality Management*, *8*(1), 37–51. doi:10.1002/tqem.3310080106

EPA. (2016). Green Infrastructure and Climate Change Collaborating to Improve Community Resiliency. EPA.

Ernst & Young. (2008). *Strategic business risk 2008: Insurance*. E&Y. https://www.ey.com/GL/en/Newsroom/News-releases/Media---Press-Release---Strategic-Risk-to-Insurance-Industry

Es'haghi, S. R., Rezaei, A., Karimi, H., & Ataei, P. (2022). Institutional analysis of organizations active in the restoration of Lake Urmia: The application of the social network analysis approach. *Hydrological Sciences Journal*, *67*(3), 328–341. doi:10.1080/02626667.2022.2026950

Eslami, Y., Dassisti, M., Lezoche, M., & Panetto, H. (2019). A survey on sustainability in manufacturing organisations: Dimensions and future insights. *International Journal of Production Research*, *57*(15-16), 5194–5214. doi:10.1080/00207543.2018.1544723

Eurostat. (2022). *Losses from climate change: €145 billion in a decade*. Eurostat. https://ec.europa.eu/eurostat/web/products-eurostat-news/-/ddn-20221024-1

Evans, S. K., Wesley, O. N., Nathan, O., & Moloto, M. J. (2019). Chemically purified cellulose and its nanocrystals from sugarcane baggase: Isolation and characterization. *Heliyon*, *5*(10), e02635. doi:10.1016/j.heliyon.2019.e02635 PMID:31687498

Fabrizio, K. R. (2013). The effect of regulatory uncertainty on investment: Evidence from renewable energy generation. *Journal of Law Economics and Organization*, *29*(4), 765–798. doi:10.1093/jleo/ews007

Fahimnia, B., Bell, M. G. H., Hensher, D. A., & Sarkis, J. (Eds.). (2015). *Green Logistics and Transportation: A Sustainable Supply Chain Perspective*. Springer International Publishing. doi:10.1007/978-3-319-17181-4

Falsarone, A. (2022). *The Impact Challenge: Reframing Sustainability for Businesses* (1st ed.). CRC Press. doi:10.1201/9781003212225

FAO. (2023). *The role of wood residues in the transition to sustainable bioenergy*. Food and Agriculture Organization.

Faraca, G., Boldrin, A., & Astrup, T. (2019). Resource quality of wood waste: The importance of physical and chemical impurities in wood waste for recycling. *Waste Management (New York, N.Y.)*, *87*, 135–147. doi:10.1016/j.wasman.2019.02.005 PMID:31109513

Fatica, S., Panzica, R., & Rancan, M. (2021). The pricing of green bonds: Are financial institutions special? *Journal of Financial Stability*, *54*, 100873. doi:10.1016/j.jfs.2021.100873

Fatoki, O. (2020). Factors influencing the purchase of energy-efficient appliances by young consumers in South Africa. *Foundations of Management*, *12*(1), 151–166. doi:10.2478/fman-2020-0012

Fauré, E., Dawkins, E., Wood, R., Finnveden, G., Palm, V., Persson, L., & Schmidt, S. (2019). Environmental pressure from Swedish consumption–The largest contributing producer countries, products and services. *Journal of Cleaner Production*, *231*, 698–713. doi:10.1016/j.jclepro.2019.05.148

Favier, V., Canova, G. R., Cavaillé, J. Y., Chanzy, H., Dufresne, A., & Gauthier, C. (1995). Nanocomposite materials from latex and cellulose whiskers. *Polymers for Advanced Technologies*, *6*(5), 351–355. doi:10.1002/pat.1995.220060514

Feng, Y., Zhang, W., Niaz, H., He, Z., Wang, S., Wang, X., & Liu, Y. (2020). Parametric analysis and thermo-economical optimization of a Supercritical-Subcritical organic Rankine cycle for waste heat utilization. *Energy Conversion and Management*, *212*, 112773. doi:10.1016/j.enconman.2020.112773

Fenlon, W. (2011, March 21). *10 Technologies Used in Green Construction*. HowStuffWorks.

Fidan, E. T. (2020). Türkiye'de Sürdürülebilir Sanayi Politikalarının Uygulanması ve Kamu, Sivil Toplum Kuruluşları ve Özel Sektörün Sürdürülebilir Sanayi Politikalarına İlişkin Yaklaşımlarının Değerlendirilmesi. *Verimlilik Dergisi*, (2), 73–100.

Finkbeiner, M., Inaba, A., Tan, R., Christiansen, K., & Klüppel, H. J. (2006). The new international standards for life cycle assessment: ISO 14040 and ISO 14044. *The International Journal of Life Cycle Assessment*, *11*(2), 80–85. doi:10.1065/lca2006.02.002

Flammer, C. (2020). Green Bonds: Effectiveness and Implications for Public Policy. *Environmental and Energy Policy and the Economy*, *1*, 95–128. doi:10.1086/706794

Flammer, C. (2021). Corporate green bonds. *Journal of Financial Economics*, *142*(2), 499–516. doi:10.1016/j.jfineco.2021.01.010

Fleming, R., & Spellerberg, A. (1999). *Using Time Use Data*. Statistics New Zealand.

Flood, E., Kapoor, S., & De Villa-Lopez, B. (2014). The Sustainability of Food Served at Wedding Banquets. *Journal of Culinary Science & Technology*, 12(2), 137–152. doi:10.1080/15428052.2013.846882

Food and Agriculture Organization (FAO). (2017). Fao and the sdgs. In *Indicators: Measuring Up to the 2030 Agenda for Sustainable Development*. Food and Agriculture Organisation of the United Nations.

Foo, M., Tan, K., Wu, T., Chan, E., & Chew, I. (2017). A Characteristic Study of Nanocrystalline Cellulose and its Potential in Forming Pickering Emulsion. *Chemical Engineering Transactions*, 60, 97–102.

Fornell, C., & Larcker, D. F. (1981). Evaluating structural equation models with unobservable variables and measurement error. *JMR, Journal of Marketing Research*, 18(1), 39–50. doi:10.1177/002224378101800104

Forsgren, L., Sahlin-Sjövold, K., Venkatesh, A., Thunberg, J., Kádár, R., Boldizar, A., Westman, G., & Rigdahl, M. (2019). Composites with surface-grafted cellulose nanocrystals (CNC). *Journal of Materials Science*, 54(4), 3009–3022. doi:10.100710853-018-3029-2

Fort, J., Sal, J., Zak, J., & Cerny, R. (2020). Assessment of wood-based fly ash as alternative cement replacement. *Sustainability*, 12(22), 1–16. doi:10.3390u12229580 PMID:35136666

Founder Institute Portfolio Companies Helping Meet the 17 UN Sustainable Development Goals. (2021, July 15). The Founder Institute. https://FI.co/insight/17-companies-helping-meet-the-17-un-sustainable-development-goals

Frank, A. G., Mendes, G. H., Ayala, N. F., & Ghezzi, A. (2019). Servitization and Industry 4.0 convergence in the digital transformation of product firms: A business model innovation perspective. *Technological Forecasting and Social Change*, 141, 341–351. doi:10.1016/j.techfore.2019.01.014

Friede, G., Busch, T., & Bassen, A. (2015). ESG and financial performance: Aggregated evidence from more than 2000 empirical studies. *Journal of Sustainable Finance & Investment*, 5(4), 210–233. doi:10.1080/20430795.2015.1118917

Frost, B., & Foster, E. J. (2019). Isolation of Thermally Stable Cellulose Nanocrystals from Spent Coffee Grounds via Phosphoric Acid Hydrolysis. *Journal of Renewable Materials*, 7, 187–203. doi:10.32604/jrm.2020.07940

Fu, B., Wang, S., Zhang, J., Hou, Z., & Li, J. (2019). Unravelling the complexity in achieving the 17 sustainable-development goals. *National Science Review*, 6(3), 386–388. doi:10.1093/nsr/nwz038 PMID:34691883

Fu, J., & Mishra, M. (2022). Fintech in the time of COVID– 19: Technological adoption during crises. *Journal of Financial Intermediation*, 50, 100945. doi:10.1016/j.jfi.2021.100945

Gabriel, I., & Gauri, V. (2019). Towards a new global narrative for the sustainable development goals. *Sustainable Development Goals: Harnessing Business to Achieve the SDGs through Finance, Technology, and Law Reform*, 53-70.

Galván-Mendoza, O., González-Rosales, V. M., Leyva-Hernández, S. N., Arango-Ramírez, P. M., & Velasco-Aulcy, L. (2022). Environmental knowledge, perceived behavioral control, and employee green behavior in female employees of small and medium enterprises in Ensenada, Baja California. *Frontiers in Psychology*, 13, 1082306. doi:10.3389/fpsyg.2022.1082306 PMID:36600723

Gangakhedkar, R., Kaur, J., & Karthik, M. (2023). Purchase intention on energy efficient household appliances-a meta-analysis of the studies based on theory of planned behaviour. *International Journal of Sustainable Economy*, 15(1), 1–25. doi:10.1504/IJSE.2023.127733

Gao, P., Zhou, Y., Meng, F., Zhang, Y., Liu, Z., Zhang, W., & Xue, G. (2016). Preparation and characterization of hydrochar from waste eucalyptus bark by hydrothermal carbonization. *Energy*, 97, 238–245. doi:10.1016/j.energy.2015.12.123

Gao, X., Gong, X., Nguyen, T. T., Du, W., Chen, X., Song, Z., Chai, R., & Guo, M. (2019). Luminescent materials comprised of wood-based carbon quantum dots adsorbed on a $Ce_{0.7}Zr_{0.3}O_2$ solid solution: Synthesis, photoluminescence properties, and applications in light-emitting diode devices. *Journal of Materials Science*, *54*(23), 14469–14482. doi:10.100710853-019-03912-y

Garbellano, S., & Da Veiga, M. D. R. (2019). Dynamic capabilities in Italian leading SMEs adopting industry 4.0. *Measuring Business Excellence*, *23*(4), 472–483. doi:10.1108/MBE-06-2019-0058

Garling, T., Book, A., & Lindberg, E. (1984). Cognitive mapping of large-scale environments: The interrelationship of action plans, acquisition, and orientation. *Environment and Behavior*, *16*(1), 3–34. doi:10.1177/0013916584161001

Gasperoni, M. (2019, June 6). The cascading use of wood: Best pratices in the wood recycling sector. *Circular Business*. https://www.rilegno.org/rapporto-2022-rilegno/

Gatzert, N., & Reichel, P. (2020). *Awareness of climate risks and opportunities: empirical evidence on determinants and value from the US and European insurance industry*. Working Paper, Friedrich-Alexander University Erlangen-Nürnberg, Nuremberg

Gaziulusoy, A. I., Boyle, C., & McDowall, R. (2013). System innovation for sustainability: A systemic double-flow scenario method for companies. *Journal of Cleaner Production*, *45*, 104–116. Scopus. doi:10.1016/j.jclepro.2012.05.013

Geissdoerfer, M., Savaget, P., Bocken, N. M., & Hultink, E. J. (2017). The Circular Economy–A new sustainability paradigm? *Journal of Cleaner Production*, *143*, 757–768. doi:10.1016/j.jclepro.2016.12.048

George, J. & Sabapathi, S.N.(2015). Cellulose nanocrystals: synthesis, functional properties, and applications. *Nanotech. Sci.Appl.*, *8*, 45-54.

Georgeson, L., Maslin, M., & Poessinouw, M. (2017). The global green economy: A review of concepts, definitions, measurement methodologies and their interactions. *Geo: Geography and Environment*, *4*(1), e00036. doi:10.1002/geo2.36

GFN, Global Footprint Network. (2023). *Ecological Deficit/Reserve dataset*. GFN. https://data.footprintnetwork.org/

Ghadimi, P., O'Neill, S., Wang, C., & Sutherland, J. W. (2021). Analysis of enablers on the successful implementation of green manufacturing for Irish SMEs. *Journal of Manufacturing Technology Management*, *32*(1), 85–109. doi:10.1108/JMTM-10-2019-0382

Ghazali, A., & Ali, G. (2019). Investigation of key contributors of CO2 emissions in extended STIRPAT model for newly industrialized countries: A dynamic common correlated estimator (DCCE) approach. *Energy Reports*, *5*, 242–252. doi:10.1016/j.egyr.2019.02.006

Ghazilla, R. A. R., Sakundarini, N., Abdul-Rashıd, S. H., Ayub, N. S., Olugu, E. U., & Musa, S. N. (2015). Drivers and barriers analysis for green manufacturing practices in Malaysian SMEs: A Preliminary Findings. *Procedia CIRP*, *26*, 658–663. doi:10.1016/j.procir.2015.02.085

Ghisellini, P., Cialani, C., & Ulgiati, S. (2016). A review on circular economy: The expected transition to a balanced interplay of environmental and economic systems. *Journal of Cleaner Production*, *114*, 11–32. doi:10.1016/j.jclepro.2015.09.007

Ghobakhloo, M. (2020). Industry 4.0, digitization, and opportunities for sustainability. *Journal of Cleaner Production*, *252*, 119869. doi:10.1016/j.jclepro.2019.119869

Ghorabaee, M. K., Amiri, M., Zavadskas, E. K., Turskis, Z., & Antucheviciene, J. (2017). Stochastic EDAS method for multi-criteria decision-making with normally distributed data. *Journal of Intelligent & Fuzzy Systems*, *33*(3), 1627–1638. doi:10.3233/JIFS-17184

Ghorabaee, M. K., Zavadskas, E. K., Amiri, M., & Turskis, Z. (2016). Extended EDAS method for multi-criteria decision-making: An application to supplier selection. *International Journal of Computers, Communications & Control*, *11*(3), 358–371. doi:10.15837/ijccc.2016.3.2557

Ghorabaee, M. K., Zavadskas, E. K., Olfat, L., & Turskis, Z. (2015). Multi-criteria inventory classification using a new method of evaluation based on distance from average solution (EDAS). *Informatica (Vilnius)*, *26*(3), 435–451. doi:10.15388/Informatica.2015.57

Giama, E., & Papadopoulos, A. M. (2020). Benchmarking carbon footprint and circularity in production processes: The case of stonewool and extruded polysterene. *Journal of Cleaner Production*, *257*, 120559. doi:10.1016/j.jclepro.2020.120559

Gianfrate, G., & Peri, M. (2019). The green advantage: Exploring the convenience of issuing green bonds. *Journal of Cleaner Production*, *219*, 127–135. doi:10.1016/j.jclepro.2019.02.022

Gilchrist, D., Yu, J., & Zhong, R. (2021). The Limits of Green Finance: A Survey of Literature in the Context of Green Bonds and Green Loans. *Sustainability (Basel)*, *13*(2), 478. doi:10.3390u13020478

Girella, L., Zambon, S., & Rossi, P. (2019). Reporting on sustainable development: A comparison of three Italian small and medium-sized enterprises. *Corporate Social Responsibility and Environmental Management*, *26*(4), 981–996. doi:10.1002/csr.1738

Giri, R. N., Mondal, S. K., & Maiti, M. (2019). Government intervention on a competing supply chain with two green manufacturers and a retailer. *Computers & Industrial Engineering*, *128*, 104–121. doi:10.1016/j.cie.2018.12.030

Global Energy Review 2021 – Analysis - IEA. (n.d.). IEA. https://www.iea.org/reports/global-energy-review-2021

Gobierno de Colombia. (2021). *Hoja de ruta del hidrogeno*. Gobierno de Colombia.

Goel, R., Singh, T., Sahdev, S. L., Baral, S. K., & Choudhury, A. (2022). Impact of AI & IOT in sustainable & green practices adopted in hotel industry and measuring hotel guests' satisfaction. In *2022 10th International Conference on Reliability, Infocom Technologies and Optimization (Trends and Future Directions) (ICRITO)* (pp. 1-5). IEEE. 10.1109/ICRITO56286.2022.9965152

Golan, M., Cohen, Y., & Singer, G. (2020). A framework for operator–workstation interaction in Industry 4.0. *International Journal of Production Research*, *58*(8), 2421–2432. doi:10.1080/00207543.2019.1639842

Golnaraghi, M. (2018). *Climate change and the insurance industry: taking action as risk managers and investors. Perspectives from C-level executives in the insurance industry*. The Geneva Association. https://www.genevaassociation.org/sites/default/files/research-topics-document-type/pdf_public//climate_change_and_the_insurance_industry_-_taking_action_as_risk_managers_and_investors.pdf

Golubchikov, O., & Thornbush, M. (2020). Artificial intelligence and robotics in smart city strategies and planned smart development. *Smart Cities*, *3*(4), 1133–1144. doi:10.3390martcities3040056

Gonzalez, A. (2021, May 24). Women entrepreneurs in DRC recover waste wood to produce clean cooking. *Forest News CIFOR*. https://forestsnews.cifor.org/72712/drc-women-entrepreneurs-recover-waste-wood-to-produce-clean-cooking-fuel?fnl=en

Gopakumar, D. A., Pottathara, Y. B., Sabu, K., Khalil, H. A., Grohens, Y., & Thomas, S. (2019). Nanocellulose-based aerogels for industrial applications. Chapter. In S. Thomas, N. Kalarikkal, & A. Abraham (Eds.), *Industrial Applications of Nanomaterials* (pp. 403–421). doi:10.1016/B978-0-12-815749-7.00014-1

Govindan, K. (2018). Sustainable consumption and production in the food supply chain: A conceptual framework. *International Journal of Production Economics*, *195*, 419–431. doi:10.1016/j.ijpe.2017.03.003

Compilation of References

Goyal, A., Agrawal, R., & Saha, C. R. (2019). Quality management for sustainable manufacturing: Moving from number to impact of defects. *Journal of Cleaner Production, 241*, 118348. doi:10.1016/j.jclepro.2019.118348

Green Economy. (n.d.). UNEP - UN Environment Programme. https://www.unep.org/regions/asia-and-pacific/regional-initiatives/supporting-resource-efficiency/green-economy#:~:text=In%20a%20green%20economy%2C%20growth,of%20biodiversity%20and%20ecosystem%20services

Green, J. M., Croft, S. A., Durán, A. P., Balmford, A. P., Burgess, N. D., Fick, S., Gardner, T. A., Godar, J., Suavet, C., Virah-Sawmy, M., Young, L. E., & West, C. D. (2019). Linking global drivers of agricultural trade to on-the-ground impacts on biodiversity. *Proceedings of the National Academy of Sciences of the United States of America, 116*(46), 23202–23208. doi:10.1073/pnas.1905618116 PMID:31659031

Grigorev, I., Shadrin, A., Katkov, S., Borisov, V., Druzyanova, V., Gnatovskaya, I., Diev, R., Kaznacheeva, N., Levushkin, D., & Akinin, D. (2021). Improving the quality of sorting wood chips by scanning and machine vision technology. *Journal of Forest Science, 67*(5), 212–218. doi:10.17221/10/2020-JFS

Grumo, J., Jabber, J., Patricio, J., Magdadaro, M., Lubguban, A., & Alguno, A. (2017). Alkali and bleach treatment of the extracted cellulose from pineapple (Ananas comosus) leaves. *Journal of Applied and Fundamental Sciences, 9*, 124-133. doi:. doi:10.4314/jfas.v9i7s.13

Gumrah Dumanli, A. (2017). Nanocellulose and its composites for biomedical applications. *Current Medicinal Chemistry, 24*(5), 512–528. doi:10.2174/0929867323666161014124008 PMID:27758719

Gunay, S., Kurtishi-Kastrati, S., & Krsteska, K. (2022). Regional green economy and community impact on global sustainability. *Journal of Enterprising Communities: People and Places in the Global Economy*.

Guppy, L., Mehta, P., & Qadir, M. (2019). Sustainable development goal 6: Two gaps in the race for indicators. *Sustainability Science, 14*(2), 501–513. doi:10.100711625-018-0649-z

Gupta, M., & Gupta, H. (2023). Sustainable Urban Development of Smart Cities in India-A Systematic Literature Review. *Sustainability, Agri. Food and Environmental Research, 11*(10), 1–20.

Hachenberg, B., & Schiereck, D. (2018). Are green bonds priced differently from conventional bonds? *Journal of Asset Management, 19*(6), 371–383. doi:10.105741260-018-0088-5

Hagos, D. A., Gebremedhin, A., & Zethraeus, B. (2014). Towards a flexible energy system – A case study for Inland Norway. *Applied Energy, 130*, 41–50. doi:10.1016/j.apenergy.2014.05.022

Hair, J. F., Babin, B. J., Anderson, R. E., & Black, W. C. (2019). *Multivariate data analysis*. http://search.ebscohost.com/login.aspx?direct=true&scope=site&db=nlebk&db=nlabk&AN=2639357

Hair, J. F., Hult, G. T. M., Ringle, C., & Sarstedt, M. (2013). *A Primer on Partial Least Squares Structural Equation Modeling (PLS-SEM)*. Sage Publications.

Halisçelik, E., & Soytas, M. A. (2019). Sustainable development from millennium 2015 to Sustainable Development Goals 2030. *Sustainable Development (Bradford), 27*(4), 545–572. doi:10.1002d.1921

Hammar, H., & Lofgren, A. (2010). Explaining Adoption of End of Pipe Solutions and Clean Technologies: Determinants of Firms' Investments for Reducing Emissions to Air in Four Sectors in Sweden. *Energy Policy, 38*(7), 3644–3651. doi:10.1016/j.enpol.2010.02.041

Han. L. & Donghui, L. (2010). *Insurance Development and Economic Growth, the Geneva Papers on Risk and Insurance-Issues and Practice, 35*(2), 183-199.

Handley, E. (2022, January 6). *How do we define green infrastructure?* Open Access Government.

Hans, R. (2022). Complete Guide to Green Manufacturing. *Deskera Blog*. https://www.deskera.com/blog/green-manufacturing/

Han, Z. M., Sun, W. B., Yang, K. P., Yang, H. B., Liu, Z. X., Li, D. H., Yin, C. H., Liu, H. C., Zhao, Y. X., Ling, Z. C., Guan, Q. F., & Yu, S. H. (2023). An All-Natural Wood-Inspired Aerogel. *Angewandte Chemie*, *135*(6), e202211099. PMID:36416072

Haraguchi, N., Martorano, B., & Sanfilippo, M. (2019). What factors drive successful industrialization? Evidence and implications for developing countries. *Structural Change and Economic Dynamics*, *49*, 266–276. doi:10.1016/j.strueco.2018.11.002

Harnal, S., Sharma, G., Malik, S., Kaur, G., Khurana, S., Kaur, P., Simaiya, S., & Bagga, D. (2022). Bibliometric mapping of trends, applications and challenges of artificial intelligence in smart cities. *EAI Endorsed Transactions on Scalable Information Systems*, *9*(4), 1–21. doi:10.4108/eetsis.vi.489

Harrison, C. (2023). [*Climate Bonds Initiative.*]. *Green Bond Pricing in the Primary Market*, H2, 2022.

Hartini, S., Ciptomulyono, U., Anityasari, M., & Sriyanto. (2020). Manufacturing sustainability assessment using a lean manufacturing tool: A case study in the Indonesian wooden furniture industry. *International Journal of Lean Six Sigma*, *11*(5), 943–971. doi:10.1108/IJLSS-12-2017-0150

Harun, S. A., Fauzi, M. A., Kasim, N. M., & Wider, W. (2022). Determinants of energy efficient appliances among Malaysian households: Roles of theory of planned behavior, social interaction and appliance quality. *Asian Economic and Financial Review*, *12*(3), 212–226. doi:10.55493/5002.v12i3.4463

Harvey, A. S. (1993). Guidelines for time use data collection. *Social Indicators Research*, *30*(2-3), 197–228. doi:10.1007/BF01078728

Hatab, A. A., Ravula, P., Nedumaran, S., & Lagerkvist, C. J. (2021). Perceptions of the impacts of urban sprawl among urban and peri-urban dwellers of Hyderabad, India: A Latent class clustering analysis. *Environment, Development and Sustainability*, *24*(11), 12787–12812. doi:10.100710668-021-01964-2

Henricksen, K., & Indulska, J. (2006). Developing context-aware pervasive computing applications: Models and approach. *Pervasive and Mobile Computing*, *2*(1), 37–64. doi:10.1016/j.pmcj.2005.07.003

Henseler, J., Ringle, C. M., & Sarstedt, M. (2015). A new criterion for assessing discriminant validity in variance-based structural equation modeling. *Journal of the Academy of Marketing Science*, *43*(1), 115–135. doi:10.100711747-014-0403-8

Herath, H. M. K. K. M. B., & Mittal, M. (2022). Adoption of artificial intelligence in smart cities: A comprehensive review. *International Journal of Information Management Data Insights*, *2*(1), 1–21. doi:10.1016/j.jjimei.2022.100076

Herawati, H. (2019). Production Technology and Utilization of Nano Cellulose. *IOP Conf. Series: Journal of Physics: Conf. Series 1295*. IOP Publishing 10.1088/1742-6596/1295/1/012051

Hering, J. G. (2017). Managing the 'monitoring imperative' in the context of SDG Target 6.3 on water quality and wastewater. *Sustainability (Basel)*, *9*(9), 1572. doi:10.3390u9091572

Herzberg, F. (2017). *Motivation to work*. Routledge. doi:10.4324/9781315124827

He, X., Huang, S. Z., Chau, K. Y., Shen, H. W., & Zhu, Y. L. (2019). A study on the effect of environmental regulation on green innovation performance: A case of green manufacturing enterprises in pearl river delta in China. *Ekoloji*, *28*(107), 727–736.

Heydari, H., Taleizadeh, A. A., & Jolai, F. (2023). Financing a two-stage sustainable supply chain using green bonds: Preventing environmental pollution and waste generation. *Engineering Applications of Artificial Intelligence*, *117*, 105583. doi:10.1016/j.engappai.2022.105583

Hjemdahl, P. W. (2020, March 17). Green Manufacturing: The Business Benefits of Sustainability. *rePurpose Global*. https://repurpose.global/blog/post/green-manufacturing-the-business-benefits-of-sustainability#:~:text=Taking%20 steps%20to%20become%20more,the%20company%20become%20more%20profitable.

Hoefnagels, R., Junginger, M., & Faaij, A. (2014). The economic potential of wood pellet production from alternative, low-value wood sources in the southeast of the US. *Biomass and Bioenergy*, *71*, 443–454. doi:10.1016/j.biombioe.2014.09.006

Holbrook, E. (2021, April 2). *JetBlue to Aim for Emission, Recycling, and Sustainable Aviation*. Environment + Energy Leader. https://www.environmentalleader.com/2021/04/jetblue-sets-big-goals-for-emissions-recycling-and-sustainable-aviation-fuel-usage/

Holling, C. S. (2001). Understanding the complexity of economic, ecological, and social systems. *Ecosystems (New York, N.Y.)*, *4*(5), 390–405. doi:10.100710021-001-0101-5

Horng, J.-S., Liu, C.-H., Chou, S.-F., Tsai, C.-Y., & Chung, Y.-C. (2017). From innovation to sustainability: Sustainability innovations of eco-friendly hotels in Taiwan. *International Journal of Hospitality Management*, *63*, 44–52. doi:10.1016/j.ijhm.2017.02.005

Hossain, M. U., & Poon, C. S. (2018). Comparative LCA of wood waste management strategies generated from building construction activities. *Journal of Cleaner Production*, *177*, 387–397. doi:10.1016/j.jclepro.2017.12.233

House, R. J., & Wigdor, L. A. (1967). Herzberg's dual-factor theory of job satisfaction and motivation: A review of the evidence and a criticism. *Personnel Psychology*, *20*(4), 369–389. doi:10.1111/j.1744-6570.1967.tb02440.x

Housing and Land Rights Network. (2018). *India's Smart Cities Mission: Smart for whom? Cities for whom?* Housing and Land Rights Network. Smart_Cities_Report_2018.pdf (hlrn.org.in)

How we feed the world today. (n.d.). OECD. https://www.oecd.org/agriculture/understanding-the-global-food-system/how-we-feed-the-world-today/

Hsu, K., & Jen-Chih, C. (2020). Economic Valuation of Green Infrastructure Investments in Urban Renewal: The Case of the Station District in Taichung, Taiwan. *Environments (Basel, Switzerland)*, *7*(8), 56. doi:10.3390/environments7080056

Hsu, P. H., Tian, X., & Xu, Y. (2014). Financial development and innovation: Cross-country evidence. *Journal of Financial Economics*, *112*(1), 116–135. doi:10.1016/j.jfineco.2013.12.002

Hua, L., & Wang, S. (2019). Antecedents of consumers' intention to purchase energy-efficient appliances: An empirical study based on the technology acceptance model and theory of planned behavior. *Sustainability (Basel)*, *11*(10), 1–17. doi:10.3390u11102994

Huang, J., Ma, X., Yang, G., & Alain, D. (2019). Introduction to Nanocellulose. In J. Huang, A. Dufresne, & N. Lin (Eds.), *Nanocellulose*. doi:10.1002/9783527807437.ch1

Huang, L., & Zhao, W. (2022). The impact of green trade and green growth on natural resources. *Resources Policy*, *77*, 102749. doi:10.1016/j.resourpol.2022.102749

Huang, Z., Liu, X., Sun, S., Tang, Y., Yuan, X., & Tang, Q. (2021). Global assessment of future sectoral water scarcity under adaptive inner-basin water allocation measures. *The Science of the Total Environment*, *783*, 146973. doi:10.1016/j.scitotenv.2021.146973 PMID:33866163

Huan, Y., Li, H., & Liang, T. (2019). A new method for the quantitative assessment of Sustainable Development Goals (SDGs) and a case study on Central Asia. *Sustainability (Basel)*, *11*(13), 3504. doi:10.3390u11133504

Hubbard, G. (2009). Measuring organizational performance: Beyond the triple bottom line. *Business Strategy and the Environment*, *18*(3), 177–191. doi:10.1002/bse.564

Hudaefi, F. A., Saoqi, A. A. Y., Farchatunnisa, H., & Junari, U. L. (2020). Zakat and SDG 6: A case study of Baznas, Indonesia. *Journal of Islamic Monetary Economics and Finance*, *6*(4), 919–934. doi:10.21098/jimf.v6i4.1144

Hussain, A., Ali, M., Ali, H. M., Sabir, M. S., & Mehboob, M. (2020). An Experimental Analysis of Waste Heat Recovery Potential from A Rotary Kiln of Cement Industry. *The Nucleus*, *57*(1), 33–38.

Hutton, G., & Chase, C. (2016). The knowledge base for achieving the sustainable development goal targets on water supply, sanitation, and hygiene. *International Journal of Environmental Research and Public Health*, *13*(6), 536. doi:10.3390/ijerph13060536 PMID:27240389

Hydrogen Tech. (2021). *Conference Agenda 2021*. Hydrogen Tech. https://www.hydrogen-worldexpo.com/2021-conference-agenda/. Https://Www.Hydrogen-Worldexpo.Com/2021-Conference-Agenda/

Hyzon Motors. (2022, July). *Hyzon to Build First Commercial Scale MEA Production line*. Hyzon. https://www.hyzonmotors.com/in-the-news/hyzon-to-build-us-first-commercial-scale-mea-production-line

Hyzon Vehicles. (2022, July). *Camiones Hyzon*. Hyzon.

IAEG-SDGs (United Nations Inter-agency and Expert Group on SDG Indicators). (2018). *Tier Classification for Global SDG Indicators*. UN. https://unstats.un.org/sdgs/iaeg-sdgs/

Iberdrola. (2021, April 22). *Green Or Sustainable Buildings*. Iberdrola; Iberdrola.

Ibisch, P. L., Hobson, P., & Vega, A. E. (2010). Mutual mainstreaming of biodiversity conservation and human development: towards a more radical ecosystem approach. In *Interdependence of biodiversity and development under global change* (pp. 15–34). Secretariat of the Convention on Biological Diversity.

Ibrahim, M., & Vo, X. V. (2021). Exploring the relationships among innovation, financial sector development and environmental pollution in selected industrialized countries. *Journal of Environmental Management*, *284*, 112057. doi:10.1016/j.jenvman.2021.112057 PMID:33581497

Idtechex. (2022). *The Hydrogen Economy, Fuel Cells, and Hydrogen Production Methods*. Idtechex. Https://Www.Idtechex.Com/En/Research-Report/the-Hydrogen-Economy-Fuel-Cells-and-Hydrogen-Production-Methods/744

Ihaka, R., & Gentleman, R. (1996). R: a language for data analysis and graphics. *Journal of Computational and Graphical Statistics*, *5*(3), 299–314.

Ihnat, V., Lubke, H., Russ, A., Pazitny, A., & Boruvka, V. (2018). Waste agglomerated wood materials as a secondary raw material for chipboards and fibreboards part II. Preparation and characterisation of wood fibres in terms of their reuse. *Wood Research*, *63*(3), 431–442.

Ilyas, R. A., Sapuan, S. M., Ibrahim, R., Atikah, M. S. N., Atiqah, A., Ansari, M. N. M., & Norrrahim, M. N. F. (2020). Production, Processes and Modification of Nanocrystalline Cellulose from Agro-Waste: A Review. *Nanocrystalline Materials*. doi:10.5772/intechopen.87001

IMARC Group. (n.d.). *Indian Pesticides Market Size, Share, Trends & Forecast 2023-2028*. IMARK Gorup. https://www.imarcgroup.com/indian-pesticides-market

IMD Smart City Observatory. (2021). *Smart City Index 2021*. IMD. https://www.imd.org/smart-city-observatory/home/#_smartCity

Institution of Chemical Engineers. (2023). Sustainable production and consumption. *Journal of the European Federation of Chemical Engineering, 39*.

Intellis. (2021, July 31). *What is Green Building Technology? Plus: The Top 5 Green Tech Trends Transforming Facility Management Right Now!* Intellis.

International Energy Agency (IEA). (2021). *Pathways to Net Zero: The Impact of Clean Energy Research*. IEA. https://www.iea.org/reports/net-zero-by-2050

International Insurance Society. (2010), *Sustainable Insurance Society*. International Insurance Society. http://www.iisoline.org/forum/markettrends/sustainable-insurance/e-insurance/

Introduction to the green economy. (2013, March 5). Why Green Economy? https://whygreeneconomy.org/introduction-to-the-green-economy/

Ioelovich, M. (2017). Characterization of Various Kinds of Nanocellulose. In Handbook of Nanocellulose and Cellulose Nanocomposites. John Wiley & Sons.

Ioelovich, M. (2017). Zero-discharge Technology for Production of Nanocrystalline Cellulose. *Research Journal of Nanoscience and Engineering, 1*(1), 29–33.

IPCC. (2014). Climate Change 2014 Part A: Global and Sectoral Aspects. In Climate Change 2014: Impacts, Adaptation, and Vulnerability. Part A: Global and Sectoral Aspects. Contribution of Working Group II to the Fifth Assessment Report of the Intergovernmental Panel on Climate Change. Retrieved from papers2://publication/uuid/B8BF5043-C873-4AFD-97F9-A630782E590D

IPCC. (2022). IPCC Sixth Assessment Report Impacts, Adaptation and Vulnerability. *IPCC Sixth Assessment Report*. IPCC.

Iqbal, M. (2021). Smart city in practice: Learn from Taipei City. *Journal of Governance and Public Policy, 8*(1), 50–59. doi:10.18196/jgpp.811342

Israel, G. D. (2013). *About*. Institute of Food and Agricultural Sciences (IFAS), University of Florida. https://edis.ifas.ufl.edu/pd006

Issock, I. P. B., Mpinganjira, M., & Roberts-Lombard, M. (2018). Drivers of consumer attention to mandatory energy-efficiency labels affixed to home appliances: An emerging market perspective. *Journal of Cleaner Production, 204*, 672–684. doi:10.1016/j.jclepro.2018.08.299

Issock, I. P. B., & Muposhi, A. (2023). Understanding energy-efficiency choices through consumption values: The central role of consumer's attention and trust in environmental claims. *Management of Environmental Quality, 34*(1), 250–270. doi:10.1108/MEQ-01-2022-0012

Iyer, L. S. (2021). AI enabled applications towards intelligent transportation. *Transportation Engineering*, 1-11. https://doi.org/ doi:10.1016/j.treng.2021.100083

Jaeger, B., & Upadhyay, A. (2020). Understanding barriers to circular economy: Cases from the manufacturing industry. *Journal of Enterprise Information Management, 33*(4), 729–745. doi:10.1108/JEIM-02-2019-0047

Jakubiec, J. A., & Reinhart, C. F. (2012). The 'adaptive zone'–A concept for assessing discomfort glare throughout daylit spaces. *Lighting Research & Technology, 44*(2), 149-170.

Jamil, K., Dunnan, L., Awan, F. H., Jabeen, G., Gul, R. F., Idrees, M., & Mingguang, L. (2022). Antecedents of consumer's purchase intention towards energy-efficient home appliances: An agenda of energy efficiency in the post COVID-19 era. *Frontiers in Energy Research*, *10*, 863127. doi:10.3389/fenrg.2022.863127

Jankovic, I., Vasic, V., & Kovacevic, V. (2022). Does transparency matter? Evidence from panel analysis of the EU government green bonds. *Energy Economics*, *114*, 106325. doi:10.1016/j.eneco.2022.106325

Jarre, M., Petit-Boix, A., Priefer, C., Meyer, R., & Leipold, S. (2020). Transforming the bio-based sector towards a circular economy-What can we learn from wood cascading? *Forest Policy and Economics*, *110*, 101872. doi:10.1016/j.forpol.2019.01.017

Jasim, A., Ullah, M. W., Shi, Z., Lin, X., & Yang, G. (2017). Fabrication of bacterial cellulose/polyaniline/single-walled carbon nanotubes membrane for potential application as biosensor. *Carbohydrate Polymers*, *163*, 62–69. doi:10.1016/j.carbpol.2017.01.056 PMID:28267519

Jha, A. K., Ghimire, A., Thapa, S., Jha, A. M., & Raj, R. (2021). A review of AI for urban planning: Towards building sustainable smart cities. In *Proceedings of the 6th International Conference on Inventive Computation Technologies*, (pp. 937-944). IEEE. 10.1109/ICICT50816.2021.9358548

Jia, P., Diabat, A., & Mathiyazhagan, K. (2015). Analyzing the SSCM practices in the mining and mineral industry by ISM approach. *Resources Policy*, *46*, 76–85. doi:10.1016/j.resourpol.2014.04.004

Ji, J., Xie, Z., Li, C., & Ji, F. (2022). The influence of the manufacturing agglomeration heterogeneity on the green economic efficiency in China. *Electronic Commerce Research*, 1–25. doi:10.100710660-022-09641-w

Johansson, G., & Winroth, M. (2010). Introducing Environmental Concern in Manufacturing Strategies Implications for the Decision Criteria. *Management Research Review*, *33*(9), 877–899. doi:10.1108/01409171011070305

Johnson, M. P., & Schaltegger, S. (2016). Two Decades of Sustainability Management Tools for SMEs: How Far Have We Come? *Journal of Small Business Management*, *54*(2), 481–505. doi:10.1111/jsbm.12154

Johnston, K. (2019). A comparison of two smart cities: Singapore and Atlanta. *Journal of Comparative Urban Law and Policy*, *3*, 191–206.

Joshi, G., Sen, V., & Kunte, M. (2020). Do Star Ratings Matter?: A qualitative study on consumer awareness and inclination to purchase energy-efficient home appliances. *International Journal of Social Ecology and Sustainable Development*, *11*(4), 40–55. doi:10.4018/IJSESD.2020100104

Joshi, G., Sheorey, P. A., & Gandhi, A. V. (2019). Analyzing the barriers to purchase intentions of energy-efficient appliances from a consumer perspective. *Benchmarking*, *26*(5), 1565–1580. doi:10.1108/BIJ-03-2018-0082

Joshi, Y., & Rahman, Z. (2015). *Factors affecting green purchase behaviour and future research directions*. International. *Strategic Management Review*, *3*(1-2), 128–143.

Julsrud, T. E., & Krogstad, J. R. (2020). Is there enough trust for the smart city? exploring acceptance for use of mobile phone data in oslo and tallinn. *Technological Forecasting and Social Change*, *161*, 1–11. doi:10.1016/j.techfore.2020.120314 PMID:32981976

Kagermann, H., Lukas, W. D., & Wahlster, W. (2011). Industrie 4.0: Mit dem Internet der Dinge auf dem Weg zur 4. industriellen Revolution. *VDI nachrichten*, *13*(1), 2-3.

Kahle, L. R., & Gurel-Atay, E. (Eds.). (2013). *Communicating sustainability for the green economy*. ME Sharpe.

Compilation of References

Kahraman, C., Ghorabaee, M. K., Zavadskas, E. K., Onar, S. C., Yazdani, M., & Oztaysi, B. (2017). Intuitionistic fuzzy EDAS method: An application to solid waste disposal site selection. *Journal of Environmental Engineering and Landscape Management*, 25(1), 1–12. doi:10.3846/16486897.2017.1281139

Kaluarachchi, Y. (2021). Potential advantages in combining smart and green infrastructure over silo approaches for future cities. *Front. Eng. Manag.*, 8(1), 98–108. doi:10.100742524-020-0136-y

Kaluarachchi, Y. (2022). Implementing data-driven smart city applications for future cities. *Smart Cities*, 5(2), 455–474. doi:10.3390martcities5020025

Kamble, S. S., Gunasekaran, A., & Gawankar, S. A. (2018). Sustainable Industry 4.0 framework: A systematic literature review identifying the current trends and future perspectives. *Process Safety and Environmental Protection*, 117, 408–425. doi:10.1016/j.psep.2018.05.009

Kararach, G., Nhamo, G., Mubila, M., Nhamo, S., Nhemachena, C., & Babu, S. (2018). Reflections on the Green Growth Index for developing countries: A focus of selected African countries. *Development Policy Review*, 36, O432–O454. doi:10.1111/dpr.12265

Kargarzadeh, H., Ahmad, I., Abdullah, I., Dufresne, A., Zainudin, S.Y., Sheltami, R.M. (2012). Effects of hydrolysis conditions on the morphology, crystallinity, and thermal stability of cellulose nanocrystals extracted from kenaf bast fibers. *Cellulose*, 19(3), 855-660. doi:10.1007/s10570-012-9684-6

Karim, S., Naeem, M. A., Hu, M., Zhang, D., & Taghizadeh–Hesary, F. (2022). Determining dependence, centrality, and dynamic networks between green bonds and financial markets. *Journal of Environmental Management*, 318, 115618. doi:10.1016/j.jenvman.2022.115618 PMID:35949085

Karlin, B., Davis, N., Sanguinetti, A., Gamble, K., Kirkby, D., & Stokols, D. (2014). Dimensions of conservation: Exploring differences among energy behaviors. *Environment and Behavior*, 46(4), 423–452. doi:10.1177/0013916512467532

Kashmanian, R. M. (2015). Building a Sustainable Supply Chain: Key Elements: Building a Sustainable Supply Chain. *Environmental Quality Management*, 24(3), 17–41. doi:10.1002/tqem.21393

Keong, C. Y. (2020). *Global environmental sustainability: Case studies and analysis of the united nations' journey to sustainable development* (1st ed.). Elsevier.

Keskisaari, A., & Karki, T. (2018). The use of waste materials in wood-plastic composites and their impact on the profitability of the product. *Resources, Conservation and Recycling*, 134, 257–261. doi:10.1016/j.resconrec.2018.03.023

Key messages. (n.d.). Food and Agriculture Organization of the United Nations. https://www.fao.org/about/meetings/soil-erosion-symposium/key-messages/en/

Khan, H. ur R., & Khan, Z. R. (2020). Green Product Innovation and Financial Resource Availability: Multi-Actor Model Approach. In S. A. R. Khan (Ed.), Advances in Logistics, Operations, and Management Science (pp. 111–133). IGI Global. doi:10.4018/978-1-7998-2173-1.ch006

Khan, S. A. R., Sharif, A., Golpîra, H., & Kumar, A. (2019). A green ideology in Asian emerging economies: From environmental policy and sustainable development. *Sustainable Development (Bradford)*, 27(6), 1063–1075. doi:10.1002d.1958

Khan, S. A. R., Yu, Z., & Umar, M. (2022). A road map for environmental sustainability and green economic development: An empirical study. *Environmental Science and Pollution Research International*, 29(11), 1–9. doi:10.100711356-021-16961-1 PMID:34643866

Khan, S. A. R., Zhang, Y., & Golpîra, H. (2018). The Impact of Green Supply Chain Practices in Business Performance: Evidence from Pakistani FMCG Firms. *Journal of Advanced Manufacturing Systems*, *17*(02), 267–275. doi:10.1142/S0219686718500166

Khare, A. P., Dwivedi, N., & Haq, S. (2023). Potential, Challenges, and Application for Wood–Plastic Composite Fabricated with Several Additives. In G. Du & X. Zhou (Eds.), Wood Industry - Past, Present and Future Outlook (pp. 1-18). IntechOpen, UK.

Khoshnava, S. M., Rostami, R., Zin, R. M., Štreimikienė, D., Yousefpour, A., Strielkowski, W., & Mardani, A. (2019). Aligning the criteria of green economy (GE) and sustainable development goals (SDGs) to implement sustainable development. *Sustainability (Basel)*, *11*(17), 4615. doi:10.3390u11174615

Kim, J. K., & Pal, K. (2010). *Recent advances in the processing of wood-plastic composites*. Springer.

Kim, T. W., Cha, S., & Kim, Y. (2018). Space choice, rejection and satisfaction in university campus. *Indoor and Built Environment*, *27*(2), 233–243. doi:10.1177/1420326X16665897

Kleindorfer, P. R., Singhal, K., & Wassenhove, L. N. (2009). Sustainable Operations Management. *Production and Operations Management*, *14*(4), 482–492. doi:10.1111/j.1937-5956.2005.tb00235.x

Klöckner, C. A. (2013). A comprehensive model of the psychology of environmental behavior—A meta-analysis. *Global Environmental Change*, *23*(5), 1028–1038. doi:10.1016/j.gloenvcha.2013.05.014

Kohtamäki, M., Parida, V., Patel, P. C., & Gebauer, H. (2020). The relationship between digitalization and servitization: The role of servitization in capturing the financial potential of digitalization. *Technological Forecasting and Social Change*, *151*, 119804. doi:10.1016/j.techfore.2019.119804

Kotler, P. T., Bowen, J. T., Makens, J., & Baloglu, S. (2016). *Marketing for Hospitality and Tourism*. Pearson Education.

Kotsantonis, S., & Serafeim, G. (2019). Four Things No One Will Tell You About ESG Data. *The Bank of America Journal of Applied Corporate Finance*, *31*(2), 50–58. Advance online publication. doi:10.1111/jacf.12346

Krawchuk, F. T. (2017). Collaboration in a VUCA environment. In *Visionary Leadership in a Turbulent World* (pp. 133–154). Emerald Publishing Limited. doi:10.1108/978-1-78714-242-820171007

Kroyer, G. (1995). *Impact of food processing on the environment--an overview*. AGRIS: International Information System for the Agricultural Science and Technology. https://agris.fao.org/agris-search/search.do?recordID=US201301513547

Kulkarni, S. J. (2016). Downstream processing in biotechnology: Research and studies. *International Journal of Science and Healthcare Research*, *1*(3), 8–10.

Kulkarni, S., O'Reilly, K., & Bhat, S. (2017). No relief: Lived experiences of inadequate sanitation access of poor urban women in India. *Gender and Development*, *25*(2), 167–183. doi:10.1080/13552074.2017.1331531

Kumar, A., Kapoor, N. R., Arora, H. C., & Kumar, A. (2022). Smart cities: A step toward sustainable development. In Smart Cities, 1-43, CRC Press. https:// doi:10.1201/9781003287186-1

Kumar, R., Hu, F., Hubbell, C. A., Ragauskas, A. J., & Wayman, C. E. (2013). Comparison of laboratory delignification methods, their selectivity, and impacts on physiochemical characteristic cellulosic biomass. Bioresour 130, 372-381.

Kumar, A., Negi, Y. S., Choudhary, V., & Bhardwaj, N. K. (2014). Characterization of Cellulose Nanocrystals Produced by Acid-Hydrolysis from Sugarcane Bagasse as Agro Waste. *Journal of Materials Physics and Chemistry*, *2*(1), 1–8. doi:10.12691/jmpc-2-1-1

Kumar, L., Nadeem, F., Sloan, M., Restle-Steinert, J., Deitch, M. J., Ali Naqvi, S., Kumar, A., & Sassanelli, C. (2022). Fostering green finance for sustainable development: A focus on textile and leather small medium enterprises in Pakistan. *Sustainability (Basel)*, *14*(19), 11908. doi:10.3390u141911908

Kumar, S. (2000). Technology Options for Municipal Solid Waste-to-energy Project. *TERI Information Monitor on Environmental Science*, *5*(1), 1–11.

Kuo, Y. H., Leung, J. M., & Yan, Y. (2023). Public transport for smart cities: Recent innovations and future challenges. *European Journal of Operational Research*, *306*(3), 1001–1026. doi:10.1016/j.ejor.2022.06.057

Kupiec, B. (2021). *Legal status of a renewables self-consumer under Polish law in light of Directive (EU) 2018/2001* European Parliament.

Kusiak, A. (2018). Smart manufacturing. *International Journal of Production Research*, *56*(1-2), 508–517. doi:10.1080/00207543.2017.1351644

Kusi-Sarpong, S., Gupta, H., & Sarkis, J. (2019). A supply chain sustainability innovation framework and evaluation methodology. *International Journal of Production Research*, *57*(7), 1990–2008. doi:10.1080/00207543.2018.1518607

Kyriakou, S. (2017) Green bond investors demand transparency. *Financial Times*. https://www.ftadviser.com/investments/2017/06/14/green-bond-investors-demand-transparency/.

Lagas, B. (2019). *Five Benefits of Embracing Sustainability and Green Manufacturing*. NIST. https://www.nist.gov/blogs/manufacturing-innovation-blog/five-benefits-embracing-sustainability-and-green-manufacturing

Lai, O. (2023). Deforestation in Southeast Asia: Causes and Solutions. *Earth.Org*. https://earth.org/deforestation-in-southeast-asia/

Larcker, D. F., & Watts, E. M. (2020). Where's the greenium? *Journal of Accounting and Economics*, *69*(2–3), 101312. doi:10.1016/j.jacceco.2020.101312

Lattimore, B., Smith, C., Titus, B. D., Stupak, I., & Egnell, G. (2009). Environmental factors in woodfuel production: Opportunities, risks, and criteria and indicators for sustainable practices. *Biomass and Bioenergy*, *33*(10), 1321–1342. doi:10.1016/j.biombioe.2009.06.005

Lavrinenko, O., Rybalkin, O., Danileviča, A., & Sprūde, M. (2022). Green economy: Content and methodological approaches. *Entrepreneurship and Sustainability Issues*, *10*(2), 635–652. doi:10.9770/jesi.2022.10.2(40)

Le Hesran, C., Ladier, A. L., Botta-Genoulaz, V., & Laforest, V. (2020). A methodology for the identification of waste-minimizing scheduling problems. *Journal of Cleaner Production*, *246*, 119023. doi:10.1016/j.jclepro.2019.119023

Lebelle, M., Lajili Jarjir, S., & Sassi, S. (2022). The effect of issuance documentation disclosure and readability on liquidity: Evidence from green bonds. *Global Finance Journal*, *51*, 100678. doi:10.1016/j.gfj.2021.100678

Lee, C. C., Wang, C. W., & Ho, S. J. (2022). The dimension of green economy: Culture viewpoint. *Economic Analysis and Policy*, *74*, 122–138. doi:10.1016/j.eap.2022.01.015

Lee, S. Y., Sankaran, R., Chew, K. W., Tan, C. H., Krishnamoorthy, R., Chu, D. T., & Show, P. L. (2019). Waste to bioenergy: A review on the recent conversion technologies. *Bmc Energy*, *1*(1), 1–22. doi:10.118642500-019-0004-7

Leigland, J., Trémolet, S., & Ikeda, J. (2016). *Achieving Universal Access to Water and Sanitation by 2030: The Role of Blended Finance*. World Bank. doi:10.1596/25111

Leong, W. D., Lam, H. L., Ng, W. P. Q., Lim, C. H., Tan, C. P., & Ponnambalam, S. G. (2019). Lean and green manufacturing—a review on its applications and impacts. *Process integration and optimization for sustainability*, *3*, 5-23.

Lešić, V. (2021). *Rapid Plant Development Modelling System for Predictive Agriculture Based on Artificial Intelligence.* 2021 16th International Conference on Telecommunications (ConTEL), Zagreb, Croatia. 10.23919/ConTEL52528.2021.9495972

Li, G., Lim, M. K., & Wang, Z. (2020). Stakeholders, green manufacturing, and practice performance: Empirical evidence from Chinese fashion businesses. *Annals of Operations Research*, *290*(1-2), 961–982. doi:10.100710479-019-03157-7

Li, G., Li, W., Jin, Z., & Wang, Z. (2019). Influence of environmental concern and knowledge on households' willingness to purchase energy-efficient appliances: A case study in Shanxi, China. *Sustainability (Basel)*, *11*(4), 1073. doi:10.3390u11041073

Li, K., Zhang, X., Leung, J. Y. T., & Yang, S. L. (2016). Parallel Machine Scheduling Problems in Green Manufacturing Industry. *Journal of Manufacturing Systems*, *38*, 98–106. doi:10.1016/j.jmsy.2015.11.006

Lillemo, S. C. (2014). Measuring the effect of procrastination and environmental awareness on households' energy-saving behaviors: An empirical approach. *Energy Policy*, *66*, 249–256. doi:10.1016/j.enpol.2013.10.077

Lin, P.-H., & Chen, W.-H. (2022). Factors That Influence Consumers' Sustainable Apparel Purchase Intention: The Moderating Effect of Generational Cohorts. *Sustainability (Basel)*, *14*(14), 8950. doi:10.3390u14148950

Lirn, T.-C., Wong, C. W. Y., Shang, K.-C., & Li, Y.-T. (2019). Identifying Green Assessment Criteria for Shipping Industries. In X. Liu (Ed.), *Environmental Sustainability in Asian Logistics and Supply Chains* (pp. 21–44). Springer Singapore. doi:10.1007/978-981-13-0451-4_2

Liu, L., Zhang, M., & Ye, W. (2019). The adoption of sustainable practices: A supplier's perspective. *Journal of Environmental Management*, *232*, 692–701. doi:10.1016/j.jenvman.2018.11.067 PMID:30522074

Liu, S., Wu, G., Syed-Hassan, S. S. A., Li, B., Hu, X., Zhou, J., Huang, Y., Zhang, S., & Zhang, H. (2022). Catalytic pyrolysis of pine wood over char-supported Fe: Bio-oil upgrading and catalyst regeneration by CO_2/H_2O. *Fuel*, *307*, 121778. doi:10.1016/j.fuel.2021.121778

Liu, X. (Ed.). (2019). *Environmental Sustainability in Asian Logistics and Supply Chains*. Springer Singapore. doi:10.1007/978-981-13-0451-4

Liu, X., & Bae, J. (2018). Urbanization and industrialization impact of CO2 emissions in China. *Journal of Cleaner Production*, *172*, 178–186. doi:10.1016/j.jclepro.2017.10.156

Liu, Z., He, M., Ma, G., Yang, G., & Chen, J. (2019). Preparation and Characterization of Cellulose Nanocrystals from Wheat Straw and Corn Stalk. *Korean Society of Pulp and Paper Engineers Pulp & Paper Technology Academic Journals Pulp and Paper Technology*, *51*(2), 40–48. doi:10.7584/JKTAPPI.2019.04.51.2.40

Li, X., Ozturk, I., Majeed, M. T., Hafeez, M., & Ullah, S. (2022). Considering the asymmetric effect of financial deepening on environmental quality in BRICS economies: Policy options for the green economy. *Journal of Cleaner Production*, *331*, 129909. doi:10.1016/j.jclepro.2021.129909

Llach, J., Alonso-Almeida, M. D. M., Martí, J., & Rocafort, A. (2016). Effects of quality management on hospitality performance in different contexts. *Industrial Management & Data Systems*, *116*(5), 1005–1023. doi:10.1108/IMDS-06-2015-0235

Lonsdale, K., Pringle, P., & Turner, B. (2015). *Transformative adaptation: What it is, why it matters and what is needed.* Academic Press.

Lööf, H., Martinsson, G., & Mohammadi, A. (2017). *Finance and Innovative Investment in Environmental Technology: The Case of Sweden (No. 445).* Royal Institute of Technology, CESIS-Centre of Excellence for Science and Innovation Studies.

Luckey, D., Fritz, H., Legatiuk, D., Dragos, K., & Smarsly, K. (2021). Artificial intelligence techniques for smart city applications. In *Proceedings of the 18th International Conference on Computing in Civil and Building Engineering*, (pp. 1-14). Springer International Publishing. 10.1007/978-3-030-51295-8_1

Luken, R., Van Rompaey, F., & Zigova, K. (2008). The Determinants of EST Adoption by Manufacturing Plants in Developing Countries. *Ecological Economics*, *66*(1), 141–152. doi:10.1016/j.ecolecon.2007.08.015

Lutterodt, G., Akuffo, F. O., & Donkoh, S. A. (2019). Improving water security through sustainable water management practices. *Journal of Cleaner Production*, *222*, 376–388.

Lv, C., Bian, B., Lee, C. C., & He, Z. (2021). Regional gap and the trend of green finance development in China. *Energy Economics*, *102*, 105476. doi:10.1016/j.eneco.2021.105476

Lv, Z., Qiao, L., Kumar Singh, A., & Wang, Q. (2021). AI-empowered IoT security for smart cities. *ACM Transactions on Internet Technology*, *21*(4), 1–21.

MacAskill, S., Roca, E., Liu, B., Stewart, R. A., & Sahin, O. (2021). Is there a green premium in the green bond market? Systematic literature review revealing premium determinants. *Journal of Cleaner Production*, *280*, 124491. doi:10.1016/j.jclepro.2020.124491

Macchi, M., Savino, M., & Roda, I. (2020). Analysing the support of sustainability within the manufacturing strategy through multiple perspectives of different business functions. *Journal of Cleaner Production*, *258*, 120771. doi:10.1016/j.jclepro.2020.120771

Machado, C. G., Winroth, M. P., & Ribeiro da Silva, E. H. D. (2020). Sustainable manufacturing in Industry 4.0: An emerging research agenda. *International Journal of Production Research*, *58*(5), 1462–1484. doi:10.1080/00207543.2019.1652777

Madaleno, M., Dogan, E., & Taskin, D. (2022). A step forward on sustainability: The nexus of environmental responsibility, green technology, clean energy and green finance. *Energy Economics*, *109*, 105945. doi:10.1016/j.eneco.2022.105945

Mahapatra, S., Cole, D., Pal, R., & Webster, S. (2021). Towards a Unified Understanding and Management of Closed Loop Operations. In C. Chen, Y. Chen, & V. Jayaraman (Eds.), *Pursuing Sustainability* (Vol. 301, pp. 219–237). Springer International Publishing. doi:10.1007/978-3-030-58023-0_9

Mahendra, I.P., & Wirjosentono, B., Tamrin, I. H., & Mendez, J.A. (2019). Oil Palm-Based Nanocrystalline Cellulose In The Emulsion System Of Cyclic Natural Rubber. *Rasayan Journal of Chemistry*, *12*(2), 635–640. doi:10.31788/RJC.2019.1225089

Mahmood, H., Alkhateeb, T. T. Y., & Furqan, M. (2020). Industrialization, urbanization and CO2 emissions in Saudi Arabia: Asymmetry analysis. *Energy Reports*, *6*, 1553–1560. doi:10.1016/j.egyr.2020.06.004

Mainali, B., Luukkanen, J., Silveira, S., & Kaivo-oja, J. (2018). Evaluating synergies and trade-offs among Sustainable Development Goals (SDGs): Explorative analyses of development paths in South Asia and Sub-Saharan Africa. *Sustainability (Basel)*, *10*(3), 815. doi:10.3390u10030815

Make in Inida. (n.d.). *Schemes that would reduce food waste, benefit farmers*. Make In India. https://www.makeinindia.com/6-schemes-would-reduce-food-waste-benefit-farmers

Maksimovic, M. (2018). Greening the Future: Green Internet of Things (G-IoT) as a Key Technological Enabler of Sustainable Development. In N. Dey, A.E. Hassanien, C. Bhatt, A. S. Ashour & S.C. Satapathy. (Eds.), *Internet of Things and Big Data Analytics Toward Next-Generation Intelligence* (pp 238-313). Springer Cham Ministry of the Environment. https://ym.fi/en/wood-building

Malhotra, N. K. (2010). *Marketing research: An applied orientation* (6th ed.). Pearson.

Maltais, A., & Nykvist, B. (2020). Understanding the role of green bonds in advancing sustainability. *Journal of Sustainable Finance & Investment*, 1–20. doi:10.1080/20430795.2020.1724864

Mangla, S. K., Govindan, K., & Luthra, S. (2017). Prioritizing the barriers to achieve sustainable consumption and production trends in supply chains using fuzzy Analytical Hierarchy Process. *Journal of Cleaner Production*, *151*, 509–525. doi:10.1016/j.jclepro.2017.02.099

Maniam, G., Poh, P. E., Htar, T. T., Poon, W. C., & Chuah, L. H. (2021). Water Literacy in the Southeast Asian Context: Are We There Yet? *Water (Basel)*, *13*(16), 2311. doi:10.3390/w13162311

Manyika, J., Sinclair, J., & Dobbs, R. (2012). *Manufacturing the Future: The Next Era of Global Growth and Innovation*. Mckinsey Global Institute.

Mao, Y., & Wang, J. (2019). Is green manufacturing expensive? Empirical evidence from China. *International Journal of Production Research*, *57*(23), 7235–7247. doi:10.1080/00207543.2018.1480842

Marcos, M., Nadia, E. K., & Dufresne, A. (2018). Cellulose nanomaterials: Size and surface influence on the thermal and rheological behavior. *Polímeros*, *28*(2), 93–102. doi:10.1590/0104-1428.2413

Mariano, M., Kissi, N., & Dufresne, A. (2014). Cellulose Nanocrystals and Related Nanocomposites: Review of some Properties and Challenges. *Journal of Polymer Science. Part B, Polymer Physics*, *52*(12), 791–706. doi:10.1002/polb.23490

Marinova, D., & Bogueva, D. (2019). Planetary health and reduction in meat consumption. *Sustainable Earth*, *2*(1), 3. doi:10.118642055-019-0010-0

Marke, A. (Ed.). (2018). *Transforming climate finance and green investment with blockchains* (1st ed.). Elsevier., doi:10.1016/C2017-0-01389-7

Marrewijk, V. M. (2003). Concepts and Definitions of CSR and Corporate Sustainability: Between Agency and Communion. *Journal of Business Ethics*, *44*(2), 95–105. doi:10.1023/A:1023331212247

Martinez, F. (2019). Process excellence the key for digitalisation. *Business Process Management Journal*, *25*(7), 1716–1733. doi:10.1108/BPMJ-08-2018-0237

Martínez-Luévanos, A., Perez Berumen, C., Ceniceros, A., Owoyokun, T., & Sifuentes, L. (2021). Cellulose Nanocrystals: Obtaining and Sources of a Promising Bionanomaterial for Advanced Applications Taiwo. *Biointerface Research in Applied Chemistry*, *11*, 11797–11816.

Martiradonna, M., Romagnoli, S., & Santini, A. (2023). The beneficial role of green bonds as a new strategic asset class: Dynamic dependencies, allocation and diversification before and during the pandemic era. *Energy Economics*, *120*, 106587. doi:10.1016/j.eneco.2023.106587

Maruthi, G. D., & Rashmi, R. (2015). Green Manufacturing: It's Tools and Techniques that can be implemented in Manufacturing Sectors. *Materials Today: Proceedings*, *2*(4-5), 3350–3355. doi:10.1016/j.matpr.2015.07.308

Mason, I. G., Page, S. C., & Williamson, A. G. (2010). A 100% renewable electricity generation system for New Zealand utilising hydro, wind, geothermal and biomass resources. *Energy Policy*, *38*(8), 3973–3984. doi:10.1016/j.enpol.2010.03.022

Matebie, B.Y., Tizazu, B.Z., Kadhem, A.A., & Prabhu, S.V. (2021). Synthesis of Cellulose Nanocrystals (CNCs) from Brewer's Spent Grain Using Acid Hydrolysis: Characterization and Optimization. *Journal of Nanomaterials*. doi:10.1155/2021/7133154

Compilation of References

Matthew Klippenstein. (2022). *Hydrogen is not the solution, the efficiency is too low. Canadian Hydrogen and Fuel Cell Association.* CHFCA.

Mazlita, Y., Lee, H. V., & Hamid, S. B. A. (2016). Preparation of Cellulose Nanocrystals Bio-Polymer from Agro-Industrial Wastes: Separation and Characterization. *Polymers & Polymer Composites*, *24*(9), 719–728. doi:10.1177/096739111602400907

Mazzucato, M., & Semieniuk, G. (2018). Financing renewable energy: Who is financing what and why it matters. *Technological Forecasting and Social Change*, *127*, 8–22. doi:10.1016/j.techfore.2017.05.021

McIntosh, A. C., Makin, I., Paw, T. G., Dhamasiri, C., Thapan, A., Rivera, P., & White, M. (2014). *Urban water supply and sanitation in Southeast Asia: a guide to good practice.*

McKibben, B., & McKibben, S. D. S. B. (2007). *Deep economy: The wealth of communities and the durable future.* Macmillan.

Meadows, D. H., Meadows, D. H., Randers, J., & Behrens, W. W. III. (1972). The limits to growth: A report to the club of Rome (1972). *Google Scholar*, *91*, 2.

Mealy, P., & Teytelboym, A. (2022). Economic complexity and the green economy. *Research Policy*, *51*(8), 103948. doi:10.1016/j.respol.2020.103948

Mena, C., Christopher, M., Johnson, M., & Jia, F. (2007). *Innovation in Logistics Services.*

Mendonca, M., Jacobs, D., & Sovacool, B. K. (2009). *Powering the green economy: The feed-in tariff handbook.* Earthscan.

Menendez, M., & Ambuhl, L. (2022). Implementing design and operational measures for sustainable mobility: Lessons from Zurich. *Sustainability (Basel)*, *14*(2), 625. doi:10.3390u14020625

Mensah, J. (2019). Sustainable development: Meaning, history, principles, pillars, and implications for human action: Literature review. *Editorial Manager*, *5*(1). doi:10.1080/23311886.2019.1653531

Metcalf, L., & Benn, S. (2013). Leadership for Sustainability: An Evolution of Leadership Ability. *Journal of Business Ethics*, *112*(3), 369–384. Scopus. doi:10.100710551-012-1278-6

Migliorelli, M. (2021). What Do We Mean by Sustainable Finance? Assessing Existing Frameworks and Policy Risks. *Sustainability (Basel)*, *13*(2), 975. doi:10.3390u13020975

Mijalkovski, S., Despodov, Z., Mirakovski, D. & Mijalkovska, D. (2012a). Rational selection of mining excavation methods. *Natural resources and technology*, *6*(6), 15-23.

Mijalkovski, S., Despodov, Z., Mirakovski, D., Adjiski, V. & Doneva, N. (2022b). Application of UBC methodology for underground mining method selection, *Underground mining engineering*, *40*(1), 15-26.

Mijalkovski, S., Despodov, Z., Mirakovski, D., Adjiski, V., Doneva, N. & Mijalkovska, D. (2021b). Mining method selection for underground mining with the application of VIKOR method. *Underground mining engineering*, *39*(2), 11-22.

Mijalkovski, S., Despodov, Z., Mirakovski, D., Adjiski, V., Doneva, N., & Mijalkovska, D. (2021a). Mining method selection for underground mining with the application of PROMETHEE method. *3st International Multidisciplinary Geosciences Conference (IMGC 2021), Mitrovica, October 2021*, (pp. 84-91). Science Direct.

Mijalkovski, S., Despodov, Z., Mirakovski, D., Hadzi-Nikolova, M., Doneva, N. & Gocevski, B. (2012b). Mining method selection by integrated AHP and PROMETHEE method. *PODEKS-POVEKS 2012, Stip*, 121-127.

Mijalkovski, S., Peltecki, D., Despodov, Z., Mirakovski, D., Adjiski, V. & Doneva, N. (2021). Methodology for underground mining method selection. *Mining science, 28*, 201-216.

Mijalkovski, S., Efe, O. F., Despodov, Z., Mirakovski, D., & Mijalkovska, D. (2022). Underground mining method selection with the application of TOPSIS method. *GeoScience Engineering, 68*(2), 125–133. doi:10.35180/gse-2022-0075

Mijalkovski, S., Peltechki, D., Zeqiri, K., Kortnik, J., & Mirakovski, D. (2020). Risk assessment at workplace in underground lead and zinc mine with application of Fuzzy TOPSIS method. *Journal of the Institute of Electronics and Computer, 2*, 121–141.

Mijalkovski, S., Zeqiri, K., Despodov, Z., & Adjiski, V. (2022a). Underground mining method selection according to Nicholas methodology. *Natural Resources and Technology, 16*(1), 5–11. doi:10.46763/NRT22161005m

Mills, E. (2009). A Global Review of Insurance Industry Responses to Climate Change. *The Geneva Papers on Risk and Insurance. Issues and Practice, 34*(3), 323–359. doi:10.1057/gpp.2009.14

Mining and Energy Planning Unit (UPME). (2015). *Integracion de las energías renovables no convencionales en Colombia*. UPME.

Ministerio de Hacienda y Crédito Público de Colombia. (2022). *decreto 895 del 2022*. MHCP.

Ministry of Housing and Urban Affairs. (2023). [Data set]. Ministry of Housing and Urban Affairs. https://smartcities.data.gov.in/cities

Mirza, N., Umar, M., Afzal, A., & Firdousi, S. F. (2023). The role of fintech in promoting green finance, and profitability: Evidence from the banking sector in the euro zone. *Economic Analysis and Policy, 78*, 33–40. doi:10.1016/j.eap.2023.02.001

Mitra, A., & Mehta, B. (2011). Cities as the engine of growth: Evidence from India. *Journal of Urban Planning and Development, 137*(2), 171–183. doi:10.1061/(ASCE)UP.1943-5444.0000056

Mittal, V. K., & Sangwan, K. S. (2014). Prioritizing Barriers to Green Manufacturing: Environmental, Social and Economic Perspectives. *Procedia CIRP, 17*, 559–564. doi:10.1016/j.procir.2014.01.075

Modak, P. (2018). *Environmental management towards sustainability*. Taylor & Francis. doi:10.1201/9781315156118

Mohamadi, A., Heidarizadi, Z., & Nourollahi, H. (2016). Assessing the desertification trend using neural network classification and object-oriented techniques (Case study: Changouleh watershed-Ilam Province of Iran). *Istanbul Üniversitesi Orman Fakültesi Dergisi, 66*(2), 683–690.

Mohammed, N., Rokiah, H., Othman, S., & Mohammad, A. (2017). Nanocellulose: Preparation methods and applications. In C.-R. N. Composites (Ed.), *In Woodhead Publishing Series in Composites Science and Engineering* (pp. 261–276). Mohammad Jawaid, Sami Boufi, Abdul Khalil H.P.S. doi:10.1016/B978-0-08-100957-4.00011-5

MoIT (Turkish Ministry of Industry and Technology). (2022). *T.C. Sanayi ve Teknoloji Bakanlığı 2021 Yılı Faaliyet Raporu*. T.C. Sanayi ve Teknoloji Bakanlığı.

Moktadir, M. A., Rahman, T., Rahman, M. H., Ali, S. M., & Paul, S. K. (2018). Drivers to sustainable manufacturing practices and circular economy: A perspective of leather industries in Bangladesh. *Journal of Cleaner Production, 174*, 1366–1380. doi:10.1016/j.jclepro.2017.11.063

Mol, A. P. (2002). Ecological modernization and the global economy. *Global Environmental Politics, 2*(2), 92–115. doi:10.1162/15263800260047844

Compilation of References

Momberg, D., Jacobs, B., & Sonnenberg, N. (2012). The role of environmental knowledge in young female consumers' evaluation and selection of apparel in South Africa. *International Journal of Consumer Studies*, *36*(4), 408–415. doi:10.1111/j.1470-6431.2011.01061.x

Monica Mendieta, C., Elizabet Cardozo, R., Esteban Felissia, F., Martin Clauser, N., Vallejos, M. E., & Area, M. C. (2021). Bioconversion of Wood Waste to Bio-ethylene: A Review. *BioResources*, *16*(2), 4411–4437. doi:10.15376/biores.16.2.Mendieta

Monika, B., & Sharma, K. (2018). Environmental consciousness and consumer lifestyle. *Business Analyst Journal*, *39*(2), 57–76.

Moon, J. S., Park, J. H., Lee, T. Y., Kim, Y. W., Yoo, J. B., Park, C. Y., Kim, J. M., & Jin, K. W. (2005). Transparent conductive film based on carbon nanotubes and PEDOT composites. *Diamond and Related Materials*, *14*(11-12), 1882–1887. doi:10.1016/j.diamond.2005.07.015

Moon, R., Beck, S., & Rudie, A. (2013). Cellulose Nanocrystals – A Material with Unique Properties and Many Potential Applications. In *Production and Applications of Cellulose Nanomaterials* (pp. 9–13). Ed. Robert Moon, Stephanie Beck and Alan Rudie Michael T. Postek Robert J. Moon Alan W. Rudie and Michael A. Bilodeau. TAPPI PRESS.

Mori, H., & Fujita, H. (2015). *Application of EPSO to designing a contract model of weather derivatives in smart grid*. In *2015 IEEE Congress on Evolutionary Computation (CEC)*. IEEE. https://www.climatepolicyinitiative.org/publication/global-landscape-of-climate-finance-a-decade-of-data/, doi:10.1109/CEC.2015.7256909

Morone, P. (2019). *Food waste: Challenges and opportunities for enhancing the emerging bio-economy*. AGRIS: International Information System for the Agricultural Science and Technology. https://agris.fao.org/agris-search/search.do?recordID=US201900212695

Morseletto, P. (2020). Restorative and regenerative: Exploring the concepts in the circular economy. *Journal of Industrial Ecology*, *24*(4), 763–773. doi:10.1111/jiec.12987

Moshood, T. D., Nawanir, G., Mahmud, F., Mohamad, F. B., Ahmad, M. S., & AbdulGhani, A. (2022). Biodegradable plastic applications towards sustainability: A recent innovations in the green product. *Cleaner Engineering and Technology*, *6*, 100404. doi:10.1016/j.clet.2022.100404

MoSIT (Turkish Science, Ministry of Industry and Technology). (2015b). *Türkiye Sanayi Stratejisi Belgesi 2015-2018*. T.C. Bilim, Sanayi ve Teknoloji Bakanlığı, Ankara.

MoSIT. (2015a). (*Turkish Ministry of Science, Industry and Technology*). İklim Değişikliği ve Sanayi. T.C. Bilim, Sanayi ve Teknoloji Bakanlığı.

MoT (Turkish Ministry of Trade). (2020). *Yeşil Mutabakat Eylem Planı*. T.C. Ticaret Bakanlığı.

MoTF (Turkish Ministry of Treasury and Finance). (2020). *Yeni Ekonomi Programı 2021-2023*. T.C. Hazine ve Maliye Bakanlığı.

Mouloudj, K., & Bouarar, A. C. (2021). The impact of word of mouth on intention to purchase green products: An empirical study. *Revue Algérienne d'Economie de gestion*, *15*(1), 871-890.

Mouloudj, K., & Bouarar, A. C. (2023). Investigating predictors of medical students' intentions to engagement in volunteering during the health crisis. *African Journal of Economic and Management Studies*. doi:10.1108/AJEMS-08-2022-0315

Mouloudj, K., Bouarar, A. C., & Mouloudj, S. (2023). Extension of the theory of planned behaviour (TPB) to predict farmers' intention to save energy. *AIP Conference Proceedings*, *2683*, 020002. doi:10.1063/5.0125022

Muhamat, A., Jaafar, M., Basri, M., Alwi, S., & Mainal, A. (2017). Green Takaful (Insurance) as a Climate Finance Tool. *Advanced Science Letters*, *23*(8), 7670–7673. doi:10.1166/asl.2017.9549

Mukhopadhyay, T., & Kekre, S. (2002). Strategic and Operational Benefits of Electronic Integration in B2B Procurement Processes. *Management Science*, *48*(10), 1301–1313. doi:10.1287/mnsc.48.10.1301.273

Mura, M., Longo, M., & Zanni, S. (2020). Circular economy in Italian SMEs: A multi-method study. *Journal of Cleaner Production*, *245*, 118821. doi:10.1016/j.jclepro.2019.118821

Musa, A., Ahmad, M.B., Hussein, M.Z., Izham, S.M. (2017). Acid Hydrolysis-Mediated preparation of Nanocrystalline Cellulose from Rice Straw. *Int J Nanomater Nanotechnol Nanomed*, *3*(2), 51-56. doi:10.17352/2455-3492.000021

Mussatto, S. I., Machado, E. M. S., Martins, S., Teixeira, J. A. (2011). Production, composition, and application of coffee and its industrial residues. *Food and Bioprocess Technology*, *4*(5), 661–672. . 32. doi:10.1007/s11947-011-0565-z

Mussatto, S. I., Carneiro, L. M., Silva, J. P. A., Roberto, I. C., & Teixeira, J. A. (2011). A study on chemical constituents and sugars extraction from spent coffee grounds. *Carbohydrate Polymers*, *83*(2), 368–374. doi:10.1016/j.carbpol.2010.07.063

Mutezo, G., & Mulopo, J. (2021). A review of Africa's transition from fossil fuels to renewable energy using circular economy principles. *Renewable & Sustainable Energy Reviews*, *137*, 110609. doi:10.1016/j.rser.2020.110609

Muttarak, R., & Wilde, J. (2022). *The World at 8 Billion*. Population Council. doi:10.31899/pdr2022.1000

Nadaleti, W. C., de Souza, E. G., & Lourenço, V. A. (2022). Green hydrogen-based pathways and alternatives: Towards the renewable energy transition in South America's regions–Part B. *International Journal of Hydrogen Energy*, *47*(1), 1–15. doi:10.1016/j.ijhydene.2021.05.113

Nam, T. (2019). Technology usage, expected job sustainability, and perceived job insecurity. *Technological Forecasting and Social Change*, *138*, 155–165. doi:10.1016/j.techfore.2018.08.017

Nam, T., & Pardo, T. A. (2011). Conceptualizing smart city with dimensions of technology, people, and institutions. In *Proceedings of the 12th Annual International Digital Government Research Conference: Digital Government Innovation in Challenging Times*, (pp. 282-291). 10.1145/2037556.2037602

Napp, T., Gambhir, A., Hills, T. P., Florin, N., & Fennell, P. S. (2014). A Review of the Technologies, Economics and Policy Instruments for Decarbonising Energy-Intensive Manufacturing Industries. *Renewable & Sustainable Energy Reviews*, *30*, 616–640. doi:10.1016/j.rser.2013.10.036

Nardo, M., Saisana, M., Saltelli, A., Tarantola, S., Hoffman, A., & Giovannini, E. (2005). Handbook on constructing composite indicators. In *OECD Statistics Working Paper 2005/3*. OECD Publishing.

NASA. (2021). *Lessons from 50 years of UN sustainable development policy The Road to Sustainable Transport Key Messages and Recommendations*. International Institute for Sustainable Development.

Nascimento, D. L. M., Alencastro, V., Quelhas, O. L. G., Caiado, R. G. G., Garza-Reyes, J. A., Rocha-Lona, L., & Tortorella, G. (2019). Exploring Industry 4.0 technologies to enable circular economy practices in a manufacturing context: A business model proposal. *Journal of Manufacturing Technology Management*, *30*(3), 607–627. doi:10.1108/JMTM-03-2018-0071

Nasir, M. A., Canh, N. P., & Lan Le, T. N. (2021). Environmental degradation & role of financialisation, economic development, industrialisation and trade liberalisation. *Journal of Environmental Management*, *277*, 111471. doi:10.1016/j.jenvman.2020.111471 PMID:33049616

Nassiry, D. (2019). The role of fintech in unlocking green finance. In *Handbook of Green Finance* (pp. 315–336). Springer. doi:10.1007/978-981-13-0227-5_27

Natterodt, J. C., Petri-Fink, A., Weder, C., & Zoppe, J. O. (2017). Cellulose Nanocrystals: Surface Modification, Applications and Opportunities at Interfaces. *Chimia*, *71*(6), 376–383. doi:10.2533/chimia.2017.376 PMID:28662741

Navarathna, P. J., & Malagi, V. P. (2018). Artificial intelligence in smart city analysis. In *Proceedings of the International Conference on Smart Systems and Inventive Technology*, (pp. 44-47). IEEE.

Nayak, B., Bisoyi, B., & Pattnaik, P. K. (2023). Data center selection through service broker policy in cloud computing environment. *Materials Today: Proceedings*, *80*, 2218–2223. doi:10.1016/j.matpr.2021.06.185

Nenavath, S. (2022). Impact of fintech and green finance on environmental quality protection in India: By applying the semi-parametric difference-in-differences (SDID). *Renewable Energy*, *193*, 913–919. doi:10.1016/j.renene.2022.05.020

Ng, T. H., & Tao, J. Y. (2016). Bond financing for renewable energy in Asia. *Energy Policy*, *95*, 509–517. doi:10.1016/j.enpol.2016.03.015

Nguyen, C. T. X., Bui, K. H., Truong, B. Y., Do, N. H. N., & Le, P. T. K. (2021). Nanocellulose from Pineapple Leaf and Its Applications towards High-value Engineering Materials. *Chemical Engineering Transactions*, *89*, 19–24.

Nguyen-Viet, B. (2022). Understanding the influence of eco-label, and green advertising on green purchase intention: The mediating role of green brand equity. *Journal of Food Products Marketing*, *28*(2), 87–103. doi:10.1080/10454446.2022.2043212

Nhamo, G., Nhamo, S., & Nhemachena, C. (2018). What gets measured gets done! Towards an Afro-barometer for tracking progress in achieving Sustainable Development Goal 5. *Agenda (Durban, South Africa)*, *32*(1), 60–75. doi:10.1080/10130950.2018.1433365

Nhamo, G., Nhemachena, C., & Nhamo, S. (2019). Is 2030 too soon for Africa to achieve the water and sanitation sustainable development goal? *The Science of the Total Environment*, *669*, 129–139. doi:10.1016/j.scitotenv.2019.03.109 PMID:30878921

Nhemachena, C., Matchaya, G., Nhemachena, C. R., Karuaihe, S., Muchara, B., & Nhlengethwa, S. (2018). Measuring baseline agriculture-related sustainable development goals index for Southern Africa. *Sustainability (Basel)*, *10*(3), 849. doi:10.3390u10030849

Nhemachena, C., Matchaya, G., Nhlengethwa, S., & Nhemachena, C. R. (2018). Exploring ways to increase public investments in agricultural water management and irrigation for improved agricultural productivity in Southern Africa. *Water S.A.*, *44*(3), 474–481.

Nike Corporate Social Responsibility (CSR) and Sustainability. (n.d.). *Nike Corporate Social Responsibility (CSR) and Sustainability*. Nike. https://www.thomasnet.com/articles/other/nike-csr/

Nikje, M. M. A., Diarjani, E., & Haghshenas, M. (2012). Nanoclay-Flexible Polyurethane Nanocomposites Formulated by Recycled Polyether Polyols. *Cellular Polymers*, *31*(5), 257–267. doi:10.1177/026248931203100502

Nobanee, H., Alqubaisi, G. B., Alhameli, A., Alqubaisi, H., Alhammadi, N., Almasahli, S. A., & Wazir, N. (2021). Green and sustainable life insurance: A bibliometric review. *Journal of Risk and Financial Management*, *14*(11), 563. doi:10.3390/jrfm14110563

Nordhaus, W. (2018). Projections and Uncertainties about Climate Change in an Era of Minimal Climate Policies †. *American Economic Journal. Economic Policy*, *10*(3), 333–360. doi:10.1257/pol.20170046

Odegard, I., Croezen, H., & Bergsma, G. (2012). *Cascading of Biomass. 13 Solutions for a Sustainable Bio-based Economy. Making Better Choices for Use of Biomass Residues, By-products and Wastes* (Report No. CE-12266552). CE Delft, Netherlands.

OECD. (2020). *Biodiversity and the economic response to COVID-19: Ensuring a green and resilient recovery*. OECD. https://www.oecd.org/coronavirus/policy-responses/biodiversity-and-the-economic-response-to-covid-19-ensuring-a-green-and-resilient-recovery-d98b5a09/

Ogbonnaya, C., Abeykoon, C., Nasser, A., Turan, A., & Ume, C. S. (2021). Prospects of integrated photovoltaic-fuel cell systems in a hydrogen economy: A comprehensive review. In Energies (Vol. 14, Issue 20). MDPI. doi:10.3390/en14206827

Ojagh, S. M., Rezaei, M., Razavi, S. H., & Hosseini, S. M. H. (2010). Development and evaluation of a novel biodegradable film made from chitosan and cinnamon essential oil with low affinity toward water. *Food Chemistry*, *122*(1), 161–166. doi:10.1016/j.foodchem.2010.02.033

Okereke, C., Coke, A., Geebreyesus, M., Ginbo, T., Wakeford, J. J., & Mulugetta, Y. (2019). Governing green industrialisation in Africa: Assessing key parameters for a sustainable socio-technical transition in the context of Ethiopia. *World Development*, *115*, 279–290. doi:10.1016/j.worlddev.2018.11.019

Olawumi, T. O., & Chan, D. W. (2018). A scientometric review of global research on sustainability and sustainable development. *Journal of Cleaner Production*, *183*, 231–250. doi:10.1016/j.jclepro.2018.02.162

Oliveira, P. E., Petit-Breuilh, X., Rojas, O. J., & Gracitua, W. (2020). Production of cellulose nanostructures from Chilean bamboo, Chusquea quila. *Agronomy Research (Tartu)*, *18*(4), 2520–2534. doi:10.15159/AR.20.193

Olszewski, A., Kosmela, P., & Piszczyk, Ł. (2022). Synthesis and characterization of biopolyols through biomass liquefaction of wood shavings and their application in the preparation of polyurethane wood composites. *Holz als Roh- und Werkstoff*, *80*(1), 57–74. doi:10.100700107-021-01755-6

Organización para la Cooperación y el Desarrollo Economico del Pais. (2011). *Harnessing Variable Renewables*. OECD., doi:10.1787/9789264111394-

Orji, I., & Wei, S. (2016). A detailed calculation model for costing of green manufacturing. *Industrial Management & Data Systems*, *116*(1), 65–86. doi:10.1108/IMDS-04-2015-0140

Ortigara, A. R. C., Kay, M., & Uhlenbrook, S. (2018). A review of the SDG 6 synthesis report 2018 from an education, training, and research perspective. *Water (Basel)*, *10*(10), 1353. doi:10.3390/w10101353

Otoo, M., & Drechsel, P. (Eds.). (2018). *Resource recovery from waste: business models for energy, nutrient and water reuse in low-and middle-income countries*. Routledge. doi:10.4324/9781315780863

Ozili, P. K. (2021). Digital finance, green finance and social finance: Is there a link? *Financial Internet Quarterly*, *17*(1), 1–7. doi:10.2478/fiqf-2021-0001

Ozili, P. K. (2022). Green finance research around the world: A review of literature. *International Journal of Green Economics*, *16*(1), 56–75. doi:10.1504/IJGE.2022.125554

Packalen, T., Karkkainen, L., & Toppinen, A. (2017). The future operating environment of the Finnish sawmill industry in an era of climate change mitigation policies. *Forest Policy and Economics*, *82*, 30–40. doi:10.1016/j.forpol.2016.09.017

Pandey, S. (2022). Wood waste utilization and associated product development from under-utilized low-quality wood and its prospects in Nepal. *SN Applied Sciences*, *4*(6), 168. doi:10.100742452-022-05061-5

Pang, R., & Zhang, X. (2019). Achieving Environmental Sustainability in Manufacture: A 28-Year Bibliometric Cartography of Green Manufacturing Research. *Journal of Cleaner Production*, *233*, 84–99. doi:10.1016/j.jclepro.2019.05.303

Panigrahi, A. K., Saha, A., Shrinet, A., Nauityal, M., & Gaur, V. (2020). A case study on Zomato – The online Foodking of India. *Journal of Management Research and Analysis*, *7*(1), 25–33. doi:10.18231/j.jmra.2020.007

Panivivat, R., Kegley, E. B., Pennington, J. A., Kellogg, D. W., & Krumpelman, S. L. (2004). Growth performance and health of dairy calves bedded with different types of materials. *Journal of Dairy Science*, *87*(11), 3736–3745. doi:10.3168/jds.S0022-0302(04)73512-2 PMID:15483157

Pardo-Alonso, S., Solórzano, E., Brabant, L., Vanderniepen, P., Dierick, M., Van Hoorebeke, L., & RodríguezPérez, M. A. (2013). 3D Analysis of the progressive modification of the cellular architecture in polyurethane nanocomposite foams via X-ray microtomography. *European Polymer Journal*, *49*, 999-1006, doi:10.1016/j.eurpolymj.2013.01.005

Parkinson, T., Candido, C., & de Dear, R. (2013). *Comfort Chimp": a Multi-Platform IEQ Questionnaire Development Environment. CLIMA 2013: Energy Efficient*, Smart and Healthy Buildings.

Parzonko, A. J., Balińska, A., & Sieczko, A. (2021). Pro-Environmental Behaviors of Generation Z in the Context of the Concept of Homo Socio-Oeconomicus. *Energies*, *14*(6), 1597. doi:10.3390/en14061597

Patnaik, P. (2022). Personalized Product Recommendation and User Satisfaction: Theory and Application. In M. Pejic-Bach & Ç. Doğru (Eds.), (pp. 35–67). Advances in Logistics, Operations, and Management Science. IGI Global. doi:10.4018/978-1-7998-7793-6.ch002

Patnaik, R. (2018). Impact of Industrialization on Environment and Sustainable Solutions – Reflections from a South Indian Region. *IOP Conference Series. Earth and Environmental Science*, *120*, 012016. doi:10.1088/1755-1315/120/1/012016

Paul, J., Modi, A., & Patel, J. (2016). Predicting green product consumption using the theory of planned behavior and reasoned action. *Journal of Retailing and Consumer Services*, *29*, 123–134. doi:10.1016/j.jretconser.2015.11.006

Pearce, D. (1992). Green economics. *Environmental Values*, *1*(1), 3–13. doi:10.3197/096327192776680179

Peiró, L. T., Polverini, D., Ardente, F., & Mathieux, F. (2020). Advances towards circular economy policies in the EU: The new Ecodesign regulation of enterprise servers. *Resources, Conservation and Recycling*, *154*, 104426. doi:10.1016/j.resconrec.2019.104426 PMID:32127729

Pejić-Bach, M., & Dogru, C. (Eds.). (2022). *Management strategies for sustainability, new knowledge innovation, and personalized products and services*. Business Science Reference. doi:10.4018/978-1-7998-7793-6

Peña-García, N., Gil-Saura, I., Rodríguez-Orejuela, A., & Siqueira-Junior, J. R. (2020). Purchase intention and purchase behavior online: A cross-cultural approach. *Heliyon*, *6*(6), e04284. doi:10.1016/j.heliyon.2020.e04284 PMID:32613132

Peng, B. L., Dhar, N., Liu, H. L., & Tam, K. C. (2011). Chemistry and Applications of Nanocrystalline Cellulose and its Derivatives: A Nanotechnology Perspective. *Canadian Journal of Chemical Engineering*, *9999*(5), 1–16. doi:10.1002/cjce.20554

Pennington's Law. (2021). *Green retrofit: what is it and what does it mean for the development industry?* Penningtonslaw.com.

Pereira, P. H. F., Waldron, K. W., Wilson, D. R., Cunha, A. P., de Brito, E. S., Rodrigues, T. H. S., Rosa, M. F., & Azeredo, H. M. C. (2017). Wheat straw hemicelluloses added with cellulose nanocrystals and citric acid. Effect on film physical properties. *Carbohydrate Polymers*, *164*, 317–324. doi:10.1016/j.carbpol.2017.02.019 PMID:28325332

Pham, L., & Luu Duc Huynh, T. (2020). How does investor attention influence the green bond market? *Finance Research Letters*, *35*, 101533. doi:10.1016/j.frl.2020.101533

Piercy, N., & Rich, N. (2015). The relationship between lean operations and sustainable operations. *International Journal of Operations & Production Management*, *35*(2), 282–315. doi:10.1108/IJOPM-03-2014-0143

Pinho, G. C., & Calmon, J. L. (2023). LCA of Wood Waste Management Systems: Guiding Proposal for the Standardization of Studies Based on a Critical Review. *Sustainability (Basel)*, *15*(3), 1854. doi:10.3390u15031854

Pradhan, P., Costa, L., Rybski, D., Lucht, W., & Kropp, J. P. (2017). A systematic study of sustainable development goal (SDG) interactions. *Earth's Future*, *5*(11), 1169–1179. doi:10.1002/2017EF000632

Praharaj, S., Han, J. H., & Hawken, S. (2018). Urban innovation through policy integration: Critical perspectives from 100 smart cities mission in India. *City, culture and society*, *12*, 35-43.

Prakash, G. (2019). Exploring Innovation and Sustainability in the Potato Supply Chains. In X. Liu (Ed.), *Environmental Sustainability in Asian Logistics and Supply Chains* (pp. 97–120). Springer Singapore., doi:10.1007/978-981-13-0451-4_6

Prakash, G., & Pathak, P. (2017). Intention to buy eco-friendly packaged products among young consumers of India: A study on developing nation. *Journal of Cleaner Production*, *141*, 385–393. doi:10.1016/j.jclepro.2016.09.116

Prasad, S., Khanduja, D., & Sharma, S. K. (2016). An Empirical Study on Applicability of Lean and Green Practices in the Foundry Industry. *Journal of Manufacturing Technology Management*, *27*(3), 408–426. doi:10.1108/JMTM-08-2015-0058

Preuss, L. (2005). *The green multiplier: A study of environmental protection and the supply chain*. Palgrave Macmillan.

Principle for Investments. (2022). *Statement on ESG in credit risk and ratings*. UNPRI. https://www.unpri.org/credit-risk-and-ratings/statement-on-esg-in-credit-risk-and-ratings-available-in-different-languages/77.article

Proskurina, S., Rimppi, H., Heinimo, J., Hansson, J., Orlov, A., Raghu, K., & Vakkilainen, E. (2016). Logistical, economic, environmental and regulatory conditions for future wood pellet transportation by sea to Europe: The case of Northwest Russian seaports. *Renewable & Sustainable Energy Reviews*, *56*, 38–50. doi:10.1016/j.rser.2015.11.030

Prudential Regulation Authority. (2019). *Enhancing banks' and insurers approaches to managing the financial risks from climate change, policy statement 11/19*. PRA. https://www.bankofengland.co.uk

Pupo-Roncallo, O., Campillo, J., Ingham, D., Hughes, K., & Pourkashanian, M. (2019). Large scale integration of renewable energy sources (RES) in the future Colombian energy system. *Energy*, *186*, 115805. doi:10.1016/j.energy.2019.07.135

Purohit, P., & Chaturvedi, V. (2018). Biomass pellets for power generation in India: A techno-economic evaluation. *Environmental Science and Pollution Research International*, *25*(29), 29614–29632. doi:10.100711356-018-2960-8 PMID:30141169

Putra, A. S., & Warnars, H. L. H. S. (2018). Intelligent traffic monitoring system (ITMS) for smart city based on IoT monitoring. In *Proceedings of the Indonesian Association for Pattern Recognition International Conference*, (pp. 161-165). IEEE. 10.1109/INAPR.2018.8626855

Radonjic, G., & Tominc, P. (2007). The Role of Environmental Management System on Introduction of New Technologies in the Metal and Chemical/Paper/Plastics Industries. *Journal of Cleaner Production*, *15*(15), 1482–1493. doi:10.1016/j.jclepro.2006.03.010

Rahman, M. M., Nepal, R., & Alam, K. (2021). Impacts of human capital, exports, economic growth and energy consumption on CO2 emissions of a cross-sectionally dependent panel: Evidence from the newly industrialized countries (NICs). *Environmental Science & Policy*, *121*, 24–36. doi:10.1016/j.envsci.2021.03.017

Compilation of References

Rahul Verma. (2021). Sustainable and Responsible Entrepreneurship and Key Drivers of Performance. Sustainopreneurship Rahul Verma (Delhi University, India). doi:10.4018/978-1-7998-7951-0.ch005

Raihan, A., Muhtasim, D. A., Farhana, S., Pavel, M. I., Faruk, O., Rahman, M., & Mahmood, A. (2022). Nexus between carbon emissions, economic growth, renewable energy use, urbanization, industrialization, technological innovation, and forest area towards achieving environmental sustainability in Bangladesh. *Energy and Climate Change*, *3*, 100080. doi:10.1016/j.egycc.2022.100080

Ralston, P., & Blackhurst, J. (2020). Industry 4.0 and resilience in the supply chain: A driver of capability enhancement or capability loss? *International Journal of Production Research*, *58*(16), 5006–5019. doi:10.1080/00207543.2020.1736724

Ramani, V. (2020). *Addressing Climate as a Systemic Risk*. Ceres. https://www.ceres.org/sites/default/files/reports/202006/Financial%20Regulators%20FULL%20FINAL.pdf

Ramaprasad, A., Sánchez-Ortiz, A., & Syn, T. (2017). A unified definition of a smart city. In *Proceedings of the 16th International Conference, EGOV*, (pp. 13-24). Springer International Publishing. 10.1007/978-3-319-64677-0_2

Ramires, E. C., Megiatto, J. D. Jr, Dufresne, A., & Frollini, E. (2020). Cellulose Nanocrystals versus Microcrystalline Cellulose as Reinforcement of Lignopolyurethane Matrix. *Fibers (Basel, Switzerland)*, *8*(4), 21. doi:10.3390/fib8040021

Ramkissoon, H., & Nunkoo, R. (2010). Predicting tourists' intention to consume genetically modified food. *Journal of Hospitality Marketing & Management*, *20*(1), 60–75. doi:10.1080/19368623.2010.514557

Rasul, G. (2016). Managing the food, water, and energy nexus for achieving the Sustainable Development Goals in South Asia. *Environmental Development*, *18*, 14–25. doi:10.1016/j.envdev.2015.12.001

Rattanamanee, T., & Nanthavanij, S. (2019). Multiple-Trip Vehicle Routing with Physical Workload. In X. Liu (Ed.), *Environmental Sustainability in Asian Logistics and Supply Chains* (pp. 261–274). Springer Singapore. doi:10.1007/978-981-13-0451-4_15

Reboredo, J. C., Ugolini, A., & Ojea-Ferreiro, J. (2022). Do green bonds de-risk investment in low-carbon stocks? *Economic Modelling*, *108*, 105765. doi:10.1016/j.econmod.2022.105765

Reefke, H., & Sundaram, D. (2021). Decision Support for Sustainable Supply Chain Management. Pursuing Sustainability: OR/MS Applications in Sustainable Design, Manufacturing, Logistics, and Resource Management, 43-70.

Rehman, M. A., Seth, D., & Shrivastava, R. L. (2016). Impact of green manufacturing practices on organisational performance in Indian context: An empirical study. *Journal of Cleaner Production*, *137*, 427–448. doi:10.1016/j.jclepro.2016.07.106

Reinhart, C. F., Mardaljevic, J., & Rogers, Z. (2006). Dynamic daylight performance metrics for sustainable building design. *Leukos*, *3*(1), 7–31. doi:10.1582/LEUKOS.2006.03.01.001

Repinski, C. (2017). *Unlocking the potential of green fintech*. Stockholm Green Digital Finance. https://static1.squarespace.com/static/59b29215c027d84ada066d3b/t/5a4f73e6e4966b7a764114ba/1515156458061/stockholm-green-digital-finance-insight-brief-no1-2017.pdf.

Reysen, S., Chadborn, D., & Plante, C. N. (2018). Theory of planned behavior and intention to attend a fan convention. []. Routledge.]. *Journal of Convention & Event Tourism*, *19*(3), 204–218. doi:10.1080/15470148.2017.1419153

Ringe, W.-G. (2021). Investor-led Sustainability in Corporate Governance. SSRN *Electronic Journal*. https://doi.org/doi:10.2139/ssrn.3958960

Ripple, W., Wolf, C., Newsome, T., Barnard, P., Moomaw, W., & Grandcolas, P. (2019). World Scientists' Warning of a Climate Emergency. *Bioscience*, 1–5. doi:10.1093/biosci/biz088

Robinson, T., Schulte-Herbrüggen, H., Mácsik, J., & Andersson, J. (2019). *Raingardens for stormwater management: Potential of raingardens in a Nordic climate. DIVA.* Trafikverket.

Roehrich, J. K., Hoejmose, S. U., & Overland, V. (2017). Driving green supply chain management performance through supplier selection and value internalisation: A self-determination theory perspective. *International Journal of Operations & Production Management, 37*(4), 489–509. doi:10.1108/IJOPM-09-2015-0566

Routa, J., Brannstrom, H., Anttila, P., Makinen, M., Janis, J. and Asikainen, A. (2017). Wood extractives of Finnish pine, spruce and birch–availability and optimal sources of compounds. *Natural resources and bioeconomy studies, 73*, 55.

Roy, A., & Pramanick, K. (2019). Analyzing progress of sustainable development goal 6 in India: Past, present, and future. *Journal of Environmental Management, 232*, 1049–1065. doi:10.1016/j.jenvman.2018.11.060 PMID:33395757

Ruggieri, R., Ruggeri, M., Vinci, G., & Poponi, S. (2021). Electric mobility in a smart city: European overview. *Energies, 14*(2), 315. doi:10.3390/en14020315

Rusinko, C. (2007). Green manufacturing: An evaluation of environmentally sustainable manufacturing practices and their impact on competitive outcomes. *IEEE Transactions on Engineering Management, 54*(3), 445–454. doi:10.1109/TEM.2007.900806

Saarikko, T., Westergren, U. H., & Blomquist, T. (2020). Digital transformation: Five recommendations for the digitally conscious firm. *Business Horizons, 63*(6), 825–839. doi:10.1016/j.bushor.2020.07.005

Saastamoinen, P., Mattinen, M.-L., Hippi, U., Nousiainen, P., Sipilä, J., Lille, M., Suurnäkki, A., & Pere, J. (2012). Laccase aided modification of nano fibrillated cellulose with dodecyl gallate. *BioResources, 7*(4), 5749–5770. doi:10.15376/biores.7.4.5749-5770

Sachs, J. (2015). The end of poverty: Economic possibilities for our time. Penguin Books.

Sachs, D. J. (2012). From millennium development goals to sustainable development goals. *Lancet, 379*(9832), 2206–2211. doi:10.1016/S0140-6736(12)60685-0 PMID:22682467

Sachs, J. D., Woo, W. T., Yoshino, N., & Taghizadeh-Hesary, F. (2019). Importance of green finance for achieving sustainable development goals and energy security. In *Handbook of Green Finance* (pp. 3–12). Springer., doi:10.1007/978-981-13-0227-5_13

Sachs, J., Schmidt-Traub, G., Kroll, C., Durand-Delacre, D., & Teksoz, K. (2016). *SDG Index and Dashboards - Global Report. Bertelsmann Stiftung and Sustainable Development Solutions Network.* SDSN., https://www.sdgindex.org/reports/sdg-index-and-dashboards-2016/

Saha, B. C. (2003). Hemicellulose bioconversion. *Journal of Industrial Microbiology & Biotechnology, 30*(5), 279–291. doi:10.100710295-003-0049-x PMID:12698321

Sahasranaman, A. (2012). Financing the development of small and medium cities. *Economic and Political Weekly, 47*(24), 59–66.

Sainorudin, M.H., Mohammad, M., Kadir, N.H.A., Abdullah, N.A., Yaakob, Z. (2018). *Characterization of several microcrystalline cellulose (MCC)-based agricultural wastes via x-ray diffraction method.* Trans Tech Publications Ltd.

Saisana, M., Saltelli, A., & Tarantola, S. (2005). Uncertainty and sensitivity analysis techniques as tools for the quality assessment of composite indicators. *Journal of the Royal Statistical Society. Series A, (Statistics in Society), 168*(2), 307–323. doi:10.1111/j.1467-985X.2005.00350.x

Compilation of References

Salmi, A., Jussila, J., & Hamalainen, M. (2022). The role of municipalities in the transformation towards more sustainable construction: The case of wood construction in Finland. *Construction Management and Economics*, *40*(11–12), 934–954. doi:10.1080/01446193.2022.2037145

Samsudin, M. H., Hassan, M. A., Yusoff, M. Z. M., Idris, J., Farid, M. A. A., Lawal, A. B. A., Norrrahim, M. N. F., & Shirai, Y. (2022). Production of nanopore structure bio-adsorbent from wood waste through a self-sustained carbonization process for landfill leachate treatment. *Biochemical Engineering Journal*, *189*, 108740. doi:10.1016/j.bej.2022.108740

Sánchez-Flores, R. B., Cruz-Sotelo, S. E., & Ojeda-Benitez, S. (2020). Green Practices in Supply Chain Management to Improve Sustainable Performance. In S. A. R. Khan (Ed.), (pp. 45–71). Advances in Logistics, Operations, and Management Science. IGI Global. doi:10.4018/978-1-7998-2173-1.ch003

Sangiorgi, I., & Schopohl, L. (2021). Why do institutional investors buy green bonds: Evidence from a survey of European asset managers. *International Review of Financial Analysis*, *75*, 101738. doi:10.1016/j.irfa.2021.101738

Sangwan, K. S., & Choudhary, K. (2018). Benchmarking Manufacturing Industries Based on Green Practices. *Benchmarking*, *25*(6), 1746–1761. doi:10.1108/BIJ-12-2016-0192

Santamouris, M., & Vasilakopoulou, K. (2021). *Present and future energy consumption of buildings: Challenges and opportunities towards decarbonisation. e-Prime-Advances in Electrical Engineering*. Electronics and Energy. doi:10.1016/j.prime.2021.100002

Santo, R., Kim, B. F., Goldman, S. E., Dutkiewicz, J., Biehl, E., Bloem, M. W., Neff, R. A., & Nachman, K. E. (2020). Considering Plant-Based Meat Substitutes and Cell-Based Meats: A Public Health and Food Systems Perspective. *Frontiers in Sustainable Food Systems*, *4*, 134. doi:10.3389/fsufs.2020.00134

Santos, F. A., Lulianelli, G. C. V., & Tavares, M. I. B. (2017). Effect of microcrystalline and nanocrystals cellulose fillers in materials based on PLA matrix. *Polymer Testing*, *61*, 280–288. doi:10.1016/j.polymertesting.2017.05.028

Santos, R. M., Flauzino Neto, W. P., Silvério, H. A., Martins, D. F., Dantas, N. O., & Pasquini, D. (2013). Cellulose nanocrystals from pineapple leaf, a new approach for the reuse of this agro-waste. *Industrial Crops and Products*, *50*, 707–714. doi:10.1016/j.indcrop.2013.08.049

Sarkar, R. (2020). Association of urbanisation with demographic dynamics in India. *GeoJournal*, *85*(3), 779–803. doi:10.100710708-019-09988-y

Sauvé, S., Bernard, S., & Sloan, P. (2016). Environmental sciences, sustainable development and circular economy: Alternative concepts for trans-disciplinary research. *Environmental Development*, *17*, 48–56. doi:10.1016/j.envdev.2015.09.002

SBB (T.R. Presidential Strategy and Budget Department). (2021). *T.C. Cumhurbaşkanlığı Strateji ve Bütçe Başkanlığı*. Orta Vadeli Program. https://www.sbb.gov.tr/wp-content/uploads/2021/09/Orta-Vadeli-Program-2022-2024.pdf

Scarpellini, S., Marín-Vinuesa, L. M., Aranda-Usón, A., & Portillo-Tarragona, P. (2020). Dynamic capabilities and environmental accounting for the circular economy in businesses. *Sustainability Accounting. Management and Policy Journal*, *11*(7), 1129–1158.

Schaumann, D., Pilosof, N. P., Date, K., & Kalay, Y. E. (2016). A study of human behavior simulation in architectural design for healthcare facilities. *Annali dell'Istituto Superiore di Sanita*, *52*(1), 24–32. PMID:27033615

Schmidt, J., Cancella, R., & Pereira, A. O. Jr. (2016a). An optimal mix of solar PV, wind and hydro power for a low-carbon electricity supply in Brazil. *Renewable Energy*, *85*, 137–147. doi:10.1016/j.renene.2015.06.010

Schmidt, J., Cancella, R., & Pereira, A. O. Jr. (2016b). The role of wind power and solar PV in reducing risks in the Brazilian hydro-thermal power system. *Energy*, *115*, 1748–1757. doi:10.1016/j.energy.2016.03.059

Schuler, D., Rasche, A., Etzion, D., & Newton, L. (2017). <i>Guest Editors' Introduction:</i> Corporate Sustainability Management and Environmental Ethics. *Business Ethics Quarterly*, *27*(2), 213–237. doi:10.1017/beq.2016.80

Seddiqi, H., Oliaei, E., Honarkar, H., Jin, J., Geonzon, L. C., Bacabac, R. G., & Klein-Nulend, J. (2021). Cellulose and its derivatives: Towards biomedical applications. *Cellulose (London, England)*, *28*(4), 1893–1931. doi:10.100710570-020-03674-w

Sedlak, M., & Nancy, W. Y. H. (2004). Production of Ethanol from Cellulosic Biomass Hydrolysates Using Genetically Engineered Saccharomyces Yeast Capable of Cofermenting Glucose and Xylose. *Applied Biochemistry and Biotechnology*, *113–116*(1-3), 403–416. doi:10.1385/ABAB:114:1-3:403 PMID:15054267

Senseware. (2022). *Top 10 Retrofit Methods for Sustainable Buildings*. Attuneiot.com.

Seow, C. N., & Hamid, N. A. A. (2017, June). Green manufacturing performance measure for automobile manufacturers. In *2017 International Conference on Industrial Engineering, Management Science and Application (ICIMSA)* (pp. 1-5). IEEE. 10.1109/ICIMSA.2017.7985589

Septevani, A. A., Annamalai, P. K., & Martin, D. J. (2017). Synthesis and characterization of cellulose nanocrystals as reinforcing agent in solely palm based polyurethane foam. In *Proceedings of the 3rd International Symposium on Applied Chemistry 2017*. AIP Publishing. 10.1063/1.5011899

Seth, D., Shrivastava, R. L., & Shrivastava, S. (2016). An Empirical Investigation of Critical Success Factors and Performance Measures for Green Manufacturing in Cement Industry. *Journal of Manufacturing Technology Management*, *27*(8), 1076–1101. doi:10.1108/JMTM-04-2016-0049

Setyaningsih, I., & Indarti, N., & Ciptono, W. S. (2018). Green Manufacturing's adoption by Indonesian smes: A conceptual model. *2018 IEEE International Conference on Industrial Engineering and Engineering Management (IEEM)*. IEEE. https://doi.org/10.1109/IEEM.2018.8607389

Setyaningsih, I., Ciptono, W. S., Indarti, N., & Kemal, N. I. V. (2019). What is green manufacturing? A quantitative literature review. In *E3S Web of Conferences* (Vol. 120, p. 01001). EDP Sciences.

Sezen, B., & Cankaya, S. Y. (2013). Effects of green manufacturing and eco-innovation on sustainability performance. *Procedia: Social and Behavioral Sciences*, *99*, 154–163. doi:10.1016/j.sbspro.2013.10.481

Shahbandeh, M. (2021). *Global pineapple production 2002-2019*. Statista. https://www.statista.com/statistics/298517/global-pineapple-production-by-leading-countries/

Shanmugarajah, B., Kiew, P. L., Chew, I. M. L., Choong, T. S. Y., & Tan, K. W. (2015). Isolation of nanocrystalline cellulose (NCC) from palm oil empty fruit bunch (EFB): Preliminary result on ftir and dls analysis. *Chemical Engineering Transactions*, *45*, 1705–1710. doi:10.3303/CET1545285

Sharifi, A., Allam, Z., Feizizadeh, B., & Ghamari, H. (2021). Three decades of research on smart cities: Mapping knowledge structure and trends. *Sustainability (Basel)*, *13*(13), 1–23. doi:10.3390u13137140

Sharma, S. (2014). *Competing for a sustainable world: Building capacity for sustainable innovation*. Greenleaf.

Sharma, S., & Henriques, I. (2005). Stakeholder influences on sustainability practices in the Canadian forest products industry. *Strategic Management Journal*, *26*(2), 159–180. doi:10.1002mj.439

Sherpa, M. L., Sharma, L., Bag, N., & Das, S. (2021). Isolation, Characterization, and Evaluation of Native Rhizobacterial Consortia Developed From the Rhizosphere of Rice Grown in Organic State Sikkim, India, and Their Effect on Plant Growth. *Frontiers in Microbiology*, *12*, 713660. doi:10.3389/fmicb.2021.713660 PMID:34552571

Compilation of References

Shimova, O. (2019). Belarus on the way to sustainable development: circular economy and green technologies. In *Modeling economic growth in contemporary Belarus* (pp. 89–106). Emerald Publishing Limited. doi:10.1108/978-1-83867-695-720191007

Shi, R., Bi, J., Zhang, Z., Zhu, A., Chen, D., Zhou, X., Zhang, L., & Tian, W. (2008). The effect of citric acid on the structural properties and cytotoxicity of the polyvinyl alcohol/starch films when molding at high temperature. *Carbohydrate Polymers*, *74*(4), 763–770. doi:10.1016/j.carbpol.2008.04.045

Shi, R., Zhang, Z., Liu, Q., Han, Y., Zhang, L., Chen, D., & Tian, W. (2007). Characterization of citric acid/glycerol co-plasticized thermoplastic starch prepared by melt blending. *Carbohydrate Polymers*, *69*(4), 748–755. doi:10.1016/j.carbpol.2007.02.010

Shivaprakash, K. N., Swami, N., Mysorekar, S., Arora, R., Gangadharan, A., Vohra, K., Jadeyegowda, M., & Kiesecker, J. M. (2022). Potential for Artificial Intelligence (AI) and Machine Learning (ML) applications in biodiversity conservation, managing forests, and related services in India. *Sustainability (Basel)*, *14*(12), 1–20. doi:10.3390u14127154

Shlieout, G., Arnold, K., & Muller, G. (2002). Powder and mechanical properties of microcrystalline cellulose with different degrees of polymerization. *AAPS PharmSciTech*, *3*(2), 45–84. doi:10.1208/pt030211 PMID:12916948

Shojaeiarani, J., Bajwa, D., & Chanda, S. (2021). Cellulose nanocrystal based composites: A review. *Composites Part C: Open Access*, *5*, 100164. https://doi.org/.2021.100164 doi:10.1016/j.jcomc

Shokri, J., & Adibkia, K. (2013). Application of Cellulose and Cellulose Derivatives in Pharmaceutical Industries. In T. a. de Ven & L. Godbout (Eds.), *Cellulose - Medical, Pharmaceutical and Electronic Applications*. IntechOpen. doi:10.5772/55178

Shoukat, A., Wahid, F., Khan, T., Siddique, M., Nasreen, S., Yang, G., Ullah, M. W., & Khan, R. (2019). Titanium oxide-bacterial cellulose bioadsorbent for the removal of lead ions from aqueous solution. *International Journal of Biological Macromolecules*, *129*, 965–971. doi:10.1016/j.ijbiomac.2019.02.032 PMID:30738165

Shrivastava, S., & Shrivastava, R. L. (2017). A Systematic Literature Review on Green Manufacturing Concepts in Cement Industries. *International Journal of Quality & Reliability Management*, *34*(1), 68–90. doi:10.1108/IJQRM-02-2014-0028

Shukla, S.K., Nidhi, S., Pooja, N., Charu, A., Silvi, M., Bharadvaja, A., & Dubey, G. C. (2013). Preparation and Characterization of Cellulose Derived from Rice Husk for Drug Delivery. *Adv. Mat. Lett*, *4* (9), 714-719.

Shura. (2019). *Türkiye'de Enerji Dönüşümünün Finansmanı*. Sabancı Üniversitesi. https://shura.org.tr/turkiyede_enerji_donusumunun_finansmani/

Singh, J., Singh, C. D., & Deepak, D. (2022). Impact of green manufacturing parameters on strategic success in Indian manufacturing industries. *International Journal of Competitiveness*, *2*(2), 91–111. doi:10.1504/IJC.2022.125747

Singh, T., Solanki, A., Sharma, S. K., Nayyar, A., & Paul, A. (2022). A Decade Review on Smart Cities: Paradigms, Challenges and Opportunities. *IEEE Access : Practical Innovations, Open Solutions*, *10*, 68319–68364. doi:10.1109/ACCESS.2022.3184710

Single-use plastics: A roadmap for sustainability. (n.d.). UNEP - UN Environment Programme. https://www.unep.org/resources/report/single-use-plastics-roadmap-sustainability

Sisodia, G., Joseph, A., & Dominic, J. (2022). Whether corporate green bonds act as armour during crises? Evidence from a natural experiment. *International Journal of Managerial Finance*.

Smartcity. (2021, November 15). 4 Reasons to Invest in Smart and Green Infrastructure. *Smartcity press*.

Smerek, R. E., & Peterson, M. (2007). Examining Herzberg's theory: Improving job satisfaction among non-academic employees at a university. *Research in Higher Education*, *48*(2), 229–250. doi:10.100711162-006-9042-3

Smith, M. J. (2018). Getting value from artificial intelligence in agriculture. *Animal Production Science*, *60*(1), 46–54. doi:10.1071/AN18522

Soeiro, V. S., Tundisi, L. L., Novaes, L. C. L., Mazzola, P. G., Aranha, N., Grotto, D., Junior, J. M. O., Komatsu, D., Gama, F. M. P., Chaud, M. V., & Jozala, A. F. (2021). Production of bacterial cellulose nanocrystals via enzymatic hydrolysis and evaluation of their coating on alginate particles formed by ionotropic gelation. *Carbohydrate Polymer Technologies and Applications*, *2*, 100155. doi:10.1016/j.carpta.2021.100155

Solar PV – Analysis - IEA. (n.d.). IEA. https://www.iea.org/reports/solar-pv

Som, T. (2021). Sustainability in Energy Economy and Environment: Role of AI Based Techniques. In *Computational Management: Applications of Computational Intelligence in Business Management* (pp. 647–682). Springer International Publishing. doi:10.1007/978-3-030-72929-5_31

Song, K., Zhu, X., Zhu, W., & Li, X. (2019). Preparation and characterization of cellulose nanocrystal extracted from *Calotropis procera* biomass. *Bioresources and Bioprocessing*, *6*(1), 45. doi:10.118640643-019-0279-z

Sosiati, H., Muhaimin, M., Purwanto, Wijayanti, D.A., & Triyana, K. (2014). Nanocrystalline Cellulose Studied with a Conventional SEM. In *2014 International Conference on Physics (ICP 2014)*. Atlantis Press. 10.2991/icp-14.2014.3

Sovereign Wealth Fund Institute. (2021). *Top 100 Insurers*. Sovereign Wealth Fund Institute. https://www.swfinstitute.org/fund-rankings/

Srivastava, S. K. (2007). Green supply-chain management: A state-of-the-art literature review. *International Journal of Management Reviews*, *9*(1), 53–80. Scopus. doi:10.1111/j.1468-2370.2007.00202.x

Staniškis, J. K. (2022a). Socio-Environmental-Economic Transformations Towards Sustainable Development. In J. K. Staniškis, E. Staniškienė, Ž. Stankevičiūtė, A. Daunorienė, & J. Ramanauskaitė, Transformation of Business Organization Towards Sustainability (pp. 81–165). Springer International Publishing. doi:10.1007/978-3-030-93298-5_3

Staniškis, J. K. (2022b). Sustainability Challenges in an Business Organisation. In J. K. Staniškis, E. Staniškienė, Ž. Stankevičiūtė, A. Daunorienė, & J. Ramanauskaitė, Transformation of Business Organization Towards Sustainability (pp. 3–14). Springer International Publishing. doi:10.1007/978-3-030-93298-5_1

Staniškis, J. K. (2012). Sustainable consumption and production. *Clean Technologies and Environmental Policy*, *14*(6), 1013–1014. doi:10.100710098-012-0517-y

Starik, M., & Kanashiro, P. (2013). Toward a Theory of Sustainability Management: Uncovering and Integrating the Nearly Obvious. *Organization & Environment*, *26*(1), 7–30. doi:10.1177/1086026612474958

StateUp. (2021, April 22). *Why digital innovation in the built environment is integral to a Green Recovery*. StateUp.

Statista (2023). *India: Degree of urbanization from 2011 to 2021*. Statista. https://www.statista.com/statistics/271312/urbanization-in-india/#:~:text=In%202021%2C%20approximately%20a%20third,a%20living%20in%20the%20cities

Steffen, B. (2018). The importance of project finance for renewable energy projects. *Energy Economics*, *69*, 280–294. doi:10.1016/j.eneco.2017.11.006

Stekelorum, R., Laguir, I., Gupta, S., & Kumar, S. (2021). Green supply chain management practices and third-party logistics providers' performances: A fuzzy-set approach. *International Journal of Production Economics*, *235*, 108093. doi:10.1016/j.ijpe.2021.108093

Sterling, S. (2004). Higher education, sustainability, and the role of systemic learning. *Higher education and the challenge of sustainability: Problematics, promise, and practice*, 49-70.

Stevic, Z., Vasiljevic, M., Zavadskas, E. K., Sremac, S., & Turskis, Z. (2018). Selection of Carpenter Manufacturer using Fuzzy EDAS Method. *The Engineering Economist*, *29*(3), 281–290.

Strubell, E., Ganesh, A., & McCallum, A. (2019). Energy and policy considerations for deep learning in NLP. *arXiv preprint arXiv:1906.02243*. doi:10.18653/v1/P19-1355

Subramanian, N. (2007). Sustainability-Challenges and solutions. *Indian Concrete Journal*, *81*(12), 39.

Sulaiman, H. S., Chan, C. H., Chia, C. H., Zakaria, S., & Sharifah Nabihah Syed Jaafar, S. N. S. (2015). Isolation and Fractionation of Cellulose Nanocrystals from Kenaf Core. *Sains Malaysiana*, *44*(11), 1635–1642.

Sun, B., Li, J., Zhong, S., & Liang, T. (2023). Impact of digital finance on energy-based carbon intensity: Evidence from mediating effects perspective. *Journal of Environmental Management*, *327*, 116832. doi:10.1016/j.jenvman.2022.116832 PMID:36462482

Sun, H., Edziah, B. K., Sun, C., & Kporsu, A. K. (2019). Institutional Quality, Green Innovation and Energy Efficiency. *Energy Policy*, *135*, 111002. doi:10.1016/j.enpol.2019.111002

Sun, Y., Kexin, B., & Shi, Y. (2020). Measuring and Integrating Risk Management into Green Innovation Practices for Green Manufacturing under the Global Value Chain. *Sustainability (Basel)*, *12*(2), 545. doi:10.3390u12020545

Sureeyatanapas, P., Poophiukhok, P., & Pathumnakul, S. (2018). Green initiatives for logistics service providers: An investigation of antecedent factors and the contributions to corporate goals. *Journal of Cleaner Production*, *191*, 1–14. doi:10.1016/j.jclepro.2018.04.206

Sureeyatanapas, P., & Yang, J.-B. (2021). Sustainable Manufacturing and Technology: The Development and Evaluation. In C. Chen, Y. Chen, & V. Jayaraman (Eds.), *Pursuing Sustainability* (Vol. 301, pp. 111–140). Springer International Publishing. doi:10.1007/978-3-030-58023-0_5

Sustainable Development. (2023, March 23). *Home*. Sustainable Development. https://sdgs.un.org/

Sustainable lifestyles. (n.d.). UNEP - UN Environment Programme. https://www.unep.org/explore-topics/resource-efficiency/what-we-do/sustainable-lifestyles

SwissRe. (2020). *Insurance Sustainable Development Goals (iSDGs)*. SwissRe. https://www.swissre.com/institute/conferences/sustainability-leadership-in-insurance/sustainability-leadership-ininsurance-live-session-3.html#abouttheevent

Tahir, D., Karim, M. R. A., Hu, H., Naseem, S., Rehan, M., Ahmad, M., & Zhang, M. (2022). Sources, Chemical Functionalization, and Commercial Applications of Nanocellulose and Nanocellulose Based Composites: A Review. *Polymers*, *14*(21), 4468. doi:10.3390/polym14214468 PMID:36365462

Taiwo, F. A. T. (2017). Preparation and Fundamental Characterization of Cellulose Nanocrystal from Oil Palm Fronds Biomass. *Journal of Polymers and the Environment*, *25*(3), 1–9. doi:10.100710924-016-0854-8

Tamasiga, P., Onyeaka, H., & Ouassou, E. H. (2022). Unlocking the Green Economy in African Countries: An Integrated Framework of FinTech as an Enabler of the Transition to Sustainability. *Energies*, *15*(22), 8658. doi:10.3390/en15228658

Tan, PSupachok, W. (2017, April 26). All-cellulose composite laminates prepared from pineapple leaf fibers treated with steam explosion and alkaline treatment. *Journal of Reinforced Plastics and Composites*.

Tan, C.-S., Ooi, H.-Y., & Goh, Y.-N. (2017). A moral extension of the theory of planned behavior to predict consumers' purchase intention for energy-efficient household appliances in Malaysia. *Energy Policy, 107*(C), 459–471. doi:10.1016/j.enpol.2017.05.027

Tang, D. Y., & Zhang, Y. (2020). Do shareholders benefit from green bonds? *Journal of Corporate Finance, 61*, 101427. doi:10.1016/j.jcorpfin.2018.12.001

Tan, Z., Sadiq, B., Bashir, T., Mahmood, H., & Rasool, Y. (2022). Investigating the Impact of Green Marketing Components on Purchase Intention: The Mediating Role of Brand Image and Brand Trust. *Sustainability (Basel), 14*(10), 5939. doi:10.3390u14105939

Tarraço, E. L., Borini, F. M., Bernardes, R. C., & Della Santa Navarrete, S. (2021). The differentiated impact of the institutional environment on eco-innovation and green manufacturing strategies: A comparative analysis between emerging and developed countries. *IEEE Transactions on Engineering Management*.

Tartarini, F., Miller, C., & Schiavon, S. (2022). *Cozie Apple: An iOS mobile and smartwatch application for environmental quality satisfaction and physiological data collection.* arXiv preprint arXiv:2210.13977.

Teng, C.-C., & Wang, Y.-M. (2015). Decisional factors driving organic food consumption Generation of consumer purchase intentions. *British Food Journal, 117*(3), 1066–1081. doi:10.1108/BFJ-12-2013-0361

Teoh, C. W., Khor, K. C., & Wider, W. (2022). Factors influencing consumers' purchase intention towards green home appliances. *Frontiers in Psychology, 13*, 927327. doi:10.3389/fpsyg.2022.927327 PMID:35846659

The Scope of Sustainability. (n.d.). Net Impact. https://netimpact.org/blog/scope-sustainability

The United Nations Environment Programme Finance Initiative. (2012). *Principles for Sustainable Insurance a global sustainability framework and initiative of the United Nations Environment Programme Finance Initiative.* UN. https://www.unepfi.org/psi/wp-content/uploads/2012/06/PSI-document.pdf

The World Bank. (2023a). *Climate Change dataset.* The World Bank. https://data.worldbank.org

The World Bank. (2023b). *Economy & Growth dataset.* The World Bank. https://data.worldbank.org

The World in 2050. (2018). *Transformations to Achieve the Sustainable Development Goals Report prepared by The World in 2050 initiative.* The World in 2050. www.twi2050.org

Thistlethwaite, J., & Wood, M. O. (2018). Insurance and climate change risk management: Rescaling to look beyond the horizon. *British Journal of Management, 29*(2), 279–298. doi:10.1111/1467-8551.12302

Thomas. (n.d.). Green Manufacturing: The Business Benefits Of Sustainability. *Thomas Blog.* https://blog.thomasnet.com/green-manufacturing-sustainability-benefits

Thomsen, M. (2005). Complex media from processing of agricultural crops for microbial fermentation. *Applied Microbiology and Biotechnology, 68*(5), 598–606. doi:10.100700253-005-0056-0 PMID:16082554

Thoorens, G., Fabrice, K., Bruno, L., Brian, C., & Brigitte, E. (2014). Microcrystalline cellulose, a direct compression binder in a quality by design environment-A review. *International Journal of Pharmaceutics, 473*(1), 64–72. doi:10.1016/j.ijpharm.2014.06.055 PMID:24993785

Thornton, P. K. (2010). Livestock production: Recent trends, future prospects. *Philosophical Transactions of the Royal Society of London. Series B, Biological Sciences, 365*(1554), 2853–2867. doi:10.1098/rstb.2010.0134 PMID:20713389

Tien, J. M. (2017). Internet of things, real-time decision making, and artificial intelligence. *Annals of Data Science, 4*(2), 149–178. doi:10.100740745-017-0112-5

Tiwari, S. (2022). Supply Chain Innovation in the Era of Industry 4.0. In Handbook of Research on Supply Chain Resiliency, Efficiency, and Visibility in the Post-Pandemic Era (pp. 40-60). IGI Global.

Tiwari, S. (2023a). Industry 4.0: Managing the Circular Supply Chain. In Handbook of Research on Designing Sustainable Supply Chains to Achieve a Circular Economy (pp. 164-185). IGI Global.

Tiwari, S., Bahuguna, P. C., & Srivastava, R. (2022a). Smart manufacturing and sustainability: a bibliometric analysis. Benchmarking: An International Journal. doi:10.1108/BIJ-04-2022-0238

Tiwari, S. (2015). Framework for adopting sustainability in the supply chain. *International Journal of Automation and Logistics*, *1*(3), 256–272. doi:10.1504/IJAL.2015.071724

Tiwari, S. (2020). Supply chain integration and Industry 4.0: A systematic literature review. *Benchmarking*, *28*(3), 990–1030. doi:10.1108/BIJ-08-2020-0428

Tiwari, S. (2023b). Smart warehouse: A bibliometric analysis and future research direction. *Sustainable Manufacturing and Service Economics*, *2*, 100014. doi:10.1016/j.smse.2023.100014

Tiwari, S., Dubey, R., & Tripathi, N. (2011). The journey of lean. *Indian Journal of Commerce and Management Studies*, *2*(2), 200–210.

Tiwari, S., & Raju, T. B. (2022). Management of Digital Innovation. In *Promoting Inclusivity and Diversity Through Internet of Things in Organizational Settings* (pp. 128–149). IGI Global. doi:10.4018/978-1-6684-5575-3.ch007

Tiwari, S., & Tripathi, N. (2012). Lean Manufacturing Practices and Firms Performance Measurement—A Review Paper. *Journal of Supply Chain Management Systems*, *1*(1), 44.

Tiwari, V., & Thakur, S. (2021). Environment sustainability through sustainability innovations. *Environment, Development and Sustainability*, *23*(5), 6941–6965. doi:10.100710668-020-00899-4

Tomitsch, M., & Haeusler, M. H. (2015). Infostructures: Towards a complementary approach for solving urban challenges through digital technologies. *Journal of Urban Technology*, *22*(3), 37–53. doi:10.1080/10630732.2015.1040296

Tortorella, G. L., Vergara, A. M. C., Garza-Reyes, J. A., & Sawhney, R. (2020). Organizational learning paths based upon industry 4.0 adoption: An empirical study with Brazilian manufacturers. *International Journal of Production Economics*, *219*, 284–294. doi:10.1016/j.ijpe.2019.06.023

Trache, D., Tarchoun, A. F., Derradji, M., Hamidon, T. S., Masruchin, N., Brosse, N., & Hussin, M. H. (2020). Nanocellulose: From Fundamentals to Advanced Applications. *Frontiers in Chemistry*, *8*, 392. doi:10.3389/fchem.2020.00392 PMID:32435633

Tran, Q. H. (2022). The impact of green finance, economic growth and energy usage on CO2 emission in Vietnam–a multivariate time series analysis. *China Finance Review International*, *12*(2), 280–296. doi:10.1108/CFRI-03-2021-0049

Trivedi, S., Negi, S., & Tiwari, S. (2023). Sustainability in the Aviation Industry in the Post-COVID-19 Era. In Challenges and Opportunities for Aviation Stakeholders in a Post-Pandemic World (pp. 235-244). IGI Global. doi:10.4018/978-1-6684-6835-7.ch012

Tseng, M. L., Tan, K. H., Geng, Y., & Govindan, K. (2016). Sustainable consumption and production in emerging markets. *International Journal of Production Economics*, *181*, 257–261. doi:10.1016/j.ijpe.2016.09.016

TSKB. (2021). *Türk Sanayicisinin Yeşil Dönüşümü*. TSKB. https://www.tskb.com.tr/uploads/file/ece618e406ec1b452e-0c7a9e3359ee18-1639386053562.pdf

TTGV. (2010). *Türkiye'de Temiz Üretim Uygulamalarının Yaygınlaştırılması için Çerçeve Koşulların ve Ar-Ge İhtiyacının Belirlenmesi Projesi Sonuç Raporu.* TTGV. https://www.ttgv.org.tr/tur/images/publications/612e1c28d6114.pdf

Tukker, A., Emmert, S., Charter, M., Vezzoli, C., Stø, E., Andersen, M. M., Geerken, T., Tischner, U., & Lahlou, S. (2008). Fostering change to sustainable consumption and production: An evidence based view. *Journal of Cleaner Production, 16*(11), 1218–1225. doi:10.1016/j.jclepro.2007.08.015

Types of Green Infrastructure - DEP. (2023). Nyc.gov.

Ullah, M. W., Manan, S., Ul-Islam, M., Revin, V. V., Thomas, S., & Yang, G. (2021) Introduction to Nanocellulose. Nanocellulose: Synthesis, Structure, Properties and Applications, 1-50. doi:10.1142/9781786349477_0001

Umar, M., Khan, S. A. R., Zia-ul-haq, H. M., Yusliza, M. Y., & Farooq, K. (2022). The role of emerging technologies in implementing green practices to achieve sustainable operations. *The TQM Journal, 34*(2), 232–249. doi:10.1108/TQM-06-2021-0172

Unal, E., Urbinati, A., Chiaroni, D., & Manzini, R. (2019). Value Creation in Circular Business Models: The case of a US small medium enterprise in the building sector. *Resources, Conservation and Recycling, 146*, 291–307. doi:10.1016/j.resconrec.2018.12.034

UNDP. (2021). *TEVMOT Project E-Bulletin is Online.* UNDP. https://www.undp.org/turkiye/news/tevmot-project-e-bulletin-online

UNEP. (1996). *Cleaner Production: A Training Resource Package, Industry and Environment.* UNEP Publications.

UNEP. (2017). *Green Industrial Policy: Concept, Policies, Country Experiences.* Geneva, Bonn: UN Environment, German Development Institute. https://wedocs.unep.org/bitstream/handle/20.500.11822/22277/Green_industrial_policy.pdf?sequence=1&isAllowed=y

UNESCAP (2018). *SDG 6: Clean water and sanitation: ensure availability and sustainable management of water and sanitation for all.* UNESCAP. https://www.unescap.org/resources/sdg6-goal-profile

UNFCCC. Conference of the Parties (COP). (2015). *Adoption Of The Paris Agreement - Conference Of The Parties Cop 21.* UNFCC. https://doi.org/FCCC/CP/2015/L.9/Rev.1

Unidad Planeación Minero Energetica. (2016). *U.* UPME-PAI.

UNIDO. (2008). *The CP Concept: What is Cleaner Production?* UNIDO Publications.

UNIDO. (2011). *Industrial Development Report 2011. Industrial Energy Efficiency for Sustainable Wealth Creation: Capturing Environmental.* Economic and Social Dividends UNIDO Publications.

UNIDO. (2016). *Overview: Industrial Development Report 2016: The Role of Technology and Innovation in Inclusive and Sustainable Industrial Development.* UNIDO Publications.

UNIDO-UNEP. (2010). *Taking Stock and Moving Forward. Sustainable production in practice in developing and transition countries.* The UNIDO-UNEP National Cleaner Production Centers.

United Nations Development Programme (UNDP). (2016). Human development report 2016. In *Human Development for Everyone.* United Nations Development Programme.

United Nations Economic and Social Commission for Asia and the Pacific. (2020). *Water Security in Asia and the Pacific: Progress, Challenges, and Prospects.* UNESCAP. https://www.unescap.org/sites/default/files/publications/Water-Security-in-Asia-and-the-Pacific-Progress-Challenges-and-Prospects.pdf

United Nations Environment Programme Finance Initiative. (2012). *PSI Principles for sustainable insurance*. UN. https://www.unepfi.org/psi/wp-content/uploads/2012/06/PSI-document.pdf

United Nations World Population Prospects. (2022). *Development*. UN. https://www.un.org/development/desa/pd/sites/www.un.org.development.desa.pd/files/wpp2022_summary_of_results.pdf

United Nations. (2015). *Transforming our World: The 2030 Agenda for Sustainable Development*. United Nations Secretariat, New York. https://sdgs.un.org/2030agenda

United Nations. (2018a). *Sustainable Development Goal 6 Synthesis Report 2018 on Water and Sanitation*. United Nations, New York https://www.unwater.org/publications/sdg-6-synthesis-report-2018-water-and-sanitation

United Nations. (2022). *The Sustainable Development Goals Report*. UN.

United Nations. (n.d.). *Climate Reports*. United Nations. https://www.un.org/en/climatechange/reports

Unsplash. (2023). *Beautiful Free Images & Pictures*. Unsplash.

Urban, J., & Scasny, M. (2012). Exploring domestic energy-saving: The role of environmental concern and background variables. *Energy Policy*, *47*, 69–80. doi:10.1016/j.enpol.2012.04.018

US EPA. (2014, October 28). *Geothermal Heating and Cooling Technologies*. US EPA.

Usubiaga-Liano, A., & Ekins, P. (2021). Monitoring the environmental sustainability of countries through the strong environmental sustainability index. *Ecological Indicators*, *132*, 108281. doi:10.1016/j.ecolind.2021.108281

Van Benthem, M., Leek, N., Mantau, U., & Weimar, H. (2007). Markets for recovered wood in Europe; case studies for the Netherlands and Germany based on the BioXchange project. In *Proc. of the 3rd European COST E31 Conf*. IEEE.

Van Wynsberghe, A. (2021). Sustainable AI: AI for sustainability and the sustainability of AI. *AI and Ethics*, *1*(3), 213–218. doi:10.100743681-021-00043-6

Vanalle, R. M., Ganga, G. M. D., Godinho Filho, M., & Lucato, W. C. (2017). Green supply chain management: An investigation of pressures, practices, and performance within the Brazilian automotive supply chain. *Journal of Cleaner Production*, *151*, 250–259. doi:10.1016/j.jclepro.2017.03.066

Varela, L., Araújo, A., Ávila, P., Castro, H., & Putnik, G. (2019). Evaluation of the relation between lean manufacturing, industry 4.0, and sustainability. *Sustainability (Basel)*, *11*(5), 1439. doi:10.3390u11051439

Varsei, M., Soosay, C., Fahimnia, B., & Sarkis, J. (2014). Framing sustainability performance of supply chains with multidimensional indicators. *Supply Chain Management*, *19*(3), 242–257. doi:10.1108/SCM-12-2013-0436

Vedachalam, S., MacDonald, L.H., Shiferaw, S., Seme, A., & Schwab, K.J. (2017). Underreporting of high-risk water and sanitation practices undermines progress on global targets. *PLoSOne*, *12*(5), e0176272. . doi:10.1371/journal.pone.0176272

Venter, Z. S., Barton, D. N., Martinez-Izquierdo, L., Langemeyer, J., Baró, F., & McPhearson, T. (2021). Interactive spatial planning of urban green infrastructure – Retrofitting green roofs where ecosystem services are most needed in Oslo. *Ecosystem Services*, *50*, 101314. doi:10.1016/j.ecoser.2021.101314

Verma, Y. K., Mazumdar, B., & Ghosh, P. (2021). Thermal energy consumption and its conservation for a cement production unit. *Environmental Engineering Research*, *26*(3).

Vinuesa, R., Fdez. de Arévalo, L., Luna, M., & Cachafeiro, H. (2016). Simulations and experiments of heat loss from a parabolic trough absorber tube over a range of pressures and gas compositions in the vacuum chamber. *Journal of Renewable and Sustainable Energy*, *8*(2), 023701. doi:10.1063/1.4944975

Vis, M., Mantau, U., & Allen, B. (Eds.). 2016. Study on the optimized cascading use of wood. No 394/PP/ENT/RCH/14/7689. Final report. Brussel.

Visual feature: The Emissions Gap Report 2022. (n.d.). UNEP. https://www.unep.org/interactive/emissions-gap-report/2022/

Vlachos, I., & Huaccho Huatuco, L. ShakirUllah, G., & Roa-Atkinson, A. (2019). A Systematic Literature Review on Sustainability and Disruptions in Supply Chains. In X. Liu (Ed.), Environmental Sustainability in Asian Logistics and Supply Chains (pp. 85–96). Springer Singapore. doi:10.1007/978-981-13-0451-4_5

Voda, A. I., & Radu, L. D. (2018). Artificial intelligence and the future of smart cities. *Broad Research in Artificial Intelligence and Neuroscience*, *9*(2), 110–127.

Voorhees, C. M., Brady, M. K., Calantone, R., & Ramirez, E. (2016). Discriminant validity testing in marketing: An analysis, causes for concern, and proposed remedies. *Journal of the Academy of Marketing Science*, *44*(1), 119–134. doi:10.100711747-015-0455-4

Waheed, A., Zhang, Q., Rashid, Y., Tahir, M. S., & Zafar, M. W. (2020). Impact of green manufacturing on consumer ecological behavior: Stakeholder engagement through green production and innovation. *Sustainable Development (Bradford)*, *28*(5), 1395–1403. doi:10.1002d.2093

Wang, C. H. (2019). How organizational green culture influences green performance and competitive advantage: The mediating role of green innovation. *Journal of Manufacturing Technology Management*, *30*(4), 666–683. doi:10.1108/JMTM-09-2018-0314

Wang, C., Ghadimi, P., Lim, M. K., & Tseng, M. (2019). A literature review of sustainable consumption and production: A comparative analysis in developed and developing economies. *Journal of Cleaner Production*, *206*, 741–754. doi:10.1016/j.jclepro.2018.09.172

Wang, C., & Pu-yan, N. (2017). Green insurance subsidy for promoting clean production innovation. *Journal of Cleaner Production*, *148*, 111–117. doi:10.1016/j.jclepro.2017.01.145

Wang, K., Gao, S., Lai, C., Xie, Y., Sun, Y., Wang, J., Wang, C., Yong, Q., Chu, F., & Zhang, D. (2022). Upgrading wood biorefinery: An integration strategy for sugar production and reactive lignin preparation. *Industrial Crops and Products*, *187*, 115366. doi:10.1016/j.indcrop.2022.115366

Wang, K., Zhao, Y., Gangadhari, R. K., & Li, Z. (2021). Analyzing the adoption challenges of the Internet of things (Iot) and artificial intelligence (ai) for smart cities in China. *Sustainability (Basel)*, *13*(19), 1–35. doi:10.3390u131910983

Wang, L., Chen, S. S., Tsang, D. C., Poon, C. S., & Shih, K. (2016). Value-added recycling of construction waste wood into noise and thermal insulating cement-bonded particleboards. *Construction & Building Materials*, *125*, 316–325. doi:10.1016/j.conbuildmat.2016.08.053

Wang, L., Toppinen, A., & Juslin, H. (2014). Use of wood in green building: A study of expert perspectives from the UK. *Journal of Cleaner Production*, *65*, 350–361. doi:10.1016/j.jclepro.2013.08.023

Wang, N., Zhan, H., Zhuang, X., Xu, B., Yin, X., Wang, X., & Wu, C. (2020). Torrefaction of waste wood-based panels: More understanding from the combination of upgrading and denitrogenation properties. *Fuel Processing Technology*, *206*(511), 106462. doi:10.1016/j.fuproc.2020.106462

Wang, Q., & Su, M. (2019). The effects of urbanization and industrialization on decoupling economic growth from carbon emission – A case study of China. *Sustainable Cities and Society*, *51*, 101758. doi:10.1016/j.scs.2019.101758

Wang, Q., Su, M., & Li, R. (2018). Toward to economic growth without emission growth: The role of urbanization and industrialization in China and India. *Journal of Cleaner Production*, *205*, 499–511. doi:10.1016/j.jclepro.2018.09.034

Compilation of References

Wang, R., Zheng, X., Wang, H., & Shan, Y. (2019). Emission drivers of cities at different industrialization phases in China. *Journal of Environmental Management*, *250*, 109494. doi:10.1016/j.jenvman.2019.109494 PMID:31514002

Wang, S., & Altiparmak, S. O. (2022). Framing climate strategy of the oil industry of China: A tailored approach to ecological modernization. *Zhongguo Renkou Ziyuan Yu Huanjing*, *20*(4), 324–331. doi:10.1016/j.cjpre.2022.11.003

Wang, S., Zhang, L., Liu, C., Liu, Z., Lan, S., Li, Q., & Wang, X. (2021). Techno-economic-environmental evaluation of a combined cooling heating and power system for gas turbine waste heat recovery. *Energy*, *231*, 120956. doi:10.1016/j.energy.2021.120956

Wang, Z., Rasool, Y., Zhang, B., Ahmed, Z., & Wang, B. (2020). Dynamic linkage among industrialisation, urbanisation, and CO2 emissions in APEC realms: Evidence based on DSUR estimation. *Structural Change and Economic Dynamics*, *52*, 382–389. doi:10.1016/j.strueco.2019.12.001

Wang, Z., Sun, Q., Wang, B., & Zhang, B. (2019). Purchasing intentions of Chinese consumers on energy-efficient appliances: Is the energy efficiency label effective? *Journal of Cleaner Production*, *238*, 117896. doi:10.1016/j.jclepro.2019.117896

Wang, Z., Wang, X., & Guo, D. (2017). Policy implications of the purchasing intentions towards energy-efficient appliances among China's urban residents: Do subsidies work? *Energy Policy*, *102*, 430–439. doi:10.1016/j.enpol.2016.12.049

Wang, Z., Zhang, B., & Li, G. (2014). Determinants of energy-saving behavioral intention among residents in Beijing: Extending the theory of planned behavior. *Journal of Renewable and Sustainable Energy*, *6*(5), 1–18. doi:10.1063/1.4898363

Waris, I., & Ahmed, W. (2020). Empirical evaluation of the antecedents of energy-efficient home appliances: Application of the extended theory of planned behavior. *Management of Environmental Quality*, *31*(4), 915–930. doi:10.1108/MEQ-01-2020-0001

Waris, I., & Hameed, I. (2020a). An empirical study of purchase intention of energy-efficient home appliances: The influence of knowledge of eco-labels and psychographic variables. *International Journal of Energy Sector Management*, *14*(6), 1297–1314. doi:10.1108/IJESM-11-2019-0012

Waris, I., & Hameed, I. (2020b). Promoting environmentally sustainable consumption behavior: An empirical evaluation of purchase intention of energy-efficient appliances. *Energy Efficiency*, *13*(8), 1653–1664. doi:10.100712053-020-09901-4

WEF. (2022b, May 20). *Here's why green manufacturing is crucial for a low-carbon future*. World Economic Forum. https://www.weforum.org/agenda/2019/01/here-s-why-green-manufacturing-is-crucial-for-a-low-carbon-future/

Westbrook, R. A. (1987). Product/consumption-based affective responses and post-purchase processes. *JMR, Journal of Marketing Research*, *24*(3), 258–270. doi:10.1177/002224378702400302

Weststrate, J., Dijkstra, G., Eshuis, J., Gianoli, A., & Rusca, M. (2019). The sustainable development goal on water and sanitation: Learning from the millennium development goals. *Social Indicators Research*, *143*(2), 795–810. doi:10.100711205-018-1965-5

WGIN-mockup. (2021, April 12). *Key Definition: Green Infrastructure - World Green Infrastructure Network*. World Green Infrastructure Network.

Wijaya, C. J., Ismadji, S., Aparamarta, H. W., & Gunawan, S. (2019). Optimization of cellulose nanocrystals from bamboo shoots using Response Surface Methodology. *Heliyon*, *5*(11), e02807. doi:10.1016/j.heliyon.2019.e02807 PMID:31844732

Williams, A., Kennedy, S., Philipp, F., & Whiteman, G. (2017). Systems thinking: A review of sustainability management research. *Journal of Cleaner Production*, *148*, 866–881. doi:10.1016/j.jclepro.2017.02.002

Wirjosentono, B., Zulnazri, Tarigan, A.S., Naomi, T., & Nasution, D.A. (2021). Preparation of palm oil empty fruit bunches nanocellulose-filled polyvinyl alcohol-polyacrylic acid biohydrogel. AIP Conference Proceedings, 2342. doi:10.1063/5.0046399

Wojnarowska, M., Sołtysik, M., & Prusak, A. (2021). Impact of eco-labelling on the implementation of sustainable production and consumption. *Environmental Impact Assessment Review*, *86*, 106505. doi:10.1016/j.eiar.2020.106505

Wongchai, A., Shukla, S. K., Ahmed, M. A., Sakthi, U., Jagdish, M., & kumar, R. (2022). Artificial intelligence-enabled soft sensor and internet of things for sustainable agriculture using ensemble deep learning architecture. *Computers & Electrical Engineering*, *102*, 108128. doi:10.1016/j.compeleceng.2022.108128

Woo, J., & Edirisinghe, R. (2018). Enhancing students' experience in real-time data collection and utilisation: A cloud-based post-occupancy evaluation app. ASA.

World Bank Group, Enersinc, & Korea Green Growth Partnership. (2017). Energy Demand situation in Colombia. World Bank.

World Bank Group. (2018, September 24). *Global Waste to Grow by 70 Percent by 2050 Unless Urgent Action is Taken: World Bank Report*. World Bank. https://www.worldbank.org/en/news/press-release/2018/09/20/global-waste-to-grow-by-70-percent-by-2050-unless-urgent-action-is-taken-world-bank-report

World Bank. (2018). *World Bank Development Indicators (WDI)*. World Bank, Washington DC https://datacatalog.worldbank.org/dataset/world-development-indicators

World Commission on Environment and Development. (n.d.). *Brundtland Report*. Encyclopedia Britannica. https://www.britannica.com/topic/Brundtland-Report

World Economic Forum. (2022). *Reducing the carbon footprint of the manufacturing industry through data sharing*. World Economic Forum. https://www.weforum.org/impact/carbon-footprint-manufacturing-industry/

Wu, X. (2016). *Conductive Cellulose Nanocrystals for Electrochemical Applications* [Thesis]. University of Waterloo. https://core.ac.uk/download/pdf/144149343.pdf

Wu, Y. C., Sun, R., & Wu, Y. J. (2020). Smart city development in Taiwan: From the perspective of the information security policy. *Sustainability (Basel)*, *12*(7), 2916. doi:10.3390u12072916

Wu, Z., Zhu, P., Yao, J., Zhang, S., Ren, J., Yang, F., & Zhang, Z. (2020). Combined biomass gasification, SOFC, IC engine, and waste heat recovery system for power and heat generation: Energy, exergy, exergoeconomic, environmental (4E) evaluations. *Applied Energy*, *279*, 115794. doi:10.1016/j.apenergy.2020.115794

WWF. (2016). *Mapping Study on Cascading Use of Wood Products*. World Wildlife Fund.

Xie, S., Zhang, X., Walcott, M. P., & Lin, H. (2018). Applications of Cellulose Nanocrystals: A Review. *Engineering and Science*, *2*, 4–16.

Xie, S., Zhang, X., Walcott, M., & Lin, H. (2018). Cellulose Nanocrystals (CNCs) Applications: A Review. *Engineering and Science*, *2*, 4–16. doi:10.30919/es.1803302

Xincheng, M. (2022). *Research on Influencing Factors of Chinese Public Renewable Energy Acceptance Intention: Based on Theory of Planned Behavior Approach* [Doctoral dissertation, Pukyong National University].

Yadav, P., Hasan, S., Ojo, A., & Curry, E. (2017). The role of open data in driving sustainable mobility in nine smart cities. In *Proceedings of the 25th European Conference on Information Systems*, (pp. 1248-1263). IEEE.

Compilation of References

Yadav, R., & Kumar, J. (2021). Engineered wood products as a sustainable construction material: A review. In M. Gong (Ed.), *Engineered Wood Products for Construction* (pp. 25–38).

Yakovleva, N. & Vazquez-Brust, D. (2021, April 2). *Circular Economy, Degrowth and Green Growth as Pathways for Research on Sustainable Development Goals: A Global Analysis and Future Agenda*. ScienceDirect. doi:10.1016/j.ecolecon.2021.107050

Yanarella, E. J., Levine, R. S., & Lancaster, R. W. (2009). Research and Solutions: "Green" vs. Sustainability: From Semantics to Enlightenment. *Sustainability (New Rochelle, N.Y.)*, 2(5), 296–302. doi:10.1089/SUS.2009.9838

Yan, C., Wang, J., Kang, W., Cui, M., Wang, X., Foo, C. Y., Chee, K. J., & Lee, P. S. (2014). Highly stretchable piezoresistive graphene-nanocellulose nanopaper for strain sensors. *Advanced Materials*, 26(13), 2022–2027. doi:10.1002/adma.201304742 PMID:24343930

Yang, H. (2016). *Multifunctional hairy nanocrystalline cellulose* [Thesis]. McGill University. https://escholarship.mcgill.ca/concern/theses/2n49t4752

Yang, C. C., Brockett, P. L., & Wen, M. M. (2009). Basis risk and hedging efficiency of weather derivatives. *The Journal of Risk Finance*, 10(5), 517–536. doi:10.1108/15265940911001411

Yang, Y., Su, X., & Yao, S. (2021). Nexus between green finance, fintech, and high-quality economic development: Empirical evidence from China. *Resources Policy*, 74, 102445. doi:10.1016/j.resourpol.2021.102445

Yan, Q., Li, J., & Cai, Z. (2021). Preparation and characterization of chars and activated carbons from wood wastes. *Carbon Letters*, 31(5), 941–956. doi:10.100742823-020-00205-2

Yavuz, V. A. (2010). Sürdürülebilirlik Kavramı ve İşletmeler Açısından Sürdürülebilir Üretim Stratejileri/Concept of Sustainability and Sustainable Production Strategies for Business Practices. *Mustafa Kemal Üniversitesi Sosyal Bilimler Enstitüsü Dergisi*, 7(14), 63–86.

Yigitcanlar, T. (2021). Smart City Beyond Efficiency: Technology–Policy–Community at Play for Sustainable Urban Futures. *Housing Policy Debate*, 31(1), 88–92. doi:10.1080/10511482.2020.1846885

Yiğit, S. (2014). İnovasyonun Çevreci Yüzü ve Türkiye. *Yönetim ve Ekonomi*, 21(1), 251–265.

Yıldız, H. (2016). Sürdürülebilirlik Bağlamında Sağlık Sektöründe İnovatif Uygulamalar: Yeşil Hastaneler. *Kafkas Üniversitesi İktisadi ve İdari Bilimler Fakültesi Dergisi*, 7(13), 323–340.

Yoshino, N., & Taghizadeh-Hesary, F. (2019). Optimal credit guarantee ratio for small and medium-sized enterprises' financing: Evidence from Asia. *Economic Analysis and Policy*, 62, 342–356. doi:10.1016/j.eap.2018.09.011

Yuan, H., Feng, Y., Lee, C. C., & Cen, Y. (2020). How does manufacturing agglomeration affect green economic efficiency? *Energy Economics*, 92, 104944. doi:10.1016/j.eneco.2020.104944

Yücel, M. (2011). Çeşitli Endüstrilerde Temiz Üretim Sistemi Uygulamalarının İşletme Ekonomilerine Sağladığı Faydalar. *Elektronik Sosyal Bilimler Dergisi*, 10(35), 150–166.

Yue, B., Sheng, G., She, S., & Xu, J. (2020). Impact of consumer environmental responsibility on green consumption behavior in China: The role of environmental concern and price sensitivity. *Sustainability (Basel)*, 12(5), 2074. doi:10.3390u12052074

Yu, L., Zhao, D., Xue, Z., & Gao, Y. (2020). Research on the use of digital finance and the adoption of green control techniques by family farms in China. *Technology in Society*, 62, 101323. doi:10.1016/j.techsoc.2020.101323

Zahra, Z. G., Seyed Nematollah, M., & Bahaeddin, N. (2019). Economic Evaluation of the Effects of Exerting Green Tax on the Dispersion of Bioenvironmental Pollutants Based on Multi-Regional General Equilibrium Model (GTAP-E). *Energy Sources. Part A, Recovery, Utilization, and Environmental Effects*, 1–12. doi:10.1080/15567036.2019.1679912

Zameer, H., Wang, Y., Yasmeen, H., & Mubarak, S. (2022). Green innovation as a mediator in the impact of business analytics and environmental orientation on green competitive advantage. *Management Decision*, *60*(2), 488–507. doi:10.1108/MD-01-2020-0065

Zazzini, P. & Grifa, G. (2018, October 29). *Energy Performance Improvements in Historic Buildings by Application of Green Walls: Numerical Analysis of an Italian Case Study*. ScienceDirect. doi:10.1016/j.egypro.2018.08.028

Zhang, C., Dan, Y., Peng, J., Turng, L., Sabo, R., & Clemons, C. (2014). Thermal and Mechanical Properties of Natural Rubber Composites Reinforced with Cellulosic Nanocrystals from Southern Pine. *Advances in Polymerv Tech.*, 1-7. doi:10.1002/adv.21448

Zhang, D., Zhang, Z., & Managi, S. (2019). A bibliometric analysis on green finance: Current status, development, and future directions. *Finance Research Letters*, *29*, 425–430. doi:10.1016/j.frl.2019.02.003

Zhang, Y., Xiao, C., & Zhou, G. (2020). Willingness to pay a price premium for energy-efficient appliances: Role of perceived value and energy efficiency labeling. *Journal of Cleaner Production*, *242*, 1–12. doi:10.1016/j.jclepro.2019.118555

Zhang, Z., Wang, Y., Meng, Q., & Luan, X. (2019). Impacts of green production decision on social welfare. *Sustainability (Basel)*, *11*(2), 453. doi:10.3390u11020453

Zhao, L., Chau, K. Y., Tran, T. K., Sadiq, M., Xuyen, N. T. M., & Phan, T. T. H. (2022). Enhancing green economic recovery through green bonds financing and energy efficiency investments. *Economic Analysis and Policy*, *76*, 488–501. doi:10.1016/j.eap.2022.08.019

Zheng, G. W., Siddik, A. B., Masukujjaman, M., & Fatema, N. (2021). Factors affecting the sustainability performance of financial institutions in Bangladesh: The role of green finance. *Sustainability (Basel)*, *13*(18), 10165. doi:10.3390u131810165

Zheng, J., Jiang, P., Qiao, W., Zhu, Y., & Kennedy, E. (2016). Analysis of air pollution reduction and climate change mitigation in the industry sector of Yangtze River Delta in China. *Journal of Cleaner Production*, *114*, 314–322. doi:10.1016/j.jclepro.2015.07.011

Zhou, H., Yang, Y., Chen, Y., Zhu, J., & Shi, Y. (2021). DEA Application in Sustainability 1996–2019: The Origins, Development, and Future Directions. In C. Chen, Y. Chen, & V. Jayaraman (Eds.), *Pursuing Sustainability* (Vol. 301, pp. 71–109). Springer International Publishing. https://stats.oecd.orghttp://eurlex.europa.eu, doi:10.1007/978-3-030-58023-0_4

Zhu, B., & Thøgersen, J. (2023). Consumers' intentions to buy energy-efficient household appliances in China. *ABAC Journal*, *43*(1), 1–17. doi:10.14456/abacj.2023.1

Zhu, X., Ren, M., Chu, W., & Chiong, R. (2019). Remanufacturing subsidy or carbon regulation? An alternative toward sustainable production. *Journal of Cleaner Production*, *239*, 117988. doi:10.1016/j.jclepro.2019.117988

Zhu, Z., Liu, Y., Tian, X., Wang, Y., & Zhang, Y. (2017). CO2 emissions from the industrialization and urbanization processes in the manufacturing center Tianjin in China. *Journal of Cleaner Production*, *168*, 867–875. doi:10.1016/j.jclepro.2017.08.245

Zikeli, F., Vinciguerra, V., Annibale, A. D., Capitani, D., Romagnoli, M., & Scarascia Mugnozza, G. (2019). Preparation of lignin nanoparticles from wood waste for wood surface treatment. *Nanomaterials (Basel, Switzerland)*, *9*(2), 281. doi:10.3390/nano9020281 PMID:30781574

Compilation of References

Zink, T., & Geyer, R. (2017). Circular economy rebound. *Journal of Industrial Ecology*, *21*(3), 593–602. doi:10.1111/jiec.12545

Ziolo, M., Bak, I., & Cheba, K. (2020). THE ROLE OF SUSTAINABLE FINANCE IN ACHIEVING SUSTAINABLE DEVELOPMENT GOALS: DOES IT WORK? *Technological and Economic Development of Economy*, *27*(1), 45–70. doi:10.3846/tede.2020.13863

Zona, R., Roll, K., & Law, Z. (2014). *Sustainable/Green Insurance Products,* pp. 165–72. Casualty Actuarial Society E-Forum.

Zuliat, F. A., Suardi, M., & Djamaan, A. (2020). CNC (Cellulose Nanocrystals) Isolationfrom Various Agriculture and Industrial Waste Using Acid Hydrolysis Methods. *IOSR Journal of Pharmacy and Biological Sciences*, *15*(6), 42–58.

Zulnazri, Z., Daud, M., & Sylvia, N. (2021). Synthesis of cellulose nanocrystals (CNCS) from oil palm empty fruit bunch by hydrothermal with pre-treatment sonication. *AIP Conference Proceedings*, *2342*, 030003. doi:10.1063/5.0046000

About the Contributors

Richa Goel is Associate Professor-Economics and International Business at SCMS Noida, Symbiosis International Deemed University, Pune. She is a Gold Medalist in her Master of Economics with dual specialization at master level accompanied with an MBA in HR and also with dual specialization at graduate level with Gold Medalist in Economics Honors also with Bachelor of Law. She is Ph.D. in Management where she had worked for almost 6 years on area of Diversity Management. She has a journey of almost 21+ years in academic. She is consistently striving to create a challenging and engaging learning environment where students become life-long scholars and learners. She has to her credit many Scopus Indexed Books including Research Papers in UGC, SCOPUS, ABDC publications in reputed national and international journals accompanied with hundreds of Research participation in International/National Conferences including FDP, MDP and Symposiums. She is serving as a member of review committee for conferences and journals. She is handling many Scopus International Peer Reviewed Journals as Lead Editor for regular and special issue journals. She is acting as the Associate Editor & special issue Editor of Journal of Sustainable Finance and Investment, JSFI is abstracted and indexed in the Chartered Association of Business Schools Academic Journal Guide (2018 edition) and Scopus, Print ISSN: 2043-0795 Online ISSN: 2043-0809. According to SCImago Journal Rank (SJR), this journal is ranked 0.52 under Q1 category. Her area of interest includes Development & Sustainable Economics, Economics Business Restructuring, Fusion of Technology with International Business.

Sukanta Kumar Baral, working as Professor, Department of Commerce, Faculty of Commerce & Management at Indira Gandhi National Tribal University (A Central University of India), Amarkantak, Madhya Pradesh, India Specialisation: Marketing Management, Human Resource Management, Entrepreneurship & Strategic Management. As an active academician, he has been closely associated with several Indian and foreign Universities. He is an accredited Management Teacher recognised by AIMA, New Delhi, India. He is a NAAC assessor, Ministry of HRD, Government of India. He has earned 6 Indian copyrights and 5 Patents in his favour, authored 15 books (reference & text) for Commerce, Economics & Management students, edited 06 books and contributed 149 research articles in different national and international journals.

***

Biju A. V. is an Assistant Professor at the Department of Commerce, School of Business Management and Legal Studies, University of Kerala. His research interests include digital payments, crypto market, ESG, green bonds, and behavioural economics. He is a Research Sans Frontier (RSF) member in Dubai; this research association aims to contribute to society through quality research and building a bridge

About the Contributors

between industry and academia. He takes guest lectures at the University of Wollongong, Dubai, and Jain University, Cochin. He is the managing editor of the Journal of Commerce and Business Researcher, published by the Department of Commerce, University of Kerala. He also serves as a review member of the Journal of the Knowledge Economy, SN Business and Economics, International Journal of Applied Management Science, International Journal of E-business Research (IJEBR), and International Journal of Business Analytics (IJBAN). He received the best paper award from the IIM Nagpur conference in 2022. His papers have appeared in Quality & Quantity, Employee Responsibilities and Rights, IJHCITP, Springer Digital Finance, etc.

Korhan Arun is a professor in Faculty of Economics and Administrative Sciences at Tekirdag Namik Kemal University since 2010. He received his BA degree in Business Administration and Organization; MA and PhD degrees in Management and Organization from Atatürk University. His research interests include management and strategic management. Saniye Yildirim Ozmutlu, Department of Management and Organization, Tekirdag Namik Kemal University, Turkey.

Radhakrishna Batule is a Senior Faculty member at the Department of Management at Vishwakarma University, a State Private University under the Govt of Maharashtra, Pune, India. Have been a faculty of Marketing & Branding with 17 years of Experience in Teaching & Research.

Bhubaneswari Bisoyi is an Assistant Professor, Sri Sri University, Cuttack, India.

Das Biswajit is a Professor at School of Management, KIIT University, Bhubaneswar, India

David Blekhman is a Professor in the Sustainable Energy and Transportation at California State University Los Angeles. He is 2021-2022 recipient of the Outstanding Professor Award at Cal State LA and the 2019-2020 Fulbright Distinguished Chair in Alternative Energy Technology at Chalmers University. Dr. Blekhman is the Technical Director and the founding member for the Cal State LA Hydrogen Research and Fueling Facility. Bringing emerging green jobs opportunities to his students, Dr. Blekhman is actively developing his program by offering cutting-edge courses such as Electric and Hybrid Vehicles, Fuel Cell Applications, Photovoltaics, Advanced Engine Design, etc. Dr. Blekhman received his B.S.-M.S. in Thermal Physics and Engineering from St. Petersburg State Technical University, Russia, and a Ph.D. in Mechanical Engineering from SUNY Buffalo.

Ahmed Chemseddine Bouarar, Professor, Department of Commerce Science, Faculty of Economic Sciences, University of Medea, Algeria.

Elif Çaloğlu Büyükselçuk was born in 1978. In 1999. She received her bachelor's degree from Yıldız Technical University, Environmental Engineering Department. Then she got her master's degree from Boğaziçi University, Environmental Technologies Department. In 2017, she completed her doctorate in Marmara University, Engineering Management program. She has been working as the head of the Department of Industrial Engineering at Fenerbahçe University since 2019.

Shibu C. is currently pursuing Ph.D. Forestry (Forest Products and Utilization) from Kerala Agricultural University.

Sunandani Chandel received her bachelors degree, B.Sc. (Hons.) Forestry from Dr. Y. S. Parmar University of Horticulture and Forestry, Nauni, Solan (India). Than she got her Masters degree from Navsari Agricultural University, Navsari, Gujarat (India). Presently she is a Ph.D. Forestry (Forest Products and Utilization) Research Scholar at Kerala Agricultural University, Vellanikkara, Thrissur, Kerala (India). She is a recipient of Best Blog Award at XV World Forestry Congress held at South Korea in 2022.

Yukta Chawla, Economics, Mahatma Jyotiba Phule Rohilkhand, Uttar Pradesh, India

Bibi Zaheenah Chummun is an Associate Professor at the University of KwaZulu-Natal (UKZN) Graduate School of Business and Leadership (GSB&L) based on Westville Campus in Durban - South Africa. Prof. Chummun has published several papers in the field of management, microenterprises, microfinance, microinsurance and financial inclusion. She is supervising Masters and PhD students in the field of management She is a Chartered Insurer from the Chartered Insurance Institute in UK. She obtained her MBA from Nelson Mandela Metropolitan University (NMMU- South Africa) in 2010 and her PhD is from North West University (NWU-South Africa). Prof. Chummun is originally from the island of Mauritius.

Ömer Faruk Efe graduated from Selçuk University, Department of Industrial Engineering in 2008. He received the M.Sc. degree in Industrial Engineering from Selçuk University. He received Ph.D. degree in Industrial Engineering from Sakarya University. His research interests are Multi-criteria decision making, fuzzy logic, lean production, ergonomics, occupational health and safety. He has been working as an Associate Professor in Bursa Technical University.

Sreelekshmi G. is a research scholar at the Department of Commerce, School of Business Management and Legal Studies, University of Kerala. Her research interests include sustainable finance, green fintech, and green bonds.

Burhan Rasheed Kalshekar has completed his graduation in Gharda Institute of Technology, Maharashtra. He has done internship at Gharda Chemicals and other chemical plants. He is currently working in a chemical company in Mahad, Maharashtra, India. He has done projects on dissolved oxygen content of wastewater and removal of heavy metals from wastewater. He has presented papers in many national and international conferences. The papers on conversion of waste into useful products presented at Advanced materials and processing for sustainable application, a national conference, was well appreciated. His recent investigation is based on applications of waste cellulosic feedstock for useful products. He has synthesized and characterized the microcrystalline cellulose from various agricultural waste namely cassava waste, rice husk and pineapple waste.

Tarun Kanade is a young author, who has given his contribution in many book chapters and research papers. Passionate about travelling, exploring new things, and giving them a documented face for educational purposes.

Ayush Khandelwal, Mahatma Jyotiba Phule Rohilkhand University, Uttar Pradesh, India

About the Contributors

Akamsha Krishnan is a Bachelor of Arts (honours) Economics student at Amity University. She has a keen interest in economics and finance and seeks to pursue a career in the same field. She is passionate about learning and exploring economics and finance topics, as well as their practical applications in the real world. She is interested in behavioral economics, international economics and economic growth models. She hopes to use her knowledge and skills to make a positive contribution to the economy and the society at large.

Sunil J. Kulkarni has completed his PhD from Sant Gadge baba Amravati University and Masters in Chemical Engineering from Tatyasaheb Kore Institute of Engineering and Technology, Warananagar. He has worked as Assistant Professor in Chemical Engineering Department of Datta Meghe College of Engineering, Airoli, Navi Mumbai, India for 13 years. He has 20 years of teaching and research experience. Dr. Sunil is involved with different academic activities across the universities in Maharashtra. His area of investigation in doctoral studies is phenol and heavy metal removal from waste water. He has also worked on kinetics and isotherms of various sorption operations. His area of research includes adsorption, clean technology, and environmental biotechnology. He is on the reviewer board of many international journals and reviewed many international papers. He is also governing body member, promotional editor and executive member of many reputed international journals.Currently he is working as Associate Professor in chemical engineering at GIT, Lavel, India.

Jeffrey León is passionate about business models supported by green processes, technology, process industry and the advancement of humanity towards a sustainable industrial revolution. Professional in Chemical Engineering (UIS-Co), MSc. and PhD. in Chemical Engineering (UNICAMP-Br), expertise in Direction, Lidership and Management arround the industrial processes, chemical process and education sector. Expert in process and product development. Skills: C2C, Business StartUp, Chemical Process, Oil&Gas, Biofuels, Food, Process Design, Energy Approach, Intensification Process, Water Treatment, Industrial Safety, Intellectual Property, Modeling&Simulation, Technology Transfer and Environment Projects.

Asma Makhlouf, is a Research Scholar, Department of Commerce Science, Faculty of Economic Sciences, University of Medea, Algeria.

Abhiraj Malia is a Research Scholar, KIIT School of Management, KIIT University.

Pooja Mehra is faculty in statistics and economics at Amity School of Economics, Amity University, Noida. She is actively researching in the areas of fruits and vegetable processing, water management, and sustainable development of resources. To her credit she has 8 journal publications and 2 book chapters. She regularly attends and presents at sustainability related seminars and academic conferences. She is currently pursuing PhD in "Linkages between farmers and processing industry in fruits and vegetables".

Shivani Mehta is an Assistant Professor at Amity School of Economics, Amity University, Noida. She pursued her bachelors in economics (honours) from Delhi University and went ahead to complete her MA in Economics from Banasthali University, Rajasthan, where she was a gold medallist. She also pursued her M.Sc., Development Economics from School of Oriental & African Studies, University of London, where her dissertation was titled "Drivers of FDI in the Indian Economy - A study of Indian

Automobile Sector". She recently completed her PhD from Amity University, Noida with her Thesis on "Women Empowerment through Entrepreneurship: Step towards Sustainable Development Goals (Case of Delhi)". Dr. Shivani has been involved in various presentations and seminars and has had 17 papers, 5 book chapters, and 2 books published. Her research fields include development economics, gender economics, and sustainable development. At amity university, she is involved in teaching various courses like environmental economics, comparative economic development, economic growth models, economic system and society, agricultural economics, and international economics. Dr. Shivani Mehta has also been involved in a funded project under NASF-ICAR titled 'Pork Marketing Chains in North East India for Sustainable Livelihood of Tribal Women (Assam, Meghalaya and Nagaland)' as CO-PI which received a total funding of INR 1.21 cr.

Stojance Mijalkovski graduated from "St. Kiril and Metodij" University, Department of Underground mining in 2007. He received the M.Sc. degree in Underground mining from "Goce Delcev" University. He received Ph.D. degree in Underground mining from "Goce Delcev" University. His research interests are Multi-criteria decision making, fuzzy logic, mining, risk assessment, occupational health and safety. He has been working as an Associate Professor in "Goce Delcev" University.

Kamel Mouloudj has examined the relationship between constructs of theory of planned behavior and intentions to implement green practices and tourist's intention to stay in green hotels; green food purchase intentions; intention to use online food delivery services; and students' intention to use online learning system. More broadly, the concepts of word-of-mouth, online learning, green hotel and green food. More recently, he has focused on the Impacts Of COVID-19 Pandemic.

Smail Mouloudj is a Research Scholar, Department of Commerce Science, Faculty of Economic Sciences, University of Medea, Algeria.

Pablo Cesar Ocampo Velez is an Industrial Engineer at Autonoma University of Colombia. Master in global supply chain management of Ecole Polytechnique Federal de Lausanne (EPFL) Switzerland. International Institute of Logistics Management, IML. Phd Process engineering at EAN University, Bogota, Colombia, southamerica. Certify by European Logistics Association, ELA. Associate professor in Engineering Faculty at EAN University. Activities and Associations: Guidance to supply chain management (OGCA) or supply chain guidance (SCO) in supplier management (supply management) to support the performance of value networks or management of the supply chain in Bogotá, Colombia. Articles published in indexed journal.

Ameya Patil is Assistant Professor of Finance and International Business at School of Business, Dr.Vishwanath Karad MIT World Peace University, Pune, India. He has research interest in the areas of Financial Analysis, Behavioural Finance and Banking. His research works have been published in reputed journals and books in these areas

Atmika Patnaik (formerly, Witkin) was awarded at UC Davis. B.A.LLB. early graduate, Jindal Global Law School, O.P. Jindal Global University. L.L.M, King's College London (currently pursuing).

About the Contributors

B. C. M. Patnaik is a Professor at KIIT University for Economics and Finance. Specialised in Rural development, Developmental Economics, Behavioral Economics and Micro-Finance.

Pranjnya Pradhan is a Research Scholar, KIIT School of Management, KIIT University.

Ipseeta Satpathy is a Senior Professor at KIIT University. Specializes in Psychology, Behavioral Science, and Organisational Behaviour.

Anahita Sawhney is an avid learner and is a final year student at Amity University, where she is pursuing Bachelors of Arts (Honours) in Economics. She has a keen interest in the subject and has always aspired to build a career in the same. She often finds herself reading and learning more about the fields of behavioral and development economics. Anahita has an inclination towards researching and believes in asking questions revolving around what and why. She reckons that her love for writing, questioning, and the subject matter of economics can be put to great use in the field of research.

Harshit Saxena MVSc Scholar- Medicine Division, ICAR-IVRI Deemed University, Izzatnagar, Bareilly, India.

Rajeev Sengupta is Associate Professor of Finance at School Business, Dr. Vishwanath Karad MIT World Peace University, Pune, India. His research focuses on the BFSI sector, bancassurance and the technological applications in the area. Prior to joining Academics, he had held leadership roles in various MNC Insurance companies for over two decades.

Nikita Sharma is Bachelor's of Economics (Honours) student at Amity University, Noida. She has keen interest in economics, international economics and data analysis. She is a data analyst aspirant aiming for expanding her knowledge in the relevant field.

Pushpam Singh is a Research Scholar, Department of Commerce, Indira Gandhi National Tribal University, Madhya Pradesh, India.

Adyasha Swain is an adviser for thesis projects at Jönköping University; previously pursued doctoral studies there for 2 years from 2020 until 2022; and obtained a master's degree from Luleå University of Technology.

Saurabh Tiwari has more than 15 years of teaching experience in the field of logistics and supply chain management and three years in the manufacturing sector. He has several publications in reputed international journals and completed his Ph.D. in the field of lean manufacturing practices in India. He currently has diversified research interests in transportation, sustainable manufacturing, Industry 4.0, and innovation. He is an Associate Professor in the field of logistics and supply chain management at the School of Business, University of Petroleum and Energy Studies, Dehradun.

Preeti Vats is an M.Sc -Forestry student in the department of Forest Products and Utilization in College of Forestry, Kerala Agricultural University, Thrissur.

Madhuri Yadav, Commerce, Indira Gandhi National Tribal University, Research Scholar, Department of Commerce, Indira Gandhi National Tribal University, Madhya Pradesh, India.

İrem Yalkı is an assistant professor at İstanbul Okan University, where she has been a Department of International Trade member since 2009. She received her Ph.D. in Economics from İstanbul University in 2014. She lectures macroeconomics, data analysis, operations research, and sustainability at the undergraduate level; and managerial economics,, statistical analysis and decision-making, and sustainability at the graduate level. Her fields of interest include economic development, and quantitative research methods; especially econometrics of panel data and optimization technics. She is specialized in sustainable development, environmental economics, the economics of energy, and renewable energy.

Saniye Yildirim Özmutlu is a lecturer in Vocational School of Social Sciences at Tekirdag Namik Kemal University since 2011. She received her BA degree from Suleyman Demirel University in 2007, her MA degree from Suleyman Demirel University in 2011 and PhD degrees in Management and Organization from Yildiz Technical University. Her research interests include management and strategic management.

Kemajl Zeqiri is graduated from University of Prishtina, Faculty of Mining and Metallurgy Department of Mining Enginering, in 2004. He received the M.Sc. degree in University of Prishtina, in field of Geotechnics and Mine Management. Mr. Zeqiri, received Ph.D. degree in Mining Engineering at University "Ss Cyril and Methodius" in Skopje. His main research interests are mining enginering, mining economics, mine management, mining safety, socio-environmental isusses in mining and post-mining activities. Actualy he is working as an Associate Professor in University of Mitrovica, Department of Mining Engineering.

Index

A

Alpha Cellulose 384, 387, 389-396
Alternative (A) 56
Analytic Hierarchy Process (AHP) 56
antimicrobial properties 283-284, 289, 291
Artificial Intelligence (AI) 142, 158-159, 328, 333, 337, 399

B

Battery electric truck (BET) 32
Behavioral Intentions 59-60, 73, 183, 271
Biodiversity 5, 101, 122, 138, 158, 161, 170-171, 201, 213, 215, 217, 224-225, 227, 231, 235, 237, 240, 254, 258, 261, 304-306, 308, 310, 321, 329, 342, 345, 372-373, 377, 400

C

Carbon Emissions 3, 25, 31, 61, 105, 122, 126, 135, 214, 219-220, 224, 227, 231, 240-241, 243-244, 248, 251, 253-254, 331, 346-348, 351, 353-354, 363, 373
Carbon Footprint 39, 139, 161, 248, 253-254, 256-257, 301, 370, 412
Cellulose 283-289, 291-300, 363, 367, 384-387, 389-397
circular economy (CE) 223, 398
Clean technology 84, 121, 132
Cleaner Production 24-26, 71-73, 86-87, 90, 105, 121-127, 129-130, 132, 134-135, 137-139, 175, 196, 211, 248, 260, 262, 325-326, 341-342, 357, 378-380, 383, 405, 412-415
climate bonds 161-162, 169, 175
Climate Change 1-3, 5, 7-8, 22-26, 29-31, 59, 61, 70, 74, 78, 91-94, 96-100, 102-105, 124, 126-129, 131-133, 135-136, 153, 161, 166, 168, 170-171, 174, 176, 213-214, 216-217, 219, 224, 233, 245, 253-254, 259, 266, 301, 304-306, 321, 323-324, 327-328, 330-332, 335-336, 344-350, 353-354, 365, 381
CO_2 Emissions 1-7, 12-13, 23-26, 28-29, 36, 217-219, 254, 258
Composite index 198, 203-205, 207, 210
composites 283-284, 293-296, 298-300, 359, 365-366, 378, 380-381, 396-397
Conservation behavior 58
Criteria (C) 56
Cropland 1, 3, 8, 12-13, 23, 26
Crystallinity index 283, 286, 288-289, 291

D

descarbonisation 27
Descriptive Analysis 1-2, 8, 23, 81, 265
Digital Transformation 119, 128, 141, 154, 403-404, 412

E

Eco-Friendly 58-59, 69, 73, 84-85, 87, 91-92, 105, 142-143, 146, 168, 180-181, 192-193, 195-196, 213, 226-227, 232-233, 235, 244, 248, 256-257, 259, 266, 269, 272-273, 278, 280, 301, 307-308, 310, 327, 349, 352, 365-367
Eco-Friendly Products 58-59, 193, 266, 273, 278, 280, 352
Economic Development 24, 29, 93, 122, 171, 176, 201, 213, 248, 250-252, 255, 262, 328-329, 353, 357, 409
EDAS method 42, 44, 46-50, 55-56
Elimination and Choice Translating Reality (ELECTRE) 56
Energy Consumption 1-2, 4, 8-9, 16-19, 23, 25-26, 28, 37-38, 58-59, 63, 67-68, 81, 98, 128, 133, 143, 153, 158, 218, 234, 252, 329, 338-339, 353, 382
Energy-efficient appliances 58-63, 66-73

Energy-efficient Household Appliances 72-73
Environment Knowledge 190, 194, 196
Environmental Awareness 43, 58, 60, 63-68, 71, 258, 266, 268, 272, 278-279
Environmental Consciousness 71, 178, 181, 183-184, 188, 190-191, 193-194, 197
Environmental Degradation 1-5, 7, 9-11, 22-24, 26, 179, 266, 324, 327, 372
Environmental Impact 5, 36, 44, 91, 105, 127, 165, 194, 217-218, 225, 248, 250-254, 257-259, 263, 345, 359, 362-364, 374, 377-378
Environmental Knowledge 61-63, 69-70, 73, 178, 181, 184-185, 188, 190-191, 193-194, 196, 265, 269, 271-273, 276, 278-279, 282
Environmental Sustainability 25, 28, 74-78, 80, 82-90, 97, 132, 138, 152, 171, 180, 182, 185, 196, 198, 220, 253, 262, 270, 302, 323, 328, 330, 336-337, 340, 343, 346, 352-353, 365, 410, 412
Environmental sustainability management 74, 82-84
Eradicate unemployment 213
Estimation based on the Distance from the Average Solution (EDAS) 56
Exploratory Factor Analysis 178, 187-189, 265, 275-277

F

Fintech 344-345, 352-357
food industry 301-303, 305-307, 309-311, 321, 395
Forest Products 3, 8, 12-13, 382
fossil fuel energy consumption 2, 9, 23
FTIR 288, 298, 384, 391, 393-394
Fuel cell electric truck 27, 31-32

G

Global Village 327
Green Bonds 160-166, 168-176, 344-348, 353-357
Green Clothes 178, 182, 193-194
Green Consciousness 265, 267-268, 273, 276, 278-279, 282
Green Consumer Behaviors 73
Green Consumerism 266, 282
Green creativity 91, 102-103, 105
Green Finance 160, 170, 173, 175-176, 225, 263, 344-348, 351-357
Green Growth 41, 122, 128, 133-134, 137, 203, 211, 213, 215, 223, 228, 260-261
Green Infrastructure 104, 133, 160, 162-163, 223, 230-232, 235-239, 242-246, 347
Green Insurance 91, 93-99, 102-103, 105, 344, 347, 349, 354, 357
green labels 279
Green Loans 175, 344, 347-348
Green Manufacturing 84, 105, 126, 137-139, 247-263, 357
Green Products 60-61, 66, 71, 91-94, 97-99, 102, 180-182, 185, 194, 254, 256-258, 266, 269-272, 274, 278-282, 302, 332, 340, 349, 412
Green Purchase Intention 183, 188, 190, 193, 197, 265, 267-268, 270-274, 276, 278-279, 281
Green supply chain management 74-75, 85-86, 89-90
Green transformation 121-122, 127-128, 131-132, 134, 136
Greener Economy 160, 162-163, 168, 247, 327
green-kitchen 301

H

Health Consciousness 265, 267-268, 273, 276, 279, 282
hydrogen economy 27, 32-36, 40
hydrogen supply chain Management 27

I

India's Growing Population 141, 143
Industrialization 1-9, 15, 20-26, 132, 136, 179, 258, 332
Industry 4.0 (I4.0) 398
Insurance Providers 92-98, 101-102, 106
Irrational behavior 58
Irrational Human Behavior 73

M

market orientation 33-34, 39
mining method 42-46, 48, 52-57
Multi Criteria Decision Making (MCDM) 42, 44, 46, 52-55

N

Natural disaster 327
NICs 1-3, 7-23, 25
nudge theory 301

O

Organic Food Knowledge 282

P

Perceived Behavioral Control 58-59, 66, 68, 70, 178,

Index

183-184, 188, 190-191, 193-194, 196-197, 271, 282
Pineapple Leaves 285, 294, 384, 386-388, 393-396
POE 107-108, 111-118
Pollution 3, 24-25, 30-31, 69, 74-75, 78, 81-85, 94, 96, 100-101, 105, 123-126, 130, 132, 134, 143, 154, 161, 175, 179, 209, 213, 216, 221, 223, 225, 227, 232-233, 236, 240-241, 248, 250, 252-253, 255-259, 261-262, 306, 308, 328-329, 345, 352, 359, 362, 382, 386
Poverty alleviation 213
Preference Ranking Organization METHod for Enrichment Evaluations (PROMETHEE) 56
Purchase Intention 60-63, 66-72, 178, 181-185, 188, 190, 192-194, 196-197, 265, 267-274, 276, 278-279, 281

R

Resource use and energy conservation 76, 78, 82-85
Resource-Efficient 122, 127, 214-215, 250, 379
responsible production and consumption 160, 171
Retrofitting 141, 147, 153, 155, 230, 232-233, 243-244, 246
Rice husk 384, 396-397

S

SDG 160-162, 165, 169-172, 174, 198-205, 207-212, 220, 229, 256, 327, 329-330, 334-335
SDG 12 160-162, 165, 171-172, 220, 327
SDG6 198-200, 202, 204-205, 207-209
Smart City 141-159, 341
Smartphones Android Application 107
Student Satisfaction Rating 107
Subjective Norms 58-59, 62, 64, 66, 68, 181, 183-185, 188, 190-191, 193-194, 197, 265, 268, 271-273, 276, 278-279
Sustainable Business 73, 95, 122, 398, 405, 410
sustainable business models (SBM) 398
Sustainable Development (SD) 4, 26, 37, 59, 71, 74, 76, 85, 88-89, 92-93, 95-96, 103, 105, 128, 131, 135, 137, 157, 160-162, 166, 169, 171, 174, 176, 180, 185, 198-201, 207, 209-212, 213-216, 221-224, 227-229, 245, 251, 257-258, 260, 262-263, 266, 280, 282, 301-302, 304, 311, 323, 327-332, 334-336, 340-342, 345-347, 352-356, 358, 374, 378, 381, 398-400, 409-410, 414
Sustainable Development Goals 37, 93, 96, 105, 161, 174, 176, 180, 198, 200-201, 209-212, 215, 221, 223-224, 228, 251, 266, 302, 323, 328, 334-336, 340-342, 345, 347, 353, 356, 358, 378
Sustainable Insurance 91-95, 97, 99, 103-106, 349
Sustainable manufacturing (SM) 398
sustainable Utilization 358, 365, 367-369, 372-373, 375-377

T

Technique for Order Preference by Similarity to Ideal Solution (TOPSIS) 57
The Ecological Footprint 1, 3, 8-11, 22, 26, 302
The ecological footprint per capita 9, 11, 26
Theory Of Planned Behavior 58-59, 69-72, 178, 183, 196, 265, 267, 281
Theory of Reasoned Actions 178
Time Use Survey 107, 112
Turkish industry 121, 127, 129, 131-132, 134

U

University of British Columbia (UBC) 57
Urban Innovation 141-142, 154, 157

V

Value addition 358, 365, 367
VIsekriterijumskog KOmpromisnog Rangiranja (VIKOR) 57
VUCA 327, 331, 342

W

Waste management and recycling companies 74, 78, 80-81, 83, 85
Water and sanitation 170, 198, 200-203, 208-212
Water Stress 198-200, 202, 204, 329

Recommended Reference Books

IGI Global's reference books are available in three unique pricing formats:
Print Only, E-Book Only, or Print + E-Book.

Order direct through IGI Global's Online Bookstore at
www.igi-global.com or through your preferred provider.

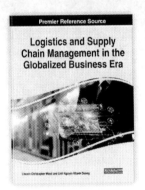

ISBN: 9781799887096
EISBN: 9781799887119
© 2022; 413 pp.
List Price: US$ 250

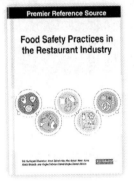

ISBN: 9781799874157
EISBN: 9781799874164
© 2022; 334 pp.
List Price: US$ 240

ISBN: 9781668440230
EISBN: 9781668440254
© 2022; 320 pp.
List Price: US$ 215

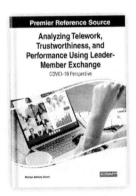

ISBN: 9781799889502
EISBN: 9781799889526
© 2022; 263 pp.
List Price: US$ 240

ISBN: 9781799885283
EISBN: 9781799885306
© 2022; 587 pp.
List Price: US$ 360

ISBN: 9781668455906
EISBN: 9781668455913
© 2022; 2,235 pp.
List Price: US$ 1,865

Do you want to stay current on the latest research trends, product announcements, news, and special offers?
Join IGI Global's mailing list to receive customized recommendations, exclusive discounts, and more.
Sign up at: **www.igi-global.com/newsletters**.

Publisher of Timely, Peer-Reviewed Inclusive Research Since 1988

Ensure Quality Research is Introduced to the Academic Community

Become an Evaluator for IGI Global Authored Book Projects

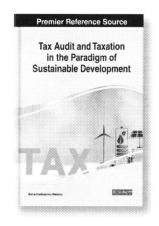

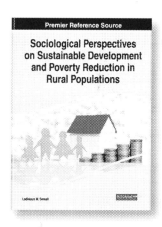

The overall success of an authored book project is dependent on quality and timely manuscript evaluations.

Applications and Inquiries may be sent to:
development@igi-global.com

Applicants must have a doctorate (or equivalent degree) as well as publishing, research, and reviewing experience. Authored Book Evaluators are appointed for one-year terms and are expected to complete at least three evaluations per term. Upon successful completion of this term, evaluators can be considered for an additional term.

If you have a colleague that may be interested in this opportunity, we encourage you to share this information with them.

Easily Identify, Acquire, and Utilize Published Peer-Reviewed Findings in Support of Your Current Research

IGI Global OnDemand

Purchase Individual IGI Global OnDemand Book Chapters and Journal Articles

For More Information:
www.igi-global.com/e-resources/ondemand/

Browse through 150,000+ Articles and Chapters!

Find specific research related to your current studies and projects that have been contributed by international researchers from prestigious institutions, including:

- Accurate and Advanced Search
- Affordably Acquire Research
- Instantly Access Your Content
- Benefit from the InfoSci Platform Features

"*It really provides* an excellent entry into the research literature of the field. *It presents a manageable number of* highly relevant sources *on topics of interest to a wide range of researchers. The sources are* scholarly, but also accessible *to 'practitioners'.*"

— Ms. Lisa Stimatz, MLS, University of North Carolina at Chapel Hill, USA

Interested in Additional Savings?

Subscribe to
IGI Global OnDemand *Plus*

Acquire content from over 128,000+ research-focused book chapters and 33,000+ scholarly journal articles for as low as US$ 5 per article/chapter (original retail price for an article/chapter: US$ 37.50).

7,300+ E-BOOKS.
ADVANCED RESEARCH.
INCLUSIVE & AFFORDABLE.

IGI Global e-Book Collection

- Flexible Purchasing Options (Perpetual, Subscription, EBA, etc.)
- Multi-Year Agreements with No Price Increases Guaranteed
- No Additional Charge for Multi-User Licensing
- No Maintenance, Hosting, or Archiving Fees
- Continually Enhanced & Innovated Accessibility Compliance Features (WCAG)

Handbook of Research on Digital Transformation, Industry Use Cases, and the Impact of Disruptive Technologies
ISBN: 9781799877127
EISBN: 9781799877141

Handbook of Research on New Investigations in Artificial Life, AI, and Machine Learning
ISBN: 9781799886860
EISBN: 9781799886877

Handbook of Research on Future of Work and Education
ISBN: 9781799882756
EISBN: 9781799882770

Research Anthology on Physical and Intellectual Disabilities in an Inclusive Society (4 Vols.)
ISBN: 9781668435427
EISBN: 9781668435434

Innovative Economic, Social, and Environmental Practices for Progressing Future Sustainability
ISBN: 9781799895909
EISBN: 9781799895923

Applied Guide for Event Study Research in Supply Chain Management
ISBN: 9781799889694
EISBN: 9781799889717

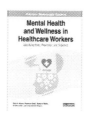

Mental Health and Wellness in Healthcare Workers
ISBN: 9781799888130
EISBN: 9781799888147

Clean Technologies and Sustainable Development in Civil Engineering
ISBN: 9781799898108
EISBN: 9781799898122

Request More Information, or Recommend the IGI Global e-Book Collection to Your Institution's Librarian

For More Information or to Request a Free Trial, Contact IGI Global's e-Collections Team: eresources@igi-global.com | 1-866-342-6657 ext. 100 | 717-533-8845 ext. 100

Are You Ready to Publish Your Research?

IGI Global offers book authorship and editorship opportunities across 11 subject areas, including business, computer science, education, science and engineering, social sciences, and more!

Benefits of Publishing with IGI Global:

- Free one-on-one editorial and promotional support.
- Expedited publishing timelines that can take your book from start to finish in less than one (1) year.
- Choose from a variety of formats, including Edited and Authored References, Handbooks of Research, Encyclopedias, and Research Insights.
- Utilize IGI Global's eEditorial Discovery® submission system in support of conducting the submission and double-blind peer review process.
- IGI Global maintains a strict adherence to ethical practices due in part to our full membership with the Committee on Publication Ethics (COPE).
- Indexing potential in prestigious indices such as Scopus®, Web of Science™, PsycINFO®, and ERIC – Education Resources Information Center.
- Ability to connect your ORCID iD to your IGI Global publications.
- Earn honorariums and royalties on your full book publications as well as complimentary content and exclusive discounts.

Join Your Colleagues from Prestigious Institutions, Including:
- Australian National University
- Massachusetts Institute of Technology
- Johns Hopkins University
- Tsinghua University
- Harvard University
- Columbia University in the City of New York

Learn More at: www.igi-global.com/publish
or Contact IGI Global's Aquisitions Team at: acquisition@igi-global.com

Individual Article & Chapter Downloads
US$ 29.50/each

Easily Identify, Acquire, and Utilize Published Peer-Reviewed Findings in Support of Your Current Research

- Browse Over **170,000+ Articles & Chapters**
- **Accurate & Advanced** Search
- Affordably Acquire **International Research**
- **Instantly Access** Your Content
- Benefit from the **InfoSci® Platform Features**

> It really provides *an excellent entry into the research literature of the field.* It presents a manageable number of *highly relevant sources* on topics of interest to a wide range of researchers. The sources are *scholarly, but also accessible* to 'practitioners'.
>
> - Ms. Lisa Stimatz, MLS, University of North Carolina at Chapel Hill, USA

Interested in Additional Savings?

Subscribe to **IGI Global OnDemand Plus**

Acquire content from over 137,000+ research-focused book chapters and 33,000+ scholarly journal articles for as low as US$ 5 per article/chapter (original retail price for an article/chapter: US$ 29.50).

Printed in the United States
by Baker & Taylor Publisher Services